HAVELOK

For over seventy years there has been no new English edition of the lively and vigorously written Middle English verse romance of *Hauelok*, despite the need of a text to meet modern standards of editing. In this thorough edition of the poem, Professor Smithers has done much to elucidate the text. Cruces are solved and other textual problems unravelled, and the edition contains a great deal that is new. The extensive and helpful apparatus includes a detailed glossary, textual notes, and an introduction that contains an account of the principal manuscript and of the Cambridge fragments, of the relation of *Hauelok* to the other main versions of the story, of the language, the sources, the date of composition, and what the poem is about. There is also a full commentary, which goes well beyond those of previous editions in range, scale, and detail, and which takes account of the author's practical interest in social, feudal, and legal institutions and in local administration, and of his connections with Lincoln.

The author's treatment of the story has been closely and fully compared with those of the other main versions, so as to bring out his individual methods and achievement. The summary discussion of his language takes in words of locally restricted distribution, and other evidence, and concludes that beyond a doubt it is a written variety of Lincolnshire English.

Professor G. V. Smithers was formerly Professor of English Language at the University of Durham, and previously a professorial Fellow of Merton College, Oxford. He has edited, among other works, *Kyng Alisaunder*, volumes I and II, and (with J. A. W. Bennett and Norman Davis) *Early Middle English Verse and Prose*.

F<small>IG</small>. 1. The Seal of Grimsby:

SIGILLVM COMMUNITATIS GRIMEBYE
HAB[?UE]LOC GRYEM GOLDEBVRGH

HAVELOK

EDITED BY

G. V. SMITHERS

CLARENDON PRESS · OXFORD

1987

Oxford University Press, Walton Street, Oxford OX2 6DP
Oxford New York Toronto
Delhi Bombay Calcutta Madras Karachi
Petaling Jaya Singapore Hong Kong Tokyo
Nairobi Dar es Salaam Cape Town
Melbourne Auckland
and associated companies in
Beirut Berlin Ibadan Nicosia

Oxford is a trade mark of Oxford University Press

Published in the United States
by Oxford University Press, New York

British Library Cataloguing in Publication Data
Havelok.
I. Smithers, G. V.
821'.1 PR2065.H3
ISBN 0-19-811939-9

Library of Congress Cataloging-in-Publication Data
Havelok the Dane.
Havelok.
Bibliography: p.
Includes index.
1. Romances, English. I. Smithers, G. V.
II. Title.
PR2065.H3 1987 821'.1 86-23480
ISBN 0-19-811939-9

Set by Joshua Associates Limited, Oxford
Printed in Great Britain
at the University Printing House, Oxford
by David Stanford
Printer to the University

PREFACE

T HIS edition has had to be reduced, because of costs, by the omission from the Introduction of sections on the versification, the style, and the literary interest of *Hauelok*. The substance of the first of these is however available in my paper 'The Scansion of *Hauelok* and the Use of ME -*en* and -*e* in *Hauelok* and by Chaucer';[1] and the other two are being reserved for publication elsewhere.

In preparing the edition I have had generous help from many scholars, including notably Mr C. Ball, Dr A. Bell, Professor M. Benskin, Professor N. Davis, Dr A. I. Doyle, Dr A. J. Forey, Dr R. F. Frame, Professor D. Gray, Mr T. A. Heslop, Dr M. Laing, Professor A. McIntosh, Mr J. S. McKinnell, Dr K. Major, Mr P. Mussett, Professor H. S. Offler, Dr M. B. Parkes, Mr A. J. Piper, Miss E. M. Rainey, Mr M. C. Snape, Mrs A. Squires, Professor M. Stokes, Dr E. Stone, and Mr V. E. Watts, to all of whom I express warm thanks. I am also very grateful for help, in the form of excellent photostats of the Cambridge Fragments, from the Photography Department of the Cambridge University Library; to the staff of the University of Durham Library and of the Bodleian Library in Oxford; the Conservateur en chef of Manuscripts of the Bibliothèque Nationale; Mr J. Wilson, Archivist in charge of the South Humberside Area Record Office. Thanks are also due to the Great Grimsby Borough Council for permission to photograph and publish the Grimsby seal, and to the National Galleries of Scotland, Edinburgh, for similar permission regarding the watercolour (D5023/50) 'The Devil's Hole' by Peter de Wint; and to the British Academy and the Leverhulme Trust for grants towards the cost of the research.

G. V. SMITHERS

---

[1] In *Middle English Studies Presented to Norman Davis* (ed. D. Gray and E. G. Stanley, Clarendon Press 1983), pp. 195–234.

CONTENTS

ILLUSTRATIONS

ABBREVIATIONS

AL	*Archivum Linguisticum*
ANTS	Anglo-Norman Text Society
Archiv	*Archiv für das Studium der neueren Sprachen*
Bosworth–Toller	J. Bosworth and T. N. Toller, *An Anglo-Saxon Dictionary* (Oxford, n.d.)
CFMA	Classiques français du moyen âge
EETS	Early English Text Society; os Original Series; es Extra Series; ss Supplementary Series
EGS	*English and Germanic Studies* (now *English Philological Studies*)
EHR	*English Historical Review*
EMEVP	*Early Middle English Verse and Prose*, ed. J. A. W. Bennett and G. V. Smithers, with Glossary by N. Davis (2nd edn. rev., Oxford, repr. 1985)
English Feudalism	F. M. Stenton, *The First Century of English Feudalism 1066–1166* (Oxford, 1954)
ES	*Essays and Studies*
EWNT	J. Franck, *Etymologisch Woordenboek der nederlandsche Taal* (2nd edn., rev. N. van Wijk, The Hague, 1929)
FEW	W. von Wartburg, *Französisches etymologisches Wörterbuch* (Tübingen, 1948; 2nd edn. in progress)
Godefroy	F. Godefroy, *Dictionnaire de l'ancien langue française* (Paris, 1881–1902)
Hav.	*Hauelok*
LSE	*Leeds Studies in English*
MÆ	*Medium Ævum*
MED	*Middle English Dictionary*, ed. H. Kurath, S. Kuhn, J. Reidy (Ann Arbor, 1956; in progress)
MGH	*Monumenta Germaniae Historica* (Hanover, 1826–), SS Scriptores
NDEW	H. Falk and A. Torp, *Norwegisch-dänisches etymologisches Wörterbuch* (Heidelberg, 1910–11)
N&Q	*Notes and Queries*
OED	*The Oxford English Dictionary*
O&N	*The Owl and the Nightingale*, ed. E. G. Stanley (London, 1960)
Pet. Chron.	*The Peterborough Chronicle*
PMLA	*Publications of the Modern Language Association*
Pollock and Maitland	Pollock and Maitland, *The History of English Law before the Time of Edward I*, 2 vols. (Cambridge, 1898)

RES	*Review of English Studies*
REW	W. Meyer-Lübke, *Romanisches etymologisches Wörterbuch* (3rd edn., Heidelberg, 1935)
RS	Rolls Series
SATF	Société des Anciens Textes Français
SMP	*So meny people longages and tonges*, Essays presented to A. McIntosh, ed. M. Benskin and M. L. Samuels (Edinburgh, 1981)
TLS	*The Times Literary Supplement*
Tobler–Lommatzsch	A. Tobler and E. Lommatzsch, *Altfranzösisches Wörterbuch* (Berlin, 1925; in progress)
TPS	*Transactions of the Philological Society*
WGS	H. Falk and A. Torp, *Wortschatz der germanischen Spracheinheit*, pt. III of A. Fick, *Vergleichendes Wörterbuch der indogermanischen Sprachen* (Göttingen, 1909)

See also the Abbreviations listed at the head of the Glossary.

INTRODUCTION

I. THE MANUSCRIPTS

I. L: MS Laud Misc. 108 of the Bodleian Library (Summary Catalogue No. 1486). Parchment; folios iii + 239 + i (the MS numbering has 170*a* and 170*b* instead of 170). The leaves are mostly *c.*280 × 175 mm.

For a recent description of the whole MS (which is a composite one) see M. Görlach, *The Textual Tradition of the South English Legendary*, p. 88.[1] Fos. 1–198 contain *The South English Legendary*, preceded by *temporale* texts,[2] viz. *The Life and Passion of Christ* and *The Infancy of Christ* (fos. 1ra and 11ra; Brown and Robbins, *The Index of M.E. Verse*, Nos. *15 and 1550). Since these are numbered 8 and 9, seven items have been lost, as well as part of item 8 up to the opening line of fo. I^r:

And spatte a luyte on is fingur. and into is erene it schok.

The Saints' Legends are followed by *The Sayings of St Bernard* fo. 198^r,[3] *The Vision of St Paul* fo. 199rb,[4] and *The Debate of the Body and the Soul* fos. 200^v–203^v.[5]

Hauelok occurs in the last part of the MS, which is separated from the preceding parts by a narrow vertical strip of parchment between fos. 203^v and 204ra. This section is a clear example (see Collation below) of what has been defined and explained by Miss P. R. Robinson as a 'booklet',[6] along with similar units that existed separately before being combined with other material in a composite MS.

The contents of this part of the MS are as follows (the item numbers written in the MS being added here in square brackets):

1. [71] *Hauelok* fos. 204ra–219va.
2. [72] *King Horn* fos. 219va–228rb (the lower half of which is blank).

---

[1] Leeds Texts and Monographs, NS 6 (1974). For earlier descriptions, see C. Horstmann, *Leben Jesu* (Münster, 1873), pp. 1–7 and 'Die Legenden des Ms. Laud 108', *Archiv*, 49 (1872), 395–414; J. Hall, *King Horn* (Oxford, 1901), pp. viii–x.

[2] See *OED temporal* sb.[1] 2. For a list of the contents pertaining to the *Legendary* see C. Horstmann, *The Early South-English Legendary* (EETS, OS 87, 1887), p. xiii.

[3] See J. E. Cross, *RES* NS 9 (1958), 1 ff.

[4] Brown and Robbins, 3089.

[5] Brown and Robbins, 351.

[6] In her unpublished thesis (B.Litt. of Oxford, 1972) 'Some Aspects of the Transmission of Middle English Texts'. See her paper '"The Booklet"' in *Codicologica*, ed. A. Gruys and J. P. Gombert (*Litterae Textuales*, Leiden), 3 (1980), 46–69.

These are both written in a compact 'textura'[7] hand of the early fourteenth century.

3. [73] *The Life and Passion of St Blaise* fos. 228ᵛ–230ᵛ.
4. [74] *The Life and Passion of St Cecilia* fos. 230ᵛ–233ᵛ.
5. [75] *The Life of St Alexius* fos. 233ᵛ–237ʳᵃ.
6. [76] *Somer Soneday*[8] fos. 237ʳᵃ–237ᵛ.

These are written in a late fourteenth-century hand of the same type and date ('Anglicana'[9]) as that of MS Magdalene College Pepys 2498 and MS Laud Misc. 622.[10] The hand of the latter two, though extraordinarily like that of the four items here, is not identical with it: the letter *a* in interior position is consistently different.

7. Four lines of ME verse in rhymed couplets (Old and New Testament paradoxes), fo. 238 (top) in a fifteenth-century hand:

Byholde merueylis: a mayden is moder;	*Isaye* vij
Here sone her fader ys and broder	*Isaye* ix
Lyfe faw3t wiþ deþe, and deþe is slayne.	*Osee* xiij
Most hi3 was lowe; he sty3e agayne.	*Philipens[es]* ij[11]

8. Two pieces of verse, fo. 238ᵛ, in a fifteenth-century hand, beginning respectively:

(*a*) [A]llas deceyte, þat in truste ys nowe
(*b*) Be þou nou3t to bolde to blame.[12]

Collation

Quire 1: 12 leaves, fos. 204–214 (with catchwords at the foot of 214ᵛ). It lacks one leaf, which was evidently 9, since one has been cut out after fo. 211. This is established by the stub still visible after fo. 211, and by the lacuna in the text between l. 1445 (at the end of fo. 211ᵛᵇ) and l. 1626 (at the beginning of fo. 212ʳᵃ), which would have been contained in four columns of forty-five lines each (the actual number of lines to the column in *Hav.* and *King Horn*).

Quire 2: 12 leaves, fos. 215–226 (with catchwords at the foot of 226ᵛ, and leaf signatures at the foot of the recto sides of 215–219 inclusive).

Quire 3: 5 single leaves, fos. 227–231, leaves 6–12 having been cut away.

Quire 4: 6 single leaves, fos. 232–237. There is sewing between 234

---

[7] For this term see M. B. Parkes, *English Cursive Book Hands 1250–1500* (Oxford, 1969), pp. xiii, xvii–xviii.

[8] Brown and Robbins, 3838.   [9] See Parkes, op. cit., pp. xiv–xviii.

[10] For facsimiles of these see *Kyng Alisaunder*, vol. i (EETS, os 227, 1961), Plate I, and J. Pålsson, *The Recluse* (Lund Universitets Årsskrift, NF, Avd. I, Bd. 6, nr. 1, 1911).

[11] References as read by Dr A. I. Doyle.   [12] Brown and Robbins, 145 and 477.

and 235. Another narrow strip of vellum between fos. 231 and 232 is conjugate with 238, which was the end leaf and was wrapped round the last quire.

Hauelok and *King Horn* are written in two columns on each side of a leaf, and with 45 lines to the column; fos. 228ᵛ–233ᵛ in one column of 44 to 46 long lines; 233ᵛ–234ʳ (*St Alexius*, in tail-rhyme stanzas) with the short line after, and not below, the couplets; and 234ᵛ–237ᵛ in two columns of *c.* 50 lines to the column.

The written space in *Hauelok* and *King Horn* is 230 × 130 mm. There are double vertical bounding-lines on the left and the right of the main written area, and in the middle. Line-initials are written in the space contained between the bounding-lines on the left of each column; they are touched in with red on fos. 204ʳ–208ᵛ, 214ᵛ–215ʳ, 219ᵛ–220ʳ, and 226ᵛ–228ᵛ. In *Hauelok* there are many, and in *King Horn* some, large initials (of the type known as 'lombards') in blue, filled in and flourished in red, which mark the beginning of individual short sections of the text.

The ink in which the item numbers have been written in arabic numerals in the margin is the same as that used in the copying of the additional items that follow *King Horn*. The man who supplied the numbers and copied the additional texts (items 73–6, on fos. 228ᵛ– 237ᵛ) was probably the man who combined the various parts of the whole MS into one volume; and he may well have done the latter at the same time.[13]

On fo. 1ʳ (top) there is the press-mark K 60, in a seventeenth-century hand, as there also is on guard-leaf iii. At the bottom of fo. 1ʳ is written:

Liber Guillelmi Laud Archiepiscopi Cantuariensis et Cancellarii Vniuersitatis Oxoniæ 1633.

The MS is one of the 'First Donation' of Laud, which was sent on 22 May 1635.[14]

An earlier owner is attested on fo. 238ᵛ, in a hand of *c.* 1450–75 (as dated by Dr Doyle):

Iste liber constat Henrico Perueys, testantibus Iohanni Rede presbitero, Willelmo Rotheley, et aliis.

The name *Henrico Perueys* has been written on an erasure; the underlying name cannot now be deciphered, even in ultraviolet light.

In *Perueys* the *u* is written just like *n*, and might be so read. But the

[13] The observations and conclusions in this section are due to Dr M. B. Parkes.

[14] See H. O. Coxe, *Bodleian Library Quarto Catalogues*, vol. ii, *Laudian Manuscripts*, corrected edn. by R. W. Hunt (Oxford, 1973), pp. ix, xxxv.

same applies to *u* in *truste* and *turnyng* in lines 1, 5, 7, and 2 of the verses, labelled (*a*) above, higher up on fo. 238ᵛ. The word must be read as *Perueys*, since a Henry Perveys and a William Wrotheley are both attested in London documents of the middle and the later fifteenth century.[15] William Rotheley was Warden of the Goldsmiths' Company in 1444, 1450, 1459, and 1465,[16] and is mentioned as being a goldsmith in a deed of gift of 1445,[17] and again in 1450, 1457, and 1458.[18] He is named in 1466, with others, in a bond for £200 to be paid to the use of Thomas Eyre, on his coming of age, the sum having been left to the said orphan by his grandfather Simon Eyre.[19] And by another bond, of 15 October 1437, the executors of John Perneys (ed.: 'or *Perueys*') are to pay £200 for the latter's son *Henry, now apprenticed to Simon Eyr, draper*, when Henry Perueys reaches his majority or marries.[20]

This last document shows that William Rotheley, through his link with the Eyre family, may well have known Henry Perueys. It is thus highly probable or virtually certain that William Rotheley and Henry Perueys of the documents cited above are the persons so named in the statement of ownership on fo. 238 of MS Laud Misc. 108: the variation between *Rotheley* and *Wrotheley* is admissible.

The latest record of William Rotheley is in 1480, when he is mentioned as a city tax collector. Henry Perueys, a draper, was still alive in 1476. His father, John Perueys, who was a fishmonger, and an alderman of London from 1416 to 1434, died in 1434.[21]

II. C: Cambridge University Library MS Add. 4407 (19) is a batch of four fragmentary leaves, each with writing on both sides. Each side is now marked with a different index letter, *a/b, c/d, e/f*, and *g/h*, for the recto and the verso respectively of each leaf. Sides *d, e*, and *f* were first identified by Skeat as portions of a copy of *Hav*.[22] These are printed below on pages facing the corresponding passages in the Laud MS, which are as follows:

---

[15] I owe this item of information, and a number of references to documents (only the most pertinent of which are mentioned below), to the kindness of Dr Doyle.

[16] T. F. Reddaway, *The Early History of the Goldsmiths' Company, 1327–1509* (London, 1975), index.

[17] P. E. Jones, *Calendar of Pleas and Memoranda Rolls AD 1437–1457* (Cambridge, 1954), p. 88.

[18] R. R. Sharpe, *Calendar of Letter-books of the City of London*: Letter-Book K (London, 1911), pp. 333, 383, 393.

[19] Sharpe, op. cit.: Letter-Book L (London, 1912), p. 63.

[20] P. E. Jones, op. cit., p. 1.

[21] For information regarding these two, and three other members of the Perueys family, see S. L. Thrupp, *The Merchant Class of Medieval London* (Chicago, 1948), p. 360.

[22] 'A New "Havelok" MS', *MLR* 6 (1911), 455–7.

1. Side *d*: ll. 174–83 (i.e. 10 lines)
2. Side *e*: ll. 341–51, then two lines not in the Laud MS, then ll. 356–64 (22 lines in all)
3. Side *f*: ll. 537–44, then 10 lines not in Laud, then ll. 545–51 (25 lines in all).

The contents of the remaining fragments are as follows:

4. Sides *a*, *b*, and *c*: respectively ll. 6–12, 20–9 (with 24 omitted), and 83–8 of the *Elegy on the Death of Edward I*,[23] which is otherwise recorded only in MS Harley 2253.
5. Side *h*: ll. 2–6 and 15–36 (all written continuously) of *The Proverbs of Hendyng*,[24] a copy of which is also contained in MS Harley 2253.
6. Side *g*: 23 lines from a poem which has not been traced in any other copy or identified, and which is reminiscent of the elegiac piece variously called *An Old Man's Prayer* by G. L. Brook[25] and *Le regret de Maximian* by Carleton Brown.[26]

The latter is modelled on the first elegy of Maximian,[27] a contemporary of Boethius.

Rubrics in the margin before ll. 7, 15, and 23 show that each of these was the first line of an eight-line stanza, which rhymes *ab ab ab ab*. Thus the first line on side *g* cannot be the opening line of the poem. It runs: *On folie was myn silwyr leyd*. Lines 7–14 were printed by Skeat;[28] I hope soon to make the fragment available in full.

All the fragments of text are in one and the same hand—an 'Anglicana' of the second half of the fourteenth century—and in the same ink, and are thus all from one and the same codex. It was one of paper (which was not in common use for the copying of literary texts before 1400). It must have been a quarto, since the disposition of the writing in relation to the 'mould lines'[29] shows that the original sheet was folded twice. The signature *e* is written at the bottom of side *b*.

The original size of the leaves (among which side *a*, at least, is shown by stains to have been used in a binding or the like) must have

---

[23] Ed. K. Böddeker, *Altenglische Dichtungen des MS. Harl. 2253* (Berlin, 1878), pp. 140–3; R. H. Robbins, *Historical Poems of the XIVth and XVth Centuries* (New York, 1959), pp. 21–4.

[24] Ed. Morris and Skeat, *Specimens of Early English*, vol. 11, pp. 35–42.

[25] *The Harley Lyrics* (2nd edn., Manchester, 1956), pp. 46–8.

[26] *English Lyrics of the XIIIth Century* (Oxford, 1932), pp. 92–100.

[27] Ed. E. Baehrens, *Poetae Latini Minores*, vol. v (Leipzig, 1883), pp. 316–29. See *MÆ* 28 (1959), 8–11.

[28] 'Elegy on the Death of King Edward I', *MLR* 7 (1912), 149–52, at 151.

[29] i.e. the lines traced on the paper by the mould in which it was formed. See P. Gaskell, *A New Introduction to Bibliography* (Oxford, 2nd impression, 1974), pp. 8, 57–61, and Fig. 26.

been over 180 × 100 mm. Leaves *a/b* and *c/d* have had the upper (and larger) part cut off, so that respectively 7, 9, 9, and 10 lines of writing are left, along with the bottom margin. Leaves *e/f* and *g/h* have had the lower (and smaller) part trimmed away, so that respectively 24, 24, 23, and 24 lines of writing are left, along with the top of the leaf. Thus the portions of text written on *a/b* and *c/d* end those sides, and the portions written on *e/f* and *g/h* begin these sides.

Since side *d* ends with *Hav.* l. 183 and side *e* begins with *Hav.* l. 341, the missing ll. 183–340 (*c.* 157 lines) must have been contained on a leaf or leaves between *d* and *e*. And since side *e* has *Hav.* 341–64, and side *f* begins with *Hav.* 537, the first few lines of the missing sequence 365–536 must have been contained on the missing lower part of *e*, and the rest on a leaf or leaves between *e* and *f*. The missing ll. 1–173 must have been written on a leaf or leaves between *c* and *d*.

These facts, and the distribution of the other sections of texts written on sides *a*, *b*, *c*, *g*, and *h*, have not availed to establish the number of lines originally contained in a column or in a leaf (beyond the fact that it was more than 24). What is clear is that the MS was a fairly substantial one (since over 2900 lines of *Hav.* are missing, if this was a complete copy); and that its contents were heterogeneous, and similar in character to those of MS Harley 2253 and Royal 12 C. xii[30] (in the former of which the inclusion of the romance *King Horn* matches that of *Hav.* here).

II. OTHER VERSIONS OF THE STORY

Since the Laud MS of *Hav.* is usually assigned, on palaeographical criteria, to a date about or soon after 1300, and the poem is almost certain to have been composed before 1310 (see VI, 3), it is the early versions of the story that matter here. There are six to be noticed:

1. An AN one of 816 octosyllabic lines in rhymed couplets, by Geoffrey Gaimar,[31] which opens his *L'Estoire des Engleis* in three of the four MSS of the latter. The *Estoire* is the second part of a work the first part of which has not survived; the latter, according to his epilogue (6522–3), began with events in Troy and was thus evidently a *Brut*.

The story of Havelok is not contained in Gaimar's main source, the OF *Brut* of Wace. Bell has therefore argued (convincingly) that it is an

---

[30] On both of these see N. R. Ker, *Facsimile of British Museum MS. Harley 2253* (EETS, os 255; 1965), pp. ix–xvi, xx–xxiii; E. J. Hathaway, P. T. Ricketts, C. A. Robson, and A. D. Wilshere, *Fouke le Fitz Waryn* (ANTS 26–8, Oxford, 1975), pp. xxxvii–liii.

[31] Ed. A. Bell, *L'Estoire des Engleis*, ANTS 14–16 (Oxford, 1960), ll. 1–816, and *Le Lai d'Haveloc and Gaimar's Haveloc Episode* (Manchester, 1925).

addition to the original *Estoire* and that Gaimar himself composed it; *L'Estoire* itself was composed *c.* 1135–40.[32] Gaimar might have had an opportunity to learn of the story of Havelok (as one centred on Lincoln) through his patron Constance, the wife of Ralf Fitzgilbert, who held lands in Lincolnshire as well as Hampshire in the twelfth century.[33]

A notable point about Gaimar's version is that the story has been brought into association with Arthur. Gaimar says that Arthur invaded and conquered Denmark to enforce payment of tribute that had been withheld (408–9), and that Arthur enabled a usurper to kill Havelok's father Gunter. It is important to be aware that this episode has been transferred to Arthur from a story of Geoffrey of Monmouth[34] about an entirely different king, Gurguint Barbtruc, the son and successor of Belinus, who invaded Denmark because the king had withheld tribute. The British king fought and killed the latter, and subjugated the country. Moreover, Aschis, whom Gaimar mentions as the brother of the Danish usurper and as having been killed fighting on Arthur's side against Modred (522), is Geoffrey of Monmouth's 'Aschil(lus), king of the Danes'.[35]

Another important point is that Gaimar sets his story of Haveloc in the reign of Constantine, the nephew of Arthur (ll. 2 and 33). And he says that Haveloc and his wife ruled for 20 years, *till the year 495* and the arrival of Cerdic.

These facts are essential aids towards some understanding of how the extant versions of the story of Havelok came into being, and especially of its ostensibly Arthurian connections in Gaimar and the *Lai d'Haveloc* (2 below).

Gaimar's account of Havelok runs as follows (in necessarily summary form):

When Britain was ruled by Constantine, Arthur's nephew and successor, there was a King Adelbriht, a Dane, who held by conquest Norfolk and the land from Colchester to Holland [in Lincs.] and had four counties in Denmark. A King Edelsi, a Briton, ruled Lincoln and Lindsey, and the land from Humber to Rutland.

Adelbriht had married Edelsi's sister Orwain, and had a daughter Argentille. When Adelbriht died, his widow (who was ill) committed the kingdom

---

[32] Bell, ed. cit., p. lii.

[33] See *L'Estoire* 6430 ff. and pp. ix–x.

[34] *Historia Regum Britanniae*, ed. E. Faral, *La Légende Arthurienne* (Paris, 1929), iii, ch. 45, p. 119 (see ii, pp. 137–40); trans. L. Thorpe, *Geoffrey of Monmouth: The History of the Kings of Britain* (Penguin Classics, 1979), Bk. iii, ch. 11. See R. H. Fletcher, *The Arthurian Material in the Chronicles* (New York, repr. Burt Franklin, n.d.), pp. 126, 84, and 141–2.

[35] Faral, ed. cit., chs. 156, 168, 171, 178 (pp. 244, 264, 268, 278).

and their daughter to Edelsi. Orwain died a few days later, and Argentille was brought up in Lincoln and Lindsey, since she had no kin on her father's side.

Edelsi coveted his niece's heritage, and therefore 'mismarried' her to a scullion in his household named Cuaran, who was handsome, cheerful, brave, strong, generous, and very popular. Cuaran had with him two lads whom he mistakenly believed to be his brothers; but he was high-born (unknown to Edelsi).

Cuaran puzzled his wife by habitually sleeping on his face, and (in his ignorance) paying no attention to her in bed. When their marriage was in due course consummated, Argentille had a dream, in which she was with Cuaran between the sea and a forest, the haunt of a bear (attended by foxes) which was bent on devouring Cuaran. A boar killed the bear; and other boars slew some of the foxes, some of the rest of which submitted to Cuaran. The sea now threatened to engulf him; he climbed a large tree; two lions slew many of the animals in the forest, then came and knelt before Cuaran.

The hubbub woke Argentille. She turned to Cuaran, embraced him, and then, seeing a flame issuing from his mouth, roused him, thinking that he was on fire; she told him of this and of the dream. The latter he naively interpreted as the preparations for a banquet of the King's, next day; but he could not explain the flame, which he said he always emitted when asleep. She then urged that they should seek out his kinfolk (whom he reported as being in Grimsby), rather than go on living in shameful circumstances in Lincoln.

At Grimsby they found Grim's daughter and her husband, a fisherman [*sic* l. 319], who recognized the three young men as Cuaran and the two sons of Grim and decided, after consulting his wife, that Haveloc [now first thus named in the action of the story] should be told of his true identity as a king's son, his origins, and his early history. Haveloc was found to believe that Grim was his father, Grim's wife Sebruc his mother, Grim's daughter Kelloc his sister, and the two boys (with whom he had gone to Lincoln when Grim and his wife died) his brothers.

Kelloc told Haveloc that a well-provisioned ship was about to leave for the country where he would find his own kin and friends, and that she and her husband [a merchant ll. 455, 481, 601] would provide him with clothes and funds if he wished to go there with her two brothers. Haveloc, she said, was the son of Gunter, the hereditary King of Denmark, and of Alvive (the daughter of a King Gaifier), who had brought her up. But Arthur had invaded Denmark to exact tribute that had been withheld, and Gunter was killed in battle; and Arthur had bestowed the land as he chose.

The queen and Haveloc (as the rightful heir to Denmark) had to flee in Grim's ship; but pirates killed all on board except Grim, his family, and Haveloc. Once arrived in England, Grim cut the damaged ship in half to make a house, and earned a living as a fisherman and later a salt-merchant. Kelloc had married a merchant, who when recently in Denmark had heard people saying that, if Haveloc could be found, he should come and claim the kingdom. Haveloc now said that, if he recovered his heritage, he would reward Grim's family.

Once in Denmark, Haveloc's party took lodgings in a town where Sigar Estalre, the former seneschal and justiciar of King Gunter, lived. He hated the usurping King Odulf for having killed Gunter with the help of Arthur, whom he had treasonably called in. Haveloc's party were attacked, because of his wife's beauty, by six young men, who carried her off; but Haveloc snatched up an axe in the house, pursued them, killed three and wounded the others, and recovered her. The hue and cry was now up, so he and his party took refuge in the tower of a church and defended themselves. Sigar arrived, saw Haveloc raining down stones on the attackers, noticed his resemblance to Gunter, called off the attack, and took them back to his hall, where he questioned Haveloc about his name, his parentage, and his wife.

Haveloc disclaimed knowledge of his origins, but recounted his story, and reported his name as *Haveloc* in childhood and *Cuaran* at Lincoln. Sigar remembered both the name *Haveloc* and the matter of the flame (of which a nurse of the boy had told him); that night he had the sleeping Haveloc watched, and the flame was duly seen and reported to him. Sigar now knew that his suspicion about Haveloc's identity was confirmed; and he saw the flame for himself.

Next day Sigar had Haveloc brought into the hall before all his men. He fetched in Gunter's horn, and offered a gold ring with life-saving properties to anyone who could sound it (which could in fact be done only by a king or the heir of a king). Haveloc alone succeeded, and Sigar acclaimed him as the rightful heir to Denmark. Sigar then summoned all his men and swore fealty to Haveloc along with them; all his barons, likewise, were summoned, and did the same.

They then marched against Odulf, and defeated him; and two princes who had supported him now sought mercy, along with the common people, and swore fealty to Haveloc, whom one and all made their lord and king. A great feast was held.

Haveloc next invaded England in force, and demanded from Edelsi the surrender of Argentille's heritage, but had to exact it by victory on the field of battle. Edelsi yielded, and the realm from Holland to Colchester was surrendered to Haveloc, who held a feast where all the barons did him homage. Edelsi died just afterwards; and Haveloc and Argentille ruled his kingdom for twenty years.

2. The *Lai d'Haveloc* is a version in 1112 octosyllabic lines of rhymed couplets, composed (in Bell's view) between *c.* 1190 and *c.* 1220.[36] We shall for convenience call it 'Anglo-Norman'—though linguistically it differs little from continental OF—mainly because it seems likely to have been composed in England. One of the two extant copies is in the College of Arms MS Arundel XIV (fos. 125ʳ–132ʳ), of the later fourteenth century. This MS also contains the fourth extant copy of Gaimar's *Estoire*, minus his version of the story of Haveloc, which the

[36] Ed. cit., pp. 25 ff.

Lai was therefore evidently meant to replace. The *Lai* is dependent on Gaimar,[37] according to the abundant evidence assembled by Bell:[38] whole lines and even couplets agree verbatim. The reverse relation is excluded by evidence of various kinds that the *Lai* is later in time.[39]

Bell has argued convincingly that the references to Arthur are based on Gaimar's.[40] These Arthurian associations, such as they are, may well have been what moved the author of this work to dress it up as a 'Breton *lai*'. He did so by means of the two standard devices of (*a*) an introductory statement (here very summary, 19–23) that the story is about an adventure, and that the Bretons named it after the hero, and (*b*) an ending of three lines according to which *li ancien* made a *lai* about Haveloc's victory. The content of the story shows that the *Lai d'Haveloc* has nothing in common with the 'strictly defined'[41] Breton *lais* in OF, and very little with any other works so styled by their authors. This is why we may warrantably doubt that the alleged Breton *Lai* of 19–23 in the *Lai d'Haveloc* ever existed.

Since the only reason for calling the ME version of the story of Havelok *The Lay of Havelok the Dane* was the existence of the so-called *Lai d'Haveloc*, and since both the scale and the story-pattern of the former are altogether different from those of the Breton *lais*, there is no basis for that misleading editorial title for the ME poem.

The *Lai d'Haveloc* runs (in summary form) as follows:

The Bretons made a *lai* about the adventure of a king called both Aveloc and Cuarant, and gave it both these names. He was the son of King Gunter of Denmark, in the time of Arthur, who invaded the land seeking tribute, fought and vanquished Gunter, and gave the kingdom to the traitor Odulf, who killed Gunter. Sigar Estalre, a powerful baron and the head of a disaffected group, had the keeping of a horn which could be sounded only by the rightful heir to the kingdom.

A baron named Grim had charge of Gunter's queen and his son, who was two years old, and from whose mouth, when he was asleep, there issued a flame with an exquisite aroma. To save the heir's life, Grim put to sea with them and his household; but pirates killed all on board save Grim (whom they knew), his wife and children, and Aveloc. They made land at Grimsby (then uninhabited, and thus named because Grim was the first to dwell there). Grim cut the ship in half and made a house out of it, and earned their living as a fisherman and by buying and selling salt. Grim changed Aveloc's name so that his identity should not be known, and everyone took him to be Grim's child.

---

[37] Ibid., pp. 32–58. [38] Ibid., pp. 34–8, especially p. 51.
[39] Ibid., Introd. pp. 21 ff. and *passim*. [40] Ibid., pp. 50–1.
[41] This conception is grounded in the recurrence, in several OF examples, of three distinctive and closely-related story-patterns. See G. V. Smithers, 'Story-Patterns in some Breton Lays', *MÆ* 22 (1953), 61–92.

Aveloc was precociously strong, and enterprising and mettlesome. Believing that he would yet come into his heritage, Grim decided that Aveloc must go elsewhere to fit himself for life, and sent him off to Lincoln with his own two sons, to find employment in which he could use his great physical strength. All three believed themselves to be brothers.

Lincoln and all Lindsey, Rutland, and Stamford were the domain of a British king Edelsi. The area towards Surrey was ruled by a King Achebrit, who had married Edelsi's sister Orwein and had a daughter named Argentille. Achebrit fell mortally ill, sent for Edelsi, and put his domains and his daughter in Edelsi's charge, after making him swear to bring her up and finally to give her in marriage to the strongest man who could be found. Achebrit died, as Orwein did just after him.

Aveloc was employed as a scullion in Edelsi's household at Lincoln, because he could lift heavy loads, cut wood, and carry water. Everyone called him Cuaran, since that was the Breton word for 'scullion'. Because of his strength he was often made to wrestle in public, and no one was a match for him. Edelsi, who wanted Argentille's heritage for himself, forcibly married her to Cuaran (as manifestly the 'strongest' man to be found).

Argentille felt humiliated by the marriage; and Aveloc slept on his face so that she should not see the flame (by which he felt embarrassed). But when the marriage had been consummated, and Aveloc forgot to do this, Argentille had a dream [almost exactly as in Gaimar's version]. She awoke in fear at it, to see her sleeping husband apparently on fire; and she roused him. He misexpounded the dream [just as in Gaimar's account] and could not explain the flame. A hermit whom Argentille then consulted about the dream said that it was prophetic: her husband was of royal birth and would be a king, and she would be a queen. She was to get him to take her to his kin, and she would learn the truth.

She and Cuaran accordingly went to Grimsby, taking the two sons of Grim, and found that Grim and his wife were dead. His daughter, Kelloc, now married to a merchant, learnt from Cuaran who his wife was, and revealed to him his own parentage, earlier history, and true name; and she said that on first arriving at Grimsby her family had changed his name to Cuaran. Her husband would take him and his party to Denmark, where the powerful Sigar Estalre (whose wife was of Aveloc's kin) still opposed the usurping king.

Once in Denmark, Kelloc's husband fitted them out with new clothes, and directed them to the court of the seneschal, Sigar Estalre. He instructed Aveloc to go to Sigar's castle and ask for lodging and a meal; and Argentille's beauty would thus impel those who saw them at Sigar's table to ask who he was and who had given him such a wife. The seneschal gave them dinner, and sent them to a lodging. On the way Argentille was carried off by six squires who had served at the meal and had been inflamed by her beauty. Aveloc at once pursued them, killed five and wounded one, recovered his wife, and took refuge with the others in a church tower, whence he rained stones on the attackers raised by the hue and cry.

The seneschal came to the scene, and noticed Aveloc's resemblance to Gunter. He stopped the assault, accepted Aveloc's account of the matter and elicited from him his previous history (which he said he had learnt from Grim), and his two names. Sigar recalled that *Aveloc* was the name of Gunter's son, and almost recognized him, but was doubtful. He lodged them in his castle, and had the sleeping Aveloc watched (since he knew of the flame from a former nurse of Aveloc's), was duly told of it, and rejoiced to have recovered the lawful heir of Gunter.

The next day Sigar assembled all his men, and brought Aveloc and Argentille before them. He sent for Gunter's horn, and promised a gold ring to anyone who sounded it. When Aveloc alone did so, Sigar presented him to the company as the rightful heir, and did homage to him, as all the others then did. They knighted Aveloc; Sigar assembled an army; they met Odulf in the field; and Aveloc insisted on single combat with him, killed him, and pardoned his followers. The Danes then made Aveloc king.

After reigning three years, Aveloc invaded England at his wife's request, to recover her heritage; he landed at Carleflod [a port near Saltfleet, in Lincs., that apparently ceased to exist in the thirteenth century]; and Edelsi yielded on the field of battle, and died fifteen days later. The Danes now ruled, from Holland to Colchester. Aveloc held a feast in the city; and he governed Lincoln and all Lindsey, and reigned twenty years. People long ago made a *lai* to commemorate his victory.

3. A ME account of 82 long lines in rhymed couplets, which has been interpolated in MS Lambeth 131 of Robert Mannyng's *Chronicle of England* and (by comparison with the two AN metrical versions) is a very compressed but remarkably circumstantial one. It tells the history of Havelok and Argill in the same order as the *Lai*. It says nothing of an oath sworn by Edelsye to Argill's dying father, or of the flame from Havelok's mouth, the radiant cross on his right shoulder (which is contained only in *Hav.*), or any process by which he was recognized, or of his wife's dream; but this might be by mere omission in a streamlined version.

It agrees closely enough otherwise with Gaimar and the *Lai* to have been based on a version very like theirs, and it gives little further help in the study of *Hav.* E. K. Putnam has argued[42] that it derives, not from Gaimar or the *Lai*, but from a version earlier than either, which was in French, was the common antecedent of all three, but which is very unlikely to have been the source of *Hav.*

> Forþ wente Gounter & his folk al in to Denemark.
> Sone fel þer hym vpon a werre styth & stark,
> þurgh a Breton kyng, þat out of Ingeland cam
> & asked þe tribut of Denmark, þat Arthur whylom nam.

4 þe: *suprascript*

[42] 'The Lambeth Version of *Havelok*', *PMLA* 15 (1900), 1–16.

þey wyþseide hit schortly, and non wolde þey ȝelde,   5
But raþer þey wolde dereyne hit wyþ bataill y þe felde.
Boþ partis on a day to felde come þey stronge:
Desconfit were þe Danes; Gounter his deþ gan fonge.
When he was ded þey schope brynge al his blod to schame.
But Gatferes doughter þe kyng, Eleyne was hure name,   10
Was kyng Gounteres wyf, and had a child hem bytwene,
Wyþ wham scheo scepade vneþe al to þe se wiþ tene.
þe child hym highte Hauelok, þat was his moder dere.
Scheo mette wiþ Grym atte hauene, a wel god marinere.
He hure knew, and highte hure wel to help hure wiþ his might,   15
To brynge hure saf out of þe lond wyþinne þat ilke night.

When þey come in myd-se, a gret meschef gan falle:
þey metten wyþ a gret schip, lade wyþ outlawes all.
Anon þey fullen hem apon, & dide him mikel peyne,
So þat wyþ strengþe of þeir assaut ded was quene Eleyne.   20
But ȝyt ascapede from hem Grym, wyþ Hauelok & oþer fyue,
& atte þe hauene of Grymesby, þer þey gon aryue,
þer was brought forþ child Hauelok, wyþ Grym & his fere,
Right also hit hadde be þer owen, for oþer wyste men nere,
Til he was mykel & mighti, & man of mykel cost,   25
þat for his grete sustinaunce nedly serue he most.
He tok leue of Grym & Seburc, as of his sire & dame,
And askede þer blessinge curteysly; þer was he nought to blame.

þenne drow he forþ norþward, to kynges court Edelsie,
þat held fro Humber to Rotland þe kyngdam of Lyndesye.   30
þys Edelsy, of Breton kynde, had Orewayn his sister bright
Maried to a noble kyng of Norþfolk, Egelbright.
Holly for his kyngdam he held in his hand
Al þe lond fro Colchestre right in til Holand.
þys Egelbright, þat was a Dane, & Orewayne þe quene,   35
Hadden gete on Argill, a doughter, hem bytwene.
Sone þen deyde Egelbright, and his wyf Orewayn,
& þerfore was kyng Edelye boþe joyful & fayn.
Anon þeir doughter & here eyr, his nece dame Argill,
& al þe kyngdam he tok in hande, al at his owene will.   40

þer serued Hauelok as quistron, & was ycald Coraunt.
He was ful mykel & hardy, & strong as a geaunt.
He was bold, curteys, & fre & fair, & god of manere,
So þat alle folk hym louede þat anewest hym were.
But for couetise of desheraison of damysele Argill,   45
& for a chere þat þe kyng sey scheo made Coraunt till,

He dide hem arraye ful symplely, & wedde togydere boþe.
For he ne rewarded desparagyng were manion ful wroþe.

A while þey dwelt after in court, in ful pore degre;
þe schame & sorewe þat Argill hadde hit was a deol to se. 50
þen seyde scheo til hure maister 'Of whenne, sire, be ȝe?
Haue ȝe no kyn ne frendes at hom, in ȝoure contre?
Leuer were me lyue in pore lyf wyþoute schame & tene
þan in schame & sorewe lede the astat of quene'.
þenne wente þey forþ to Grymesby, al by his wyues red, 55
& founde þat Grym & his wyf weren boþe ded.
But he fond þer on Aunger, Grymes cosyn hend,
To whom þat Grym & his wyf had teld, word & ende,
How þat hit stod wyþ Hauelok, in all manere degre.
& þey hit hym telde, & conseilled to drawe til his contre, 60
T'asaye what grace he mighte fynde among his frendes þere,
& þey wolde ordeyne for þeir schipynge, and al þat hem nede were.

When Aunger hadde yschiped hem, þey seilled forþ ful swyþe,
Ful but intil Denemark, wyþ weder fair & liþe.
þer fond he on sire Sykar, a man of gret pouste, 65
þat hey styward somtyme was of al his fader fe.
Ful fayn was he of his comyng, & god help hym bihight
To recouere his heritage of Edulf kyng & knyght.
Sone asembled þey gret folk of his sibmen & frendes;
Kyng Edulf gadered his power, & ageyn þem wendes. 70
Desconfyt was þer kyng Edulf & al his grete bataill,
& so conquered Hauelok his heritage, saunz faille.

Sone after he schop hym gret power in toward Ingelond—
His wyues heritage to wynne ne wolde he nought wonde.
þat herde þe kyng of Lyndeseye, he was come on þat cost, 75
& schop to fighte wyþ hym sone, & gadered hym gret host.
But atte day of bataill Edelsy was desconfit,
& after, by tretys, gaf Argentill hure heritage al quit.
& for scheo was next of his blod, Hauelokes wyf so feyr,
He gaf hure Lyndesey after his day, & made hure his eyr. 80
& atte last so byfel þat vnder Hauelokes schelde
All Norþfolk & Lyndesey holy of hym þey helde.

4. The unpublished AN prose *Brut* (i.e. a history of Britain, which in practice means a history of its kings) contains a summary but well-told version. In its earlier extant form this work ends with the year 1272, and survives in four MSS: (*a*) MS fonds fr. 14640, fos. 1–49b (the earliest MS, written *c.* 1300); (*b*) MS Nouvelle Acquisition 4267, fos. 9–14 (copied 1337; incomplete, and begins with the reign of John), both of the Bibliothèque Nationale; (*c*) Additional 35092, fos. 5–144 (mid-

fourteenth-century); (d) Cotton Tiberius A. vi, fos. 121–142 (c. 1420; incomplete), both of the British Museum.

This *Brut* was carried chronologically further, first in a continuation up to 1307; then in another up to c. 1333 (the battle of Halidon Hill), in two different forms termed the 'Short' and the 'Long' versions.[43]

The story of Havelok in the first-stage form of the AN prose *Brut* is a condensed version, a main feature of which is that it makes no mention of Grim. It has been printed from the earliest MS by Brie.[44] But this MS embodies one disastrous corruption, produced by a scribe or redactor who misunderstood a formally ambiguous context and wrote that Cuaran was the son of Havelok (which was reproduced in the ME prose *Brut*,[45] for which see 5 below). Another fundamental error (also reproduced in the ME translation) is the statement that Havelok was killed by Danes and Saxons, and was buried at Stonehenge. This has been transferred to him from Constantine, of whom it is said by Geoffrey of Monmouth.[46] The story is therefore reproduced here from MS Rawlinson D. 329, which—even though it represents the later continuation of the *Brut* to 1333—offers a more accurate and better text than that printed by Brie (see *Geschichte und Quellen*, p. 21):

55ᵛ   Cesti Constantin qe regna apres la mort Arthur estoit noble chiualer e
56ʳ vaillant de corps. . . . En tens Cesti Roi Constantin y aueient deux rois en
Bretanie. L'un aueit a noun Athelbright e feust Daneis, et tent tut le pais de
Norffolk e Suffolk; l'autre aueit a noun Edelsi, e feust breton, e tent Nicole,
Lyndeseie, e tote la terre iesqes a Humbre.   5
Ces deux rois s'entreguerrerent e mult se entreheierent; mes puis furent
acordez, e s'entre-amerent taunt com ils eussent esté freres d'une ventre. Le
roi Edelsi aueit vne soer q'aueit a noun Orwenne, e la dona par graunt amité
au roi Athelbright a feme; et il engendra de lui vne fille q'aueit a noun Goldeburgh. E le quint an apres, vne greeue maladie lui prist, e deueit morir; e 10
maunda le roi Edelsi, son frere en lei, qu'il vensit oue lui parler, et il vient
volenters. Donqe lui pria le roi Athelbright e li coniura el noun de Dieu q'il
apres sa mort preist sa fille Goldeburgh e sa terre, e la feit bien garder e nurrir
en sa chambre; et qaunt ele serreit d'age, q'il la dust marier au plus fort home e
plus vaillant qu'il poeit trouer, e la rendisist donqe sa terre. Edelsi lui graunta 15
e par serment afferma sa priere. Qant Edelbright fu mort et enterrée, Edelsi

---

[43] By F. W. D. Brie, *Geschichte und Quellen der mittelenglischen Prosachronik The Brute of England* (Marburg, 1905), pp. 13 ff. For further details on Bodleian MSS, see P. D. Record, *Summary Catalogue of Western MSS in the Bodleian Library* (Oxford, 1953), Index: 'Chronicles—Brut chronicles'.

[44] In 'Zum Fortleben der Havelok-sage', *Englische Studien* 35 (1905), 362–3.

[45] Ed. F. Brie, *The Brut, or The Chronicles of England*, vol. i (EETS, os 131, 1906), p. 92, ll. 22–3.

[46] Ed. Faral, ch. 180; cf. Thorpe, op. cit., xi. 4.

prist la damoisele e la nurrist en sa chaumbre, et ele deuent la plus bele
creature q'ome saueit. fo.

20 Le roi Edelsi son vncle pensa treiterousement en son queor coment il purra
la terre sa nece auer pur touz iours, e malueisement, encountre soun serment,
la pensa deceiure e trahir. E la maria a vn quistron de sa quisine, qe feust
appellé Kuarran; e si esteit il le plus haut, le plus fort, e le plus vaillant de
corps q'ome saueit en nule part. E la quidast hountousement auer marie, pur
auer eu sa terre a remenaunt. Mes il feust deceu, car cesti Kuarran fust le fiz le
25 roi Birkebain de Denmarz qe feust puis roi de Denmarz et appellé Hauelok. E
puis conquist la terre sa femme en Bretaigne, et occist le roi Edelsi, vncle sa
femme, et aueit tote la terre, *si com aliours est troué plius pleinement en l'estorie*.

Cesti Constantin ne regna qe .xx. aunz, car Sessons e Daneis li occirent; e
ceo feust graunt doel a tote Bretaigne. Brutons lui porterent a Stonheng et
30 illoqes l'enterrerent.[47]

27 *l'estorie*: MS lostorie

The fact that this account has been set in Constantine's reign shows
that it is based on Gaimar.[48] The name *Birkabeyn* in MS BN fonds fr.
14640 might have been substituted for Gaimar's *Gunter* by a scribe
(since the MS is of *c.* 1300, by which time he might have had access to the
extant *Hav.*), just as *Goldeburgh* in the fourteenth-century MS Rawlinson D. 329 is only too likely to have been substituted for *Argentille* of the
first form of the *Brut* by a scribe. But the use of Goldeburgh in an earlier
passage of the *Brut* (see pp. lxvii–lxix), in both the Additional and the
BN MSS, requires a different explanation, and is very important.

The italicized clause in the antepenultimate sentence is potentially
important, but is ambiguous. *L'estorie* might denote either the AN
prose *Brut* itself, or its source. If the former is meant, the reference
must be to the short statement (at an earlier point in the *Brut*) about
Havelok's title to rule England by his marriage to the lawful heir that
is discussed below (pp. lxviiff.). But the phrase *plius pleinement* (either
'more plainly' or 'more fully') may imply a full form of the story, rather
than an outline such as this one in the AN prose *Brut*. On the whole,
this seems the more probable interpretation.

A gloss of sorts on our reference is available in a very summary
version of the story of Havelok in an anonymous Latin prose chronicle

---

[47] *Variant readings of MS BN fr. 14640*:
    4, 8, 15, 16: Edelsi: Edelfy   8: amité: admyrabilite
    9–10, 13: Goldeburgh: Argentille   11: Edelsi: Edelfi
    15: trouer: Arouer   18: saueit: purreyt trouer
    19: Edelsi: Edelphi   23: saueit: oy parler
    24–5: Car cesti Curran fu a Hauelok fyz le roy Birkebeyn ke puis
        fu roy de Denemarz
[48] Brie, 'Zum Fortleben der *Havelok*-sage', p. 363.

in MS Cotton Domitian ii, fos. 130–141, which begins with Arthur and ends with the year 1292, and is palaeographically dated *c.* 1300. Brie judged this version to be derived from Gaimar;[49] and he may well have been right, since it not only sets the story in the reign of Constantine, but tells it of two local kings (respectively a Dane and a Briton), and uses the names *Argentille* and *Gunter*. But he also stated that it has no direct connection with the AN prose *Brut*. We must, therefore, note (as he did not) that the final sentence in it corresponds quite closely to the italicized clause above in the *Brut*, and sounds like a reproduction of it or of something like it:

Fuerat enim filius Dacie [regis] vocatus Hauelocke, cuius pater vocabatur Gunter, qui ab Arthuro fuerat interfectus. *Huius* [i.e. Hauelok's] *hystoria patet alibi, et qualiter conquesiuit regnum suum primo in Dacia, posterea in Anglis*, vbi regnauit xx annis.

1 [regis]: not in MS

The phrase *patet alibi* is a trifle vague, and possibly evasive: the writer himself may not have understood just which work was meant. But for what it is worth, the italicized sentence sounds more like a reference to the full form of the story than not.

5. The ME *Brute of Englande*,[50] the first part of which to 1333 is a translation of the AN prose *Brut*, contains the story of Havelok in a form that corresponds closely to the version of the latter. It is thus of no independent interest in connection with *Hav.*; but it is included here as a handy means of reference in the absence so far of an edition of the AN prose *Brut*.

6. A brief account of certain main points in the story of Havelok is contained in the unpublished AN prose chronicle *Le Petit Bruit*, which (according to the author's own statement, fo. 1ʳ) was composed in 1310 at the request of Henry de Lacy, Earl of Lincoln, by Meistre Rauf de Bohun, of whom nothing more is known.[51] This work is preserved in only one copy, in MS Harley 902, fos. 1–11ᵛ, in a hand of the later fifteenth century (commonly but mistakenly reported as a seventeenth-century one). What it says of Havelok is as follows:

Apres ceo vient Adelwold son fitz [of Edmund] que reigna xvj [aunz] et demie; si engendroit ij feiz et iij filis, dount trestoutz murrirent frechement

1 [aunz]: not in MS

---

[49] 'Zum Fortleben der *Havelok*-Sage', p. 364.   [50] Ed. F. Brie (see above, n. 15).
[51] See M. D. Legge, *Anglo-Norman Literature and its Background* (Oxford, 1963), pp. 280–3.

fors que sa puné file. Le out a nom Goldburgh, del age de vj aunz kaunt son
pere Adelwold morust.

5 Cely Roy Adelwold, quant il doit morir, comaunda sa file a garder a vn Count
de Cornewayle, al houre kaunt il [le] quidou*t* hountousment auoir deparagé,
quant fit Hauelok fitz le Roy Byrkenbayne de Denmarche esposer le encountre
sa volunte, que primis fuit Roy d'Engleterre et de Denmarch tout a vn foitz. Par
quele aliaunce leis Daneis queillerent grendre mestrie en Engleterre, et long
10 temps puise le tindrunt, si cum vous nouncie *L'Estorie de Grimesby* come Grime
primiz nurist Hauelok en Engleterre depuis cel houre q'il feut chasé de Denmarch etc., deqis al houre q'il vint au chastell de Nichole, que cely auauntdit
traitre Goudrich out en garde, en quel chastel il auauntdit Hauelok espousa
l'auauntdit Goldeburgh que fuit heir d'Engleterre.

15 Et par cel reson tynt cely Hauelok la terre de Denmarch auxi comme son
heritage, et Engleterre auxi par mariage de sa femme. Et si entendrez vous,
que par la reson que ly auauntdit Gryme ariua primez kaunt il amena l'enfaunt
Hauelok hors de Denmark, par meyme la reson reseut cele vile son nom de
Grime, quel noun ly tint vnquore Grimisby.

20 Apres ceo regna meyme cely Hauelok, que mult fuit prodhomme et
droiturell, et bien demenoit son people en reson et ley. Cel Roy Hauelok
reigna xli aunz; si engendroit ix fitz et vij filis, dount trestoutz murreround ainz
que furunt d'age, fors soulement iiij de ses feitz, dont l'un out a noum Gurmound, cely que entendy auoir son heir en Engleterre. Le secound out a noum
25 Knout, q'en fitz feffoit son pere en le regne de Denmarch quant il estoit del
age de xviij aunz, et ly misme se tynt a la coroune d'Engleterre, quel terre il
entendy al oeps son ainez fitz Gurmound auoir gardé. Mes il deb*r*isa son col
auxi comme il feu mounté vn cheval testous que poindre voileyt, en l'an de son
regne xxiij entrant.

30 Le tiers fitz out a non Godard, que son pere feffoit de la Seneschacie
d'Engleterre que n'auout taunt com ore fait ly quart. Et le puisnez fitz de toutz
out a noum Thorand, que espousa la Countesse de Hertouwe en Norwey. Et
par la reson que cely Thorand feut enherité en la terre de Norwey, ly et ses
successours sont enheritez ieces en sa par*t*e. Toutdis puis y auoit affinité de
35 alliaunce entre ceulx de Denmarch et ceulx de Norwey, a checun venue que
vnkes firent en ceste terre pur chalenge ou cleyme mettre, iekes a taunt que
lour accion feut en *f*eyne destrut par vn noble chevaller Guy de Warwike etc.
Et tout ensy feffoit Hauelok sez quatre fitz; si gist a priorie de Grescherch en
Loundrez. [fo. 6ᵛ ends]

40　6 [le]: *not in MS*　quidout *C. A. Robson*: MS qui douie　27 deb*r*isa: *MS*
debusa　34 par*t*e: *MS* parce　37 en *f*eyne: *MS* enseyne

Rauf's main source for the work as a whole is unknown. He says (fo. 1ʳ)
that it has been *abbreggé hors du grant Bruit*; but the latter work has not
been identified.[52] The main point of interest for our purpose here is

[52] See F. Madden, *The Ancient English Romance of Havelok the Dane* (Roxburghe Club,
1828), p. 20.

that, alone among our early authors, he uses the same names for the main characters as *Hav.* does. What is especially significant and revealing is that these include the name *Godrich* and his title, which are peculiar to *Hav.* among these early versions and are likely to be inventions by the author of *Hav.* (for reasons explained in 178 n. and 1608 n.). Moreover, in his sequel on the four sons of Havelok, the Danish usurper has been transformed into one of them, who is *named Godard*, and whom Havelok made *the seneschal* of England. These two points imply knowledge of the form of story that was available only in *Hav.* among the previous versions.

Furthermore, in his statement (fo. 2^r) about the four royal roads of Britain, Rauf introduces Roxburgh and Dover as the terminal points of one of these roads. These two places are not represented in any other form of the traditional statement transmitted in chronicles, and must surely derive from *Hav.* 139 and 265 (in the second of which they are named as the extremities of *a* route through England, though nothing is said of any other three).

Rauf's version of the story says nothing of the Danish usurper, nor of the hero's father, nor of his being a scullion in the castle at Lincoln (which, in a summary account, are all no doubt mere omissions). One symptom that Havelok's status in Lincoln as a scullion has simply been left out is that its absence leaves the 'disparagement' ('being given in marriage to someone below one's station') of Goldeburgh both unexplained and unmotivated. In this account, she is made to marry someone described only as the King of Denmark's son—which is no 'disparagement' at all—and there is no hint that it is done in order that Goudrich may seize the kingdom for himself. Rauf does mention Grim as having got Havelok out of Denmark and brought him up, and as the founder of Grimsby. This, like the personal names, shows that Rauf's source cannot have been the AN prose *Brut*.

There is thus enough in Rauf's account to suggest that he used *Hav.* as his source. Apart from the foregoing evidence for this, the work he calls *L'Estorie de Grimesby* (l. 10) has usually been taken to be *Hav.* What speaks for this view is his immediately following summary of the early history of Havelok (up till his marriage) as told in *L'Estorie*. It agrees with *Hav.*, since it includes the names *Goudrich* and *Goldeburgh* (which are not those used by Gaimar and the *Lai*). And Grim's alleged role as the founder of Grimsby, which was named after him according to *Hav.* 744–7, shows at least this element in the story of *Hav.* to be a 'founding-legend'.[53] Moreover,

[53] See H. Matter, *Englische Gründungssagen von Geoffrey of Monmouth bis zur Renaissance*

this aspect of it is confirmed by the extraordinary fact that the town seal of Grimsby (of the thirteenth century) should depict and name the three main characters in the story of *Hav.* Clearly, the point and the meaning of the seal are to state the founding-legend: *L'Estorie de Grimesby* is not so arbitrary a name as it might seem.[54]

In any case, however, Rauf's version is valuable in providing a later limit of 1310 for the composition of *Hav.*, and a clear association of the poem with Lincoln.

The table given below of the personal names in each version shows that all but two in *Hav.* are distinctive, and that Rauf's are likely to derive from the corresponding ones there.

The two different sets of names are not enough to constitute two different traditions, i.e. to imply that there were two different antecedents for *Hav.* on the one hand and the first four versions on the other. For one thing, several of the divergent names in *Hav.* are undeniably innovations or inventions (see pp. lx–lxi and lxix–lxxi).

It is a striking fact that all the other versions except the *Lai* are contained in chronicles; and, as we have noted, the *Lai*, in one of the two extant MSS, looks like having been substituted for Gaimar's version (since it immediately follows a copy of *L'Estoire* in that MS). This is a useful hint that they are all essentially akin (viz. in being accounts of dynastic history), and is a clue to the kind of interest that the author of *Hav.* may have found in the story (see pp. lvi ff.).

The interrelations of some or all of the first three versions above,[55] and their relation to *Hav.*, have been explored over the years;[56] but where *Hav.* is concerned, finality has not been reached and is hardly possible. The main issue regarding *Hav.* (as prescribed by the relative chronology of the various versions) is whether it derives from Gaimar or the *Lai* (or both), or is independent of them. This, as a particular question, is dealt with below under *Sources*: the comparative analysis of Gaimar, the *Lai*, and *Hav.* (III below) suggests that the author of *Hav.* need not have had a main source or sources beyond these two.

(Anglistische Forschungen, 66, Heidelberg, 1922), pp. 241–80, for an illuminating analysis of the origins of the whole story of Havelok.

[54] For the seal of Grimsby, see our frontispiece, and Sisam's edition §12 and n. 1, and our Appendix B.
[55] See e.g. M. Kupferschmidt, 'Die Haveloksage bei Gaimar und ihr Verhältniss zum Lai d'Haveloc', Böhmer's *Romanische Studien*, 4 (1880), 411–30, especially 429–30; E. K. Putnam, op. cit., n. 12 above; and especially A. Bell, *Le Lai d'Haveloc and Gaimar's Haveloc Episode*, pp. 29–79.
[56] e.g. H. E. Heyman, *Studies on the Havelok-Tale*, pp. 139–48; E. Fahnestock, *A Study of the Sources and Composition of the Old French Lai d'Haveloc* (Bryn Mawr diss., 1915; New York, pp. 25–57 (a useful table of parallel passages, with comments).

Gaimar	*Lai*	Lambeth	AN *Brut*	*Hav.*	Rauf de Bohun
Adelbriht, Albriht	Achebrit	Egelbright	Athelbright	Aþelwold	Adelwold
Or(e)wain	Orwein	Orewayn	Orwenne	——*	——
Argentille	Argentille	Argill, Argentille	Argentille	Goldeborw	Gold(e)burgh
Edelsi(s)	Edelsi(s)	Edelsie	Edelsi	Godrich, Earl of Cornwall	Goudriche, Count of Cornwall
Guntier	Gunter(s)	Gounter	Birkebein	Birkabeyn	Byrkenbayne
Alvive	——	Eleyne	——	——	——
Gaifier	——	Gatfer	——	——	——
Odulf	Odulf	Edulf	——	Godard	[Godard]
Haveloc Cuaran(t)	Aveloc Cuaran(t)	Hauelok Coraunt	Hauelok Kuarran	Hauelok [——]	Hauelock [——]
——	——	——	——	Swanborw	——
				Elfled	
Sigar Estalre	Sigar Estal	Sykar	——	Ubbe	——
Grim	Grim	Grym	——	Grim	Grime
Sebruc	Seburc	Seburc	——	Leue	——
Kelloc	Kelloc	——	——	Gunnild	——
——	——	——	——	Leuiue	——
[——]	[——]	——	——	Robert þe Rede	——
[——]	[——]	——	——	Huwe Rauen	——
——	——	——	——	William Wendut	——
Algiers	——	Aunger	——	——	——
[——]	——	——	——	Reyner, Earl of Chester	——
[——]	——	——	——	Earl Gunter	——
——	——	——	——	Griffin Galle	——

* A dash here means that neither the name nor the person is represented; a dash in square brackets, that a corresponding person occurs but not the (or a) name; and a name in square brackets, that the role of the person thus named has been modified or blurred.

A main general question is whether some or all of the first three versions in our table derive (as was argued by Kupferschmidt and accepted by others) from a lost AN romance in rhymed couplets. Bell has challenged and refuted this view, where Gaimar and the *Lai* are concerned. What we must ask here is whether Gaimar's version, the *Lai*, the Lambeth Interpolation, and the AN prose *Brut*, or any of these, on the one hand, or *Hav.* on the other, give any signs of being genetically the earlier.

In general, *Hav.* is much more remote than all these versions are from an 'original' stage (if there was an antecedent form of the story earlier than any of them, and one from which they might all ultimately derive), since so much in it is demonstrably due to innovations that might well be by the author of the extant *Hav.* (see IV, 3), e.g. most of the names. As their names are independent of those in *Hav.*, one might think that the story too, as told in these versions, might be independent of *Hav.* and thus genetically as well as chronologically older.

III. THE RELATION OF *HAUELOK* TO THE OTHER MAIN VERSIONS

The first step towards understanding the distinctive literary character and qualities of *Hav.* is to compare the way in which the action is handled in all these three works. The 'action', which is essentially the 'story', in practice sometimes inevitably takes in the motivation, i.e. it becomes (intermittently) the 'plot'.

1. Gaimar and the *Lai*, in presenting the story as one that concerned two local kings of eastern England, one of whom ruled over Lincoln and Lindsey, may have picked up at least one scrap of archaic tradition. There really was, in the historic period, an ancient line of kings of Lindsey, which went back to the Anglo-Saxon conquest. It ended with one *Aldfrið*, who can be identified with an *Ealdfrid rex*, of whom all that is known is that he attested (evidently as an under-king) a confirmation by Offa of Mercia of a grant of land in an undated Sussex charter.[57] It appears, from various clues, that Aldfrið probably did not outlive the eighth century. The name of the fourth member of the line (omitting such persons as Woden) is the hybrid *Caedbaed*, with the OE *-baed* plus the British word *cad* 'battle': it must, therefore, be assumed to imply that by his time there had been some contact (and perhaps intermarriage) between the Anglo-Saxon invaders and an indigenous Celtic population.[58] We should accordingly note that according to Gaimar (59), Edelsi of Lindsey *esteit Bretun* 'was a Briton', and accord-

---

[57] Birch, *Cartularium Saxonicum*, vol. i, No. 262, pp. 365–6.

[58] These facts and conclusions have been elicited from an early ninth-century genealogy in MS Cotton Vespasian B. vi by F. M. Stenton, 'Lindsey and its Kings', in *Preparatory to Anglo-Saxon England*, ed. D. M. Stenton (Oxford, 1970), pp. 127–35.

ing to the *Lai* (202) *esteit Brez par linage* 'was an inhabitant of *Britaine*'.[59] Adelbriht was of Danish descent, according to Gaimar (58).

Gaimar and the author of the *Lai* were content to place their story in an earlier time than their own; in this regard they probably followed the received form of it. The author of *Hav.*, writing a hundred and fifty years after Gaimar, and a century after the *Lai* was composed, has modernized it: he presents a single ruler of all England, and a usurper (Godrich), who consequently has had to be reduced from the royal status that he has in Gaimar's version and the *Lai*: he is an earl, as the next best thing. As Earl of Cornwall, however, he recalls a great personage of that title in real life, who was King Henry III's brother Richard (1209–72)[60] and was made earl in 1227. The differences in status are likely, and the startling choice of this illustrious earldom virtually certain, to be innovations in *Hav.*

2. The structure of the individual histories of Hauelok and his wife in each version can be summarized thus:

I. Gaimar
   1. Begins with the story of Argentille, which he tells economically up to the point where Edelsi (*a*) has brought her up in Lincoln and Lindsey (but without ill-treating her as Godrich did Goldeborw), and (*b*) married her against her will to a scullion named Cuaran.
   2. Then gives a brief account of Cuaran—but only from the point where he was already established in Edelsi's service.
   3. Does not disclose the previous history of Havelok (up till he left Grimsby for Lincoln) till he and Argentille have returned to Grimsby, when Havelok himself first learns it, from the lips of Grim's daughter Kelloc.

II. The *Lai*
   1. Begins with the story of Havelok, told from the outset till the point when he and Grim's two sons left Grimsby for Lincoln (= G 3).
   2. Then deals with Argentille up to the point when she passed into Edelsi's charge (= G 1(*a*)).
   3. Next, gives a sketch of Cuaran at Edelsi's court in Lincoln (= G 2).
   4. Recounts the forced marriage (= G 1(*b*)).
   5. Repeats 1 and 4 in Havelok's account of himself to Sigar Estal.

III. *Hauelok*
   1. Begins with the story of Goldeborw, up to her imprisonment in the castle at Dover, 316–30 (= G 1(*a*) and *Lai* 2).
   2. Tells Havelok's story continuously up till and including his triumph at putting the stone.
   3. Shows how Godrich formed the plan of marrying Goldeborw to Havelok, had her brought to Lincoln, told her of his intention and coerced her and Havelok by menaces into complying.

---

[59] The terms are ambiguous; but see A. Bell, ed. cit., p. 261.   [60] See 178 n.

4. Repeats Havelok's early history (up till his upbringing at Grimsby) in (*a*) his account of it to the three sons of Grim (1401–35), and (*b*) Ubbe's virtually identical account to the Danes (2205–40).

After Havelok's return to Grimsby, the ordering of events is linear in all three versions. His departure for Denmark launched the process by which the two long drawn out crises (in his fortunes and Goldeborw's respectively) were gradually unravelled. The pattern of the action is much the same in all three works. The following summary, for convenience, presents the version of *Hav.*; its divergences from the other two are set in square brackets and are discussed below:

5. Havelok [masquerading as a merchant] and his party made their way to [the *iustise*] Ubbe, who gave them a meal and sent them out to a lodging for the night.

6. After the party [at the house of the town *greyue*, who had given them lodging at Ubbe's request] was attacked unsuccessfully [by a gang of murderous robbers], Ubbe lodged them the next night in his castle. As a result, he discovered, by the flame emitted from Havelok's mouth in his sleep, that the young man was the heir to the throne of Denmark; and he then realized how strongly Havelok resembled Birkabeyn. Havelok was alarmed [by the joyous response of Ubbe's men, in kissing his feet].

7. Ubbe made his followers and all the loyal adherents of the dead king (in two successive stages) do homage and swear fealty to Havelok. Ubbe dubbed him knight and made him king; and there was feasting [and games for forty days].

[8. Havelok knighted the three sons of Grim, made them barons, and gave them land and possessions.]

9. Havelok then sent a strong force [under Robert the Red to find and capture the Danish usurper] by which the latter was duly defeated, [brought back, sentenced by a court of Havelok's assembled subjects, flayed and hanged for his treason].

[10. Havelok took seisin of all Godard's possessions and at once transferred them to Ubbe.]

[11. Havelok vowed to found a priory of Black Monks in memory of Grim, and duly did so in Grimsby.]

12. The English usurper [having learnt that Havelok had invaded England in force] mustered his army, [which included Reyner the Earl of Chester, at Lincoln], did battle [near Grimsby], and was overcome by Havelok in person.

13. Havelok pardoned the defeated English fighting-men. [They acknowledged Goldeborw as queen; and Havelok made them sentence Godrich, who was burnt at the stake.]

14. The Englishmen all did homage and swore fealty to Havelok,

[15. who then gave Grim's two daughters in marriage to the Earl of

Chester and Bertram, the Earl of Cornwall's cook, respectively, and made Bertram Earl of Cornwall.]

16. Havelok bestowed lands and property on his Danish followers, and then went to London to be crowned.

[17. Havelok charged Ubbe with the rule of Denmark as his *iustise* and the Danes returned there.]

18. Havelok remained in England with Goldeborw, and they reigned for [sixty] years [in idyllic happiness and had fifteen children, who all became kings or queens].

There is thus a main difference between *Hav.* on the one hand and Gaimar and the *Lai* on the other. The two latter both recount the history of Havelok in two separate parts. Both divide it into his experiences up till he set out for Lincoln, and those at Edelsi's court, but in a different sequence, which in the *Lai* is chronological, but in Gaimar's telling is reversed. In *Hav.*, the hero's whole history (up to the pivotal point of his return to Grimsby, which is the starting-point for his experiences in Denmark), is told in one piece, and in chronological order.

The two separate histories of Havelok and Goldeborw (up to the time when they converged) could evidently be ordered in at least two ways. The narrator could either (*a*) take one of them close to the point of convergence and then mark time with it while he told the other, or (*b*) pick up the thread of one at about the point of convergence and tell the previous part of it later by casting back in time. The *Lai* and *Hav.* have followed the first method, and Gaimar the second.

The arrangement in *Hav.*, however, alone among the three, has the advantage of continuity in the story of the hero and is, on the whole, more effective, in this instance at least (though that might be partly or wholly for quite other reasons, such as the author's use of opportunities for invention of whole scenes, or of motivation, or of dialogue). One slight reservation to be made is that when the narrator in *Hav.* marks time with the story of Goldeborw, he does so by leaving her imprisoned in the castle at Dover, for what must have been a long time—right up till her forced marriage, when Godrich has her fetched to Lincoln. It seems more natural to leave her (as Gaimar and the *Lai* do) being brought up in Edelsi's household at Lincoln.

A third point is that Ubbe, who in 2207–20 had been recalling matters of common knowledge, then (2221–40) recounted the details of Havelok's escape from death and his flight with Grim by sea—including the remarkable one that Godard had been moved by pity not to kill the boy himself. The question is how Ubbe knew all this: no one is said to have told him. Presumably, authorial omniscience has here been allowed to spill over into Ubbe's discourse to the Danes because he had briefly assumed the part of the narrator.

But these things are altogether overshadowed by the author's inspired stroke in making Goldeborw bring out the central idea of the story and the unconscious irony in what Godrich planned, by swearing that she would marry only a king or a king's heir (1112–17)—which was just what she was being made to do, without knowing it.

3. The symmetry in the accounts of Aþelwold and Birkabeyn in *Hav.* is especially pronounced in the more dramatic moments of the action. Birkabeyn died, not in battle as his equivalent Gunter did, but in bed—and is of course provided with a death-bed scene like that of Aþelwold (if briefer). The parallelism is carried into the depiction of the Danish usurper Godard (whose un-Danish name has the same first element as the English usurper's): not only is he presented (like Godrich) as an earl, but he is similarly entrusted with the king's children and the duty of securing the heir's succession. He, likewise, is thus able to get his hands on them. And he matches and goes beyond what Godrich had done to Goldeborw, when he butchers Havelok's two little sisters and arranges for the murder of Havelok.

Neither Gaimar nor the *Lai* mentions sisters of Havelok. If they have been added in the ME version, as seems likely, it was presumably done to heighten the pathos of Havelok's situation and the wickedness of Godard. On the other hand, *Hav.* does not mention either Goldeborw's or Havelok's mother. The only function of Argentille's mother Orwain was to provide the link of kinship between Edelsi and Argentille; and of Havelok's mother to have the initial keeping of the heir and make him safe from Odulf. In *Hav.*, Goldeborw is not represented as Godrich's niece. But the kinship might be thought to be implied in Godrich's status as Earl of Cornwall, if this really is some sort of allusion to Henry III's brother Richard of Cornwall. On the other hand, Godard is explicitly said to be King Birkabeyn's kinsman (*frende* 375 seems less likely here to mean 'friend') though without further definition: it would not be untypical of *Hav.* for this to have been transferred from the English to the Danish usurper.

As for Havelok's mother, the different use made of Grim in *Hav.* (as a thrall who was intended to murder the heir: see 5 below) perhaps made it difficult to accommodate her in the action. In any case, the two royal mothers may have been left out in the interests of economy: they do very little in the other two versions and are very soon got out of the way.

One other difference in the number of subsidiary kin is that in *Hav.*

Grim has three sons and two daughters, instead of two sons and one daughter. Moreover, in *Hav.* the hero goes to Lincoln alone, without the complication of having to look after two sons of Grim there.

4. The parallelism has made an opening for one piece of what is surely felicitous invention, and a gain on any showing. The scene (450–522) in which Havelok had to stand by and see his two sisters barbarously murdered, and then pleaded for his own life, contrives a neat psychological sketch of how the blackest heart could veer briefly towards compassion before relapsing into cruelty. What is striking in it is Havelok's remarkably sophisticated conduct in offering never to reveal that he was the son and heir of the Danish king or to take up arms against the usurper: he could not have been an infant of two years, as in the *Lai* 70 (where, however, the v.l. vii occurs).

But what matters is that, thus early in the story, the author has (on the surface, smoothly) disposed of the pivotal issue (which has given some trouble in the AN versions) of when Havelok first knew of his royal birth. This is clearly an alteration, since it has elicited consequential changes, and indeed two or three slight inconsistencies, in the action of *Hav.* (see 8 below).

In Gaimar's version and the *Lai*, Havelok first learnt of his royal descent and of his history before going to Lincoln, from Grim's daughter Kelloc, after returning to Grimsby. The immediate reason for this is that he was too young to know when he was brought away from Denmark. But the knowledge of his identity, in himself and others, has in the AN versions become entangled with attempts to use his byname (i.e. that of the tenth-century Viking Anlaf Sihtricsson, no longer understood to be a byname) as a pseudonym.

Gaimar, beginning Havelok's story at the point where he was already a scullion in Edelsi's household, presents him as Cuaran, without explaining why he was so called, and first introduces his true name in Kelloc's account (420) of his earlier history. Havelok took this a little further by telling Sigar Estalre (809–11) that at court he was called Cuaran, but as a small boy at Grimsby (as he had recently been informed) Haveloc. At no point, however, does Gaimar say anything to explain why Havelok had two names.

It is clear that neither Havelok nor Grim's two sons (whom he took with him to Lincoln) had any inkling of his identity; yet Kelloc knew of it. Grim must, therefore, presumably have kept the facts from the three youths, but revealed them to Kelloc. This is faintly surprising, and raises doubts: is the order in which Gaimar recounts Havelok's experiences an alteration of an earlier or original pattern?

In the *Lai*, the story opens with an account of Havelok's life from the earliest stage. But Grim is here said to have changed the boy's name after they reached Grimsby in order that Havelok should not be known (149–50), i.e. in order to protect him. The fact of this change was repeated by Kelloc, when enlightening Havelok. Neither of them said outright that the new name was Cuaran (though it surely must have been). But the author in his own person says that all at the court in Lincoln called the young man Cuaran, *because that was the Breton word for 'scullion'*. It was nothing of the kind, but a Celtic (Irish and Gaelic) word for 'sock, legging'. The statement is a transparent attempt to provide a reason for the curious fact that the hero had two names; and it is all but explicitly irreconcilable with the previous information that (*a*) Grim had changed Havelok's name (*b*) for quite a different reason, and with Kelloc's later mention of the change (615–16).

In *Hav.* the name *Cuaran* is never mentioned; the handling of Havelok's identity is in consequence simple and straightforward. One cannot help wondering whether someone among the servants in the castle would not have been bound to notice the flame, and the cross on Havelok's shoulder, at some time when he was asleep. But the story required that his royal birth should remain unknown to Godrich and to all connected with the usurper, since the point of the forced marriage was Havelok's supposed low birth. Thus it also required that Havelok should not be known by his real name at Godrich's court: calling him *Cuaran* at that stage must have been a means of disguising him, and must therefore (in the story) have been Grim's doing (as the *Lai* represents it). This means was to hand because the two names would have been received as a combined name (since the byname *Cuaran* could not have been evolved independently of *Anlaf*; see p. lv). The author of *Hav.* (or an antecedent version) apparently cut the knot by simply letting Havelok go under the same name all the time.

5. The demotion of Godard to the status of earl (from that of his equivalent Odulf as king), as a main example of how Godard has been assimilated to the English usurper, has issued in a muffled inconsistency that affects the status of Ubbe. The gist of it is that Ubbe, as the equivalent of Sigar Estal(re), must in an earlier form of the story (even if that form is represented only in Gaimar and the *Lai*) have been the seneschal of Denmark under Birkabeyn. The author of *Hav.*, however, has thought fit to present Godard (as a non-royal usurper of supreme power) as the seneschal: he calls Godard by the equivalent native term once, in speaking of him as [*of*] *Denmark stiward* (667).

The implicit inconsistency in Ubbe's status is that in *Hav.* there are properly two seneschals—Ubbe being a displaced one (though this is not mentioned), and Godard a usurping one. The author was evidently aware of this inconsistency, since he refrains from ever referring to Ubbe as seneschal (or *steward*). But Gaimar makes it explicitly clear (505–6, quoted below) that Ubbe had been seneschal under Havelok's father. And the point is made still clearer and more explicit in ll. 165–6 of the interpolation in the Lambeth MS of Mannyng's *Chronicle* (in which the story is essentially the same as in Gaimar and the *Lai*, and independent of *Hav.*, as e.g. the personal names show):

> . . . sire Sykar, a man of gret pouste,
> That *hey styward somtyme was of al his fader fe*.

This view is prescribed by the collective testimony of all the three early versions. In the *Lai*, Sigar Estal is repeatedly referred to as 'seneschal' (e.g. 649–50, 665, 671, 689, 737, 767, 807)—indeed, more often than by name. And Gaimar gives him the same office, with an important addition:

> *Seneschal* ert al rei Guntier
> E *de sa terre justisier*.   (505–6)

Moreover, according to the *Lai*, Havelok's party, in order to meet Sigar Estal, had to make their way to his *curt*:

> . . . *la curt* al *seneschal*
> K'um apellot Sigar Estal.   (649–50)

They duly found him there; and it was in his castle:

> . . . La ou li *seneschals* maneit.
> Al chastel alerent tut dreit;
> Le seignur en *sa curt* troverent.   (655–7)

Things are very much the same in the equivalent situation in *Hav.* When the hero and his party were to eat a meal with Ubbe, they too went to his 'court', which is here called *þe heye curt* (1686). In the context of the episode, this phrase may seem ambiguous. But *curt* is more likely to refer to a part of the castle or its precincts (as in OF *basse court* 'ground level area in which cattle or horses are kept (within a castle)') than to a court of law, and *heye* to be a concrete use 'upper' than the figurative 'of high status'. They found him in his hall (1695), and took a meal there with him; and they were later lodged in sleeping-quarters in the 'high tower' (2074).

Ubbe clearly could not be presented in *Hav.* as the *steward* of Denmark, as that was what Godard had already been declared to be

(667). But the author has left Ubbe with the rest of what Gaimar and the *Lai* attributed to Sigar Estal(re). He was a *iustise* (1629 and 2203), and finally Havelok's (i.e. a king's) *iustise* (2959). This probably means 'chief justiciar', since the context in 2959 shows that he was to have the supreme power in Denmark because Havelok would be residing in England, and since Gaimar's phrase *de sa terre justisier* seems to imply jurisdiction of the realm. On the whole, Ubbe's status is less clearly defined than that of Sigar Estal(re). The term Estalre itself (ME *stallere*, LOE *steallere*, ON *stallari*) does not recognizably clarify matters, as a word meaning 'high official in the king's household'.

6. The role given Godard in *Hav.* ruled out the use of Grim as a trusted adherent of the Danish king to whom the care of the queen and the heir could safely be entrusted (as in the *Lai* 57 ff.) and in whose ship she and Havelok could flee the country (as in Gaimar 421–2 and the *Lai* 89 ff.). Godard's intended murder of Havelok called for the services of someone of servile status, who could be expected not to withstand a command to commit murder or to resist the bait of manumission for it, and could then be repudiated as lying if he invoked his lord's bidding as an excuse. But the story required that Havelok should survive; Grim has, therefore, been used for two purposes, since he still carried out what must have been his original function in the story and saved Havelok's life by getting him away from Denmark.

One result of all this is an inconsistency in the conduct and even the character of Grim in *Hav.* He had been willing to murder a small (if surprisingly articulate) boy for the mercenary motive of gaining his freedom and a cash reward; but he suddenly showed an overwhelming care and concern for the boy's welfare when he learnt who he was. The inconsistency may even be implied in Havelok's report to the three sons of Grim (1422 ff.): what Grim had done for him was warmly acknowledged, but Grim's intention of drowning him, and his brutal handling of Havelok before getting to that point, were revealingly passed over in silence (perhaps because they did not accord with the rest of what Havelok had to say about Grim).

7. The status of Grim as Godard's thrall has had important consequences in the handling of the story. It is clear that Grim did not know the identity of the boy whom he was about to murder (*þis child* 532, *þis knaue* 559). The extreme change that was required in his behaviour required in turn that he should, at this stage, discover who Havelok was. Hence the supernatural signs of Havelok's royal birth (the flame from his mouth and the blazing cross on his right shoulder) were first introduced as an efficient cause in the action here (592 and 605)—

earlier than Gaimar and the *Lai* mention the flame. It is potentially of
some interest that Ubbe, in his first speech to the Danes about
Havelok, mentioned that Grim learnt that he was the rightful heir to
the throne of Denmark (2236), but not the means by which Grim came
to know this.

In any case, the alteration (as it looks like being) was well-judged,
since it was plainly necessary for Grim to learn at this point who
Havelok was, in order that he should enable Havelok to survive. The
radiant cross on the sleeping boy's right shoulder (which is peculiar to
Hav.) might be thought to be labouring the point which the flame was
enough to make: why have *two* supernatural signs? It may be that the
author was trying to be logical: Havelok was, after all, to be king of two
realms. This explanation accords with one of the comments that Grim
made immediately after seeing both the flame (592) and the *kynemerk*
(605) on Havelok's right shoulder:

> He shall hauen in his hand
> Al Denemark *and Engeland*.   (610–11)

Grim had otherwise no means of knowing that Havelok would rule
England. This remark, therefore, if read in isolation, is either a
strangely prescient one (and hence perhaps a sign that the narrative
sequence has been altered), or an inadvertent anticipation by the
author of an outcome necessarily known to him.

The angel who spoke to Goldeborw immediately after she saw both
the flame and the cross admittedly mentioned only the cross as the
sign that Havelok was the son and heir of a king, and that he would
rule both Denmark and England. Thus, where the first point is concerned, the cross undeniably duplicates the function of the flame. But,
according to the angel, the cross meant in addition that Havelok
would rule both Denmark and England:

> Jt bikenneth more—þat he shal
> Denemark hauen *and Englond* al.
> He shal ben king strong and stark
> *Of Engelond* and Denemark.   (1270–3)

In the third instance, when Ubbe and over a hundred of his men
saw the brilliant light diffused by Havelok in his sleep, they interpreted both signs in conjunction as meaning that he was of royal birth
(2144) and Birkabeyn's son and heir. And (rather strangely) they were
convinced that he was Birkabeyn's son and heir only after seeing
Havelok's great likeness to him (2155–8). Perhaps strangely again, it
was only on the ground of this resemblance, and without any mention
of the flame or the cross, that Ubbe presented Havelok to the knights,

constables, and sheriffs from all over Denmark as the heir of Birkabeyn:

> Lokes nou hw he is fayr:
> Sikerlike he is hise eyr.   (2301–2)

To be fully intelligible, this needs to be filled out by the earlier passage (expressing the reaction of Ubbe's men to the sight of the sleeping Havelok) which it echoes, and which explicitly states how alike Havelok and Birkabeyn are:

> For it was neuere yet a broþer
> Jn al Denemark so lich anoþer,
> So þis man, þat is so fayr
> Als Birkabeyn: he is his eyr!   (2155–8)

In his stated reason for identifying Havelok as Birkabeyn's heir, Ubbe was consistent at one point, at least. In reporting how Grim got Havelok away from Denmark, and all that had happened to the boy, Ubbe represented Grim as discovering Havelok's identity, not by the flame and the cross (which again he did not mention here), but solely by his likeness to Birkabeyn, stated in the same elliptical terms (which refer only to his good looks) as in 2301–2 (quoted above):

> Hwan Grim saw þat he was so fayr
> And wiste he was þe rith eir . . .   (2235–6)

Ubbe says nothing of Havelok as the prospective king of England. He was thus apparently unaware that the radiant cross marked Havelok as such, though Grim had realized it. This may be an appropriate way of representing the situation in which Ubbe had just discovered the heir of Birkabeyn. Ubbe would hardly have been interested (especially when conveying this momentous fact to the assembled Danes) in an aspect of Havelok's destiny that would take him away from Denmark to rule England, even if Ubbe had known of it.

Gaimar and the *Lai* use two objective criteria, the flame and the horn, to establish Havelok's identity as the rightful heir to the kingdom of Denmark; neither criterion is given any connection with his later rule over England. Gunter's horn, which Havelok alone succeeded in blowing, in effect duplicates the function of the flame. It is faintly reminiscent of a magical device found not only in wonder-tales[61] but in literary use in the Arthurian cycle, notably in the First Continuation of Chrétien's *Li Contes du Graal*,[62] and in a 'Breton lay',

---

[61] See Stith Thompson, *Motif-Index of Folk Literature*, vol. iii (Copenhagen, 1955–8), H 411, 4.

[62] Ed. W. Roach, *The Continuations of the Old French* Perceval *of Chrétien de Troyes*, vol. i (Philadelphia, 1949), pp. 231–8.

the Anglo-Norman *Lai du Cor* (composed by *c.* 1200),[63] in both of
which a horn is put to a quite different use as a test of chastity in
women, and of jealousy and cuckoldry in men. But in these works the
object used is a drinking horn, the contents of which spill over anyone
who fails the test of trying to drink from it. In fact, the horn in the *Lai
du Cor* may well be a quite distinct conception.

The subjective criterion of Havelok's resemblance to Gunter is
used by Gaimar and the *Lai* at an earlier stage than its equivalent in
Hav. Each represents Sigar as noticing the likeness when he arrived at
the scene of the attack on the church and saw Havelok throwing stones
from the tower at his assailants. In each, Sigar then (*a*) learnt
Havelok's name by questioning him, (*b*) remembered that it was the
name of Gunter's son, (*c*) set a watch for the flame (of which he had
learnt long before from the boy's nurse), and had it duly reported to
him, and (*d*) applied the test of the horn. All these things are done in
identical order in the two works. The only discrepancy is that in the
Lai, Sigar, after learning Havelok's name, 'nearly' recognized him, but
was still not quite sure of his identity. This is surely a sign of the
author's embarrassment that two more tests of the hero's identity were
to be made, and is an attempt to motivate them.

It is also an attempt to have Sigar avoid an irrational failure to iden-
tify Havelok from his name alone. In fact, the evidence of Havelok's
name had to take second place—in this world of legendary fiction—to
the two supernatural tests that would prove his identity. And this
shows that in *Hav.* there is a lapse in everyday logic that goes a little
further. Since Ubbe used Havelok's name when he entertained him
and Goldeborw to a meal (1718), he must have learnt it at their very
first meeting, the account of which has been partly lost in the lacuna in
the MS (1446–625).

We have seen (5 above) how and why Ubbe's original function as
Birkabeyn's seneschal has been suppressed. Even so, as a high official
of the king's, he surely would have known Havelok's name of old, and
therefore have realized his identity on first hearing his name. Another
way of putting this is that Havelok's name has been revealed to Ubbe
too early. This is a slight inconsistency; and it is of course due to the
primacy of the supernatural signs as the means of identifying the heir.
It probably implies that this whole episode in which Havelok met
Ubbe before going to his castle is an innovation, and an alteration of
the arrangement in Gaimar and the *Lai*.

The upshot of all this is that the processes by which Havelok's

---

[63] Ed. C. T. Erickson, ANTS 24 (Oxford, 1973).

identity was established are not fully coherent in any of the three works under consideration. So far as *Hav.* is concerned, it is clear that the radiant cross is an addition to the received form of the story. Since it is strictly speaking superfluous, the best explanation for it is that the author simply took it over from *Richars li Biaus*, in which the hero is exposed at birth, and found and rescued by a count. The latter's wife, on unwrapping the infant's clothes, observes both a brilliant radiance in his face, from which she concludes that he is highborn, and two crosses on his right shoulder, from which she instantly deduces that he is destined to be king:

> L'enfant regarde enmi la chiere
> Que resplendist si con lumiere.
> Dist la dame: 'Ie ne puis croire
> Que chilz ne soit de haute estoire;
> Il est dignes de haute table.'
> Puis regarde desour l'espale;
> Dessour la diestre uoit .ii. crois.
> 'Dieus!' dist elle, 'chilz sera rois!'[64]

This explanation is substantially reinforced by Dr M. Mills's recent discovery (see 11 below) that the episode of the attack on Havelok's party at the *greyue*'s house was remodelled after one in *Richars li Biaus* 3296–466. *In conjunction*, the modifications of the episode in *Hav.* and the radiant cross (which is rare in ME and in OF literature) are much more likely to derive from *Richars li Biaus* than the radiant cross in isolation would be; and the use of this work as a model for the episode is virtually assured. Adoption of the radiant cross from *Richars* is chronologically feasible, since that work is thought to have been composed *c.* 1250–75 if it is by the same author as *Blancandin et l'orgueilleuse d'Amour* (one MS of which was written in 1288), or *c.* 1275–1300 if it is not.[65] The most recent editor of *Blancandin*, however, believes (on grounds that are not explicitly clear to me) that the latter was composed in the first third of the thirteenth century.[66]

8. The process by which Goldeborw learnt of Havelok's royal birth and his destiny differs in one substantial point, and in minor preliminaries, from the account of Gaimar and the *Lai*. Havelok and his wife left Lincoln for Grimsby immediately after the wedding (1187–203)— not as a result of any prophetic dream of Goldeborw's, but because they

[64] Ed. W. Foerster (Vienna, 1874), pp. 663–70.
[65] Foerster, ed. cit., pp. xxi–xxii.
[66] F. P. Sweetser, *Blancandin et l'orgueilleuse d'Amour*, Textes littéraires français (Geneva, 1964), p. 41.

realized that Godrich was ill-disposed to them, and because Havelok
was concerned lest she should incur shame or blame (for the implications of which see 83–4). It is difficult to see a reason for this difference, other than that it accords with the attribution of the dream to
Havelok (see below): the first gives the initiative, the second the focus
of interest, to Havelok instead of Goldeborw.

Goldeborw accordingly did not see the flame and the cross till
their first night in Grimsby (their first together), 1252 ff. Then
came the intervention of the angel (see 7 above) to explain matters to
her; in the *Lai* this function is given to a hermit, while Gaimar does
not provide an interpretation of the dream at all. Clearly, in the
action as arranged in *Hav.*, there was no need for Goldeborw to have
a revelatory dream about Havelok: he was perhaps the appropriate
person to have one about his own destiny. In any case, the author (or
a forerunner) has provided one that was an unmistakably plain
expression of what was in store for Havelok (1284 ff.). Argentille's
dream in Gaimar's version and the *Lai*, on the other hand, with its
symbolic wild animals representing Havelok's enemies and supporters, is slightly mystifying.

These things are likely to be innovations in *Hav.*: the young
couple's departure for Grimsby seems a little less convincingly motivated than by the dream in the AN versions. And there is one main
point behind all this that has been judged an inconsistency.[67] Since the
hero in *Hauelok* knew from the outset about his own descent, why did
he not reveal it to Goldeborw before the angel did—especially as this
would have met her strong objection to being 'disparaged' in this
marriage to a scullion?

The answer to this question is that the facts of Havelok's identity
and royal birth could not be revealed at least till the marriage had
taken place, since the plot required that Godrich should believe
Havelok to be of low birth. And the interval between the marriage and
Havelok's dream was minimal. The author might, of course, have
represented Havelok as confiding the facts to Goldeborw as a secret—
but there was hardly time for him to do so before the wedding, and
very little time after it. In the circumstances, the inconsistency is
surely not a glaring and serious one.

Nevertheless, to explain why it arose and to show that it is only a
modest one, is not to eliminate the inconsistency. The fact is that it
would not have arisen if Havelok had been ignorant of his royal birth
(as he was in the AN versions till informed of it at Grimsby by Grim's

[67] By H. L. S. Creek, 'The Author of "Havelok the Dane"', *Englische Studien*, 48
(1915), 193–212, at 200.

daughter). It follows that in *Hav.* the hero's knowledge of the facts from the outset is an innovation.

Another symptom of this is the way Grim's children reacted when Havelok and Goldeborw returned to Grimsby: they did not need to be told who he was (or to tell him), but greeted him as their lord, expressed their devotion (on their knees), promised their service to him and Goldeborw, and even tried to get him to settle there with them. And they did not suggest that he should return to Denmark to claim his heritage. Clearly, they had from the outset known all about Havelok's identity and royal birth, because he himself had done. The author of *Hav.* has thus handled the matter straightforwardly, without tortuous implications such as that Grim (and Havelok) had originally concealed the facts from Grim's children. Yet this little scene, too, has introduced an inconsistency:[68] Goldeborw could hardly have witnessed it without realizing that Havelok was of more exalted rank than he had seemed.

A further result of Havelok's knowledge of his true identity throughout the story is his address to the three sons of Grim. It was, of course, meant to get them to go to Denmark with him; the expression of this (1441–5) was called for, and roughly corresponds to a detail in Gaimar (462–3) and the *Lai* (634). But the preceding section is otiose, since 'all five children' of Grim had clearly shown that they knew of Havelok's royal descent and therefore presumably his whole history (1206 ff.), including their father's part in it. Indeed, Havelok began by acknowledging that they knew of it all:

> 'Louerdinges, Ich wile you shaue
> A þing of me þat ye wel knawe.'   (1402–3)

He was evidently recapitulating the known facts, in order to make the full case for their going to Denmark with him.

This part of Havelok's speech should therefore probably not be regarded as an inconsistency. However, an important point is involved. Havelok here for the first time overtly showed that he knew his true identity and the history of how Grim saved his life. But, as was pointed out by Creek,[69] the author represented him as doing so simply because these facts were recounted at the corresponding point in the AN versions (Gaimar 376 ff., *Lai* 601 ff.) by Grim's daughter to Havelok himself—who in those versions had till then not known them (see 9 below). The author of *Hav.* could not present them in this way, since in his version the hero at all times knew of his origins and what

---

[68] Detected by Creek, ibid., p. 200.   [69] Ibid., p. 200.

Grim had done. He therefore transferred the exposition of the facts to Havelok.

This utterance of Havelok's thus makes two things clear: his previous knowledge of his royal descent and of his rescue by Grim is due to an alteration in the ME version, and one that presupposes a form of the story (as in the AN versions) in which he did not know of them till he returned to Grimsby.

9. Havelok's pretence of being a merchant when he arrived in Denmark is unconvincing, since nothing whatever came of it, and not a word more was said of it. It is likely to have been suggested by the presence, in the AN versions, of a merchant as the husband of Grim's daughter Kelloc, who by his calling was able to provide Havelok's party with a passage to Denmark and with directions when they arrived.

The lacuna in the Laud MS (1446–625) covers the part of the text within which a reference to an accompanying merchant would have occurred, if there was one. But it is clear that even if there was a merchant, he could not have been the husband of either of Grim's daughters. There is no mention of a husband of either daughter when Havelok and Goldeborw reached Grimsby; Havelok himself married off both Grim's daughters at the end of the story, to the Earl of Chester (2865–8) and Bertram the cook respectively (2913–15); and it is Goldeborw (1336–52), instead of Grim's daughter, who urges and persuades Havelok to go to Denmark.

In fact, the five children of Grim tried to persuade Havelok to take up his abode with them as their lord and with Goldeborw as their lady. This is charming (as a simple heartfelt expression of their devotion), but suspect as a step in the action. This doubt is confirmed by the passage in which they first transferred to Havelok all their possessions (1222–9), including money that Grim had left with them for Havelok, livestock, and (significantly) a ship, and then brought out food and drink for a feast, including a goose, a hen, a duck, and a drake. This is heart-warming behaviour. But it looks much like an alteration by the author of *Hav.* of the process by which Grim's daughter Kelloc offered to supply Havelok and Goldeborw with provisions, clothes, and money for the journey to Denmark, as well as the sea-passage, and which has much more point in the context. And it was of course the ship belonging to Grim's sons (1351; cf. 1223) that was evidently used for the passage, since this was what Goldeborw suggested to Havelok (1351) in the speech of advice that in the other two versions was delivered by Kelloc.

Thus there seems to be no scope for a merchant in the action of *Hav.* hereabouts; and this may well be the result of alterations.

10. One other point associated with Havelok's masquerade as a merchant raises doubts and looks like an innovation. The gold ring, the gem in which was alone worth a hundred pounds, and by the gift of which Havelok induced Ubbe to let him move from borough to borough and vill to vill buying and selling, is not represented at this point in Gaimar or the *Lai*. This may have been a historically accurate gesture (in order that a soi-disant merchant might get himself, as an alien, exemption from the payment of local tolls). But it arouses a fleeting suspicion that the author of *Hav.* got the idea from the gold ring that Sigar offered to anyone who could sound Gunter's horn (Gaimar 686 ff.; *Lai* 885–6). The whole passage in *Hav.* concerning the ring turns out to make sense on this assumption.

In the *Lai* nothing is said of the nature of the ring. But, according to Gaimar (689–92) it had magical properties: the wearer would not drown if he fell into the sea, nor be harmed by fire, nor be wounded by any weapon. Thus Sigar understandably said that it was worth more than a castle (presumably with an implied comparison of two kinds of life-saver). This is tolerably similar to the statement in *Hav.* (1644–5) that Ubbe would not have parted with the ring on any account, *not even for the* borw ('*castle*') *and everything that went with it*. Sigar's assessment of the ring is close enough to have been the model for an otherwise somewhat tamely grounded equivalent in *Hav.* and to account for it. The pleasure that Ubbe, as a man of exalted rank (and hence wealth) took in possessing a gold ring, however valuable, has less point than it would have had if the ring had had the power to preserve life against water, fire, and weapons (which it may be assumed to have had in the received form of the story).

A magical device such as Sigar's ring would have been altogether out of keeping with the author of *Hav.*'s relish for real life and for building it into the fabric of his story. To represent Havelok as offering Ubbe a very valuable gift, and Ubbe as accepting it, was a bold stroke that expresses the author's vision of life. It may not in the thirteenth century have been thought improper to give a high official an inducement ostensibly to exempt one from local tolls for foreign merchants. But the author of *Hav.* has apparently seen fit to hint (1638–40) that what the hero really gained by it was an opening (through access to Ubbe, who of course could not know what was to come of it) that led to his recognition as the rightful heir to Denmark. This (if we have interpreted it correctly) was at least an attempt to strengthen the rationale of the story in realistic terms.

The effect of the passage as a whole is slightly cryptic. The most natural explanation of this is that, in making over Sigar's ring to a different use and excising the irrelevant magic, the author presented the matter in a slightly elliptic form. His use of the ring (according to the above analysis) does not imply that Gaimar was his source, since Gaimar's account of it might well go back to a common antecedent of all three works. In any case, the incident of the ring has all the marks of an alteration by the author of *Hav.*, and a characteristic one.

11. The episode in which the house of Bernard Brun the *greyue* was attacked just after he had taken Havelok's party in for a night's lodging is, within the narrative sequence, an equivalent of the assault by six young men and the abduction of Argentille in Gaimar (531 ff.) and the *Lai* (683 ff.). But it has been built up into something substantially different, and elaborated to astonishing proportions.

The author has given the episode *c.* 235 lines (1767–926, 1952–2008, 2013–33), most of which are taken up with details of the fighting. The assailants were thieves bent on plundering the *greyue* (1956–60) and murdering him and his dependants, instead of abductors of Argentille as in Gaimar (531–40) and the *Lai* (679–86, 761–2), in which latter they were explicitly bent on rape. In *Hav.*, the attack was not originally aimed at Havelok and his party at all. The assailants have been multiplied *by ten* to sixty-one (1769), and more according to Bernard Brun (1957), plus a leader, or seventy according to the bystanders (2027).

This episode has been analysed, and certain divergences from Gaimar and the *Lai* satisfactorily explained, by M. Mills,[70] who shows that it has been remodelled on a passage in *Richars li Biaus*[71] or some cognate version of this, in a degree such as leads him to regard it as an 'interpolated episode', the scale of which he believes to be due to the length of this model (p. 28).

The most important symptom (as Dr Mills has made clear) of this recasting is one particular lapse in rationale as a result of the suture between the received episode and the material adapted from *Richars li Biaus*. The escort of ten knights and sixty other armed men whom Ubbe sent to take Havelok's party to the *greyue*'s house (1747–50) were to mount guard over them during the night (1755–6). But nothing is said of them during the fight, or of their having returned to Ubbe. Soon after, the sixty-one marauders (called *laddes*) appear (1768–9).

[70] 'Havelok's Return', *MÆ* 45 (1976), 20–35, at 24–8.
[71] Ed. W. Foerster, 3295–492.

But in the report given to Ubbe, the latter are termed sixty-one of his best men-at-arms (*sergeaunz* 1929–30). The exact correspondence of the number sixty-one in each group shows that the escort has been turned into the band of marauders; and the discrepant total of seventy mentioned to Ubbe by the bystanders is probably due to conflation with the ten knights and sixty armed men who were said in 1747–9 to make up the escort. Clearly, the *sergeaunz* of 1929–30 belong to an earlier form of the story. And Ubbe, in assuring Havelok (2083–6) that, when they lodge with him the following night, no one will attempt to molest Havelok's wife, is perhaps attesting that the earlier form of the attack, with the motive of abduction and rape, was contained in the version received by the author of Hauelok. A reasonably assured trace of this motif is the statement that Huwe Rauen:

> . . . þowthe wel þat men misferde
> with his louerd *for his wif*.   (1869–71)

Two other main changes made by him call for notice. By making the *greyue* Havelok's host for his first night in the town, Ubbe put the matter on an appropriately official basis, since the *greyue* was apparently (as a Northern equivalent of the town reeve elsewhere) a local official and headman of the community. And, in his detailed picture of the fighting, the author has given the three sons of Grim a large part.

Having introduced the *greyue*, he has likewise put him to use, and involved him in the action, by having him report to Ubbe what had happened, and above all how Havelok had acquitted himself. This is done in terms laudatory beyond what any author could possibly have represented Havelok as using about himself, though not beyond verisimilitude. And the retelling is done in such a way as to avoid otiose repetition. It is a great advance on having the barest outline of the facts reported to Sigar by Havelok (as is done in the *Lai*, 757–66) or not at all (as by Gaimar). To use the bystanders to corroborate the *greyue*'s account (2013–33) typically enlarges the scope and the human interest of the episode.

In the version received by the author of *Hav.* (if it is fairly represented by Gaimar and the *Lai*) Havelok's prowess and prominence in the fracas were already amply emphasized. The author's reasons for his alterations must therefore have to do with his personal tastes and interests. Two suggest themselves: a strong interest in the maintenance of law and order (and hence in outrageous breaches of them); and a relish for the details of daily life within the administrative framework of a community.

The matters to be discussed from this point are among those covered in the summary (Nos. 5–18 above) of the action in the second half of the story:

12. Havelok's alarm (6), being unlikely to be of independent origin in all three versions, is one of the more surprising correspondences with Gaimar and the *Lai*, and is thus probably from a common antecedent. But in these two it is differently contrived (see the translations above). The hero's reaction in *Hav.* is perhaps less convincingly motivated, and less warrantable in its context. But a more interesting aspect of it is that the author's explanation is a naturalistic one, and Havelok's behaviour more obviously human.

13. The feasting (2321–46) is contained in Gaimar's account at a later point, after the Danish usurper had been defeated (755).

14. In advancing the three sons of Grim (2347–54), Havelok had remembered, and was carrying out, the promise he had made them at Grimsby when he asked them to come to Denmark with him (1441–5). The promise appears in Gaimar's account (468) and in the *Lai* (638–9), though in the latter it was uttered by Argentille. But it was not explicitly carried out, and therefore remains a loose end in these two.

15. The judicial execution of Godard (2465–511), and later that of Godrich (2811–42), along with Havelok's action in assembling a court to sentence each of them, are clear examples of the author's taste for parallelism in the telling of his story, and of his interest in legal institutions. Gaimar says nothing of what happened to Odulf, beyond his defeat (740); and in the *Lai*, Havelok killed him in single combat (962–4). The account in *Hav.* is virtually certain to be an innovation.

16. The British usurper Edelsi, in the account of Gaimar (799–800) and of the *Lai* (1083–92), was not put to death. He merely surrendered Argentille's heritage, after the stratagem of propping up the dead men on the battlefield had led him to believe that further resistance was useless. He died, in the course of nature, within fifteen days.

This outcome is not merely tame in itself, but seems a surprisingly limp way of dealing with what, by contemporary standards in real life, was an extremely grave crime. The customary penalty for treason and *felonye* was a horrible and shameful death.[72] The version of *Hav.* (without necessarily being accurate at all points) is much closer to actuality and makes vastly more of an impact.

[72] See 2477–512 n. and 2821–42.

17. The special mention of the Earl of Chester and an Earl Gunter as allies of Godrich is a revealing example of the author of *Hav.*'s methods. These two are to be equated with Gaimar's *dous princes* (743) who were allies of the Danish usurper: the author of *Hav.* has transferred them to the English usurper and to the battle against him, and has bestowed on one of them an authentic English earldom which was held, in the twelfth and the thirteenth century respectively, by two men prominent in public life. As for the Earl Gunter, the author of *Hav.*, if he had access to either of the other two versions, would have been quite capable of reusing the name borne by Havelok's father in them to give the second prince an identity.

There is no mention of the two *princes* in the *Lai*. But they are represented symbolically by the two lions of Argentille's prophetic dream, which knelt to Havelok in submission, and which are mentioned in the *Lai* (425–6 and 433–6) as well as by Gaimar (227–8, 233–4). If this interpretation is correct, they must, in one form or another, go back to an antecedent version common to all three extant ones.

The treatment of these two figures in *Hav.* differs revealingly and typically from that of Gaimar or the *Lai*. Even in Gaimar's account, which does at least follow up the symbolic lions of the dream, the two princes are unidentified, colourless, and functionless. The equivalent figures in *Hav.* have names (one of them of ringing renown), and hence immediacy, and substance in some degree. And one of them— since Havelok gave him the hand of one of Grim's daughters—has been drawn into the circle of those linked with the hero.

Why, it must be asked, did the author of *Hav.* bring in the Earl of Chester? This question applies equally to the Earl of Cornwall (see 1 above). The two answers, which must be sought independently, are interdependent.[73] Neither question is answerable except by reference *in conjunction* to (*a*) Ranulf de Blundeville, who was Earl of Lincoln (from 1217) as well as Earl of Chester (and thus would account for the presence of an Earl of Chester at Lincoln in *Hav.*), and died in 1232, and (*b*) Richard of Cornwall, the brother of Henry III, who was in revolt against the king in 1227 with a group of earls led by the Earl of Chester, though the quarrel was patched up.[74]

---

[73] See 178 n. and 2608 n.
[74] See F. M. Powicke, *King Henry III and the Lord Edward* (Oxford, 1966), vol. 1, pp. 50 n. 1, 83 and n. 1, 138 n. 1; N. Denholm-Young, *Richard of Cornwall* (Oxford, 1947), pp. 10–13, 16–17, 24–5.

IV. THE SOURCE OR SOURCES OF *HAUELOK*

Since *Hav.* thus corresponds closely and extensively to the two AN versions, especially in the action but sometimes in details, and since the differences are such as might be due to alterations by the author of *Hav.* himself, it must derive ultimately from the same form of the story.

It is at first sight remarkable that the changes made in the story as a whole have not left a trail of incoherence such as would beyond question show *Hav.* to be derived from one or (when the two AN versions agree) both of these. This is partly because Gaimar and the *Lai* agree at most points in the action and differ (in content) relatively seldom and slightly. But it is also very largely due to the author of *Hauelok*'s skill in making changes and innovations without creating disorder. The inconsistencies brought out by a detailed comparison with the AN versions are unobtrusive: they do not come instantly into view in the course of ordinary reading, and have to be searched for. They are in fact slight; and they seem to be such as might have arisen in a careful recasting of the story as available in a written form, but hardly in an oral one.

Perhaps the most valuable pointers to the nature of the main source of *Hav.* are those structural features, or scenes, or motifs, or details (already discussed above for other purposes) that presuppose a rather different form from what they actually have in the AN versions. The symptom of this is that in *Hav.* they are intelligible as alterations of the AN version(s) and that the converse does not hold. They are as follows (numbers in square brackets refer to sections above):

(*a*) the reverberations set up by the change in the status of Godard and in the role of Grim, and in the distribution (among the characters) of the knowledge of Havelok's true identity;

(*b*) that Havelok had not told Goldeborw of his descent before she learnt it from the angel implies that there was an antecedent form of story in which he did not know it himself;

(*c*) Havelok unnecessarily informs Grim's sons of his own history (1402–35), because in a form of the story in which he did not know it this information had been given at this point (to Havelok) by Grim's daughter [8];

(*d*) the action of Grim's family in turning over to Havelok all their possessions (including a ship) [9];

(*e*) Havelok's masquerade as a merchant [9];

(*f*) and his gift of the gold ring to Ubbe [10];

(g) the two different forms of motivation used for the attack on the *greyue*'s house, as against one of these in the AN versions [11];

(h) the somewhat undefined status of Ubbe [5].

It is just conceivable that the author of *Hav.* altered the sequence of the early history of Havelok and Goldeborw from the way in which it was ordered by Gaimar and the *Lai*. He could assuredly have hit on the idea of Havelok's masquerade as a merchant (by 'contiguity') either from Gaimar's account, in which Havelok was accompanied to Denmark by merchants in two ships (494–500), or from that of the *Lai*, in which Kelloc's husband, who was a merchant, sailed to Denmark with Havelok (619–20, 645–50).

But the author of *Hav.*'s use of the Earl of Chester and the Earl Gunter (see 17 above) rules out the *Lai*—which does not mention the two *princes* of Gaimar 743—as an immediate source *at this point*. Likewise, since the meal that Havelok's party took with Ubbe (1715 ff.) is missing from Gaimar's version (by a simple error, indicated by ll. 666–8 in Gaimar), the author of *Hav.* cannot have used the extant version of Gaimar *at this point*. He might nevertheless have had recourse to both the AN versions, without necessarily following one or the other, or both, at all points.

The only warrantable conclusion from all this is that the author of *Hav.* used a version of the story that was at many points identical with both the AN ones, was very close to them as a whole (if we make due allowance for the substantial and numerous changes that he made), and may well have been written in AN. It is conceivable that Gaimar and the *Lai* were his main sources, in a form not quite identical with the extant copies. There is some evidence to show that there was an antecedent ME version (not definable to any extent).[75]

Among subsidiary sources, the AN prose *Brut*, though merely a potential rather than an assured instance, must not be passed over in silence:

1. One, especially, of the two references in *Hav.* to Dover and Roxburgh as extreme points of the realm (for *travellers*: see 264–5 and n.), which rest on the tradition of the four royal roads of Britain, can have been suggested only by a chronicle or by *The Laws of Edward the Confessor* or the *Leis Willelme*.[76]

2. In *Hav.*, the author's emphasis on the fact that Goldeborw was the 'rightful heir' to the kingdom of England (see pp. lvii–lviii) reverses that of Gaimar and the *Lai*, which is on Havelok's status as the

---

[75] See pp. lxvii–lxix.   [76] See *SMP* pp. 191 ff.

'rightful heir' to the kingdom of Denmark. The author of *Hav.*'s procedure is reminiscent of the standard statement in chronicles that Havelok came to rule England through his marriage to Goldeborow, who was the 'rightful heir' (see pp. lvii–lviii).

Since both these points occur in immediate succession in the AN prose *Brut*,[77] it seems just conceivable that the author used that work. This suggestion is perhaps somewhat less frail than may at first appear. The AN prose *Brut* was the only chronicle (other than Gaimar's) in being by *c.* 1300 that contained an account of the story of Havelok; and the dynastic history of England (which is the subject of any *Brut*) was the context to which, for the author of *Hav.*, the story belonged.

3. The felicitous pun on *heye* (see 199 n. and pp. lxvi–lxvii) might conceivably be an inspired elaboration of a simple non-punning use of AN *haut* in the sense 'of high rank, eminent'. It is therefore worth recalling that the AN prose *Brut* has the only early version of the story of Havelok in which the work *haut* itself is used of the hero (see p. lxvi); though his height is also mentioned in a different phrase (*ot. . . bele estature*) in the *Lai* 739.

4. The name *Ubbe* may also have come the author's way from a chronicle such as the AN prose *Brut* (see p. lx).

Another subsidiary source is the OF romance *Richars li Biaus*, knowledge of which would satisfactorily account for two major innovations in *Hav.*—the treatment of the attack on the *greyue*'s house, and the radiant cross on Havelok's shoulder (see pp. xliv and xlix–l).

It is convenient to notice here the arresting fact that the hero of the Havelok story bears a name that can be equated with that of a historical figure among the Scandinavian rulers of York in the earlier tenth century. The received view turns on two points:

1. *Haueloc* (the form of the name on the Grimsby seal) = MW *Abloec*, *Abloyc* = OIr. *Amlaib* = OIcel. *Óláf-r* < *Áleif-r* = OE *Anláf*.
2. Anlaf Cwaran, the son of Sigtrygg, is clearly the source of the alternative name under which Havelok is known in Gaimar and the *Lai*. Anlaf Cwaran (ON Ólafr kváran in e.g. *Ólafs Saga Truggvasonar*, *Flateyjarbók*, i, pp. 164 and 239, ed. S. Nordal, 1944) = *Hauelok* alias *Kuarran*, *Cuaran(t)*, *Coraunt* in the AN and Lambeth versions; and the second name is likely to have been shed from the ME version.

Anlaf Cwaran had succeeded his father Sigtrygg as king of York *c.* 925, but ruled only intermittently in the intervals of exile, rejection,

---

[77] e.g. MS Rawlinson D. 329, fo. 23^{r-v}.

or being in Dublin; he was last ruling in Northumbria in 949.[78] There is not enough in what is known of him to make him a model for the story of *Hav.* All that seems clear is that a form of the story was known among the Welsh of Cumberland and passed from them to the Anglo-Danish inhabitants of Lincoln.

V. WHAT *HAUELOK* IS ABOUT

The author did not have occasion to say or suggest what kind of work he believed *Hav.* to be, and what he saw as the main point of the story. For certain writers of his own time, at least, the story was history, and specifically dynastic history. This much appears e.g. from the interpolation of the story into the Lambeth MS of Mannyng's *Chronicle*.

But another and more specific significance was extracted from it. As one among the chronicles of England, the AN prose *Brut* not only includes a summary version of the story as told by Gaimar and the *Lai* (see pp. xxiv–xxvii), but makes a brief allusion to it elsewhere, as a pendant to an account of how a Danish king named Guthlak was forced to pay tribute to the British king Belinus after being captured and becoming his vassal. This runs as follows in MS Rawlinson D. 329, fo. 23[r–v]:

Et en ceste manere furent departiz le Roi Guthlak e s'amie e ses genz, e retournerent en Denmarz. E touz iours apres furent les couenantes tenues e le truage rendu, taunt que au temps *Hauelok, qe feust Roi de Denmarz e de ceste terre auxi, par Goldeburgh qu'il aueit espose, que feust dreit heir de ceste terre*.

The ME prose *Brut* (translated from the AN one) has a similar account.[79]

The substance of the episode derives from a corresponding one about a Danish king Guithlacus in Geoffrey of Monmouth's *Historia Regum Britanniæ*;[80] but Geoffrey does not say anything about continuance of the tribute or about Havelok. A different but comparable allusion to Havelok occurs in *Le Petit Bruit* (which contains a version of his story in a summary form and closely modelled on the ME one: see II, 6 above), hitched on to one Frederick, the son and successor of a Danish king Gurmound. The latter, after the death of the British king Cassibelin without an heir, is said to have successfully claimed the realm of

---

[78] For his tangled history see A. Campbell, *The Battle of Brunanburh* (London, 1938), pp. 50–2; Gwyn Jones, *A History of the Vikings* (Oxford, 1968), pp. 236–9; F. M. Stenton, *Anglo-Saxon England*, pp. 340, 351–8, 361–3.

[79] Ed. Brie, vol. i, p. 26, ll. 2–6.

[80] Ed. E. Faral, *La Légende Arthurienne*, vol. iii, pp. 109–12, chs. 35–8; see vol. ii, pp. 119–22, and Thorpe, op. cit., iii. 2–4, pp. 91–3.

Britain as the son of the eldest daughter of Belyn and of her husband
Thorand king of Denmark:

... par cel prime venue de auauntd[it] roy Gormound ... si fu le rancour de
Daneis vers nous enpendaunt, et le regne par cel primer accion vers nous
enchalangount plus de sept C. ans apres, *ieke* ['until'] *a la venue Haneloke, fitz le
roy Birkenebayne de Dannemarche, qe le regne par mariage entra de sa femme.* [MS
Harley 902, fo. 2ᵛ]

The absence of any mention of tribute from this last passage brings
out the point of the allusion to Havelok and Goldeborw in all three
still more clearly. The one thing that is always mentioned is that
Havelok became king of England through his marriage to Goldeborw
(and, explicitly in the other two texts, *because she was the rightful heir*).
The implication is plain: Havelok's own rule over England was therefore by lawful right. Thus the original aim of this comment was apparently to show that Danish rule over England (by Cnut) was legitimate.

This aim is not necessarily to be attributed to all the chroniclers who
made the comment; but it looks like having been in origin a piece of pro-
Danish propaganda. Havelok, as an essentially legendary figure (perhaps tenuously linked to an actual tenth-century Dane and an actual
historical situation in northern England: see IV, 4 above), has been
treated as a parallel case to Cnut, the historical Dane who really did
come to rule England after succeeding to the kingdom of Denmark.

This matter turns out to be directly relevant to *Hav.* In it Goldeborw is three times described as *(þe) riht(e) eir* 'the lawful heir' to
England,[81] and three times as the *eir*,[82] and Havelok once as *þe rihte eir*
(2235), and five times simply as the *eir*,[83] of Birkabeyn. But Gaimar
applies the phrase five times,[84] and the noun alone (once, 68) only to
Havelok, apart from naming him and Goldeborw (i.e. Argentille) in
conjunction as *eir ... dreiturier* (pl.) to England (809). The *Lai* calls
Havelok *dreiz eir* to Denmark four times,[85] and reproduces from
Gaimar the expression *eir ... dreiturer* (1101) for him and his wife.

The fact that Goldeborw and Havelok are heirs by lawful right to
England and Denmark respectively is so clamantly obvious as (one
might think) hardly to need mentioning. But the author of Hav. under-
lines it by repetition, and thus implies that he regards it as important.
And since he has emphasized Goldeborw's right of succession more
than Gaimar and the *Lai* had done, it is conceivable that he had had

[81] 289, 2540, 2770.
[82] 110, 1096, 2806.
[83] 410, 607, 1268, 2158, 2302.
[84] *dreit (dreiz) eir(s)* 418, 519, 676–7, 723.
[85] 49, 92, 840, 813.

access to the statement of the AN prose *Brut* (see p. lvi) according to which the crucial fact was that Goldeborw *feust dreit heir de ceste terre* (hence, in the ME prose *Brut, for she was þe ryȝt heire of þis lande*).

In itself, this is hardly more than a possibility. But it becomes much more if we recall that the foregoing comment on the climax of Havelok's story in the two prose *Bruts* is immediately followed by the passage on the four royal roads of Britain, and that this latter tradition must (for contextual and other reasons: see 263–5) have been the source of the two references in *Hav.* to Roxburgh and Dover as extreme geographical points of the realm. If it was the AN prose *Brut* that gave the author of *Hav.* the idea of mentioning Dover and Roxburgh, he would have been likely to notice in that text also the immediately preceding passage on the hero's accession to the English throne through his wife as the *dreit heir*.

This seems more likely than that the author either (*a*) took over the idea of the 'rightful heir(s)' from Gaimar and the *Lai*, but shifted the emphasis to Goldeborw's right of succession, as in the two prose *Bruts* (which would be a coincidence), or (*b*) that his use of it was entirely independent (which would be still more of a coincidence). The author of *Hav.* was probably aware anyway of the significance of Goldeborw's hereditary right as the ground for Havelok's own accession to the realm of England. He does not expressly say so; but he may have shown himself aware of it by concluding his story of Havelok with an account of his coronation (2943 ff.) as king of England.

What *Hav.* is about is very much more than this. A dispossessed king's son rises, by his natural gifts as well as his birth, from cruel ill-treatment, exile, and adversity to the pinnacle of prosperity and happiness: the story of *Hav.* appeals to the same human instincts as wonder-tales do. As to its subject, a strong interest in kingship is undeniably implicit in the poem: this is partly why Aþelwold is extolled at such length as an ideal king. But, where Havelok is concerned, as distinct from Aþelwold, it is kingship, not in isolation, nor solely as a political institution, but in its social and human aspect as well: what sort of person did his subjects find the king to be, and how did he treat them?

In *Hav.* the personality of the king is crucially important to his fellows in society, because of the kind and the extent of his powers in an Anglicized feudal system, and because he is the apex of the system of government, and hence the guardian of law and order, and (as the idealized picture of Aþelwold shows) the exemplar of what the Church expected and required the king to be. And Havelok himself is manifestly an exemplary figure. But the well recognized plebeian sympathies of the author suggest that Havelok is an exemplary popular hero as well as an exemplary king in the making. The author is interested in him not only in his public aspect as the man born to be king, but in his private aspect as a person. In fact, the view that *Hav.* is 'a handbook for princes'[86] is perhaps a trifle narrow.

If the poem has such a thing as 'a' theme (rather than 'themes'), it is not solely the institution of kingship.[87] *Hav.* is about the triumph of right over wrong, and of the lawful right of succession to a kingdom; the importance of law and order in feudal England of the thirteenth century; the power of goodness, and the governance and the protection of the good man by God.

Hav. cannot be regarded as a political document; it was beyond doubt meant primarily to entertain. But the author has brought into it so much of the legal and feudal processes and of the local administration of his time as to have built up a picture worth having of the way life was ordered. This is what is altogether distinctive in *Hav.* and makes it an unusual example of the genre to which (for lack of a more precise term than 'romance') we may go on assigning it. The author of such a work was no minstrel. *Hav.* bears the impress of an individual literary talent, and conveys the presence of a distinct and vigorous personality—and the latter is rare in earlier ME narrative fiction.

Hav. is nowadays apt to leave two delusive impressions—of savagery and a streak of cruelty in the author, and of a crudity in his outlook and in his writing. But one need only read contemporary reports of the punishment visited on traitors and of the standard modes of judicial execution (see 2477–512 n. and 2821–42) to realize that the savagery of *Hav.*, in two horrifying instances, is essentially that of the law in the author's own time (and also considerably later). Flaying alive admittedly is not among the standard judicial penalties. And one undeniable instance of blood-curdling cruelty (among the author's additions to the story) is Godrich's murder of Havelok's two small sisters; yet this is surely intended to underline the usurper's villainy.

Analysis of the author's literary style shows that he was an unobtrusively sophisticated writer, and certainly not a minstrel. His lively writing does much to give *Hav.* its especially vigorous and uninhibited tone. But it is the sense of closeness to real life that makes this romantically improbable story so acceptable in *Hav.* This is due especially to the settings he has created for many points in the action. What is almost as important in conveying the flavour of real life is the

---

[86] D. S. Staines, 'Havelok the Dane: A Thirteenth-century Handbook for Princes', *Speculum*, 51 (1976), 602–23.

[87] For Judith Weiss, the author's central concern is 'the land and its rulers', 'Structure and Characterisation in *Havelok the Dane*', *Speculum*, 44 (1969), 247–57, at 249.

author's relish for treating even subsidiary or minor figures in the story as individuals. He does it in the first instance by giving them names, and hence identities.

Since the author was evidently willing to devise the new names *Godrich* and *Godard* for the two usurpers, to fit his own purposes (see 178 n.), he would certainly have been capable of changing the received names of other characters. Hence *Ubbe* for *Sigar* of the AN versions is also likely to be an innovation. *Ubbe* is extremely rare as a personal name in Lincolnshire after the Conquest,[88] and occurs only in the place-name *Obthorpe* there (cf. *Ubbeston* in Suffolk, from 1086). In *Hav.*, given the Danish context, *Ubbe* is probably of Scandinavian origin, rather than < OE *Ubba*. And, given the connections of the story with prose chronicles (see II, 3–6), it might have been suggested to the author by the Dane who with his brother Inwær did such damage as an invader in Alfred's time, and who is duly mentioned in the ME prose *Brut*,[89] though in the spelling *Hubba* (with inorganic *h* before an initial vowel) as in the *Anglo-Saxon Chronicle*. Ubbe's wife is not named, though she is at least mentioned.

If the names *Leue*, *Gunnild*, and *Leuiue* were adopted from the *Life of St William of Norwich*, as suggested below,[90] they must have entered the story after 1172–3. They might be innovations by the author either of the extant *Hav.* or of the ME antecedent that has had to be posited below (pp. lxvii–lxix).

The three sons of Grim, too, have been given names in *Hav.*, in contrast to their unnamed counterparts in the other versions. In all three instances a byname is added to a personal name: *Robert þe Rede* (the mod. E surname *Reid*), *Huwe Rauen* (perhaps, like *þe Rede*, referring to the coour of the man's hair), and *William Wendut*. This last is of special interest, since the whole name recurs in William of Canterbury's *Miracula S. Thomae* (i.e. the miracles wrought by Becket; composed soon after 1171), as the name (fittingly) of a mariner ('William Given-to-going-overseas'):

Guillelmus cognomento *Wendhut*, per loca maritima ex suo nomine notus.[91]

Mr V. E. Watts has kindly drawn my attention to a *Robert Wendout* attested in 1346 in Newton-by-the-Sea (E. Bateson, *A History of*

---

[88] See G. F. Jensen, *Scandinavian Personal Names in Lincolnshire and Yorkshire* (Copenhagen, 1968), p. 319.

[89] Ed. Brie, vol. i, pp. 105 ff.

[90] See pp. lxix–lxxi.

[91] Ed. J. C. Robertson, *Materials for the History of Thomas Becket*, vol. i (RS 67. i; 1875), p. 324. This was noticed by B. Dickins, 'The Name of Grim's Children in the Havelok Story', in *A Philological Miscellany presented to Eilert Ekwall*, ed. S. B. Liljegren and J. Melander (*Studia Neophilologica*, 14 and 15; Uppsala, 1942), i. 114.

Northumberland, vol. ii (Newcastle-upon-Tyne, 1895), pp. 87–8). In the genealogy of his family (ibid., p. 89), his son John (d. 1367) and grandson Robert (d. 1379) show that the byname had become a surname. The only other instance known to me of the name *Wend-ut* is recorded in the fifteenth century,[92] and is thus not to be reckoned with here. The recurrence of the whole name in *Hav.* therefore suggests that the author adopted it from the *Life*—especially since the sobriquet is not obviously appropriate to one among three brothers whose experiences are not differentiated.

Bernard Brun (mod. E *Brown*) and *Griffin Galle* are of the same class. These last five names are of a familiar contemporary type which (in East Anglia, at least) had virtually replaced the single male personal name by *c.* 1250.[93] *Ubbe* is an understandable exception, if the explanation suggested above is valid, or in any case because the main characters are not given surnames. *þe Rede* and *Brun* both recur as surnames in two London documents respectively of 1292 and 1319, as *Iohn le Rede* (and with the synonymous OF adj., as *John le Rous* in 1295) and *William Broun c.* 1319.[94]

The names of the two exalted supporters of Godrich, Earl *Reyner* of Chester and the Earl *Gunter*, are probably of literary origin. Both belong to the large stock of personal names used in OF epics; *Reyner* is extremely common in these works;[95] and, since both occur in the AN *Gui de Warewic*,[96] the author of *Hav.* may have adopted them from it.

Among the characters invented in *Hav.*, Godrich's cook has been given the unelaborated personal name *Bertram* towards the end of the story (perhaps because he was about to become Earl of Cornwall). On the other hand, the six earls who fetched Goldeborw to Grimsby are anonymous (perhaps because there were too many of them to name). The hero's two sisters *Swanborw* (on whose name see p. lxx) and *Elfled*, *Bernard Brun* the *greyue*, and *Griffin Galle*, the leader of the robbers, all of whom were Danes living in Denmark, have been given English-style names (see 2030 n.).

The invention of names for characters in a romance was not an original stroke: it was not unknown as one of the procedures of literary

[92] Thomas Wyndoute, mercer and alderman of London. See C. L. Kingsford, *Chronicles of London* (Alan Sutton; repr. 1977), p. 219, l. 7 (AD 1497) and p. 225, l. 16 (1498).

[93] See Seltén, *The Anglo-Saxon Heritage in Middle English Personal Names: East Anglia 1100–1399* (Lund Studies in English, 43, Lund, 1972), p. 169.

[94] E. Ekwall, *Two Early London Subsidy Rolls* (Lund, 1951), pp. 158, 279.

[95] See E. Langlois, *Table des noms propres . . . dans les chansons de geste* (Paris, 1904), s. vv. *Gontier*, *Renier*.

[96] Ed. A. Ewert, CFMA 74 and 75 (Paris, 1932–3).

composition. A notable example is the AN *Romance of Horn*.[97] But this practice, like other methods used in *Hav.*, has produced an atmosphere utterly alien to the stylized representations of life and human beings that make the weaker ME metrical romances bloodless and wearisome. Rare examples of extravagance in *Hav.* are the number of men slain (especially by the hero) in the assault on the *greyue*'s house, the number of children (viz., fifteen) born to Havelok and Goldeborw as king and queen of England, and the statement that all the sons became kings and all the daughters queens. But the first is a type of exaggeration common in OF epics and in ME works of the same kind. In general, the universally acknowledged 'realism' of *Hav.* (which goes further than has been generally recognized) makes it seem somewhat inappropriate to call this work a 'romance'. The title *Vita Hauelok* inscribed at the head of the Laud text suggests that Havelok was regarded as a secular Christian hero; and the point of the story, for certain thirteenth- and fourteenth-century chroniclers, might be called political (see p. lvii).

There is no secure criterion for judging whether the morality expressed in *Hav.* is conventional or indirectly represents the author's own outlook. The main figures in the story are rendered as extremes of character: Havelok, like Aþelwold, is totally noble, virtuous, and without blemish; Ubbe is, as a man in authority, appropriately commanding, and is totally loyal and devoted to his hereditary lord (as Grim is, once he knows who Havelok really is); Godrich and Godard are totally wicked. Godrich is shown to be the true type of self-destructive evil by his pointless and involuntary persistence in rejecting good, when he scorns Havelok's offer of pardon (2723 ff.). All these figures, and Goldeborw with them, are types of good and evil respectively, and to that extent the kind of fictive human beings who might be thought characteristic of a romantic tale. But the author of *Hav.* has gone well beyond the conventions of medieval romantic fiction in making credible human beings out of these types.

The extent to which he has filled his story with facts, events, and institutions of the real life of his own time goes far beyond what is normally found in medieval romances. On the other hand, his treatment of them is not stylized as such things commonly are in OF epics: it is all done so naturally as to be easy to overlook. Not all of it is from our author's hand. The much slighter AN versions provided the suggestions for the parliament at Lincoln (1000 ff.); for the list of fish that Grim habitually took (758 ff.); for Godard (displacing Ubbe) as the

---

[97] See Pope and Reid, vol. ii, pp. 18–19.

steward, i.e. seneschal, of Denmark, and for the (here more frequent and authentic) references to formal acts of homage and fealty. But to have the Archbishop of York as the celebrant of Hauelok's wedding was his own idea, like that prelate's factually true presence at the parliament in Lincoln (1179–81).

He is responsible for bringing in, by way of official persons, the itinerant justices, the sergeants of the peace, and the beadles freshly appointed by the new regent (263–73); Ubbe as the person whom Hauelok bribes (sc. to get exemption from tolls as a foreign merchant intending to move about the country with his wares (1627–40)); and Bernard Brun the *greyue* (1750 ff.). And this is to say nothing of the Earl of Chester, and of the creation of other named and subsidiary characters such as Bertram the earl Godrich's cook (881, 2899) and the brigand chief Griffin Galle (2029–30).

The author of *Hav.* is also responsible for adding official acts performed or in prospect, such as the manumission of Grim by charter (530, 628–32), a very rare phenomenon in medieval literature; the likewise rare account of a wedding as a money payment (1173–6); the formal establishment of Ubbe as the feudal ruler of Denmark in Hauelok's projected absence, and the ceremonial use of the staff to do it (2513–20); the oath taken by the bystanders to support the *greyue*'s account of the attack by brigands (2013–16); and the setting up of a court to try both the traitors (2465 ff., 2811–14).

The author further shows unusual knowledge of legal facts or documents in turning to advantage the mixed marriage of a free wife (and her 'disparagement') and a supposedly unfree husband as the reason (for Godrich) why he would be able to cheat Goldeborw out of her inheritance (1090–1100). His use of the writ of military summons is another impressive example (2549–66), like his sense of the importance of the offence of *felonye, tresoun, and tricherye* to one's lord (444 n.). In the ecclesiastical sphere, the anathema reminiscent of the 'Great Sentence' (426–36 and n.) is hardly to be matched in the medieval literature of entertainment. His knowledge of social and feudal institutions also appears in his echoes of formulae from documents—'till the day he could live and die' (257 n.); 'woods and fields', apropos of rights of tenure in the wording of a grant of land (1444–5).

A similar procedure is his exceptional use of local colour in his settings from real life, as with the green on the southern side of Lincoln, or 'the bridge' [sc. on the Witham, and hence the same as the surviving 'High Bridge'] and its fish market.

All this (apart from other things in the poem) makes *Hav.* an intensely realistic work. A man with these resources must have been familiar at first hand with the institutions and documents in question, and is therefore likely to have been a clerk, and one of some distinction.

VI. THE DATE OF COMPOSITION

There is more and better evidence for the dating of *Hav.* than for that of most ME romances. The case rests on three main points,[98] two of which are discussed at the appropriate places below and cannot be fully re-traversed here. As it happens, these matters lead into a related issue, which is accordingly dealt with below (pp. lxvii–lxix): was there an earlier ME version of *Hav.*?

1. The reference to Roxburgh (139 and 265) is an idiosyncratic variant of a traditional mode of reference to the two terminal points of one of the four 'royal' roads of Britain.[99] But its traditional character does not matter here, since it explicitly equates this route with the length of England (264) instead of Britain (which, in the more usual pattern of the type, the four roads are said to traverse).

Of the two periods when the castle of Roxburgh was in English hands,[100] the later accords much better (though this is a matter of individual judgement) with other indications of the approximate date of composition of *Hav.* The anterior limit of 1295 or 1296 is contingent on our ruling out altogether the other period between 1174 and 1189— which latter was actually preferred by M. Deutschbein[101] (as it has been by at least one other person since), because he believed that the idealistic picture of Aþelwold (27–109) was more likely—though he himself had shown it to be of a traditional type—to have been modelled on Henry II than on Edward I. But this is not a substantial point.

2. The references in 1007 and 1180 to a *parlement* at Lincoln carry considerable weight, for a reason that has not in the past been given the attention that it deserves. See 1179–80 n.

3. The most clear-cut piece of evidence for a later limit is one so far generally passed over—the unpublished *Le Petit Bruit* of Rauf de Bohun, on which, and for the relevant passage of the text, see Introduction II, 6. The author's statement that he composed his work in

---

[98] See 265 n. and 1179 n.; and *SMP* pp. 191–201.
[99] See *SMP* pp. 191 ff.
[100] See *SMP* p. 196.
[101] *Studien zur Sagengeschichte Englands*, vol. i (Cöthen, 1906), pp. 165–6.

1310 means almost certainly that *Hav.* must have been composed before that date.

4. It is unavoidable to notice here, because of what has been made of it (and in revised form recently; see notes 106 and 107 below), another fact, which calls for more critical assessment. The unpublished AN prose *Brut* which is the source of the ME prose *Brut*[102] is extant (in four MSS) in a form that ends in 1272. It was in due course carried chronologically further (in a form preserved in other MSS[103]), e.g. to 1333 (the date of the battle of Halidon Hill); and the ME translation goes on to 1377 (and thereafter in two different translations).

The first form of the AN work already contains a summary but skilfully told version of the story of Havelok.[104] This account agrees substantially enough with those of Gaimar and the *Lai* to be recognizably the same type of version, and probably (or, as Brie thinks, certainly) derives from Gaimar. Among other things, the names of persons in the story (with one exception, discussed below) are as in Gaimar and the *Lai*. But Brie remarked that this version had 'features' which it shared with *Hav.*.[105] And since he believed that the extant *Hav.* could not have been composed before 1301 (the year of the parliament at Lincoln), he concluded (p. 364) that there must have been an earlier (ME) version of *Hav.* from which the AN prose *Brut* got the 'features' in question, and hence that a ME *Hav.* was in being by 1272 (when the AN *Brut* in its first form ends).

This conclusion has been taken further in the two recent studies of H. Meyer-Lindenberg[106] and G. B. Jack.[107] They do not believe that the *parlement* of *Hav.* 1007 and 1180 owes anything to the actual parliament of 1301 at Lincoln; and being thus free not to set an anterior limit of 1301, they conclude that the version of *Hav.* available to the author of the AN prose *Brut* (as they believe one to have been, in accordance with Brie's views) was the extant poem. Mr Jack accordingly thinks that the latter must have been composed by 1272 or soon after.

What does not seem to have been realized is that the evidence for this important conclusion is thin. The 'features' noted by Brie as correspondences between the AN prose *Brut* in its first form (as in the best MS, BN fonds fr. 14640, of *c.* 1300) and *Hav.* are only two in

---

[102] Ed. F. Brie, EETS, os 131 (1906) and 136 (1908).
[103] See F. Brie, *Geschichte und Quellen der mittelenglischen Prosachronik The Brute of England*, especially pp. 13–17, 51.
[104] Printed by F. Brie, 'Zum Fortleben der *Havelok*-sage', 358–371, at 362–3.
[105] Ibid., p. 363.
[106] 'Zur Datierung des Havelok', *Anglia*, 86 (1968), 89–112.
[107] 'The Date of Havelok', *Anglia*, 95 (1977), 20–33.

number—the pledge that the dying king exacted from his brother-in-law (as he is in the 'French' form of the tradition) to bring up his daughter and in due course see her suitably married; and the name *Birkabeyn* for Havelok's father. The AN *Brut* in a further continuation represented in MS Rawlinson D. 329 (*c.* 1350) provides another correspondence with *Hav.*, in replacing the name *Argentille* for the heroine with *Goldeburgh*. Brie points out ('Zum Fortleben der *Havelok*-sage', p. 363 n. 6) that the same has happened in all the other MSS of the AN prose *Brut* in the 'Shorter Version' (by which he means the continuation till just before the battle of Halidon Hill), while *Argentille* is retained in the MSS of the 'Longer Version', which ends at a point just after the battle.

This is an apt illustration of the principle that a name can enter a story, or replace another, or be dropped, independently of the story-pattern—e.g. by contamination with another version. And if contamination can operate at one point, how can one know that it has not operated at another? The only reasonably secure criterion (which, even so, may not always be conclusive) for the direct dependence of one version of a story on another is the occurrence in each of a sequence of logically indispensable steps in the action.

It is important to note that the one other point cited by Brie as a correspondence between the AN prose *Brut* in its first form and *Hav.* is not peculiar to them: if it occurred nowhere else it would carry much more weight. The *Lai* (216–32) contains an altogether explicit version of the scene in which the dying king exacted from Edelsi (Godrich in *Hav.*) the pledge to care for the king's daughter and her inheritance. It does not necessarily follow that the *Lai* was the source of this point in the AN prose *Brut*, but merely that the point is not really conclusive evidence for the dependence of the *Brut* on *Hav.* and hence for 1272 or soon after as the later limit for the composition of *Hav.*

There is one so far unnoticed quasi-correspondence that does seem to be peculiar to the AN prose *Brut* and *Hav.* AN *haut* is used of Havelok in the former (once only), as the ME equivalent *heie* is in *Hav.* in all instances but one,[108] to mean 'tall'. But at the point where the dying king enjoins Godrich to bestow Goldeborw on the man 'of highest rank [or 'birth']' (199), the AN prose *Brut* says merely:

al plus fort home e plus vayllaunt ... (ed. Brie, 'Zum Fortleben der *Havelok*-sage', p. 362)

[108] In 988, 1072, 1081–2, 1084; cf. 983–4. In 199 the sense is crucially different (see 199–200 n.).

It is when the author of the AN prose *Brut* recounts how Edelsi married Argentille to his scullion that he describes the latter as:

> le *plus haut*, le plus fort, e le plus vaylaunt de cors (ibid.).

This context, in which *de cors* perhaps modifies all three preceding adjectives, requires the sense 'tall'; and there are no other applications of *haut* to Havelok in the story as told in the AN prose *Brut*.

In that work, accordingly, there is no explicit example of such punning on two senses of *haut* as there is on two senses of *heie* in *Hav.* (notably 1081–4). And it seems unlikely that there ever was—that e.g. *haut* in the sense 'of high rank' might have dropped out of the first passage above. For instance, the ME *Brute* (ed. Brie, vol. i, p. 92) reads thus in the two passages from the AN prose *Brut*:

> ... done here bene marede to *þe strengest and worþieste* man ... (l. 7)

> ... mariede here to a knaf of his kechyne þat me callede Curan; and he bicome *þe worþiest* man & *strongest of body* ... (l. 19).

Significantly, in the *Lai* the word on which Edelsi's pledge to the king and his breach of it turn is not one that means 'tall': Edelsi chooses the scullion Cuaran as the heroine's husband (363–73) because Cuaran is demonstrably the 'strongest' of men in the literal sense. Edelsi is thus able in effect to carry out an 'ambiguous oath'. But the play on two senses of *fort*—if there is one—is relatively feeble, since the semantic contrast of 'physically strong' to 'mighty' (which is what the dying king presumably meant by *fort*) is hardly a vibrant one.

The pun in *Hav.* on *hei(e)* in the senses 'of high rank or birth' and 'tall' is much neater, since the point about Havelok was precisely that he was a king's son, though at first not known to be such. The pun has thus been skilfully integrated into the action, and has been underlined by repetition; and it is not matched in any other version. It therefore seems likely to be an individual and original stroke. And the solitary use of *haut* (as 'tall') in the first form of the AN prose *Brut*, if derived from it, would be a jejune and inept reduction of such a pun. It seems correspondingly unlikely that *Hav.* was the model for it, and hence that *Hav.* had been (on this evidence) composed by 1272.

One fact that has to be fitted into all this has been universally overlooked in Brie's time and since.[109] The AN prose *Brut* in its earliest form (i.e. ending with the year 1272) contains not only a version of the story of Havelok, but (at an earlier point) a summary

---

[109] e.g. by me, *SMP* pp. 196–8.

statement about his having become king of England because of his marriage to the 'lawful heir':

E touz iours apres furent les couenauntes tenues e le truage rendu, tanqe a temps de Hauelok, qe fu Roi de Denmarz e de ceste terre auxi par Goldeburgh, q'il auoit espuse, qe fu dreit heir de ceste terre.

(MS Additional 35092, fo. 20ᵛ)[110]

This statement recurs in other chronicles, e.g. Rauf de Bohun (see Brie, 'Zum fortleben . . .' p. 369 and II, 6). The preoccupation with the grounds for Havelok's rule over England (as distinct from his title to Denmark) is foreshadowed in Gaimar's comment (reproduced verbatim in the *Lai* 1101–2):

> Il n'ot nul eir si dreiturier
> Cum Haveloc e sa muillier. (809–10)

Moreover, the statement in the AN prose *Brut* may well be based on knowledge of the whole story of Havelok, since it makes three points— that he was king of Denmark, that he married the lawful heir to 'this land', and that he ruled 'this land' as a result. And these climactic points summarize what would have been seen as the essential significance of the story for dynastic history.

The phrase 'this land' is enough to show that the statement cannot be based on Gaimar (whose story of Havelok was the source of that in the AN prose *Brut*) or the *Lai*, since both these represent the domains of Havelok and his wife as the two local kingdoms (roughly Norfolk and Suffolk, and Lincoln and Lindsey respectively) previously ruled by Adelbriht and Edelsi. In other words, 'this land' means 'England'. The matter is spectacularly clinched by the use of the name *Goldeburgh* for Havelok's wife, in contrast to that of Argentille in the actual story of Havelok as told not only in the AN prose *Brut* itself, but by Gaimar and the *Lai*. *Goldeburgh* is (up to *c.* 1300) otherwise peculiar to *Hav.* and this statement in the AN prose *Brut*.

All this means that the statement must derive from a form of the story that was identical with *Hav.* in two points—the fundamental one of the modernized political setting (the kingdom of England), as well as one more exposed to scribal interference (the name of Havelok's wife). The implications are far-reaching.

It seems unlikely that the entry was added by a scribe in a lost

---

[110] Kindly transcribed for me by Prof. D. Gray. The text of MS BN fr. 14640, fo. 6ᵛ (a transcript of which has been very kindly provided by the Conservateur of the Cabinet des Manuscrits) is identical, apart from differences of spelling, as is that of the continuation to 1333 in MS Rawlinson D. 329, fo. 23ʳ.

common antecedent of the two complete MSS of the AN prose *Brut* in its earliest form—i.e. somewhat before 1300 (the palaeographical date of MS BN fonds fr. 14640). Thus it confronts us with what looks like a conflict of evidence, if we accept the following assumptions in the argument:

1. That the statement naming Goldeburgh was based on the whole story of Havelok, and not on a summarizing formula;
2. that the AN prose *Brut* was compiled very soon after the date of the events with which the record ends, i.e. 1272; and
3. that the version of *Hav.* in question was the extant one, which (there is reason to think) was composed between 1295–6, or even 1301, and 1310 (see pp. xxvii–xxx and 265 n.).

The dilemma is contained in (2) and (3), which cannot both be true. The simplest course is to assume—as Brie had concluded, on other grounds that could not sustain the case[111]—that a ME version of *Hav.* was in being by *c.* 1272; and that it was not the extant one, but an antecedent of it, minus at least the references to Roxburgh and perhaps to the *parlement* at Lincoln (ll. 1007 and 1180), that provided the material for this statement about Havelok and Goldeburgh in the AN prose *Brut*.

These two important conclusions are henceforward (in this edition) necessarily assumed to be valid—but only with the utmost reserve, since they are founded on just one fact, and its interpretation, and are accordingly highly vulnerable. There is, for instance, no means of being certain that the earliest extant form of the AN prose *Brut* would necessarily have been put together immediately or soon after the date at which the record ends.

The foregoing considerations do not take us very far back in time; and they do not avail to show that the story was first composed in English. There are signs that the name *Goldeburgh* was rare in real life.[112] It is not recorded in OE, in which names with *Gold-* as first element are all but unknown.[113] Only two examples in ordinary usage are known to me so far. One is recorded in a Latin document of *c.* 1160–5, which is a confirmation by a London goldsmith Peter Merevin of a grant by him and his wife *Goldburga*, in her last will, of 12*d.* annually from land of theirs to Southwark Priory.[114] The other is attested for a woman *Goldburga* who

---

[111] See pp. lxvff.
[112] See Bo Seltén, *The Anglo-Saxon Heritage in Middle English Personal Names: East Anglia 1100–1399*, pp. 15, 33–6.
[113] See M. Boehler, *Die altenglischen Frauennamen* (Germanische Studien, 98, Berlin, 1930), p. 80.
[114] G. F. Warner and H. J. Ellis, *Facsimiles of Royal and Other Charters in the British Museum*, vol. i (London, 1903), charter 47.

was the subject of one of the miracles in the Latin *Life and Miracles of St William of Norwich*,[115] composed *c.* 1172–3,[116] which contains twenty-three female personal names current in ordinary usage.

But where *Hav.* is concerned, the background and the origin of the name *Goldeborw* are more complicated; and its immediate origin may be literary. Only six female personal names are used in *Hav.*; and it is a remarkable fact that no less than four of them occur in this *Life*. Apart from *Goldburga*, there are *Leuiua* (for someone who, as the boy saint's aunt, is one of the main figures in his story),[117] *Gunnilda*, and *Leua*[118] (for two women who are the subject of other miracles)—and these, in the equivalent ME forms, are the names of Grim's two daughters and his wife in *Hav.* Second, *Goldeburc* and *Swanburc* occur in the AN *Romance of Horn* (composed *c.* 1170)[119] as the names of the hero's grandmother and mother respectively—and *Swanborw* is the name of one of the hero's two sisters in *Hav.*

Leofgifu, *Gunnhild*, and *Leofa* were all in use in OE, and *Leofgifu* was common at least by 1086.[120] Nevertheless, the occurrence of the four female names *Goldburga*, *Leuiua*, *Gunnilda*, and *Leua* both in the *Life* and (in the corresponding ME forms) in *Hav.* cannot be by chance. If the name *Goldeburgh* was already in the form of the story that was received by the author of the extant *Hav.*, he may have been responsible for bringing the other three names into his own version as a result of finding all four in the *Life*. Similarly, he may well have taken over *Swanborw* from the AN *Horn* because it occurred there along with *Goldeburc* and in the same specific context (of the hero's close female kin). It is not recorded in OE: the only female name in *Swan-* is *Swanhild* (twelfth century).[121] The OE antecedent of the name of Havelok's other sister *Elfled* is very common.[122]

The statement about Havelok and his title to rule England through his marriage to Goldeborw as the rightful heir does not appear in Geoffrey of Monmouth's *Historia Regum Britanniae*, Gaimar's *Estoire*, or Wace's *Brut* (composed 1155) at the usual point (2577–98). The name *Goldeborw* cannot have been introduced into the story of Havelok by the author of the extant *Hav.*, since it occurs in the brief passage in the AN prose *Brut* (i.e. by or a little later than 1272). It may conceivably have been first adopted in the antecedent ME version of

---

[115] Ed. A. Jessopp and M. R. James (Cambridge, 1896), p. 156.
[116] Ibid., p. liii. [117] Ibid., pp. 40–4.
[118] Ibid., pp. 273 and 266.
[119] Ed. M. K. Pope and T. B. W. Reid, vol. i, l. 257 and *passim*.
[120] See O. von Feilitzen, *The Pre-Conquest Personal Names of Domesday Book* (Nomina Germanica No. 3, Uppsala, 1937), pp. 312, 277, 310.
[121] Boehler, op. cit., p. 118. [122] Boehler, op. cit., p. 15.

Hav. that we have now been obliged to posit provisionally—i.e. after 1172–3, if it was suggested by either or both of the examples in the *Life of St William* and the AN *Romance of Horn*. In that case, the other three names *Leuiue*, *Gunnild*, and *Leue* may have been introduced either in that antecedent ME version or the extant one; and the same must be said of the name *William Wendut* (see pp. lx–lxi).

Since the five versions of the story of Havelok up to *c.* 1300 do not differ widely in the action (as distinct from adjuncts to it), a lost ME antecedent of *Hav.* would probably have agreed substantially with them in this regard. A work on such a subject would at this time (after 1172–3) have been in verse. In any case, it is conceivable that another writer wishing to tell the story at the end of the thirteenth century might have chosen to rework, paraphrase, or otherwise take over some material from an earlier version in his own.

Such a process might preserve whole sections of the antecedent work; but it would be liable to produce inconsistencies or other symptoms of adaptation. In *Hav.*, one case above all that would be open to this explanation is the episode of the attack on the *greyue*'s house (see III, 11). A process of reworking might be expected to leave plain traces in rhymes implying more than one variety of ME; and little of this sort is noticeable in *Hav.* In an extreme form of the process, the later of two versions might be a recension or expansion of the earlier; while this cannot be ruled out for *Hav.*, there is no evidence of it.

The hypothetical ME antecedent of *Hav.* (which is likely to have contained the name *Goldeborw*) cannot go back nearer to Gaimar than a point over fifty years later than his version. The story is not to be found in Geoffrey of Monmouth or even (after Gaimar) in Wace; but Gaimar cannot have invented it. The nature of his source, and the language in which it was expressed, are not ascertainable.

5. The parallels in Mannyng's *Handlyng Synne* (composed 1303), ll. 5611–2 and 5809–10, to *Hav.* 680–1 and 820–1 respectively are commonly regarded as direct imitations by Mannyng of the latter.[123] Sisam remarks that it is difficult to establish imitation in ME romances because they abound in conventional phrases, but in this instance admits it because of 'Mannyng's special connexion with the *Hauelok* story' (by which he presumably means the knowledge of it that Mannyng shows in his *Chronicle of England*, composed in 1330[124]).

These two parallels are superficially impressive, since the rhyme-

[123] See 821 n., and Skeat–Sisam, ed. cit., p. xxiii and n. 1.
[124] Ed. T. Hearne, *Peter Langtoft's Chronicle* (as illustrated and improved by Robert of Brunne) (Oxford, 1725), vol. i. 25–6; see Skeat–Sisam, ed. cit., p. xvi.

words in both couplets are the same as in *Hav.*; the second is perhaps the more impressive because of the phrase *a ferþing(es) nok*. But there is no knowing whether this colloquial-sounding expression might not have had wider currency without getting into general literary use (in which case Mannyng might have picked it up elsewhere). The sort of expression that would carry weight in this connection is something highly unusual, or even aberrant, and therefore highly personal. Since the two parallels in question are not recognizably of that order, they can hardly rank as proof that Mannyng had read *Hav.*, or heard it read or recited, by the time he composed *Handlyng Synne*, and that *Hav.* had therefore been composed by 1303. A third parallel (not mentioned by Skeat–Sisam or Holthausen in their editions) is a more convincing instance of what might well be imitation by Mannyng.[125] But it occurs in his *Chronicle* (4117–8), of 1330; it is thus of less interest for the dating of *Hauelok* than the other two passages might have been, since there is already evidence for a later limit of 1310 (VI, 3 above).

6. So far as the language of *Hav.* is concerned, as a guide to the date of composition, the seductively clear analysis and firm conclusions of Skeat[126] regarding the much more extensive use of the final vowel (in pronunciation) that is written *-e* in *Hav.* than in *Handlyng Synne* deserve to be pondered on their own merits. But they cannot be taken into account here, simply because:

(*a*) the accidence of a given variety of ME might be radically remodelled in a short time, since it was shaped by the needs of the system as a whole and hence partly by systemic processes such as the workings of analogy. The example of the *Ormulum* (which on the palaeographical evidence of the autograph MS must have been composed by *c.* 1200) shows how a given variety of ME accidence may be more 'advanced' than that of a near-contemporary variety such as in the 'Katherine Group'.

(*b*) rates of change in the accidence of individual varieties of ME were accordingly not the same.

Thus the difference of scale in the pronunciation of final *-e* as between *Hav.* and *Handlyng Synne* cannot safely be treated as a purely chronological one. Skeat's conclusion, on the evidence of final *-e* in each, that 'the first draft of the poem must surely have been composed earlier than 1300' might (if we had access to the whole truth) happen to be right, notwithstanding the potential significance of the references to a *parlement* at Lincoln. But there is no secure means of establishing

---

[125] See 744–5 n.   [126] Skeat–Sisam, ed. cit., pp. xxiv–xxv.

it by comparison of the treatment of final *-e* with that in *Handlyng Synne*.

For certain essentials under this head see 'The Scansion of *Hauelok*', in *Middle English Studies Presented to Norman Davis* (ed. D. Gray and E. G. Stanley, Oxford, 1983), pp. 195–234. The following must be added here:

The main example of phonetically incomplete correspondences in rhyme in *Hav.* is assonances. There is a ME system of at least ten classes of assonance that are based on phonetic affinity. Any member of the following may assonate with another in its class:

1. voiceless plosives
2. voiced plosives
3. voiceless fricatives
4. voiced fricatives
5. nasals
6. liquids
7. nasals + voiced plosives
8. liquids + voiced plosives
9. nasals and voiced fricatives
10. liquids and voiced fricatives
11. nasals + voiced plosives and nasals + voiced affricates

Thus in *Hav.*:

1. *shop*: *hok* 1102–3; *fet*: *ek* 1304–5; *maked*: *schaped* 1647–8
2. none
3. *bouth* (i.e. presumably for *boht*): *oft* 884–5
4. See 13 below
5. *rym*: *fyn* 21–2; *yeme*: *quene* 182–3
6. *yer*: *del* 1334–5
7. *longe*: *Engelonde* 172–3
8. *(-)feld*: *swerd* 1825–6, 2635–6
9. none
10. none
11. *fonge*: *gronge* 764–5
12. (not among the common ME types) voiceless dental plosive and voiceless dental fricative: *oth*: *wot* 2527–8
[13.] Since the rhyme *awe* 1293: *lowe* implies that /ɣ/ had > /w/, the following rhymes are apparently assonances of /v/ on /w/:

   drawe: *haue* 1298–9;   *knaue*: *plawe* 950–1;   *ofslawen*: *Rauen* 2677–8; *serued*: *werwed* 1915–6.

But this is not one of the customary types of ME assonance. And it is striking that similar rhymes are used by Mannyng: *awe* n.:*saue* (other MS *haue*), *drawen* p.p.:*hauen* n., in *Chronicle* 7150 and 7722.

Accordingly, Boerner (*Die Sprache Roberd Mannyngs of Brunne* §53, n. 2) treats the latter (perhaps rightly) as assonances of /v/ on /ɣ/, with a second phonetic development by which /ɣ/ remained, alongside the regular one to /w/ (for which see Boerner further §196). In *Hav.*, likewise, this would require us to assume that there were two different pronunciations of /ɣ/.

The rhyming technique in *Hav.* is on the whole phonetically exact. Among the infrequent exceptions is the rhyming of slack /oː/ on tense /oː/, for examples of which see below, Language, I Phonology, 13. 1(*a*)–(*c*). Since at least two or three of these latter cannot be explained away, rhyming of slack /eː/ on tense /eː/ must also be reckoned with, and is more likely than raising of the former before dentals (except when the early mod. E evidence establishes it). This view is confirmed by ll. 87–105, which must be meant to be monorhymed, but in which the rhyme-words include /eː/ of various origins and potentially varying quality.

Another (and occasional) irregularity is the rhyming of a short vowel on a long one, as in:

on:*don* 116–17, *shon* 860–1, 970–1; *wiþe*:*siþe* n. 1052–3; *syþes*:*liþes* 2163–4.

In the very common rhymes of *wel* adv. on *del* (13 examples), and that on *tel* n. 190–1, there is probably a long vowel in *wel*, since this is attested by the spelling *wel* in the *Ormulum*, e.g. 1033, 1691 etc.

The rhyming in ll. 87–105 of a block of nineteen lines on a variety (more probably, more than one variety) of /eː/ throughout must be meant as a sequence on a single vowel of approximately the same quality. I know of no parallel in ME rhymed couplet verse. The nearest thing to it in OF is the rare use of octosyllabic lines grouped in short 'tirades' (stanzas of variable length), on a single rhyme in each tirade. The three known examples are the fragmentary OProv. *Alexandre* of Alberic, *La Chancon de Sainte Foy*, and *Gormont & Isembart*.[127] The tirades may be of six to *c.* 15 lines (in the *Chancon* mostly eleven).

The passage in *Hav.* can be read as something tacked on to what goes before; and the content divides it into two parts of ten and nine lines respectively. But why the author (or for that matter a hypothetical interpolator) should have launched into anything of this kind at this point is an impenetrable mystery.

---

[127] Ed. respectively A. Foulet, *The Medieval French Roman D'Alexandre*, vol. iii, Elliott Monographs 38 (Princeton, 1949), pp. 37–41; A. Fabre (Rodez, 1940); A. Bayot, *CFMA* 14** (3rd edn., Paris, 1931).

The following account of the language of *Hav.* has had to be most drastically streamlined and pruned to the bare essentials, with minimal examples. But this is based on a full study which may be published elsewhere. In both accounts, only words or forms established by rhymes are normally used as evidence for the phonology and the accidence.

I. *Phonology*

A. *Vowels and Diphthongs of Stressed Syllables*

1. The reflex of early OE /a/ rhymes
   on OF /a/ in *shame*: *blame* 2425.
2. The reflex of early OE /æ/ rhymes
   (*a*) on OE /a/ in -*bare* a.: *ware* n. 767;
   (*b*) when subject to breaking and *i*-mutation before a lengthening consonant-group, on /e/ or /e:/ in *weldes*: *feldes* 1360;
   (*c*) when subject to smoothing before *r* + consonant, perhaps on /e/ in -*merk*: *serk* 605;
   (*d*) before front /g/, in a closed monosyllable, on the reflex of OE /e/ in *tayl*: *seyl* 2507 (in which the diphthong is shown by the Early mod. E development to have been /ai/).
3. The reflex of early OE /e/ rhymes
   (*a*) when subject to diphthongization by a preceding palatal consonant, on /e/ or /e:/ in *yelde*: *elde* 2713;
   (*b*) when subject to breaking and smoothing, on /e/ in *werkes*: *clerkes* 34;
   (*c*) see 2(*d*).
4. The reflex of early OE /i/ rhymes
   (*a*) when subject to breaking and followed by palatal consonant group + prim. OE *i, j*, on /i:/ in *swire*: *sire* 311;
   (*b*) when subject to back-mutation, on /i/ in the OA-derived *milk* (: *suilk* 644).
5. The reflex of early OE /y/ rhymes on /i/ in *sinne*: *blinne* 2376.
6. For OE /a:/, see 13 below.
7. The reflex of early OE $æ^1$ rhymes
   (*a*) on slack /e:/ in *red* n.: *bred* 827;
   (*b*) on tense /e:/ in *wede*: *fede* 323;
   (*c*) on the reflex of $æ^2$ in *wede*: *lede* 2826;
   (*d*) when shortened in OE, on /a/ and /e/ in *adrad*: *bad* 1049, : *bed* 1259.

8. The reflex of early OE $\bar{æ}^2$ rhymes
   (a) predominantly on that of OE tense /e:/, e.g. *lede*: *mede* 687;
   (b) when shortened in OE, on /e/ in *ledde*: *fedde* 786, and /a/ in *cladde*: *radde* 1355.
9. The reflex of early OE $\bar{y}$ rhymes on /i:/ in *fyr*: *shir* 916.
10. The reflex of early OE $\bar{e}a$ rhymes
    (a) on /e:/, probably slack, $< \bar{æ}^1$ in *bred*: *red* n. 826;
    (b) on tense /e:/ in *leue*: *reue* 1627;
    (c) when subject to *i*-mutation in OE, on tense /e:/ in *leues*: *þeues* 1782;
    (d) before OE /χ/, or /ɣ/ + vowel, on /i:/ in *hey*: *fri* 1072, and /e:/ or /i:/ in *eye* 'eye': *fleye* inf. 1813;
    (e) when shortened, on OE /e/ in *þrette*: *lette* 1164, *sette* 2405.
11. The reflex of early OE $\bar{e}o$ rhymes
    (a) on tense /e:/ in *tre*: *he* 2033;
    (b) on the reflex of OE $\bar{e}a$ + /ɣ/ in *fleye* v.: *eye* 'eye' 1828;
    (c) when stress-shifted, on tense /o:/ in *sho*: *do* 1233, and before w, on /u:/ in *yow*: *now* 160.
12. The reflex of early OE $\bar{i}o$ (> OM, OWS $\bar{e}o$) rhymes
    (a) when subject to *i*-mutation, on tense /e:/ in *dere* a.: *here* v. 2883;
    (b) when subject to *i*-mutation before /w/, on tense /e:/ in *newe*: *grewe* 2975.
13. The reflex of OE /a:/ rhymes
    (i) (a) on the reflex of OE tense /o:/ in *more*: *swore* 2307; *oth*: *soth* 2010; *þore*: *swore* 2013 (if OE *þāra*, not ON *þár*, is the etymon);
       (b) on ME tense /o:/ in *hom*: *grom* 790. Though *grom* is of unknown etymology, the /u/ in pres. E *groom* implies an antecedent ME tense /o:/, which > /u:/ by the Vowel Shift and was later shortened. As *grom* rhymes on tense /o:/ in *dom* 2473, one of these rhymes must be a phonetically inexact one, of slack /o:/ on tense /o:/.
          For *boþen*: *utdrowen* 2659 cf. VII *Note on Versification*, Assonances 13.
       (c) after /w/, on the reflex of OE /o:/ in *swo*: *to* 324, 2138, 2961, *undo* 2739; *two*: *do* 1805, 2731; *wo*: *to* 2746. The pres. E pronunciation of *two*, *who* shows that in these two words, at least, the root-vowel had been raised in ME by the preceding lip-rounded consonant to tense /o:/.
    (ii) (a) on /a/ in *baþe* (whether < ON *bāðir* or OE *bāðā*): *raþe* adv. 2595, 2937;

(b) on OF /a/ followed by a nasal in *anan*:*Iohan* 176 (see n.), 1112, 2563;

(c) on MDu. /a:/ in *rore*:*gore* 2497 (see *EGS* 3 (1949–50), 69–72). MDu. *gaer*, *gare*, *gere* appears in ME and later E only as *gare* (*OED* sb.², from 1606) and *OED* s.v. *gere*, first in Chaucer). Thus *gore* here is probably a scribe's mechanical alteration of *gare*.

(d) before medial /w/ < the OE back fricative /ɣ/, as in *awe* (< OE *āgan*):: *lowe* (*hlāw*) 1293, on OE /a/ in *þrawe* (OE *þrāge*) : *lawe* (OE *lagu*) 1216; *sawe* pt. pl. 1183: *lawe*; and on ON /a/ in *þrawe*:*awe* n. 276.

Hence the other rhymes of *sawe* pt. pl. on *hawe* (OE *āgan*) 1188, *wowe* (OE *wāge*) 1963, must also contain either /a:/ or /a/, as likewise those on *lawe*, *lowe* a. and adv. (OE *lag(e)*) 958, 2079, 2144, 2431, 2767, 2945.

The unique rhyme of *sowen* pt. pl. 1056 on tense /o:/ in *lowen* may therefore be a rhyme on the unstressed syllable. The rare OM *gesāgun*,[128] beside normal OA *sǣgon* (ME *seyen*, *syen*), or alternatively OSw. *sagho*, would be ante-cedents compatible with the other type above. Infiltration of a WS-derived type (OE *sāwon*) is in *Hav.* less probable.

(e) before medial /w/ < OE *w*, on unrounded or non-rounded /a:/, or on /a/ shortened < /a:/, in *lowe* (OE *hlāw*): *shawe*** 1700 (OE *scāwian*, < *sceāwian* < *scēawian*, with stress shifted from the first element of *ēa* to the second). What excludes slack /o:/ in *lowe* and *shawe* (by rounding of OE /a:/) is the two rhymes of *þrawe* on /a/ in (d) above, since *awe* (< *āgan*), which rhymes in 1293 on *lowe* (< *hlāw*), is in the same phonological category as *þrawe*:*lowe* and *shawe* must therefore likewise have /a:/ or /a/.

It follows that *shawe* must have /a:/ or /a/ in the rhymes *inter se* in 1402*, 1854*, 2057*, 2207, 2785, and hence that the rhyme-words *knawe* v., *mowe* (< OE *mawan*) can be added to our list of words with /a:/ or /a/ < OE /a:/.

The shortening of /a:/ to /a/ that is directly attested in (d) and indirectly in (e) is part of the process by which new ME diphthongs were developed from OE sequences of long (as well as short) vowels, + OE *w*, or the palatal fricative *ġ* (EME /j/), or the velar fricative /ɣ/, which latter > ME /w/ at a rate that differed in individual varieties of

---

[128] Recorded thrice in the Rushworth text of *Matthew* (XXV. 37, 38, and 44, ed. W. W. Skeat, *The Holy Gospels in Anglo-Saxon* (Cambridge, 1871–87).

ME. Cf. Orm's *eȝȝe* < OE *ege* and *clawwess* (OE nom. sg. *clawu*, nom. acc. pl. *clēa*): in his system of spelling the medial consonant could not have been doubled unless it belonged to the same syllable as the preceding vowel.

The treatment of EME /a:/ + /w/ or /ɣ/ (> later ME /w/) is matched in nineteenth-century dialect in north Lincs., where ME *āw* and *aw* have coalesced;[129] and (in ME) in the language of Robert Mannyng of south Lincs. In the language of *Hav.*, at least, OE /a:/ was never rounded to slack /o:/ before /ɣ/ or /w/: see below.

The author's treatment of the reflex of OE /a:/ in rhyme is the most important and revealing feature of the whole system of sounds in his variety of ME. What seems at first sight to be an inconsistency and a conflict of evidence between 1(*a*), (*b*), and (*c*) on the one hand, and 2(*a*) and (*b*) on the other, is to be interpreted as meaning that he knew and used not one, but two, pronunciations of the reflex of OE /a:/— both the non-rounded /a:/ and the rounded slack /o:/ which are in general characteristic of Nth. and non-Nth. ME respectively. These rhymes are in fact phonetically significant, and represent facts of living speech rather than an amalgam in a hypothetical 'literary' form of ME.

This conclusion is assured by the evidence of place-names, as mustered and analysed by E. Ekwall, whose results have been confirmed by G. Kristensson[130] in a further analysis extended to include personal names. The presence of at least six rhymes implying an unconditioned /a:/ or /a/ in *Hav.*, besides five that prescribe unconditioned slack /o:/, is not the puzzling anomaly that it at first seems. Though what is often loosely called 'the Humber–Ribble line' is the boundary (more closely defined by Ekwall)[131] between ME slack /o:/ and ME /a:/, the relevant Lincs. place-names confirm and account for the rhymes in *Hav.* They include forms with ME /a:/ in such numbers as to show that in Lindsey and Kesteven, at least, /a:/ was the indigenous ME reflex of OE /a:/,[132] though /o:/ might have been the type proper to Holland. The *o*-type evidently spread northwards from neighbouring areas of the Midlands, e.g. Notts., Northants., Norfolk. The process can be seen in miniature in *Whaplode* (OE *-(ge)lād*), spelt

---

[129] See J. Wright, *The English Dialect Grammar* (Froude, 1905) §§123–4 and 63; K. Luick, *Untersuchungen zur englischen Lauteschichte* (Strasburg, 1896), p. 24, §39.

[130] See respectively 'The Middle English *ā/ō*-boundary', *English Studies*, 20 (1938), 147–65, and *A Survey of Middle English Dialects 1290–1350*, Lund Studies in English, 35 (Lund, 1967), pp. 17–38, 241–6, and maps 10–17.

[131] Op. cit., pp. 160–3, 166–7.

[132] e.g. *Aby*, *Ailby*, *Aisby* (OScand. *Ā-byr*, *Āli*, *Āsi*), *Cabourn* (ME *cā*) in Lindsey, all recorded from 1086 in Domesday Book), beside *Beltisloe* (OE *-hlāw*), *Boston* (OE *-stān*), *Cuxwould* (OE *-wāld*). See Ekwall, op. cit., pp. 162–3.

Copelade 1086, *Quappelad(e)* 1202, 1235, 1250, 1296, but *Quap(p)elode* 1232 and 1254; and in *Cuxwold*, *Stixwold*, *Syston*, which are spelt with -*a* well into the 13th century. Hence the *o-* rhymes in *Hav.*, and likewise e.g. in the Northern *Sir Tristrem*,[133] and the Lincs. place-names with -*o-*. This accords with the findings of the Middle English Dialect Survey.[134]

B. *Consonants*

1. /ɣ/ has > /w/ in *awe* v. 1293 : *lowe*. Since the change must be posited in all examples in *Hav.*, it follows that rhymes such as *serued* : *werewed* 1915–16, *knaue* : *plawe* 950–1 are assonances of /v/, not on /ɣ/, but on /w/.

2. There is a noticeable bias in rhyme towards the non-assibilated forms of /k/ and (once) /g/ as against the variant type with /tʃ/ and /dʒ/ respectively:

   recke 3 pr. sg. subj. 2048, 2758; /k/ otherwise solely in adverbial -*like* : *hertelike* 1348, *shamelike* 2463, *sikerlike* 422, *unkyndelike* 1251, apart from *kunerike* 2085 and (corrupted to -*riche*) 2401.

   Provided that the text in question shows a strong Scandinavian influence (as *Hav.* does), the non-assibilated forms can be attributed to the currency of ON cognates, e.g. *hrygg-r*, *ríki*, and the adverbial -*lik* which is thought to have been remodelled in -*lega*[135] along with a group of formations such as *líki* 'shape', *lík-r* a., *líklig-r*. Verbs, however, offer so many possibilities for internal analogy as to be explicable in those terms: the syncopated forms of the 2 and 3 pr. sg. *recst*, *recþ* prevented assibilation.

II. *Accidence*

In the type of authorial ME represented in *Hav.*, as in that of Orm and Chaucer, there is no longer a true system of inflexions. What survives as a grammatical ending is the phonetically substantial and therefore serviceable -*es* (syllabic and otherwise) < OE -*as* to mark the plural of virtually all nouns, in virtually all the old grammatical cases. The analogous pattern of accidence in Orm and Chaucer suggests that -*es* (< OE -*es*) had likewise been analogically generalized in *Hav.* to mark the genitive sg. of virtually all types of noun, though the only

---

[133] See E. Kölbing, *Sir Tristrem* (Heilbronn, 1882), pp. lxiv, lxxi–lxxiv, lxxvii, and the other material noticed by A. Brandl, *Thomas of Erceldoune* (Berlin, 1880), pp. 49–52.

[134] As I am kindly informed by Prof. A. McIntosh.

[135] A. Noreen, *Altisländische und altnorwegische Grammatik* (4th edn., Halle, 1923), §248 n. 4.

examples in rhyme are *swines* 782 and *greyues* 1750, the first of which is historically regular, but the second is by origin (ON *greifi*), like the native cognate *gerefa*, a weak noun.

   In the other grammatical cases of the singular of nouns, where all the vowel-endings and -*e* < OE -*an* had been reduced to a single ME written form -*e* (which scansion shows to have been extensively 'elided' and thus 'lost' in *Hav.*), the work of inflexions was now not merely duplicated, but taken over, by prepositions and to some degree word-order. For the arresting exception by which in monosyllabic adjectives syllabic inflexional -*e* was retained and used in an astonishingly consistent and regular way to mark the inherited difference between a 'definite' (i.e. old 'weak') and 'indefinite' (old 'strong') sense,[136] and the plural of all adjectives, see 'The Scansion of *Havelok*'.[137] With that main exception, final -*e* had ceased to be an inflexion in the language of *Hav.*, and survived partly in a rhythmic function, as a handy means of preventing a sequence of two successive full stresses (in speech as in the four-beat and five-beat verse).

A. Nouns

The following minimally illustrates both the inherited and the analogical use of pl. -*es*:

1. OE *stān*-type (strong *o*-declension): nom. *þeues* 2105, obj. *sypes* (after numeral) 2163. *Syþe* 779, 1247, 2190, 2844 (all after *fele*) is a fossilized gen. pl., preserved because, as part of a collocation, it escaped analysis and because plurality was sufficiently expressed by *fele*.

2. OE *bearn*-type (neuters with long root-syllable): nom. *barnes* 1913; obj. *liues* 698; prep. *wiues* 1309. *þinge* obj. 1141, prep. 71 is in collocations with *alle* and *none kines*.

3. Nouns with OE nom. acc. pl. ending in a vowel: nom. *quenes* 2983; obj. *feldes* 1361; prep. *speres* 2323. In prep. *hend* (: nom. sg. *fend* 505, 1413, 2229, and :prep. *frend* 2070) the ON *i*-mutated nom. acc. pl. *hend-r* has been treated like native *i*-mutation nouns.

4. Old weak nouns: obj. *þrotes* 471; prep. *sides* 1851. The historically regular *(bi here) siden* 371 is a scribe's form, since the rhyme-word is an inf. (which in the author's ME had shed -*n*).

Hine 621 is an old gen. pl. (*hīgna*), in which the -*n* was 'metanalysed' as belonging to the stem instead of the ending. It is an implied collective, and hence singular in form. Another collective (and singular form) has been corrupted in the historically regular

---

[136] My attention was kindly drawn to the significance of this distinction in meaning, as a potential reason for the survival of both types, by Mr M. Benskin.

[137] In *Middle English Studies presented to Norman Davis* (Oxford, 1983), pp. 195–234.

(but hypermetrical) pl. *hosen* 970 within the line. In *shon* obj. 861, 970 the *-n* has survived, as widely in ME, in a monosyllabic form ending in a vowel (cf. *Infinitive* below).

Ladden : *stareden* 1039, beside *laddes* within the line at various points, is probably corrupt, since the pt. pl. of verbs is shown by rhymes to have shed *-n* at least at that point in the verse. A pl. *ladde* is difficult to account for, unless, here and in the pl. *grom* (: *dom* obj. sg. 2473)—if this latter is not a collective—the author used a rhyme with discrepant unstressed syllables (see *Kyng Alisaunder*, ii. 149–50 n.), i.e. *laddes*: *starde*; *gromes*: *dom*.

B. *Adjectives*

An instructive major exception to the operation of apocope is the inflexion of adjectives. As in some other forms of ME (including Chaucer's), the use of syllabic final *-e* has been strikingly systematized, in order to mark the distinction between the old 'weak' (definite) and 'strong' (indefinite) types of inflexion. This could now be effectively done only in the singular, because of the coalescence of final vowels in the plural and the loss of final *-n*. But it was done so consistently as to override the operation of apocope.

The following is a minimal sample of the material given on pp. 210–12 of 'The Scansion of *Havelok*', stripped of all the niceties there included.

Words with a monosyllabic OE antecedent, and preceded by the definite article or a demonstrative or a possessive:

1. 1. *Nom. Sg.*
   tĕ bést̆e knĭth 87; *þat fúl̆e fénd* 506; *þi fáyr̆e wíf* 1663.
   In superlatives, there is no syllabic *-e* if it would have produced a trisyllable: *þe stránğest* 1082.
2. *Obj. Sg.*
   þĕ shárp̆e swérd 2646; *þis fáyr̆e génğe* 1736; *his gód̆e swérd* 2734.
   In superlatives, there is no syllabic *-e* if it would have produced a trisyllable: *þe faír̆est þíng* 2866.
3. *Prep. Sg.*
   þĕ gód̆e bóru 774; *þat ílk̆e grén̆e* 2841.
   Again, superlatives do not normally have syllabic *-e* that would make them trisyllabic: *þe fáyr̆est wýmm̆an* 1157.

The plural has *-e* in all grammatical cases: nom. *þe héld̆e mén* 2473, *þo fóul̆e þéŭes* 2045; obj. *mín̆e gód̆e kníht̆es* 2707; prep. *álþerbést̆e mén* 2416.

In the strong-type inflexion the singular is endingless and the plural ends in syllabic -*e*, in accord with the OE model in the nom. sg. and the nom. and acc. pl. respectively:

1. *Nom.* *án gŏd clérk* 1178; *strŏng mán* 1072
2. *Obj.*   *á gŏd tré* 1883; *gód chĭld* 2984
3. *Prep.* *án ŏld séyl* 2508; *gŏd líf* 2934

Plural

1. *Nom.* *gódĕ métĕs* 2341, *míklĕ* 2015
2. *Obj.*   *grétĕ díntĕs* 1438
3. *Prep.* *állĕ mén* 435, *gódĕ bówĕs* 1749.

C. Pronouns

The main points of interest are as follows:

1. The only form, and the only example, of the 3 pers. nom. sg. fem. in rhyme is *sho* 1233. The obj. sg. is *hire* 1231.
2. The nom. pl. of the 3 pers. (once only in rhyme) is *he* 555, also used within the line.
3. The obj. pl. of the 3 pers. is occasionally rendered by the agglutinated -*(e)s* 785 (within the line 971), which is spelt *as* and *ys* as an independent form within the line in 1175. Otherwise the form used (within the line) is *hem*, with *here* as gen. 2069 and *hem* as dative.

   The Scandinavian type of pl. is represented only in *þey*, and perhaps *þere* gen. 1351; *þe(i)m* is not used in *Hav*.

D. Verbs

As the pr. pl., inf., pt. pl. strong and weak and pt. sg. weak, and the past participle are prime instances of -*en* and -*e* as endings, and hence of the variation between syllabic -*en* and -*e* and zero as established and illustrated in 'The Scansion of *Havelok*', pp. 203 ff., only the forms need be registered here, with one or two examples.

Pr. Indic. Sg. 2: -*es*: *wenes* 599
　　　　　　　　 3. -*es*: *weldes* 1360
　　　　　　 Pl. 2. -*e*: *rothe* 2818
　　　　　　　　 3. -*e*: *calle* 746* (the only available example, in an assured emendation)

Pret.-presents

Pr. Indic. Pl. 1. -*e*: *mone* 841
　　　　　　　　 3. -*e*: *kunne* 435

'To be'

Pr. Indic. Sg. 3. *es* 2700*
          Pl. 2. *are* 1629
              3. *are* 1339 (scribal *-n* in *aren* 1350)

Infinitive

1. *calle* (: *alle* a. pl.) 230, 2859; *gonge* 856 (MS *-n*); *holden* (scribal *-n*) : *holde* a. pl. 29; *do* 17, 252, but *don* 117; *go* 125, 542, 2849; *slo* 512.

2. Weak verbs of class II have no *-i-* in the infinitive, and hence (we may assume) in the present stem: *loke* 376, *were* 2153, *wone* 247; and in class VI (strong) *swere* 1418.

Preterite

1. *Strong*: Pl. with syllabic ending e.g. *wrúngĕn*, *wépĕn* 152 and probably *stode* 2609 (: *wode* a. pl.)

2. *Weak*: Sg. 2. *dedes* 2394
              3. *cóupĕ* 131 (syllabic)
          Pl. 3. *préydĕn* 153

But there are many non-syllabic endings, e.g.:

3. sg. *déyĕdĕ bĭfórn* 231; pl. *Hĕ grétĕŋ ănd góulĕdĕŋ ănd góuĕŋ ḫĕm íllĕ* 164; *séydĕŋ ănón* 176; *hăuĕdĕŋ of* 181 (cf. *háuĕdĕn* 241).

Past Participle

1. *Strong*: syllabic *-en* does occur as the normal type (in which *-n* is preserved): *grauen* 2529 (: *nauen*, MS *name*); *ofslawen* 2677 (: *Rauen*). After *r* ending a stem, the spelling *-n* in *born* 461, *forlorn* 771. Besides *don* 2355, 2525, *do* is used 1806.

2. *Weak*: *-ed*, syllabic in e.g. *páyĕd* 184.

3. Scansion shows that all verbs had discarded the prefix spelt *y*, *i*, e.g. *browt* 58, *comen* 161, *hoten* 106. But there is a very occasional *-i*, confirmed as syllabic by scansion in e.g. *ĭgrét* 163, *ĭgrótĕn* 285.

III. *Vocabulary*

Two strands in the vocabulary of *Hav.* are striking. There are (*a*) at least a dozen words or phrases that are closely restricted in distribution to Northerly (and occasionally EMidl. or NW) areas, and several of them are adoptions from ON; and (*b*) notable adoptions from ON that are not necessarily restricted in distribution. Both bear on the localization of *Hav.*, and must therefore be noticed here.

A. Words of restricted distribution[138]

1. *coupe* 'buy' 1801, 2006 (ON *kaupa*). Recorded only once otherwise, except in glossaries as Nth. and Scots (1691–1855).
2. *a ferþinges nok* 'a scrap of money' 821. Only in *The Legend of Gregory* and *RM* (twice).
3. *fyle* 'repulsive creature' 2500 (ON *fýla*). Before 1400, only in *RM* and *CM*.
4. *goule* v. 'howl' 164, 454 (ON *gaula*). Otherwise only Nth. and Scots (*PC*, *SLS*, *Minor Poems of the Vernon MS*, etc.); modern dialect of Whitby and Lakeland.
5. *greyue* 'headman of a town' 266 (ON *greifi*). Used in parts of Yorks. and Lincs., and in Lancs., Norfolk, and Suffolk.
6. *polk* 'puddle' 2686 (dim. of OE *pōl*). Only *Sir Tristram* and *Promptorium Parvulorum*; later Nth. and EAnglian dialect.
7. *rowte* 'bellow' 1912 (ON *rauta*). In ME, only Rolle and *Catholicon Anglicum*; then Nth. and Sc. dialect.
8. *strie* 'incubus' 999 (med. L *striga*). Only *YP* and *TP*.
9. *teyte* 'cheerful' 1842 (ON *teit-r*). Only *Gaw.* group, Henryson, Dunbar, and Douglas; as noun, in *Gaw.* group and *Wars of Alexander* only.
10. *þarne* 'lose' 1914 (ON *þarfna*). Only *O*, *CM*, *PC*, *SLS*, *YP*, *TP*.
11. *þerne* 'girl' 298 (ON *þerna*). Only *RM* and the MK *Poems of Shoreham* and the *Ayenbite*.
12. *wrobberes* 'persons who stir up strife' 39. The only example; the cognate verb *wrobbe* occurs only in *Thomas of Erceldoune*, and the apophonic variant *wrabbe* only in *O* (in a fragment published by N. R. Ker, *TLS* 1936, p. 928).

B. Main Scandinavian Elements in the Language of Hav.

1. *Grammatical forms*: the uninflected plurals *frend* 326, 2069 (ON *frænd-r*) and *hend* 505 etc. (ON *hænd-r*); the 3 pr. sg. *es* 'is' 2700* (ON *es*, later *er*); the auxiliary *mone* 'must' 841; the p.p. *keft* 'paid for' 2006 (ON *keypt-r*).
2. *Idioms* (see Commentary under each): *gouen hem ille* 164; *made . . . gouen* 218–20, 365; *wiþ neues under hernes set* 1918; *wil of* 1043.

---

[138] Titles of works are abbreviated thus: *CM Cursor Mundi*; *Gaw. Sir Gawain and the Green Knight*; *O Ormulum*; *PC Prick of Conscience*; *RM Robert Mannyng of Brunne's* works; *SLS Scottish Legends of Saints*; *TP Towneley Plays*; *YP York Plays*.

3. *ON cognates* used for common native words: *bleike* 470; *frest* 1338; *grate*, *grote passim*; *leyke* 469; *loupe* 1802; *ok* 1082; *þeþen* 2630; *þrinne passim*; *wayke* 1013.
4. Specifically *EN forms*: *bon*, in *o-bon* 2356, 2572; *tro* 2863, 2339*.
5. *Notable adoptions* in the vocabulary, most of which pertain to everyday life:

   (*a*) *Nouns*:   *are-dawes*, *blome*, *brenne*, *gaddes*, *gate*, *grene*, *greyue*, *hernes*, *keuel*, *kiste*, *nihter-tale*, *rippe*, *seckes*, *stith*.

   (*b*) *Verbs*:   *felede*, *frie*, *gete*, *keft*, *mele*, *route*, *yat*.

   (*c*) *Adjectives*: *bloute*, *kaske*, *kunrik*, *mirke*, *spannewe*, *witer(like)*.

C. Separable Compounds

Hav. contains no less than 37 verbs that have been registered in the *OED* as separable compounds (i.e. under their unseparated form as the head-word). The class is of the first importance in the evolution of the English vocabulary, since they are the source of the throngs of 'phrasal verbs' (*lead out*, *stand by*, etc.)—first, by direct descent for some, and then (already in ME) as a model for the formation of new ones. Those recognized in *Hav.* by the *OED* are:

again-come, *-go*, *-stand*; *at-gonge*; *away-bear*, *-go*; *down-fall*; *forth-bring*, *-come*, *-draw*, *-nim*; *in-let*; *on-come*, *-lay*; *out-brayd*, *-draw*, *drive*, *-lead*, *-spread*, *-thrust*; *over-fare*, *over-fly*, *-go*; *through-fare*, *-go*; *to-come*; *up-bear*, *-break*, *-come*, *-draw*, *-heave*, *-lead*, *-leap*, *-lift*, *-rise*, *-sit*, *-start*.

The editors of the *OED* usually define the foregoing words by the phrases 'In ME commonly two words', '(In ME) properly two words', which are not altogether felicitous, since such verbs may perfectly well occur as 'two words' in OE. They have used the term 'separable compound' s.vv. *away-bear*, *away-go* (see *away* adv. V), and *on-come*.

   The main criteria for classifying OE and ME verbs as separable compounds are:

1. the word-order (see 3 below)
2. a recorded OE antecedent (which incidentally gives a further opportunity for both separated and unseparated forms to occur)
3. Germanic cognates—among other things, because in e.g. German, Dutch, and Afrikaans the practice even of the present day is that:
   (*a*) in a main clause, 'simple' (non-compound) tenses are used in separated form, with the verb first and the particle later in the clause;
   (*b*) in a subordinate clause, the verb is used in unseparated form (i.e. with the particle first), commonly at the end of the clause.

The rule is traceable in ME, e.g. in *Ormulum* 14789:

> . . . he toc þatt follc
> Annd *ledde* hemm *ut* off lande

beside 14776:

> þatt he shollde
> *Utledenn* off Egippte land
> Hiss follc . . .

If at least one of these criteria is met, the ME verb in question is admissible as a separable compound, whether an ancient one or newly formed in ME. The evidence is often skimpy, since a given verb may simply not be used often enough (even in 2802 lines) to occur in both main types of syntactic conditions. And even the *OED*'s material is not necessarily complete by any means.

The *OED* attests *through-go* (from Ælfric, Orm, the *Early E. Psalter*, and *Isumbras*) solely in the unseparated form; a separated form occurs in *Hav.* 849. Similarly, OE *þurhfaran* is recorded by Bosworth–Toller only in the unseparated form (in several examples); but the separated form appears in *Hav.* 264. The record for OE *ofermæg*, ME *ouermai* is likewise thin.[139]

However, even if the recorded evidence is not complete in an individual instance, a verb of this type might have had an OE antecedent. In another, one prefix might be replaced by a synonym: the ME formations in *d(o)un-* (< LOE *adūn-* < *of dūne*) have apparently replaced OE ones with the inherited (Gmc) particle *niðer*, as demonstrated in 889 n. Since *down-fall* v. is rightly registered in this form in the *OED*, *down-fell*, *-renne*, *-sette*, *-sitte* in *Hav.* must also be recognized as separable verbs—though their date of origin must await documentation from texts, as there is no trace of unseparated forms in *OED* or *MED*.

Among the verbs without OE antecedents, at least some (in their unseparated forms) are likely to have been struck out in ME, on the immanent pattern of the inherited combination of unseparated and separated forms in other individual verbs. A specially clear (though admittedly special) case is *ūt-bēde** 2549, beside 3 pt. sg. *bead ut* in the *Peterborough Chronicle* (see 2549 n.). This (as a special use, applied to the 'calling out' of military levies) is probably a calque on ON *bjóða út* (which the related n. *útboð* shows to have been originally a separable compound), rather than < a lost OE *ūt-bēodan. If so, an unseparated ME infinitive has been created *on the native model* (since in ON the

---

[139] See *EMEVP* p. xxxiii, for the recognition of this as a separable compound.

infin. of the equivalent class of verbs was already fixed in the separated form). New formations of the class may be distinguished from older ones as 'quasi-separable', and are so defined in the Glossary here.

The *OED* omits to mention that there are OE antecedents for about ten verbs in the list above:

forth-come, *-nim*; *in-let*; *on-come*, *-lay*; *out-draw*, *out-drive*, *out-lead*; *to-come*; *up-sit*.

On the other hand, there are about eleven verbs in *Hav.* (without OE antecedents, and not registered in *OED*) that qualify as quasi-separable compounds (apart from the three in *d(o)un-* above):

in-laye; *of-fleye*, *of-plette*; *on-haue*; *up-kippe*; *ut-bede*, and *ut-kippe* (whether an adoption of MDu. *utekippen* or not).

One other important set of innovations in the vocabulary of English directly depends on the existence of separated forms of separable compounds, with the particle immediately followed by a prepositional phrase. It was clearly this type of sequence that engendered the new compound prepositions of English (as distinct from older ones such as *ymbe* < **um bi*), the main instances being *into* (and in *Hav.* its variants *intil*, *until*, *unto*), *out of*, *upon*, which are already well established in the language of *Hav.*, and have emerged a century earlier in *Ormulum*. Some of the contexts in *Hav.* are either inconclusive or incompatible with such an analysis. But some avail to show that a new independent preposition has developed, as in the use of *into* 203, 265, 1086, 2873, *intil* 251, 438, 1311, 1394, 2238, 2688; *upon* 1776, 2597, 2641, 2822, 2635; *ut of* 155, 725, 1179, 1277, 1947, 2122. Formally ambiguous contexts (in which the adverb might still be tied mainly to the verb) are *lep up on a stede* (1943, 2193)—with a verb attested in OE as a separable compound—and *cam in til Ubbe* 1927.

In one remarkable instance, both types of relation between the adverb and the preposition are illustrated (in a verb first traceable in EME, but not in forms that would show it to have been a separable compound). In the phrase *nam until his lond* 2931, 'set out for his own domain', which is the key to the crux *Nim in . . . to Denemark* 1337, *until* is undeniably an independent preposition. The sole other example of the idiom so far known to me is compatible with either analysis. But the separation of the preposition from the adverb in *Nim in . . . to* 1337 suggests that here they were not merged in a single syntactic function. In 1967–8:

> And *driue* hem *ut* . . .
> So dogges *ut of* milne-hous

the duplication of *ut* of the separable compound in *ut of* implies that the latter was felt as a unit (independent of *ut* in 1967).

Note on Spelling

About three main points are to be noted in the spelling system of *Hav.*:

1. the letter 'yogh' is not used at all.
2. The letter *ð* is not used at all.
3. The character 'wynn' survives or is traceable in a very few instances.

The work normally done by 'yogh' (3) partly concerns the voiced fricative /j/, which is written *y* in *Hav.* (*yung* 30), and the voiceless palatal fricative /ç/, which in the consonant group /çt/ is here very variously spelt. By far the commonest graphy for the latter is: (*a*) the unusual and baffling *th*: *brouth* 57, *douther* 280. Others are

(*b*) *ct*: *þoucte* 694, *micte* 571. This is virtually dropped after l. 957 (*aucte* 2788).

(*c*) *cth*: *nicth* 143. This too (which looks like a blend of *ct* and *th* is virtually dropped after the first few hundred lines (*knicthes* 2665).

(*d*) *t*: *browt* 58, *þoute* 905; mainly after a diphthong.

(*e*) *ht*: this standard graphy is very rare through most of the text, but becomes more frequent in the last 500 lines (*douhtres* 2216).

(*f*) *cht*: relatively rare (*tonicht* 533).

One oddity is the spelling of the fricative /ç/ as *th* in *þuruth* 52, *þoruth* 1066, 2787, *þoruthlike* 681, the only variants of which are *þoru*, *þorw*.

The absence of *ð* means that *þ* is used for both /θ/ and /ð/. But there is a striking tendency to use *th* for the voiceless member of the pair, especially in final position in monosyllabic forms: *cloth* 1145, *oth* 314 beside *cloþe* v. 1199, *oþes* 419 (cf. *forth* 553, *grith* 61, *wroth* 1118; *suereth* 648).

Th is also used for /t/, again mostly in final position in monosyllabic forms: *greth* 1026, *leth* 252, *neth* 809, *uth* 1179, *woth* 654; *nouthe* 1333.

/ʃ/ is spelt *sh* virtually without exception, i.e. *sch* does not occur. The solitary *schaped* 1648 may be on the same footing as other variants so rare as probably to be errors: *same* 1952; *she* 519, *shotshipe* 2100.

OE *hw* is represented commonly by *w* and *wh* (*wat* 453, *hwan* 1132, etc.) and very occasionally by *qu*: *quanne* 134, 162, 204, *quan* 240. The *-wh-* in *newhen* 1867 is a puzzle.

Two examples of 'wynn' occur in *Ꝥe* 1059, *ƿerpen* 1427. Traces of it occur four times, in the 'thorn' of *þitdrow* 502, *forþi* 2579, *þith uten* 425, and *þit* 998, for words that would in later ME be spelt *forwi*, *withuten*, and *with*. *Y* is commonly difficult to distinguish from 'thorn', since it is often undotted, e.g. in *deye* 168, *preye* 169, *curteysye* (2) 194, *yeue* 198, *yeme* 209, *you yeue* 485 etc.

IX. PROVENANCE

The language of the main MS of *Hav.* will not be noticed here, since it has been discussed by Prof. A. McIntosh and assigned to Norfolk.[140] The language of the author can be localized with certainty and in fairly specific terms.

The relatively advanced accidence of *Hav.* is of an EMidl. type, in a Northerly variety. It has things in common with that of the *Peterborough Chronicle*, Orm, and Chaucer—notably the virtually uniform *-es* as the pl. ending of nouns. As for the 3 pr. sg. *-es* and pl. *-e*, Orm's and Chaucer's sg. *-eþ* is best regarded as an earlier type (alongside Chaucer's three examples of *-es*), while Orm's pl. *-en* is self-evidently an earlier stage of *-e*. The 3 pers. fem. pron. *sho*, and *es* and *are* as the 3 pr. sg. and pl. of the verb 'to be', are distinctly Northerly-looking within the EMidl. area, without being Northern.

One profoundly important criterion is the phonological peculiarity of the dual reflex of OE /a:/. This is decisive for Lincs. (see I, A, 13 above), and is happily confirmed by the non-linguistic evidence that consists in the author's knowledge of Lincoln.[141] Useful confirmation of a general kind is provided by Robert Mannyng, and by links with his vocabulary as well as his phonology and accidence.

The language of *Hav.* is English of Lincolnshire, quite possibly of a man of Lincoln itself. Though it must embody many individual choices and preferences of the author in vocabulary, syntax, and idiom, the core of it is surely close to English speech of that area and time, and not a bookish or literary product. There is no direct mention of a single literary work in the poem. The style admittedly shows that the author was thoroughly versed in the 'epic style' as available in OF and AN, at least. But this need mean only that he was influenced in some of the things that he chose to say, and only in a restricted degree in the words that he used to say them.

---

[140] 'The Language of the Extant Versions of *Havelok the Dane*', M.Æ 45 (1976), 36–49.
[141] See notes on 754–60, 876, 2829–30.

X. SELECT BIBLIOGRAPHY

A. Editions of Hauelok

1828 F. Madden, *The Ancient English Romance of Havelok the Dane* (Roxburghe Club).

1868 W. W. Skeat, *The Lay of Havelok the Dane*, EETS, es 4.

1901 F. Holthausen, *Havelok* (London).

1902 W. W. Skeat, *The Lay of Havelok the Dane* (Oxford).

1915 W. W. Skeat, *The Lay of Havelok the Dane*, 2nd edn., rev. K. Sisam (Oxford).

1928 F. Holthausen, *Havelok*, 3rd edn. (Heidelberg).

1973 W. W. Skeat, *The Lay of Havelok the Dane*, 2nd edn., rev. K. Sisam, new impression (Oxford).

1980 A. V. C. Schmidt and N. Jacobs, *Medieval English Romances*, vol. i (London), pp. 7–15, 37–121, 172–87.

B. Studies

1889 J. W. Hales, 'The Lay of Havelok the Dane', *The Athenaeum*, No. 3200, 23 Feb., pp. 244–5.

1900 F. Schmidt, *Zur Heimatbestimmung des Havelok*, Diss. Göttingen.

1903 H. E. Heyman, *Studies on the Havelok-Tale* (Uppsala).

1905 F. W. Brie, 'Zum Fortleben der *Havelok*-Sage', *Englische Studien*, 35, 359–71.

1906 M. Deutschbein, *Studien zur Sagengeschichte Englands*, vol. i (Cöthen), 96–168.

1915 H. L. S. Creek, 'The Author of "Havelok the Dane"', *Englische Studien*, 48, 193–212.

1923 J. H. Kern, *De taalvormen van 't middelengelse gedicht Havelok*, Mededeelingen der koninkl. akad. van wetensch., afd. letterkunde, deel 55, serie A, no 2 (Amsterdam), pp. 19–53.

1949 C. T. Onions, 'Comments and Speculations on the Text of Havelok', *Philologica*, The Malone Anniversary Studies, ed. T. A. Kirby and H. B. Woolf (Baltimore), 154–63.

1969 J. Weiss, 'Structure and Characterisation in *Havelok the Dane*', *Speculum*, 44, 247–57.

1977 G. B. Jack, 'The Date of *Havelok*', *Anglia*, 95, 20–33.

1983 G. V. Smithers, 'The Scansion of *Hauelok* and the use of ME -*en* and -*e* in *Hauelok* and by Chaucer', *Middle English Studies presented to Norman Davis*, ed. E. G. Stanley and D. Gray.

C. OE and ME Texts

B. Thorpe, *Homilies of Ælfric*, Ælfric Society (London, 1844–5).

K. Wildhagen, *Der Cambridger Psalter* (Bibliothek der angelsächsischen Prosa, VII, Hamburg 1910).

J. Earle and C. Plummer, *Two Saxon Chronicles Parallel* (Oxford, 1892 and 1899).

J. A. W. Bennett and G. V. Smithers, *Dame Sirith*, in *EMEVP* VI, pp. 77 ff.

C. Horstman, *The Gast of Gy*, in *Yorkshire Writers* (see below), vol. ii (London, 1896), pp. 292–333.

J. R. R. Tolkien and E. V. Gordon, *Sir Gawain and the Green Knight* rev. N. Davis (Oxford, 1967).

O. S. Arngart, *The Middle English Genesis and Exodus*, Lund Studies in English, 36 (1968).

J. Zupitza, *Guy of Warwick (15th-c. version)*, EETS, ES 25 and 26 (London, 1875 and 1876).

J. Zupitza, *Guy of Warwick (14th-c. version)*, EETS, ES 42 (1883), 49 (1887), and 59 (1891).

K. Böddeker, *Altenglische Dichtungen des MS. Harl[ey] 2253* (Berlin, 1878).

S. Nevanlinna, *The Northern Homily Cycle*, vol. i (Helsinki, 1972).

E. V. Gordon, *Pearl* (Oxford, 1953).

C. Clark, *The Peterborough Chronicle* (2nd edn., Oxford, 1970).

J. W. Bright and R. L. Ramsay, *Liber Psalmorum: the West Saxon Psalms* [Pss. 1–50] (Boston, 1907).

G. P. Krapp, *The Paris Psalter and the Meters of Boethius* [Pss. 51–150], The Anglo-Saxon Poetic Records, vol. v (London, 1933).

Richard Coeur de Lion: K. Brunner, *Die mittelenglische Versroman über Richard Löwenherz* (Vienna, 1913).

W. A. Wright, *The Metrical Chronicle of Robert of Gloucester* (RS, 1887).

Robert Mannyng's *Chronicle*: F. J. Furnivall, *The Story of England by Robert Manning of Brunne*, vols. i and ii (RS, 1887).

Sir Tristrem: E. Kölbing, *Die nordische und die englische Version der Tristan-Sage*, vol. ii (Heilbronn, 1882).

C. Horstman, *Yorkshire Writers*, vols. i–ii (London, 1895–6).

Other Works

E. Einenkel, *Historische Syntax, Geschichte der englischen Sprache*, in Paul's *Grundriss der germanischen Philologie* (3rd edn., Strasburg, 1916).

T. Mustanoja, *A Middle English Syntax*, vol. i (Helsinki, 1960).

Bo Seltén, *The Anglo-Saxon Heritage in Middle English Personal Names: East Anglia 1100–1399*, Lund Studies in English, 43 (Lund, 1972).

D. Old French and Anglo-Norman

L. Brandin, *La Chanson d'Aspremont*, vols. i–ii, CFMA (Paris, 1923–4).

L. Demaison, *Aymeri de Narbonne*, vol. ii, SATF (Paris, 1887).

W. Foerster, *Erec und Enide*, text-edn. (Halle, 1934).

A. Bell, *L'Estoire des Engleis by Gaimar*, ANTS (Oxford, 1960).

Li Contes del Graal, ed. A. Hilka, *Der Percevalroman* (Halle, 1932).

H. Suchier, *La Chançun de Guillelme* (Halle, 1911).

D. McMillan, *La Chanson de Guillaume*, SATF (Paris, 1949–50).

J. Willem-Wathelet, *Recherches sur La Chanson de Guillaume*, vols. i and ii, Bibliothèque de la Faculté de Philosophie et Lettres de l'Université de Liège, ccx (Paris, 1975); edition in vol. ii.

A. Bell, *Le Lai d'Haveloc and Gaimar's Haveloc Episode* (Manchester, 1925).

M. K. Pope, *The Romance of Horn*, vol. i, ANTS 9–10 (Oxford, 1955).

M. K. Pope and T. B. W. Reid, *The Romance of Horn*, vol. ii, ANTS 12–13 (Oxford, 1964).

W. Foerster, *Richars li Biaus* (Vienna, 1874).

T. A. Jenkins, *La Chanson de Roland* (Boston, 1924).

Le Roman de toute Chevalerie, ed. B. Foster, *The Anglo-Norman Alexander*, ANTS 29–31 (London, 1976–7).

T. B. W. Reid, *Yvain* (Manchester, 1952).

J. Morawski, *Proverbes français antérieurs au XVe siècle*, CFMA (Paris, 1925).

A. Tobler, *Vermischte Beiträge zur französischen Grammatik* (Leipzig, 1902–12).

E. General

W. de Gray Birch, *Cartularium Saxonicum*, vols. i–iii (London, 1883–93).

L. J. Downer, *Leges Henrici Primi* (Oxford, 1972).

F. L. Ganshof, *Feudalism*, trans. P. Grierson, 3rd English edn. (Longman's, 1964).

J. W. F. Hill, *Medieval Lincoln* (Cambridge, 1948).

J. E. A. Jolliffe, *The Constitutional History of Medieval England* (London, 1948).

F. Liebermann, *Die Gesetze der Angelsachsen* (Halle, 1898–1916).

Pollock and Maitland, *The History of English Law before the Time of Edward I* (Cambridge, 1898).

A. L. Poole, *From Domesday Book to Magna Carta* (Oxford, 1951).

F. M. Powicke, *The Thirteenth Century, 1216–1307* (Oxford, 1953).

XI. EDITORIAL PROCEDURE

1. The text is punctuated in accordance with present English usage. The spelling of the MS has been retained. But:

(*a*) capitals are used as in present English;

(*b*) long *i* has been printed *j*;

(*c*) abbreviations have been expanded without notice, except that the *titulus* has been printed in italic as *n* or *m* (whichever is required), in order to distinguish between the abbreviated and the unabbreviated *-n* in the hypermetrical *-en* (for which see 2 below);

(*d*) since the spaces between words in the MS vary in size, and it is often impossible to know whether the scribe regarded two successive elements as two words or one, word-division has been standardized, on sometimes (unavoidably) arbitrary criteria. *For to*, as the present English style, has been preferred to *forto* (both being numerous).

Two elements separated in the MS have been hyphenated in

the compound forms of separable verbs, and in indefinite pronouns and adverbs such as *wo-so*, *hwore-so*, and combinations of *þer* with following preposition, or if attested as a compound in earlier or in present English, or to avoid visually awkward sequences, as in *euere-ilc*.

2. Emendations are marked by square brackets for added letters, and by italic for those substituted for others. Corrupt rhymes are generally not emended unless the author's forms (which cannot all be known with certainty) are philologically important or regionally distinctive.

There are within the line not less than 213 examples of *-en* as an inflexion or a suffix that are hypermetrical and corrupt.[142] But they have been retained in order to let the reader see how abundant they are. The following list displays them more economically than the footnotes would do:

10, 12, 18, 21, 26, 29, 43, 56, 57, 68, 69, 88, 102, 116, 145, 161, 164 (3 examples), 175, 176, 181, 190, 195, 201, 203, 220, 227, 242, 244, 255, 257, 260, 270, 287, 295, 325, 335, 346, 348, 369, 370, 379, 417, 439, 441, 448, 461, 463, 464, 470, 493, 516, 518, 519, 521, 530, 531, 536, 562, 564, 582, 602, 623, 659, 671, 696, 699, 722, 732, 741, 748, 763, 783, 792, 798, 801, 803, 812, 843, 846, 861, 890, 902, 915, 932, 942, 951, 953, 970, 982, 1013, 1021, 1029, 1031, 1032, 1033, 1038, 1058, 1083, 1084, 1094, 1122, 1123, 1124, 1132, 1168, 1171, 1182, 1186, 1187, 1188, 1193, 1195, 1198, 1203, 1204, 1211, 1231, 1234, 1239, 1245, 1247, 1251, 1257, 1271, 1304, 1322, 1347, 1348, 1421, 1630, 1632, 1641, 1684, 1695, 1709, 1718, 1737, 1738, 1767, 1770, 1825, 1833, 1838, 1839, 1845, 1863, 1867, 1877, 1890, 1897, 1908, 1911, 1916, 1917, 1930, 1954, 1965, 1967, 1978, 2002, 2017, 2021, 2027, 2046, 2085, 2099, 2104, 2119, 2134, 2138, 2140, 2148, 2162, 2163, 2167, 2175, 2197, 2260, 2270, 2271, 2291, 2305, 2307, 2380, 2413, 2414 (twice), 2427, 2436, 2468, 2475, 2523, 2548, 2557, 2565, 2583, 2590, 2592, 2617, 2659, 2670, 2711, 2775, 2776, 2791, 2807, 2813, 2832, 2854, 2896, 2952, 2974, 2987, 2988.

3. The Cambridge Fragments have been edited from photostats; D in the apparatus criticus designates readings of the MS contributed by Dr A. I. Doyle.

4. Since it is editorial policy here to reproduce the MS use of *i*, *j* and *u*, *v* as each being capable of denoting a vowel or a consonant, the spelling *Hauelok* is obligatory in the text and in all citations from or references to it, except that in the much used abbreviated form of the name *Hav.* has been preferred, and *Havelok* is used on the title-page.

---

[142] See 'The Scansion of *Havelok*', p. 202.

HAUELOK

Herknet to me, gode men—
Wiues, maydnes, and alle men—
Of a tale þat Ich you wile telle,
Wo-so it wile here and þer-to duelle.
þe tale is of Hauelok imaked: 5
Wil he was litel he yede ful naked.
Hauelok was a ful god gome—
He was ful god in eueri trome;
He was þe wicteste man at nede
þat þurte riden on ani stede.   10
þat ye mowen nou yhere,
And þe tale ye mowen ylere.
At þe biginni[n]g of vre tale,
Fil me a cuppe of ful god ale,
And wile drinken her Y spelle   15
þat Crist vs shilde alle fro helle.
Krist late vs heuere so for to do
þat we moten comen him to,
And wit þat it mote ben so,
Benedicamus Domino!   20
Here Y schal biginnen a rym:
Krist us yeue wel god fyn!
þe rym is maked of Hauelok—
A stalworþi man in a flok.
He was þe stalworþeste man at nede   25
þat may riden on ani stede.

It was a king bi are-dawes
þat in his time were gode lawes
He dede maken an ful wel holden.

At top of page, in red ink, and preceded by two words that have been mostly trimmed off:
    . . . elok qu . . . Rex Anglie *[then a line filler]* Et Denemarchie.
Independently interpreted by Dr A. I. Doyle as:
       Incipit vita Hauelok quondam Rex Anglie et Denemarchie,
as by Skeat—Sisam and Holthausen.

Hym louede yu*n*g, him louede holde—   30
Erl and barun, dreng and þayn,
Knict, bondema*n*, and swain,
Wydues, maydnes, prestes, and clerkes,
And al for hise gode werkes.
He louede God with al his micth,   35
And Holi Kirke, and soth ant ricth.
Ri*c*thwise men he louede alle,
And oueral made hem for to calle.
Wreieres and wrobberes made he falle,
And hated he*m* so ma*n* doth galle;   40
Vtlawes and theues made he bynde,
Alle þat he micthe fynde,
And heye he*n*gen on galwe-tre—
For hem ne yede gold ne fe!
Jn þat time a man þat bore   45

· · · · · · · · · ·

Of red gold upon hijs bac,   fo. 204rb
Jn a male with or blac,
Ne funde he non þat him misseyde
N[e] with iuele on hond leyde.   50
þa*n*ne micthe chapme*n* fare
þuruth Englond wit here ware,
And baldelike beye and selle*n*
Oueral þer he wilen dwellen—
Jn gode burwes and þer-fram   55
Ne fu*n*den he non þat dede he*m* sham,
þat he ne were*n* sone to sorwe brouth
An pouere maked and browt to nouth.
þa*n*ne was Engelond at hayse—
Michel was svich a king to preyse   60
þat held so Englond in grith!
Krist of heuene was him with—
He was Engelondes blome.
Was non so bold lo*u*[er]d to Rome
þat durste upon his [londe] bringhe   65
Hunger ne here—wicke þinghe.
Hwan he felede hise foos,

31 þayn *Skeat: MS* kayn   37 Ri*c*thwise: *MS* Rirth wise   46 *no gap in the*
MS   64 lo*u*[er]d *Craigie: MS* lond   65 [londe]: *not in MS*

He made he*m* lurke*n* and crepe*n* i*n* wros—
þe[i] hidde*n* he*m* alle and helde*n* he*m* stille,
And diden al his herte wille.   70
Ricth he louede of alle þinge—
To wronge micht hi*m* noma*n* bri*n*ge
Ne for siluer ne for gold,
So was he his soule hold.
To þe faderles was he rath—   75
Wo-so dede hem wrong or la*t*h,
Were it cler*c* or were it k*ni*cth,
He dede hem sone to haue*n* ricth.
And wo dide widuen wrong,
Were he neure knicth so strong   80
þat he ne made hi*m* sone kesten
And in feteres ful faste festen.
And wo-so dide maydne shame
Of hire bodi or brouth i*n* blame
(Bute it were bi hire wille)   85
*H*e made him sone of limes spille.
*H*e was te beste knith at nede
þat heuere micthe ride*n* on stede,
Or wepne wagge or folc vt-lede.
Of kn*i*th ne hauede he neuere drede,   90
þat he ne spro*n*g forth so sparke of glede
And lete him [shewe] of hise hand-dede,   fo. 204va
Hw he couþe with wepne spede;
And oþer he refte hi*m* hors or wede,
Or made him sone ha*n*des sprede   95
And 'Louerd, merci!' loude grede.
He was large and no-wicth gnede:
Hauede he non so god brede
Ne on his bord no*n* so god shrede
þat he ne wolde þor-wit fede   100
Poure þat on fote yede,
Forto haue*n* of Him þe mede
þat for vs wolde on rode blede—

---

76 la*t*h: *MS* lach   77 cler*c*: *MS* clert   k*ni*cth: *MS* kincth   79 dide: *MS*
didē   *H*e: *MS* ke   87 *H*e: *MS* ke   90 kn*i*th: *MS* knrth   99 n*on*:
MS n̄

Crist, þat al kan wisse and rede
þat euere woneth i*n* ani þede.   105

þe ki*n*g was hoten Aþelwold;
Of word, of wepne, he was bold.
Jn Engeland was neure knicth
þat betere hel[d] þe lond to ricth.
Of his bodi ne hauede he eyr   110
Bute a mayden swiþe fayr,
þat was so yung þat sho ne couþe
Gon on fote ne speke wit mouþe.
þan him tok an iuel strong,
þat he we[l] wiste and underfong   115
þat his deth was comen hi*m* on,
And seyde, 'Crist, wat shal Y don?
Louerd, wat shal me to rede?
J woth ful wel Ich haue mi mede.
[H]w shal nou mi douhter fare?   120
Of hire haue Ich michel kare.
Sho is mikel in mi þouth—
Of meself is me rith nowt.
No selcouth is þou me be wo:
Sho ne ka*n* speke ne sho kan go.   125
Yif scho couþe on horse ride,
And a thousande me*n* bi hire syde,
And sho were com*en* intil helde
And Engelond sho couþe welde,
And don hem of þar hire were queme,   130
An hire bodi couþe yeme,
Ne wolde me neuere iuele like,
*N*e þou Ich were i*n* heueneriche.'

Quanne he hauede þis plei*n*te maked,
þer-after stro*n*glike quaked,   135
He sende writes sone onon
After his erles euere-ichon,   fo. 204vb
And after hise baru*n*s, riche and poure,
Fro Rokesburw al i*n*to Douere,
þat he shulde*n* comen swiþe   140

Til him þat was ful vnbliþe,
To þat stede þe[r] he lay
Jn harde bondes nicth and day.
He was so faste wit yuel fest
þat he ne mouthe hauen no rest: 145
He ne mouthe no mete hete,
Ne he ne mouchte no lyþe gete,
Ne non of his iuel þat couþe red—
Of him ne was nouth buten ded.
Alle þat þe writes herden   150
Sorful an sori til him ferden.
He wrungen hondes and wepen sore,
And yerne preyden Cristes hore—
þat he [wolde] turnen him
Vt of þat yuel þat was so grim.   155
þanne he weren comen alle
Bifor þe king into þe halle
At Winchestre þer he lay,
'Welcome' he seyde 'be ye ay!
Ful michel þank kan [Y] yow   160
þat ye aren comen to me now.'

Quanne he weren alle set
And þe king aueden igret,
He greten and gouleden and gouen hem ille;
And he bad hem alle ben stille   165
And seyde þat 'greting helpeth nouth,
For al to dede am Ich brouth.
Bute nov ye sen þat I shal deye,
Nou Ich wille you alle preye
Of mi douther, þat shal be   170

154 [wolde]: *Skeat–Sisam*   160 [Y]: *Skeat–Sisam*

(edited from photostats; *D* in footnotes designates readings of the
MS contributed by Dr A. I. Doyle)

Til sche be womman of elde
þat sche it may here selwe welde   175
. e andswerde and seyd anon
be jesu crist and sen jon
. e erl godric of cornualie
. e is trewe man wyt outen faile
Wis man of . ed and of dede   180
. an men haued of mekel drede
. . d he may here best ȝeme
. . . . of hym þinket queme

Yure leuedi after me,
Wo may yemen hire so longe,
Boþen hire and Engelonde,
Til þat she [be] wman of helde,
And þa[t] she mowe [hir] yemen and welde?'   175
He ansuereden and seyden anan
Bi [Iesu] Crist and Seint Io[ha]n,
þat þerl Godrigh of Cornwayle
Was trewe man wituten faile,
Wis man of red, wis man of dede,   180
And men haueden of him mikel drede—
'He may hire alþerbest yeme   fo. 205ra
Til þat she mowe wel ben quene.'
þe king was payed of þat rede.
A wol fair cloth bringen he dede,   185
And þer-on leyde þe messe-bok,
þe caliz and þe pateyn ok,
þe corporaus, þe messe-gere.
þer-on he garte þe erl suere
þat he sholde yemen hire wel,   190
Withuten lac, wituten tel,
Til þat she were tuelf winter hold
And of speche were bold,
And þat she covþe of curteysye,
Gon and speken of luue-drurye,   195
And til þat she louen muthe
Wom-so hire to gode þoucte,
And þat he shulde hire yeue
þe heste man þat micthe liue,
þe beste, fayreste, þe strangest ok   200
(þat dede he him sweren on þe bok),
And þanne shulde he Engelond
Al bitechen into hire hond.
Quanne þat was sworn on his wise,
þe king dede þe mayden arise,   205
And þe erl hire bitaucte

---

174 [be]: *Zupitza*   [hir]: *Holthausen*   176 anan: *MS* anon   177 [Iesu]:
Ellis   and Seint: *MS* and bi seint   180 red: *followed by medial point*
196 muthe: *MS* mithe   199 heste: *MS* beste, *Skeat* hexte   204 Quanne: *MS*
Ouanne

And al þe lond he euere awcte—
Engelonde, eueri del—
And preide he shulde yeme hire wel.
þe king ne mowcte don no more, 210
But yerne preyede Godes ore
And dede him hoslen wel and shriue,
J woth, fif hundred siþes and fiue,
An ofte dede him sore swinge
And wit hondes smerte dinge, 215
So þat þe blod ran of his fleys
þat tendre was and swiþe neys.
He made his quiste swiþe wel
And sone gaf it euere-il del.
Wan it was gouen, ne micte men finde 220
So mikel men micte him in winde
Of his in arke ne in chiste
Jn Engelond, þat noman wiste,
For al was youen faire and wel
þat him was leued no catel. 225
þanne he hauede ben ofte swu[n]gen,
Ofte shriuen and ofte dungen, fo. 205rb
'Jn manus tuas, Lou[er]d' he seyde.
Her þat he þe speche leyde,
To Iesu Crist bigan to calle, 230
And deyede biforn his heymen alle.
þan he was ded, þere micte men se
þe meste sorwe þat micte be:
þer was sobbing, siking, and sor,
Handes wringing and drawing bi hor. 235
Alle greten swiþe sore
Riche and poure þat þere wore,
An mikel sorwe haueden alle—
Leuedyes in boure, knictes in halle.

Quan þat sorwe was somdel laten 240
And he haueden longe graten,
Belles deden he sone ringen,
Monkes and prestes messe singen,
And sauteres deden he manie reden,

218–9 *transposed in MS* 228 Lou[er]d: *MS* loude

þat God self shulde his soule leden   245
Jnto heuene biforn his sone,
And þer wituten hende wone.
þan he was to þe erþe brouth,
þe riche erl ne foryat nouth
þat he ne dede al Engelond   250
Sone sayse intil his hond,
And in þe castels leth he do
þe knictes he micte tristen to,
And alle þe Englis dede he swere
þat he shulden him ghod fey beren: 255
He yaf alle men þat god þoucte,
Liuen and deyen til þat he moucte,
Til þat þe kinges dowter wore
Tuenti winter hold and more.

þanne he hauede taken þis oth   260
Of erles, baruns, lef and loth,
Of knictes, cherles, fre and þewe,
Justises dede he maken newe
Al Engelond to faren þorw,
Fro Douere into Rokesborw.   265
Schireues he sette, bedels and greyues,
Grith-sergeans wit longe gleyues,
To yemen wilde wodes and paþes
Fro wicke men þat wolde don scaþes,
And for to hauen alle at his cri,   270
At his wille, at hise merci,
þat non durste ben him ageyn—   fo. 205va
Erl ne barun, knict ne sweyn.
Wislike for soth was him wel
Of folc, of wepne, of catel: 275
Soþlike, in a lite þrawe
Al Engelond of him stod awe—
Al Engelond was of him adrad,
So his þe beste fro þe gad.

þe kinges douther bigan þriue   280
And wex þe fayrest wman on liue.

257 he *Skeat*: MS him

Of alle þewes w[as] she wis
þat gode weren and of pris.
þe mayden Goldeboru was hoten;
For hire was mani a ter igroten!   285
Quanne þe Erl Godrich him herde
Of þat mayden hw we[l] he ferde,
Hw wis sho was, [h]w chaste, hw fayr,
And þat sho was þe riþe eyr
Of Engelond, of al þe rike,   290
þo bigan Godrich to sike.
And seyde 'Weþer she sholde be
Quen and leuedi ouer me?
Hweþer sho sholde al Engelond
And me and mine hauen in hire hond?   295
Daþeit hwo it hire thaue!
Shal sho it neuere more haue.
Sholde Ic yeue a fol, a þerne,
Engelond, þou sho it yerne?
Daþeit hwo it hire yeue   300
Euere more hwil I liue!
Sho is waxen al to prud,
For gode metes and noble shrud
þat Hic haue youen hire to offte—
Hic haue yemed hire to softe.   305
Shal it nouth ben als sho þenkes:
Hope maketh fol man ofte blenkes!
Jch haue a sone, a ful fayr knaue:
He shal Engelond al haue—
He shal [ben] king, he shal ben sire,   310
So brouke I euere mi blake swire!'
Hwan þis trayson was al þouth,
Of his oth ne was him nouth.
He let his oth al ouer-ga—
þer-of ne yaf he nouth a stra,   315
Bute sone dede hire fete,
Er he wolde heten ani mete,   fo. 205vb
Fro Winchestre þer sho was,
Also a wicke traytur Iudas,

And dede lede*n* hire to Doure, 320
þat standeth on þe seis oure,
And þer-hinne dede hire fede
Pourelike in feble wede.
þe castel dede he yemen so
þat non ne micte come*n* hire to 325
Of hire frend, with to speke*n*,
þat heuere micte hire bale wreke*n*.
Of Goldeborw shul we nou laten,
þat nouth ne bli*n*neth for-to grate*n*
þer sho liggeth i*n* prisoun. 330
Jhesu Crist, þat Lazarun
To liue broucte fro dede-bondes,
He lese hire wit hise hondes,
And leue sho mo[te] him yse
Heye ha*n*gen on galwe-tre 335
þat hire haued i*n* sorwe brouth,
So as sho ne misdede nouth.

Sa]ye] we nou forth i*n* hure spelle!
Jn þat time so it bifelle
Was in þe lon[d] of Denemark 340

328 *Of*: MS Qf

a riche king strong and starc   341
his name it was birkebein
he hauede mani knigth and swen
he was fayr man and wyth
and is body þe beste knigth   345
þat euere mith . e . . . to werre
Riden on stede or handelen spere
þre childre he hauede be
þat he louede so . s l . f
he hadde a sone and doutr. to   350
swiþe fayre and fellet s .
þan he was in is best . . . ynt
juel hym toke in eueri gonyt   355
þat he was so wyth euel bunde   a
þat he ne mith liuen non stunde   b
þan he mith no longere liuen
for siluir þat he mithe giuen
þan he þat wiste he dede senden
after prestis fer and henden
after chanons munkes boþen   360
hym to wissen and to roþen
hym to husselen and to schriue
Quiles þat he were o liue
Quan he was husseled and wel

346 *one letter illegible immediately before* e *and two or three immediately after it*
348 *tear in MS has obliterated an unascertainable number of letters after* be   349 *about six
letters illegible at end of line*   352 *about two letters illegible before* ynt   353 gonyt: n
perhaps subpuncted   355 b: ne *above line*   360 chanons: o *above line*
364 *several letters trimmed off after* wel

A riche king and swyþe stark;
þ[e] name of him was Birkabeyn.
He hauede mani knict and sueyn.
He was fayr man and wicth:
Of bodi he was þe beste knicth   345
þat euere micte leden uth here,
Or stede on-ride or handlen spere.
þre children he hauede bi his wif—
He hem louede so his lif.
He hauede a sone, douhtres two,   350
Swiþe fayre, as fel it so.
He þat wile non forbere,
Riche ne poure, king ne kaysere,
(Deth) him tok þan he bes[t] wolde
Liuen, but hyse dayes were fulde,   355
þat he ne moucte no more liue
For gol[d] ne siluer ne for no gyue.
Hwan he þat wiste, raþe he sende
After prestes, fer an hende—
Chanounes gode and monkes baþe,   360
Him for to wisse and to raþe,
Him for to hoslen an for to shriue,   fo. 206ra
Hwil his bodi were on liue.
Hwan he was hosled and shriuen,
His quiste maked and for him gyuen,   365
Hise knictes dede he alle site,
For þorw hem he wolde wite
Hwo micte yeme his children yunge
Til þat he kouþen speken wit tunge,
Speken and gangen, on horse riden,   370
Knictes an sweynes bi here siden.
He spoken þer-offe, and chosen sone
A riche man þat under mone
Was þe trewest, þat he wende—
Godard, þe kinges oune frende—   375
And seyden he moucthe hem best loke
Yif þat he hem vndertoke,

347 on-: *MS* onne   360 baþe: *MS* boþe   361 for to wisse: *MS* fort hm to
wisse *with* hm *sub-puncted*   raþe: *MS* rede   362 hoslen: *MS* hoslon
373 þat: *MS* was

Til his sone mouthe bere
Helm on heued and leden vt here,
Jn his hand a spere stark, 380
And king ben maked of Denemark.
He wel trowede þat he seyde,
And on Godard handes leyde,
And seyde 'Here biteche I þe
Mine children alle þre, 385
Al Denemark, and al mi fe,
Til þat mi sone of helde be,
But þat Ich wille þat þo[u] suere
On auter and on messe-gere,
On þe belles þat men ringes, 390
On messe-bok þe prest on singes,
þat þou mine children shalt we[l] yeme,
þat hire kin be ful wel queme,
Til mi sone mowe ben knicth.
þanne biteche him þo his ricth: 395
Denemark and þat þer-til longes—
Casteles and tunes, wodes and wonges.'
Godard stirt up an swor al þat
þe king him bad, and siþen sat
Bi þe knictes þat þer ware, 400
þat wepen alle swiþe sare
For þe king þat deide sone.
Iesu Crist, þat makede mone
On þe mirke nith to shine,
Wite his soule fro helle-pine, 405
And leue þat it mote wone
Jn heueneriche with Godes sone! fo. 206rb

Hwan Birkabeyn was leyd in graue,
þe erl dede sone take þe knaue
(Hauelok, þat was þe eir), 410
Swanborow, his sister, Helfled þe toþer,
And in þe castel dede he hem do,
þer non ne micte hem comen to
Of here kyn, þer þei sperd were.
þer he greten ofte sore 415
Boþe for hunger and for kold,

Or he weren þre winter hold.
Feblelike he gaf hem cloþes.
He ne yaf a note of hise oþes—
He hem cloþede rith ne fedde, 420
Ne hem ne dede richelike bebedde.
þanne Godard was, sikerlike,
Vnder God þe moste swike
þat eure in erþe shaped was,
Þithuten on—þe wike Iudas! 425
Haue he þe malisun today
Of alle þat eure speken may—
Of patriark and of pope,
And of prest with loken kope,
Of monekes and hermites boþe . . . 430
And of þe leue holi rode
þat God himselue ran on blode!
Crist warie him with his mouth!
Waried wrþe he of norþ and suth,
Offe alle men þat speken kunne, 435
Of Crist þat maude mone and sunne!
þanne he hauede of al þe lond
Al þe folk tilled intil his hond,
And alle haueden sworen him oth,
Riche and poure, lef and loth, 440
þat he sholden hise wille freme
And þat he shulde him nouth greme,
He þouthe a ful strong trechery,
A trayson and a felony,
Of þe children for to make— 445
þe deuel of helle him sone take!

Hwan þat was þouth, onon he ferde
To þe tour þer he woren sperde,
þer he greten for hunger and cold.
þe knaue, þat was sumdel bold, 450
Kam him ageyn, on knes him sette,
And Godard ful feyre he þer grette, fo. 206va
And Godard seyde 'Wat is yw?

Hwi grete ye and goule*n* nou?'
'For us hu*n*greth swiþe sore'—   455
Seyden he [he] wolden more:
'We ne haue to hete, ne we ne haue
Her-inne neyþer knith ne knaue
þat yeueth us drinke*n* ne no mete,
Halue*n*del þat we moun ete—   460
Wo is us þat we weren born!
Weilawei! nis it no korn,
þat men micte make*n* of bred?
*W*s hungreth—we aren ney ded!'
Godard herde here wa—   465
þer-offe yaf he nouth a stra,
But tok þe maydnes boþe same*n*
Al so it were upon hiis game*n*,
Al so he wolde with he*m* leyke
þat were*n* for hu*n*ger grene and bleike.   470
Of boþen he karf on two here þrotes,
And siþen he*m* al to grotes.
þer was sorwe, wo-so it sawe,
Hwan þe children bi þ[e] wawe
Leyen and spraulede*n* i*n* þe blod!   475
Hauelok it saw and þe[m] bi-stod—
Ful sori was þat seli knaue.
Mikel dred he mouthe haue,
For at hise hert he saw a knif
For to reuen him hise lyf.   480
But þe k[n]aue, þat litel was,
He knelede bifor þat Iudas,
And seyde 'Louerd, merci nov!
Ma*n*rede, louerd, biddi you:
Al Denemark I wile you yeue,   485
To þat forward þu late me liue.
Here Hi wile on boke swere
þat neuremore ne shal I bere
Ayen þe, louerd, shel[d] ne spere,
Ne oþer wepne bere þat may you dere.   490
Louerd, haue merci of me!
Today I wile fro Denemark fle,

464 *W*s: *MS* þs

Ne neueremore comen ageyn:
Sweren Y wole þat Bircabein
Neuere yete me ne gat.'   495
Hwan þe deuel he[r]de þat,
Sumdel bigan him for to rewe—   fo. 206vb
With-drow þe knif, þat was lewe
Of þe seli children blod.
þer was miracle fair and god   500
þat he þe knaue nouth ne slou,
But fo[r] rewnesse him þit-drow—
Of Auelok rewede him ful sore,
And þoucte he wolde þat he ded wore,
But on þat he nouth wit his hend   505
Ne drepe him nouth, þat fule fend.
þoucte he als he him bi-stod,
Starinde als he were wod,
'Yif Y late him liues go,
He micte me wirchen michel wo—   510
Grith ne get Y neueremo;
He may [me] waiten for to slo.
And yf he were brouct of liue,
And mine children wolden þriue,
Louerdinges after me   515
Of al Denemark micten he be.
God it wite, he shal ben ded—
Wile I taken non oþer red!
J shal do casten him in þe she:
þer I wile þat he drenth be,   520
Abouten his hals an anker god,
þad he ne flete in þe flod.'
þer anon he dede sende
After a fishere þat he wende
þat wolde al his wille do,   525
And sone anon he seyde him to:
'Grim, þou wost þu art mi þral:
Wilte don mi wille al
þat I wile bidden þe?
Tomorwen shal [I] maken þe fre   530
And aucte þe yeuen and riche make,

502 þit-drow: _MS_ þitdrow   512 [me]: _Skeat_   530 [I]: _Skeat_

Grim toke þe cheld and bond wel faste   537
Quiles þe bondes mith laste
þat was a foul strong line
. anne was haueloc in mekel pine   540
Wiste he neuere er of wo
. ut jesu crist þat made to go
þe alte and þe dumme for to speke
Haueloc þout of godard wreke   544
and þat he do him al quic flo   a
Wyt schame and pine and mekel wo   b
for he it seruede on fele manere   c
Als ye schuln forwar here   d
He was traitur in mani a kas   e
and he it aboute þat he swilc was   f
he broute þe child in mechel sorwen   g
yet wurth is soule neuere borwen   h
he bad grim don is comaundemet   j
and þerfore was he ate þe laste schent   k
    or þanne grim hadde him faste bounde   545
    and sithen in an old cloþe wnden
he þriste in his muth wel faste
a corner of an old cloþe ful him wraste
þat he ne mith speken ne greden
Quider so he wolde hym leden   550
            dde   d h . m so

545–6 space left at beginning of these lines for illuminated capital away   551 *mostly trimmed*

With þan þu wilt þis child take
And leden him with þe tonicht,
þan þou sest þe mone lith,
Jn to þe se and don him þer-inne.   535
Al wile taken on me þe sinne.'
Grim tok þe child, and bond him faste
Hwil þe bondes micte laste,
þat weren of ful strong line.
þo was Hauelok in ful strong pine—   540
Wiste he neuere her wat was wo!
Jesu Crist, þat makede to go   fo. 207ra
þe halte and þe doumbe speken,
Hauelok, þe of Godard wreken!

Hwan Grim him hauede faste bounden,   545
And siþen in an eld cloth wnden,
[He þriste in his muth wel faste]
A keuel of clutes ful unwraste,
þat he mouthe speke ne fnaste
Hwere he wolde him bere or lede.   550
Hwan he hauede don þat dede,
Hwan þe swike him hauede heþede
þat he shulde him forth [lede]
And him drinchen in þe se—
þat forwarde makeden he—   555
Jn a poke ful and blac
Sone he caste him on his bac,
Ant bar him hom to hise cleue,
And bitaucte him dame Leue,

534 þan: *MS* þai   þe: *MS* se   547 *supplied from Cambridge fragments*
553 [lede]: *Skeat*

And seyde 'Wite þou þis knaue,   560
Al so þou wi[l]t mi lif haue [saue]!
J shal dreinchen him in þe se:
For him shole we ben maked fre,
Gold hauen ynou and oþer fe—
þat hauet mi louerd bihoten me.'   565

Hwan dame [Leue] herde þat,
Vp she stirte and nouth ne sat,
And caste þe knaue so harde adoun
þat he crakede þer his croune
Ageyn a gret ston þer it lay.   570
þo Hauelok micte sei 'Weilawei
þat euere was I kinges bern—
þat him ne hauede grip or ern,
Leoun or wlf, wluine or bere,
Or oþer best þat wolde him dere!'   575
So lay þat child to middel-nicth,
þat Grim bad Leue bringen lict
For to don on his cloþes:
'Ne þenkeste nowt of mine oþes
þat Ich haue mi louerd sworen?   580
Ne wile I nouth be forloren:
J shal beren him to þe se—
þou wost þat [bi]houes me—
And I shal drenchen him þer-inne.
Ris up swiþe an go þu binne,   585
And blou þe fir and lith a kandel.'
Als she shulde hise cloþes handel
On for to don, and blawe þe fir,   fo. 207rb
She saw þer-inne a lith ful shir,
Al so brith so it were day,   590
Aboute þe knaue þer he lay.
Of hise mouth it stod a stem
Als it were a sunne-bem;
Al so lith was it þer-inne
So þer brenden cerges inne.   595

561 wi[l]t: *MS* with   haue: *two raised dots after* e   [saue]: *Holthausen*
566 [Leue]: *Skeat*   568 so harde adoun *Skeat*: *MS* adoun so harde
569 *Skeat*: *MS* þat hise croune he þer crakede   588 þe: *MS* þer

'Jesu Crist!' wat dame Leue,
'Hwat is þat lith in vre cleue?
*R*is up, Grim, and loke wat it menes!
Hwat is þe lith, as þou wenes?'
He stirte*n* boþe up to þe knaue   600
(For ma*n* shal god wille haue),
Vnkeuelede*n* him and swiþe unbou*n*de*n*,
And sone anon [upon] him fu*n*den,
Als he tiruede*n* of his serk,
On hise rith shuldre a kynemerk—   605
A swiþe brith, a swiþe fair.
'Goddot!' quath Grim 'þis ure eir,
þat shal [ben] louerd of Denmark!
He shal be*n* king strong and stark—
He shal haue*n* i*n* his hand   610
A[l] Denemark and Engeland.
He shal do Godard ful wo—
He shal him hangen or quik flo,
Or he shal him al quic graue.
Of him shal he no merci haue.'   615
þus seide Grim, and sore gret,
And sone fel him to þe fet,
And seide 'Louerd, haue merci
Of me and Leue, þat is me bi!
Louerd, we aren boþe þine—   620
þine cherles, þine hine.
Lowerd, we shole*n* þe wel fede
Til þat þu cone ride*n* on stede,
Til þat þu cone ful wel bere
Helm on heued, sheld and spere.   625
He ne shal neuere wite, sikerlike
(Godard, þat fule swike).
þoru oþer ma*n*, louerd, þa*n* þoru þe
Sal I neuere frema*n* be.
þou shalt me, louerd, fre[man] make*n*,   630
For I shal yeme*n* þe and wake*n*—
þoru þe wile I fredom haue.'
þo was Haueloc a bliþe knaue!   fo. 207va

---

598 *R*is *Skeat: MS* Sir   603 [upon]: *Skeat*   630 fre[man] make*n*: *MS* fremaken *with hairline between* e *and* m

He sat him up and crauede bred,
And seide 'Ich am ney ded,   635
Hwat for hunger, wat for bondes,
þat þu leidest on min hondes,
And for [þe] keuel at þe laste,
þat in my mouth was þrist faste.
Y was þe[r]-with so harde prangled   640
þat I was þe[r]-with ney strangled!'
'Wel is me þat þu mayth hete!
Goddoth,' quath Leue 'Y shal þe fete
Bred an chese, butere and milk,
Pastees and flaunes—al with suilk   645
Shole we sone þe wel fede,
Louerd, in þis mikel nede.'
Soth it is þat men seyt and suereth:
þer God wile helpen nouth ne dereth.

þanne sho hauede brouth þe mete,   650
Haueloc anon bigan to ete
Grundlike, and was ful bliþe.
Couþe he nouth his hunger miþe—
A lof he het, Y woth, and more,
For him hungrede swiþe sore.   655
þre dayes þer-biforn, I wene,
Et he no mete—þat was wel sene!
Hwan he hauede eten and was fed,
Grim dede maken a ful fayr bed,
Vncloþede him, and dede him þer–inne,   660
And seyde 'Slep, sone, with muchel winne!
Slep wel faste and dred þe nouth—
Fro sorwe to ioie art þu brouth!'
Sone so it was lith of day,
Grim it undertok þe wey   665
To þe wicke traitour Godard
þat was [of] Denema[r]k stiward,
And seyde 'Louerd, don Ich haue
þat þou me bede of þe knaue:
He is drenched in þe flod,   670
Abouten his hals an anker god—

638 [þe]: *Skeat*   667 [of] Denema[r]k: *MS* Denemak a

He is witerlike ded.
Eteth he neueremore bred:
He liþ drenched in þe se.
Yif me gold [and] oþer fe,   675
þat Y mowe riche be,
And with þi chartre make fre;
For þu ful wel bihetet me   fo. 207ᵛᵇ
þanne I last spak with þe!'
Godard stod and lokede on him   680
þoruthlike, with eyne grim,
And seyde 'Wiltu ben erl?
Go hom swiþe, fule drit-cherl!
Go heþen, and be eueremore
þral and cherl als þou er wore—   685
Shal[tu] haue non oþer mede.
For litel I do þe lede
To þe galues, so God me rede!
For þou haues don a wicke dede.
þou mait stonden her to longe,   690
Bute þou swiþe eþen gonge!'

Grim þoucte to late þat he ran
Fro þat traytour, þa[t] wicke man,
And þoucte 'Wat shal me to raþe?
Wite he him on liue he wile [us] baþe   695
Heye hangen on galwe-tre.
Betere us is of londe to fle
And berwen boþen ure liues,
And mine children and mine wiues.'
Grim solde sone al his corn,   700
Shep wit wolle, neth wit horn,
Hors and swin, [geet] wit berd,
þe gees, þe hennes of þe yerd—
Al he solde þat outh douthe,
þat he eure selle moucte,   705
And al he to þe peni drou.
Hise ship he greyþede wel inow:
He dede it tere an ful wel pike

þat it ne doutede sond ne krike,
þer-inne dide a ful god mast,   710
Stronge kables and ful fast,
Ores gode an ful god seyl—
þer-inne wantede nouth a nayl
þat euere he sholde þer-inne do.
Hwan he hauedet greyþed so,   715
Hauelok þe yunge he dede þer-inne,
Him and his wif, hise sones þrinne,
And hise two doutres þat faire wore.
And sone dede he leyn in an ore,
And drou him to þe heye se   720
þere he mith alþerbest fle.
Fro londe woren he bote a mile,
Ne were neuere but ane hwile   fo. 208ra
þat it ne bigan a wind to rise
Out of þe north men calleth 'bise',   725
And drof hem intil Engelond,
þat al was siþen in his hond,
His þat Hauelok was þe name.
But or he hauede michel shame,
Michel sorwe and michel tene,   730
And þrie he gat it al bidene,
Als ye shulen nou forthwar[d] here
Yf þat ye wilen þer-to here.
In Humber Grim bigan to lende,
Jn Lindeseye rith at þe north ende.   735
þer sat is ship upon þe sond;
But Grim it drou up to þe lond,
And þere he made a litel cote
To him and to hise flote.
Bigan he, þere for to erþe,   740
A litel hus to maken of erþe,
So þat he wel þore were
Of here herboru herborwed þere.
And for þat Grim þat place aute
þe stede of Grim þe name laute,   745
So þat Grimesbi it calle
þat þer-offe speken alle;

719 *Skeat omits* he, *metri causa*   746 it calle *Skeat*: *MS* calleth alle

And so shulen men callen it ay
Bituene þis and Domesday.

Grim was fishere swiþe god 750
And mikel couþe on þe flod—
Mani god fish þer-inne he tok,
Boþe with neth and with hok.
He tok þe sturgiun and þe qual,
And þe turbut and lax withal; 755
He tok þe sele and þe hwel—
He spedde ofte swiþe wel.
Keling he tok, and tumberel,
Hering and þe makerel,
þe butte, þe schulle, þe þornebake. 760
Gode paniers dede he make,
On til him, and oþer þrinne
Til hise sones, to beren fishe inne,
Vp o londe to selle and fonge—
Forbar he neyþe[r] tun ne gronge 765
þat he ne to-yede with his ware.
Kam he neuere hom hand-bare,
þat he ne broucte bred and sowel fo. 208rb
Jn his shirte or in his couel,
Jn his poke benes and korn— 770
Hise swink ne hauede he nowt forlorn.
And hwan he tok þe grete laumprei,
Ful we[l] he couþe þe rithe wei
To Lincolne, þe gode boru;
Ofte he yede it þoru and þoru, 775
Til he hauede wol wel sold
And þer-fore þe penies told.
þanne he com þenne he were bliþe,
For hom he brouthe fele siþe
Wastels, simenels with þe horn, 780
Hise pokes fulle of mele an korn,
Netes flesh, shepes and swines,
And hemp to maken of gode lines,
And stronge ropes to hise netes—
Jn þe se-weres he ofte setes. 785

785 se-weres: *MS* se werē

þus-gate Grim him fayre ledde:
Him and his genge wel he fedde
Wel twelf winter oþer more.
Hauelok was war þat Grim swank sore
For his mete, and he lay at hom— 790
þouthe 'Ich am nou no grom!
Jch am wel waxen, and wel may eten
More þan euere Grim may geten.
Jch ete more, bi God on liue,
þan Grim an hise children fiue! 795
Jt ne may nouth ben þus longe.
Goddot, Y wile with þe[m] gange
For to leren sum god to gete.
Swinken Ich wolde for mi mete—
Jt is no shame for to swinken! 800
þe man þat may wel eten and drinken
þat nouth ne haue but on swink long—
To liggen at hom it is ful strong.
God yelde him, þer I ne may,
þat haueth me fed to þis day! 805
Gladlike I wile þe paniers bere—
Jch woth ne shal it me nouth dere,
þey þer be inne a birþene gret
Al so heui als a neth.
Shal Ich neuere lengere dwelle— 810
Tomorwen shal Ich forth pelle.'

On þe morwen, hwan it was day,
He stirt up sone and nouth ne lay, fo. 208ᵛᵃ
And cast a panier on his bac
With fish giueled als a stac. 815
Al so michel he bar him one,
So he foure, bi mine mone!
Wel he it bar and solde it wel;
þe siluer he brouthe hom il del,
Al þat he þer-fore tok— 820
With-held he nouth a ferþinges nok.
So yede he forth ilke day
þat he neuere at home lay—
So wolde he his mester lere.

Bifel it so a strong dere 825
Bigan to rise of korn of bred,
þat Grim ne couþe no god red
Hw he sholde his meine fede.
Of Hauelok hauede he michel drede,
For he was strong and wel mouthe ete 830
More þanne heuere mouthe be gete;
Ne he ne mouthe on þe se take
Neyþer lenge ne þornbake,
Ne non oþer fish þat douthe,
His meyne feden with he mouthe. 835
Of Hauelok he hauede kare,
Hwil-gat þat he micthe fare;
Of his children was him nouth—
On Hauelok was al hise þouth,
And seyde 'Hauelok, dere sone, 840
J wene þat we deye mone
For hunger: þis dere is so strong,
And hure mete is uten long.
Betere is þat þu henne gonge
þan þu here dwelle longe— 845
Heþen þou mayt gangen to late.
þou canst ful wel þe ricthe gate
To Lincolne, þe gode borw—
þou hauest it gon ful ofte þoru.
Of me ne is me nouth a slo. 850
Betere is þat þu þider go,
For þer is mani god man inne:
þer þou mayt þi mete winne.
But wo is me þou art so naked:
Of mi seyl Y wolde þe were maked 855
A cloth þou mithest inne gongen,
Sone, no cold þat þu ne fonge.'

He tok þe sh[e]res of þe nayl fo. 208ᵛᵇ
And made him a couel of þe sayl,
And Hauelok dide it sone on. 860
Hauede neyþer hosen ne shon,
Ne none kines oþe[r] wede:
To Lincolne barfot he yede.

Fɪɢ. 2. View of High Bridge, Lincoln: 'The Devil's Hole', by Peter de Wint,
D 5027/50 of the National Galleries of Scotland, Edinburgh

Hwan he kam þe[r] he was ful wil—
Ne hauede he no frend to gangen til.   865
Two dayes þer fastinde he yede,
þat non for his werk wolde him fede.
þe þridde day herde he calle:
'Bermen, bermen, hider forth alle!'

.   .   .   .   870

Sprongen forth so sparke on glede.
Hauelok shof dun nyne or ten
Rith amidewarde þe fen,
And stirte forth to þe kok

.   .   .   .   875

þat he bouthe at þe brigge.
þe bermen let he alle ligge,
And bar þe mete to þe castel,
And gat him þere a ferþing wastel.

þet oþer day kepte he ok   880
Swiþe yerne þe erles kok,
Til þat he say him on þe b[r]igge,
And bi him mani fishes ligge.
þe herles mete hauede he bouth
Of Cornwalie, and kalde oft: 885
'Bermen, bermen, hider swiþe!'
Hauelok it herde, and was ful bliþe
þat he herde 'Bermen!' calle:
Alle made he hem dun-falle
þat in his gate yeden and stode—   890
Wel sixtene laddes gode.
Als he lep þe kok til,
He shof hem alle upon an hyl—
Astirte til him with his rippe
And bigan þe fish to kippe.   895
He bar up wel a carte-lode
Of segges, laxes, of playces brode,
Of grete laumprees and of eles.
Sparede he neyþer tos ne heles
Til þat he to þe castel cam,   900
þat men fro him his birþene nam.

870 *no gap in MS*   875 *no gap in MS*

þan men haueden holpen him doun
With þe birþene of his croun,
þe kok stod and on him low,
And þoute him stalworþe man ynow,   fo. 209ra
And seyde 'Wiltu ben wit me?   906
Gladlike wile Ich feden þe.
Wel is set þe mete þu etes,
And þe hire þat þu getes!'

'Goddot!' quoth he 'leue sire,   910
Bidde Ich you non oþer hire,
But yeueþ me inow to ete—
Fir and water Y wile you fete,
þe fir blowe an ful wel maken.
Stickes kan Ich breken and kraken,   915
And kindlen ful wel a fyr,
And maken it to brennen shir.
Ful wel kan Ich cleuen shides,
Eles to-turuen of here hides;
Ful wel kan Ich dishes swilen,   920
And don al þat ye euere wilen.'
Quoth þe kok 'Wile I no more!
Go þu yunder and sit þore,
And Y shal yeue þe ful fair bred,
And make þe broys in þe led.   925
Sit now doun and et ful yerne—
Daþeit hwo þe mete werne!'

Hauelok sette him dun anon
Al so stille als a ston,
Til he hauede ful wel eten;   930
þo hauede Hauelok fayre geten!
Huan he hauede eten inow,
He kam to þe welle, water up-drow,
And filde þe[r] a michel so—
Bad he non ageyn him go,   935
But bitwen his hondes he bar it in,
A[l] him one, to þe kichin.

Bad he non him water to fett,
Ne fro b[r]igge to bere þe mete.
He bar þe turues, he bar þe star, 940
þe wode fro þe brigge he bar,
Al þat euere shulden he nytte
Al he drow and al he citte—
Wolde he neuere hauen rest
More þan he were a best. 945
Of alle men was he mest meke,
Lauhwinde ay and bliþe of speke.
Euere he was glad and bliþe—
His sorwe he couþe ful wel miþe.
Jt ne was non so litel knaue fo. 209rb
For to leyken ne for to plawe, 951
þat he ne wode with him pleye.
þe children þat y[e]den in þe weie
Of him he deden al he[re] wille,
And with him leykeden here fille. 955
Him loueden alle, stille and bolde,
Knictes, children, yunge and holde—
Alle him loueden þat him sowen,
Boþen heye men and lowe.
Of him ful wide þe word sprong, 960
Hw he was mike, hw he was strong,
Hw fayr man God him hauede maked,
But on þat he was almest naked;
For he ne hauede nouth to shride
But a kouel ful unride, 965
þat [was] ful and swiþe wicke—
Was it nouth worth a fir-sticke.
þe cok bigan of him to rewe,
And bouthe him cloþes al span-newe:
He bouthe him boþe hosen and shon, 970
And sone dide him dones on.
Hwan he was cloþed, osed, and shod,
Was non so fayr under God
þat euere yete in erþe were,
Non þat euere moder bere. 975
Jt was neuere man þat yemede

966 [was]: *Skeat*

Jn kinneriche þat so wel semede
King or cayser for to be,
þan he was shrid, so semede he.
For þanne he weren alle samen   980
At Lincolne at þe gamen,
And þe erles men woren al þore,
þan was Hauelok bi þe shuldren more
þan þe meste þat þer kam.
Jn armes him noman nam   985
þat he doune sone ne caste.
Hauelok stod ouer hem als a mast.
Als he was heie, al[s] he was long
He was boþe stark and strong—
Jn Engelond non hise per   990
Of strengþe þat euere kam him ner.
Als he was strong so was he softe:
þey a man him misdede ofte,
Neueremore he him misse[y]de
Ne hond on him with yuele leyde.   fo. 209ᵛᵃ
Of bodi was he mayden clene: 996
Neuere yete in game ne in grene
Ƿit hire ne wolde leyke ne lye
Nomore þan it were a strie.
Jn þat time al Hengelond   1000
þerl Godrich hauede in his hond,
And he gart komen into þe tun
Mani erl and mani barun,
And alle þat liues were
Jn Englond þanne wer þere,   1005
þat þey haueden after sent
To ben þer at þe parlement.
With hem com mani chambioun,
Mani with ladde, blac and brown,
An fel it so þat yungemen,   1010
Wel abouten nine or ten,
Bigunnen þe[re] for to layke.
þider komen boþe stronge and wayke,
þider komen lesse and more

---

995 missse[y]de *Skeat*: MS misdede   998 Ƿit hire: MS þithire
1008 chambioun: *or* chanbioun (*MS* chābioun)

þat in þe borw þanne weren þore—   1015
Chaunpiouns and starke laddes,
Bondemen with here gaddes
Als he comen fro þe plow.
þere was sembling inow;
For it ne was non horse-knaue,   1020
þo þei sholden in honde haue,
þat he ne kam þider þe leyk to se.
Biforn here fet þanne lay a tre,
And pulten with a mikel ston
þe starke laddes, ful god won.   1025
þe ston was mikel and ek greth,
And al so heui so a neth:
Grundstalwrþe man he sholde be
þat mouthe liften it to his kne—
Was þer neyþer clerc ne prest   1030
þat mithe liften it to his brest.
þer-wit putten þe chaunpiouns
þat þider comen with þe barouns.
Hwo-so mithe putten þore
Biforn anoþer an inch or more,   1035
Wore he yung, wore he hold,
He was for a kempe told.
Al so þe[y] stoden an ofte stareden,
þe chaunpiouns and ek þe ladden,
And he maden mikel strout   fo. 209vb
Abouten þe alþerbeste but,   1041
Hauelok stod and lokede þer-til,
And of puttingge he was ful wil;
For neuere yete ne saw he or
Putten þe ston or þanne þor.   1045
Hise mayster bad him gon þer-to—
Als he couþe, þer-with do.
þo hise mayster it him bad,
He was of him sore adrad:
þer-to he stirte sone anon,   1050
And kipte up þat heui ston
þat he sholde puten wiþe.
He putte at þe firste siþe

1030 clerc: MS clert

Ouer alle þat þer wore
Twel[ue] fote and sumdel more.　　　　　　1055
þe chaunpiouns þat put sowen:
Shuldreden he ilc oþer and lowen.
Wolden he nomore to putting gange,
But seyde 'Þe dwellen her to longe!'
þis selkouth mithe nouth ben hyd:　　　　1060
Ful sone it was ful loude kid
Of Hauelok, hw he warp þe ston
Ouer þe laddes euerilkon,
Hw he was fayr, hw he was long,
Hw he was with, hw he was strong.　　　　1065
þoruth England yede þe speke
Hw he was strong and ek meke.
Jn þe castel, up in þe halle,
þe knithes speken þer-of alle,
So þat Godrich it herde wel,　　　　　　1070
þe speke of Hauelok, eueri del—
Hw he was strong man and hey,
Hw he was strong and ek fri,
And þouthte Godrich 'þoru þis knaue
Shal Ich Engelond al haue,　　　　　　　1075
And mi sone after me,
For so I wile þat it be!
þe king Aþelwold me dide swere
Vpon al þe messe-gere
þat I shude his douthe[r] yeue　　　　　1080
þe hexte [man] þat mithe liue,
þe beste, þe fairest, þe strangest ok—
þat gart he me sweren on þe bok.
Hwere mithe I finden ani so hey
So Hauelok is, or so sley?　　　　　　fo. 210ra
þou Y southe heþen into Ynde,　　　　　1086
So fayr, so strong, ne mithe Y finde.
Hauelok is þat ilke knaue
þat shal Goldeborw haue!'
þis þouthe with trechery,　　　　　　　1090
With traysoun and wit felony:

1066 speke *Skeat*: *MS* speche　　1071 speke *Owen*: *MS* spekē　　1081 [man]: *Skeat*

For he wende þat Hauelok wore
Sum cherles sone and no more,
Ne shulde he hauen of Engellond
Onlepi forw in his hond   1095
With hire þat was þer-of eyr,
þat boþe was god and swiþe fair.
He wende þat Hauelok wer a þral—
þer-þoru he wende hauen al
Jn Engelond þat hire rith was.   1100
He was werse þan Sathanas
þat Iesu Crist in erþe shop—
Hanged worþe he on an hok!

After Goldebo[r]w sone he sende,
þat was boþe fayr and hende,   1105
And dide hire to Lincolne bringe.
Belles dede he ageyn hire ringen,
And ioie he made hire swiþe mikel;
But neþeles he was ful swikel.
He seyde þat he sholde hire yeue   1110
þe fayreste man þat mithe liue.
She answerede and seyde anan,
Bi [Iesu] Crist and Seint Iohan,
þat hire sholde noman wedde
Ne noman bringen to hire bedde   1115
But he were king or kinges eyr,
Were he neuere man so fayr.

Godrich þe erl was swiþe wroth
þat she swor swilk an oth,
And seyde 'Hwor þou wilt be   1120
Quen and leuedi ouer me?
þou shalt hauen a gadeling—
Ne shalt þou hauen non oþer king!
þe shal spusen mi cokes knaue—
Ne shalt þou non oþer louerd haue.   1125
Daþeit þat þe oþer yeue
Eueremore hwil I liue!
Tomo[r]we ye sholen ben weddeth

1112 anan: *MS* anon   1113 [Iesu]: *Skeat*   and Seint: *MS* and bi seint

And maugre þin togidere beddeth.'

Goldeborw gret and *yaf* hire ille;   fo. 210rb

She wolde ben ded, bi hire wille.   1131

On þe morwen, hwan day was sprungen,

And day-belle at kirke rungen,

After Hauelok sente þat Iudas

þat werse was þanne Sathanas,   1135

And seyde 'Mayster, wilte wif?'

'Nay!' quoth Hauelok, 'bi my lif!

Hwat sholde Ich with wif do?

J ne may hire fede ne cloþe ne sho.

Wider sholde Ich wimman bringe?   1140

J ne haue none kines þinge—

J ne haue hws, Y ne haue cote,

Ne I ne haue stikke, Y ne haue sprote,

J ne haue neyþer bred ne sowel,

Ne cloth but of an hold with couel.   1145

þis cloþes þat Ich onne-haue

Aren þe kokes and Ich his knaue!'

Godrich stirt up and on him dong,

.   .   .   .

And seyde 'But þou hire take   1150

þat Y wole yeuen þe to make,

J shal hangen þe ful heye,

Or Y shal þristen vth þin heie!'

Hauelok was one and was odrat,

And grauntede him al þat he bad.   1155

þo sende he after hire sone,

þe fayrest wymman under mone,

And seyde til hire, [fel] and slike

(þat wicke þral, þat foule swike):

But þu þis man understonde   1160

J shal flemen þe of londe,

Or þou shal to þe galwes renne,

And þer þou shalt in a fir brenne!'

Sho was adrad for he so þrette,

And durste nouth þe spusing lette,   1165

But þey hire likede swiþe ille,

þouthe it was Godes wille—

1130 *yaf Stratmann*: MS þas *or* pas   1149 *no gap in MS*   1158 [fel]: *Skeat*

God þat makes to growen þe korn,
Formede hire wimman to be born.
Hwan he hauede don him, for drede, 1170
þat he sholde hire spusen and fede,
And þat she sholde til him holde,
þer weren penies þicke tolde
Mikel plente upon þe bok—
He ys hire yaf and she as tok. 1175
He weren spused fayre and wel: fo. 210ᵛᵃ
þe messe he dede, eueri del
þat fel to spusing, an god cle[r]k—
þe erchebishop uth of Yerk,
þat kam to þe parlement, 1180
Als God him hauede þider sent.

Hwan he weren togydere in Godes lawe,
þat þe folc ful wel it sawe,
He ne wisten hwat he mouthen
Ne he ne wisten wat hem douthe— 1185
þer to dwellen or þenne to gonge.
þer ne wolden he dwellen longe,
For he wisten and ful wel sawe
þat Godrich hem hatede—þe deuel him hawe!
And yf he dwelleden þer outh— 1190
þat fel Hauelok ful wel on þouth—
Men sholde don his leman shame,
Or elles bringen in wicke blame,
þat were him leuere to ben ded.
Forþi he token anoþer red, 1195
þat þei sholden þenne fle
Til Grim, and til hise sones þre—
þer wenden he alþerbest to spede,
Hem for to cloþe and for to fede.
þe lond he token under fote— 1200
Ne wisten he non oþer bote—
And helden ay þe rith [sti]
Til he komen to Grimesby.
þanne he komen þere þanne was Grim ded—
Of him ne haueden he no red. 1205

1177 dede: *MS* deden   1178 an: *MS* and   1201 [sti]: *Skeat*

But hise children alle fuye
Alle weren yet on liue,
þat ful fayre ayen hem neme
Hwan he wisten þat he keme,
And maden ioie swiþe mikel—   1210
Ne weren he neuere ayen hem fikel.
On knes ful fayre he hem setten
And Hauelok swiþe fayre gretten,
And seyden 'Welkome, louerd dere,
And welkome be þi fayre fere!   1215
Blessed be þat ilke þrawe
þat þou hire toke in Godes lawe!
Wel is hus we sen þe on lyue.
þou mithe us boþe selle and yeue;
þou mayt us boþe yeue and selle,   1220
With þat þou wilt here dwelle.   fo. 210ᵛᵇ
We hauen, louerd, alle gode—
Hors, and neth, and ship on flode,
Gold, and siluer, and michel auchte,
þat Grim ure fader us bitawchte.   1225
Gold and siluer and oþer fe
Bad he us bitaken þe.
We hauen shep, we hauen swin;
Bileue her, louerd, and al be þin!
þo[u] shalt ben louerd, þou shalt ben syre   1230
And we sholen seruen þe and hire.
And hure sistres sholen do
Al þat euere biddes sho:
He sholen hire cloþen washen and wringen,
And to hondes water bringen: 1235
He sholen bedden hire and þe,
For leuedi wile we þat she be.'
Hwan he þis ioie haueden maked,
Sithen stikes broken and kraked,
And þe fir brouth on brenne,   1240
Ne was þer spared gos ne henne,
Ne þe hende ne þe drake.
Mete he deden plente make—
Ne wantede þere no god mete.
Wyn and ale deden he fete   1245

And made hem glade and bliþe;
Wesseyl ledde*n* he fele siþe.

On þe nith als Goldeborw lay,
Sory and sorwful was she ay,
For she wende she were biswike,   1250
þat she [we]re yeue*n* unkyndelike.
O nith saw she þer-inne a lith,
A swiþe fayr, a swiþe bryth—
Al so brith, al so shir,
So it were a blase of fir.   1255
She lokede no[r]þ and ek south,
And saw it come*n* ut of his mouth
þat lay bi hire in þe bed.
No ferlike þou she were adred!
þouthe she 'Wat may þis bimene?   1260
He beth heyma*n* yet, als Y wene—
He beth heyma*n* er he be ded!'
On hise shuldre, of gold red,
She saw a swiþe noble croiz.
Of an angel she herde a uoyz: 1265

'Goldeborw, lat þi sorwe be!   fo. 211ra
For Hauelok, þat haueþ spuset þe,
He [is] kinges sone and ki*n*ges eyr—
þat bike*n*neth þat croiz so fayr.
Jt bikenneth more—þat he shal   1270
Denemark haue*n* and Englond al.
He shal ben king strong and stark
Of Engelond and Denemark—
þat shal þu wit þin eyne sen,
And þo[u] shalt quen and leuedi ben.'   1275

þanne she hauede herd þe steuene
Of þe angel uth of heuene,
She was so fele siþes bliþe
þat she ne mithe hire ioie mythe,
But Hauelok sone anon she kiste,   1280
And he slep and nouth ne wiste

1251 she [we]re: *MS* shere

Hwa*t* þat aungel hauede seyd.
Of his slep anon he brayd,
And seide 'Le*m*ma*n*, slepes þou?
A selkuth drem dremede me nou—   1285

Herkne nou hwat me haueth met.
Me þouthe Y was i*n* Denemark set,
But on on þe moste hil
þat euere yete kam I til.
Jt was so hey þat Y wel mouthe   1290
Al þe werd se, als me þouthe.
Als I sat up-on þat lowe
J bigan Denemark for to awe,
þe borwes and þe castles stronge;
And mine armes were*n* so lo*n*ge   1295
þat I fadmede al at ones
Denemark with mine lo*n*ge bones.
And þa*n*ne Y wolde mine armes drawe
Til me and hom for to haue,
Al þat euere in Denemark liueden   1300
On mine armes faste clyueden,
And þe stronge castles alle
On knes bigunne*n* for to falle—
þe keyes felle*n* at mine fet.
Ano þer drem dremede me ek   1305
þat Ich fley ouer þe salte se
Til Engeland, and al with me
þat euere was in Denemark lyues
But bo*n*deme*n* and here wiues,
And þat Ich kom til Engelond—   1310
Al closede it i*n*til min hond,   fo. 211rb
And, Goldeborw, Y gaf [it] þe.
Deus, le*m*man! hwat may þis be?'
Sho answerede and seyde sone
'Jesu Crist, þat made mone,   1315
þine dremes turne to ioye . . .
þat wite þw þat sittes i*n* trone!
Ne non stro*n*g ki*n*g ne caysere
So þou shalt be, fo[r] þou shalt bere

Jn Engelond corune yet.   1320
Denemark shal knele to þi fete;
Alle þe castles þat aren þer-inne
Shaltow, lemman, ful wel winne—
J woth so wel so Ich it sowe.
To þe shole comen heye and lowe,   1325
And alle þat in Denemark wone—
Em and broþer, fader and sone,
Erl and baroun, dreng an[d] þayn,
Knithes and burgeys and sweyn—
And [bes] mad king heyelike and wel.   1330
Denemark shal be þin euere-ilc del—
Haue þou nouth þer-offe douthe,
Nouth þe worth of one nouthe!
þer-offe with-inne þe firste yer
Shalt þou ben king of euere-il del.   1335
But do nou als Y wile rathe:
Nim in wit l[i]þe to Denema[r]k baþe,
And do þou nouth on frest þis fare—
Lith and selthe felawes are—
For shal Ich neuere bliþe be   1340
Til I with eyen Denemark se,
For Ich woth þat al þe lond
Shalt þou hauen in þin hon[d].
Prey Grimes sones alle þre
þat he wenden forth with þe;   1345
J wot he wilen þe nouth werne—
With þe wende shulen he yerne,
For he louen þe hertelike.
þou maght tel he aren quike,
Hwore-so he o worde aren;   1350
þere ship þou do hem swiþe yaren,
And loke þat þou dwelle nouth—
Dwelling haueth ofte scaþe wrouth!

Hwan Hauelok herde þat she radde,
Sone it was day, sone he him cladde,   1355
And sone to þe kirke yede   fo. 211ᵛᵃ

1328 an[d] þayn: *MS* an kayn   1337 wit l[i]þe: *MS* witl þe   1349 tel:
MS til   1352 dwelle: *MS* dwellē *i.e.* dwellen

Or he dide ani oþer dede,
And bifor þe rode bigan falle,
'Croiz' and 'Crist' bi[gan] to kalle,
And seyde 'Louerd, þat al weldes—   1360
Wind and water, wodes and feldes—
For þe holi milce of you
Haue merci of me, Louerd, nou!
And wreke me yet on mi fo
þat Ich saw biforn min eyne slo   1365
Mine sistres with a knif,
And siþen wolde me mi lyf
Haue reft, for in þe se
Bad he Grim haue drenched me.
He [haldes] mi lond with mikel vnrith,   1370
With michel wrong, with mikel plith,
For I ne misdede him neuere nouth,
And haued me to sorwe brouth.
He haueth me do mi mete to þigge
And ofte in sorwe and pine ligge.   1375
Louerd, haue merci of me,
And late wel passe þe se,
þat Ihc haue þer-offe douthe and kare,
Withuten stormes ouer-fare
þat Y ne drenched [were] þer-ine   1380
Ne forfaren for no sinne,
And bringge me wel to þe lond
þat Godard haldes in his hond,
þat is mi rith eueri del—
Jesu Crist, þou wost it wel!'   1385

þanne he hauede his bede seyd,
His offrende on þe auter leyd,
His leue at Iesu Crist he tok
And at his suete moder ok,
And at þe croiz þat he biforn lay,   1390
Siþen yede sore grotinde awey.
Hwan he com hom he wore yare,
Grimes sones, for to fare
Jnto þe se fishes to gete,

1370 [haldes]: *Skeat*

þat Hauelok mithe wel of ete. 1395
But Auelok þouthe al anoþer:
First he ka[l]de þe heldeste broþer,
Roberd þe Rede bi his naue[n],
Wiliam Wenduth and H[uwe R]auen—
Grimes sones alle þre— 1400
And sey[d]e 'Liþes nou alle to me! fo. 211ᵛᵇ
Louerdinges, Ich wile you shaue
A þing of me þat ye wel knawe.
Mi fader was king of Denshe lond—
Denemark was al in his hond 1405
þe day þat he was quik and ded.
But þanne hauede he wicke red,
þat he me and Denemark al
And mine sistres bitawte a þral—
A deueles lime hus bitawte, 1410
And al his lond and al hise authe.
For Y saw þat fule fend
Mine sistres slo with hise hend:
First he shar a two here þrotes,
And siþen hem al to grotes, 1415
And siþen bad in þe se
Grim youre fader drenchen me.
Deplike dede he him swere
On bok þat he sholde me bere
Vnto þe se an drenchen ine, 1420
And wolde taken on him þe sinne.
But Grim was wis and swiþe hende—
Wolde he nouth his soule shende.
Leuere was him to be forsworen
þan drenchen me and ben forlorn. 1425
But sone bigan he for to fle
Fro Denemark for to berþen me,
For yif Ich hauede þer ben funden,
Hauede ben slayn, or harde bunden,
And heye ben henged on a tre— 1430
Hauede go for him gold ne fe.
Forþi fro Denemark hider he fledde,

1398 naue[n] Sisam: MS name   1399 H[uwe R]auen Skeat: MS hauen
1402 shaue: MS sheue   1403 knawe: MS knewe   1428 yif: MS yis

And me ful fayre and ful wel fedde,
So þat [her] vnto þis day
Haue Ich ben fed and fostred ay.   1435
But nou Ich am up to þat helde
Cume*n* þat Ich may wepne welde,
And Y may grete di*n*tes yeue,
Shal I neuere hwil Ich lyue
Ben glad til þat Ich Denemark se!   1440
J preie you þat ye wende with me,
And Ich may mak you riche men:
Jlk of you shal haue castles ten
And þe lond þat þor-til longes—
Borwes, tunes, wodes, and wo*n*ges . . .   1445

With swilk als Ich byen shal.   fo. 212ra
þer-of biseche you nou leue   1627
(Wile Ich speke with non oþer reue
But with *yo*[u] þat iustise are)
þat Y mithe seke*n* mi ware   1630
Jn gode borwes up and doun,
And faren Ich wile fro tun to tun.’
A gold ring drow he forth anon—
An hundred pu*n*d was worth þe ston—
And yaf it Ubbe for to spede.   1635
He was ful wis þat first yaf mede!
And so was Hauelok ful wis here:
He solde his gold ring ful dere—
Was neuere non so dere sold
F*ro* chapme*n* neyþer yung ne old.   1640
þat sho*le*n ye forthward ful wel here*n*
Yif þat ye wile þe storie heren.

Hwa*n* Ubbe hauede þe gold ring,
Hauede he youenet for no þing,
Nouth for þe borw euere-il del.   1645
Hauelok bihel[d] he swiþe wel,

1439 Shal: *MS* S shal   1445 *After fo. 211*^vb, *which ends here, a leaf has been cut out of the MS. Since each leaf has two columns of writing on the recto and two on the verso, and since there are regularly 45 lines in each column, the lost section of the text must have contained 180 lines* 1629 *yo*[u] *Holthausen: MS* þe   *art written and subpuncted by the scribe after* þat 1640 F*ro Holthausen: MS* For   1641 sho*le*n: *MS* shorē

Hw he was wel of bones maked,
Brod in þe sholdres, ful wel schaped,
þicke in þe brest, of bodi long—
He semede wel to ben wel strong.   1650
'Deus!' hwat Ubbe, 'Qui ne were he knith?
J woth þat he is swiþe with:
Betere semede him to bere
Helm on heued, sheld and spere,
þanne to beye and selle ware—   1655
Allas, þat he shal þer-with fare!
Goddot, wile he trowe me,
Chaffare shal he late be.'
Neþeles, he seyde sone:
'Hauelok, haue þi bone!   1660
And Y ful wel rede þ[e]
þat þou come and ete with me
Today, þou and þi fayre wif
þat þou louest al so þi lif.
And haue þou of hire no drede—   1665
Shal hire no man shame bede.
Bi þe fey þat Y owe to þe
þer-of shal I meself borw be.'

Hauelok herde þat he bad,
And thow was he ful sore drad   1670
With him to ete, for hise wif;   fo. 212rb
For him wore leuere þat his lif
Him wore reft þan she in blame
Felle or lauthe ani shame.
Hwanne he hauede his wille yat,   1675
þe stede þat he onne-sat
Smot Ubbe with spures faste
And forth awey, but at þe laste,
Or [þat] he fro him ferde,
Seyde he, þat his folk herde: 1680
'Loke þat ye comen baþe,
For Ich it wile and Ich it raþe.'

Hauelok ne durste, þe[i] he were adrad,
Nouth withsitten þat Ubbe bad.
His wif he dide with him lede—   1685
Vnto þe heye curt he y[e]de.
Roberd hire ledde, þat was red,
þat haue[de] þoled for hire þe ded
Or ani haue[de] hire misseyd
Or hand with iuele onne-leyd.   1690
Willam Wendut was þat oþer
þat hire ledde, Roberdes broþer,
þat was with at alle nedes.
Wel is him þat god man fedes!
þan he weren comen to þe halle   1695
Biforen Ubbe and hise men alle,
Vbbe stirte hem ageyn,
And mani a knith and mani a sweyn,
Hem for to se and for to shawe.
þo stod Hauelok als a lowe   1700
Aboven þat þer-inne wore,
Rith al bi þe heued more
þanne ani þat þer-inne stod.
þo was Ubbe bliþe of mod
þat he saw him so fayr and hende: 1705
Fro him ne mithe his herte wende,
Ne fro him ne fro his wif—
He louede hem sone so his lif.
Weren non in Denemark þat him þouthe
þat he so mikel loue mouthe: 1710
More he louede Hauelok one
þan al Denemark, bi mine wone.
Loke nou hw God helpen kan
O mani wise wif and man!

Hwan it was comen time to ete,   1715
Hise wif dede Ubbe sone in fete,   fo. 212va
And til hire seyde al on gamen:
'Dame, þou and Hauelok shulen ete samen,
And Goldeboru shal ete wit me
þat is so fayr so flour on tre—   1720

1688 þoled: *MS* þarned   1699 shawe: *MS* shewe

Jn al Denemark [n]is wimman
So fayr so sche, bi Seint Iohan.'
þanne [he] were set and bord leyd,
And þe beneysun was seyd,
Biforn hem com þe beste mete 1725
þat king or cayser wolde ete:
Kranes, swannes, ueneysun,
Lax, lampreys, and god sturgun,
Pyment to drinke and god clare,
Win hwit and red, ful god plente— 1730
Was þer-inne no page so lite
þat euere wolde ale bite.
Of þe mete for to telle
Ne of þe *win* bidde I nout dwelle;
þat is þe storie for to lenge— 1735
Jt wolde anuye þis fayre genge.
But hwan he haueden þe kilþing de[y]led,
And fele siþes haueden wosseyled,
And with gode drinkes seten longe,
And it was time for to gonge 1740
Jl man to þer he cam fro,
þouthe Ubbe 'Yf I late hem go
þus one foure, withuten mo,
So mote Ich brouke finger or to,
For þis wimman bes mike wo! 1745
For hire shal men hire louerd slo.'
He tok sone knithes ten,
And wel sixti oþer men
Wit gode bowes and with gleiues,
And sende him unto þe greyues— 1750
þe beste man of al þe toun,
þat was named Bernard Brun—
And bad him als he louede his lif
Hauelok wel y[e]men and his wif,
And wel do wayten al þe nith 1755
Til þe oþer day þat it were lith.
Bernard was trewe and swiþe with—
Jn al þe borw ne was no knith
þat betere couþe on stede riden,

1723 [he]: *Skeat*   1734 *win Skeat: MS* metes

Helm on heued ne swerd bi side.   1760
Hauelok he gladlike understod   fo. 212ᵛᵇ
With mike loue and herte god,
And dide greyþe a super riche
(Al so he was no-with chiche)
To his bihoue eueril del,   1765
þat he mithe supe swiþe wel.

Al so he seten and sholde soupe,
So comes a ladde in a ioupe,
And with him sixti oþer stronge,
With swerdes drawen and kniues longe,   1770
Jlkan in hande a ful god gleiue,
And seyde 'Undo, Bernard þe greyue!
Vndo swiþe and lat us in,
Or þu art ded, bi Seint Austin!'
Bernard stirt up, þat was ful big,   1775
And caste a brinie upon his rig,
And grop an ax þat was ful god—
Lep to þe dore so he wore wod,
And seyde 'Hwat are ye þat are þer-oute,
þat þus biginnen for to stroute?   1780
Goth henne swiþe, fule þeues!
For bi þe Louerd þat man on leues,
Shol Ich casten þe dore open,
Summe of you shal Ich drepen,
And þe oþre shal Ich kesten   1785
Jn feteres and ful faste festen!'
'Hwat haue ye seid?' quoth a ladde,
'Wenestu þat we ben adradde?
We shole at þis dore gonge
Maugre þin, carl, or outh longe!'   1790
He gripen sone a bulder-ston,
And let it fleye, ful god won,
Agen þe dore, þat it to-rof.
Auelok it saw, and þider drof,
And þe barre sone vt-drow,   1795
þat was unride and gret ynow,
And caste þe dore open wide

1764 chiche: *MS* chinche   1777 ax: *MS* ar

And seide 'Her shal Y now abide!
Comes swiþe vnto me—
Daþeyt hwo you henne fle!'   1800
'No!' quodh on, 'þat shaltou coupe!'
And bigan til him to loupe,
Jn his hond his swerd ut-drawe
(Hauelok he wende þore haue slawe),
And with [him] comen oþer two   1805
þat him wolde of liue haue do.   fo. 213ra
Hauelok lifte up þe dore-tre,
And at a dint he slow hem þre:
Was non of hem þat hise hernes
Ne lay þer ute ageyn þe sternes.   1810
þe ferþe, þat he siþen mette,
Wit þe barre so he him grette
Bifor þe heued þat þe rith eye
Vt of þe hole made he fleye,
And siþe clapte him on þe crune   1815
So þat he stan-ded fel þor dune.
þe fifte þat he ouertok
Gaf he a ful sor dint ok
Bitwen þe sholdres þer he stod,
þat he speu his herte-blod.   1820
þe sixte wende for to fle,
And he clapte him with þe tre
Rith in þe fule necke so
þat he smot hise necke on to.
þanne þe sixe weren doun-feld,   1825
þe seuenþe brayd ut his swerd,
And wolde Hauelok riht in þe eye;
And Haue[lok] le[t þe] barre fleye
And smot him sone ageyn þe brest,
þat hauede ne neuere sch[r]ifte of prest   1830
(For he was ded on lesse hwile
þan men mouthe renne a mile).
Alle þe oþere weren ful kene:
A red þei taken hem bitwene
þat he sholde him bihalue,   1835

1799 *MS has* daþeit *at the end of this line as well as* Daþeyt *at the beginning of the next*
1805 [him]: *Skeat*   1828 Haue[lok] le[t þe] *Skeat: MS* haue le

at hym wolde of liue tune do
auelok liste up þe dore ne
nd at a dint he slow þe þre
as non of hem þat hise hiues
le say þer ute ageyn þe sternes
e kerte þat he siyen mette
it þe laine so hebin gine
þor þe heued þat þe nith ese
t of þe hole made he sleye
nd siye clapte hym on þe crune
o þat he stunded fel word dune
e fifte þat he ouer tok
af he aful fordint oli
riþen þe sholdres þer he stod
at he siyen his herte blod
e sixte wende forto fle
nd he clapte hym with þe tre
rith in þe fule necke so
at he smot hise necke on to
ane þe sixe weren doun feld
e seuenþe brayd ut his sword
nd wolde hauelok siþir iþe eye
ud hauele lane sleye
nd smot hym sone ageyn þe brest
at hauede he neue schitte of part
or he was ded on lesse hwile
an me mouthe rene a mile
Ne þe oþere weren ful kene
red þei taken hem bi twene
at he sholde hym bi halue
nd brise so þat wit no salue
e sholde hym helen leche non
ey drowen ut swerdes ful god won
nd shoten on hym so don on here
ogges þat wolden hym to tere
ane men doth þe bere lyre
e laddes were kabre and teyte
nd un bi yeden hym illron
u smot with tre and su wit ston
ime putte with gleynie thur and sde
nd yene wundes longe and wide
u siwenti stedes and wel mo

or þe blod ran of his sides
o water þat fro þe welle glides
ut þane bigan he for to molwe
ith þe laine and ler þem þewe
we scholde cowþe sore smite
or was þer non long nelite
at he mouthe ouer take
at he ne gaue his crune kniue
o þat on a litel stund
elde he twenti to þe grund
o bigan grer dine to rise
for þe laddes on ilke wise
im a sayleden wit grete dintes
to ser he sloden hym with flintes
nd gleyues schote hym for serue
or drepen hym he wolden yerne
ut durste he ne wie hym no more
ane he for or leu wore
ulde raue þat dine heide
And wolbche wel þat me mul sende
ith his louerd for his wif
nd grop an ore and a long knif
nd yider drof also an herit
nd cham þer on a litel sterr
nd salw holk þe ladder wode
auelok his louerd umbi stode
nd bete on hym so doth þe smith
ith þe hamer on þe stith
Allas hwat haue þat y was lore
at eule er ich bred of koren
at ich here þis sorwe se
oberd william hwate ar þe
riþeth euer unker a god tre
nd late we nouth þise dogel fle
il ure louerd wreke
ometh swiþe and folwer me
ch haue in honde a ful gyd ore
avett wo ne sinte sore
ya leue ya quod wberd sone
we haue ful god slith of þe mone
Roberd grop a staf strong and gret
at mouthe ful wel bere a net

FIG. 3. *Hauelok*, lines 1806–92: MS Laud Misc. 108, fo. 213^r,
Bodleian Library, Oxford

And brise*n* so þat wit no salue
Ne sholde him helen leche non.
þey drowen ut swerdes, ful god won,
And shoten on him so don on bere
Dogges þat wolden him to-tere,   1840
þa*n*ne men doth þe bere beyte.
þe laddes were kaske and teyte
And v*m*biyeden him ilkon:
Su*m* smot with tre, and su*m* wit ston,
Su*m*me putte*n* with gleyue i*n* bac and side   1845
And yeue*n* wundes longe and wide
Jn twenti stedes, and wel mo,
Fro þe croune til þe to.
Hwan he saw þat, he was wod,
And was it ferlik hw he stod!   1850
For þe blod ran of his sides   fo. 213rb
So water þat fro þe welle glides.
But þa*n*ne bigan he for to mowe
With þe barre, and let hem sha*we
Hw he cowþe sore smite;   1855
For was þer non, long ne lite,
þat he mouthe ouertake,
þat he ne garte his croune krake,
So þat on a litel stund
Felde he twenti to þe grund.   1860

þo bigan gret dine to rise,
For þe laddes on ilke wise
Him asaylede*n* wit grete dintes.
Fro fer he sto[n]den him with flintes,
And gleyues schote*n* him fro ferne,   1865
For drepen him he wolden yerne;
But dursten he newhe*n* him nomore
þa*n*ne he bor or leu*n* wore.

Huwe Raue*n* þat dine herde,
And þowthe wel þat men misferde   1870
With his louerd for his wif,
And grop an ore and a long knif,

1843 v*m*biyeden *Skeat*: *MS* vnbiyeden   1854 sha*we: *MS* shewe

And þider drof al so an hert,
And cham þer on a litel stert,
And saw how þe laddes wode   1875
Hauelok his louerd umbistode,
And beten on him so doth þe smith
With þe hamer on þe stith.

'Allas' hwat Hwe 'þat Y was boren!
þat euere et Ich bred of koren!   1880
þat Ich here þis sorwe se!
Roberd, Willam, hware ar ye?
Gripeth eþer unker a god tre,
And late we nouth þise doges fle
Til ure louerd wreke [be]!   1885
Cometh swiþe, and folwes me:
Jch haue in honde a ful god ore—
Daþeit wo ne smite sore!'
'Ya, leue, ya!' quod Roberd sone,
'We hauen ful god lith of þe mone.'   1890
Roberd grop a staf strong and gret
þat mouthe ful wel bere a net,
And Willam Wendut grop a tre
Mikel grettere þan his þre,
And Bernard held his ax ful faste   1895
(J seye, was he nouth þe laste!)   fo. 213ᵛᵃ
And lopen forth so he weren wode
To þe laddes þer he stode,
And yaf hem wundes swiþe grete.
þer mithe men wel se boyes bete,   1900
And ribbes in here sides breke,
And Hauelok on hem wel wreke.
He broken armes, he broken knes,
He broken shankes, he broken thes,
He dide þe blod þere renne dune   1905
To þe fet rith fro þe crune,
For was þer spared heued non.
He leyden on heuedes ful god won,
And made croune breke and crake
Of þe broune and of þe blake.   1910

1885 [be]: *Skeat*

He made*n* here backes al so bloute
Als he[re] wombes and made he*m* rowte
Als he weren kradel-barnes,
So dos þe child þat moder þarnes.

Daþeit þe recke! for he it seruede.   1915
Hwat dide he þore? were*n* he werewed!
So longe haude*n* he but and bet,
With neues under hernes set,
þat of þo sixti men and on
Ne wente þer awey liues non.   1920

On þe morwe*n*, h*w*an it was day,
Jlc on oþer wirwed lay
Als it were dogges þat were*n* he*n*ged,
And su*m*me leye i*n* dikes slenget,
And su*m*me in gripes bi þe her   1925
Drawen ware and late*n* þer.
Sket cam tiding intil Ubbe
þat Hauelok hauede with a clubbe
Of hise slawen sixti and on—
Sergaunz, þe beste þat mithe*n* gon.   1930
'Deus!' quoth Ubbe, 'hwat may þis be?
Betere his I nime miself and se
þat þis baret on hwat is wold
þa*n*ne I sende yunge or old;
For yif I sende him unto,   1935
J wene me*n* sholde him shame do,
And þat ne wolde Ich for no þing.
J loue him wel, bi heueneking—
Me wore leuere I wore lame
þa*n*ne men dide him ani shame,   ·   1940
Or tok or onne handes leyde   fo. 213vb
Vnornelike, or same seyde.'
He lep up on a stede lith,
And with him mani a noble knith,
And ferde forth unto þe tun,   1945
And dide calle Bernard Brun
Vt of his hus, wan he þer cam;

1921 h*w*an: *MS* hhan

And Bernard sone ageyn-nam,
Al to-tused and al to-torn,
Ner al so naked so he was born,   1950
And al to-brised bac and þe.
Quoth Ubbe, 'Bernard, hwat is þe?
Hwo haues þe þus ille maked,
þus to-riuen and al mad naked?'

'Louerd, merci!' quot he sone,   1955
'Tonicht, al so ros þe mone,
Comen her mo þan sixti þeues
With lokene copes and wide sleues,
Me for to robben and to pine,
And for to drepe me and mine.   1960
Mi dore he broken up ful sket,
And wolde me binden hond and fet.
Wan þe godemen þat sawe
(Hauelok and he þat bi þe wowe
Leye), he stirten up sone onon,   1965
And summe grop tre, and sum grop ston,
And driue hem ut, þei he weren crus,
So dogges ut of milne-hous.
Hauelok grop þe dore-tre,
And [at] a dint he slow hem þre.   1970
He is þe beste man at nede
þat eueremar shal ride stede—
Als helpe God, bi mine wone
A þhousend of men his he worth one!
Yif he ne were Ich were nou ded—   1975
So haue Ich don mi soule red!
But it is of him mikel sinne:
He maden him swilke woundes þrinne
þat of þe alþerleste wounde
Were a stede brouht to grunde.   1980
He haues a wunde in þe side
With a gleyue, ful unride;
And he haues on þoru his arum
(þer-of is ful mikel harum);
And he haues on þoru his þhe—   1985

þe vnrideste þat men may se.
And oþe[r] wundes haues he stronge,
Mo þan twenti, swiþe longe.
But siþen he hauede lauth þe sor
Of þe wundes, was neuere bor   1990
þat so fauth so he fauth þanne!
Was non þat hauede þe hernpanne
So hard þat he ne dede al to-cruhsse,
And al to-shiuere, and al to-frusshe.
He folwede hem so hund dos hare!   1995
Daþeyt on he wolde spare,
þat ne made hem euerilkon
Ligge stille so doth þe ston.
And þer nis he nouth to frie,
For oþer sholde he make hem lye   2000
Ded, or þei him hauede slawen,
Or al to-heuen or al to-drawen.

Louerd, haui nomore plith
Of þat Ich was þus greþed tonith.
þus wolde þe þeues me haue reft;   2005
But, God þank, he hauenet sure keft!
But it is of him mikel scaþe—
J woth þat he bes ded ful raþe.'

Quoth Ubbe: 'Bernard, seyst þou soth?'
'Ya, sire, þat I ne leye oth!   2010
Yif Y, louerd, a word leye,
Tomorwen do me hengen heye!'
þe burgeys þat þer-bi stode þore
Grundlike and grete oþes swore,
Litle and mikle, yunge and holde,   2015
þat was soth þat Bernard tolde—
Soth was þat he wolden him bynde,
And trusse al þat he mithen fynde
Of hise in arke or in kiste,
þat he mouthe in seckes þriste.   2020
'Louerd, he haueden al awey born
His þing, and himself al to-torn,

2010 leye: *MS* lepe

But als God self barw him wel
þat he ne tinte no catel.
Hwo mithe so mani stonde ageyn,   2025
Bi nither-tale, knith or swein?
He weren bi tale sixti and ten—
Starke laddes, stalworþi men,
And on þe mayster of hem alle,
þat was þe name G[r]iffin Galle.   2030
Hwo mouthe agey[n] so mani stonde,   fo. 214ʳᵇ
But als þis man of ferne londe
Haueth hem slawen with a tre?
Mikel ioie haue he!
God yeue him mikel god to welde,   2035
Boþe in tun and ek in felde:
We[l] is set he etes mete!'
Quoth Ubbe 'Doth him swiþe fete,
þat Y mouthe his woundes se,
Yf þat he mouthen holed be;   2040
For yf he mouthe couere yet
And gangen wel upon hise fet,
Miself shal dubbe him to knith,
Forþi þat he is so with.
And yif he liuede, þo foule þeues   2045
(þat weren of Kaym[es] kin and Eues),
He sholden hange bi þe necke—
Of here ded daþeit wo recke,
Hwan he yeden þus on nithes
Tobinde boþe burgmen and knithes!   2050
For bynderes loue Ich neueremo—
Of hem ne yeue Ich nouht a slo!'

Hauelok was bifore Ubbe browth,
þat hauede for him ful mikel þouth
And mikel sorwe in his herte,   2055
For hise wundes þat we[re] so smerte.

But hwan his wundes weren shawed,
And a leche hauede knawed
þat he hem mouthe ful wel hele,

2046 Kaym[es] *Skeat*: *MS* Kaym   2057 shawed: *MS* shewed

Wel make him gange and ful wel mele, 2060
And wel a palefrey bistride,
And wel upon a stede ride,
þo let Ubbe al his care
And al his sorwe ouer-fare,
And seyde, 'Cum now forth with me, 2065
And Goldeboru þi wif with þe,
And þine seriaunz alle þre!
For nou wile Y youre warant be:
Wile Y non of here frend
þat þu slowe with þin hend 2070
Mouthe wayte þe [to] slo
Al so þou gange to and fro.
J shal lene þe a bowr
þat is up in þe heye tour,
Til þou mowe ful wel go 2075
And wel ben hol of al þi wo. fo. 214ᵛᵃ
Jt ne shal noþing ben bitwene
þi bour and min, al so Y wene,
But a fayr firrene wowe—
Speke Y loude or spek Y lowe, 2080
þou shalt ful wel heren me,
And þan þu wilt þou shalt me se.
A rof shal hile us boþe o nith,
þat none of mine, clerk ne knith,
Ne sholen þi wif no shame bede 2085
No more þan min, so God me rede!'

He dide unto þe borw bringe
Sone anon, al with ioiinge,
His wif and his serganz þre
(þe beste men þat mouthe be!). 2090
þe firste nith he lay þer-inne,
Hise wif and his serganz þrinne,
Aboute þe middel of þe nith
Wok Ubbe and saw a mikel lith
Jn þe bour þar Hauelok lay, 2095
Al so brith so it were day.

2071 [to]: *Skeat*   2081 shalt: *MS* sahalt, *with second* a *subpuncted instead of the first*
2085 bede: *MS* beden *with* n *subpuncted*   2088 ioiinge: *MS possibly* ioiynge (*with undotted* y)   2095 þar: *MS* þat

'Deus!' quoth Ubbe, 'hwat may þis be?
Betere is I go miself and se
Hweþer he sitten nou and wesseylen,
Or of ani shotshipe to-deyle   2100
þis tid nithes also foles;
þan birþe men casten hem in poles,
Or in a grip, or in þe fen—
Nou ne sitten none but wicke men,
Glotuns, reures, or wicke þeues,   2105
Bi Crist þat alle folk onne leues!'

He stod and totede in at a bord
Her he spak anilepi word,
And saw hem slepen faste ilkon,
And lye stille so þe ston,   2110
And saw al þat mikel lith
Fro Hauelok cam þat was so brith.
Of his mouth it com il del—
þat was he war ful swiþe wel.
'Deus!' quoth he, 'hwat may þis mene?'   2115
He calde boþe arwe men and kene,
Knithes and serganz swiþe sleie,
Mpo þan an hundred, withuten leye,
And bad hem alle comen and se
Hwat þat selcuth mithe be.   2120

Als þe knithes were comen alle   fo. 214vb
þer Hauelok lay ut of þe halle,
So stod ut of his mouth a glem
Rith al swilk so þe sunne-bem,
þat al so lith wa[s] þare, bi heuene,   2125
So þer brenden serges seuene
And an hundred serges ok
(þat durste Hi sweren on a bok!).
He slepen faste, alle fiue,
So he weren brouth of liue,   2130
And Hauelok lay on his lift side,
Jn his armes his brithe bride:
Bi þe pappes he leyen naked—

2095 þar: MS þat

So faire two weren neuere maked
Jn a bed to lyen samen. 2135
þe knithes þouth of hem god game*n*,
Hem for to shewe and loken to.
Rith al so he stode*n* alle so,
And his bac was toward he*m* wen*t*,
So were*n* he war of a croiz ful gent 2140
On his rith shuldre, sw[iþ]e brith
(Brithter þan gold ageyn þe lith),
So þat he wiste, heye and lowe,
þat it was kunrik þat he sawe.
Jt sparkede and ful brith shon 2145
So doth þe gode charbucle-ston,
þat men mouthe se by þe lith
A peni chesen, so was it brith!
þa*n*ne bihelden he him faste,
So þat he knewe*n* at þe laste 2150
þat he was Birkabeynes sone,
þat was here king, þat was he*m* wone
Wel to yeme and wel were
Ageynes uten-laddes here—
'For it was neuere yet a broþer 2155
Jn al Denemark so lich anoþer,
So þis man, þat is so fayr,
Als Birkabeyn; he is hise eyr!'

He fellen sone at hise fet.
Was non of hem þat he ne gret— 2160
Of ioie he weren alle so fawen
So he him haueden of erþe drawen!
Hise fet he kisten an hundred syþes,
þe tos, þe nayles, and þe liþes,
So þat he bigan to wakne 2165
And wit he*m* ful sore to blakne; fo. 215ra
For he wende he wolde*n* him slo,
Or elles binde him and do wo.

Quoth Ubbe, 'Louerd, ne dred þe nowth!
Me þinkes þat J se þi þouth. 2170

2139 wen*t*: *MS* wend   2145 brith: *MS perhaps* krith

Dere sone, wel is me
þat Y þe with eyn se!
Manred, louerd, bede Y þe—
þi man auht I ful wel to be,
For þu art comen of Birkabeyn,   2175
þat hauede mani knith and sweyn.
And so shalt þou, louerd, haue:
þou þu be yet a ful yung knaue
þou shalt be king of al Denemark—
Was þer-inne neuere non so stark!   2180
Tomorwen shaltu manrede take
Of þe brune and of þe blake,
Of alle þat aren in þis tun,
Boþe of erl and of barun,
And of dreng and of thayn,   2185
And of knith and of sweyn;
And so shaltu ben mad knith
Wit blisse, for þou art so with.'

þo was Hauelok swiþe bliþe,
And þankede God ful fele siþe.   2190
On þe morwen, wan it was lith,
And gon was þisternesse of þe nith,
Vbbe dide upon a stede
A ladde lepe, and þider bede
Erles, barouns, drenges, theynes,   2195
Klerkes, knithes, bu[r]geys, sweynes,
þat he sholden comen a-non
Biforen him sone euerilkon,
Al so he loue[de]n here liues,
And here children and here wiues.   2200

Hise bode ne durste he non atsitte,
þat he ne neme for to wite
Sone hwat wolde þe iustise;
And bigan anon to rise,
And seyde sone 'Liþes me,   2205
Alle samen, þeu and fre!

2177 þou: *MS* you   2199 loue[de]n Skeat: *MS* louē   2202 neme: *MS*
meme

A þing Ich wile you here shauwe
þat ye alle ful wel knawe.
Ye witen wel þat al þis lond
Was in Birkabeynes hond   2210
þe day þat he was quic and ded,   fo. 215rb
And how þat he, bi youre red,
Bitauhte hise children þre
Godard to yeme, and al his fe.
Hauelok his sone he him tauhte,   2215
And hise two douhtres and al his auhte.
Alle herden ye him swere,
On bok and on messe-gere,
þat he shulde yeme hem wel,
Withuten lac, withuten tel.   2220

He let his oth al ouer-go—
Euere wurþe him yuel and wo!
For þe maydnes here lif
Refte he boþen with a knif,
And him shulde ok haue slawen—   2225
þe knif was at his herte drawen.
But God him wolde wel haue saue:
He hauede reunesse of þe knaue,
So þat he with his hend
Ne drop him nouth, þat sor[i] fend,   2230
But sone dide he a fishere
Swiþe grete oþes swere,
þat he sholde drenchen him
Jn þe se þat was ful brim.

Hwan Grim saw þat he was so fayr,   2235
And wiste he was þe rith eir,
Fro Denemark ful sone he fledde
Jntil Englond, and þer him fedde
Mani winter, þat til þis day
Haues he ben fed and fostred ay.   2240
Lokes hware he stondes her!
Jn al þis werd ne haues he per—

2208 ye: *MS* he   þat: *MS* yat   2230 sor[i] *Skeat*: *MS* sor
2231 fishere: *MS* sishere

Non so fayr, ne non so long,
Ne non so mikel, ne non so strong.
Jn þis middelerd nis no knith   2245
Half so strong ne half so with.
Bes of him ful glad and bliþe,
And cometh alle hider swiþe
Manrede youre louerd for to make,
Boþe brune and þe blake—   2250
J shal miself do first þe gamen,
And ye siþen alle samen.'

O knes ful fayre he him sette—
Mouthe noþing him þer-fro lette—
And bicam is man rith þare,   2255
þat alle sawen þat þere ware.   fo. 215ᵛᵃ

After him stirt up laddes ten
And bicomen hise men,
And siþen euerilk a baroun
þat eurere weren in al þat toun,   2260
And siþen drenges, and siþen thaynes,
And siþen knithes, and siþen sweynes,
So þat, or þat day was gon,
Jn al þe tun ne was nouth on
þat it ne was his man bicomen—   2265
Manrede of alle hauede he nomen.

Hwan he hauede of hem alle
Manrede taken in þe halle,
Grundlike dide he hem swere
þat he sholden him god feyth bere   2270
Ageynes alle þat woren on liue.
þer-yen ne wolde neuer on striue
þat he ne maden sone þat oth—
Riche and poure, lef and loth.
Hwan þat was maked, sone he sende   2275
(Ubbe) writes fer and hende
After alle þat castel yemede,
Burwes, tunes, sibbe an fremde,

2258 *after* men, *MS* beye *in a different hand in the margin*   2274 Riche: *MS* Rithe

þat þider sholden comen swiþe
Til him, and heren tiþandes bliþe   2280
þat he hem alle shulde telle.
Of hem ne wolde neuere on dwelle,
þat he ne come sone plattinde.
Hwo hors ne hauede com gangande,
So þat withinne a fourtenith   2285
Jn al Denemark ne was no knith,
Ne conestable, ne shireue,
þat com of Adam and of Eue,
þat he ne com biforn sire Ubbe—
He dredden him so þhef doth clubbe.   2290

Hwan he haueden alle þe king gret
And he weren alle dun-set,
þo seyde Ubbe 'Lokes here
Vre louerd swiþe dere,
þat shal ben king of al þe lond   2295
And haue us alle under hond,
For he is Birkabeynes sone—
þe king þat was vmbe stou[n]de wone
[Us] for to yeme and wel were
Wit sharp swerd and longe spere.   2300
Lokes nou hw he is fayr: fo. 215vb
Sikerlike he is hise eyr.
Falles alle to hise fet—
Bicomes hise men ful sket!'
He weren for Ubbe swiþe adrad,   2305
And dide sone al þat he bad.
And yet deden he sumdel more:
O bok ful grundlike he swore
þat he sholde with him halde,
Boþe ageynes stille and bolde   2310
þat euere wo[l]de his bodi dere.
þat dide hem o boke swere.

Hwan he hauede manrede and oth
Taken of lef and of loth,
Vbbe dubbede him to knith   2315

2289 Ubbe: MS Ulbe   2290 þhef: MS þhes   2299 [Us]: supplied Skeat

With a swerd ful swiþe brith,
And þe folk of al þe lond
Bitauhte him al in his hond,
þe cunnriche eueril del,
And made him king heylike and wel.   2320
Hwan he was king, þer mouthe men se
þe moste ioie þat mouhte be—
Buttinge with sharpe speres,
Skirming with taleuaces þat men beres,
Wrastling with laddes, putting of ston,   2325
Harping and piping ful god won,
Leyk of mine, of hasard ok,
Romanz-reding on þe bok.
þer mouthe men here þe gestes singe,
þe glevmen on þe tabour dinge;   2330
þer mouhte men se þe boles beyte
And þe bores, with hundes teyte;
þo mouthe men se eueril gleu;
þer mouthe men se hw grim greu—
Was neuere yete ioie more   2335
Jn al þius werd þan þo was þore.
þer was so mike yeft of cloþes
þat, þou I swore you grete othes,
J ne wore nouth þer-offe trod.
þat may I ful wel swere, bi God: 2340
þere was swiþe gode metes,
And of wyn þat men fer fetes
Rith al so mik and gret plente
So it were water of þe se.
þe feste fourti dawes sat—   2345
So riche was neuere non so þat!   fo. 216ra
þe king made Roberd þere knith,
þat was ful strong and ful with,
And Willam Wendut hec, his broþer,
And Huwe Rauen, þat was þat oþer,   2350
And made hem barouns alle þre,
And yaf hem lond and oþer fe,
So mikel þat ilker twent[i] knihtes
Hauede of genge, dayes and nithes.

2339 *t*rod *Sisam*: *MS* croud

Hwan þat feste was al don, 2355
A thousand knihtes ful wel o-bon
With-held þe king with him to lede,
þat ilkan hauede ful god stede,
Helm, and sheld, and brinie brith,
And al þe wepne þat fel to knith. 2360
With hem fiue thusand gode
Sergaunz þat weren to fyht wode
With-held he al of his genge—
Wile I namore þe storie lenge.
Yet hwan he hauede of al þe lond 2365
þe casteles alle in his hond,
And conestables don þer-inne,
He swor he ne sholde neuere blinne
Til þat he were of Godard wreken,
þat Ich haue of ofte speken. 2370
Hal[f] hundred knithes dede he calle,
And hise fif thusand sergaunz alle,
And dide sweren on þe bok
Sone, and on þe auter ok,
þat he ne sholde neuere blinne, 2375
Ne for loue ne for sinne,
Til þat he haueden Godard funde
And brouth biforn him faste bunde.

þanne he haueden swor þis oth,
Ne leten he nouth, for lef ne loth, 2380
þat he ne foren swiþe rathe
þer he was, unto þe paþe
þer he yet on hunting for,
With mikel genge and swiþe stor.
Robert, þat was of al þe ferd 2385
Mayster, was girt wit a swerd,
And sat upon a ful god stede
þat vnder him rith wolde wede.
He was þe firste þat with Godard
Spak, and seyde 'Hede, cauenard! 2390
Wat dos þu here at þis paþe? fo. 216rb
Cum to þe king swiþe and raþe!
þat sendes he þe word and bedes,

þat þu þenke hwat þu him dedes
Hwan þu reftes with a knif   2395
Hise sistres here lif,
An siþen bede þu in þe se
Drenchen him; þat herde he—
He is to þe swiþe grim!
Cum nu swiþe unto him,   2400
þat king is of þis kuneriche,
þu fule man, þu wicke swike,
And he shal yelde þe þi mede,
Bi Crist þat wolde on rode blede!'

Hwan Godard herde þat [he] þer þrette,   2405
With þe neue he Robert sette
Biforn þe teth a dint ful strong,
And Robert kipt ut a knif long,
And smot him þoru þe rith arum—
þer-of was ful litel harum!   2410

Hwan his folk þat sau and herde,
Hwou Robert with here louerd ferde,
He haueden him wel-ner browt of liue,
Ne were his two breþren and oþre fiue
Slowen of here laddes ten   2415
Of Godardes alþerbeste men.
Hwan þe oþre sawen þat, he fledden,
And Godard swiþe loude gredde:
'Mine knithes, hwat do ye?
Sule ye þus-gate fro me fle?   2420
Jch haue you fed and yet shal fede—
Helpe me nu in þis nede,
And late ye nouth mi bodi spille,
Ne Hauelok don of me hise wille!
Yif ye it do, ye do you shame   2425
And bringeth youself in mikel blame!'
Hwan he þat herden, he wenten ageyn,
And slowen a knit and a sweyn·

2414 were: *MS* werē   2405 [he]: *Skeat*   2425 i*t*: *MS* id   2428 and²:
MS and and

Of þe kinges oune men,
And woundeden abuten ten.   2430

þe kinges men, hwan he þat sawe,
Scuten on hem, heye and lowe,
And euerilk fot of hem slowe,
But Godard one, þat he flowe
So þe þef men dos henge,   2435
Or hund men sholen in dike slenge.   fo. 216va
He bunden him ful swiþe faste
Hwil þe bondes wolden laste,
þat he rorede als a bole
þat wore parred in an hole   2440
With dogges for to bite and beite.
Were þe bondes nouth to leite—
He bounden him so fele sore
þat he gan crien Godes ore,
þat he sholde of his hend plette;   2445
Wolden he nouht þer-fore lette
þat he ne bounden hond and fet.
Daþeit þat on þat þer-fore let,
But dunten him so man doth bere,
And keste him on a scabbed mere,   2450
Hise nese went unto þe crice.
So ledden he þat ful swike
Til he was biforn Hauelok brouth,
þat he haue[de] ful wo wrowht,
Boþe with hungre and with cold.   2455
Or he were twel[ue] winter old,
And with mani heui swink,
With poure mete and feble drink,
And [wiþ] swiþe wikke cloþes,
For al hise manie grete othes.   2460
Nu beyes he his holde blame:
Old sinne makes newe shame!
Wan he was [brouth] so shamelike
Biforn þe king (þe fule swike!)

2440 þat wore: *MS* þat he wore   2443 *so: MS* fo
2455 hungre: *MS* hungred   2459 [wiþ]: *Skeat*
2463 [brouth]: *Skeat* (*transferred from beginning of* 2464)
2451 crice: *MS* crite   2461 beyes: *MS* beþes

þe king dede Ubbe swiþe calle   2465
Hise erles and hise barouns alle,
Dreng and thein, burgeis and knith,
And bad he sholden demen him rith,
For he kneu þe swikedam;
Eueril del God was him gram!   2470
He setten hem dun bi þe wawe,
Riche and pouere, heye and lowe,
þe helde men and ek þe grom,
And made þer þe rithe dom,
And seyden unto þe king anon,   2475
þat stille sat so þe ston:
'We deme þat he be al quic flawen,
And siþen to þe galwes drawe
At þis foule mere tayl,
þoru is fet a ful strong nayl,   2480
And þore ben henged wit two feteres;   fo. 216vb
And þare be writen þise leteres:
"þis is þe swike þat wende wel
þe king haue reft þe lond il del,
And hise sistres with a knif   2485
Boþe refte here lif"—
þis writ shal henge bi him þare.
þe dom is demd—seye we namore.'

Hwan þe dom was demd and giue,
And he was wit þe prestes shriue,   2490
And it ne mouhte ben non oþer,
Ne for fader ne for broþer,
[But] þat he sholde þarne lif,
Sket cam a ladde with a knif
And bigan rith at þe to   2495
For to ritte and for to flo;
And he bigan for to rore
So it were grim or gore,
þat men mithe þeþen a mile
Here him rore, þat fule file!   2500
þe ladde ne let nowith forþi,

2469 swikedam: *MS possibly* swike dam   2477 flawen: *MS*   slawen
2493 [But]: *Skeat*

þey he criede 'merci, merci!'
þat ne flow [him] eueril del
With knif mad of grunde*n* stel.
þei garte bringe þe mere sone,   2505
Skabbe*d* and ful iuele o-bone,
And bunde*n* him rith at hire tayl
With a rop of an old seyl,
And drowe*n* him unto þe galwes
(Nouth bi þe gate but ouer þe falwes),   2510
And henge þore bi þe hals—
Daþeit hwo recke: he was fals!

þanne he was ded, þat Sathanas,
Sket was seysed al þat his was
Jn þe kinges hand il del—   2515
Lond and lith, and oþer catel—
And þe king ful sone it yaf
Vbbe i*n* þe hond wit a fayr staf,
And seyde 'Her Ich sayse þe,
Jn al þe lon*d*, in al þe fe.'   2520
þo swor Hauelok he sholde make,
Al for Grim, of monekes blake
A priorie to seruen inne ay
Jesu Crist til Domesday,
For þe god he hauede him don   2525
Hwil he was pouere and *iu*e[l] o-bon.   fo. 217ra
And þer-of held he wel his oth,
For he it made, God it woth,
Jn þe tun þer Grim was graue*n*,
þat of Grim yet haues þe na*u*e[n]—   2530
Of Grim bidde Ich namore spelle.
But wan Godrich herde telle,
Of Cornwayle þat was erl
(þat fule traytour, þat mixed cherl!)
þat Hauelok, was king of Denemark,   2535
And ferde with him, strong and stark,
Comen Engelond with-inne,
Engelond al for to winne,

2503 [him]: *Skeat*   2506 Skabbe*d*: *MS* Skabbeb   2525 hauede: *MS*
haueden   2526 *iu*e[l]: *MS* we   2530 na*u*e[n] *Sisam*: *MS* name

And þat she þat was so fayr,
þat was of Engelond rith eir, 2540
Was comen up at Grimesbi,
He was ful sorful and sori,
And seyde 'Hwat shal me to raþe?
Goddoth, I shal do slon hem baþe!
J shal don hengen hem ful heye, 2545
So mote Ich brouke mi rith eie,
But yif he of mi lond fle.
Hwat! wenden he to deserite me?'
He dide sone ferd ut-bede,
þat al þat euere mouhte o stede 2550
Ride or helm on heued bere,
Brini on bac, and sheld and spere
Or ani oþer wepne bere,
Hand-ax, syþe, gisarm, or spere,
Or aunlaz and god long knif, 2555
þat als he louede leme or lif
þat þey sholden comen him to,
'With ful god wepne ye ber[e]', so
To Lincolne, þer he lay,
Of Marz þe seuentenþe day, 2560
So þat he couþe hem god þank.
And yif þat ani were so rank
þat he þanne ne come anan,
He swor bi Crist and Seint Johan
þat he sholde maken him þral, 2565
And al his ofspring forthwithal.

þe Englishe þat herde þat
Was non þat euere his bode sat,
For he him dredde swiþe sore,
So runci spore, and mikle more. 2570
At þe day he come sone fo. 217rb
þat he hem sette, ful wel o-bone,
To Lincolne with gode stedes
And al þe wepne þat knith ledes.

2541 Was: *MS* þat was   2549 bede: *MS* bidde   2558 ber[e] so: *MS*
þeberso *with first* þe *subpuncted by scribe for deletion*
2563 anan: *MS* anon   2562 rank: *MS* rang

Hwa*n* he wore come, sket was þe erl *y*are 2575
Ageynes Denshe men to fare,
And seyde 'Lyþes nu, alle samen!
Haue Ich gadred you for no game*n*,
But Ich wile seyen you for*p*i.
Lokes hware here at Grimesbi 2580
His uten-laddes here comen,
And haues nu þe priorie numen—
Al þat euere mithen he finde,
He bre*n*ne kirkes and prestes binde;
He strangleth mo*n*kes and nu*n*nes ba*þ*e. 2585
Wat wile ye, frend, her-offe ra*þ*e?
Yif he regne þus-gate longe,
He moun us alle ouer-gange—
He moun vs alle quic henge or slo,
Or þral maken and do ful wo, 2590
Or elles reue us ure liues
And ure children and ure wiues.
But dos nu als Ich wile you lere,
Als ye wile be with me dere:
Nimes nu swiþe forth and raþe, 2595
And helpes me and yuself baþe,
And slos upo þe dogges swiþe!
For [I] shal neueremore be bliþe,
Ne hoseled ben ne of prest shriuen,
Til þat he ben of londe driuen. 2600
Nime we swiþe and do hem fle,
And folwes alle faste me!
For Ich am he, of al þe ferd,
þat first shal slo with drawe*n* swerd—
Daþeyt hwo ne stonde faste 2605
Bi me hwil hise armes laste!'
'*Y*e, lef, *y*e!' *qu*oth þe erl Gunter;
'Ya!' quoth þe erl of Cestre, Reyner,
And so dide alle þat þer stode,
And stirte forth so he were wode. 2610
þo mouthe me*n* se þe brinies brihte

2575 *y*are: *MS* þare   2579 for*p*i: *MS* forþi   2581 His: *MS* Hise
2585 ba*þ*e: *MS* boþe   2586 ra*þ*e: *MS* rede   2607 *Y*e[1]: *MS* þe   *y*e[2]: *MS*
þe   *qu*oth *Skeat*: *MS* couth

On backes keste and la*c*e rithe,
þe helmes heye on heued sette.
To armes al so swiþe plette
þat þei wore on a litel stunde   2615
Greþet als me*n* mithe telle a pund,   fo. 217va
And lopen on stedes sone anon;
And toward Grimesbi, ful god won,
He foren softe bi þe sti,
Til he come ney at Grimesbi.   2620

Hauelok, þat hauede spired wel
Of here fare eueril del,
With al his ferd cam hem ageyn.
Forbar he noþer knith ne sweyn:
þe firste knith þat he þer mette   2625
With þe swerd so he him grette,
For[þ] his heued of he plette—
Wolde he nouth for sinne lette.
Roberd saw þat dint so hende—
Wolde he neuere þeþe[n] wende   2630
Til þat he hauede anoþer slawen
With þe swerd he held ut-drawen.
Willa*m* Wendut his swerd vt-drow,
And þe þredde so sore he slow
þat he made upon þe feld   2635
His lift arm fleye with þe swerd.

Huwe Raue*n* ne forgat nouth
þe swerd he hauede þider brouth:
He kipte it up, and smot ful sore
An erl þat he saw priken þore   2640
Ful noblelike upon a stede
þat with him wolde al quic wede.
He smot him on þe heued so
þat he þe heued clef a two,
And þat bi þe shudre-blade   2645
þe sharpe swerd [he] let wade
þorw þe brest unto þe herte.
þe dint bigan ful sore to smerte,

2612 la*c*e: *MS* late

þat þe erl fel dun anon
Al so ded so ani ston.   2650
Quoth Ubbe 'Nu dwelle Ich to longe!'
And leth his stede sone gonge
To Godrich, with a god spere
þat he saw anoþer bere,
And smoth Godrich and Godrich him   2655
Hetelike with herte grim,
So þat he boþe felle dune
To þe erþe, first þe croune.
þanne he woren fallen dun boþen,
Grundlike here swerdes ut-drowen   2660
þat weren swiþe sharp and gode,   fo. 217vb
And fouhten so þei woren wode
þat þe swot ran fro þe crune

.   .   .   .

þer mouthe men se *t*[w]o knicthes bete   2665
Ayþer on oþer dintes grete,
So þat with [þ]alþerlest dint
Were al to-shiuered a flint.
So was bitwenen hem a fiht,
Fro þe morwen ner *to* þe niht,   2670
So þat þei nouth ne bl*u*nne
Til þat to sette bigan þe su*n*ne.
þo yaf Godrich þorw þe side
Vbbe a wunde ful unride,
So þat þorw þat ilke wounde   2675
Hauede ben brouth to þe grunde
And his heued al of-slawen,
Yif God ne were and Huwe Rauen,
þat drow him fro Godrich awey
And barw him so þat ilke day.   2680
But er he were fro Godrich drawen,
þer were a þousind knihtes slawen
Bi boþe halue and mo ynowe.
þer þe ferdes togidere slowe,
þer was swilk dreping of þe folk   2685
þat on þe feld was neuere a polk

2655 *second* Godrich: *MS* .G.   2664 *no gap in MS*   2665 *t*[w]o: *MS* co
2670 *to*: *MS* co   2671 bl*u*nne: *MS* blinne

þat it ne stod of blod so ful
þat þe stem ranintil þe hul.
þo tarst bigan Godrich to go
Vpon þe Danshe and faste to slo,　　　　　　　2690
And forthrith, also leun fares
þat neuere kines best ne spares,
þanne his gon, for he garte alle
þe Denshe men biforn him falle.
He felde browne, he felde blake,　　　　　　　2695
þat he mouthe ouertake.
Was neuere non þat mouhte þaue
Hise dintes, noyþer knith ne knaue,
þat he feldem so dos þe gres
Biforn þe syþe þat ful sharp es.　　　　　　　2700
Hwan Hauelok saw his folk so brittene
And his ferd so swiþe littene,
He cam driuende upon a stede,
And bigan til him to grede,
And seyde 'Godrich, wat is þe,　　　　　　　2705
þat þou fare þus with me
And mine gode knihtes slos?　　　　　　　fo. 218ra
Sikerlike, þou misgos!
þou wost ful wel, yif þu wilt wite,
þat Aþelwold þe dide site　　　　　　　2710
On knes and sweren on messe-bok,
On caliz and on *pateyn* hok,
þat þou hise douhter sholdest yelde,
þan she were wimman of elde,
Engelond eueril del.　　　　　　　2715
Godrich þe erl, þou wost it wel!
Do nu wel withuten fiht
Yeld hire þe lond, for þat is rith:
Wile Ich forgiue þe þe lathe,
Al mi dede and al mi wrathe,　　　　　　　2720
For Y se þu art so with
And of þi bodi so god knith.'
'þat ne wile Ich neueremo',
Quoth erl Godrich, 'for Ich shal slo

2691 leun *Holthausen*: MS leuin　　　2700 *e*s: MS is　　　2712 *pateyn Skeat*: MS
messe

þe, and hire forhenge heye! 2725
J shal þrist ut þi rith eye,
þat þou lokes with on me,
But þu swiþe heþen fle!'
He grop þe swerd ut sone anon,
And hew on Hauelok ful god won, 2730
So þat he clef his sheld on two.
Hwan Hauelok saw þat shame do
His bodi þer biforn his ferd,
He drow ut sone his gode swerd,
And smot him so upon þe crune 2735
þat Godrich fel to þe erþe adune.
But Godrich stirt up swiþe sket—
Lay he nowth longe at hise fet—
And smot him on þe sholdre so
þat he dide þare undo 2740
Of his brinie ringes mo
þan þat Ich kan tellen fro,
And woundede him rith in þe flesh,
þat tendre was and swiþe nesh,
So þat þe blod ran til his to. 2745
þo was Hauelok swiþe wo,
þat he hauede of him drawen
Blod and so sore him slawen.
Hertelike til him he wente
And Godrich þer fulike shente, 2750
For his swerd he hof up heye,
And þe hand he dide of-fleye fo. 218rb
þat he smot him with so sore—
Hw mithe he don him shame more?

Hwan he hauede him so shamed, 2755
His hand of-plat and yuele lamed,
He tok him sone bi þe necke
Als a traytour (daþeyt wo recke!),
And dide him binde and fetere wel
With gode feteres al of stel, 2760
And to þe quen he sende him,

2725 *raised medial point after* þe   2747 drawen: *MS* drawem   2748 *raised medial point after* Blod

þat birde wel to him ben grim,
And bad she sholde don him gete,
And þat non ne sholde him bete
Ne shame do, for he was knith,   2765
Til knithes haueden demd him rith.
þan þe Englishe men þat sawe,
þat þei wisten, heye and lawe,
þat Goldeboru þat was so fayr
Was of Engeland rith eyr,   2770
And þat þe king hire hauede wedded,
And haueden ben samen bedded,
He comen alle to crie 'merci',
Vnto þe king at one cri,
And beden him sone manrede and oth   2775
þat he ne sholden, for lef ne loth,
Neueremore ageyn him go
Ne ride, for wel ne for wo.

þe king ne wolde nouth forsake
þat he ne shulde of hem take   2780
Manrede þat he beden and ok
Hold-oþes sweren on þe bok.
But or bad he þat þider were brouth
þe quen for hem (swilk was his þouth)
For to se and for to shawe   2785
Yif þat he hire wolde knawe—
þoruth hem witen wolde he
Yif þat she aucte quen to be.

Sixe erles weren sone yare
After hire for to fare: 2790
He nomen onon and comen sone,
And brouthen hire, þat under mone
Jn al þe werd ne hauede per
Of hendeleik, fer ne ner.
Hwan she was come þider, alle   2795
þe Englishe men bigunne to falle
O knes, and greten swiþe sore,   fo. 218va
And seyden 'Leuedi, K[r]istes ore

And youres! We haue*n* misdo mikel,
þat we ayen you haue be fikel,   2800
For Englond auhte for to ben
Youres, and we youre me*n*.
Js non of us, yung ne old,
þat *h*e ne wot þat Aþelwold
Was king of þis kunerike   2805
And ye his eyr, and þat þe swike
Haues it halden with mikel wro*n*ge—
God leue him sone to honge!'

Quot Hauelok 'Hwan þat ye it wite,
Nu wile Ich þat ye doun-site;   2810
And after Godrich haues wrouht,
þat haues in sorwe himself brouth,
Lokes þat ye deme*n* him rith
(For dom ne spare𝛿 clerk ne knith),
And siþen shal Ich understonde   2815
Of *y*ou, after lawe of londe,
Manrede and holde-oþes boþe,
Yif ye it wilen and ek rothe.'
Anon þer dune he hem sette,
For non þe dom ne durste lette,   2820
And demden him to binde*n* faste
Vpon an asse swiþe unwraste
(Andelong, nouht ouerþwert,
His nose went unto þe stert)
And so to Lincolne lede,   2825
Shamelike in wicke wede;
And, hwan he cam unto þe borw,
Shamelike ben led þer-þoru,
Bi-souþe þe borw unto a grene
þat þare is yet, als Y wene,   2830
And þere be bunde*n* til a stake,
Aboute*n* him ful gret fir make,
And al to dust be brend rith þere.
And yet demde*n* he þer more,

2801–2 *Holthausen*; *MS* For Englond auhte for to ben youres | And we youre men and
youres   2804 *h*e: *MS* we   2814 spare𝛿: *MS* spared   2816 *y*ou: *MS*
þou

Oþer swikes for to warne: 2835
þat hise children sulde þarne
Eueremore þat eritage
þat his was, for hise utrage.

Hwan þe dom was demd and seyd,
Sket was þe swike on þe asse leyd,   2840
And [led] huntil þat ilke grene
And brend til asken, al bidene.   fo. 218ᵛᵇ
þo was Goldeboru ful bliþe—
She þanked God fele syþe
þat þe fule swike was brend   2845
þat wende wel hire bodi haue shend,
And seyde 'Nu is time to take
Manrede of brune and of blake
þat Ich se ride and go,
Nu Ich am wreke of mi fo!'   2850

Hauelok anon manrede tok
Of alle Englishe on þe bok,
And dide hem grete oþes swere
þat he sholden him god feyth bere,
Ageyn alle þat woren liues   2855
And þat sholde ben born of wiues.

þanne he hauede sikernesse
Taken of more and of lesse,
Al at hise wille, so dide he calle
þe erl of Cestre, and hise men alle,   2860
þat was yung knith wituten wif,
And seyde 'Sire erl, bi mi lif,
And þou wile mi conseyl tro,
Ful wel shal Ich with þe do!
For Ich shal yeue þe to wiue   2865
þe fairest þing þat is o liue,
þat is Gunnild of Grimesby,
Grimes douther, bi Seint Dauy,
þat me forth-broute and wel fedde,
And ut of Denemark with me fledde   2870

2841 [led] huntil: *Skeat* led until, *MS* him til   2857 hauede: *MS* haueden

Me for to burwe fro mi ded.
Sikerlike, þoru his red,
Haue Ich liued into þis day—
Blissed worþe his soule ay!
J rede þat þu hire take,   2875
And spuse and curteyse make,
For she is fayr, and she is fre,
And al so hende so she may be.
þer-tekene she is wel with me;
þat shal Ich ful wel shewe þe,   2880
For Ich giue þe a giue
þat, eueremore hwil Ich liue,
For hire shaltu be with me dere—
þat wile Ich þat þis folc al here.'
þe erl ne wolde nouth ageyn   2885
þe king be, for knith ne sweyn,
Ne of þe spusing seyen nay,   fo. 219ra
But spusede þat ilke day.
þat spusinge was god time maked,
For it ne were neuere, clad ne naked,   2890
Jn a þede samened two
þat cam togidere, liuede so
So þey dide al here liue:
He geten samen sones fiue,
þat were þe beste men at nede   2895
þat mouthe riden on ani stede.
Hwan Gunnild was to Cestre brouth,
Hauelok þe gode ne forgat nouth
Bertram, þat was þe erles kok,
þat he ne dide callen ok,   2900
And seyde 'Frend, so God me rede,
Nu shaltu haue riche mede,
For wissing and þi gode dede
þat tu me dides in ful gret nede!
For þanne Y yede in mi cuuel,   2905
And Ich ne haue[de] bred ne sowel,
Ne Y ne hauede no catel,
þou feddes and claddes me ful wel.
Haue nu forþi of Cornwayle

þe erldom il del, withuten fayle,   2910
And al þe lond þat Godrich held,
Boþe in towne and ek in feld.
And þer-to wile Ich þat þu spuse
(And fayre bring hire until huse)
Grimes douther, Leuiue þe hende,   2915
For þider shal she with þe wende.
Hire semes curteys for to be,
For she is fayr so flour on tre:
þe heu is swilk in hire ler
So þe rose in roser   2920
Hwan it is fayr sprad ut newe,
Ageyn þe sunne brith and lewe'—
And girde him sone with þe swerd
Of þe erldom, biforn his ferd,
And with his hond he made him knith,   2925
And yaf him armes, for þat was rith,
And dide him þere sone wedde
Hire þat was ful swete in bedde.

After þat he spused wore,
Wolde þe erl nouth dwelle þore,   2930
But sone nam until his lond
And seysed it al in his hond,   fo. 219rb
And liuede þer-inne, he and his wif,
An hundred winter in god lif,
And gaten mani children samen,   2935
And liueden ay in blisse and gamen.
Hwan þe maydens were spused boþe,
Hauelok anon bigan ful rathe
His Denshe men to feste wel
Wit riche landes and catel,   2940
So þat he weren alle riche,
For he was large and nouth chiche.

þer-after sone, with his here,
For he to Lundone for to bere

2934 _the line after this in the MS contains the words_ For he saw þat he: _but they have been crossed out, and the word_ va cat (_divided into two sections thus_) _has been written at the beginning and the end of the line respectively. The deleted words are an anticipation of line 2955_ 2942 chiche: _MS_ chinche

Corune, so þat it sawe 2945
Henglische and Denshe, heye and lowe,
Hwou he it bar with mikel pride,
For his barnage þat was unride.

þe feste of his coruni[n]g
Laste[de] with gret ioying 2950
Fourti dawes and sumdel mo.
þo bigunnen þe Denshe to go
Vnto þe king to aske leue;
And he ne wolde hem nouth greue,
For he saw þat he woren yare 2955
Jnto Denemark for to fare,
But gaf hem leue sone anan,
And bitauhte hem Seint Johan,
And bad Ubbe, his iustise,
þat he sholde on ilke wise 2960
Denemark yeme and gete so
þat no pleynte come him to.

Hwan he wore parted alle samen,
Hauelok bilefte wit ioie and gamen
Jn Engelond, and was þer-inne 2965
Sixti winter king with winne,
And Goldeboru quen, þat I wene
So mikel loue was hem bitwene
þat al þe werd spak of hem two.
He louede hire and she him so 2970
þat neyþer oþe[r] mithe be
Fro oþer ne no ioie se
But yf he were togidere boþe.
Neuere yete ne weren he wroþe,
For here loue was ay newe— 2975
Neuere yete wordes ne grewe   fo. 219ᵛᵃ
Bitwene hem hwar-of ne lathe
Mithe rise ne no wrathe.

2950 Laste[de] *Skeat: MS* Laste   2957 anan: *MS* anon   2973 togidere:
MS to gidede

He geten children hem bitwene
Sones and douthres rith fiuetene,   2980
Hwar-of þe sones were kinges alle,
So wolde God it sholde bifalle,
And þe douhtres alle quenes.
Him stondes wel þat god child strenes!
Nu haue ye herd þe gest al þoru   2985
Of Hauelok and of Goldeborw;
Hw he weren born and hw fedde,
And hwou he woren with wronge ledde
Jn here youþe, with trecherie,
With tresoun, and with felounye,   2990
And hwou þe swikes haueden tit[h]
Reuen hem þat was here rith,
And hwou he weren wreken wel,
Haue Ich sey[d] you eueril del,
And forþi Ich wolde biseken you   2995
þat hauen herd þe rim nu,
þat ilke of you, with gode wille,
Seye a Pater Noster stille
For him þat haueth þe rym maked,
And þer-fore fele nihtes waked,   3000
þat Iesu Crist his soule bringe
Biforn his Fader at his endinge.
A———m———e———n

2991 tit[h]: *MS* thit

COMMENTARY

1–26. ME romances commonly begin with a formal exordium that conforms in varying degree with a set pattern. The device was taken over from the OF epics and romances on which the genre of ME romance was modelled; but individual examples vary greatly in sophistication according to the literary culture and the talent of their authors. The notably elaborate one of *Kyng Alisaunder* 1–40 (modelled in part on that of its source, *Le Roman de toute Chevalerie*) contains two *sententiae*, an *exemplum*, an exhortation to listen, a recommendation of the story to come, and a statement of the theme, but (untypically) no prayer on behalf of the assembled company. For others, see *Sir Gawain and the Green Knight* 23–36, and *Sir Degrevant* 1 ff. and n. For OF examples see *Aymeri de Narbonne*, ii. 1–67; *Li Coronnemenz Loois* (ed. E. Langlois, CFMA 1925), 1–11; *Le Charroi de Nimes* (ed. J.-L. Perrier, CFMA 1931), 1–13; *Le Siège de Barbastre* (ed. J.-L. Perrier, CFMA 1926), 1–5, 41 ff.

In *Hav.*, the repetitive style of the exordium masks the formal design: an exhortation to listen, a statement of the subject, praise of the hero, and a prayer are all standard elements. C. T. Onions has argued that the exordium is not the author's work, since l. 5 is repeated in l. 23, and ll. 9–10 in 25–6 respectively, and since it contains three examples of the prefix *i-* (5, 11, 12), which is likely to be alien to the author's usage.[1] However, the author himself was willing to use the couplet of 9–10 and 25–6 no less than three times (87–8, 1971–2, 2895–6); and it would have been unorthodox to do without an exordium.

1. *tó me*: the use of unstressed forms of personal pronouns for the purposes of rhyme is not uncommon in ME. Cf. *O&N* 545–6 *dome : to me*, 1671–2 *come* (pt. pl.) : *to me*; and *Prologue to Cant. Tales* 671–2 *Rome : to me*, *Squire's Tale* 675–6 *yowthe : allow the*.

4. *Wo-so*: a common ME usage, in which the indefinite pronoun (lit. 'whoever') has conditional force and means 'if anyone'. The formal model was OE *(swā) hwā swā*. But the ME use illustrated here and in 473 is not recorded, whether with or without *þat*, till 1297 (without *-so*), in Robert of Gloucester's *Metrical Chronicle* 2235:

> þat I nolde noȝt abbe uorsake þat lond,
> *Wo* me adde ibroȝt þerto.

It may thus be a calque on the corresponding use of OF *qui* as 'if anyone', e.g. *Li Dis dou Vrai Aniel* (ed. A. Tobler, 3rd edn., Leipzig, 1912), 10–11:

> Je ne sai si grant richete
> Com de grant sens, *ki* bien en use.

See E. Einenkel, *Historische Syntax*, p. 125, §47 γ.

[1] *Philologica*, 154–6.

10. *þurte*: wrongly registered in *OED* under *dare* v. The historically irregular *-u-* (OE *þorfte*) is due either to a systemic analogy proceeding from the other pret.-presents *schulde*, *durste* (with *-u-* from the pres. pl. *schulen*, *durren*), or to adoption of ON *þurfti* (which in *Hav.* is just as likely). The form is also attested in Mannyng's *Chronicle* 4145: 'Ne neuere *þurt* hem haue drad no tyde.'

15. Skeat's insertion of *Y* before *wile*, to provide an explicit subject for the latter, is unnecessary and unjustified, since the MS reading is entirely idiomatic. There is a common ME and early Mod. E usage in which a pronominal subject or object need not be expressed if the subject has occurred (whether as a noun or a pronoun) in any oblique case in a preceding clause of the same sentence. For other examples in *Hav.* see 1167, 1330, 1421, 1429, 2204, and 2676; for ample other ME examples, see Zupitza's note on *Guy of Warwick* (15th-c. version) 10; and for a simple Shakespearean one, *The Winter's Tale*, IV. iv. 168–9:

> They call him Doricles, and boasts himself
> To have a worthy feeding.

There is another category of cases in which the apparent (but delusive) 'omission' of a pronominal subject may be due not to a syntactic process but a phonetic one, in which e.g. *he* has been agglutinated with and absorbed by a final vowel in the preceding word. Instances of this are commonly ambiguous; see however 710, 791, 998, and 2312. For 1090 see note ad loc.

Genuine omission of a pronominal subject is probable in 1723 and 2405, and almost certain (*metri causa*) in 2646.

20. *Benedicamus Domino*: this is a versicle in the Mass; see W. L. Smoldon, *The Music of the Medieval Church Dramas* (Oxford, 1980), p. 60, e.g. for musical elaboration of it in the Roman service book version as at Lauds on Solemn Feasts.

The only other literary example known to me is used by the highly literate Philippe de Thaün, in his *Bestiaire*[2] (dedicated to Henry I's second wife Adeliza, and hence composed between 1121 and 1135), as the last line in his account of the pearl, of which he had said that it symbolizes Jesus (3065):

> Union est Pere e Fiz,
> Union est Sainz Espiriz,
> Union est cumencement,
> Union est definemenz,
> Union est alpha e ω.
> Benedicamus domino!   (3163–8)

27–86. A notably extensive example of a traditional kind of eulogy of kings by chroniclers, e.g. of William the Conqueror and Henry I in the *Anglo-Saxon Chronicle*. See Earle and Plummer, *Two Saxon Chronicles Parallel*, vol. i, pp. 219–20 (especially p. 220, ll. 12–18) and p. 263, ll. 8–12, and M. Deutschbein, *Studien zur Sagengeschichte Englands*, vol. i (Cöthen 1906), pp. 162–4.

[2] Ed. E. Walberg (Lund and Paris, 1900): the earliest Anglo-Norman poet whose works have come down to us (p. xvii).

28. *þat... his*: this substitute for an inflected relative 'whose' was inherited from the OE pattern *þe... his, þe... hine* etc., in which the personal pronoun was used to supply the grammatical meaning of 'case' that was not expressed in the indeclinable relative. Cf. *The Wanderer* (ed. Dunning and Bliss, London, 1969), 9–11 for the dative 'to whom':

> *þe* ic *him* modsefan minne durre sweotule asecgan.
>
> nis nu cwicra nan
> minne durre

On the replacement of *þe* by *þat* in ME, see A. McIntosh, *EGS* 1 (1947–8), 73–87.

31. *dreng*: see Appendix D.

39. *wrobberes*: see Appendix A.

50. *on... leyde*: amply clear evidence is available to show that this is a separable compound verb of the common-Gmc (and indeed older) type, and one of which an unseparated form occurs in 1690. The OE antecedent is attested in the gerundial adj. *onlecgende* 'to be laid upon' (a *hapax legomenon*), and implied in the corresponding noun *onlegen* 'poultice', lit. 'that which is laid upon' (which is inseparable, like all nouns formed on separable compound verbs). And these are vouched for by the cognate ON *leggja á* 'to lay upon' and the noun *álǫg* 'spell', lit. 'something laid upon', and corresponding MDu. pair *aenleggen* v., *aenlage* n.

In the post-Conquest period the unseparated forms of these separable verbs were being replaced, at varying rates in various types of ME, by the separated ones, which proliferated into the very large and productive class of 'phrasal verbs' in present English. See further *EMEVP*, pp. xxxii–xxxiv.

Three ME examples of unseparated forms of *onleyen* are available in *Cursor Mundi*: 8807–8, 16723–4, 29161–2. The example in 995 of the idiom represented here in *Hav.* shows that *on* in 50 governs *him* ('understood' from 49). Cf. also *Firumbras* 551 and *Ywain and Gawain* 715, beside *Firumbras* 20.

61. On the distinction between *grið* and *frið* in OE laws, see J. E. A. Jolliffe, *The Constitutional History of Medieval England*, pp. 59 and 114; and cf. *grith-sergeans* 267 and 263–9 n.

64. *lou[er]d*: Craigie's emendation of MS *lond* is palaeographically very probable, if we assume that -*er*- was abbreviated in the standard way and written above the two minims (joined by a diagonal upward left-to-right hairline) that might in some ME hands represent *n* and be misread as *u* or vice versa.

It is set beyond doubt by the common use in OF of such expressions as *jusqu'a* 'as far as', *deci qu'a* 'from here as far as' as in *Aymeri de Narbonne* 1351:

> 'Je n'en sai nule en France n'en Berri,
> Ne *jusqu'a Rome* ...'

and *La Mort Aymeri de Narbonne* 1372: '*Deci a Rome* en oïst en parler' (ed. Couraye du Parc, SATF, 1884). The same type of locution is represented in *Hav.* 1086: *heþen into Ynde*'.

66. *Hunger ne here*: first recognized by B. Dickins (*LSE* 4. 75–6) as an example of an OE alliterative phrase used at least three times by Wulfstan. *wicke þinge* is very unconvincing and almost certainly corrupt: an asyndetic use of such a phrase in this context would be altogether untypical in ME.

67. *felede*: see C. T. Onions, *Philologica* 157–8.

74. *his soule hold*: this unusual expression recurs in *Ywain and Gawain* 887, where it refers to the concern of the knight of the fountain's widow for the soul of her dead husband:

> *Upon his sawl* was sho ful *hulde*:
> Opon a sawter al of gulde
> To say þe salmes fast sho began.

87–90. These four lines recur (intact, except that *wagge* 89 and *knith* 90 are represented by *welde* or *bere* and by *mon* respectively) in the account of King Arthur in three MSS (and in the original version) of the *Anonymous Short English Metrical Chronicle of England* 245 ff. (p. 11, and p. 247 n.); see Zettl's *Introduction* p. lxiii and n. 2. It seems likely that the passage was imitated by the author of the *Chronicle* from *Hav.*, since (as a somewhat similar case) *Hav.* 264–7 and 270–1 have palpably been imitated in at least one MS of that work (see 264 n.).

89. *folc vt-lede*: the sense of *folc* as 'army' is established by the use of *here* in the obviously synonymous *leden ut here* in precisely similar contexts in 346 and 379. It is a sense recorded in OE: see Bosworth–Toller *Supplement*, *folc* I. (1a).

92. [*shewe*]: supplied here on the model of *let hem shawe* 1854.

hand-dede: the sole example in post-Conquest English; and it is (by chance) not recorded in OE, though implied by one of the agent nouns mentioned below. But it is a relatively ancient word, since it occurs in other early WG languages; and it implied 'violence' (OHG and MHG *hant-tat*, MDu. *hant-daet* 'violent deed'), and sometimes 'criminal violence' (in OE *riht-handdæda* 'the actual perpetrator of a crime' and MDu. *hant-dadige* 'one who perpetrates a criminal or violent act'). Thus in *Hav.* (where criminality is not in question) the imputation is of violence.

116. *comen ... on*: this is shown by the cognates in ON and MDu. (see Glossary) to be a separable compound. An unseparated form of the antecedent OE *on-cuman* occurs in *Genesis* 1041:

> hine *on-cymeð*
> æfter þære synne   seofonfeald wracu
> 'Seven-fold vengeance will descend upon him ...'

The verb has been recognized and correctly registered as a separable compound in *OED* s.v. *on-come* v. (along with the related noun *oncome*). The example in *Pearl* 644 (included there) has been misinterpreted in the edition of E. V. Gordon.

130. The following parallels are helpful here: *Vices & Virtues* (ed. Holthausen, EETS, OS, 89, 1888), p. 131, l. 7:

> Swa me scal *don of* hem ðe grið ne willeð

and *Cursor Mundi* 19040:

> ... Befor þe apostels fete it broght,
> þar *of* to *do quat þaim god thoght*.

The first attests *don of* as a prepositional verb in the sense 'do regarding, do with' and governing *hem*, and hence suggests that *of* in *Hav.* is a delayed preposition governing *hem* there. The second is all but a syntactic equivalent of the whole line in *Hav.*, and *quat ... thoght* is synonymous with the second half of that line: it follows that *þar* in *Hav.* does not fit and is likely to be a corruption of *þat* (as the common reduction of *þat þat* 'that which').

131. *hire body*: a calque (not uncommon in ME) on a standard OF periphrasis in which a possessive pronoun + *cors* 'body' is the equivalent of a personal or reflective pronoun plain and simple in the appropriate grammatical case, as in *Yvain* 3798: 'Qu'autretant l'aim come *mon cors*' ('For I love him as myself'). For ME examples see T. F. Mustanoja, *A Middle English Syntax*, vol. i (Helsinki, 1960), pp. 148–9, and *Sir Gawain and the Green Knight* 353 n., and 1237 and n.

C's *here selwe* (l. 175) establishes this as the correct interpretation.

139. *Fro Rokesburw ... Douere*: see 265 n.

148. Metrically difficult. The line would just scan with *of his* and *iuel* as monosyllabic; but reduction of *his* to a non-syllabic element, though theoretically admissible, would not be normal practice in *Hav.*

160. *þank kan*: OE *þonc cunnan* 'to be (feel) grateful', paralleled not only in other Gmc languages, but in the OF phrase *savoir gré*. A comparable idiomatic use of a verb normally meaning 'to know' is that of OE *witan* in certain collocations, e.g. the rare *myne witan* 'to feel love' (giverning an objective genitive) in *Beowulf* 169 and *The Wanderer* 27 ([*min*] *myne*).

164. *gouen hem ille*: a remarkable example of a calque on a Scandinavian idiom MSw. *giva sik illa* 'to be distressed', and first satisfactorily explained by C. T. Onions, 'On *Havelok*, lines 164, 1129', *RES* 5 (1929), 328–30. There are at least nine other examples in Nth. ME, and a corrupt one in *Hav.* 1130.

166. This way of introducing direct speech by means of *þat* is not uncommon in ME. Cf. *Troilus und Criseyde* V. 99–100:

> But natheles this thoughte he wel ynough
> That 'certaynly I am aboute nought ...'

169–209. This is much more than a prudent (if obvious) course of action aptly devised by the author to fit the king's situation. Aþelwold is in fact acting as feudal law required for minors in real life, in arranging for the wardship of his daughter (and hence of the lands to which she is heir), just as Birkabeyn, in his closely parallel situation, does for his three children (367–97).

What the kings do, by making Godrich and Godard respectively the guardians of their children, is to put these two magnates in the same position as any feudal lord in relation to the underage children (as heirs) of a deceased vassal of his. He had the legal right to give an heiress in marriage, and even to sell the marriage, as the great 13th-century jurist Henry de Bracton attests (*De*

Legibus et Consuetudinibus Angliae, Bk. ii. 3: fo. 87, ed. G. E. Woodbine and trans. S. E. Thorne (Harvard UP, 1986), vol. ii, p. 252):

> ... plenam habet dispositionem ... in mulieribus maritandis et maritagiis vendendis.

But according to the demands of the Barons that were conceded in Magna Carta, wards were not to be married below their social status (there was to be no 'disparagement'); and the advice of their kindred was to be taken (*Articles of the Barons* (1215), ch. 3, in Stubbs, *Select Charters* (9th edn.), p. 286):

> ... ut haeredes ita maritentur ne disparagentur, et per consilium propinquorum de consanguinitate sua.

This was conceded in Magna Carta ch. 6 (Stubbs, ibid., p. 294):

> Haeredes maritentur absque disparagatione, ita tamen quod, antequam contrahatur matrimonium, ostendatur propinquis de consanguinitate ipsius haeredis.

Moreover, the guardian was required to maintain his wards on a scale befitting their status (Bracton, loc. cit.):

> ... Heredes autem quamdiu fuerint in custodia pro quantitate hereditatis honorifice exhibebunt.

It is thus very much to the point that both Godrich and Godard are explicitly represented as flouting the third of these obligations (314–23; 415–21), and Godrich the first (1088–100). Moreover, the mention of the kindred in each case (324–7; 392–3 and 413–14), though not in connection with marriage of the heirs, clearly implies a breach of the formal requirement that the kindred should be satisfied with the treatment of the wards. See Pollock and Maitland, *The History of English Law before the Time of Edward I*, i. Bk. II, ch. 1 §8: Wardship and Marriage.

174–5. This couplet is evidently one of those loosely stereotyped formulas that could easily be adapted, with slight changes anywhere except in the rhyme-words, to various contexts. There are at least four other examples of it in ME romances, one in a Breton lay, and one other:

> And whan þow ert of swich *elde*
> þat þow miȝt þeself *wilde*

(*Sir Beues of Hamtoun* 367–8, and ibid. 19–20), *The Seven Sages of Rome* (Nth. version, ed. K. Campbell, Boston, 1907, 4273–4), *Guy of Warwick* (15th-c. version), 877–8, *Sir Degarre* (ed. G. Schleich, Heidelberg, 1929), 119–20, *Cursor Mundi* 585–6. The formula also appears in slightly different forms: for one that amounts to a variant see 1436–7 and n.

The point of noticing these six passages is that they are crucial for the recognition of what has happened to the text of *Havelok* here. First, *here selwe* in C is vindicated, at least as a purely formal pattern, by the reflexive use of *welde* in all seven. Even *it* makes sense, since it evidently refers to *Engelonde* 173. But it requires the reflexive pronoun (*here selwe*) to be the subject (in part) of *welde*, instead of the object as in the above passages; and it may therefore have been introduced by a scribe.

The Laud line 175 scans satisfactorily, since there is a mass of conclusive metrical evidence that the author's form of infinitive had shed the final -*n*. But the lack of a grammatical object for *yemen and welde* is a bad sign; and the recurrence of *yemen* just after 172 is slightly suspicious. And *yemen* 172 points us straight back to the similarly phrased sequence in 128–31, which is notably coherent, and in which 128–9 are a convincing variation on the pattern of our formula as authenticated above, and as attested for *Hav.* by C 175. Since C 175 squares (except for *it*) with all the examples of the formula, it is likely that the author wrote something like *And þat she mowe hir-selwe welde*.

That form of the line corresponds in all essentials (if we allow for the equivalence of *hir-selue* and *hire bodi*: see 131 n.) with 131, except for the rhyme-word. It accordingly explains how *yemen* (and accordingly *and*) might have got into L 175 as a corruption. A scribe, having just previously written 131, now absently reproduced it, *rhyme-word and all*, in 175, and then duly wrote the proper rhyme-word for 175, viz. *welde*. This in turn explains how and why *hir-selwe* dropped out: the corrupt antecedent form of L 175 was now grossly hypermetrical; something had to go; and this could not be either the correct rhyme-word or the one that had intruded from 131, nor the subject of the clause.

177. The two successive stresses at the beginning of the line as transmitted in L are metrically unusual and probably a sign that something has gone wrong. Another suspicious point is that the rhyme-word *Ion* occurs in the disyllabic form *Iohan* in 1113, 1722, and 2564. Line 1113 can just be scanned, e.g. as:

Bí Crı̆st ańd bı̆ Seı́nt Ĭŏhán

or

Bı̆ Crı́st ańd bı́ Seı́nt Ĭŏhán.

But 1722 and 2564 are metrically impeccable; and in 2564, which contains the same double invocation as 177 and 1113, *bi* is used only once, before *Crist* (just as in C 177).

We may conclude that:

1. As the disyllabic *Iohan* is metrically obligatory in 1722, and the author is unlikely to have used both this and *Ion*, he will have written *Iohan* in all four passages.

2. Ellis's [*Iesu*] in 177 has the not altogether negligible support of the Cambridge fragment. And if the disyllabic *Iohan* is substituted for *jon* in C 177, the latter scans immaculately. Thus the second *bi* in the Laud text of 177 will have been added, and *Iesu* omitted, by a scribe; so that, except for *jon*, the text of C 177 is nearer to what the author wrote.

3. Accordingly, the best way to deal with 1113 is to insert *Iesu* before *Crist* (on the model and the authority of C 177), and to excise the second *bi* (as being

spurious), just as in 177. This makes the double invocation uniform in 177 and 1113, and solves all the metrical difficulties.

As C. T. Onions has pointed out (*Philologica* 158), the use of the disyllabic *Iohan* by the author requires the rhyme-word *anon* in 176, 1112, and 2563 to have the Nth-type non-rounded /aː/ as the reflex of OE *ā* in the stressed syllable.

178. *perl of Cornwayle*: the author has taken the extraordinary step of giving two figures in the action of his story (which was almost from first to last a fiction) the titles and the status of the two most illustrious earldoms of England in the reign of Henry III. The other figure is *þe erl of Cestre* 2608.

The regent–guardian–traitor–usurper was in the received story (see Introduction, pp. xxxiii and xxxvi), but not as the Earl of Cornwall. The career of Henry III's younger brother Richard (1209–72) resembles that of Godrich at three main points. Richard was made Earl of Cornwall in 1225, co-regent with the queen after she joined him in 1254, and guardian of Lord Edward's children during his absence abroad and just before his accession in 1272. But the author of *Hauelok* has planted a more striking clue of his own. He has virtually duplicated the Earl Godrich in the Earl Godard, the Danish usurper; and it is thus hardly by chance that their names (in which the identical first elements cancel each other out) have second elements that combine to make the name *Richard*.

From the accounts of the historians of the time Richard emerges as a great personage, skilled and distinguished in the affairs of the realm, financial management, and negotiation, who from 1230 was much relied on by his brother and was finally King of the Germans from 1257 till his death in 1272. But he had previously been at odds with his brother more than once, and in 1227 in armed rebellion that finally subsided without their coming to blows, and once more in 1238.[3]

This makes it a little less startling that the author of *Hauelok* should have dared to glance at Richard in his depiction of the traitor Godrich. But the political situation in the sixth decade of the 13th century in any case amply accounts for it. As a result of the baronial war that led up to the battle of Lewes in 1264, a very different view of Richard from that of contemporary historians was taken in other quarters. An anonymous clerical partisan of the barons' cause produced the Latin poem known as *The Song of Lewes*,[4] a political tract in which Simon de Montford is eulogized, and the king, his son Edward, and Richard are condemned along with their supporters (who are accused of fornication with seven hundred women on the night before the battle, ll. 152–3).

Moreover, Richard was singled out for special and startling vituperation as the subject of the ME poem *Song against the King of Almaigne*,[5] in which he like-

---

[3] See N. Denholm-Young, *Richard of Cornwall* (Oxford, 1947), pp. 1–38.
[4] Ed. C. L. Kingsford (Oxford, 1890) with a translation.
[5] Ed. E. Mätzner, *Altenglische Sprachproben*, i. 1 (Berlin, 1867), pp. 152–4; K. Böddeker, *Altenglische Dichtungen des MS. Harl[ey] 2253*, pp. 95–100.

wise is accused of fornication (l. 9), but also specifically of being *trichard* 'one who breaks faith':[6]

> Richard, þau þou be euer trichard,
> tricchen shalt þou neuermore.

This is not an isolated instance: the word is applied to Richard as his sole name in the 13th-century OF mime *La Paix aux Anglais*,[7] which burlesques the arrogance of the English and their barbaric French, and was probably inspired by the treaty of Paris in 1259:

> Le bon rai d'Ingleter se trama a .i. part,
> Li et Trichart sa frer irrous comme lipart.

This charge reinforces the case stated above for thinking that Godrich was styled Earl of Cornwall in *Hav.* because the author was glancing at Richard.

There is some conflict in the internal evidence for the date of the piece against Richard, which deals with the battle of Lewes and events soon after it. The entrenched opinion (because of allusions in ll. 34 and 40 that seem to imply the absence of the Earl of Surrey and Hugh de Bigot in France) is that it was composed before May 1265 (when they returned), i.e. during Richard's lifetime. But the preterite in the words *Richard of Alemaigne, whil þat he wes kyng* (8) surely implies a date after 1272. If, nevertheless, the former allusions have been correctly interpreted, we must assume that the author of *Hav.* might equally have dared to hint opprobriously at Richard during his lifetime.

This is likely to be a matter of historical reminiscences rather than historical allusions; they might have been suggested by written sources, and need not have been topical. No precise conclusions regarding the date when *Hav.* was composed can safely be drawn from them, beyond the almost otiose one that it must have been after 1227 (when Richard became Earl of Cornwall).

192. *tuelf winter hold*: inconsistent with *tuenti* 259. In Bracton's formulation of the matter, the age differed according to types of tenure; but a female ward could marry at twelve (*De Legibus et Consuetudinibus Angliae*, Bk. ii. 3, ch. 37, fo. 86; Woodbine and Thorne, ed. cit., ii. 251–2).

195. Since *gon and speken* is in its literal use 'to walk about and have the power of speech' a common formula in ME, the phrase may be interpreted here as a similar case to that of *liuen and deyen* in 257: each is used in a syntactic connection to which only one of its members is appropriate, because it is a formula and hence syntactically a unit, which is no longer precisely analysed by speakers. The phenomenon is especially clear in an example in *Pearl* 149: '*Abowte me* con I *stote and stare*' ('I stopped and looked about me'); similarly *Cursor Mundi* 22724 (which is identical with *Cursor Mundi* 204). Thus *Hav.* 194–5 might be interpreted: 'And until she was versed in courtly behaviour, and in the procedures and the converse proper to polite dalliance'.

199–200. The repetition of *beste* is not in itself a sure sign of corruption. But

---

[6] For the corresponding sense in the verb *trichier* in AN see the *Romance of Horn*, i. 1. 4126, 4721, 5184.

[7] Ed. E. Faral, *Mimes français du XIIIe Siècle* (Paris, 1910), pp. 31–47, ll. 29–30.

if it is emended (as by Skeat) to *hexte*, the whole couplet is identical with
1081–2 (apart from the palpable error, on the metrical test, by which *man* has
been omitted from 1081), and in particular contains the same four epithets, in
the same order, as are applied to Havelok there. On top of this, *hey* is used of
him in 1072 and 1084, where it must mean 'tall', as the unambiguous mention
of his great height in 983–4 and 987 shows, and since Godrich, like those who
use the word of Havelok in 1072, did not then know of his royal descent. And
hexte in 199 (where king Aþelwold would of course have meant it in the sense
'noblest by birth') would make Godrich's designation of Havelok in 1084 as
hey, in the sense 'of towering stature', a cynical pun by which he claimed to be
carrying out his oath to the king (cf. 199–204 and 1078–83) while actually
breaking it.

In fact, this example of an 'ambiguous oath' is reminiscent of the ancient
folktale *The Equivocal Oath*, of Indian origin, which is best known nowadays
from the literary use of it in the story of Tristan and Iseult, and which is also
represented in Olcel. literature, in *Grettis Saga* ch. LXXXIX (ed. Guðni Jónsson, *Íslenzk Fornrit* vii, 1936), by the story of Spes and her lover þorsteinn. In
the folktale and its offshoots the oath is sworn by a woman to clear herself
(successfully) from her husband's charge (which is true) of infidelity. There is
thus a great difference in the application of the idea; what the motif in *Hav.*
has in common with the folktale is the use of ambiguity in the formulation of
an oath, in the service of a lie. See A. Aarne and S. Thompson, *The Types of the
Folktale* 1418 (FF Communications No. 184, Helsinki, 1961); G. Schoepperle,
Tristan and Isolt, vol. i (London, 1913), pp. 223–6.

Our emendation to *heste* (as a slight refinement on Skeat's *hexte*) is both
philologically and palaeographically probable: the Anglian-derived *heste* is
the form proper to the author's NE-Midland ME; the letters *h* and *b*, in
some ME hands, are not dissimilar; and *heste* and MS *beste* are otherwise
identical.

211–31. The king (*a*) utters a prayer for God's mercy, (*b*) receives the
Eucharist, (*c*) makes his confession, (*d*) is scourged and beaten (by way of
penance), (*e*) makes his testament and bestows all his goods, (*f*) commends his
spirit to God with the words *In manus tuas*, (*g*) calls on Christ while he still has
the power of speech, and (*h*) is explicitly said to expire.

This account corresponds in all essentials but the scourging, and in certain
details (though the king is not directly said to expire voluntarily), with what is
said in *The Book of the Craft of Dying* about the procedure to be followed by and
on behalf of a dying man.[8] This late ME work is one of the vernacular versions
of the *Ars Moriendi*. The latter is extant in a great many 15th-century MSS and
in printed editions of the 15th and 16th centuries, both in Latin and in the ver-
naculars of Western Europe. It exists in a longer and a shorter form, which
Sister M. C. O'Connor terms respectively CP and QS (after the opening
words *Cum de presentis* and *Quamvis secundum*).[9] It cannot antedate the first

[8] Ed. C. Horstman, *Yorkshire Writers*, vol. ii. 414, 27–415, 2 and 416, 19–24 (see
218–9 n.).

[9] *The Art of Dying Well: The Development of the Ars Moriendi* (New York, 1966), p. 7.

decade of the 15th century, since the main source is the *De Arte moriendi* (called by P. Glorieux *Medicine de l'âme*[10]) of Gerson (1363–1429), which he included in his *Opus tripartitum* (or *Doctrinale*) as the third of its three parts[11] (*Tertia pars hujus opusculi, de Scientia Mortis*).

What remains unexplained is how, and in what form, this material came to be available to the author of *Hav.* by *c.* 1300. See further L. Gougaud, 'Étude sur les "Ordines Commendationis Animae"', *Ephemerides Liturgicae*, 49, NS 9 (1935), 3–27.

214–15. Cf. 226–7. Scourging was an established form of voluntary penitential discipline from the middle of the 11th century. For a native literary example of it (within the life of a cloister, but apparently voluntary), cf. *St Editha* 1041–4 (ed. C. Horstmann, Heilbronn, 1883). The reason why the king underwent scourging and buffeting, even on the point of death, was in order to conform to the experience of Christ in his Passion (for this point, with reference to the meaning of penance in general, see *New Catholic Encyclopedia* (New York, 1967), 5, s.v. *Flagellation*; *Lexikon für Theologie und Kirche*, vol. ii (Freiburg, 1958), s.v. *Bussübungen*, and vol. iv (1960), s.v. *Geisselung*).

218–19. *The Book of the Craft of Dying* prescribes that every man who is sick or in any danger should make his peace with God and receive the sacraments, *ordeynynge and makynge his testament* (ed. cit., ii. 416, 19–24). For another example of a man who does this last (orally) on his death-bed, see *The Tale of Gamelyn* (ed. W. W. Skeat, Oxford, 1884), 53–66.

Made, gaf/gouen, as in *maked* . . . *gyuen* 365. Since there is a corresponding MSw. phrase (as pointed out by C. T. Onions, *Philologica* 159), the collocation of *made* and a form of *gyuen* looks very much like a calque on that phrase, which (in Onions' example) likewise refers to a 'testament' and in *göra* v. has a literal equivalent of *maken*:

þetta war *giuit oc gört* vndir mit inzighle ['seal'].[12]

But the MSw. formula was not restricted to testamentary use. It occurs e.g. in a grant of privileges (dated 1347, and in an original MS) by King Magnus:

þættæ bref var *gyort ok giuit* i varom garþe viþ Husæby kirkio.[13]

Quiste here and in 365 are the only recorded examples with -*i*-, alongside three with -*e*- (dated *c.* 1400, 1418, 1478) in *OED* s.v. *quest* sb.[2]. But the /i/ is also recorded once in *byquyste*, beside /e/ in *byqueste*. And if *OED* is right in referring the word to an OE *(bi-)cwiss* (with analogical use of the suffix -*t*-, after *hest* < OE *hǣs* < *hǣtt-), the -*i*- form is the earlier one.

223. *þat noman wiste*: not an adjectival clause. The OE equivalent of this use

[10] 'La Vie et les Œuvres de Gerson', *Archives d'histoire doctrinale et littéraire du Moyen Âge*, 18 (1950–1), 166–7. See also P. Glorieux, *Jean Gerson, Œuvres Complètes*, vii (Paris, 1966), pp. 404–7.

[11] Ed. Ellies du Pin, *Joannis Gersonii Opera Omnia* (Antwerp, 1706), i. 447–50.

[12] *Svenskt Diplomatarium*, ed. B. E. Hildebrand, 5, 568, see also 5, 160 (dated 1343) and 6, 181, and Söderwall, *Ordbok öfver svenska medeltids-språket* (Lund, 1884–1918), s.v. *giva*.

[13] A. Noreen, *Altschwedisches Lesebuch* (2nd edn., Halle, 1904), p. 25.

of *þat* was *þæs þe*; as in *Dialogues of Gregory* (ed. H. Hecht), p. 47, l. 14: '*þæs þe*
ic ongyte, þes wæs mycel wer' and prose Boethius XXVI. i. 29 ff. (ed. Sedgefield). For the ME collocation with a verb meaning 'know', which survives
today (commonly in the form *that I know (of)*), see *Ste. Iuliene* l. 138: 'Ne Ich nes
neuer, *þet Ich wite*, 3et wið him icnawen', and *Troilus and Criseyde* iii. 839–40
and *Towneley Plays* xxi. 238–9. It corresponds closely to the common OF idiom
of the type *que je sache*, as in *Yvain* 430 (and 573 and 6489):

> Ja, *que je sache*, a esciant
> Ne vos en mantirai de mot.

In OF, the verb is normally in the subjunctive if the main clause expresses
negation, otherwise in the indicative. The first ME example above conforms
to this rule, while the other two are compatible with it (since the pret. *wiste*
may be either a subj. or an indic. form). Given the difference in the OE way of
putting it, this establishes that the ME idiom is a calque on the OF one.

The OF idiom in turn derives from the corresponding L type *quod sciam* 'so
far as I know'. The main point about all three is that they are absolute uses, as
T. B. W. Reid has recognized for the OF one.[14] The *þat* is classed as a relative
pron. in *OED* (6 b. and *know* v. 18 c), and OF *que* as a relative by Tobler, as L
quod is by Lewis and Short (*A Latin Dictionary*, *qui* I, II E a. I). There is, however, a case for regarding it as an indefinite pronoun, like *who* (and the corresponding OF use of *qui*) in the idiom in *Hav.* 4 (see n.). [Prof. Reid kindly told
me, at the time when this note was written, that he concurred.]

noman: 'anyone'. The irrational negative is due to the established use of
multiple negatives in early English up to the time of Shakespeare. The double
(i.e. reinforced) negative *Ne ... noman* was orthodox and common within a
single clause: that sufficiently accounts for its distribution into separate
clauses here.

225. The point of this is made clear by Jean Gerson's brief *Testamentum
peregrini tendentis in paradisum* in the OF version:[15]

> Et car je suis nez tout nudz au ventre ma mere et nudz retourneray en terre,
> je laisse toutes choses temporelles aulx temporels et mortels telx ou teles
> etc.

228. C. T. Onions argues (*Philologica* 159) for MS *loude* 'loudly', against
Skeat's emendation to *Louerd* after *The Reeve's Tale* 4287, since the former
would represent the phrase *voce magna* in the passage of Luke 23: 46 from which
the formula comes: 'Et clamans *voce magna*, Iesus ait: *Pater, in manus tuas* com-
mendo spiritum meum.' Not surprisingly, Chaucer's line (put in the mouth of
the Miller's wife) is not a complete rendering of Jesus' utterance. But the latter
is translated in full, without any equivalent of *voce magna*, and with *Lord God* in
place of *Pater*, in a passage and a context specially relevant to the deathbed
scene in *Hav.*, in *The Book of the Craft of Dying*, where Jesus' actions on the

[14] *Yvain*, Glossary s.v. *que* pron. interr. and 430 n. See also A. Tobler, *Vermischte Beiträge zur französischen Grammatik*, i. 17, pp. 117–23.

[15] Published by P. Glorieux, p. 68 of 'Comment Gerson préparait son père à la mort',
Mélanges de science réligieuse, 14 (1957), 63–70.

Cross are prescribed for imitation by a dying man, who is to say, 'Lord God, into þin handis I commende my spirit' (p. 414, l. 46).

Moreover, there is a modified version[16] (meant for monks and nuns) of St Anselm's *Questions to the Dying*[17] that runs thus at a corresponding point (while the original does not contain the crucial word), 'Deinde dicat ter: "In manus tuas, *Domine*, comendo spiritum meum"'. This last parallel tilts the balance in · favour of Skeat's emendation, since *Domine* follows *in manus tuas*, as MS *loude* does in *Hav*. The palaeographical explanation of the error is as for *louerd*, MS *lond*, in 64.

234. *sobbing*: the verb is not recorded in OE. For the clear signs that it is an ideophonic formation, see 39 and Appendix A on the parallel case of *wrobben*, *wrabben*. The root-vowel -*o*- in *sobben* has the usual ideophonic variant -*a*- (as is typical in Gmc ideophonic verbs) in Fris. *sabje* (beside *sobje*) 'suck; slaver (in eating); kiss' and Du. *zabbelen* 'slaver'.

For words formed on the Gmc base **suƀ*- 'sip (audibly)' and their cognates, see Falk and Torp, *WGS* (*suf*) and *NDEW suk*. The -*eu*- grade of the root is represented in OE *sēofian* 'to sigh; to lament'.

243. *sauteres*: i.e. (in the light of 214–15 and 226–7) specifically the penitential psalms, viz. 6, 32, 38, 51, 102, 130, 143 (in the Vulgate 6, 31, 37, 50, 101, 131, 142). They were seven in number because they were regarded as antidotes for the seven deadly sins (*The Gast of Gy* 1144–9):

> þe seuyn psalmes and þe letany
> Forto say er moste souerayne
> Vnto þe saules þat suffers payne
> For þai er ordand more and myn
> Euer a psalme ogaynes a sin;
> So þai destroy þe sines seuyn.

For what is probably another instance of their use on behalf of someone who has just died, see *Ywain and Gawain* 888–9 (in 74 n. above).

245–7. This prayer expresses (e.g. by the use of the word *lede*) the immemorial conception of the soul's journey after death,[18] which is specifically termed one in a prayer in *The Book of the Craft of Dying* (p. 420, 26–7): 'Alle þe contrarie [legions] and mynystres of Sathanas be not so hardy to lett þi iornaye.'

The journey commonly requires a guide or *psychopompos*: in Greek mythology Hermes *psychopompos* conducts souls of the dead to or from Hades (*Odyssey* xxiv. 1–2) or to Elysion.[19] In the Christianized form of the conception,

[16] See *Facsimile of British Museum MS. Harley 2253*, ed. N. R. Ker (EETS, os 255), fo. 137ᵛ, item 113.

[17] Ed. F. S. Schmitt, *Beiträge zur Geschichte der Philosophie und Theologie des Mittelalters*, 33. 3 (1936), 5–6.

[18] See M. W. Bloomfield, *The Seven Deadly Sins* (Michigan, repr. 1967), pp. 12–58; P. A. Recheis, *Engel Tod und Seelenreise*, Temi e Testi, 4 (Rome, 1958), pp. 17–137.

[19] Aeschylus, *Persae* (ed. H. W. Smyth, *Aeschylus* i, Loeb Classical Library, repr. 1973), 623 ff.; *Orphic Hymns* (ed. W. Quandt, *Orphei Hymni*, Berlin, 1955), 57. 6; cf. *Aeneid*, vi. 749, and see the notes of R. G. Austin and H. E. Butler on this line in their editions.

the guide is commonly an angel, notably the archangel Michael, as in another prayer in *The Book of the Craft of Dying* (p. 419, 15 ff.). But the guide may be Christ, who 'leads' the soul into the bosom of the Father, as in the passage below from Clement, and in *Hav.* 3001–2; cf., in the first prayer cited above: 'Crist Goddis sonn *brynge þe* to ioyes of mery Paradyse' (p. 420, 28–9).

What is remarkable, and difficult to explain, in the prayer in *Hav.* is that it is God who is envisaged as 'leading' the soul of King Aþelwold into the presence of Christ. *Biforn his sone* suggests the Day of Judgement. But the conflation of this with the death of Aþelwold is not a difficulty, since the Fathers do sometimes visualize the last end of either the individual or of all mankind in one and the same image. In remarking on this, Recheis[20] adds that Origen has applied one and the same passage of *Jeremiah* (16: 16) at one point to the spiritual destiny of the souls of the good (Homily XVI, on Jer. 16: 4),[21] and at another to the end of the world (*Commentary on Song of Songs*, iii).[22]

The immediate interest of the prayer, however, is that it explains why the author has so insistently emphasized the king's penance and so particularly specified the rest of what he did on his deathbed (see 214–15 n. and 244 n.). The prayer is an integral part of the whole procedure that is followed by the king and laid down in *The Book of the Craft of Dying*; and it can have the intended result only because of the king's penance, as a passage in Clement of Alexandria's homily *Quis diues saluetur* makes clear (after a lacuna that has not destroyed the sense):

> . . . [the angels] with jocund faces, rejoicing, singing praises, laying open the heavens. In advance of them all the Saviour himself comes to meet him, greeting him with his right hand; from the Saviour emanates an unshadowed and unremitting radiance, as he leads the way into the arms of the Father, into eternal life, into the kingdom of heaven. . . . The man who has received the angel of repentance in this life will not do penance when he leaves his body, nor be shamed when he sees the Saviour in his glory, and the heavenly hosts, approaching him; nor will he fear the flames.[23]

It is worth noticing that in *Ywain and Gawain*, after the knight of the fountain has been buried, his widow is represented as reciting *þe psalmes* from a psalter, in her concern for his soul (887–9; see 244 n. above), and as uttering on his behalf a prayer to God (857 ff.) that in general corresponds to the prayer in *Hav.* and has the same rhyme-words:

> Of his sins do hym pardowne . . .
> God grant þe grace þou mai won
> In hevyn with his owyn son.

---

[20] Op. cit., pp. 66 and 84, and 107 n. 174.

[21] Ed. P. Nautin, *Origène: Homélies sur Jérémie*, ii (Sources Chrétiennes, 238, Paris, 1977), pp. 138–40.

[22] Ed. W. A. Baehrens, *Origenes Werke*, viii (Die griechischen christlichen Schriftsteller der ersten drei Jahrhunderte, Leipzig, 1925), p. 205, ll. 17–28.

[23] Text and translation in G. W. Butterworth, *Clement of Alexandria* (Loeb Classical Library). Ed. L. Früchtel, *Clemens Alexandrinus* (2nd edn., 1970), iii. 190. 20–191. 3, in Die griechischen christlichen Schriftsteller der ersten drei Jahrhunderte.

Both points were contributed by the English author; they are not in *Yvain* (1152 ff., and 1206 ff.), which was his source.

254. The author's familiarity with feudal institutions appears in the phrase *ghod fey beren* (with an indirect object in the dative), which is used in the oath of fealty for the act of homage in the jurist Bracton's formulation: see 2203–14 n.

257. This curious expression is a variant of *þe day þat he was quik and ded* 1406, which occurs in virtually the ame couplet in 2211. Both spectacularly attest the author's first-hand knowledge of legal documents, since they echo a Latin formula used in royal charters and writs of the 13th c., as when Stephen confirms charters for Abingdon Abbey: '. . . sicut tenuerunt die qua rex Henricus *fuit vivus et mortuus* et die qua primum coronatus fui' (*Regesta Regum Anglo-Normannorum 1066–1154*, ed. Cronne & Davis, vol. iii, p. 3, No. 10). For other examples see ibid., p. 176, No. 472, and p. 262, No. 713. In other than juridical contexts, *live and die* is a fixed collocation up to the time of Shakespeare (*As You Like It* III. v. 7); see C. T. Onions, 'Die and Live', *RES*, NS, 7 (1956), 174–6.

For the syntax of 257, see 195 n. and especially 1038–9 n.: *til þat* properly belongs to only one of the two co-ordinate verbs. MS *him* conceals a corruption of the plural of the personal pronoun, which (since *mouhte* is not an impersonal verb) must have been in the nominative form.

263–9. This passage is remarkable (and most unusual in a ME romance) as a thumb-nail sketch of the machinery of local government in England in the 13th century. The justices in eyre, who existed in the reign of Henry I, had come to function systematically by the time of Henry II in the court of each county, to collect taxes and revenues due to the king and to hear cases.[24] The sheriff was a very powerful agent of the king, who had to arrest criminals, execute writs, empanel juries and distrain goods in respect of debts, collect taxes and various dues, and hold the county court, and the sheriff's 'tourn' in individual hundreds.[25] The *bedels* were among the sheriff's underlings, and assistants of the bailiffs of the hundred. They carried out the sheriff's orders in the company of the bailiffs, and collected dues and distrained goods.

Literary instances of the word *bedel(s)* in this sense represent them, along with bailiffs, as oppressors robbing and despoiling the community by their extortions. A *locus classicus* is *The Song of the Husbandman* in MS Harley 2253,[26] which vividly indicts such officials and their exactions (see ll. 37–40, 45–56). It mentions the chief beadle 'fierce as a boar' and his catchpolls (*cachereles* 50) who come with 'green wax' demands, i.e. the mandates from the Exchequer to collect monies due to the king at Easter and Michaelmas, and who extort them many times over. In the *Ayenbite of Inwyt* (repr. 1965, vol. i, p. 37), reeves, provosts, and beadles are cited as robbing and oppressing the poor (p. 39), and as embezzling the rents due to their lords (p. 37). Walter Map, in more precise terms, cites as oppressors the justices, sheriffs, under-sheriffs, and beadles

---

[24] See F. W. Maitland, *The Constitutional History of England* (Cambridge, 1913), pp. 43, 63, 69, 89, 127, 137–8, 210.

[25] For a most helpful account of his office and powers see H. M. Cam, *The Hundred and the Hundred Rolls* (London, 1930), especially pp. 59 ff.

[26] Ed. K. Böddeker, *Altenglische Dichtungen*, pp. 102–5.

whom the court sends out to make inquisitions (sc. into revenues due to the king from rents and pleas).[27]

The *greyue* (as l. 1751 indicates[28]) was the headman (*praepositus*) of a village, and therefore evidently the same official as denoted by the native word *reeve* (OE *gerefa*). When the itinerant justices visited the county, he, along with four leading fellow-citizens, had to appear before them to represent the community. The word *greyue* (ON *greifi*) is attested in Lay Subsidy Rolls and Feet of Fines for Yorks., Lancs., Lincs., Norfolk, and Suffolk, and was thus obviously restricted to areas of strong Scandinavian influence.[29]

The collocation here with *bedels* (which is matched in *Ormulum* 18365, in an apparently incongruous context) suggests that the *greyue* was involved, like them, in policing duties among others. The context as a whole implies approval of all these officials and their activities, which is a view the opposite of that illustrated above and sounds like that of a man who was himself inside the system. Likewise significantly, it is the *greyue* to whom Ubbe sends Havelok's party for a safe night's lodging (1750): he is not in question in the other versions, and is clearly an invention.

Grith-sergeans 267 is the sole recorded example of the word in literary use; and it is otherwise attested only once by *OED* and twice by *MED*. Revealingly, there are four more examples in mainly 13th-century documents printed by R. Stewart-Brown in *The Serjeants of the Peace in Medieval England and Wales*.[30] The serjeants of the peace were the nearest approach to police in the 13th century; they had the duty of perambulation and the power to arrest, and indeed to behead robbers taken in the act.

A striking point in the whole passage is the implication that in appointing these officials Godrich was making some sort of clean sweep (*Justises . . . newe* 263). It recalls the reforms of administration, justice, and law and order that Edward I launched in and after 1274 (when he returned to England). The inquest of 1274 elicited a mass of evidence not only of rents and revenues due to the king, and of franchises, but of corruption and extortion, which was duly set down in the Hundred Rolls.[31] But there was also Edward's drastic purge, in 1289, of the justices, some ten of whom were dismissed, or imprisoned, or fined, and of others.[32]

It has in fact been suggested that the measures described in *Hav.* echo the provisions of the First Statute of Westminster I (1275) and the Commissions of

[27] *De Nugis Curialium*, ed. M. R. James (*Anecdota Oxoniensia*, Medieval and Modern Series, 14, Oxford, 1914), *Distinctio* I, ch. X; composed between 1181 and 1193.

[28] *þe beste man of al þe toun*.

[29] See B. Thuresson, *Middle English Occupational Terms* (Lund Studies in English, 19, 1950), p. 100; *reeve* is used in Suffolk, Surrey, Sussex, Hants., etc., and Lancs. (ibid., p. 101).

[30] (Manchester, 1936), Appendix III, pp. 129 (III), 130 (34), 135 (45), 136 (46); and *grith servientem* in 132 (37).

[31] As so vividly analysed and illuminated by H. M. Cam, *The Hundred and the Hundred Rolls* (London, 1930), *passim*.

[32] See F. M. Powicke, *The Thirteenth Century*, 361 ff.

Trailbaston (1305).[33] But the inquest of 1274 and the Second Statute of Westminster (1285)[34] also seem in general potentially relevant; and 1305 is a little late as an earlier limit for the date of composition of *Hav.*

264. Lines 264–7 and 270–1 recur, in a debased form, in MS F of the *Anonymous Short English Metrical Chronicle* 334–9 (p. 78):

> Alle þis londe thrugh and thrugh
> Fro Douer in to Rokesburgh
> She dide schereves to make
> And serians hire londe to take
> For to do alle hire cry
> At hire wille and at hire mercy.

Since the pasage occurs in only one MS, and that one is (according to the editor's stemma, p. xlv) genetically later than one other extant MS, we can hardly posit its presence in the original version of the *Chronicle* (notwithstanding the fairly well assured case of *Hav.* 87–90: see note ad loc.).

In any event, this is a clear case of actual plagiarism (as distinct from repetition of commonplaces that might have been picked up anywhere), even if it was only by a redactor of F, rather than the author of the *Chronicle*. The specific mention, and the conjunction, of Roxburgh and Dover as the boundaries of England must be a direct imitation of *Havelok*, where they are more natural, both as an echo of the other example in 139, and because the situation of which they are used (265) matches the first. The bungling *do . . . hire cry*, for the very unusual *(hauen) at his cri*, is another tell-tale sign that this is an unauthentic and therefore potentially derivative form of the passage.

265. The mention of Dover and Roxburgh as marking the extreme limits of England, as in 139, is here in a context of peace-keeping and the king's peace. This is why the AN *Le Petit Bruit* names a road from *en long de Rokesburg jekis a Dover* as one of *les quatre royales chemyns parmy Engleterre*[35]—the four royal roads were under the king's peace, as e.g. the *Laws of William I* attest: '. . . ki en aucun de ces quatre chemins ocist aucun ki seit errant par le pais, si enfreint la pais le rei'.[36] In fact, *Le Petit Bruit* makes explicit what is only implicit in *Hav.*: the author of *Hav.* mentioned Dover and Roxburgh with the four royal roads in mind.

Moreover, *Le Petit Bruit*'s account of Havelok is the only early one that says (*a*) the road from Roxburgh to Dover is one of the four royal roads, and the only other early one (apart from *Hav.*) to say that (*b*) Godrich is Earl of Cornwall. These points both seem almost certain to derive from the extant *Hav.*; and in that case, *Hav.* must have been composed by 1310 (the date of *Le Petit Brut*).

The reference to Roxburgh as part of England provides another helpful

[33] J. W. Hales, 'The Lay of Havelok the Dane', *The Athenaeum* No. 3200, 23 Feb. 1889, p. 244.

[34] For which see F. M. Powicke, op. cit., p. 369 and Index s.v. Statutes.

[35] MS BM Harl. 902, fo. 2ʳ.

[36] Ed. F. Liebermann, *Die Gesetze der Angelsachsen* (Halle, 1898–1916), i. 510.

limit. A point after Baliol's surrender of Roxburgh, Jedburgh, and Berwick in 1295 is indicated, since the period 1174–89, when Roxburgh had otherwise been in English hands, is too early. See *SMP*, especially pp. 191–6.

277. *Al Engelond . . . stod awe*: with the ON cognate *agi* substituted for native *ege* in the OE impersonal idiom *ege(sa) stondan*, e.g. *Beowulf* 783–4:

Norð-Denum stod

atelic *egesa*.

See 1154 n.

278. *adrad*: the form of the prefix might be thought to indicate OE *ondrǣdan* or the rare *adrǣdan* as the etymon, rather than *ofdrǣdan*. But the first two of these, which mean 'to fear', do not fit the sense 'afraid' in the seven examples of *adrad*, *adred* (and *odrat* 1154) in *Hav.* as well as the causative weak verb *ofdrǣdan* does.

331–2. For other examples of this formula used in ME invocations of Christ or God, cf. *Sir Beues of Hamtoun* 2839: 'Lord, þat rerede þe Lazaroun', and (in a series of no less than five in succession) the 14th-century version of *Guy of Warwick* (Auchinleck MS), st. 252, 1–6:

'Lord' seyd Gij 'þat rered Lazeroun
& for man þoled passioun,
& on þe rode gan blede,
þat saued Sussan fram þe feloun,
& halp Daniel fram þe lyoun,
To-day wisse me & rede',

as well as the double one in *Guy and Colebrande* 157–8;[37] see also ibid. 334 ff.

For other invocations of Christ or God in *Hav.*, see 403–4, 542–5, and 1317. The device itself, and the modes of reference used in it, were learnt from OF, and specifically from the chansons de geste. For the raising of Lazarus, cf. *Le Siège de Barbastre* 1028–31, in a series of three of the stock formulae used in these invocations and prayers:

Je crieng et ain celui qui sofri pasion . . .
Et de mort au cart jor sucita Lazaron,
Et gueri seint Jonas el ventre del poison.

See E. R. Labande, 'Le "crédo" épique', in *Recueil de travaux offert à M. Clovis Brunel* (Société de l'école des Chartes, 1955), ii. 62–80; J. de Caluwé, 'La "prière épique" dans les plus anciennes chansons de geste françaises', *Olifant*, 4 (1976), 4–20.

337. *So as*: the sole example in the *OED* of the concessive use of *so as* as 'although'; and only one (17th-century) example of *so that* in the same function is recorded. The former, at least, probably derives from the rare concessive use of OE *swa* in a subordinate clause, with correlative *(swa) þeah* 'nevertheless' in the main clause, as in the only two recorded examples: *Elene* (ed. P. Gradon, London, 1958), 498–501:

---

[37] Ed. Furnivall and Hales, *Bishop Percy's Folio MS.* (London, 1867–8), ii. 527.

swa he þurh feondscipe

to cwale monige   Cristes folces
demde to deaþe,   swa þeah him Dryhten eft
miltse gefremede.

and *Genesis* 391–2:

swa he us ne mæg ænige synne gestælan,
þæt we him on þam lande lað gefremedon,   he hæfð us
þeah þæs leohtes bescyrede.

The OE usage evidently developed out of the combination of *swa* with *þeah* in the sense 'nevertheless' (originally proper only to *þeah*), which was then transferred to the *swa* in the subordinate clause. This is an example of the phenomenon which in the past was opaquely termed 'concretion of meaning'; it illustrates a category of semantic changes that Meillet classified as being due to purely linguistic factors (as in F *pas*, *personne*, *rien* in negation).[38]

342. *Birkabeyn*: a wisp of historical fact (of a sort). There is just one early Scandinavian king who, according to the Englishman Roger of Hoveden, was known by this name, since he called him by it at least five times in his Latin *Chronica*[39] (dealing with events up to 1201): *Swerus Birkebain*, i.e. Sverri King of Norway 1184–1202. This nickname, meaning 'Birch-bark-shanks', was evidently transferred to him from the followers who helped him fight his way to the kingship, and who, when they first emerged as a small fighting group and had to keep to the wilds, became so tatterdemalion that they made do with birch-bark for leggings, and were accordingly called *Birkibeinar* by the farmers.[40]

No one need be shocked that, in what clearly were not merely popular but (at some stage) oral English traditions, the nickname of a Norwegian king should have come to be used of a Danish one. From *Orkneyinga Saga* (chs. 59–60) we learn that in an episode between 1115 and 1127, Grimsby was being visited by Norwegians (among others); and that they included a future king of Norway in Harold Gilli (1130–6).

Kali, who later became Earl Rognvald Kali and ruled the Orkneys (1136–58), and was an accomplished poet, attests a visit to Grimsby (and what apparently made the greatest impression on him) in an occasional stanza composed soon afterwards on his return to Norway: 'We moved about for five weeks in appalling mud; when we were in the middle of Grimsby there was no lack of mud' (op. cit., ch. 60); see E. A. Kock, *Den norsk-isländska Skaldediktningen* (Lund, 1946–9), i, p. 235, st. 2, and A. B. Taylor's translation in *The Orkneyinga Saga* (Edinburgh, 1938), p. 226. An important piece of evidence for a Norwegian presence in Grimsby is the writ, of the reign of Henry II (1154–89),

---

[38] *Linguistique historique et linguistique générale*, vol. i (Paris, 1948), 239–40, in 'Comment les mots changent de sens', 230–71.

[39] Ed. W. Stubbs (RS 51, 1868–71), ii. 212 (s.a. 1180), 290 (1184); iii. 271 (1194); iv. 25, 162 (1197 and 1201).

[40] *Magnús Saga Erlingssonar*, ch. 36, in *Heimskringla*, ed. Finnur Jónsson (Copenhagen, 1911), p. 637.

addressed to Norwegians who came to Grimsby and to others of the king's ports in Lincolnshire.[41] And, as an instance of how Englishmen might know of Sverri's affairs, there is the fact that King John sent a force of 100 fighting men to Sverri's aid in 1201.[42]

347. *on-ride*: shown to be a separable compound by the OE nouns *onrad* '(the action of) riding on horseback' and *onrid* 'a mount', which are supported by MDu. *aen-rijden* 'ride forward (with an aim in view)'.

The extended form *onne* of the MS is hypermetrical in *on-ride* here, though it is metrically required in the other separable compounds *on-leyen* in 1690 and 1941 (see 1676 n.), *onne-sat* 1676, and *onne-haue* 1146 (see n.). It is hypermetrical in 2106 (*onne leues*), unless *alle* is a corruption of *al* (which would be an admissible form with the collective noun *folk* if the latter were treated as a singular). There is no OE or Gmc evidence for a separable compound *on-leue*. Moreover, *onne leues* occurs here in an adjectival clause, and *onne* might therefore be analysed as a preposition governing the relative *þat* (like *on* in *on singes* 391, where the relative may have been 'understood').

355. Lines 355ᵃ and 355ᵇ of the Cambridge MS: (*a*) produce an ungainly repetition in l. 356, (*b*) sound like a variation of the expression used in the parallel case of Aþelwold (144–5), and (*c*) are not represented in the Laud MS; and they are almost certainly spurious. Ll. 544ᵃ⁻ᵏ (likewise not in Laud) are in general textually unconvincing, since e.g. the construction in 544ᵃ⁻ᵇ turns on the reading *þout* 'intended' (544) for *þe* of Laud, and makes the wholly ortho-dox periphrastic invocation of Christ (for which cf. 331–2 and n.) into a plain statement. They too are thus unlikely to be by the author.

The reference to coming events in the story, in the second passage, is standard practice in OF *chansons de geste* and their AN congeners (both of which were models from which the author of *Hav.* learnt his style). It has not so far been explained just how, in such cases, a minstrel would have been able to embody as long a passage as this in an already written copy of the text; but a scribe might easily have done so. On the process of transmission of such works see M. de Riquer, *Les Chansons de geste françaises* (trans. I. Cluzel, Paris, 1957), pp. 297–321.

360–1. The rhymes *boþe : rede* here and 2585–6, and *rede : beþe* 694–5 and *beþe : rede* 1681–2, are all corrupt, by substitution of the native *red* n. and *rede* v. for ON *ráð* and *ráða* respectively. The ON n. and v. are preserved in correct forms of this very rhyme in 75 and 2543, and in 2818 respectively (apart from the ambiguous 1336, in which the adverb 'quickly' < OE *hraþe* is equally possible, and indeed more probable, in view of the reference to 'delay' in 1338).

The author's form of the corrupt rhymes is not altogether assured, since he rhymes the reflex of OE /a:/ both on /a:/ and on /ɔ:/, and since these three are rhymes *inter se* and would accordingly admit equally of *baþe : raþe* or *boþe : roþe*. The unambiguous *soth : oth* 2009–10 is the one notable instance in which the non-Nth. long slack *o* is required. But the non-rounded Nth.-type form is

[41] W. de G. Birch, *The Royal Charters of the City of Lincoln* (Cambridge, 1911), p. 18.

[42] *Sverris Saga* (ed. G. Indrebø, Kristiania, 1920), ch. 174.

called for in the rhymes *baþe*: *raþe* adv. (OE *hrǽþe*) 2596 and 2937, *ouer-ga* : *stra* n. 314–15, and *anan* : *Iohan* 176–7, 1112–13, 2563–4.

388. *But þat*: the sense 'provided that' is relatively common in the OF literal equivalent *mes que*, as in *Yvain* 4863–4:

> . . . Qu'ele cuide, que ele truisse
> Ostel, *mes que* venir i puisse,

and *Erec* 3294–5.

The synonymous use of *but þat*, however, is not recorded in *OED* or *MED*, and must therefore be presumed to be rare. At least one other example is available, in *Ywain and Gawain* 1500–2. Moreover, the expression *but on þat* 'provided only that' in *Hav.* 505 and 963 looks like a reinforced and therefore derivative form of it. This in turn recurs in *Dame Sirith* 38:

> '*Bote on þat* þou me nout bimelde . . .
> Min hernde will I to þe bede'.

Since no OE equivalent of either is recorded, both ME usages are probably calques on the OF type.

393. *hire kin*: a dative, since *queme* in this context is an unambiguously impersonal use.

403–4. Cf. 331–2 and n., 542–4, and 1317 and n.

411. The line is hypermetrical. *Toþer* is the seat of the trouble; though rhymes on inflectional and derivational syllables are admissible in ME, the occurrence of two successive unstressed elements in *þĕ* and *tŏþér* is suspect.

414. The author's form of the corrupt rhyme is not assured; cf. 360–1 and n. Here either *wāre* (< ON *wáru* > *vǫru*), or *wōre* by rounding of *ā* < OE *ā* as in native words in other than Nth. varieties of ME, is possible.

420. *cloþede . . . ne fedde*: the single negative, placed before the second of two co-ordinate words, is normal ME usage. Cf. *speke ne fnaste* 549; and *Sir Degrevant* 1755: '*Mete ne drynk* shall do me gode', and *Dame Sirith* 136–7.

426–36. This remarkable anathema can be matched, within my knowledge, only in non-literary documents. A very brief example occurs in the forged charter of 656 in the Laud MS of the *Anglo-Saxon Chronicle*.[43]

The passage in *Hav.* undeniably resembles the prose type of 'The Great Sentence (of Cursing)' represented in John Mirk's *Instructions for Parish Priests*,[44] including the reference to Judas as the pattern of the traitor. Another version occurs in the penitential manual *Jacob's Well* i, pp. 13–14.[45] In these the curse is pronounced *on the authority of* God the Father, Son, and Holy Ghost, the Virgin, the angels and archangels, St John, the patriarchs and prophets etc., while in *Hav.* it is they who are invoked to pronounce the curse.

Hav. agrees, on this last point, with a Latin formula of excommunication of *c*. 900–1100, in which likewise the cursing itself is attributed to Christ, the patriarchs etc., and in which, moreover, as in *Hav.*, the cross utters the curse:

[43] Ed. Earle and Plummer, *Two Saxon Chronicles Parallel*, i, p. 33, 4–6.
[44] Ed. G. Kristensson, Lund Studies in English, 49 (1974), pp. 106–7.
[45] Ed. A. Brandeis, EETS, os 115 (1900).

'Maledicat illum sancta crux, quam Christus pro nostra salute hostem trium-
phans ascendit . . .' (F. Liebermann, *Die Gesetze der Angelsachsen*, i, p. 439).

For a list and a discussion of the various ME prose versions of 'The Great
Sentence' (which is surprisingly not registered in *OED* even as a collocation),
see O. S. Pickering, 'Notes on the Sentence of Cursing in Middle English'
(Leeds Studies in English, NS 12 (1981), 229–44).

427. *May* might represent the OE 3 pres. pl. subj. *mægen*, since the metre in
Hav. abundantly demonstrates that both final -*n* and an -*e*- preceding it had
been extensively eliminated in the author's variety of ME. And though a disyllabic *alle* is here hypermetrical (since it produces two unstressed elements
between the full stresses on *Of* and *eure*), *al* is shown to be possible as a plural
form by the obj. pl. *al þe wepne* 2360, and by line 958, where the nom. pl. *Alle*
would if disyllabic, be similarly hypermetrical.

The line is thus grammatically ambiguous, since *al* and *may* can equally
well be singular forms (i.e. with *al* as the pronoun 'everyone', which occurs as
an obj. sg.—established by the sg. *woneth*—in 104). The almost identical line
435 is likewise ambiguous: see note.

435. This can be scanned with either disyllabic (and presumably plural)
alle or monosyllabic (unstressed) *al*, which might be either sg. or pl. *Kunne*
is likewise ambiguous, as representing OE pr. subj. sg. *cunne* or pl. *cunnen*
or the pr. indic. pl. *cunnon*. The contrast with Christ is perhaps more
pointed if 'all men' are in question, rather than 'every man'; and *al man* as a
way of saying 'every man' is much less likely in *Hav.* than *ilk man* or *euerilk
man*.

444. *felony*: all three examples of this word in *Hav.* are accompanied by
treson and trecherye to designate a single act. Here the word refers to Godard's
plan to murder all three of Birkabeyn's children, in order to seize the kingdom
for himself and his own children (513–16); in 1091, to Godrich's action in
marrying Aþelwold's heir to someone far beneath her (as he believed), for the
same purpose (1074–6); and in 2990, to both these in conjunction. In both
cases a vassal has broken a solemn oath to the king.

These contexts show that *felony* is here being used as a technical term in the
special vocabulary of feudal law, in the sense 'breach of the feudal bond', and
specifically (in *Hav.*) 'act of disloyalty to or betrayal of one's feudal lord'. This
was regarded as 'the most heinous of all crimes',[46] and was punished by death
and by the 'escheat' of the transgressor's lands and goods to the king (so that
his heirs were excluded). Both penalties were exacted from both the traitors in
Hav. (2514–15; 2836–8).

The Lat. equivalent *felonia* occurs four times in the *Leges Henrici Primi*,[47]
'the high-water-mark of English vassalism',[48] put together *c.* 1116–18 as a body
of laws current in the time of Henry I, by a justice of the King's Court.[49] In the

[46] F. W. Maitland, *The Constitutional History of England*, p. 110.
[47] Ed. L. J. Downer, chs. 43. 7; 46. 3; 53. 4; 88. 14. See pp. 11–12 for the editor's convincing explanation of an apparent inconsistency as between 43. 7 and 13. 12.
[48] Pollock and Maitland, i. 300.
[49] *English Feudalism*, p. 218.

sequence *felonia uel fide mentita* of ch. 53. 4, if *uel* is interpreted as linking two equivalents, *felonia* amounts to 'breach of the oath of fealty'.

This use has not been clearly identified in *OED* or *MED* (which have not registered the instances in *Hav.*). Nor is it attested in the dictionaries of OF, though a virtually certain example occurs in the *Chanson de Roland* [3829–]3833 (where the gravamen of the accusation in *fel* 3829 and 3833, *felonie* 3833 is that Gamelon had broken his oath of fealty to the king). *Felony* in *Hav.* may thus well be a direct adoption of the Latin legal term.

545–55. Since this *locus desperatus* is almost beyond repair, it is here printed almost as it stands. The difficulties, and the conclusions they suggest, are as follows:

1. Since the subject and the verb of the main clause (in which *a keuel of clutes* is necessarily the object) are missing, something mut have dropped out after l. 546.
2. C indicates that only one line has been lost from L. And since this line in C contains the missing verb and subject, and is moreover corroborated by l. 639 in L (where the passage is paraphrased), it has been adopted in our text.
3. But this leaves the L version with three lines, instead of two or four, rhyming on *-aste*. *Fnaste* is probably to be preferred to C's *grede*, since it is a much less common word and therefore the *lectio difficilior*, and since it is more specifically appropriate in the context, and is echoed in 641. And to adopt *grede* would merely shift the break in the couplet system down to 552.
4. MS *hepede* or *he pede* (not *he yede*, as Skeat–Sisam) is hardly interpretable other than as a form of the verb *ēpen* (OE *æðan* 'to conjure on oath; to exhort'), spelt with the inorganic *h-* before initial vowels that is common in *Hav.* (e.g. *helde* 128, 174, 387; *hende* 247; *heten* 317; *heuere* 88).

    In the sentence as it stands, a past participle is required; and the final *-e* of *hepede* (if this word is one) is presumably an error. But a rhyme on the unstressed ending of the past participle would be unparalleled in *Hav.*
5. *Hwan* 552 is not idiomatically convincing, and is likely to be corrupt, by repetition from a point in the preceding line immediately above it.
6. The missing verb in 553 may have rhymed on *-ede*, and may have been *lede* (as in the Skeat–Sisam emendation). But a scribe might have had a stronger urge to omit it if it was a word that did not rhyme on *-ede*.

C 544 a–k. These lines (not represented in L) are unlikely to be authentic; see 355 n.

578. *don on*: as usual, ME unseparated forms (in contrast to separated ones) are extremely rare: but one is available in *Confessio Amantis* ii. 2283:

> And broghte hire werk aboute so
> That Hercules this scherte *on-dede*.

But, apart from the evidence of MDu. *aendoen* 'put on (clothes etc.)', an OE separable compound is clearly attested, in the requisite sense, in the

11th-century interlinear gloss on Defensor's *Liber Scintillarum* 83, l. 6 (used figuratively):

se þe gemænsumað mid ofermodigum he *ondeð* [rendering *induet*] ofermodignysse,[50]

and the interlinear gloss on the *De Consuetudine Monachorum* l. 390:

þam adrogenum, gan gebroþru to unscrydende daegþerne scos 7 *on-don* [rendering *induantque*] nihtlice.[51]

There is likewise the cognate OE noun *ondoung* 'injection', in *Læceboc*, p. 78, l. 19:

mid smeþre *ondounge* wyrtdrences þurh horn oððe pipan sio wamb biþ to clænsianne.[52]

604. The existence of OE *oftyrfan* and *oftorfian*, both of which mean 'to pelt with stones' (originally 'with turves') shows that *tirueden of* is virtually certain to be a separable compound deriving in form from the first of these, though it must mean something like 'to peel off' (as in 919). The semantic gap is easily bridged: as the uses of the related noun show (*OED turf* sb.), a 'turf' was pared (i.e. 'stripped') from the surface of the soil. The cognate ON noun *torfa* is recorded in the sense 'scalp (i.e. with hair on it)' as well as 'turf'; and the same conjunction of senses (a 'semantic pattern') occurs in *sward* and its Gmc cognates, and is therefore evidently a natural one. The examples in *Sir Gawain and the Green Knight* 1921, *Purity* 630, and *The Wars of Alexander* 4114 of the verb registered in *OED* as the simplex *tirve* 'to strip off' etc. (of clothes and skin), which in all three is used with the adv. *of* 'off', may well be separated forms of a compound *of-tiruen*. See 919 n.

605. *kynemerk*: cf. 1263–4, 1268–9 and n., 2140–4, and Introduction III, 7. Since there is only one other recorded example of the word (see *MED kinemerk*), it is worth noting that a mild and natural corruption of it occurs in *Emaré* 503–4:

> ... A fayr chyld borne and a godele
> Hadde a dowbylle *kyngus marke*.

The nature of the *kyngus marke* is not specified in *Emaré*; but, as in *Hav.*, it is meant to attest royal birth.[53]

636. *Hwat ... wat*: common in this form, e.g. *St. Thomas à Becket* 337: '*Wat* for loue, *wat* for eiʒe . non him ne wiþsede' (ed. D'Evelyn and Mill, *The South English Legendary*, Text II (EETS, os 236, 1956), 610 ff.) and (with a following clause) *Richard Cœur de Lion* 7025–7. But the idiom is also quite common in the form that has survived today, e.g. *Arthour and Merlin* 8873–5: '*What* wiþ wristling, *wat* wiþ togging. . . .' There is an OF equivalent with the synonymous *que* ...*que*, as in *Erec* 1861, 6181, *Yvain* 6222–3.

---

[50] Ed. E. W. Rhodes (EETS, os, 93, 1889).
[51] Ed. W. S. Logemann, *Anglia*, 13 (1891), 365–454.
[52] Ed. G. Leonhardi (Bibliothek der angelsächsischen Prosa, 6; Hamburg, 1905).
[53] See E. Rickert, *The Romance of Emaré* (EETS, es 99, 1906), 504 n.

649. The only early parallels known to me are approximate ones: 'But ther our Lord woll helpe, ne dar no man doute' (*Firumbras* 1171) and 'Bien est eidiez cui Deus velt eidier' (J. Morawski, *Proverbes français antérieurs au XV* *siècle* no. 251). But the words *wile*, *woll*, and *velt* 'is willing to' clinch the correspondence. And since the OF version is attested in a MS of the end of the 13th century (Morawski, p. iii), the ME one is probably an adoption of it; for a clearer case, see 2462 n. The form of proverb after 1400 varies likewise.[54]

677. *chartre*: since few charters of manumission have survived from this period,[55] a literary reference to one is noteworthy: indeed, no other such reference is recorded. A charter was not the only means by which a serf might become a free man (purchase was another);[56] but it was the most secure. Purchase and a charter are combined in an example that concerns a villein (*nativus*) enfranchised by Emma of Dumard between 1186 and 1216.[57] It begins:

> Sciant omnes, tam praesentes quam futuri, quod ego Emma de Dumard . . . liberavi Willelmus nativum meum. . . . Et pro hac libertate & confirmatione, dedit mihi pro illo Ricardus filius Hugonis quindecim solidos argenti.[58]

695. Skeat's emendation of *on liue* to the adverbial genitive sg. *liues* is attractive, since it removes the hypermetrical unstressed element, and since the substitution of either of two equivalent expressions for the other is a very common type of scribal corruption. Cf. 1004 n.

719. *leyn in an ore*: a nautical term. The only other example of *leyn in* in a comparable context is in the remarkable description in *Patience*, 101 ff., of the procedure of a ship's crew putting out to sea:

> Then he tron on þe tres, and þay her tramme ruchen,
> Cachen vp þe crossayl; cables þay fasten,
> Wiȝt at þe wyndas weȝen her ankres,
> Sprude spak to þe sprete þe spare bawe-lyne,
>
> Gederen to þe gyde-ropes–þe grete cloþ falles.
> þay *layden in* on laddeborde, and þe lofe wynnes.
> þe blyþe breþe at her bak þe bosum he fyndes.

Happily, the cognate ON verb *leggja inn* is recorded as a nautical idiom meaning 'to set a course': *Hœnsa-þóris Saga* (ed. W. Baetke, Halle, 1953), p. 34, ll. 17–19:

> þat var eitt sumar, at skip kom af hafi í Borgarfjorð; ok lǫgðu þeir eigi *inn* í ósinn, en lǫgðu útarliga á hǫfnina.

---

[54] See M. P. Tilley, *A Dictionary of the Proverbs in England in the Sixteenth and Seventeenth Centuries* (Ann Arbor, 1950), G 263.

[55] For pre-Conquest examples see N. R. Ker, *Catalogue of Manuscripts containing Anglo-Saxon*, Index I, s.v. *Records*, *passim*.

[56] See Pollock and Maitland, i. 427–30: A. L. Poole, *Obligations of Society in the XII and XIII Centuries* (Ford Lectures, 1944), pp. 12–34, and especially pp. 28 ff.

[57] See Poole, op. cit., p. 31, for the evidence for this date, and for a translation, p. 32.

[58] Full text in T. Madox, *Formulare Anglicanum* (1702), p. 417, no. DCCLIV, whose next examples are one of the second year of Richard II and then two others of the time of Henry V and Henry VIII.

'It happened one summer that a ship put into Borgarfjorð; and they did not set
their course for the estuary, but for a point further out in the harbour.'

In this idiom the word *skip* is understood as the object of *leggja inn*, as appears
from *Njáls Saga* 155. 20 (ed. Einar Ól. Sveinsson, *Íslenzk Fornrit*, xii, 1954):

hann *lagði* skip sín *inn* á sundit ('he set his course for the fjord').

In the latter passage the ON verb is followed by the preposition *á*, just as the
ME one is followed by the cognate *on*; both are by origin separable compounds (the ME one being adopted from ON).

Up till the 14th century English, Scandinavian, and French ships were
steered with a quarter-rudder (i.e. one fixed at the right side, and not the
stern). And since this rudder was an oar, the word *ore* here in *Hav.* must be <
OE *ár* 'oar' and must mean 'starboard' (which, as the OE antecedent *stēorbord*
'steering side of the ship, rudder-side' shows, designated the quarter on which
the rudder was fixed). This interpretation has the advantage of making the
whole phrase a counterpart to that in *Patience*, which means 'set a course to
larboard (port)' and in fact clinches the meaning of *on ore* as 'to starboard'.

722–4. This construction is essentially of the type represented in 767–9 (see
n. ad loc.). The negative in 724 is thus idiomatically orthodox. Line 723, with
its unusual subjunctive (*were*) apparently means 'nor would it have been more
than [lit. 'other than'] a single hour'. The negative in 723 makes that line the
formal antecedent of 724, as is shown by the parallel of l. 80 (with its subjunctive *were*) as the antecedent of 81–2.

The rhyme *mile* : *hwile* is a stock one. The sequence in 723 consisting of a
negative + the verb 'to be' + the prep. *but* is a set syntactic pattern in ME (and
one comparable with the use of L *non nisi*, lit. 'not except', i.e. 'only'), as in
Laȝamon's *Brut* 828*a*: 'Nes hit *buten* litel wile', and *Guy of Warwick* (15th-
century version) 6513–14, which is closely echoed in *Syr Tryamowre* (ed. A. J.
Erdmann Schmidt, Utrecht, 1937), 1324–5:

> He had not redyn but a whyle,
> Not þe mowntans of a myle.

And since the sense 'only' in *but(en)* < OE *butan* '(without), except, other than'
could have developed only by reduction of its use with a preceding negative
(as in *noht bute, neuere bute*), the type illustrated above is necessarily the origin
of the variant without a negative, as in *Guy of Warwick* 2411–12 (repeated in
2809–10):

> They had redyn but a whyle,
> Vnnethe the mowntaunce of a myle.

The lines following each of these passages in *Guy of Warwick* and *Syr Tryamowre* happen to be main clauses, and are thus of no further help in the eluci-
dation of *Hav.* 724. But it is clear that *Hav.* 722–3 contain both the secondary
and the primary type respectively, in successive lines. The example in the *Brut*
is followed by a subordinate clause, introduced by *þat*, which (unlike *Hav.*
724) is not in negative form (828 b–829):

þat Goffar king com him liðen
Mid vnimete ferde   of Frenchisce folke.

731. *þrie* is in form open to only one interpretation—as an adverbial use of 'three', viz. 'thrice'; in the context, however, this is wholly obscure, since Havelok 'got possession of' (*gat*) England only once. But Holthausen's emendation *yete* (adopted by Skeat–Sisam) is palaeographically too remote from *þrie* to be satisfactory.

744–5. A suggestively similar form of words, including the same rhyme, is used by Mannyng in his *Chronicle* (4117–18) about King Lud of Britain:

> Byside his gate þey hym leyd,
> þat, for his name, Ludgate ys seyd:
> He yt made, and he yt aughte,
> Lodgate for hym þe name laughte.

754–60. Eighteen kinds of fish are mentioned here and in ll. 772, 833, 897–8. With the exception of *tumberel* and *schulle*, they are also named in early works dealing with household cuisine, e.g. *The Boke of Nurture*[59] of John Russell, the usher and marshal of Duke Humphrey of Gloucester, who names more than fifty; and Grim's catches, which were sold, were evidently for the table.

The idea of naming the fish taken by Grim may have been suggested by the brief list of six in Gaimar:

> Turbuz [e] salmuns e mulvels,
> Graspeis, porpeis, e makerels.   (443–4)

But *Hav.* does not mention mulwells or grampuses. It would be tempting to think that the author got the rest in his list from a book of household cuisine, or from a list of names of fish such as those cited by Le Grand d'Aussy in *Histoire de la vie privée des François*, ii. 70 and 80.[60] And this might account for the reference to *þe grete laumprei* 772 and 898, and the implicit distinction between this and the *lampron* or small (i.e. young) lamprey (see *OED lampern* and 772 n. below).

But first-hand observation of real life at Lincoln cannot be ruled out, since the author of *Hav.* has alluded to *þe brigge* (876 and 882) as the place where the earl's cook bought fish and meat, i.e. as a market. Thomas Sympson, writing in 1737,[61] speaks of *the fish market* 'between the Stonebow and the High Bridge' as being well furnished with sea fish on Wednesdays and freshwater fish on Fridays, the former being brought chiefly from the Yorkshire coasts, the latter taken from the Witham, 'which affords plenty of pike, carp, tench, eels, barbotts etc.'

That the author of *Hav.* regarded all the fish he named as edible appears

[59] Ed. F. J. Furnivall, *Manners and Meals in Olden Time* (EETS, os 32, 1868), pp. 117–226.
[60] Ed. J. B. B. de Roquefort (Paris, 1815).
[61] *Adversaria*, in Bodl. MS Gough Linc. I, p. 305.

from the comments (with reservations) of Moufet (writing *c.* 1604) on the more
unlikely ones:

> *Porpesses* . . . an unsavoury meat . . . yet many Ladies and Gentlemen love it
> exceedingly (p. 165). *Seales* flesh is counted as hard of digestion . . . where-
> fore I leave it to Mariners (p. 167). *Whales* flesh is the hardest of all other . . .
> yet the livers of Whales, Sturgiuns, and Dolphins . . . taste most pleasantly
> being salted (p. 173). (*Healths Improvement*, ed. C. Bennet, London, 1655.)

754. *sturgiun*: the jurist Bracton reports, regarding the privileges of the
Crown, that large fish such as the sturgeon and the whale, and other things
without an owner, belong to the king; and that the whole of the sturgeon is the
king's, but where the whale is concerned, it is enough (some say) for the king
to have the head, and the queen the tail.[62] But the king sometimes granted the
right to take these 'reserved' fish.[63]

qual: usually interpreted as 'whale' OE *hwæl*, with *qu* for /kw/ < OE /χw/,
as in *qui* 1651. The sturgeon and the whale do tend to be contextually associated. But *hwel* in 756 (see n.) seems likely to mean 'whale'; and, in a list of
fish, the author would not have repeated himself within two lines.

Qual is therefore best referred to a small group of words formed on the Gmc
base **kwel-* (IE **g^{u}el*) 'swell', such as G *Qualle*, Du. *kwal* 'jellyfish', and
shown to be old by the verb fossilized in the p.p. as OE *collen(ferhð)* 'great (in
courage)' and represented in OHG *quellan* 'swell'.[64] It may be interpreted as
the name for some kind of fish, so called after its bulbous or slimy appearance,
and evidently edible—perhaps 'basket-fish', 'starfish'. The dearth of recorded
examples is as typical of the early names of fish as is the tendency to coin
descriptive ones: see those in 758–60, where four out of seven are descriptive
(*tumberel*, *butte*, *schulle*, *þornbake*, along with *lenge* 833, *segges* 897), and some
are *hapax legomena* in English or first recorded in *Hav.* (*tumberel* and *schulle*,
and *keling*, *butte*, *lenge* respectively).

756. *hwel*: cannot represent OE *hwæl*, since the reflex of OE /æ/ is always
rhymed on /a/ in *Hav.* A form in /e/ is attested in OHG *wels* (< **hwalis*)
'whale', the cognate OE form of which would be **hwele*, and which may be
represented in *hwel* here.

758. *keling*: another name for the 'common cod' (W. Yarrell, *A History of
British Fishes* (London, 1836), ii. 143).

tumberel, as a *hapax legomenon* without a precise equivalent in any language,
may well be a nonce-formation by the author of *Hav.* The analogy of the rare
name *tumbler* for 'porpoise' (recorded 1671 and 1808–12, *OED* sb.³) shows that
tumberel likewise probably means 'porpoise' and is formed either on LOE
tumbian 'tumble; dance' or OF *tomber* 'fall', with a suffix loosely adopted
specifically from the fish-name *makerel* (since this is used in this passage) and
contained also in *pickerel* 'a young pike' (recorded 1338).

[62] *De Legibus et Consuetudinibus Angliae*, fo. 120: *De Corona* ch. 3. 5; Woodbine &
Thorne, ed. cit. ii, pp. 739–40.

[63] A. L. Poole, *From Domesday Book to Magna Carta*, p. 92.

[64] See the lucid etymological analysis of Franck–van Wijk, *EWNT* s.v. *kwalster*.

The origin and history of the suffixes in these words cannot be fully traced, since *makerel*, which is the earliest (recorded in L form as *macarellus* 13th c.) is of unknown etymology. But the two originally distinct elements are *-el*, ultimately L *-ellus* and *-ella* (which were greatly extended in use in the Romance languages, partly replacing *-ulus*, *-ula*), OF *-el* and *-elle*, and (by metanalysis of an /r/ ending the stem in some words, e.g. *lamprel* 'a young lamprey' 1526) *-rel*.[65]

760.   *butte*: equated by Yarrell, op. cit., ii. 216 with the 'Flook, or Flounder'. According to Moufet,[66] it is a name for the turbot 'whilst . . . young'. Along with MDu. *but(te)*, *bot(te)* and MLG *but* 'a fish', it can be referred to the Gmc base in MDu. *bot* adj. 'blunt, stumpy; snubnosed'.[67] It is probably an adoption of the MDu. word: so also J. F. Bense, invoking the fact that Dutch and Flemish fishermen put in at east coast ports in this period to sell their fish.[68]

schulle: a *hapax legomenon* in English, and one of the only two fish-names in *Hav.* that do not occur in the long series named in *The Boke of Nurture* (see 754–60 n.). Along with MDu. *scolle*, *sculle* and MLG *scholle*, *schulle* 'a fish', it is related to MDu. *scolle* 'clod' and cognates.[69] It is probably an adoption of the MDu. word, which is first recorded in 1316 and, like *butte*, might have been picked up from Dutch or Flemish fishermen (so also Bense, *A Dictionary* s.v. *schulle*).

765–6. It is not certain whether *to-yede* is tr. or intr. (i.e. in absolute use): if the former, 766 is an adjectival clause, but if the latter, it is a consecutive clause of the type discussed in 767–9 n. The use of *Forbar* in 765 suggests identity with the special group of examples there defined as having in the main clause a verb that implies non-fulfilment of an action; and in that case 766 is a consecutive clause.

A separable compound *to-gon* meaning 'approach', and an OE *to-gan* (*to-gangan*) 'id.', are recognized only by *OED*, s.v. *to* prep., conj., adv. D i: 'Often the separable particle of a compound verb', which may be taken to apply to its example from *The Homilies of Ælfric* (ed. B. Thorpe), ii. 182: *Gang to and arær hine*. But the existence of this verb is unmistakably implied by the OE noun *to-gang* 'approach', and by MDu. *toegang* n. and *toegaen*, *toegangen* v. 'id.'. OE *to-gan*, *to-gangan* 'disperse, etc.' are different words, with a separate prefix < IE *tis-* (L *dis-*), as is clearly shown by MDu. *te-gaen* in the same senses.

767–9. This construction, with a negative main clause, followed by a subordinate clause which is introduced by *þat* and contains a negative, is in *Hav.* a common and important one. It corresponds to the Latin use of *quin*, which is a compound of the relative (in the ablative case) and the negative *ne* (lit. 'that . . . not'), and which follows a negative main clause. The *þat* clause here is of

---

[65] See *OED -el* suff. and *-rel*; *cockerel* (*c.* 1440), which is probably a formation in AN or ME; *pickerel*; Furnivall, op. cit., pp. 215–16, n. on l. 630 of *The Boke of Nurture*.

[66] Ed. C. Bennet, *Healths Improvement* (1655), p. 173.

[67] See Franck–van Wijk, *EWNT* I *Bot*.

[68] *A Dictionary of the Low-Dutch Element in the English Vocabulary* (The Hague, 1939) s.v. *butt*; *Anglo-Dutch Relations from the Earliest Times to the Death of William the Third* (the Hague, 1925), pp. 52, 54–7, 96, 142.   [69] See Franck–van Wijk, *EWNT* s.v. II *schol*.

the 'consecutive' type: *þat* means 'so that'. When the preceding main clause contains a noun as part of the predicate, *þat* in the subordinate clause means 'such that', as in 79–82, 98–101, 1020–2, 2264–5, 2286–9, 2686–8, 2803–5.

Some of the examples in *Hav.* are in a particular category, in which the sense of the verb in the main clause implies non-fulfilment of an action: 'forget' 249–51; 'resist' 2272–3; 'spare, exempt' 765–6, 1996–8; 'omit, neglect (to), leave off' 2501–4, 2779–81. What sets the consecutive force of the subordinate clause beyond doubt is the presence of an expressed subject (e.g. *he* 768). But the subject is sometimes merely implicit (i.e. in the verb-form), as in 1997 and 2503. Lines 722–4 do not diverge from the essential pattern; for this example, and the ambiguous 765–6, see notes ad loc. For a rare variant without a negative in the subordinate clause, see 2699 and n.

The type of construction illustrated above is common in OF, e.g. *Yvain* 1760–1:

> 'Va!' fet ele, 'puez tu noiier,
> *Que* par toi *ne* soit morz mes sire?

The negation occurs there not merely in consecutive clauses (such as the ME ones above), including those that follow negative main clauses containing the sort of verbs specified above, but in clauses of comparison and in temporal clauses.[70] In consecutive clauses after a negative main clause, the negation in ME and OF, so far from being illogical or 'pleonastic' (as Einenkel has called this example in *Hav.* 724, *Historische Syntax*, §22ζ), is in fact called for.

772. *þe grete laumprei* becomes intelligible in the light of Moufet's distinction (1655 edn.), pp. 181–3: 'The little ones called Lamprons ... the great ones called Lampreys'.[71]

780. *(simenels) with þe horn*: this (the sole recorded example of this description of *simenels*) presumably refers to some sort of projecting piece of the latter.

785. *se-weres*: the MS *se werē* is due to a scribe's unfamiliarity with the rare compound *se-weres*, which is adopted in the text here on the evidence of the LOE *hapax legomenon sæ-wære*, in which the second element is *were* 'enclosure for catching fish'. The latter is often attested in association with nets (as in 784 here) from the 13th century onwards. See J. Strachey, J. Pridden, and E. Upham, *Index to the Rolls of Parliament* (1832) s.v. *wears*; R. W. Chambers and M. Daunt, *A Book of London English, 1384–1425*, p. 257, note on l. 326; *OED weir-net* s.v. *weir*.

setes: 'placed them'. The form *-(e)s* is (*a*) first recorded in ME, *c*.1200, (*b*) restricted to SE and EMidl. texts,[72] apart from Robert of Gloucester's *Chronicle*, and (*c*) occurs only in works with a conservative pronoun system as a fem. accusative singular. Its striking peculiarities are the restricted distribu-

[70] See T. B. W. Reid, *Yvain* 80 n., 3605 n., 3700 n.; A. Tobler, *Vermischte Beiträge zur französischen Grammatik*, iv (1908), pp. 26–64; E. Mätzner, *Englische Grammatik*, vol. iii (Berlin, 1885), p. 522.

[71] Furnivall, *Manners and Meals in Olden Time*, p. 157 n. 8.

[72] Respectively e.g. *Vices and Virtues*, *Kyng Alisaunder* and *Arthour and Merlin*, *Ayenbite of Inwyt*; and *The Bestiary* and *Genesis and Exodus*.

tion, and its use enclitically in forms analysable as reductions to -*s* beside another type, in independent position, that is spelt *es*, *is*, *his*, *hise*, *hes*.

Essentially the same phenomenon occurs in MDu.,[73] where the personal pronoun *se* (acc. sg. fem. and acc. pl. in all genders) is reduced to -*s* in enclitic use. In ME, when the -*s* had followed and coalesced with final -*e* (as in *setes*), new independent forms with an initial vowel were evolved. Hence the uncertainty in the quality of that vowel in the spellings *ys* and *as* in *Hav.* 1175.

The facts suggest, beyond reasonable doubt, that the two new pronouns were adopted from MDu.

786. *him... ledde*: a calque on OF *se mener* 'conduct oneself'.

791. *pouthe*: for *póuthe he*; cf. 10980, and *hauede* 861.

802. *on swink long*: 'in proportion to his work'; see C. T. Onions in *Philologica*, p. 160. The OE idiom *gelong æt* 'depending on, in accordance with' > ME *(i)long on*, *(i)long o*, whence (since the preposition *o* might be either < *on* or < *of*) the erroneous re-expanded *long of* in non-standard Mod. E., comparable with the Shakespearean *We are such stuff as dreams are made on* in *The Tempest*, IV. i. 156 for *... made of*.

815. *giueled*:

(*a*) is clearly akin in form and sense to *gavel* sb.[2] of *OED* 'a quantity of corn cut and ready to be made into sheaves' and the cognate *gavel* v. 'collect mown corn into heaps', both of which are recorded from *c.*1440 (in the EMidl. *Promptorium Parvulorum*), and survive in 19th-c. dialectal use in E. Anglia.

(*b*) these are adoptions of corresponding Nth OF words, *gavele*, *gavellee*, *gaveleis* 'a heap' and *gaveler* 'throw on the earth in heaps'—all in the 13th-c. OPicard *Doon de Maience*[74]—beside the equivalent non-Nth OF forms *javel(e)* and *javeler*, with /dž/ for the characteristic Picard and Norman /g/.[75]

(*c*) *giueled* is to be explained as an apophonic variant of OPicard *gaveler*, by the kind of process that operates in ideophonic words and that produced as *variae lectiones* the forms *peaðerep* in *Ancrene Wisse* (fo. 57va), the equivalent *paðerep* in the Nero MS of the *Ancrene Riwle* (p. 95, l. 16), and *piðerip* in Vernon (fo. 382ra), beside the etymologically regular *puðeres* of Titus (p. 69, l. 33).[76] Apophonic variants of this type are often nonce-words; and *giueled* (which is nowhere else to be found) was probably a coinage by the author of *Hav.* and never generally current. But it must have been formed on the verb-root *gauel*; and this, not being available in English, must have been the OF form.

The latter is in OF recorded solely with -*a*- in the first syllable (never -*e*- or -*i*-), which implies the phonetic development proper to unaccented GR /a/ after /g/—i.e. it was the second syllable of the verb that carried the accent.

[73] See J. Franck, *Mittelniederländische Grammatik* (2nd edn., Leipzig, 1910), pp. 177–80.

[74] Ed. M. A. Pey (Paris, 1859), in *Les Anciens Poètes de la France*.

[75] See C. T. Gossen, *Grammaire de l'ancien Picard* (Paris, 1970), pp. 100–2; von Wartburg, *FEW* s.v. **gabella*; Tobler–Lommatzsch s.v. *javeler, javelee, javeleiz, javele*.

[76] See pp. 88–91 of 'Some English Ideophones', *AL* 6 (1954), 73–111.

This would account for the very un-English stressing of the second syllable of *giueled* (in disregard of the fact that the apophonic *-i-* must be the root-syllable), that is prescribed by the metre:

> Wíth fish gĭuélĕd áls ă stác.

817. *(bi mine) mone*: since this rhymes here on the reflex of OE /aː/, it cannot (in *Hav.*) be interpreted, as by *MED* (*mone* n. 3), as ME *mŭne* 'memʘry; intention' < ON *mun-r*. In form and in the required sense 'opinion' *mone* would be congruent with an unrecorded OE *mān*, the root of *mǣnan* 'relate', *gemǣnan* 'mean; reflect' and cognate with OHG *meina*, OFris. *mene* 'opinion'. But *mōne* 'opinion' here is without parallel. It is therefore probably a blend of *mēne* v, 'believe, think' (*OED mean* v.¹) < OE *mǣnan*, with ME *wōn* (< ON *wān* > OIcel. *ván*), especially since the author of *Hav.* uses the latter in the syntactically and semantically identical phrase *bi mine wone* 'in my opinion' 1973.

821. *ferþinges*: makes the line hypermetrical at this point. The other three recorded examples of the collocation with *nok* (all ME, and two of them in the work of Robert Mannyng, who was a Lincolnshire man, like the author of *Hav.*) have *ferþyng*; and one occurs in a couplet that agrees almost verbatim with this one,[77] and that may therefore be an imitation of it (or vice versa). Thus the *-es* in *Hav.* may be corrupt.

Nok is first recorded *c.*1300, and is of unknown origin. In *The Legend of St Gregory*[78] (Vernon MS (V)) 909–10 the phrase, used of a ransom, seems to mean 'small piece':

> Heo swor he schulde ȝelden out
> Eueri peny and *ferþing nok*.[79]

Each of the other three MSS has its own variant version of l. 910. Since the Rawlinson (R) and the Cleopatra (C) MSS confirm l. 909, the quite different Auchinleck version of 909 and therefore 910 is corrupt; the R version of both is hypermetrical and therefore suspect; and in C, 910 is metrically defective (*Al þat he þer mys-toke*). Thus V may well have preserved the author's expression here. His English is of EMidl. type, with a vocabulary of a strong northerly cast (as displayed in some of the adoptions from ON).[80] *Ferþing(es) nok* was thus probably current only in a very limited area, namely Lincs.

822. To be scanned with *fórth*.

825–8. Cf. 840–3. This motivation for Havelok's departure for Lincoln—which is sufficiently explained in the *Lai* by Grim's wish that Havelok should there be able to make his way in the world (169–79)—is possibly an innovation in the ME version, though perhaps not on an imaginary basis. *The Chronicle of Bury St. Edmunds 1212–1301* (ed. A. Gransden, Nelson, 1964) attests two famines, in 1258 (p. 22) and 1294 (p. 123) respectively. In the first of these,

---

[77] *Handlyng Synne* 5810–11; the other is in Mannyng's *Chronicle* (ed. T. Hearne, 1810), 28.   [78] Ed. C. Keller, *Die mittelenglische Gregoriuslegende* (Heidelberg, 1914).
[79] See *OED nook* sb. 1*b*.
[80] Inter alia, OENse *bón* (as in *Hav.*) V 697 and C 531; 3. pr. sg. *goþ* V 620 (also C and A); unrounded /i(ː)/ for OE /y(ː)/; /oː/ for OE /aː/, beside /aː/, reflects a later stage, just as in *Hav.*

'countless' people died of hunger because an abundant corn crop had been ruined by autumn rain. In the second, there was a very severe famine and dearth (*fames et inopia*) throughout England, and in the following autumn an excessive rainfall ruined the grain.

It would have been in character for the author of *Hav.* to bring in this sort of event from real life. The second of the famines above is said to be nationwide, and is near enough to the probable limits within which *Hav.* was composed (1295–1310) to have been much the more topical. The great European famine of 1315–17 (for which see M. McKisack, *The Fourteenth Century* (Oxford, 1959), pp. 43, 49–50, and 329) is too late.

833. *lenge*: 'nothing but a long cod', Moufet (1655 edn.), pp. 154–5 (a comment that corroborates the etymological analysis of the word as a descriptive name formed on the base in the word *long*).

843. MS *uten*: OE *utan* (lit. 'from outside') is hardly in question because unsuitable in meaning; and the final -*n* in *uten* cannot be historically regular on any other terms. *Uten* is thus likely to be an adoption of either ON *úti* 'at an end' or MDu. *ute* 'used up'. In any case, the final -*n* is best taken as simply an error, of the large class of 200 odd listed under Editorial Procedure, in which -*en* is hypermetrical and corrupt—in this case, on the analogy (through rhyme-association) of pairs like *aboute / abouten*. See my 'The Scansion of *Hauelok* and the Use of ME -*en* and -*e* in *Hauelok* and by Chaucer', pp. 202–34.

864. Cf. *will of rede* 'at a loss what to do' in *Ywain and Gawain* 379 and *wil of wane*, ibid., 1643, 2115. The construction with *of* in *Hav.* 1043 is the distinctive point that establishes this type of expression as a calque on ON *vill-r* + genitive (of reference) 'all at sea with', lit. 'having lost one's way'. The word is restricted to texts with a strong Scandinavian element in the vocabulary i.e. mainly Northern and Northerly, and EMidl. ones.

866. *fastinde . . . yede*: this idiomatic use of *yede* is a calque on an OF and AN one of the synonymous *aler* 'to go' with a form of the main verb ending in -*ant*, as in the following example: 'La soe mort li *vait* molt *angoissant*' (*Chanson de Roland* 2232); see also *Le Roman de toute Chevalerie* 1729.

The OF -*ant* in this idiom is sometimes analysed as the present participle (L -*ant*-, -*ent*-), as by J. Bédier, *La Chanson de Roland (Commentaires)*, pp. 330–1. But it is shown to be by origin the gerund (L -*and*-, -*end*-)[81] by the following med. L example—in a poem of Venantius Fortunatus (*c.* 530–610)— of what is clearly the antecedent of the OF usage: 'Credas ut stellas *ire trahendo* comas' (*Opera Poetica*, ed. Leo, v. 5. 118). Similarly, in the tenth-century *Historia de Preliis* the Archipresbyter Leo uses not only L *ire* with the gerund: 'Hic Alexander nihil aliud optat facere, nisi *ire preliando* et *subiugando* sibi gentes' (3. 1), but a form of L *vadere*, which is the antecedent of the verb-forms used in many of the OF examples: 'Congregasti socios tuos et *vadis pugnando* et *dissipando* civitates' (1. 40; ed. F. Pfister, Heidelberg, 1913).

The idiomatic singularity of these usages[82] is that med. L *ire* and *vadere*, OF

---

[81] See G. and R. Le Bidois, *Syntaxe du français moderne* (Paris, 1935–8), §§788, 792–6.

[82] For examples from the other early Romance languages, see P. Aalto, *Untersuchungen über das lateinische Gerundium und Gerundivum* (Helsinki, 1949), pp. 75–6.

aler and *vait*, *vont*, etc., and ME *yede* all express the continuous and hence progressive nature of the action: Havelok 'was continuously without food'. In fact, all represent an important linguistic innovation, since they are a device to express 'aspect' in a verb (i.e. the nature, and not the tense, of an action), and specifically durative aspect.[83] In the colloquial Mod. E derivative of the idiom, as in 'Don't *go doing* anything rash!', *go* has developed a force that is sometimes 'ingressive'.

In terms of the above analysis, the present participle *fastinde* here has been substituted (whether by a scribe or by the author) for the gerund. This would sometimes have happened because in some varieties of ME both the present participle and the gerund ended in -*yng* (just as in OF they both ended in -*ant*). But it is also traceable in types of ME in which the present participle and the gerund were distinct; e.g. in the *Ayenbite of Inwyt*, in which they end respectively in -*inde* and -*ing(e)*, OF -*ant* in the common locution *en ton uiuant* has been misinterpreted as the ending of the present participle and translated *ine pine libbinde* (p. 73, l. 18).

For an entirely different view of our idiom, see T. Mustanoja, *A Middle English Syntax*, pp. 557–8, who treats the -*inde*, -*ynge* form in it as a present participle. But he does not mention the med. L usage; and for the OF equivalent he cites only G. Gougenheim, *Étude sur les périphrases verbales de la langue française* (Paris, 1929), pp. 2–36.

870. Perhaps some such line as *Alle þe laddes þat þer yede* is what is missing; cf. 886–91.

875. The lacuna must have mentioned *mete* or fish (cf. 882–4), in some such terms as *And seiȝ þe mete and fishes ok*.

876 and 882–3. See 754–60 n. above for the 18th-century fish market between the Stonebow and the High Bridge in Lincoln.

876. *þe brigge* (again 882, 939, 941) must have meant for the author a specific bridge, or he could not have spoken of it in such an apparently unspecific way. Moreover, a bridge is not a priori an appropriate place at which to buy supplies of fish, other food, and wood—unless by its position. An individual bridge is evidently in question; and there is little doubt that this was High Bridge, referred to as *pons magna* in 1146,[84] and as the *High bryg* of Lincoln in 1527.[85] Mr J. W. F. Hill unhesitatingly identifies the bridge in *Hav.* as being this one, and states (without citing evidence) that porters waited there in the 18th century to be hired.[86]

The key to this matter is that High Bridge stood (and stands now) on the river Witham, which flows down into the Wash, and which was a vital factor in the trade and the economic wealth that Lincoln enjoyed in the twelfth and thirteenth centuries.[87] Some of the fish bought by the earl's cook at *þe brigge*

---

[83] See E. Bourciez, *Éléments de linguistique romane* (Paris, 1930), §§246 (e) and 319 (c).

[84] C. W. Foster, *The Registrum Antiquissimum of the Cathedral Church of Lincoln*, vol. i (Lincoln Record Society, vol. xxvii, 1931), p. 200.

[85] C. W. Foster, *Lincoln Wills*, vol. ii (Lincoln Record Society, vol. x, 1918), p. 56.

[86] *Medieval Lincoln*, 176.

[87] See Hill, op. cit., ch. XV, and especially pp. 306 ff.

would have been deep-sea fish brought up the Witham, since this is what would have happened in real life. The other main waterway of crucial commercial importance to Lincoln was the canal known as the Fossdyke, which, according to Simeon of Durham,[88] was cut by Henry I, and on which see Hill, op. cit., 13–14, 306–7, 310–11.

It is a view under High Bridge that is shown in Peter de Wint's watercolour 'The Devil's Hole' (D5023/50 of the National Galleries of Scotland) reproduced in Figure 2. This view is no longer to be seen, since the opening under the bridge has been blocked and altered (as I am kindly informed by Mr T. Baker, of Lincoln).

For copious early examples of the name *High Bridge* after 1146, whether in Latin or English form, see K. Cameron, *The Place-Names of Lincolnshire* I (English Place-Name Society vol. LVIII, 1985), p. 26.

878. Since *þe brigge* (876 n.) and the *grene* (2829–30 n.) are pretty certainly taken straight from real life in Lincoln, *þe castel* (again 900, 1068), which is directly linked with *þe brigge*, must be the actual castle of Lincoln; and its master, at the time when *Hauelok* was composed, would have been the Earl, not of Cornwall, but of Lincoln.

For the history of Lincoln Castle, which goes back to a time soon after the Conquest, see J. W. F. Hill, *Medieval Lincoln*, 82 ff.

884–5. *þe herles mete . . . of Cornwalie*: 'the Earl of Cornwall's food'. In this variety of the common ME split genitive (with a prepositional adjunct containing *of*), *of* has replaced an inflected genitive in an OE antecedent type with a dependent genitive, as in *þæs . . . Mercna cyninges Pendan*.[89] See O. Jespersen, *Progress in Language* (1894), pp. 293–6; E. Ekwall, *Studies on the Genitive of Groups in English* (Lund, 1943), pp. 6–8, 68–9; T. Mustanoja, *A Middle English Syntax*, vol. i (1960), pp. 78–9.

bouth : *oft*: it is unnecessary to emend to *keft* (cf. 2006): *eft*, as was proposed by Kern (see *Anglia Beiblatt*, 35 (1924), 35), since any voiceless fricative may rhyme on any other in the system of assonances used in ME.

889. *dun-falle*: in this and other compound verbs in *d(o)un-* (see Glossary), the first element is < OE *adūne* < *of dūne*. *D(o)un* is thus a synthetic adverb (meaning lit. 'from the hill') of English and relatively late origin; and it has replaced, both in independent use and in separable verbs, the Gmc equivalent represented in OE *niðer*, ON *niðr*, G *nieder*, Du. *ne(d)er*.

A small series of OE separable verbs in *niðer-* is traceable in Bosworth–Toller s.v. *niþer* (though not there registered as such); and six are registered in the *Enlarged Addenda and Corrigenda* to it. The existence of a few more is implied by the nouns *niþer-gang*, *niþer-sige*, *niþer-stige*; and this is confirmed by the occurrence of *nyðer astah* in *Homilies of Ælfric* (ed. Pope) XII. 36 and 198, and *nyþer-stigaþ* in the *Salisbury Psalter*, ed. C. & K. Sisam, EETS, os 242 (1959) XXI. 30.

When such verbs are used in the separated form, the adverb follows the

[88] *Historia Regum*, vol. ii. 260, ed. T. Arnold, *Opera Omnia* (RS 75, 1882–5).
[89] Bede's *Ecclesiastical History of the English People*, iii. 18, ed. T. Miller, EETS, os 95 (1890), p. 234, l. 19.

verb; and the compound nature of the verb may be obscured or uncertain. But a sequence *He niðerasette þa mihtigan*, rendering *deposuit potentes* (*Lambeth Psalter*, Hymn 10, l. 6, ed. U. Lindelöf, *Der Lambeth-Psalter*, Acta Societatis Scientiarum Fennicae, 25 (Helsinki, 1909), p. 251) shows the verb to be a compound *niðer-asettan* (in which *a-* is an emphatic prefix). This is confirmed by the existence of OIcel. *setja niðr* (OIcel. separable verbs being by tradition always registered in dictionaries etc. under the separated form). The latter is used reflexively, just as ME *dun-set* in *Hav.* 2292 is; and *dun-set* clearly derives ultimately from an OE *niþer-(a)settan*.

In fact, OE *niþer-* and *adune-* even occur as equivalents in one and the same verb, in the following sentence of Ælfric's homily on the First Sunday in Lent (ed. H. Sweet, *Selected Homilies of Ælfric* (Oxford, 1922), p. 44, l. 92):

þæt wære swiþe gilplic dæd gif Crist *scute* þa *adun*, þeah þe he eaþe mihte butan awyrdnesse his lima *nyþer-asceotan*.

And Ælfric uses the unseparated form with *adun-* immediately afterwards, and thereby shows both to be separable verbs: 'þa nolde he *adun-asceotan*' (ibid., p. 44, l. 96).

The OE antecedent of ME *dun-falle* (*Hav.* 889) that the noun *downfall* would lead us to expect is directly attested in the same homily: 'Gif þu Godes sunu sy, *feall* nu *adun*' (p. 42, l. 17), and the latter is actually shown to be an equivalent of *adun-sceotan* in a repetition of that sentence: 'Gif þu Godes sunu sy, *sceot adun*' (p. 43, l. 71). The older form of expression is represented, again in the same homily, by the synonymous *nyþer-hreosende* 'falling down', rendering *deorsum ruens* (p. 45, ll. 140 and 135).

Thus the ME verbs with *d(o)un-* as first element belong to the ancient system of separable verb-compounds; and this is by descent, and not by some analogical process in ME.

897. *segges*: the voicing of /tš/ in OF *seche* 'cuttlefish' is paralleled in the remarkable *choger* (for OF *coucher* < L *collocare*) in *Kyng Alisaunder* 7763 (see n. there), i.e. in syllable-initial position. Taken at face value, both may imply a sporadic voicing in AN (and hence in words adopted thence into ME), as in *grudge* < OF *gruchier*. But they might be inverted spellings produced by the unvoicing of /dž/ in the Picard variety of OF: see C. T. Gossen, *Grammaire de l'ancien Picard*, §45.

919. Syntactically ambiguous. In 604, *tirueden of* is best interpreted as a separated form of a separable compound *of-tiruen* (see n.). In 919 as transmitted, *of* can be interpreted as an adverb, 'off' ('denute eels of their skins'). *Eles* is best read as a dat. of disadvantage, and *here hides* as the object of *to-turuen*.

994. Line 995 is virtually identical with 50 and 1690; and in each *leyde* rhymes on *misseyde*. Since (*a*) a rhyme of the diphthong spelt *ey* on tense or slack /e:/ (according to the variety of ME in question) would not be phonetically exact, or paralleled in *Hav.*, and since (*b*) *misdede* occurs in 993, it is virtually certain that *misdede* is a corruption of *misseyde*.

997–8. *grene*: convincingly explained by A. McIntosh (*RES* 16 (1940),

189–93) as a metathetic form of ON *girni* 'desire; lust', with the characteristic Nth. lengthening of /i/ to tense /e:/ in a disyllabic word with open root-syllable, i.e. *grīne* > *grẹ̄ne*. This is clinched by one other example of the phrase *leyke in grene* 'disport oneself sexually' in *St Oswald and the Monk* (ed. C. Horstmann, *Archiv*, 57 (1877), 290, l. 91).

Hire may be an equivalent of mod. Icel. *hýra* 'beloved', which is first recorded in the 17th century (lit. 'sweetness', cognate with *hýrr* a. = OE *hēore* 'pleasant'), or an adoption of an unrecorded OIcel. antecedent of it. A parallel in *Hav.* would be *file* 2500: this is an adoption of ON *fýla*, which, though by origin an abstract noun (lit. 'foulness'), came to be applied to human beings in an affective (derogatory) use, while in Icel. *hýra* the affective use is laudatory. Alternatively, *hire* in *Hav.* might be an early substantival use of the fem. nom. sg. of the ON adj., in the sense 'attractive young woman'.

Bradley's identification of *hire* with MDu. *huere*, and his gloss 'courtesan' (Bradley–Stratmann, *A Middle English Dictionary* s.v. *hüre* sb.², are phonologically dubious, since the recorded MDu. forms are *hoer(e)*, *hor*, and since *hueren* occurs only as a variant of *hoeren* in *hoeren-dochter*. Kölbing's emendation to *hore* ('Textkritische Bemerkungen', *Englische Studien* 19 (1894), 146–7) must be ruled out as palaeographically very improbable.

999. *strie*: only two other examples are attested by *OED*, which glosses all three as 'beldam, hag'. But none of the contexts decisively prescribes this sense: in the *York Plays*, XXIV (*The Woman taken in Adultery*), 13 and the *Towneley Plays*, XVI, 348) (on the Massacre of the Innocents) the use is substantially affective, and hence not closely definable from the contexts.

Much more specific light on the meaning of *strie* in *Hav.* is available in the use of its lineal antecedent (through OF *estrie*) L *striga*, which means both (*a*) 'nocturnal bird, viz. the screech-owl', and (*b*) 'woman who flies by night in the form of a bird, for amorous purposes or to harm children by sucking their blood',[90] beside *strix* 'owl' and Gk στρί(γ)ξ 'owl'.

An instantly luminous aid to understanding this conjunction of senses, and hence the meaning of *strie*, is a Greek story in the pseudo-Lucian work *Lucius, or The Ass*,[91] according to which the narrator was able to watch how a Thessalian woman set about turning into an owl in order to fly to *her lover* (by night):

After *intoning a charm* and *anointing herself* all over, she sprouted feathers, *turned into a bird* 'just like a night-raven' [i.e. owl], *uttered a dreadful croak* such as those birds utter, and *flew off* through a window.

The woman is not designated by any term corresponding to the sense (*b*) of L *striga* —but the story itself could hardly have conveyed the point more neatly if it had been invented for the purpose.

[90] See J. Hansen, *Zauberwahn, Inquisition und Hexenprozess im Mittelalter*, Historische Bibliothek, vol. xii (Munich, 1900, repr. 1964), pp. 14–16 and *passim*.
[91] Ed. M. D. Macleod, *Lucian*, vol. viii (Loeb Classical Library, London, 1967), 12–13, pp. 70–3.

Likewise circumstantial and therefore valuable is Ovid's account in *Fasti*, vi. 131–43,[92] the gist of which is:

> There are *birds* that *fly by night*, and *attack children who lack a nurse*[93] and defile their bodies, and are called *striges* [139], because they *screech horribly at night* [140]. Whether they are born as birds, or *become such by incantations* [*carmine* 141] and are *hags transformed into birds by a* Marsian *spell*. . . .

The difference from the tale of pseudo-Lucian is that Ovid's *striges* are seeking not nocturnal amours (sc. as a succubus would), but hapless infants on whom to prey (in a way specified by Pliny below). Ovid echoes the conception summarily in his reference (in *Amores*, i. 8, 1–14) to an old witch whom he suspected of flitting about by night in the shape of a bird. Pliny says:

> Fabulosum enim arbitror de *strigibus*, ubera eas infantium labris inmulgere. Esse in maledictis iam antiquis *strigem* iam conuenit, sed quae sit auium, constare non arbitror. (*Natural History* xi. xcv. 232, ed. Loeb (1940).)

> 'For regarding *striges*, I think it a fairy-tale that they discharge milk from their breasts into the lips of infants. It is established that *strix* occurs already in ancient curses; but I do not think it is agreed what sort of bird this may be.'[94]

A medieval example of *striga* (intermediate in time between pseudo-Lucian and *Hav.*, and less informative than the classical ones) occurs in a Latin sermon (the latest MSS of which are 9th-century) of a standard type, against pagan superstitions:

> Sunt aliqui rustici homines qui credunt quasi aliquas mulieres quod vulgum dicitur *strias* esse, debeant et *ad infantes vel pecora nocere possint*.[95]

> 'There are some country-men who believe certain women to be what is popularly called *striae*, and to have the power to harm infants and cattle.'

One other potential example occurs in a collection of maxims in Latin and OE, in Durham Cathedral MS B III 32[96] (an English MS of the mid-11th century), in the enigmatic passage:

> 'Eque confiderem liceat bene ambulasset'
> Dixit qui uidit frigas capite peregredientes.

Dixit qui: *MS* dixitque

> 'Ne swa þeah treowde þeah þu teala eode'
> Cwæþ se þe geseah hægtessan æfter heafde geo[ngan].

[92] Ed. and transl. by J. G. Frazer (London, 1929), i, p. 308. See his Commentary in vol. iv, p. 143.

[93] i.e. to suckle them (see Pliny's account below).

[94] I owe help with this translation to the kindness of Mr V. E. Watts.

[95] W. Levison, *England and the Continent in the Eighth Century* (Oxford, Ford Lectures 1943), p. 310 and n. 3.

[96] See N. R. Ker, *Catalogue of MSS. containing Anglo-Saxon* (Oxford, 1957), No. 107; O. Arngart, *The Durham Proverbs* (Lunds Universitets Årsskrift, N.F. Avd. I, Bd. 52, 1956) no. 11.

Since *frigas* is rendered *hægtessan* 'witches', it is presumably a corruption of *strigas*. This may mean that a scribe (or the translator himself) did not know what a *striga* was, and hence that the conception was not widely known in 11th-century England.

No help in this matter is to be had in OF. The example of *estrie* in *Le Roman de la Rose* 18426 is neither informative nor apropos, since it has there been associated with a quite different conception.[97]

As a whole, this material shows that *strie* in *Hav.* has much more point than the customary gloss 'hag, beldam' (*OED*) allows it. There is altogether more force in the contrast of an attractive young woman with the loathsome owl-succubus that preyed on infants. In *Hav.*, at least, the main implications of the word *strie* seem to persist: it is accordingly a remarkable survival of an ancient superstition.

1004. Skeat inserts *men* after *alle*, *metri causa*. But the replacement of the adverbial gen. *liues* by the equivalent *on liue* would do equally well (cf. 695 n.).

1020–2. See 767–9.

1021. *þei*: i.e. the *chaunpiouns* (1016) and others; Skeat's emendation to *þouh* is unnecessary.

1023. Both the occasion depicted here, and the other example in 2325 (again in a context that mentions *laddes*, which commonly means 'man of low status; fellow; servant'), might suggest that 'putting the stone' was a plebeian sport. But, so far as literary evidence goes, it was far from being so. *The Romance of Horn* ('the whole tone' of which its editor M. K. Pope characterizes as 'strongly aristocratic', ii. 2) describes at length (2567–659) how, at a feast at a royal court at Pentecost, the *bacheler* ('young men of noble birth') disported themselves either at throwing lances or at 'putting the stone' (*pierre jeter* 2568), and the king's younger son took part in a contest of the second kind, watched by the king and queen. And in the ME *Isumbras*, it is knights who are represented as going to *put the stane* 606–8 (ed. J. O. Halliwell, *The Thornton Romances*, Camden Society, 1844).

Miss Pope thinks the scene depicted in *Hav.* 1023–57 has 'a strong resemblance' to that in the AN *Horn*. The most notable points they have in common are that the contestants are young men, and that the hero is not versed in the sport but achieves the best throw. But otherwise they differ considerably.

Miss Pope (ii. 115–16) cites other references to 'putting the stone' in Wace's *Brut* 4348 and 10528 (the latter at the feast held at Arthur's coronation), and in Geoffrey of Monmouth's *Historia Regum Britanniae*, likewise at Arthur's coronation, and along with other sports (ed. Faral, *La Légende arthurienne*, vol. iii, ch. 157, ll. 45–52, and translated Thorpe ix. 14: *alii ponderosorum lapidum jactu . . . contendentes*). ME examples may be found in Mannyng's *Chronicle* 4746 (as a sport indulged in by *bachelers*, just as in the AN *Horn*); *Octavian* (Sth. version) 895 and 899; *The Lyfe of Ipomydon* 79–80; and the dance-refrain printed e.g. in *EMEVP* VIII E, Commentary, note on l. 2.

Havelok's feat is elsewhere one of two clear signs that a local legend about

[97] See the note on 18427 by E. Langlois (*Le Roman de la Rose*, vol. iv, SATF, Paris, 1922, pp. 314–16).

him had developed in Lincoln, as is directly attested by Mannyng (*Chronicle*, ed. T. Hearne, vol. i, p. 26), in explicitly distinguishing an oral and 'popular' account of Havelok from a written version (probably the extant one):

> *Men sais* in Lyncoln castelle ligges ȝit a stone
> þat Hauelok kast wele forbi euerilkone.
> & ȝit þe chapelle standes þer he weddid his wife,
> Goldeburgh þe kynges douhter. *þat saw* is ȝit ryfe.

1024. The textual status of MS *pulten* is at best dubious. It does not matter decisively that in 1032, 1034, 1045, and 1053 the word used for the same process is *putten*, since ME *pulten* is attested in the sense 'push, thrust' (*OED pilt, pult*, v.)—and this, if not an exact equivalent of *putten*, is not impossibly remote. But the ME forms of *pulten* imply /ü/ as a root-vowel (in an antecedent OE **pyltan*), which in *Hav.* is normally represented by an /i/. The only loophole left by the phonological facts is to posit a direct adoption of L *pultāre* 'beat, strike'; and this, in the vocabulary of *Hav.*, is improbable.

1038–9. K. Sisam's proposed emendation to *stadden* here is impossible. As an adoption of ON *staddr*, p.p. of *steðja* 'to place', ME *stadden* cannot (and does not anywhere else) have the sense 'looked on' which he posits on the alleged analogy of *Mani man on stad and sei* in *Cursor Mundi* 204 and 22724. For the correct syntactic analysis of the latter expression see 195 n. and the parallel in *Pearl* 149: *on* properly modifies only *sey*—'stood and looked on'—though its position has been shifted because the two verbs of the collocation came to be felt as a syntactic unit. A word meaning 'looked on' would not be happy in conjunction with *ofte* 1038; and the emendation is palaeographically untenable.

The rhyme is in fact one of *starden* on *ladden*, and implies and depends on a phonetic weakening of *r* before an alveolar consonant and assimilation to it. The phenomenon survived e.g. in the 19th-century sub-standard form *hoss* 'horse'. It is occasionally traceable in ME writings, as in *fled : wyþsperd* in Mannyng's *Chronicle* 15659–60 and *pres : trauers* ibid. 13393–4, and is well attested in OF. See *Richars li Biaus*, p. xi, and M. K. Pope, *From Latin to Modern French* (Manchester, 1934), §396.

1071. As W. J. B. Owen has pointed out,[98] the word required instead of MS *spekē* (i.e. *speken* v.) is the unassibilated form of the n. *speche* < OE *spēc, spǣc*. It is clearly prescribed by the rhyme in 1066, and is directly attested in 946 (in the same rhyme as in 1066). The MS version is syntactically odd (even with Skeat's emendation of *þe* 1071 to *þer*). *Speke* for MS *speken* produces a syntactically and idiomatically acceptable proleptic use of the pronoun *it* for a following noun object (*speke* 'report'), as in 665. A scribe might have been led to write *spekē* in 1071 as a mechanical repetition of *speken* (3 pr. pl.) in 1069.

1073. Nearly all the other ME examples of *frī*, which is a rare form of *frē* < OE *frēo*, occur in SE texts, in which it is lineally descended from OK *frīo*: OK *īo* > MK *īe*, which in final position > /iː/. But *frī* occurs also in *Sir Ferumbras* 3441 (: *cortesly*) and *Reinbrun* p. 634, st. 11 (: *presenti* inf.). The former is SW;

[98] *N&Q* 197 (1952), 468–9.

and the latter is composed in a variety of ME that is essentially (*a*) Sth., (*b*) not Anglian-derived, and (*c*) not Kentish. In both works, these are the sole examples of *frī* in rhymes; both authors otherwise use *frē*, with tense /e:/ < OE *ēo*.

Outside the SE, *frī* is best explained as a sporadic phonetic variant of *fre* (since it coexists with the latter in individual ME works), and hence as the ME derivative of OE *frig-* as in *frigne, friges*. The latter is itself a rare but orthodox phonetic variant, in which **frij-* was developed at the WG stage before a front vowel in an ending, while WG *-iu-* (> OE *īo* > *ēo*) arose in this word by the elimination of *-j-* and contraction of /i/ with a following back vowel in an ending.[99]

In *Hav.* likewise *frī* occurs (once only) alongside the normal *frē*, as would be understandable where phonetic variants are concerned.

1090. See 15 n. *þouthe* might be analysed as an agglutinated spelling of *þouth he* or *þouthe he*, since the full stress that is here required after *þouth-* cannot well fall on the final *-e* (unstressed in speech) of a 3 pt. sg. *þouthe*. If we expand the presumed agglutinated spelling, the line may be scanned:

þís þ̆outh [h]é wĭþ tréchĕrý

or:

þ̆is þóuthĕ [h]é wĭþ tréchĕrý.

A Chaucerian example of the sequence *þis þouthe he* in *Troilus and Criseyde* V. 99 is open to scansion not only as:

Bŭt náthĕlés thĭs thóughtę hĕ wél y̆nóugh

but also (with agglutination that implies a spoken form) as:

Bŭt náthĕlés thĭs thóughte˘ḫe wél y̆nóugh.

1090–1100. i.e. Havelok, as 'some churl's son' and a thrall (as Godrich imagined him to be) could not own land. On mixed marriages (between a man and a woman of free and unfree status respectively, and vice versa), see Pollock and Maitland, i. 423 ff., and P. Vinogradoff, *Villainage in England* (Oxford, 1891), pp. 61–3. For the case in which a free woman marries a serf and thereby forefeits her right and claim to land (with an example of 1277 and a ruling of 1275), see H. S. Bennett, *Life on the English Manor* (Cambridge, 1969), p. 243.

1103. *on an hok*: in the sole parallel known to me, this detail in the process of execution by hanging refers to a stage after the victim was dead. Mathew Paris reports (*Chronica Maiora*, ed. H. R. Luard (RS, 1877), iv. 196) of the execution of the pirate William Marsh in 1242, that he was 'dragged' (i.e. at the tail of a horse) from Westminster to the Tower and then:

. . . usque ad illam poenalem machinam. quae vulgariter *gibbetus* dicitur, distractus, cum ibidem miseram animam exhalasset, *super unum uncorum est suspensus*.

[99] See A. Campbell, *Old English Grammar*, §§120, (3), (c); 410, and 648; K. Luick, *Historische Grammatik der englischen Sprache*, §102.

1112–13. See 177 n.

1130. See 164 n.

1133. Cf. D. Knowles, *The Monastic Order in England* (Cambridge, repr. 1950), pp. 543–4, and the *Regularis Concordia* (ed. W. S. Logemann with the OE interlinear gloss, *De Consuetudine Monachorum*, in *Anglia*, 13 (1891), 365–454), ll. 521–8; and *Le Morte Arthur* (ed. J. D. Bruce, EETS, ES 88, 1903), 2236–7:

> Bot by the tyme of *euvyn belle*
> Launcelot party the better stode.

1146. *onne-haue*: beside the abundant separated forms (*MED Haven* v. 2 (*c*)), just one unambiguous unseparated form (in a main clause) is available in *Romaunt of the Rose* 1071: 'Richesse a robe of purpre *on-hadde*'. And the MDu. cognate (see Glossary) clinches the identification of this verb as a separable compound.

1154. The line as transmitted is not altogether convincing: 'H. was alone and was terrified'. In all the *OED*'s examples of *one* in the sense 'alone', the word is used in apposition either with a personal pronoun (as in all the other examples in *Hav.*) or with a noun.

In any case, *one* looks very much like a corruption of *awe* 'fear' (through the stages *awe > owe > oue > one*), in an originally impersonal construction synonymous with the common idiom (also originally impersonal) *awe* [or cognate *eie* < OE *ege*] *stonden*, as in 277, and recorded once in OE: '*nis me ege* mannes | for ahwæðer' (*The Paris Psalter*, Ps. 55. 4).

If one reads *awe* here for *one*, the apparently tautological expression is not a difficulty, since it is exactly matched in 277–8 (*was. . . adrad*). Since the second sentence in each passage is a personal construction, the idiom in the first sentence of each was probably no longer understood to be impersonal. This was due to the loss of final *-e*, by which the dat. sg. of many nouns in an impersonal construction became identical with the nom. sg.

This change from an impersonal to a personal construction was extended analogically to those with pronouns (in which it could not have originated, since the nom. sg. and the dat. sg. would have been so clearly distinct). Thus e.g. *Le Morte Arthur* 909: 'Off nothinge ne *stode he drede*' and *he was wo* (ibid. 2875)—beside *me ys wo* (ibid. 2783)—and Shakespeare's *I am woe for't* (*The Tempest* v. i. 139).

1158. The problem here is not just the identity and origin of *slike*, which is not recorded in OE (and on which see *OED slick* a.). An adverb would be stylistically more natural after the verb *seyde*, and before the nouns *þral* and *swike*, than an adj. parallel to Skeat's inserted *fals*. But no monosyllabic adverb of suitable meaning suggests itself.

Slike is usually interpreted as an example (admittedly, a 'doubtful' one in *OED* s.v. 3) of *slick* a. in the sense 'smooth; plausible' (i.e. as a figurative application). But this does not fit the context, since the short speech to which *slike* should refer is the last word in nakedly brutal menace.

1170–6. Cf. Gower's allusion to the marriage ceremony (*Confessio Amantis* V. 557–61):

> I wot the time is ofte cursed
> That evere was *the gold* unpursed
> The which was *leid upon the bok*,
> Whan that alle othre she forsok
> For love of him. . . .

The money 'laid on the book' is not said to be taken by the bride, as it is in *Hav.* It is nevertheless not (as Macaulay states in his note on the passage) a marriage fee paid 'to the priest and clerk', but the bride's dowry—on the evidence not only of *Hav.*, but of the following passage in the early forms of the marriage service:

> Deinde ponat vir [the bridegroom] *aurum*, *argentum*, et annulum *super* scutum vel *librum* [*þe bok* in *Hav.* and Gower],[100]

and of the words to be uttered by the bridegroom (after the ring has been sprinkled with holy water):

> With this rynge I the wed, and this gold and siluer I the geue . . .   (ibid., p. 58).

Cf. also the passage cited by Maskell (p. 58 n. 14) from MS Royal 2 A XXI (a *Manuale*, of the beginning of the 15th century, that once belonged to the parish church of South Charford[101]):

> et dato annulo dicat sacerdos: Loo, this gold and this siluer is leyd doun in signifyinge that the woman schal haue hure dower, thi goodes, ȝif heo abide aftur thy disces.[102]

1179–80. In the AN *Lai*, at the corresponding point, there is an *assemblement* (284) of the princess's vassals at her uncle's court in Lincoln to urge him to find her a suitable husband. He appoints a day to give them his answer; when they again 'assemble' (352), he instantly marries her to Havelok.

Thus the author, in introducing a *parlement* at Lincoln here and in l. 1007, was probably elaborating on something suggested to him by the received story. He may nevertheless have been led to do so by an actual *parlement* at Lincoln. Only two that were held there are in question—in 1301 and 1316;[103] and the second is a little too late to be consistent with the other evidence for the date of composition of *Hav.* (see Introduction, VI).

The surprising presence of the Archbishop of York as the celebrant of the wedding, however, was not in the received story. And the author has revealingly felt called upon to explain that the Archbishop was in Lincoln for the *parlement* (along with a characteristic reference to the agency of God). The

[100] Ed. W. Maskell, *Monumenta Ritualia Ecclesiae Anglicanae*, vol. i (2nd edn., Oxford, 1882), p. 57. I owe this reference to the kindness of the Right Revd. J. R. H. Moorman.

[101] N. R. Ker, *Medieval Libraries of Great Britain* (London, 1964), Appendix, p. 220.

[102] On the dowry, see also the statements of Bracton, *De Legibus et Consuetudinibus Angliae*, Bk. ii, fo. 92 ff.; ed. Woodbine, vol. ii, pp. 265–6).

[103] See G. O. Sayles, *The King's Parliament of England* (London, 1975), 137 ff., for lists of parliaments from 1258 (which is the earliest date for which the term is now thought to be admissible); and F. M. Powicke and E. B. Fryde, *Handbook of British Chronology* (London, 1961), 492 ff.

value of this for our purposes is that the real Archbishop of York was enjoined by an extant writ of summons[104] to attend the parliament at Lincoln on 20 January 1301.

Since the author's explanation thus fits authentic facts, the statement which it is designed to explain may well also have been an allusion to an event in real life (on which he has frequently drawn elsewhere).

1269–9. A hitherto unobserved example of this conception, in a near-contemporary story from real life, is available in Mathew Paris's account of an attempt on the life of Henry III in 1238. A man presented himself at the King's court at Woodstock, and pretended to be mad, saying to the King: 'Surrender to me the kingdom which you have usurped and long retained'; then: 'Addidit quoque, *quod signum regale gestabat in humero*': 'and added that he bore a mark of royal birth on his shoulder' (*Chronica Maiora*, ed. H. R. Luard (RS, 1876), iii. 497). That the man had been suborned to kill the king, and his claim was thus a lie, is neither here nor there: the story attests the belief that there was such a thing as a 'mark' on the shoulder attesting royal birth.

Another literary use of the idea occurs in the 13th-century OF romance *Richars li Biaus*[105] (here again in conjunction with the motif of the light (*Hav.* 592–3, 1252 ff., 2123 ff.) in the vestigial form of a radiance in the face of the boy in question (663–4): see Introduction, pp. xl–xlii. It also occurs in the related 14th-c. OF *Lion de Bourges*, along with the horn that can be blown only by the true heir, as in Gaimar 670 ff., *Lai d'Haveloc* 880 ff.[106]

1316. A lacuna must be posited after this line, not merely because *ioye* cannot rhyme with *trone*, but especially since the main clause *þat wite þw* in 1317 does not follow smoothly on 1315–16. But there is no means of knowing what has gone wrong, or what the author wrote.

The expression *þat wite þw* shows that God is being invoked: it is merely a less common form (in the second person) of the conjuration *God it wite, wite God, wite Crist* 'may God (Christ) be my witness', beside *God (it) wot* (on all of which see C. T. Onions, *RES* 4 (1928), 334–7, 5 (1929), 330). For other invocations in *Hav.* see 331–2 n. and 542–4.

One point here has gone unnoticed. The OF *trosne*, OF and AN *trone*, AN *trun* is amply attested in the senses 'firmament; heaven', as in the un-ambiguous context of *The AN Voyage of St. Brendan* 1247 (ed. E. G. R. Waters, Oxford, 1928): 'Jesu, chi moz tut le *trone*', which corresponds to '*per quem* firmamentum *et sidera moventur*' of the Latin version printed by Waters at the foot of the page. See also 674. Similarly, the sense 'throne' is excluded in the AN *Romance of Horn* 615: '*li sire de haut* trun', and 1393: '*par le seignur del* trun'.

What has bedevilled the interpretation of *trone* in the ME forms of this

---

[104] For the text, see F. Palgrave, *Parliamentary Writs and Writs of Military Summons* (London, 1827), vol. i, p. 89.

[105] Ed. W. Foerster, 665–70.

[106] See H. E. Heyman, *Studies on the Havelok-Tale* 101–7; W. W. Kibler, J.-L. G. Pich-erit, T. S. Fenster, *Lion de Bourges*, i–ii (Geneva, 1980): see I. lix–lxi and lx. 2. 3, xcii–cxix, and ll. 381–3, 437–8, 552–6, II. 32300–9, 32378–89. This work also contains an episode with brigands (10209–404) that is reminiscent of that in *Richars li Biaus* 3295–492.

invocation is that God may be named or invoked as 'seated', as in *Firumbras* 1065 (and in *Hav.*): '. . . that ilke lord that *syttyth in trone*'. In this, too, and similar forms of the expression (for examples and a discussion of which see *SMP* pp. 201–3) *trone* in some instances means 'firmament; heaven' rather than 'throne'. The *OED* glosses the phrase *in (on) throne* only as 'enthroned' (*throne* sb. 3), and does not register the sense 'firmament; heaven' in the noun at all. But it is beyond belief that the sense 'throne' is to be posited in all the abundant ME examples when 'firmament; heaven' is clearly established in comparable AN contexts.

1330. The insertion of *bes* is merely an expedient to provide the indispensable auxiliary verb. The pronominal subject *þou*, though not expressed, is implied in the preceding *þe*: see 15 n.

1332. Skeat–Sisam are mistaken in suggesting that this rhyme implies the (northerly) lengthening of /u/ in disyllabic words with open root-syllables (*hnute* here): that lengthening produced a tense /oː/, while the rhyme on *doute* here admits only of /uː/ if there had been lengthening. The rhyme is in fact one of a long vowel on a short one (see VII. Note on Versification).

1337–9. *Lith* 1339 is formally compatible with either ON *lið* 'body of men' or ME *liþ(e)* 'journeying'; and in the repetitive style of *Hav.* the latter might (as a synonym of *fare* 1338) have been the author's word.

As an emendation, *l[i]þe* 1337 has the advantage of preserving the *l* in MS *witl* as well as the MS *þe* (while the example of *witl* for *with* that Sisam invokes from 1165 is not to be found there). If *liþe* is interpreted as 'journey' in 1337, it is necessary to take *wit* as the dual 'we two' and to emend *nim in* to *nime* (since, already in OE, optative pl. forms had shed the final -*n* if followed by a pronominal subject): 'Let's both make the journey to Denmark'. Since the dual gen. *unker* occurs in 1883, there is no difficulty in positing the nom. *wit* here. But the emendation to *nime* is not palaeographically probable.

In the alternative analysis of *liþe* 1337 as 'body of men; following', *wit* must be the prep. 'with', and *nim* intransitive in the sense 'go'. This last is just traceable in OE[107] (possibly developed from *weg niman* by ellipse of the object). And *nime in* + *to* + a place-name is recorded at least once in ME: 'And *in to* Sichem, a burgt, he *nam*' (*Genesis and Exodus* 744)—'and he proceeded to a city named Sichem'. Best of all, a vital parallel is available in *Hav.* itself, in 2931: 'But sone *nam until* his land'.

The use of the parallel and synonymous pairs *intil/into* and *until/unto* in *Hav.* (see Glossary) shows that *nam until* is synonymous with *Nim in . . . to*, and that the latter is an equivalent of it. The difference that the compound prep. *in to* (developed, like others, from a sequence of adv. + prep.) is here still used in the separated form is not a material one. The appositive use of the pl. *baþe* with the understood singular subject of *nim in* is admittedly a trifle harsh; no precise parallel is as yet to hand.

---

[107] Prose *Boethius*, ed. W. J. Sedgefield (Oxford, 1899), ch. XVI, i, l. 20: v.l. *noman* for *comon*.

1349. There is no known word corresponding in form to *til* that would fit this context. Skeat's *telle*, though palaeographically not ideal as an emendation, meets the need for an expedient.

1359. *'Croiz' and 'Crist'*: Havelok's procedure here (to 1390) is not random or arbitrary. Two striking points are the prominence of the Cross (ll. 1358 and 1390), and the conjunction of the Cross and Christ in Havelok's invocation and prayer. Both points recur in conjunction in an antiphon (*antefne*) among the 'hours' and the prayers that are laid down for the anchoresses of the *Ancrene Riwle* to say between their rising and going to bed: 'Salua nos, Christe Saluator, per uirtutem sancte crucis.' This occurs after four of a series of psalms, then comes a fifth, and then the antiphon again, after which they are to cross themselves, saying: 'Qui saluasti Petrum in mari [MS mare], miserere nobis.'[108] They are to do this while meditating on the Cross and on the pains of Christ.[109]

These two Latin sentences, which are separated in the text of the *Ancrene Riwle*, are to be read continuously, since they are then identical with the antiphon prescribed in the Sarum Breviary for (*a*) the Second Nocturn of Matins of the Feast of the Holy Cross (14 Sept.), (*b*) a *Memoria de Cruce ad Vesperas*, and (*c*) the Second Vespers of the Feast *Yconiae Domini Salvatoris*.[110]

It should be noted that Havelok in his prayer asks Christ for a safe passage over the sea (1377) and for mercy (1363), since these are potential links with the content of the antiphon. The author may well have been recalling not merely the antiphon, but the whole process followed in the adoration of the Cross.

1361. Echoes a Latin formula used in legal documents, e.g. in the royal charters of Stephen: '. . . precipio quod teneat bene *in bosco et plano et pratis et aquis* . . .' (Cronne and Davis, *Regesta Regum Anglo-Normannorum* iii, p. 119, no. 312).

1365. Hypermetrical and probably corrupt; the parallel in 1412–13 does not help.

1368–9. *Haue*: the perfect is used to express an unrealized condition, intention, or wish.

1378. The combination of *þat* and *þer-offe* is syntactically dubious; but Skeat's emendation of *þat* to *þouh* is a mere rewriting. *þer-offe* is the sort of common compound that a scribe might absently have been led to build on *offe*. The omission of *þer* would make the syntax normal (*þat . . . offe* 'of which') without marring the metre.

1380. [*Were*] has the advantage over Skeat's [*be*] of being palaeographically probable, as a potential product of haplography before *þer-*.

1402–35. This passage is virtually repeated in 2207–40, where it is put in the mouth of Ubbe, and in which no less than six couplets are reproduced

---

[108] *Ancrene Wisse*, ed. J. R. R. Tolkien, p. 13, ll. 12–22 and pp. 21, l. 24–22, l. 10.

[109] On the salutations and prayers used in the *Ancrene Riwle*, see the helpful remarks by Dom Gerard Sitwell in M. B. Salu's *The Ancrene Riwle* (Orchard Books, London, 1955), pp. 193–6.

[110] *Breviarium ad usum Sarae*, ed. F. Procter and C. Wordsworth, vol. iii (Cambridge, 1886), col. 815; vol. ii (1879), col. 94. See also L. Gjerløw, *Adoratio Crucis* (Norwegian Universities Press, 1961), p. 27.

(closely or approximately) with the same rhyme-words. The correspondences are:

$$1402-3 \;=\; 2207-8$$
$$1404-5 \;=\; 2209-10$$
$$1416-17 \;=\; 2233-4 \;(\text{cf. } 1420 \text{ and } 535-6)$$
$$1410-11 \;=\; 2215-16$$
$$1432-3 \;=\; 2237-8$$
$$1434-5 \;=\; 2239-40$$

In addition, with the same content, and with one rhyme-word reproduced in each pair:

$$1418-19 \;=\; 2231-2$$

And with different rhyme-words:

$$1408-9 \;=\; 2213-14$$
$$1420-1 \;=\; 2233-4 \;(\text{combined with } 535-6)$$

Moreover, each passage opens with an adjuration of the form *Liþes . . . me*.

What is unusual, conspicuous, and remarkable here is not that so much is virtually the same in the two passages, but that so many of the rhyme-words are identical. One account is clearly a doublet of the other.

1403. MS *knewe*: in 2207–8, where the couplet is repeated, *knawe* must be the 2 pres. indic. pl., since this is required by *Ye witen wel* 2209, which is evidently a synonymous variant of it. *Knewe* must therefore have been substituted for *knawe* by a scribe to fit the rhyme-word, in which he or another scribe had evidently replaced *shawe* (< OE *scéáwian* with stress-shifted rising diphthong) with the phonetic variant and orthodox *sheue* (< OE *scéáwian* with falling diphthong). The latter type is again shown to have been substituted for the former in 1699, 1854, and 2057 by the rhyme-words *lowe*, *mowe*, and *knawed*, which admit only of *á* or slack *ó* as the vowel of the stressed syllable.

1436–7. This is a natural variant of the formula represented in 174–5 (see n.) and 128–9. Though apparently less common than that main type, it recurs at least thrice in ME romances:

> For he was fallen into elde,
> þat he my3te *non armes* welde

(*Richard Coeur de Lion* 6237–8); also *Sir Beues of Hamtoun* 4545–6 and *Arthour and Merlin* (later version, L MS) 219–20.

1444–5. The point of this expression, as of the virtually identical one in 396–7, is revealed by the stereotyped use of a certain type of formula (which these passages echo) in grants of land, as in the following one of 1135–46 by King Stephen to one John de Chesney (Cronne and Davis, *Regesta Regum Anglo-Normannorum*, iii, p. 63, no. 174):

> Precipio quod idem Johannes . . . et heredes sui teneant et habeant predictum manerium de me et heredibus meis in pace, hereditarie, et quiete, *in bosco in plano in pratis et pasturis*, aquis et mariscis, in molendinis et stangnis [*sic*], in viis et semitis et in omnibus aliis locis et rebus cum soca et saca, tol et them, et infangethef, et cum omnibus aliis pertinentibus libertatibus et

quietationibus que ad hoc pertinent cum quibus illas habui dum fuerunt in manu mea.

The carefully explicit details in this formula specify the rights of the tenant on whom the land is conferred, i.e. the financial or other benefits to be gained from them (as Prof. H. S. Offler has kindly informed me). This appears from the reference to the rights of jurisdiction given him under the names 'sake and soke', 'toll and team', and 'infangethef' (on all of which see Stenton, *English Feudalism*, pp. 99–107), and the reference to 'liberties' or immunities (from dues) which he will enjoy. In fact Havelok is here promising each of Grim's sons feudal possessions to be held of himself as their prospective lord, just as in 396–7 he is claiming the equivalent for himself as the rightful lord of all Denmark, and is doing so in at least fleetingly appropriate terms.

It is perhaps conceivable that *monges* here and in 397 is (in this sort of context) being used as the technical term for 'block of unenclosed land (a third of a furlong strip) in the open-field system'. For this use see D. M. Stenton, *English Society in the Early Middle Ages* (Penguin Books, 1951), p. 121, and *OED* s.v. *wong*. It is moreover conceivable that the mills and ponds of the above formula are echoed (along with the woods and fields) in l. 1361, where the mention of *wind and water* is altogether unusual in a periphrastic invocation of Christ or God (see 331–2 n.).

1629. The emendation is required, not so much by the medieval social convention that the plural form of the pronoun of the second person was used in address to superiors, and the singular to familiars, intimates, or inferiors, as by the plural form of the verb. The convention was evidently not consistently represented in ME writings: a surprising sustained use of the singular pronoun occurs in Ubbe's speech to Havelok (whom he calls *louerd* 2173) in 2169–85.

1636. Shown to be a proverb by the almost identical authorial comment in *Sir Tristrem* 626–7, on the bribing of a porter with a ring by the hero:

> He was ful wise, Y say,
> þat first ȝaue ȝift in land.

I cannot trace any OF examples in the valuable collection of J. Morawski, *Proverbes français antérieurs au XVᵉ siècle*. But it clearly was current in OF, on the evidence of an example in the epic *La Chanson D'Aspremont* (ed. L. Brandin, i (CFMA), 80–1), where it is explicitly presented as a proverb (of the common man):

> Car li vilains le dist en reprovier:
> 'Ne fu pas fols cil qui dona premier'.

Since no other English examples are cited by Smith and Heseltine, *The Oxford Book of English Proverbs* (s.v. *Wise*, p. 719), the two ME ones may have been adopted from OF; or the example in *Hav.* may have been adopted from OF, and imitated in *Sir Tristrem* (which contains a striking parallel to *Hav.* 2517–20: see n.).

1676. The extended form *onne* is metrically required here (as distinct from

347, where it is hypermetrical). Nevertheless, it is clearly by origin, at least, the particle of a separable compound *on-sitten* 'to ride upon', which (though not registered in *OED*) is attested once in OE as a *varia lectio* in the form *onsittend* 'rider': '*hors and upstigynd oðð̈e onsittend*', rendering '*equum et ascensorem*' (*Cambridge Psalter*, ed. K. Wildhagen, Hymn 4, l. 2).

Support for this analysis is available in *Hav.*, in the parallel case of the incontrovertible separable compound *on-leyen* 'lay upon' (see 50 n.), in which the extended *onne* is metrically required in 1690 and 1941, alongside *on* that is likewise required in 50 and 995.

1679. The insertion of *þat* in this metrically defective line rests on the equivalence of *or* and *or þat* as forms of the conjunction 'before'. Skeat's *ferre*, inserted after *he*, might have been better placed before *ferde*, as a potential opportunity for homoeoteleuton by a scribe.

1681–2. See 360–1 and n.

1686. *þe heye curt*: clearly an adoption of the equivalent OF phrase *haute cort*, only two examples of which are recorded by Tobler–Lommatzsch (s.v. *haut*). In *La Chanson de Guillaume* (ed. Suchier), 1967, William reproves his nephew for his discreditable treatment of a Saracen foe on the battlefield thus:

> cum fus unc tant osez
> que osas home   mahaigné adeser!
> *En halte curt*   te serrad reprové.

The following in *Le Siège de Barbastre* 3070–1 (not noticed by Tobler–Lommatzsch) is potentially valuable because of its reference to 'speaking':

> Se fuiant m'en aloie, l'en me devroit tuer;
> Ja mes *en haute cort n'oseroie parler*.

Both these contexts are compatible with 'pleading' in a 'court' of law. The juridical sense and the sense 'abode of a sovereign and his entourage' are both recorded in OF from the 12th century. But the epithet *haut/heye* recalls the literally contrasted and less sparsely attested OF phrase *la basse court*, as used in *Baudoin de Sebourg*, xvi. 173 (Slatkine Reprints, 1972; Valenciennes, 1841):

> Au chastel de Sebourc est venus vistement.
> *Le basse court* passa, que nuls ne lui deffent—
> Venus est a *le tour*, qui *haute* est durement.

This expression refers to a part of a castle;[111] and the contrast with the *tour* suggests that it was an outer and lower part, separated from and less secure than the 'tower'. It is conceivable that the architectural use was the starting-point, and that the applications to this part of a magnate's castle, and then to the court of law that he might hold there, were naturally evolved from it; but the evidence does not suffice to show this.

In *Hav.*, when the hero and his party make for *þe heye curt* (1686), they find Ubbe and his men assembled in the hall (1695–6). Later, Havelok and his wife are lodged (for safety) by Ubbe in a bedroom in *þe heye tour* 2074, and are said to be sleeping outside (*ut of* 2122) the hall. Thus the 'high court' apparently

[111] See Tobler–Lommatzsch s.v. *cort*.

contained or was identical with the hall, and was in the same part of the build-ings as *þe heye tour*. It was probably the inner and more secure part of the castle (*borw* 2087), and on an upper level, in relation to the *basse court*.

1690. See 1676 n. and 347 n.

1699. *shawe*: see 1402–3 and 1403 n.

1732. This apparently peculiar use of *bite* in application to a liquid is paralleled in *King Horn* 1131–2:

> No *beer* nullich *ibite*
> Bot of coppe white.

It may have developed out of a 'consociation' (or semantic conjunction that recurs) in which both food and drink were mentioned, as in *Sir Beues of Hamtoun* 1740: 'Mete ne *drink* ne *bot* I non'.

1734. This use of *bidde* (again 2531) is an idiom of which there are not less than seven other ME examples, but none in OE. The idiomatic singularity consists in (*a*) the use in the sense 'wish' of a verb that normally means 'ask; command', and (*b*) an invariable association with a negative. In the absence of a lineal OE antecedent, these two features suggest foreign origin; and they duly recur in a corresponding OF use of *rouver* 'ask' < L *rogāre*, which is clearly the source of the ME idiom. In an AN instance (Gaimar, *L'Estoire des Engleis* 3887) it occurs, just as in *Hav.*, in an *occupatio* (or pretended, and some-times actual, refusal to speak of something in detail):

> Ho! fait Gaimar, *ne rois parler*
> De sa belte pour demurer.

The OF idiom in turn derives from the use in ecclesiastical Latin of *iubēre* 'to command' in the sense 'deign, be willing', as the latter does from the epis-tolary formula *avēre iubet* of classical Latin, which was adopted into OE, as in the famous opening of the *Pastoral Care* (ed. H. Sweet, EETS, os 45, repr. 1958): *Ælfred cyning hateþ gretan Wærferþ biscep*.

For further material and explanation see 'A Middle English Idiom and its Antecedents', *EGS* 1 (1947–8), 101–13.

1737. Skeat's violent emendation of *þe kilþing* to *ilk þing* must be rejected as a re-writing that offers no means of accounting for the alleged corruption. It is less arbitrary and drastic (and to that extent better) to equate the troublesome *kil-* with the ON verb *kýla* 'fill one's belly with', as used in the phrase *kýla ǫl* 'tipple ale'. Cf. *Vatnsdæla saga* ch. II (ed. Einar Ól. Sveinsson, *Íslenzk Fornrit*, viii, 1939).

> en nú vilja ungir menn gerask heimaelskir ok sitja við bakelda ok *kýla vǫmb* sína á miði ok mungáti

> but nowadays young men want to hang about at home and sit by the fire to warm themselves and fill their bellies with mead and ale.

See *EGS* 3 (1949–50), 67–8.

1764. Both here and in 2942 a scribe has marred the rhyme on *riche* by sub-stituting the variant *chinche* for *chiche*. The *-n-* in the corresponding by-form of the OF etymon *chiche* has not been satisfactorily explained. The OF word, which by some is referred to L *cicer*[112] 'chick-pea', is probably represented also in F *pois chiche*, the source of E *chick-pea* 'dwarf pea', earlier *chich pea*.

1777. MS *ar*: an example of the standard palaeographical error, in ME hands, of the misreading and consequent miswriting of *x* and *r*, e.g. *for* for *fox* in the common antecedent of the Cotton and Jesus MSS of *O&N* 812, and *wering* for *wexing* in *The Seven Sages of Rome* 569.

1789. *at . . . gonge*: possibly < OE *ætgongan* (only in *Azarias* 183) 'approach', which is shown to have been a separable verb by ON *atganga* 'attack' beside *ganga at* 'to attack'.

Traces in E *at* of the sense 'through' (referring to entry by a door) are slight. The citation in *OED* (s.v. 10) from *The Fight at Finnsburg* 16 is mistaken, since *æt* there is not in fact associated with the verb *eodon* in the text.

There is no means of deciding whether *at . . . gonge* here means 'get at' (< OE *ætgongan*) or 'attack' (as a semantic borrowing of ON *ganga at*), or 'get in through'.

1792. *ful god won*: as in 1838 and 1908, has developed an intensive force, from the literal sense 'abundance'. The other main senses of *won* in ME are (*i*) 'hope, expectation' (as in the native cognate *wen*), (*ii*) 'expedient; remedy; course of action', (*iii*) 'wealth, riches'. The starting-point was (*i*), whence the others as individual applications of it.

1827–8. The one certainty here is that MS *haue* in 1828 is to be emended or expanded to *Hauelok*. An unfulfilled intention, condition, or wish is idiomatically expressed (in English up to and including that of Shakespeare) by a perfect infinitive, as in *wende . . . haue slawe* 1804 and *wolde . . . haue do* 1806. The analogy of these two expressions suggests that MS *haue* in 1828 may have originally stood in 1827, and that a scribe absently transposed it with *Hauelok* in 1828.

The cardinal difficulty is in the rest of 1827, which is likely to be corrupt. The main verb might be concealed in either *wolde* or *riht*; but the former is improbable, in view of the parallels in 1804 and 1806. E. J. Dobson's proposed emendations to *diht* 'maltreat' or *pliht* 'endanger, harm, injure' (*EGS* 1 (1947–8), 58) are not idiomatically or palaeographically probable.

Riht may just conceivably be another example of the very rare verb *riȝth* in *Kyng Alisaunder* 3905 'aim a blow at', which seems to be an adoption of MDu. *richten*. Both the latter are applied to an intended blow with a named weapon, as *riht* is in *Hav.*; see *Kyng Alisaunder* 3905 and n.

1864. MS *stoden* makes altogether inadequate sense, and is manifestly a corruption of *stonden* 'stoned' (from which a scribe omitted *n*, probably abbreviated by the titulus in his exemplar); see *EGS* 3 (1949–50), 68–9. *Him* 1865 is governed by *fro ferne* rather than by *schoten*: 'keeping their distance from him'.

1894. Skeat's palaeographically baseless emendation of *þre* to *þe* 'thigh' is mistaken. The MS reading preserves a rare and archaic idiom, the nature of

---

[112] See von Wartburg, *FEW* s.v. *cicer*; but Meyer-Lübke, *REW* 9653, suggests an ideophonic **čikk*.

which is made especially clear by the two following examples in the MHG
Laurin:[113] 'Werstu sterker den *diner fier*, | Sie schlugen dich vil schier' (1251–2)
'If you were stronger than *four of you* [sg.]'; 'Ich han me den *uwer dry*' (282) 'I
have more than three of you [pl.]'.

These show that *his* here is not (as Skeat supposed) the possessive adj. 'his',
but the gen. sg. of the personal pronoun used partitively, and governed by a
numeral, which it precedes, just as in OE a dependent genitive idiomatically
precedes the word governing it. A detail that makes these MHG examples still
more apt for comparison is that, just like *his þre* in *Hav.*, they follow a comparative.

This idiom is not amply attested in the dictionaries and the handbooks of
OE and ME syntax in the form with a numeral; though it is not uncommon in
OE and ME in a form in which the partitive genitive is governed by such
words as OE *eall, ægþer, sum* and ME *al, ayþer, som*. For passages that combine two instances of the idiom used with a numeral, cf. *King Horn* 823 (L MS):
'ʒef *vre on* ['one of us'] sleh *oure þre* ['three of you']' and Laʒamon's *Brut* 8140.
A stock example, in which the force of the genitive is put beyond doubt by a
Latin original, is *Ste. Katerine* 468 (ed. d'Ardenne and Dobson, EETS, ss 7,
1981): 'ʒef fifti wimmen . . . hefden wið wordes *ower an* awarpen', rendering: 'Si
quinquagene . . . femine uerbis *unum e uobis* euicissent'.

1900–2. Since *bete* and *breke* are passive infinitives, *wreke* is best interpreted thus likewise. Skeat's insertion of *be* before *wreke* is syntactically and
palaeographically improbable.

1900. *boyes*: first recorded in the 13th century, and first satisfactorily
etymologized by E. J. Dobson[114]—as an aphetic form of an AN past participle
embuié 'fettered', formed on OF *boie* < L *boia* 'fetter'.

1918. Shows, in a single example, how the vocabulary of the author of
Hauelok was enriched with idiomatic phrases from two different foreign
sources. ON *setja hnefann (við)* 'strike with the fist (against)' (as in *Hav.* 2405–6)
has been combined with the OF locution *desuz l'oie* 'under the ear', but with
oie replaced by its ON synonym *heyrn*. For the documentation and arguments
on which this interpretation is based, see *RES* 13 (1937), 458–62.

1933. This line is usually emended to produce the phrase *haueth on wold*
(*OED wield* sb. 4c) or *oweth on wold* 'signifies' (thus Skeat–Sisam and Holthausen) and *Wat* or *Hwat* for *þat*. This drastic rewriting leaves *is* un-
accounted for.

Moreover, *is wold* is suggestively like the ON use of *valdr* (or *valdi*) a.
'responsible for, the agent of' with the verb 'to be' (*þótt þú sjálfr sér þess eigi valdr,
Fornmanna Sǫgur* VI. 380. 5), and probably should not be tampered with. But the
line remains an enigma.

1953. *þe . . . ille maked*: this is shown to be an idiom (in which ON *ill-r* a.,
used substantively, has replaced a native word) by a solitary OE example of
the type (with indirect object):

---

[113] Ed. T. Dahlberg, *Zwei unberücksichtigte mittelhochdeutsche Laurin-versionen* (Lund,
1948).
[114] See *MÆ* 9 (1940), 121–54, 12 (1943), 71–6.

eac is *hearm Gode*
modsorg *gemacod*.   (*Genesis* 754–5)

For the sense 'cause to experience' see *OED make* v.[1] 9 b.

Ille here is shown to be a noun by a synonymous variant in which both words have been replaced by ON equivalents: 'In Egipt was na *ill* vs *graid*' (*Cursor Mundi*, Göttingen MS 6230), and by yet another in *ille don* 'inflict injury on' (*OED ill* a. and sb. B 4; *MED il(le)* n. I. (*b*)). The idiom is not traceable in ON.

1970. *hem þre*: there is nothing in the context (1955–69) to show who these adversaries are, though the pronoun *hem* ineluctably implies that they have been mentioned. The explanation is that in 1969–70 the author is repeating 1807–8 (since Bernard is here reporting to Ubbe the events recounted by the author in 1767 ff.); and in the latter context, *hem þre* is perfectly clear, since it refers to the three assailants mentioned in 1801 (*on*) and 1805 (*oþer two*). The author has exerted himself to be precise by specifying the total number of assailants as sixty-one in 1769, 1919, and 1929 (beside *mo þan sixti* 1957). *Hem thre* 1970 is an untypical lapse—not in his tallying, but in his control of two versions of the same events.

His repetition of 1808 at this point establishes that Skeat's insertion of *at* is right.

1977. *sinne*: see 2376 n.

1983–4. *arum, harum*: again 2409–10. These are phonetically significant spellings that directly attest a syllabic *r* in pronunciation, and are thus of practical help in scansion (i.e. when a disyllable rather than a monosyllable is metrically necessary). For other examples see *O&N* 1161–2 and 1260 (the latter within the line, but shown by the corruption to the nonsensical *atem* in MS J to derive from a common antecedent MS).

1996–8. See 767–9 n.

2010. The key to the understanding of this line is the rare OE collocation *aþ(as) a-leogan* 'be false to one's oaths' as used in *The Anglo-Saxon Chronicle* (anno 947): 'Hi hit eall *alugon*, ge wed ond eac *aþas*', and in the *Orosius* (ed. J. Bately (EETS, ss 6, 1980), III. viii, p. 67, l. 6) along with the almost identical ON equivalent *ljúga eið(a)* which is recorded only once, in the *Brot af Sigurþarkviða*, st. 2 (ed. G. Neckel and H. Kuhn, *Die Edda*, Heidelberg, 1962):

Mér hefir Sigurðr   selda *eiða*,
eiða selda,   alla *logna*

'Sigurþ gave me pledges—gave me pledges and has been false to them all.'

Leye oþ in *Hav.* may be a calque on the ON phrase rather than a survival of the OE one, since in the latter case *a-leye oþ* would have been the proper equivalent.

The juridical nature of the conception expressed in the phrase is adumbrated by the context in 2012–20, which is reminiscent of the legal function of 'oath-helpers'. See Liebermann, *Die Gesetze der Angelsachsen*, vol. ii, s.v. *Eideshelfer*; and *EGS* 2 (1948–9), 1–9.

2030. *G[r]iffin Galle*: the case for MS *Giffin* is shaky, since the only known name of this form is a surname, recorded four times in the early period,[115] from 1327 into the post-1500 period.

Griffin, which is a pet name for MW *Gruffydd*, is amply recorded by Reaney from *Domesday Book* up till 1285, in Wales, War., Staffs., and Norfolk. Three more examples are available, all of the time of Henry II[116]—one each from Notts., Leics., and Lincs., and this last as *(Griffinus) Bret* 'Breton'. Reaney regards *Griffin*, in examples from the Eastern counties, as being of Breton origin—on the strength of this third instance, and of what F. M. Stenton has described (with some striking evidence) as a 'migration' of Bretons into Lincs. from the Conquest onwards.[117]

Galle is recorded six times before 1400 by Reaney, including one example *c.* 1170 from Lincs. At least thirteen more from Lincs. are available, referring to members of one family and its branches, in numerous 12th-century charters,[118] and two 13th-century ones.[119] Thus *Galle* was clearly a well-known surname in Lincolnshire in the 12th and 13th centuries. We cannot know for how long speakers of English were aware that it meant 'foreigner' (see Reaney s.v. *Gall*). In the other examples in which it is combined with 'Christian' names, these are ordinary ones such as Arnald, Walter, etc. But in *Hav.* the combination of this surname of Celtic origin with the non-English Griffin is striking.

2046. *Kaym[es]*: there is just one recorded instance of *Kaim* (which is the OF form of the name) as an uninflected genitive singular in ME. In *Cursor Mundi* 1559, in this same common collocation with *kyn*, the Cotton and Göttingen MSS read *Kaym* (and *Caym* respectively) *kyn* (for Fairfax *Caymys* and Trinity *Kaymes*). But where this passage in *Hav.* is concerned, the metre happens to be an all but overriding argument for emending to the normal (and very common) form *Kaymes*. The uninflected one requires the line to be scanned:

þåt wérẹn ȯf Kaým˙kín aṅd Eűẹs.

This type of line, with two successive full stresses (and therefore a pause between them in the middle), is relatively uncommon; and the type produced by *Kaymes*:

þåt wérẹn ȯf Káyměs kín aṅd Eűẹs,

being a basic and very common one, is more likely to be what the author wrote here.

2069–70. *here frend þat*: 'the relatives of those whom ...'; cf. 1257.

[115] By P. H. Reaney, *A Dictionary of British Surnames* (rev. R. M. Wilson, London, 1976), s.v. *Geffen*.

[116] F. M. Stenton, *Documents Illustrative of the Social and Economic History of the Danelaw* (London, 1920), pp. cii, n. 3; 340; 385.

[117] *English Feudalism*, 24–6.

[118] Stenton *Documents* ... Index s.v. *Saltfleetby*, and pp. xxxix–xl.

[119] Peter Galle (1273) and Philip Galle (1292–3), *Placita de Quo Warranto* (Record Commission, 1818), temp. Edw. I–Edw. III, pp. 397 and 429.

2104. The hypermetrical line has manifestly been produced by a scribe's use of two negatives instead of one. *Ne* is the spurious one, since it constitutes an extra unstressed element after *Nou* (which is indispensable to the sense: cf. *nou* 2099 and *þis tid nithes* 2101).

2107. *at a bord*: i.e. at a gap between the planks in the 'wall of fir-wood' that Ubbe mentions in 2079 as all that divided his own bedroom from that of Havelok and Goldeborw.

2144. *kunrik*: emendation (as by Skeat, to *kunmerk* 'sign of royal birth') is based on the tacit assumption that the word is a noun and directly designates the supernatural light. But it is unnecessary and almost certainly mistaken to emend, since there is an ON adj. *kynrík-r* 'of exalted birth', and since an adjective (referring to Havelok) is syntactically admissible here. Moreover, the other references to the light that is emitted from Havelok's mouth in his sleep (589–93; 1252–8), and to the cross on his shoulder (603–5 and 1263–4), are immediately followed by explicit interpretation of these as signs of Havelok's exalted birth and destiny (607–11; 1261–2, 1267–71).

2166. *blakne*: superficially ambiguous, since the form is compatible either with *blåkne* 'grow dark', formed on *blåk* a. < OE *blæc* 'black' or with *blakne* 'grow pale', formed on *blāk* < OE *blāc* 'pale'. The former, however, is ruled out by 2169, which makes it clear that Havelok reacted not with anger but with fear. *Blakne* 'grow pale' is vouched for by the example of *blokne* in the Kentishman Shoreham's *Poems* (p. 3, l. 77), with the orthodox non-Nth. /ɔ:/ < OE *blāc*. *Blakne* here is thus the Nth. or Northerly form *blakne* with non-rounded /a:/.

No OE antecedent is recorded. But new formations in ME with the inchoactive suffix *-ne* (< OE *-nan*) are quite common; and the ON cognate a. *bleik-r* 'pale' has been used to form the 16th-century Scots *blaiken* 'become pale'.

2303–14. What the author is telling us here is authoritatively illustrated by the roughly contemporary account, by Henry de Bracton, of the procedure and the form of words to be used in the act of homage and the oath of fealty that always followed it:[120]

[The vassal places his hands between those of the lord and says these words:]
'*Deuenio homo vester*, de tenemento quod de vobis teneo [vel aliter: quod de vobis teneo & tenere debeo], & *fidem vobis portabo . . . contra omnes gentes* [*qui viuere poterint & mori*, secundum quosdam], salua fide debita domino regi et haeredibus suis'—et statim post, faciat domino suo sacramentum fidelitatis hoc modo:
'Hoc audis, domine N., quod *fidem vobis portabo* de vita & membris, corpore, et cattallis, & terreno honore, sic me Deus adiuuet & *hæc sancta Dei euangelia*—Et quidam hoc adiciunt: 'in sacramento, & bene, quod fideliter,

---

[120] *De Legibus et Consuetudinibus Angliae* Bk. II, *De Acquirendo rerum dominio*, ch. 35, 8, fo. 80; Woodbine and Thorne, ed. cit., p. 323.

et sine diminutione, contradictione . . .'. Terminis statutis faciet seruitium suum domino suo, et haeredibus suis.[121]

The act of homage (*manrede*) is mentioned in *Hav.* no less than eleven times (see Glossary); the procedure itself, without being named, in 2796–7; and the oath of fealty in 255, 487–90, 2269–70, 2308–11 and 2313, 2775, 2782, 2817, 2853. That they are distinct, is explicit in the phrase *manrede and oth* 2313, 2775; and that they are required by feudal law, in the phrase *after lawe of londe* 2816.

What is especially striking is that the author goes so far beyond bald statement of the two processes, and echoes cardinal phrases and details expressed in Bracton's formulation. Thus:

1. Deuenio homo vester	bicam is man 2255; cf. 2258, 2265, 2304, 2801–2, and 2174
2. fidem vobis portabo	him ghod fey beren 255
3. contra omnes gentes	ageynes stille and bolde 2310
4. qui viuere poterint & mori	liuen and deyen til þat he mouhte 257 (see n.)
5. fidem vobis portabo contra omnes gentes qui viuere poterint	. . . him god feyth bere Ageynes alle þat woren on liue 2270–1 (sim. 2854–5)
6. sic me . . . adiuuet . . . haec sancta Dei euangelia	o(n) (þe) bok(e) swere 487, 2308, 2782

For the sense of *hold-oþes* in 2782 and 2817, see 2782 n.

2204. Skeat's insertion of *he* after *And* is unnecessary and mistaken. The same syntactic principle applies here as is explained in the note on 1330: an unexpressed pronominal subject may have a noun as an antecedent (here *þe iustise* 2203).

2327. The games of *mine* and *hasard* are plentifully mentioned in OF romances, often in conjunction, though they were distinct. Cf. *Erec* 356:

> Li autre jeuent d'autre part
> Ou a la mine ou a hasart

and *Roman de la Rose* (ed. G. Servois, SATF, 1893), 498:

> Rejoent as dez, au hasart . . .
> Cil as eschez, cil a la mine.

See F. Semrau, *Würfel und Würfelspiel im alten Frankreich, Zeitschrift für romanische Philologie*, Beiheft 23 (Halle, 1910), pp. 39, 50–2, and Index s.v. *mine* and *hasart*.

2334. *grim greu*: see 2498 n., and H. Bradley, 'On *Havelok*, Line 2333', *TPS* (1903–4), 163; and *Sir Beues of Hamtoun* 1880: *þus beginneþ grim to growe*.

2337. i.e. to minstrels, as is sometimes explicitly said in OF accounts of marriage festivities and other public celebrations to which minstrels contributed their services; cf. *Chrétien's Erec* 2109 ff. (of the festivities at the hero's wedding):

---

[121] For a translation, see Pollock and Maitland, i. 297–8. On homage and fealty, see ibid., pp. 297–307; F. L. Ganshof, *Feudalism*, pp. 64–78; J. E. A. Jolliffe, *The Constitutional History of Medieval England*, p. 153.

Cel jor furent jugleor lié;
Car tuit furent a gre paiié.
Tot fu randu quanqu'il acrurent,
Et *maint bel don doné lor furent*,
Robes de ver et d'erminetes,
De conins et de violetes,
D'escarlates, de dras de soie;
Qui vost cheval, qui vost monoie,
Chascuns ot don lonc son savoir
Si buen com il le dut avoir.

The equivalent here in *Hav.* is put so tersely as to be cryptic.

2339. *trod*: nothing can be made of MS *croud*; and Sisam's palmary emendation is as certainly right as such things can be. The corruption may have begun with a scribe's attempt to replace the past part. *trod* (OEN *tróa* inf.) with that of the native *trowe*, its cognate: *trod* > *troud* > *croud*. A short vowel and a 'weak' inflection *-dd-* are attested in the MSw. forms pret. *trodde*, p.p. *trodder* (beside *tróþe*, *tró(i)t*.

2356. *o-bon*: recurs 2526, and as *o-bone* (: *sone* 'soon') 2506, 2572, in each case preceded by the adverb *wel* or *iuel(e)*. It was first satisfactorily explained by E. Ekwall,[122] who accounted for the *o* as a reduced form (by assimilation) of the ON 'expletive' particle *of* in an ODa. *(vael, illa) of bóin* 'equipped, etc.', in which OEN *bóin* corresponds to OIcel. *búinn*, past part. of *búa*. This particle occurs in ON before verbs, as an equivalent of certain unstressed prefixes in the other early Gmc languages: itself originally *inter alia* a prefix, it has in ON come to replace these others.[123]

There is no knowing precisely how the author of *Hav.* conceived of the structure of *o bon(e)*. In the roughly equivalent *iboen* in *Dame Sirith* 434, the foreign *bon* has been given the native past participle prefix. On this analogy, we may deduce that *of bon(e)* (> *o bon(e)*) was apprehended as a compound of the native class represented in OE *ofslean* etc.

2376. *sinne*: one of three exceptional uses in *Hav.* In the straightforward context of 1977, the sense is clearly 'a pity; a shame', as it is glossed in *OED sin* sb. 3*a*. In 2628 (which is not registered in *OED*) the context is not decisive, but is consistent with 'pity'. The example in 2376 is glossed 'a fear of doing wrong' in *OED sin* sb. 3*b* (obviously for the sake of retaining some sort of lien with the main sense 'sin' in *sinne*).

None of these senses is attested for OE *synn* nor explicable from its uses; and only one other example is recorded by *OED* for the first and the third (in each case from Henry's *Schir William Wallace*, *c.* 1470[124]). All this points to a semantic borrowing from another language; and the answer lies ready to hand in OF *pechié* 'sin', among the secondary senses of which 'a pity' and 'an

---

[122] 'Middle English *o bon*', *Selected Papers*, Lund Studies in English 33 (1963), 104–11.
[123] See H. Kuhn, *Das Füllwort of—um im Altwestnordischen* (Göttingen, 1929), especially pp. 126–7.
[124] Ed. J. Moir, Scottish Text Society, Edinburgh, 1889.

occasion for pity' are recorded (alongside abundant examples of the related sense 'misfortune, bad luck').[125] All are entirely natural semantic developments: the use of OF *pechiere* 'sinner' as an interjection to express pity shows that there was an emotional or affective charge in these words.

OF *pechié* is even used in a context very like that of *sinne* in *Hav.* 1977, of a hero's wounds, in *Gormont et Isembart* (ed. A. Bayot, CFMA, 1931), 324 (and in the identical line 414) to mean 'a (great) pity':

> Ses plaies prennant a sainnier,
> li cor li ment ['fails'], e Hue chiet:
> ceo fut damages e *pechié*.

Thus all three uses of *sinne* in *Hav.* are best treated as varieties of one and the same sense. 'Pity' is the appropriate one in 2376 and 2628, and 'a pity' (which is simply 'occasion for pity') in 1977.

2390. *cauenard*: this hitherto unique (and therefore suspect) spelling of a rare word otherwise recorded as ME *caynard* has now been authenticated by a second example discovered by Prof. A. McIntosh in the MS Bodl. Ashmole 42 text (fo. 199 b, 14) of the *Northern Homily Collection*. See 'Some Words in the *Northern Homily Collection*', *Neuphilologische Mitteilungen*, 73 (1972), 197.

The ME type *caynard* is apparently an adoption of French *cagnard* 'lazybones, slothful person'. The latter is not recorded till 1520 (in Jean Marot); but, as a manifestly affective expression (usually referred to a Gallo-Rom. *cania 'bitch'), and therefore likely to have been colloquial, it might well have escaped record in OF literary texts, and might likewise have existed in AN. The semantic history of the French word is complex: see von Wartburg, *FEW* *cania 1, 3*a*–*b*.

Of the three ME examples of *caynard*, those in *Handlyng Synne* 8299 and *Wife of Bath's Prologue* 235 are highly contextual uses the sense of which is difficult to define closely; *The Man in the Moon*[126] 20 alone prescribes or is compatible with the sense 'sluggard'. The rather less specific notion 'useless object; good-for-nothing wretch' might be nearer the mark for the others. The two contexts available for *cauenard* in *Hav.* and the *Northern Homily Collection* (where a fiend calls a Bishop Nonnus *þou olde* ~) likewise do not give a clue to the sense; but the notion 'slothful' is not apt in either. As an expedient for the present, 'wretch' might do as a gloss that would at least not clash with any of the contexts.

The ME form *cauenard* is difficult to account for in terms of the etymological explanation of F *cagnard* as formed on *cania 'bitch'.

2393. *þat*: best taken as the object of *sendes . . . word and bedes*, and hence as an antecedent of the noun clause introduced by *þat* 2394.

2406–7. Cf. 1918 and n.

2409–10. Cf. 1983–4 and n.

2414. Line 2415 shows that *his two breþren and oþre fiue* is the subject of *slowen*, and hence that the MS *ne werē* is a corruption (by a mechanical and mistaken use of the titulus, as in *didē* 79, *dwellē* 1352) of the ME conjunction *ne*

---

[125] See von Wartburg, *FEW pĕccare* I, 2.   [126] Ed. *EMEVP* VIII N, pp. 127–8.

were, *nere* 'had not'. This latter developed out of the construction of *ne were* 'had it not been for', which actually occurs in *Hav.* 1975 and 2678 and is inherited from OE. As a conjunction, *ne were* is a ME innovation, which apparently arose from repetition of *were* at another point in the clause (and was thus due to 'hyper-characterization'), as in the following examples (all negative conditional clauses): 'And *neore* his worþly wille *weore*' (Carleton Brown, *Religious Lyrics of the Fourteenth Century*, No. 112, 51); '*Nere* helpe *nere* þe nerre' (*þe Wohunge of Ure Lauerd*, EETS, os 241, pp. 27, 284 ff.); 'And *nere were* that he ys nat stable . . .' (Vinaver, *The Works of Sir Thomas Malory*, vol. ii. 948, 23). See further my 'Some Textual Problems in Religious Lyrics of the Fourteenth Century', *English Philological Studies* 9 (1965), 94–6.

2433. *fot*: six other examples of *fot* as 'man, person' are recorded in *MED*, ranging from the early 13th-century *Ste. Iuliene* 642 to the 15th-century *Merlin*, vol. ii, p. 274, l. 22 (ed. H. B. Wheatley, EETS, os 36 (1899)); and three are used with a negative. There is no trace of this use in OE. But both are attested for the OF synonym *piez*—the first, corresponding to the use of *fot* here, as in *Fergus* (ed. E. Martin, Halle, 1872), 6099:

> Ja Damesdius bien ne me face
> Se uns sels *piés* en escapast.

For the second, cf. *Les Enfances Guillaume* 819 (see 812–13): 'Des quinze mil n'en poist *piez* aler!' (ed. P. Henry, SATF, Paris, 1935), where the editor has misunderstood *piez* and glossed it 'de pire facon'. Thus *fot* here is clearly a calque on this use of OF and AN *piez*.

2462. Though this proverb is plentifully attested in post-medieval times,[127] the only other ME examples cited in *The Oxford Dictionary of English Proverbs* (s.v. *old*) are two later ones—from MS Douce 52 (*c.* 1350) No. 119, and Gower's *Confessio Amantis* iii. 2033. And William of Shoreham, who became vicar of Chart Sutton some time after 1320,[128] has left us a version in which, by paraphrasing the word *old*, he has sacrificed the pointed and pithy turn of phrase that is typical of proverbs: 'Senne makeþ nywe schame, | þaȝ hy forȝete be.' (p. 98, ll. 17–18).

The proverb is attested in OF, in the same MS of the end of the 13th century as is concerned in 649 n.: 'Vieulz pechiez fet novele honte' (Morawski, *Proverbes français antérieurs au XVᵉ siècle*, No. 2481). The ME equivalent is thus probably an adoption of the latter.

2469. A serious difficulty in the established interpretation of *dam* here as a separate word (representing OF *dan* < L *dominus* and meaning 'lord') is that in all the *OED*'s other six examples it is used as a title. It is therefore best treated in this passage as the unstressed form (repeatedly used by the Lincolnshire writer Robert Mannyng, in rhyme, and not uncommon in ME) of the OE suffix *-dōm*.

---

[127] See M. P. Tilley, *A Dictionary of the Proverbs in England in the Sixteenth and Seventeenth Centuries*, S 471.
[128] See M. Konrath, *The Poems of William of Shoreham* (EETS, es, 86, 1902), p. xiv.

2477–512. The savagery of the penalties described here was no mere literary fiction, but a fact of real life. Flaying alive, however, is extremely rare as a historical fact in medieval England, though commoner in France.[129]

Examples of the standard horrifying forms of execution are those of David, brother of Llewellyn of Wales, and his seneschal (1283);[130] Andrew of Harcla (1322), who was first stripped of the insignia of knighthood and of the earldom of Carlile;[131] and the two Despensers, father and son (1322).[132]

Flaying is more freely mentioned in romances, e.g. as a threat uttered to Alexander (as part of the process of execution) in *Kyng Alisaunder* 893–5. For the ignominious ride to execution (with face towards the horse's or ass's tail, *Hav.* 2451 and 2822–4) see ibid., 4701–2. For other examples see R. Mellinkoff, 'Riding Backwards: Theme of Humiliation and Symbol of Evil' (*Viator*, 4 (1973), 153–76), whose first ME example is from *Hav.*, and who does not mention *Kyng Alisaunder*.

Godrich is let off much more lightly (2821–42) than Godard. But each is explicitly called a 'traitor' (*swike* 2402, 2483, 2806, 2758); and each suffered the penalty of having his children deprived of their inheritance.

2482–7. Attaching a written statement of the offence to a criminal's body was evidently the practice in real life. The only examples known to me are two hundred and fifty years later, in *The Diary of Henry Machyn*,[133] and refer to lesser offences: 'three men put in the pillory for perjury *with paper sett over their hedes*' (1556), p. 104; '. . . a woman ryd apone [horse-back] *with a paper on her hed*, for bawdere, with a basen ryngyng' (1559), p. 220; see also pp. 74 and 251.

2496. *ritte*: the earliest recorded example; mostly Nth. and Northerly in ME—later on, Nth. and Scots. The only potential equivalents are OHG *rizzon, rezzon*, weak II (with geminated affricate compatible with Gmc *-tt-*) 'prick; tear; wound', beside OHG *rizzen*, weak I 'id.' and Sw. *rita* 'carve; write' (1600–).

OHG *rizzon, rezzon* is an acknowledged product of the 'expressive' doubling of the final consonant of a verb-stem,[134] which was very commonly used in the early Gmc tongues to form verbs of weak class II (often on a base represented in one of the principal parts of a strong verb). Those with doubled voiceless plosives are usually intensives.

Ritte, like other verbs of this type that are first recorded in ME, has escaped notice by Wissmann and Martinet only because there is no recorded OE antecedent. It is clearly an ideophonic verb, formed (like OHG *rizzon*) on the

---

[129] See W. R. J. Barron, 'The penalties for treason in medieval life and literature', *Journal of Medieval History*, 7 (1981), who gives only one English example of the sentence (and one not actually carried out), p. 191, and French ones 192 ff.

[130] John of Oxenedes, *Chronica* (ed. H. Ellis, RS, 1859), 262.

[131] *The Brut* (ed. F. Brie, EETS, os 131), vol. i (1960), pp. 226–8.

[132] Ibid., i. 240.

[133] Ed. J. G. Nichols (Camden Society, 1848).

[134] See W. Wissmann, *Nomina Postverbalia in den altgermanischen Sprachen*, vol. i (Göttingen, 1932), pp. 170–2, 190, 42, and 58, 12; A. Martinet, *La Gémination consonantique d'origine expressive dans les langues germaniques* (Paris, 1937), p. 169; 'Some English Ideophones' (*AL* 6 (1954), 73–111).

Gmc base *rit- 'incise' write' as in Sw. rita,[135] and immediately perhaps on some unrecorded verb in ON cognate with OIcel. rita (weak II), which latter is attested only in the senses 'write; reckon up'.

2498. grim: identical with grim 2334 'a fury of excitement'. It is to be equated with MDu. grimme 'bitterness, hostility', just as gore here is with MDu. gare, gaer and the phonetic variant MDu. gere 'desire; passion, fury', since both the MDu. words are used in the same collocation—met groter grimmen and met groten gare (gere)—in similar contexts.

Moreover, there is a rare ME grim, used once in the equivalent phrase with muche grym, and a gere 'fit of passion', recorded from Chaucer to 1609, of which gare sb.[2] of OED 'fit of passion' (1606–74) is obviously a phonetic variant. These are clearly identical with grim and gore respectively in Hav., and like them adoptions of the MDu. equivalents. See my 'Ten Cruces in Middle English Texts', EGS 3 (1949–50), 69–72.

2517–20. In Sir Tristrem 909–17 the hero acts likewise in a closely similar situation, after he has reconquered his hereditary domains and decides to take ship to the court of King Mark:

> Rohand he 3af þe wand
> And bad him sitt him bi,
>   þat fre:
> 'Rohand lord make Y
> To held þis lond of me!
>
> þou and þine sones fiue
> Schul held þis lond of me;
> þer-while þou art o liue
> þine owhen schal it be!'

In both passages possession of the domains is formally bestowed (as a form of feudal tenure) by the hereditary lord of the land. Sir Tristrem contributes the orthodox detail (not explicit in wit a fayre staf in Hav.) that the lord (in Hav. the king) hands the staff or rod over to the vassal.

In this ceremonial act of investiture the staf, or wand, or rod symbolized the property, as any of a number of objects might, such as a clod of earth or a glove; and investiture was always preceded by the act of homage and the oath of fealty (on which see 2303–14 n.), already carried out by Ubbe in 2251–6. The use of a staff[136] in ceremonial actions of this kind can be traced back at least to Frankish custom, whatever its precise symbolic force. In a historical instance in 787, of proceedings something like the inverse of the two ME examples, Tassilo, duke of the Bavarians, yielded up his land to Charlemagne as follows:

> reddit ei ipsam patriam cum baculo in cuius capite similitudo hominis erat scultum [et effectus est vassus eius].[137]

---

[135] See Hellquist, Svensk etymologisk ordbok s.v. rita.

[136] See Bracton, De Legibus et Consuetudinibus Angliae, Bk. ii, fo. 40; M. Bloch (trans. L. A. Manyon), Feudal Society, i. 173; Pollock and Maitland, ii on Seisin and pp. 83–90.

[137] Annales Guelferbytani, ed. G. H. Pertz, MGH SS, i, p. 43; bracketed addition from Annales Nazariani, ibid.

See the discussion by K. Hauck, in P. E. Schramm, *Herrschaftszeichen und Staatssymbolik*, i (*MGH* Schriften, 13/1, Stuttgart, 1954), pp. 192–212, and by A. Gauert, ibid., 262–70.

2521–4. Gaimar and the *Lai* know nothing of this. The author of *Hav.* might well have chosen to credit Havelok with founding a fictive priory, to mark the quasi-filial gratitude and the religious devotion of a hero whose experiences were legend and thus hardly less than fictive. To found a religious house was a conventional gesture for a main figure in a ME romance. Apart from an abbey in *Octavian*,[138] and an unspecified house in *Sir Beues of Hamtoun*, ll. 4613–16, a chantry is mentioned in *Sir Gawain and the Carl of Carlisle*[139] in words reminiscent of those in *Hav.*:

> 'And I purpose for their sake
> A chantry in this place to make,
> And 5 preists to sing for aye
> *Vntill itt be doomesday*'.[140]

The example in *Hav.* has nevertheless led editors to look for an actual model. No priory of Benedictine 'monks' is traceable at Grimsby during the thirteenth century. Wellow Abbey is sometimes mentioned—as by Holthausen, note ad loc., and (doubtfully) by Skeat in his edn. of 1868—as perhaps being the house in question. But it was a house of Augustinian canons, not of monks (*Victoria County History of Lincoln*, ii, p. 161). And the poet would not have been either so slack or so ignorant as to say 'monks' when he meant 'canons', since he mentions both (as if to imply that they were distinct) in 360, and since he shows such a strong interest in ecclesiastical matters. The house of Augustinian friars at Grimsby, founded in 1293 (D. Knowles and R. N. Hadcock, *Medieval Religious Houses in England and Wales*, p. 240), must be ruled out for the same reason.

It is therefore worth noticing that there was a Benedictine priory *at Lincoln* in the author's time, sited in the open area to the east of the city that was later known as the Monks' Liberty. This was St Mary Magdalene, a cell of the Benedictine abbey of St Mary's, York; it had been founded by 1150, for an establishment of a prior and one or two monks.[141] In view of the signs that the author knew Lincoln at first hand (see 876 n. and 2829–30 n.), he may well have chosen—in adding the foundation of a priory for Grim to the story—to make it a Benedictine one on the model of St Mary Magdalene's at Lincoln (the existence of which has been independently pointed out to me by Dr Eric Stone).

2549. *ut-bede*: this has escaped record as a separable compound in Bosworth–Toller and *OED*, though shown to be such by the ON noun *útboð*

---

[138] Northern version, ed. G. Sarrazin (Heilbronn, 1886), ll. 76 ff.

[139] Ed. A. Kurvinen (Helsinki, 1951), Additional MS, ll. 421–4.

[140] On chantries, see A. Hamilton Thompson, *The English Clergy and their Organisation in the Later Middle Ages* (Oxford, 1947), pp. 132 ff.

[141] See J. W. F. Hill, *Medieval Lincoln*, pp. 338–40; Knowles and Hadcock, op. cit., p. 69.

'summons to muster for a battle or war' beside the related verb *bjóða út* 'summon to muster for a military expedition etc.'. The one other example traceable in the dictionaries (though not registered as a separable compound) is the post-Conquest separated form *bead ut*, in a main clause introduced by the adv. *þa*, where the separated form was idiomatically obligatory in OE and hence extensively used in ME. And it is significant that this solitary other example occurs in the *Pet. Chron.* (s.a. 1071), the language of which has been strongly influenced by ON: '*þa bead* he *ut* scipfyrde and landfyrde' ('Then he ordered a naval force and a land force to muster'). Moreover, it occurs in a context virtually identical with that in which *bjóða út* is used in *Egils Saga* (ed. Finnur Jónsson (Halle, 1894)), ch. IX, l. 1: 'Haraldr konungr *bauð út* leiðangri miklum ok dró saman skipaher' ('King Harald ordered a large expeditionary force to muster and got together a naval force'). All this strongly suggests that (at least in the only two known examples) ME *ut-bede* is a calque on the ON phrase.

2549–74. The startling use of a specific date (naming month and day, but— just as oddly—not the year) in a legendary tale that mentions no other dates, is the clue to the nature of this whole passage, and shows it to be a literary version of the type of official document known as a 'writ of military summons', or a writ *De veniendo cum equis et armis*.[142] This was a formal summons of the feudal levy, issued by the king (hence the equivalent action in *Hav.* by Godrich, as regent) to his tenants-in-chief, ordering them to muster the knights whose service they 'owed' him, at a specified date and place, ready, mounted, and armed, to discharge the *servitium debitum*.

A good example, roughly of the time when *Hav.* was composed, is the writ for the first of Edward I's six summonses of the feudal host (1276, 1282, 1294, 1299, 1302, 1306), in the version addressed to the sheriffs of counties, for them to pass on to his tenants-in-chief:[143]

... precipimus quod ... cum omni celeritate clamari faciatis in comitatu predicto & in singulis Hundredis, Burgis, et villis mercatoriis per totam balliam tuam quod omnes illi ... qui de nobis tenent in capite per servicium militare ad portandum arma potentes existunt, *sicut terras et tenementa sua* quae de nobis tenent in capite *diligunt*, sint apud Wygorniam in Octavis Sancti Johannis Baptiste proximis futuris [24 June] *cum equis et armis* et cum servicio suo nobis *parati* exinde nobiscum proficisci *in expeditionem nostram* contra predictum Lewelinum. ...

A cardinal point in these writs is the requirement *cum equis et armis*. One of great interest for *Hav.* is the penalty for defaulting, which is veiled in the italicized clause above and explicit in King John's important writ of 1205:[144] landed defaulters would be disinherited, and those with no land would

---

[142] So called by Jolliffe, *The Constitutional History of Medieval England*, p. 357, because it is sometimes thus docketed.

[143] Text in F. Palgrave, *Parliamentary Writs and Writs of Military Summons*, vol. i (London, 1827), p. 196.

[144] T. D. Hardy, *Rotuli Litterarum Patentium* (London, 1835), p. 55, col. I.

become serfs, along with their heirs in perpetuity (*ipsi et heredes sui servi fient in perpetuum*). In *Hav.*, the equivalent of *cum equis et armis* is so insistently under-lined as to be unmistakably the main point; and even the penalty for defaulters is stated (2562–6). The phrase *ferd ut-bede* unequivocally shows that a muster under arms is concerned. And to clinch the correspondence, in the writs like-wise the year of the muster is commonly not mentioned in the summons itself.

By *c.* 1200, the rank and file of the feudal levy were no longer knights, but paid men-at-arms (*servientes equites* or *servientes pedites*), ME *sergeaunz*, with some knights as officers. This passage in *Hav.* specifies only knights in 2574. But other passages show that the change had already come about by the time *Hav.* was composed: cf. *knithes and serganz* 2117, and see 2356 and 2362, 2371–2.[145] For further changes up to and including the reign of Edward I, see F. M. Powicke, *The Thirteenth Century*, pp. 542–59.

It is not clear why the author of *Hav.* chose 17 March as the date of the muster. But this happens to be the date of issue of just one document (for the year 1295) among all the writs of Edward I (1272–1307).[146] Though not itself a writ of military summons, it is an inquisition for purposes of a summons to military service with the king.[147] And 1295 is curiously close to the probable earlier limit for the date of composition of *Hav.* (Introduction VI, 1). See *SMP* 203 ff. for further discussion.

2558. This reading of the line, though by far the neatest and simplest of all that have been propounded, has been passed over in silence, no doubt because it goes back to Skeat's edition of 1902 and was suppressed in Sisam's revision of that edition in 1915. A shift from indirect into direct speech without any explicit indication is common in ME (see 166 n.).

The one thing that might not be instantly clear in any reading whatever of the line is the point of *so*. It is to be interpreted as correlative with and anticipating *So (þat)* in the adverbial clause of purpose in 2561, and hence as 'in such fashion', and as summarizing the various ways of being armed that are specified in 2550–5. Line 2558 thus means ' "with altogether reliable weapons as your equipment [lit. 'that you carry']", in such fashion'.

Sisam's emendation to *þe[i]* (or *he*) *ber[e] so*, i.e. 'with which they were equipped', has the advantage of echoing the insistent use of *bere* in conjunc-tion with the weapons in 2551 and 2553, but is palaeographically somewhat frail. It is, however, less drastic than the emendation to *yb[o]re[n] so* which has been substituted for it in the 1973 impression of Skeat–Sisam, and which simply makes away with the *e* of MS *ye* without accounting for it. This had already been suggested by Skeat in 1902 as an alternative to his interpretation of the line as being in direct speech. But Skeat's first explanation is the only

---

[145] See A. L. Poole, *Obligations of Society in the XII and XIII Centuries*, pp. 36–53; F. M. Stenton, *English Feudalism*, pp. 175–9 (and especially on *expeditio*, as used in the writ above); A. E. Prince, 'The Army and Navy', in J. F. Willard and W. A. Morris, *The Eng-lish Government at Work, 1327–1336*, vol. i (Cambridge, Mass., 1940), 348–58.

[146] F. Palgrave, op. cit., i, p. 267.

[147] For its significance see M. Powicke, *Military Obligation in Medieval England* (Oxford, 1962), p. 110.

convincing one—among other things, because in this reading the line comes nearer to sounding like ME—and is likely to be right.

2568. *Sat* in the sense 'disregarded' does not occur in OE, and is recorded only in Scots from the later 15th century onwards (*OED sit* v. 34). Ekwall has therefore suggested (*Selected Papers*, p. 111) that the use here is a semantic borrowing from ON, in which this sense 'disregarded' for *sitja* 'to sit' (though rare) is attested in *Árna Saga* (ed. Guðni Jónsson, *Byskupa Sögur*, i (Reykjavík, 1948)), p. 316, ch. 33:

> Enn hafði annat bref komit til Lofts a sama sumri, ok *sat* hann bæði ('another letter had reached Loftr in the same summer, and he disregarded both').

But *sat* here is more likely to be an aphetic form of *atsitte* 'resist', since it is used with *bode* 'summons' as object, just as *atsitte* is in 2201.

2582. *þe priorie*, with the definite article, and in the singular, seems surprisingly specific. The only 13th-century priory in Grimsby was one of Augustinian canonesses, founded before 1184 (Knowles and Hadcock, *Medieval Religious Houses in England and Wales*, p. 278). There was a house of Franciscan friars, founded by 1240, and another of Austin friars, founded in 1293.

Since l. 2584 clearly refers to churches and priests at large, the monks and nuns of 2585 are not to be associated with the priory of 2582.

2607. Though *cop(e)* and *cup* are attested as spellings of *quoth* 'said', MS *couth* is not. Thus it can hardly be a merely erratic spelling of *quoth*, and is likely to be corrupt.

2607–8. These two earls, as figures in the action, correspond to two *princes* mentioned by Gaimar as allies of the *Danish* usurper (743–6), and hence to the two symbolic lions in the prophetic dream assigned to Goldeborw by Gaimar (227–34) and the *Lai d'Haveloc* 433–6 (see Introduction III, 17). They were thus evidently made available to the author of *Hav.* in the received story. But their names are innovations; for the highly specific status and title given the second of them here, see 2608 n.

2608. What (it must be asked) was the Earl of Chester doing in a battle near Lincoln, above all on the side of the reprobate Godrich? The first clue is that Ranulf de Blundeville, 'the greatest baron of the realm',[148] Earl of Chester at the time of King John's death, one of his executors, and devotedly loyal to the young King Henry III, was also Earl of Lincoln from 1217. He had been one of the leaders of the royalist army that overwhelmed the French and native forces supporting Louis the Dauphin as a claimant to succeed John at the battle of Lincoln on 20 May 1217.[149] But he was also leader of the group of earls with whom Richard of Cornwall allied himself in his violent quarrel with Henry III in 1227.[150] Thus the Earl of Chester's association with Godrich in *Hav.* is intelligible on the assumption that the latter, *qua* Earl of Cornwall, is a reminiscence of Richard of Cornwall: see 178 n.

[148] F. M. Powicke, *The Thirteenth Century*, p. 2.

[149] See F. M. Powicke, *King Henry III and the Lord Edward*, pp. 11–13, 736–8.

[150] Powicke, ibid., 50 n. 1, 83 and n. 1, 138 n. 1; N. Denholm-Young, *Richard of Cornwall*, pp. 10–13, 16–17, 24–5.

Ranulf died in October 1232, having just previously resigned the earldom of Lincoln to his sister the Countess of Winchester, who resigned it after his death to her son-in-law John de Lacy, constable of Chester. But it does not follow that *Hav.* was composed before 1232: cf. 178 n.

2611–3. The construction is as in a corresponding type of passage in OF epics which is a *locus communis* in descriptions of battle or of preparations for it, and for the normal form of which see *Aymeri de Narbonne* 826–8, 4120–3, 4212–16 and *Aliscans* 277–80. For the example in *Hav.* cf. *Aymeri de Narbonne* 1245–6:

> Lors *veisiez* ces chevax enseler,
> Metre ces frains et ces hernois trouser

and *Aliscans* 3093–100 (ed. G. Rolin, Leipzig, 1894).

2612. The emendation of MS *late* to *lace* is prescribed by the fact that corslets were laced up when being donned for combat, as the two following passages in *King Horn* show (L 718–20, O 739–41, C 716–18; and O 868–9, C 841–2):

> Wiþ armes he gon him shrede;
> His *brunie* he con *lace*
> So he shulde in to *place* ('field of battle')

> Hys *brenye* on he caste—
> *Lacede* hyt wel faste.

See Hall's note on O 841 in his edition.

For the standard scribal error of misreading and hence miswriting *c* and *t* for each other, see 2339 and n.

2614. The line is syntactically ambiguous:

(*a*) *al* might be the adv. in emphatic use before *so*; but the examples in *Hav.* (see Glossary) are all followed by *so* + adj. + *so* (correlative). It is thus more likely to be the pl. of the adj. used substantivally. The endingless form is metrically obligatory (cf. *al* 2360 as the obj. pl. of the adj.)

(*b*) if 2614 introduces a new sentence, *al* is the subject, and a nom. pl. If on the other hand 2614 is governed by *se* 2611, *al* is an obj. pl.

The first OF passage quoted in 2611–13 n. makes it clear that *keste*, *lace*, and *sette* are passive infinitives; and since *plette* is in the second analysis of 2614 an active infinitive and would break the sequence, the line is best taken as a new sentence.

plette: (1) the root-vowel *-e-* in this, and in *of . . . plette* inf. 2445 and pret. 2627, cannot represent *-æ-* in OE *plættan* 'strike someone a blow', since the reflex of OE *æ̆* in the author's variety of ME is shown by rhymes to have been *ă̆*. (2) All the other examples in *OED*, like those of the corresponding noun *plat* sb., have *-a-*, and must therefore represent OE *plættan* v. and *plætt* n. 'a buffet'. (3) The *-e-* type in *Hav.* must therefore be an adoption of MDu. *pletten* 'strike someone a blow'. (4) *Of-plat* 2756 and *plattinde* 2283 thus probably derive in form from OE *plættan*. (5) The sense 'rush, hurry' in *plattinde* and in *plette* 2614 is not attested in OE *plættan* or MDu. *pletten*. It can be explained as due to the fact that both 'a buffet' and 'rushing' are accompanied by some sort of sound, and that a verb might therefore develop the latter from the former sense. (6) Since no separable compound of the type *of-pletten*, *of-platten* is traceable elsewhere in Gmc, it is apparently a new formation in ME.

2627. Skeat's emendation of *For* to *þat* does not account for the alleged corruption of the latter to something palaeographically so remote from it. *Forþ* is palaeographically less improbable; and one known use of it that would fit this context is 'far, a good distance' (*OED forth* adv. 4).

2635–6. The rhyme, being one of the standard ME types of assonance (paralleled in *Hav.* 1825–6), is unexceptionable. The difficulty is that *with þe swerd* 2636 cannot refer to the adversary's sword, since it was the shield that was held by the left arm (see below, and *Sir Beues of Hamtoun* 2467–9). K. Sisam argues that *swerd* must be a corruption of *sheld*, on the strength of descriptions of single combat in which one of the stock details is that an adversary's left arm is cut off along with the shield (and in which, we may add, the rhyme *sheld* : *feld* 'field' is common), as in *Roland and Vernagu* 823–4.

A key passage is available in *Lybeaus Desconus* (ed. M. Mills, EETS, os 261, 1969), 1930–5:

> But Lybeauus karf adoun
> Hys scheld *wyth hys fachoun*,
> þat he tok Yrayn fro.
> Wyth-out more tale teld
> þe *left* arm *wyth þe scheld*
> Well euene he smot of þo.

This combines two relevant points: not only does the hero cut off the adversary's left arm along with the shield, but he is explicitly said to do so *with his sword* (*fachoun*). Both points recur in *Sir Beues of Hamtoun* 1767–70:

> Wiþ þat word Beues smot doun
> Grander is *scheld wiþ is fachoun*,
> And is *left* hande be þe wrest,
> Hit fleз awei þourз help of Crist.

It is thus clear that *with þe swerd* in *Hav.* 2636 can warrantably be analysed (as suggested in the textual footnotes of Skeat–Sisam) as modifying *slow* 2634, just as the equivalents *wyth hys fachoun* in *Lybeaus* 1931 and *Sir Beues of Hamtoun* 1768 modify *karf* and *smot* respectively. Thus: 'he struck the third (adversary) so hard with his sword that he caused the man's left arm to fly on to the field of battle'.

A stylistic point also calls for notice. The author has twice just before chosen to specify that a blow is dealt *with þe swerd* by Havelok and Robert (2626 and 2632), and goes on to say the same of the latter's two brothers (2633; 2638, 2646). Moreover, three times over he speaks of someone 'striking' (always with the word *slo*) with a *drawn* sword (Godrich 2604; Robert 2631–2; William 2633–4). This notably uniform mode of expression may be read either as reinforcing the above interpretation of *with þe swerd* 2636, or just conceivably as an objection to it (on the ground that, even in a ME romance, to repeat the mention of William's sword in 2633 would not be acceptable).

2666–7. The apparent oddity of the use of *bete* with *dintes* as an object is due to the neat native device (*ayþer on oþer*) for expressing its reciprocal force. This reciprocal use of *beat* is otherwise attested only once, in 1586 (cf. *OED beat* v.[1] 4*b*).

2687–8. See 767–9 n.

2688. *hul*: the passage is a version of a type of hyperbole which is a stock device in descriptions of battle in OF epics, and hence in ME romances, and which refers to the blood that is shed. Cf. *Arthour and Merlin* 5293 ff.:

> So many paiems, saun faile,
> Were yslawe at þat bataile
> þat þe blod ran *in* ['into'] *þe valaie*.

Thus *hul* may be expected to mean something like 'valley, low ground', and belong to the group of Gmc words represented in English by *hollow* and *hole*. The rhyme on *ful* shows that the vowel in *hul* must be /u/; the word therefore cannot be a form of *hole* n. 'hole etc.', as *MED* interprets it (*hol(e)* n. (2), 4 (*a*)). The only words that match it in form and (effectually) in sense are the early Da. *hul* n. (also a.) 'hole' and *hula* 'hollowness, hole' (beside *hol* and *hola*). They were produced by the levelling out, within the paradigm, of a prim. ON /u/ that was followed by /u/ in an ending, as in the nom. and acc. pl. *hulu, dat. pl. *hulum*, or by /e:/ in the dat. sg. *hule, beside /o/ before /a/, e.g. nom. and acc. sg. *hula > *hol*, by the process of *a*-mutation.[151]

Just one other probable example is available in ME, in *The Bestiary* 81 (ed. *EMEVP* XII, pp. 165 ff.):

> Caue ge ['she'] haueð to crepen in, ðat winter hire ne derie,
> Mete in hire *hule* ðat ge muge bi liuen.

Other versions of *The Bestiary*, e.g. the AN one of Philippe de Thaün, and one among the three L translations of the Greek original, though not direct sources of the ME, correspond closely enough to suggest that *hule* 81 means 'cave'. Cf. the *Physiologus Latinus* (version B),[152] pp. 22–5, especially p. 22, ll. 6–8 (= *The Bestiary* 72–7; cf. 80–9):

> Et quaerunt grana cuiuslibet seminis; cum autem inuenerint . . . apprehendunt singula grana, portantes in *spelunca* sua.

And Philippe uses *fosse* 858, *fossete* 864 and 974. Moreover, since *hole* 77 and *caue* 80, 89 are used as variants of it, the word can hardly represent OE *hulu* 'husk', which is recorded in ME in the sense 'hut, hovel; pen for animals'.

2692. *neuere kines*: the sole instance in *OED* (*never* 2 *c*) of such a use. *Neuere* here is probably a reduction of the emphatic use (for which see Glossary,

---

[151] See J. Brøndum-Nielsen, *Gammeldansk Grammatik* i (2nd edn., Copenhagen, 1950), §76, pp. 106–7; and for the comparable phenomenon in OE, K. Luick, *Historische Grammatik der englischen Sprache* §§77–83.

[152] Ed. F. J. Carmody (Paris, 1939).

neuer(e), *colloc.*) in such expressions as *neuer (n)ones. Neuere kines* is in more particular terms a variant of *none* [< *nones*] *kynes* 1141.

2693. *his*: best taken as a spelling of *is*, with the inorganic *h-* before initial vowels that is common in the Laud text of *Hav.* The subject of the verb is sufficiently indicated by *Godrich* 2689 in the first of the two co-ordinate main clauses.

2699. MS *feldem* is in itself acceptable as a spelling of an agglutinated (spoken) form of *feld(e)* 3 pt. sg. + *hem*. The difficulty is that the following clause is incompatible with this interpretation, since it requires an intransitive verb in *feldem*, and 'felled' is thus ruled out; and *-em* is miswritten for *-en* in 2747. Skeat's emendation *felden*, as the 3 pt. pl. 'fell', does accord with the following clause (and *dos* and *Biforn* in particular). But *felde* is uncomfortably rare and late in ME as a weak preterite of the strong verb *falle* 'fall'.

Happily, one other example of the simile is available, in *Richard Cœur de Lion* 6857–8:

> And slowen Sarazynes also swyþe
> As gres falliþ byfore þe syþe.[153]

It suggests that *feldem* in *Hav.* 2699 is a corruption of a verb meaning 'fell', probably *felle*. In view of *hise* 2698, the scribe's *he feldem* can mean only 'he [Godrich] laid them low'. As a corruption of *he felle* 'they fell', it is to be explained not in palaeographical terms, but as due to misinterpretation of *he* 'they' as *he* 'he' and to the consequent repetition of *felde* which the scribe had written twice in 2695 (where it is a singular, with Godrich as subject).

Holthausen and Skeat insert *ne* after *he* in 2699. The material assembled in 767–9 n. above shows beyond all doubt that ll. 2697–700 contain another instance of the construction there discussed, and that *ne* would therefore be idiomatically orthodox in 2699. But there is an ill-documented and little understood ME variant of the construction that serves to vindicate the syntax of the MS here in *Hav.* After a main clause containing a negative, the consecutive clause introduced by *þat* may occasionally lack a negative: for example, *Guy of Warwick* (14th-c. version, Auchinleck 1457–60):

> Gij wiþ spors smot þe stede . . .
> Nas þer non þat him agros.

—i.e. 'there was none [of his enemies] who was *not* panic-stricken'. And, above all, after a negative and *so* + adj. or adv. in the main clause, as in *St Gregory* (Vernon MS), 983–4:

> Nis þer non so derne dede
> þat sum tiyme hit may be seiȝen.[154]

See also *Verses on the Earthquake of 1382*, 18–19, in Carleton Brown, *Religious Lyrics of the XIV Century* No. 113; *Sir Gawain and the Green Knight* 726; *St Editha*

[153] *Byfore*, which is the reading of the *b* group of five MSS (including Auchinleck) and of the 16th-c. print, is correct, on the evidence of *Hav.*, against the *fro* (from the other group of three MSS) of Brunner's edn.

[154] So also MSS Auchinleck and Rawlinson; MS Cleopatra *nul* for *hit may*).

2301–2. In fact, the MS reading here in *Hav.* will do, if *þat* is interpreted as expressing consequence and as meaning 'so that'.

2720. *Al mi dede*: since *mi dede* recurs in the unambiguous context of 2871 (where likewise the use of *mi* before *ded(e)* is a little unexpected), *mi dede* in 2720 must also refer to the projected killing of Havelok, as planned, in the allusion of 2871, by Godard in Denmark, but in 2720 by Godrich (i.e. presumably as the purpose of the battle that the latter has here just launched against Havelok).

2748. Skeat's insertion of *ek* after *and* (on metrical grounds) gives no means of accounting for the presumed corruption. And, if something really has dropped out, it might conceivably have been *hauede*: since *hauede* and *hauede slawen* are equivalents, a scribe might have replaced the longer form (which is adequately expressed by *hauede* in 2747) with the other.

2765–6. The author again makes the action fit an important principle of feudal law. In dealing with 'the more serious pleas' in the county courts, the *Leges Primi Henrici*, ch. 31. 7, lay down that: 'Vnusquisque *per pares suos iudicandus est* et eiusdem prouincie' ('every man must be judged by men who are equal in rank to him and are from the same district'.) The right to 'judgement by one's peers' was in due course written into *Magna Carta* (ch. 39): no free man was to be arrested, or imprisoned, or dispossessed, or outlawed, or banished, 'nisi per legale judicium parium suorum vel per legem terrae'.[155] For barons this would have been in the king's court and in his presence; for all other free men, in the county court. For the reasons why the principle was vitally important to the barons, see the luminous remarks of Maitland, *The Constitutional History of England*, 169–70; also Pollock and Maitland, i. 171–3, 409, 552, 594; ii. 625 n. 2; Jolliffe, *The Constitutional History of Medieval England*, pp. 250–4; Bloch, *Feudal Society*, ii. 368–70.

2782. Since *hold-oþes* is used here in conjunction with *manrede* 'homage', and again in 2817, it must denote the oath of fealty. It occurs in this sense already in the famous and controversial statement of the *Pet. Chron.* regarding the oaths enforced by William I at Salisbury in 1086:

> And þær him comon to his witan, and ealle þa landsittende men þe ahtes wæron ofer ealle Engleland, wæron þæs mannes menn þe hi wæron; and ealle hi bugon to him and *weron his menn*, and him hold-aðas sworon þæt hi woldon *ongean ealle oðre menn him holde beon*.

This has been interpreted, e.g. by F. M. Stenton (*English Feudalism*, pp. 111–13), as attesting the act of homage; though Jolliffe has argued against this, on the ground that 'an oath of homage from mesne-tenants [i.e. sub-tenants] to the king was at that time impossible in law'.[156] It is thus worth noticing that the phrases italicized above match three fundamental ones in Bracton's form of words for the act of homage (see 2303–13 n.): *deuenio homo vester*, *contra omnes gentes*, and *fidem vobis portabo* (= *him holde beon*). On the

[155] See Pollock and Maitland, i. 173 n. 3 for the force of *vel* here and for its implications.

[156] *The Constitutional History of Medieval England* (2nd edn., 1948), p. 162, n. 2.

other hand, Bracton does not represent the words uttered in the act of homage as an oath; and Stenton interprets *hold-aðas* as 'oaths of fealty'.[157] The act of homage and the oath of fealty have apparently been conflated.

2829–30. What is arresting here is not so much the author's claim that the 'green' (mentioned again 2841) was still to be seen in his time, but the specific detail that it lay *south of the city* (and hence, clearly, outside it). He is unlikely to have invented such information, since he was dealing with a city well known in real life.

It is thus not surprising that there was indeed, from the 12th century onwards, a piece of ground known as *le grene* just outside Lincoln, a few yards beyond Bargate, and *due south of the city*. The leper hospital named the Hospital of the Holy Innocents[158] was situated very near it, and partly on a piece of ground called the Malandry; there also Edward I erected the first of the Eleanor crosses. East of *le grene* stretched an area of open ground (Canwick or South Common), on which to the east stood the city gallows. See J. W. F. Hill, *Medieval Lincoln* 343–5, for a map (fig. 23) that makes the site and the environment clear, and for helpful information.

The main interest of all this (in conjunction with the bridge in Lincoln: see 876 n.) is that a man who knew this much of the city was evidently speaking of it at first hand, and may actually have lived there.

2854–5. See 2303–14 and n.

2857. *sikernesse*: the significant thing here is that the word and what it designates follow immediately on the act of homage and the oath of fealty to Havelok by all the English. Its meaning must therefore be the same as that of the etymologically equivalent Latin word *securitatem* in the following passage of the *Chronicon Hanoniense* (composed by 1196) of Gislebert of Mons, since the latter is part of the same process of doing homage and swearing fealty: 'Comiti Hanoniensi ... faciat *fidelitatem* et *securitatem* cum *hominio*' (ed. L. Vanderkindere, *La Chronique de Gislebert de Mons* (Brussels, 1904), p. 75, ch. 43). And *securitas* is something that is sworn: 'Sibi sicut regi fidelem *securitatem* oppidanos [Corbejenses] iurare coegit' (*Miracula Adalardi* (*c.* 1095) Bk. ii, ch. I, ed. O. Holder-Egger, *MGH SS* 25, ii, p. 863).

In fact, *sikernesse* here is a technical term in the vocabulary of feudalism, and thus probably a semantic borrowing of this use of *securitas*; it is not among the senses of *sikernesse* registered in *OED*. *Securitas* in this use is defined in virtually identical terms by Ganshof (*Feudalism*, 86–7) and Niermeyer (*Mediae Latinitatis Lexicon Minus*, s.v. 5) as 'promise of fealty, in the negative sense of abstention from acts prejudicial to the person receiving the promise'. It may be rendered in *Hav.* here as 'sworn promise to refrain from prejudicial actions'.

2868. *Seint Dauy*: the 6th-century patron saint of Wales, whose name is perpetuated in that of St Davids.[159] His cult had spread early to the nearby

---

[157] Loc. cit., and *Anglo-Saxon England*, pp. 618–19.
[158] Giraldus Cambrensis, in the late 12th c., attests the foundation of the hospital (*Vita S. Remigii*, *Opera* ed. J. F. Dimock (RS, 1877), vii, p. 18.
[159] See S. Baring-Gould, *The Lives of the British Saints* (London, 1907–13), ii. 285–322.

south-western ecclesiastical centres—Sherborne, Glastonbury, and Salisbury.[160] The evidence for it is to be found in martyrologies, the *Vitae* of the
saint (which contain prayers in which he is named, and which were intended
for the mass and office of the Roman liturgy), and in the early breviaries
(which provide a special form of the daily choir services).[161] Two centres (at
first sight unexpected) at which his feast-day was celebrated were Aberdeen
and Lincoln.

It is remarkable (if only because it is so unusual) that St David should be
named in a vernacular work of entertainment such as *Hav.* There are no references at all to him e.g. in the corpus of OF epics that were in print by 1904,[162]
nor in the works of Chaucer, Langland, Gower, and Malory. The only other
known to me is (appropriately) in an Arthurian work, *Li Contes del Graal*, in
which Chrétien de Troyes puts it in the mouth of Arthur himself, who
expressly affirms the specifically Welsh celebration of the saint:.

> Puis m'a si bien a gré servi
> Que par mon seignor *saint Davi*,
> *Que l'an aore et prie an Gales* . . .   (4133–5)

Moreover, the form of the name in *Hav.* (in accord with Chrétien's) corresponds, in the loss of the final consonant, with the regularly developed OW
form *Dewi*, and not the 'learned' type *Dafydd*, and appears (in view of the root-
vowel *-a-*) to be a compromise between *Dewi* and *David*. The former appears
thrice, in the phrase *Dewi wareth* 'David, help!', in the *Vita* of St David by John
of Tynemouth, and once in John's remark: 'Sanctus . . . Dauid, quem vulgus
Dewi appellat'.[163]

How, it must therefore be asked, did the author of *Hav.* come to know of St
David, and why was he sufficiently interested in him to make his Danish hero
invoke the patron saint of Wales for no discernible contextual reason? The
answer, in general terms at least, is to be sought in certain Welsh connections
of the cathedral and the monastic community of Lincoln. The prominent
Welsh writer and churchman Giraldus Cambrensis, who wrote a *Vita* of St
David,[164] had withdrawn from court life after 1194 to go and study at Lincoln
under William of Leicester (then Chancellor of Lincoln), and was there from
at least 1196 to 1198.[165] Moreover, Gerald also wrote *Vitae* of two bishops of
Lincoln, St Remigius (1072–92) and St Hugh (1186–1200). And four of his
works are mentioned in a list, of *c.* 1200, of the books of Lincoln Cathedral.[166]

---

[160] See N. K. Chadwick and others, *Studies in the Early British Church* (Cambridge,
1958), pp. 133–4; S. M. Harris, *Saint David in the Liturgy* (Cardiff, 1940), pp. 69–72.

[161] S. M. Harris, ibid., 4 ff., 12 ff., 44 ff.

[162] E. Langlois, *Table des noms propres dans les chansons de geste* (Paris, 1904).

[163] Ed. C. Horstman, *Nova Legenda Angliae*, vol. i (Oxford, 1901), 262, ll. 13, 18, and 20;
and ibid. 254, l. 6.

[164] Ed. J. S. Brewer, *Giraldi Cambrensis Opera* (RS, 1863), iii. 377–404.

[165] *De Rebus a se Gestis* (*Opera* i, ed. J. S. Brewer, RS, 1861), iii. 3, p. 93; F. M. Powicke,
'Gerald of Wales', *Bulletin of the John Rylands Library*, 12 (1928), 389–410.

[166] R. M. Woolley, *Catalogue of the Manuscripts of Lincoln Cathedral Chapter Library*
(Oxford, 1927), pp. vii and ix.

The earliest *Vita* of St David (and the source of Gerald's and John of Tynemouth's) was composed *c.* 1092 by the Welshman Rhigyfarch.[167] It is extant in several MSS, one of which is Lincoln Cathedral MS 149. This last appears in a list compiled by Dean Honeywood (1660–82) of books that he had given to the Cathedral Library.[168] Its provenance and earlier history are unknown: it is not mentioned either in the catalogue of *c.* 1200 or the 15th-century one.[169]

It does not necessarily follow that the author of *Hav.* had read Gerald's *Vita* (or any other). But it does seem likely that he was in some fashion exposed to the ecclesiastical interest in St David at Lincoln, and therefore that he may have lived in Lincoln (as is also suggested by the signs that he knew the city at first hand: see 876 n. and 2829–30 n.).

2889. *god time*: 'in a happy hour'. The absence of a preposition is striking and curious, and recalls OF *buer* (< *bona hora*). The ME phrase is clearly a calque on the latter, since it is used likewise without a preposition and in the same sense: '"Bele!" fet il, "*buer* fussiez vos ainz nee!"' (*Aymeri de Narbonne* 4408). Cf. ibid. 1676.

The ME form with a preposition occurs in *Guy of Warwick* (14th-c. version, EETS, ES 42, 1883) 840, and its antonym *in iuel stounde* 909.

2923–4. For the use of the sword here to symbolize the governance of the earldom of Lincoln there is a historical parallel that is curiously near home and is attested by Matthew Paris: 'Veniente autem ibidem ad Lodouuicum Gileberto de Gant, comitatus Lincolniae ipsum gladio donavit' (*Historia Anglorum* (ed. F. Madden, RS, No. 44), ii. 182; see also ii. 212).

When in 1216 a party of the barons had elected Louis, son of the king of France, as king of England, Gilbert of Ghent wa among the supporters of the French prince and his forces in their campaign in England. He occupied Lincoln, but withdrew before the advance of King John; he later besieged the castle, was taken prisoner in the battle of Lincoln (1217), and was finally pardoned.

Gilbert had an uncle and namesake who had been Earl of Lincoln (from 1147 to 1148). The associations of these two with Lincoln may have suggested to the author of *Hav.* the idea of investiture 'with the sword of the earldom' of Lincoln.

2934. It was long ago noticed that the line written after this one and then deleted (by the scribe) occurs in the text twenty lines further on (both times on fo. 219rb). Earlier commentators ventured to deduce that a scribe who wrote the exemplar of MS Laud Misc. 108, on reaching the foot of a leaf, then missed a whole side of a leaf; that the MS would therefore have been written with only twenty lines on the recto and on the verso of each leaf; and that the MS would perhaps have belonged to an itinerant minstrel.[170]

---

[167] Translated, with an introduction, A. W. Wade-Evans, *Life of St. David* (London, 1923).

[168] Woolley, op. cit., pp. xviii–xx (No. II); see p. 105, no. 23.

[169] Woolley, op. cit., pp. v–ix and x–xiv.

[170] J. Zupitza, p. 155 of 'Zum Havelok', *Anglia*, 7 (1884), 145–55.

All three conclusions have been rejected by J. C. Hirsch,[171] and with them J. Hall's conclusions, on the model of this hypothesis about *Hauelok*, that the misplacing of a block of twenty lines (1462–81) of the Laud Misc. 108 text of *King Horn* should be interpreted in the same way, and that the single exemplar from which he believed the Laud text of both *Hav.* and *King Horn* to have been copied was one 'of a format such as a wandering minstrel would possess'. Hirsch has proceeded also to deny that some ME romances were composed or 'transmitted' by itinerant minstrels, and is sceptical even of their having read such works aloud.

Hirsch's own explanation of the corrected error in *Hav.* is that the scribe's eye had fallen on l. 2954, which Hirsch thinks sufficiently similar to have elicited the error, but which in fact is less than satisfactory as a basis for this. If the error was indeed due to a scribe's 'faulty return' to the copy (which is by no means certain), he could conceivably have 'returned' to a corresponding point in an adjacent column and have hit on 2955 there: this would imply that there were twenty lines to the column and two columns on each side of a leaf.

2939. *feste*: best interpreted, not as the verb 'feast' (as by *OED feast* v. 2 and *MED festen* v. (*a*)), but as an adoption of ON *festa*, the cognate of the OE causative weak verb *fæstan* (lit. 'make firm'). An undoubted instance of the native verb is applied to the pledging of oaths of fealty in a notable episode of real life: 'To þe kyng Edward hii *fasten huere fay*' (*Poem on the Death of Sir Simon Fraser* 41, ed. Böddeker, pp. 121–34). The adopted ON verb is likewise used to designate the swearing of fealty in MScots, in *Schir William Wallace* xi. 540:

> Passand thai war . . .
> Till Inglismen thair *fewte* for *to fest*.

And since the ON verb itself figures in a series of juridical phrases,[172] it was undeniably used in the special vocabulary of law.

Feste here in *Hav.* describes an action of Havelok's in relation to his Danish followers, after the defeated English followers of Godrich had done homage and sworn fealty to him (2851–5). In bestowing domains and possessions (2939) on the Danes, Havelok is manifestly acting as a feudal lord. There is thus a strong presumption that *feste* in *Hav.* is the ON word (especially as OE *fæstan* would > *faste(n)*, not *feste(n)*, in an EMidl. variety of ME), and that it means something like 'endow (as a feudal lord)'.

2942. Cf. 1764 and n.

2950. Skeat's emendation of *laste* to *lastede* is well based, since the latter is attested in early ME as a form of the preterite of *lasten* 'to last' (alongside the historically regular *lǣste* < OE *lǣstte*), and either of the two preterite forms was open to replacement by the other. As transmitted in the MS, the line has two successive full stresses (on *with* and *gret*): this not impossible type (/×/·/×/) need not be insisted on here when the overwhelmingly more common /×/×/×/ can be so convincingly posited.

[171] 'Havelok 2933', *Neuphilologische Mitteilungen*, 78 (1977), 339–49.
[172] Cleasby–Vigfusson, *An Icelandic–English Dictionary*, *festa* II, 2.

2959–63. Not in Gaimar or the Lai. But in Gaimar's version, Sigar Estalre, the person corresponding to Ubbe, held two offices:

> Seneschal ert al rei Guntier
> E de sa terre justisier.   (505–6)

The collocation with *de sa terre* perhaps implies an authority such as the justiciar in England would have wielded; and this may have suggested the statement in *Hav.* But in any case, since Ubbe is to be the regent of Denmark (2960–1), *(his) iustise* in 2959 is likely to mean not just 'a justice of the king's', but '*chief* justice', i.e. 'justiciar'.

The word *iustitiarius* (the antecedent of OF *iustisier*) in this last sense is attested only in England,[173] e.g. notably by Henry of Huntingdon, who refers s.a. 1123 to Roger, Bishop of Salisbury, thus: '. . . *justitiarius* fuit *totius Angliae et secundus a rege*'.[174] But F. West argues that Roger's position was a matter of personal authority, and that there was not as yet a formal office.[175]

Dr E. Stone has kindly pointed out to me that a literary instance of the office of justiciar at this time is anachronistic, since that office ceased to exist with Stephen of Segrave's tenure of it (1232–41). What became an anachronism when adopted from a much earlier main source is not necessarily a survival from the earlier version of *Hav.* that we have been obliged to posit (Introduction p. lxix).

þat no pleynte him come to, which sounds natural enough, is an echo, which thus shows first-hand knowledge, of a legal formula used in royal charters and writs confirming charters. Thus in one of Stephen's: '. . . *justicia mea* comes Willelmus *faciat, ne super hoc* amplius *audiam inde clamorem* [= *pleynte* in *Hav.*] pro penuria pleni recti vel justicie' (ed. Cronne and Davis, *Regesta Regum Anglo-Normannorum 1066—1154*, vol. iii, No. 472, p. 176). For another example in virtually identical form, see ibid., No. 715, p. 263. It is alternatively just conceivable that the word *pleynte* may here be an example of the technical legal use (as of its L equivalent *querela*) 'an oral or written statement of grievance to a court of law, for the purpose of obtaining redress (*OED plaint* sb. 3). See F. M. Powicke, *The Thirteenth Century*, pp. 350–5.

---

[173] Niedermayer, *Lexicon Minus* s.v. *justitiarius*, 4.
[174] *Historia Anglorum* (ed. T. Arnold, RS, 1879), vii, §35, p. 245.
[175] *The Justiciarship in England 1066–1232* (Cambridge, 1966), pp. 15–23.

APPENDIX A

WROBBERES

Wrobberes 39 is formed on *wrobbe* v., which is recorded only in *Thomas of Ercel-doune* l. 38 (ed. A. Brandl, Berlin, 1880):

> If J solde sytt to Domesdaye
> With my tonge to *wrobbe and wrye*,
> Certanely, þat lady gaye
> Neuer bese scho askryede for me.

Wrabbe, which is a varia lectio of *wrobbe* here, recurs only in the fragment of the *Ormulum* published by Dr N. R. Ker (*TLS* 1936, p. 928):

> To spaechen ifell hinden on,
> To *wreȝen annd* to *wrabben*.

The cognate OE personal names *Wrabba*, *Wrobba*, and *Wribba* or *Wrybba* are attested in the place-names *Wrabness* in Essex (first recorded in Domesday Book as *Wrabenasa*), *Robley* in Hants. (*Wrobban lea*, 909), *Rabley* in Herts. (first recorded as *Wrobele*, 1235), and *Ribden* in Somerset (first as *Wrybbedon*, 1327).

Wrabbe v. and *Wrabba* may be interpreted as formations on the Gmc base **u̯rab̄-* 'to twist' (attested in Sw. and Norw. dialect *vravla* v. 'twist, tangle'). The -*bb*- is an 'affective' doubling of *b̄*—i.e. it expresses the feeling aroused by a sense-impression (originally because the latter elicited a corresponding muscular movement of the organs of speech) associated with an action, movement, sound, taste, etc. In the very numerous words of this type in all the Gmc languages, the voiced double plosives -*bb*-, -*dd*-, and -*gg*- at the end of the root originally designated a slow, or heavy, or slack, or muffled quality in the movement or sound etc., just as the energetically produced voiceless -*pp*-, -*tt*-, -*kk*- express a quick, or light, or taut, or clear one. An individual 'base' may be used for new formations by permutations within any phonetically related group of consonants: potentially congruent consonants are the members of the homorganic series *p/b* or *b̄/ff/bb/pp*; *t/ð*, *d/þþ/dd/tt*; *k/ȝ*, *g/χχ/gg/kk*.

Wribba and *Wrobba*, *wrobbe* v. fit perfectly into the same category, since new 'expressive' words may be formed on an existing 'base', or on an 'expressive' word derived from it, by permutations of the root vowel that are likewise phonaesthetic: -*i*- stands for 'small, quick, light etc.' and -*u*- and its variant form -*o*- for 'large, slow, heavy, blunt etc.' as has been established experimentally (see H. Kronasser, *Handbuch der Semasiologie*, Heidelberg, 1952, §§121–6). Like the permutations of final consonants in an 'ideophonic' base, these variations are not explicable in terms of phonetic change: they do not fit into the patterns of vowel-gradation (see G. V. Smithers, 'Some English Ideophones', *AL* 6 (1954), 80–92).

The rare *wrabbed* 'perverse' and *warble* v. 'contend' imply a 'semantic pattern' like that attested in *writhe* v. /*wroth*/*wrath* and *twist* v./Du. *twist* n. 'quarrel' (in which the senses of the nouns and the adj. are due to application of the concrete sense 'twist' to the emotions), and hence a sense 'be contentious' for *wrabbe*, *wrobbe* (alongside 'twist' in Norw. *vravla*, and 'twist closely round' in E *wrap*, which is typically ideophonic in form, and is first recorded in ME). This is confirmed by the existence of the obviously synonymous phrase *wragge and wrye* in the *Towneley Plays* (1021, 58; 371, 143), in which *wragge* is either a substitutional variant of *wrabbe* (with an 'expressively' equivalent double voiced stop) or a formation on *wrage* v. 'anger' with affective doubling of the final consonant of the root.

Dr K. Sisam's interpretation of *wrobberes* as 'informers' (note ad loc., impression of 1973) is taken over from C. T. Onions' 'Middle English *wrabbe*, *wrobbe*', *MÆ* 10 (1941), 159–60. But Dr Onions' etymological analysis is founded mainly on modern material—Icel. and Norw. *rabba* 'babble, chatter', Norw. *robb* 'babbler', apart from the OIcel. *hapax legomenon rabba* 'babble, etc.'—and takes no cognizance of the OE personal and place names and the extensive other English material assembled in my paper (loc. cit.). Moreover, the initial -*w*- of the prehistoric ON *wrabba, *wrobba that he posits as the antecedent of *rabba* is ruled out by universally acknowledged cognates of *rabba* such as Du. *rabbelen* 'chatter, babble, LG *rabbelen* 'speak fast or unclearly', since an initial *w*- would have survived in Dutch; see Falk–Torp, *NDEW rable* I and *vrøvle*. Finally, the semantic link between 'babble' and 'inform' is not convincing.

APPENDIX B

THE GRIMSBY SEAL

A main point of interest in this seal[1] is that the legend *Sigillvm Communitatis Grimebye* attests for Grimsby a *communitas*. This is a technical term, used in charters in senses that are sometimes not easily defined. All that can be said here is that, on evidence and for reasons authoritatively presented by J. Tait,[2] the term comes to mark a particular stage in the corporate development of boroughs.[3]

The substantive step towards the independence of boroughs was the right to elect their own officers (reeves or baillifs) to pay the king's revenue into the exchequer, instead of having it collected, and of their thus being controlled, by the sheriff. This development, 'which went on rapidly during the last decade of the twelfth century and the first two of the thirteenth, was marked by the appearance of municipal seals'.[4] It is sometimes expressly laid down in borough charters that the burgesses shall have a seal, e.g. in the Coventry charter of 1345.[5] The possession of a seal is one of five criteria of an incorporated town.[6]

Since the seal of Grimsby depicts the three main characters in the story of Havelok, one of whom is named Grim, it shows the latter to be a founding-legend. This is corroborated by one other case in which a seal (not, as it happens, a municipal but a monastic one) is inscribed with a scene and a legend that refer to the central characters in a founding-story of a legendary kind. The seal of Evesham Abbey, as read by C. H. Hunter Blair,[7] bears on one scene the legend:

Eoves her [wonede ant] was swon for i [me'] clepet þis Eovishom

---

[1] On medieval seals in general see J. H. Bloom, *English Seals* (The Antiquary's Books, Methuen, 1906); W. de Gray Birch, *Seals* (The Connoisseur's Library, Methuen, 1907); G. Pedrick, *Monastic Seals of the XIIIth Century* (London, 1902); T. A. Heslop, *Seals*, in *English Romanesque Art 1066–1200* (Hayward Gallery, London, 5 April–8 July 1984), pp. 298–319.

[2] 'The Borough Community in England', *English Historical Review*, 45 (1930), 529–51, at pp. 546–51; *The Medieval English Borough* (Manchester, 1936), 237–47.

[3] The phrase *communitas burgi* 'the *communitas* of the borough' occurs e.g. in a charter of 1147–83 for Tewkesbury (A. Ballard, *British Borough Charters 1042–1216* (Cambridge, 1913), p. 140.

[4] Tait, *The Medieval English Borough*, p. 235.

[5] M. Weinbaum, *The Incorporation of Boroughs* (Manchester, 1937), pp. 47–8 and p. 48 n. 1.

[6] See F. W. Maitland, *The Constitutional History of England*, p. 54; Weinbaum, op. cit., pp. 18 ff., 21.

[7] *Catalogue of the Seals in the Treasury of the Dean and Chapter of Durham*, ii (Society of Antiquaries of Newcastle on Tyne, 1911–21), p. 561, no. 3465; also in *Archæologia Æliana*, 3rd Series, 15 (Kendal, 1918), p. 173 and n. 1.

—apparently 'Eoves lived here and was a swineherd: for that reason [reading *þi* for *i*] this is called Eovishom.' A slightly different reading is given by Bloom (op. cit., p. 195):

Eoves her wonede ant was swon for pi men clepet pis Eovishom

in which *pi* and *pis* are either misreadings or miswritings for *þi* and *þis*. For another very similar one (but mistranslated), a description, and an illustration, see Pedrick op. cit., pp. 72–5 and plate VIII. Birch's reading[8] is the same as Hunter Blair's.

Unfortunately these readings cannot be authenticated (from the Durham impression of the seal) at a crucial point. The impression is damaged to the extent that Mr A. J. Piper (of the Department of Palaeography in the University of Durham) has been able to read for me only:

Eoves [*followed by an unspecifiable number of letters*] was s. on for þi me clepet þis Eoves [*illegible letters follow*].

Wonede, if a valid reading, would suggest that the legend and the story condensed into it were based on a mistaken etymological interpretation of -*hom* or -*ham* in *Eoveshom* as *hōm* < OE *hām*. Even without that reading, this can be taken as what probably happened. The word in question is the quite different one *homm*, *hamm* 'meadow (especially one bordering on a stream)' which occurs in a mass of OE place-names,[9] and which is in any case prescribed by the OE forms of the name Evesham *(æt) Homme*, *(into) Homme* in two charters of 709 (Birch, *Cartularium Saxonicum*, i, nos. 124 and 125) in one of which, along with no. 131 of 714, the core of the saint's legend is already mentioned.[10] And since the -*es* in *Eoves-(hamm)* must be the ending of the genitive singular, the name must be OE *Eof*. Ekwall has duly etymologized the place-name as 'Eof's *hamm*':[11] the name *Eoves* for the swineherd is a nominative mistakenly reinterpreted from it.[12] Thus the part of Eoves in the saint's legend looks transparently fictitious; though St Ecgwine's own is attested already in the charter of 709, along with the place-name that developed into *Evesham*:

in loco in quo beata virgo Maria se venerabili viro Egwino manifestavit in *Homme*.

As with the story of Havelok, the reason why the story of Eoves was depicted on the seal is that it is a founding-legend. It is told in the saint's legend of Ecgwine,[13] bishop of Worcester 692.[14] According to this a man

---

[8] *Catalogue of Seals in the Department of Manuscripts in the British Museum* (London, 1892), ii, p. 83, no. 4958.

[9] See H. Middendorff, *Altenglisches Flurnamenbuch* (Halle, 1902), pp. 63–5.

[10] Birch, *Cartularium Saxonicum*, i, no. 125.

[11] *The Concise Oxford Dictionary of English Place-Names* (4th edn., Oxford, 1974).

[12] See Mawer and Stenton, *The Place-Names of Worcestershire* (Cambridge, 1927), pp. 262–3.

[13] In the Latin *Vita*, ed. C. Horstman, *Nova Legenda Angliae*, i (Oxford, 1901), pp. 372–3, which is abridged from that edited by W. D. Macray in the *Chronicon Abbatiae de Evesham*, RS 29 (1863), pp. 3 ff.

[14] On the evidence of Florence of Worcester, *Chronicon ex Chronicis* (ed. B. Thorpe, London, 1848), i, anno 692 and 717. See Birch, *Cartularium Saxonicum*, i, nos. 77, 137.

named Eoues was one day near a forest which Ecgwine had been given by king Æþelred of the Mercians, in a desolate spot in the Worcestershire area now called *Eoueshamm*. In the forest there appeared to Eoues a dazzlingly radiant female figure holding a book and singing psalms, in the company of two other holy virgins. When this was reported to Ecgwine, he himself went to the spot, prayed, and saw the three virgins, the pre-eminent one among whom held a book and a gold cross. When he reflected that this was the Lord's mother, she held out the cross and blessed him with it, and vanished. Ecgwine realized that it was God's will that the spot (called 'at Homm') be consecrated; and he founded a monastery there in honour of God and Mary.

The earliest recorded examples of municipal seals are those of Oxford (1191) and of York (between 1191 and 1206),[15] Ipswich (1200), and Exeter (1208). Thus the Grimsby seal can hardly be earlier than *c.*1200. Tait has stated (op. cit., p. 23) that, with the two doubtful exceptions of Barnstaple and Leicester, a legend of the form '"seal of the *communitas* of X"' is not known to have been used in the early part of the thirteenth century, and never became common'. The earliest charter of Grimsby is dated 1201.[16] It provides that Grimsby shall have the same liberties and free customs as the burgesses of Northampton.[17] The link between the establishment of a formal *communitas* and a specific provision in a charter for a seal is attested both in the Coventry charter of 1345 (*Calendar of Charter Rolls* (HMSO, 1916), v. 36) and in that of Hedon (ibid., pp. 87–9), as shown for both by Weinbaum;[18] though in each it is a king's seal, for the record of debts, and not a common seal of the *communitas*.

The parallel of the Evesham Abbey seal brings out another point about the Grimsby seal that without it might be missed. The story of Eoues has the character of a local legend, i.e. one that developed in and was attached to a particular locality. A still clearer example of this is the saint's legend of Kenelm, with its commemorative couplet of alliterative verse and its connection with Clent.[19] There are signs that the story of Havelok existed as a local legend by 1338 (when Mannyng completed his *Chronicle*), even if it was not one at the outset. The most definite evidence is a passage that Mannyng interpolated in the *Chronicle* (ed. T. Hearne (1725), i. 25:

> Bot þat þise lowed men upon Inglish tellis
> Right story can me not ken, þe certeynte what spellis.
> *Men sais* in Lyncoln castelle ligges *ʒit* a stone
> þat Hauelok kast wele forbi euerilkone.
> & *ʒit* þe chapelle standes þer he weddid his wife,   5
> Goldeburgh þe kynges douhter: *þat saw is ʒit rife*.
> & of Gryme a fisshere *men redes ʒit in ryme*,
> þat he bigged Grymesby, Gryme þat ilk tyme.

[15] See Tait, *The Medieval English Borough*, pp. 235–6.
[16] Ed. T. D. Hardy, *Rotuli Chartarum*, i (Record Commission, 1837), p. 91.
[17] See C. Stephenson, *Borough and Town* (Cambridge, Mass., 1933), p. 142 n. 1.
[18] *The Incorporation of Boroughs*, pp. 48 n. 1, 49, 50 n. 2, and 52. See also pp. 40–4.
[19] See *EMEVP* vii, pp. 96 ff.

Of alle stories of honoure þat I haf þorgh-souht
I fynd þat no compiloure of him tellis ouht.   10
Sen I fynd non redy þat tellis of Hauelok kynde,
Turne we to *þat story þat we writen fynde*.

What is important in this passage is that:

1. Mannyng expressly distinguishes between oral stories (told in English by uneducated men, lines 1 and 6) and a written one in rhyming verse (12 and probably 7), which may well be the extant poem. Sisam–Skeat (p. xvi) have identified the former with *Havelok*; but there is an undeniable contrast.

2. The word *saw* 6 (like the phrase *Men sais* 3) is more specific here than has apparently been supposed. It literally means 'something that is said' [also 'uttered, recounted'], i.e. orally. But here it is probably (as the helpful context suggests) as specific as the German cognate *Sage*, which means 'legend (told orally in prose)' and often 'local legend'. In fact, these two expressions here are more precise and informative than the vague 'traditions' (which conveys no implication of literary form) that is usually applied to this passage.

3. The unreliability that Mannyng complains of in the oral accounts (of Havelok etc.) by unlettered men (1–2) suggests the variations and discrepancies that would be typical of orally transmitted material.

Mannyng himself has provided a striking parallel to all this, in very similar terms, in connection with another founding-legend. He knew two versions of the origin of the name *England*; according to the one:

> For þys Engle [*a king*] þys lond þus wan
> Engelond cald hit ilka man
>   *Chronicle* 14913–14)

According to the other, Hengest arrived in England with a daughter named Ronewen (7529–30), who (Mannyng says) is claimed (*a*) by unlettered men, (*b*) who celebrated her in oral accounts (7533 and 14837), (*c*) to have been called *mayden Inge*, (*d*) but is not traceable in any written one:

> Bot *þis lewed men sey & synge*
> & telle þat *hit was mayden Inge*   (ibid. 7533–4)
>
> But *lewed men þer-of speke & crye*   (14837–8)
> & meyntene al-wey vp þat lye
>
> *Wryten of Inge no clerk may kenne*   (7535)
>
> But *of Ynge saw Y neuere nought*
> Neyþer *in boke write* ne wrought   (14835–6)

Though no town such as Grimsby is directly concerned, the reference to Inge does occur in connection with Hengest's arrival and his acquisition and founding of *þongcastre* (7523) by means of the trick of the bull's hide as in the founding of Carthage by Dido in the *Aeneid*, i. 365–8, on which see J. L. Austin, *Aeneidos*, i (Oxford, 1971), 367 n., and E. Faral, *La Légende Arthurienne*, ii, pp. 219–20. 'The castle of the thongs' must be a legendary interpretation, also offered by Wace, *Le Roman de Brut* 6913 ff., 13425 (ed. I. Arnold, SATF

1938), of a toponymical place-name *Th(w)ong* as recorded in Kent (see Ekwall, op. cit., *Thong*) which is Caister in Lincs. (as shown by Wace, *Twancastre en Lyndesie* 13425, in telling the story).

Wace does not give either version of the origin of the name of England, but correctly refers it to the name of the English (13643–52); and he gives only *Ronwen* as the name of Hengest's daughter (6929–31). Mannyng invokes one *Mayster Edmond* (14831–4) for his first explanation—i.e. an author whose identity and work are not known to us. But what he says about the tradition of Inge, and the fact that Wace does not mention it, suggest that this too was a local legend, and one naturally accessible to Mannyng as a Lincolnshire man.

It is doubtful whether *(sey & synge* 7533 implies an account in verse rather than prose. The phrase is rare in ME, and a *hapax legomenon* in OE verse (applied in *Widsiþ* 54 to *spell*).[20] In Me, *spell* is often enough contrasted with *song*[21] to be shown to mean 'narrative; discourse (in prose)'. Thus ME *(seye &) synge* need mean no more than '(utter &) intone, declaim', and does not necessarily imply that *synge* in this phrase here means 'sing' and therefore that the oral account of Inge was in verse.

Local legends differ radically from wonder-tales in being anchored to places and named persons; and they deal in individual objects as memorials and evidences of the truth of the story, which are treated as if they required explanation. This precisely applies here. The stone cast by Havelok and the chapel in which he and Goldeburgh were married are singled out as 'still' to be seen in Lincoln. And the boundary-stone that Gervase Holles mentions as being named 'Havelok's stone *to this day*' is reported by him along with a version of Havelok's story (Sisam–Skeat, ed. cit., pp. xx–xxi) that is hardly more than skeletal.

The chapel in which, according to Mannyng's report, Havelok was married to Goldeburgh (as an example of the orally circulating recollections of Havelok) is not mentioned at all in *Hauelok*. But since it is not a sheer invention—the poem does describe how Havelok and Goldeburgh were married—it implies a different form of the story, and one that was therefore possibly a distinct account and drawn from a local legend. A divergence such as that of Holles's version from the whole sequence of the opening events in *Hauelok* points in the same direction. And finally, though Grimsby must undoubtedly have been named after one *Grim*, and Evesham possibly after one *Eof*, it by no means follows that they were identical with the persons thus named in the stories considered here. We should not overlook the potential point of ll. 744–7 in *Hav.* as being meant not as information, but as explanatory, just as the statement about *Eoves* on the Evesham Abbey seal clearly is:

> And for þat Grim þat place aute
> þe stede of Grim þe name laute,
> So þat *Grimesbi* it calle
> þat þer-offe speken alle.

[20] See *OED*, *sing* v. II and *say* v. 9, and F. Norman, *The Germanic Heroic Poet and his Art*, in *German Studies presented to H. G. Fiedler* (Oxford, 1938), p. 299 n. 1.

[21] See *OED*, *spell* sb.[1].

According to the view here being presented, Havelok's stone and chapel, as reported by Mannyng, have been detached from a story of him. A parallel to this would be the spring and the chapel (each marking the miraculous powers of a saint) that are still perpetuated in the Ordnance Survey map of Worcestershire:[22] they were mentioned in the saint's life of Kenelm and have been detached from it. It is at first sight notable that Rauf de Bohun should refer to the source of his account of Havelok as *L'Estoire de Grimesby* (p. xxix above): does this title imply that it was a work quite distinct from the ME *Hav.*? But since de Bohun alone shares with *Hav.* several of the personal names and the status of Godrich as Earl of Cornwall, it is probably safest to assume that his source (i.e. *L'Estoire*) must have been the extant ME poem, rather than a now lost AN version that might (in view of its name) have been oriented rather more than *Hav.* as a local legend. The title given it by de Bohun may mean (like the dominant size and the central position of Grim on the seal) that the story was for some the founding-legend of Grimsby rather than primarily the story of Havelok.

The dates of 1201 for the earliest Grimsby charter and 1207 for the next[23] are compatible with a date of the earlier thirteenth century for the Grimsby seal. The original of the first charter is now lost; but in a translation of the copy in the Public Record Office (see n. 16 above) kindly made available to me by Mr J. F. Wilson, archivist in charge of the South Humberside Area Record Office, Grimsby is at least six times referred to as a 'borough'.

The spelling of the words inscribed on the Grimsby seal is not much help with the dating, but must be noticed. The bizarre form *Gryem* (or *Gryen*?), in which the philologically unjustifiable *-e-* may have been transposed from *Gryme*, can be left aside. The apparent *B* in Havelok's name, which is not at all like the *B* in *Goldebvrgh*, is best interpreted as a ligature of *U* and *E*: for examples of ligatures on seals, see Bloom, op. cit., pp. 13–14.

The *-gh* in *Goldebvrgh*, for the voiceless velar fricative /x/, which in final position was replaced in ME by the /w/ developed (by paradigmatic analogy) from the voiced variant in inflected forms of the same words, is at any rate the earlier type. In *Hav.* itself—the obvious potential criterion, as a rhymed work composed in Lincolnshire between 1295 or 1296 and 1310—the voiceless velar fricative /x/ in final position occurs only in rhymes *inter se*, though always spelt *w* or *u* in the Laud MS (*þorw* : *Rokesborw* 264–5; cf. *þoru* : *Goldeborw* 2985–6, *boru* 774–5, 848–9, 2827–8). The voiced velar fricative /ɣ/ between vowels had developed in *Hav.* into /w/, as attested by the single rhyme *awe* v. 1293 : *lowe* 'mound'; and this corresponds to the development in Lincolnshire place-names and surnames examined by G. Kristensson.[24] But this latter material, which mostly covers a period from c.1296 to 1332, consistently shows *-gh* spellings for the voiceless velar

---

[22] See *EMEVP*, pp. 314–15, notes on VII. 214–17 and 247–56.

[23] A. Ballard, *British Borough Charters 1042–1216*, p. xxviii. They are attested in the *Rotuli Chartarum* (for the reign of John), pp. 91 and 168 respectively.

[24] *A Survey of Middle English Dialects 1290–1350* (Lund Studies in English, 35, Lund, 1967), p. 240, no. 51.

fricative in final position.[25] The -*gh* on the Grimsby seal is thus compatible with any date up to *c.* 1332.

It should also be noted that the two letters *M* and *T* on the seal are each used there in two different forms, one which is identical in each case with the Roman capital (as still used today in English), and the other of the Lombardic type (as the letter *E* also is). Birch has pointed out that this mingling of the two types is to be found in the early seals of Richard I,[26] in the letters *A*, *E*, and *H*, and that in the seal of John this is followed by 'further alteration into Lombardic forms' (though he does not give specific details).

The first seal of Richard I, which is illustrated in *English Romanesque Art 1066–1200*, p. 304, no. 334, shows Lombardic *E* and *M*, and the second seal of Richard I (reverse), which is illustrated by Bloom, op. cit., p. 65, *M*, *A*, and *E*. The seal of John illustrated in *English Romanesque Art 1066–1200*, p. 305, no. 335, shows Lombardic *E* and *H*, and the reverse (ibid., p. 1) likewise. An early authority has said that the seal is 'at least as old as the time of Edward I' (F. Madden, *The Ancient English Romance of Havelok the Dane*, p. xliii). But I cannot trace the further statement attributed to him by Sisam–Skeat (ed. cit., §12, p. xxii) that 'the legend is written in a character which after the year 1300 fell into disuse'. Mr T. A. Heslop kindly tells me that he would assign the Grimsby seal to the later 13th century, on e.g. these grounds:

1. the use of a star-like sign at the beginning of the inscription, rather than a plain cross, is a mid-13th or late 13th-century feature;
2. the Lombardic lettering is of a type current only from *c.* 1230; but the Lombardic *M* here (with a rounded continuous top) suggests a materially later date.

We have seen (pp. lvi ff.) that the earliest form (which ends at 1272) of the AN prose *Brut* has a summarizing allusion to the story of Havelok and Goldeburgh that implies knowledge of a version like that of the extant ME poem (and not only because it used the name *Goldeburgh* of the latter and not the *Argentille* of the AN versions). As *Hav.* can be dated between 1295 or 1296 and 1310, the allusion (by 1272) in the *Brut* is likely to derive from an English version of *Hav.* earlier than 1272.

Although the Grimsby seal likewise names the heroine Goldeburgh, one detail at least in the scene points to a different version from the extant ME one: Havelok is depicted as holding a battleaxe in his right hand. This corresponds with the account in the *Lai* of his fight with the Danish usurper Odulf, in which he is said to have used an axe (963), while in *Hav.* he is never represented as wielding a battleaxe: he uses a sword against the English usurper Godrich (2751). This (if it is not merely a random variation on the seal) ought to mean that the scene on the latter was based on a version (*a*) different from *Hav.*, (*b*) that agreed in this detail with the *Lai* (composed in the early

[25] Ibid., p. 216, viii.

[26] *Seals*, pp. 36–7. On lettering see also Pedrick, op. cit., p. 21, and Bloom, op. cit., pp. 13–15.

thirteenth century in the view of Bell, ed. cit., p. 59), (*c*) that need not have been as late as *Hav.*, and (*d*) was possibly based on an oral tradition.

It is moreover curious, and potentially another discrepancy, that Grim is depicted on the seal as wielding a sword and a shield: since he never takes part in deeds of arms in *Hav.*, nor indeed in Gaimar's version or the *Lai*, this might be based on a different and lost (and perhaps oral) version. The ring that Havelok holds in his other hand, though it likewise is not mentioned in the account of his wedding in *Hav.* (1170–81), or for that matter in Gaimar's or in the *Lai*, may simply symbolize the fundamentally important fact of his marriage to Goldeburgh (to whom he is holding the ring out), since both of them are shown with a crown above their heads.

Descriptions of public festivities, on such occasions as weddings, coronations, and the like, are a standard procedure in OF romances, which commonly mention music and various sports and forms of entertainment as taking place. These literary parallels are both ample and close enough to show that they were undoubtedly models for the author of *Hauelok* here.

Two good examples of the late twelfth century are available in Chrétien's *Erec et Enide* 2035 ff. and *Le Chevalier de la Charrete* 1635–48,[1] and a slightly later one in *L'Escoufle* (composed before 1204).[2] They manifestly reproduce a standard pattern in which the same individual activities recur, if in a different order. Thus (with the titles of these texts abbreviated respectively as *EE*, *CC*, and *LE*):

1. Entertainers include acrobats and tumblers (*EE* 2041, *CC* 1647), magicians (*EE* 2041), and minstrels (*Hav.* 2330).
2. There is wrestling (*CC* 1648, *Hav.* 2325); music on various instruments (*EE* 2043–6, *LE* 8990), including the harp and the flute or the pipe (*EE* 2043–6, *Hav.* 2326), and the tabour (*EE* 2052 and—by minstrels—*Hav.* 2330); songs (*CC* 1647, *EE* 2042), and story-telling (*EE* 2042, *LE* 8994; cf. *romanz-reding* and *gestes singe* in *Hav.* 2328 and 2331).
3. There are dancing and carols (*CC* 1646), by maidens (*EE* 2047, *LE* 9000–1).
4. There are games (*CC* 1637) such as chess (*CC* 1640, *LE* 8993), *mine* (*CC* 1642, *LE* 8995), *mine* and *hasard* (*Hav.* 2327).
5. There is abundant food and wine (*EE* 2061–5, *Hav.* 2341–4);
6. and rich gifts to those who served them (*LE* 8988–9), of clothes, horses, and money to the minstrels and entertainers (*EE* 2109–18), and of clothes to minstrels (*Hav.* 2337).
7. There is jousting (*LE* 9011–13);
8. and the use of dogs to hunt boars, bears, and leopards (*LE* 9004–5), or to bait bulls and boars (*Hav.* 2331–2).
9. The occasion is one characterized by 'joy' in the highest degree (*LE* 9014–15; *Hav.* 2322 and 2335–6), which everyone vies in expressing and giving.

The things in *Hav.* that are left over are 'putting the stone' 2325 (on which see 1023 n.), 'thrusting with spears' 2323, and 'sword-play with bucklers' 2324. For the second of these, cf. the 'throwing of lances' mentioned in the *Anglo-Norman Romance of Horn* 2568 (1023 n.); but it may refer to jousting. *Skirming*

---

[1] Ed. respectively by W. Foerster (Halle, 1934) and M. Roques, CFMA 86 (Paris, 1958).
[2] Ed. H. Michelant and P. Meyer, SATF 1894.

2324 (OF *escremie*) designates both serious combat with the sword and the shield, and a sport of duelling with a wooden staff and a shield. All the pursuits in question (including those listed above) have been massively documented by A. Schultz from MHG as well as OF literature (*Das höfische Leben zur Zeit der Minnesinger* (2nd edn., Leipzig, 1889), i. 164–7, 531–79).

The style of *Hav.* was for the most part closely modelled on that of medieval epic, and notably of the *chansons de geste*. But the scale here of the topos illustrated above is emphatically characteristic of OF romances rather than *chansons de geste* (in which the examples tend to be altogether slighter).

APPENDIX D

DRENG 31

The precise status of the dreng is a crux of feudal and social history; the term is of foreign origin (ON *dreng-r* 'a young man', adopted before the Conquest). See J. E. A. Jolliffe, 'Northumbrian Institutions', *EHR* 41 (1926), 1–42; R. R. Reid, 'Barony and Thanage', *EHR* 35 (1920), 189, n. 4; S. Aakjær, 'Old Danish Thegns and Drengs', *Acta Philologica Scandinavica*, 2 (1927–8), 1–30 (which takes account of English usage); and especially F. M. Stenton, *English Feudalism*, 145–8 ('the *dreng* of the eleventh century was the Scandinavian equivalent of the English *cniht*', p. 146).

A notable point in *Hav.* is that all six examples (see Glossary) are immediately followed by *þayn* in a collocation which is itself used in a catalogue of six or (twice) seven or (once) eight elements. The collocation is invariably preceded (in *Hav.*) by *erl(es) (and) baroun(es)*, and followed by *knith(es) (and) swayn(es)*, these latter being twice separated by *burgeys* (1328 and 2195). Thus the order is apparently fixed; though *þayn* and *swayn* are needed (and therefore fixed) as rhyme-words. But there is no obvious reason why one or other should be the first rhyme-word unless the order of the elements implied and was fixed by a social hierarchy (as in the sequence, here fixed, of *erl(es) (and) baroun(es)*). This would imply that the *dreng* was of higher status than the thane.

GLOSSARY

This glossary is designed both to record and explain the author's individual usage in some detail and to give an insight into the main features and some of the niceties of ME usage in general. With this in view, phrasal idioms above all, grammatical forms, the semantic and the syntactic range of prepositions and conjunctions, of 'basic' verbs such as *be*, *bring*, *do*, *have*, *make*, *set*, *take*, and the verbs here termed 'separable' and 'quasi-separable compounds' have been more fully recorded than is commonly done in editions of ME texts.

In the alphabetic sequence:

1. initial *þ* follows initial *t*, and the here very rare initial *th* is entered under *þ*;
2. *y* denoting (*a*) the vowel /i/ is registered as an alternative spelling under *i* (except that *y* < OE *ge-* is entered under *y*), and (*b*) the semi-vowel /j/ under *y*;
3. *i* representing the consonant /dž/ is entered under *i*;
4. *u* and *v* representing the vowel /u/ both come under *u*;
5. *u* representing the consonant /v/ (here only in *ueneysun* and *uoyz*) is entered under *u*.

In the etymologies, quantity is marked in OE words, except before the lengthening groups *ld*, *mb*, *nd*, *ng*, *rd*, *rð* (since both lengthened and unlengthened forms could obtain as paradigmatic variants in a single word).

The forms of a verb are normally entered under the infinitive, which is enclosed in square brackets if it does not occur in *Hav.*, and which is also marked with an asterisk if it is not recorded in OE or ME. But if a verb occurs only in one grammatical form, it is entered under that form. Verbs derived from OE separable compounds, or newly formed in ME on the inherited pattern (and registered here as respectively 'separable' and 'quasi-separable verbs') are entered under the unseparated form of the infinitive, even if this does not occur in *Hav.* For the rationale of this procedure, see the discussion of the separable compounds in *Hav.* under Vocabulary (pp. lxxxv–lxxxviii).

The following abbreviations are used in the Glossary and elsewhere:

a. adjective	*art.* article
absol. absolute	*attrib.* attributive
acc. accusative	*auxil.* auxiliary
ad. adoption of	*bef.* before
adj. gen. adjectival genitive	*bes.* beside
ad loc. at that point (L *ad locum*)	*card.* cardinal
adv. adverb(ial); advantage	*caus.* causative
agglut. agglutinated	*cf.* compare (L*confer*)
anal. analogy	*cl.* clause
antec. antecedent	*cogn.* cognate
aph. (*f.*) aphetic (form of; from)	*coll.* collective
apoph. apophonic	*colloc.* collocation
appos. apposition	*comp.* comparative

conj. conjunction
cons. consonant
consec. consecutive
co-ord. co-ordinating
correl. correlative
cpd. compound
dat. dative
def. definite
dem. demonstrative
dep. dependent
dial. dialect
dim. diminutive
diphth. diphthong
dir. direction
disadv. disadvantage
disj. disjunctive
distrib. distribution
disyll. disyllabic
emph. emphatic
encl. enclitic
esp. especially
excl. exclamation
expr. expressing, expressed
f. form; formed on
fem. feminine
fig. figurative
foll. following; followed
freq. frequentative
fut. future
gen. genitive
ger. gerund(ial)
gramm. grammatical
ibid. in the same place (L *ibidem*)
id. the same (L *idem*)
ideo. ideophone, ideophonic
imper. imperative
impers. impersonal
indecl. indeclinable
indef. indefinite
indic. indicative
indir. indirect
inf. infinitive
infl. inflected
instr. instrument(al)
interj. interjection
interr. interrogative
intr. intransitive
introd. introducing
lit. literally
loc. location
masc. masculine
modif. modification
n. note; noun

neg. negative
neut. neuter
nom. nominative
num. numeral
obj. objective (case)
obl. oblique
obsc. obscure(ly)
om. omitted
opt. optative
ord. ordinal
orig. originally
p.p. past participle
part. participle
pass. passive
perf. perfect
perh. perhaps
periphr. periphrasis, periphrastic
pers. personal
phon.var. phonetic variant
phr. phrase(s)
pl. plural
poss. possessive (case)
pr. present
prec. preceding, preceded
predic. predicative
pref. prefix
prep. preposition(al case)
pret.-pres. preterite-present
prim. primitive
prob. probably
pron. pronoun
pt. preterite
q.v. see this (L *quod vide*)
recipr. reciprocal
red. reduced, reduction of
refl. reflexive
reinf. reinforcing
rel. relative; related
repl. replacing
sb. substantival (use)
sc. understand (L *scilicet*)
sep. separable
sg. singular
sim. similarly
str. strong
subj. subjunctive
subord. subordinating
subst. substitution
suff. suffix
superl. superlative
s.v. under entry (L *sub voce*)
synon. synonymous
temp. temporal

tr. transitive
unassib. unassibilated
unstr. unstressed
var. variant

v. verb; vowel
vbl.n. verbal noun
voc. vocative
wk. weak

A	Anglian varieties of OE	MScots	Middle Scots
AN	Anglo-Norman	MSw.	Middle Swedish
Da.	Danish	MW	Middle Welsh
Du.	Dutch	NE	North-East
EME	Early Middle English	Nth.	Northern
EMidl.	East Midland	OA	Old Anglian
EN(se)	East Norse	ODa.	Old Danish
F	French	OE	Old English
Fris.	Frisian	OEN	Old East Norse
G	German	OF	Old French
Gallo-Rom.	Gallo-Roman	OFris.	Old Frisian
Gk	Greek	OHG	Old High German
Gmc	Germanic	OIcel.	Old Icelandic
Goth.	Gothic	OK	Old Kentish
Icel.	Icelandic	OM	Old Mercian
K	Kentish	ON	Old Norse
L	Latin	ONF	Northern Old French
LG	Low German	ONth.	Old Northumbrian
LL	Late Latin	OPicard	Old Picard
LOE	Late Old English	OProv.	Old Provencal
LONth.	Late Old Northumbrian	OS	Old Saxon
MDu.	Middle Dutch	OScand.	Old Scandinavian
ME	Middle English	OW	Old Welsh
med.	medieval	OWM	Old West Mercian
MFlem.	Middle Flemish	OWN	Old West Norse
MHG	Middle High German	Sth.	Southern
MK	Middle Kentish	WG	West Germanic
MLG	Middle Low German	WS	West Saxon
Mod.	modern		

> became
< derived (deriving) from
= corresponding to
~ as last form cited
* (before a form) unrecorded and reconstructed

* (after a form) emended
† the first recorded example
‡ the only recorded example
+ compounded with
× blended with

a¹, **an** *indef.art.* (1) **a** (*normally bef. initial cons.*) a 3, 7, 21, 24, *etc.*; *with num.*: ~ *thusand* 1974, 2356, 2682. (2) **an** (*normally bef. initial vowel*) an 114, 671, 1145, 1178, *etc.*; *bef. initial* **h**: 893, 1103, 1873 (*and num.*) ~ *hundred* 1634, 2118, 2127, 2163, 2934; *nom.sg.* **an** 671, 1178; *obj.sg.* **an** 1035, 1119; *prep.sg.* **an** 1103 [OE *ān* < *ān* 'one']
a²: *see* **on** *prep.*
a³: *see* **on** *num.*

abide *v.intr.* wait 1798 [OE *abīdan*]
aboven *prep.* towering above 1701 [ME *a* (< OE *on*) + OE *bufan*]
aboute(n), abuten prep. round 521, 591, 671, around 2832; (*temp.*) at about 2093; (*num.*) approximately 1011, 2430; regarding 1041 [OE *onbūtan*]
adoun, adune *adv.* down 568, 2736 [OE *of dūne* lit. 'off the mountain']
adrad *p.p.a.* afraid 278, 1049, 1164, 1683; **adred** 1259; *pl.* **adradde** 1788, **adrad**

2305. See **odrat**. [OE *ofdrǽdd*, *ofdrĕdd p.p.* of *ofdrǽdan*, *ofdrēdan*]

after *prep.* after 2257, in succession to 171, 515, 1076; with *v.* of motion: summoning (*see* **sende**) 137, 138, 359, 524, 1006, 1104, 1156, to fetch 2790; in accordance with 2816; *conj.* according as 2811 [OE *æfter*]

ageyn, aye(y)n (1) *adv.* back 493, 2427 (2) *prep.* facing 1810, 2922, reflecting 2142; towards 2800; (*with v. of motion*) to meet 1697 (*see* **ageyn-come, -go, -nime, -stonde**); against 272 (*see* **be(n)**), 570 [OE *ongegn, ongǣgn*]

[**ageyn-come**] *sep.v.* come to meet: *3 pt.sg.* **kam him ageyn** 451; advance to encounter: *3 pt.sg.* **cam hem ageyn** 2623 [OE *ongǣgn-cuman*]

ageynes *prep.* against 2154, 2271, 2310 [ME *ageyn* + -*es*, on model of OE *tō-gēanes*]

[**ageyn-go**] *quasi-sep.v.* go to meet; *inf.* **ageyn him go** 935 [ME *ageyn* + *go*]

[**ageyn-, ayen-nime**] *quasi-sep.v.* go to meet: *3 pt.pl.* **ageyn-nam** (*intr.*) 1948; *3 pt.pl.* **ayen . . . neme** 1208. *Cf.* **ageyn-come** [ME *ageyn, aye(y)n* + *nime*]

[**ageyn-stonde**] *sep.v.* resist; *inf.* **stonde ageyn** 2025, **ageyn . . . stonde** 2031 [OE *age(a)n-, ongean-standan*]

al (1) *a.* all; *nom.sg.* **al** 224, 278, 1342, 1405, 2884, *etc.*; *obj.sg.* **al** 250, 386, 700, 954, 1271, 2893, *etc.*; *prep.sg.* **al** 35, 290, 2179, 2264, 2365, 2603, *etc.*; *dat.sg.* **al** 277; *nom.pl.* **alle** 236, 401, 747, 958, 980, 2795, 2963, *etc.*; *obj.pl.* **alle** 169, 270, 366, 1344, 2589, 2693, *etc.*, **al** 2360; *poss.pl.* **alþer**- (*only in cpds.: see* ~**beste**, ~**leste**); *prep.pl.* **alle** 71, 282, 427, 946, *etc.*; *dat.pl.* **alle** 256. (2) *n.* everyone 104, 2614, everything 1099, 1360; *obj.sg.* **al** 104, 1099, 1360 [OE *all bes. eall* **a.**, whence subst. use]

al *adv.* entirely 34, 727, 937, 1311, 1415, 2221, *etc.*; completely 312; fully 614, 2477, 2363 (? *a.obj.pl.*); altogether 969 (with foll. **to** *adv.*) 302, *etc.*; *see* **quic**. *See* **almest, al so, oueral, withal, forthwithal** [OE *eal*]

ale *n.* ale; *obj.sg.* ~ 1245, 1732; *prep.sg.* ~ 14 [OE *ealu, alu*]

allas *interj.* alas; ~ *þat* . . . 1879 [OF *alas*]

almest *adv.* very nearly 963 [OE *eal mǣst*, bes. *mǣst eal*]

al so, als *A. conj.*; (1) *manner:* **al so** just as if 468, 469, **als** as if 593, 1913, as best 1047, **als** as 1291 (2) *temp.*: **al so** while 1038, when 1956, 2072; *correl.*: ~ . . . **so** when . . . then 1767, 2138, **als . . . so** when . . . then 2121–3; **als** as 507, 1292, when 587, 604, 1018, 1248, 1292, while 2616. *B. adv.* (1) *manner:* **al so** like 1873, **als** 987; *correl.*; **al so . . . als** just as . . . as 929, 1911–12, ~ . . . **so** 816–17, just as . . . as if 590, 594–5, 1254–5, 2096 **als . . . so** just as . . . so 992 [OE *eal swā*, red. to ME *als, as*; *correl.* OE *ealswā . . . swā*]

alþerbeste *a.* best of all 1041, very best 2416; *adv.* **alþerbest** best of all 182, 721, 1198 [OE gen.pl. *ealra, alra* + superl. *betsta* a., *betst* adv.]

alþerlest(e) *a.* slightest of all 1979, 2667 [OE gen.pl. *ealra* + superl. *lǣsta*]

am: *see* **be(n)**

amidewarde *prep.* in the middle of 873 [OE *on middan* + *w(e)ard*]

anan: *see* **anon**

and, ant, an *conj.*; **and** and 31, 115, 215, 320, 416, 514, *etc.*; if 2863; **ant** and 36, 558; **an** and 29, 58, 151, 214, 238, 362, 371, 644, 708, 712, 795, 1010, *etc.* [OE *and*]

andelong *adv.* lengthways 2823 [OE *andlang* a. 'the whole length of', *andlang* prep. 'along']

angel, aungel *n.* angel; *nom.sg.* **aungel** 1282; *prep.sg.* **angel** 1265, 1277 [OF *angele*, AN *aungle*]

ani *a.* any; *nom.sg.* ~ 2650; *obj.sg.* ~ 317, 1357, 1674, 1940, 2553; *prep.sg.* ~ 10, 26, 105, 2896; *pron.* ~ any man; *nom.sg.* ~ 1689, 2562; *obj.sg.* ~ 1703 [OE *ǽnig*]

anilepi, onlepi *a.* a single; *obj.sg.* **onlepi** 1095, **anilepi** 2108 [OE *ānlēpig*]

anker *n.* anchor 521, 671 [OE *ancor*]

anon, onon, anan* *adv.* immediately 176,* 1112,* 1633, 2204, 2563,* 2938, *etc.* (*very frequent*); **sone** ~ at once 136, 1050, 1965, 2088, 2617, 2729, *etc.* (*very frequent*) [OE *on ān*]

anoþer *a.* a second 1305, another 2156; a different 1195; *nom.sg.* ~ 1305; *obj.sg.* ~ 1195; *dat.sg.* ~ 2156 [OE *an ōþer*]

anoþer *pron.* somebody else 1035, 2654; a second (one) 2631; *obj.sg.* ~ 2631, 2654; *prep.sg.* ~ 1035 [OE *ān ōþer*]

anoþer *adv.*; (*al*) ~ (very) differently 1396 [perh. < neut. form of OE *oþer* a.]

answerede *3 pt.sg.* replied 1112, 1314; *3 pt.pl.* **ansuereden** 176 [OE *andswerian*]

anuye *v.tr.* bore 1736 [OF *anuier, enuier*]

are-dawes *n.* days of yore; *prep.pl.* ~ 27 [ON *ár-dagar* pl.]

are(n): *see* **be(n)**

arise *v.intr.* stand up 205 [OE *arīsan*]

arke *n.* coffer; *prep.sg.* ~ 222, 2019 [OE *arc*]

arm *n.* arm; *obj.sg.* ~ 2636; *prep.sg.* **arum** 1983, 2409; *nom.pl.* **armes** 1295; *obj.pl.* **armes** 1298; *prep.pl.* **armes** 985, 1301 [OE *earm*]

armes *n.* arms (for battle); *phr.* to ~ to arm themselves 2614; *nom.pl.* **armes** 2606; *obj.pl.* **armes** 2926 [OF *armes*]

arwe *a.* timorous; ~ *and kene* (timorous and brave) one and all 2116; *obj.pl.* ~ 2116 [OE *earg*]

as *pron.*: *see* **-es** *pron.*

as *adv.*: *see* **al so** *and* **so** *adv.*

asayleden *3 pt.pl.tr.* attacked 1863 [OF *asaillir*]

aske *v.tr.* ask; ~ *leue* ask permission (to depart) 2953 [OE *ascian*]

asken *n.* ashes; *prep.pl.* ~ 2842 [ON *aska*]

asse *n.* ass; *prep.sg.* ~ 2822, 2840 [OE *assa*]

astirte *3 pt.sg.intr.* leapt 894 [ME verb-pref. *a-* < OE *a-* + ME *stirten* v.]

at *prep.*; *loc.* (1) at 735, 876, ~ *mine* (*hise*) *fet* 1304, 2159, 2738, ~ *hom* 790, 823, (assembled) at 981 (2) through 2107 (3) *motion*: *dir.*: to 2620, ~ *his herte* aimed at 479, close to 2226 (4) *circumstances*: ~ *hayse* in a good state 59, ~ *nede* in a tight corner 9, 25, 1971, 2895, ~ *alle nedes* in all (warlike) crises 1693 (5) *manner*: ~ *one cri* with one voice 2774, ~ *a dint* with one blow 1808, 1970* (6) *pers. relation*: ~ *his cri* (*merci*) at his command (mercy) 270, 271, ~ *his wille* to do with as he pleased 271, as he pleased 2859 (7) *temp.*: ~ *ones* at one and the same time 1296, ~ *þe laste* finally 1678, 2150, ~ *þe firste siþe* at the outset 1053. *See* **at-gonge, atsitte** [OE *æt*]

[at-gonge] ?(*quasi-*)*sep.v.*; *inf.* **at ... gonge** 1789 (*see* n.) [OE *ætgangan* 'approach' or ad. ON *ganga at* 'attack']

atsitte *v.tr.* oppose 2201 [OE *ætsittan*]

auhte *n.* property 531, possessions 1224, 1411, 2216; *obj.sg.* **aucte** 531, **auchte** 1224, **authe** 1411, **auhte** 2216 [OE *æht*]

aunlaz *n.* dagger; *obj.sg.* ~ 2555 [unknown]

auter *n.* altar; *prep.sg.* ~ 389, 1387, 2374 [OF *auter*]

awcte: *see* **awe** v.

awe *n.* fear 277; *see* **stonden** [ON *agi*]

awe, hawe, owe v. (1) *tr.* own 744, rule over 207, take possession of 1293; take 1189, owe 1667; *1 pr.sg.* **owe** 1667; *3 pr.sg.subj.* **hawe** 1189; *inf.* **awe** 1293; *3 pt.sg.* **awcte** 207, **aute** 744 (2) *intr.* ought; *as a present* (*in form,* < OE *pt.subj.*): **auht** 2174, **auhte** 2801, **nouth** (*ne ouhte*) 802; *as a pt.*, **aucte** 2788 [OE *āgan* 'possess']

awey *adv.* away; (*with v. of motion*) 2679; (*with ellipse of v.*) *forth* ~ 1678 [OE *onweg*]

[awey-bere] *sep.v.* carry off; *p.p.* **awey-born** 2021 [OE *aweg-beran*]

[awey-go] *quasi-sep.v.* go away; *pt.sg.* **yede ... awey** 1391 [ME *awey* + *go*]

[awey-wende] *quasi-sep.v.* go away; *pt.sg.* **wente ... awey** 1920 [ME *awey* + *wende*]

ax *n.* axe; *obj.sg.* ~ 1777*, 1895 [OE *æx*]

ay *adv.* at all times 159, 947, 2936; for ever 748, perpetually 2523, 2874, 2975; continuously 1202, 1435 [ON *ei*]

ayþer, eþer *pron.* (1) each (*of two*) 1883 (*see* **unker**) (2) **ayþer ... oþer** each ... the other 2666 [OE *ægþer*]

bac *n.* back; *obj.sg.* (*of reference*) ~ 1951; *prep.sg.* ~ 47, 557, 1845; *obj.pl.* **backes** 1911; *prep.pl.* **backes** 2612 [OE *bæc*]

baldelike *adv.* securely 53. *See* **bold** [OE *baldlīce*]

baret *n.* fighting 1933 [OF *barat*]

barfot *a.* unshod 863 [OE *bærfot*]

barnage *n.* king's vassals of high rank; *prep.sg.* ~ 2948 [OF *barnage*]

barre *n.* bar used to fasten a door securely; *obj.sg.* ~ 1795, 1828; *prep.sg.* ~ 1812, 1854 [OF *barre*]

barun *n.* noble (of the lowest rank) 31, 273, 2259; *prep.sg.* ~ 2184; *obj.pl.* **barouns** 2195, 2466; *prep.pl.* **baruns** 138, 261 [AN *barun*]

baþe: *see* **boþe** a. *and* adv.

bed *n.* bed; *obj.sg.* ~ 659; *prep.sg.* **bedde** 1115, 2928, **bed** 2135 [OE *bedd*]

bedden *v.tr.* lodge in bed (as man and wife) 1236; *p.p.* **beddeth** 1129, **bedded** 2772 [OE *beddian*]

bede *n.* prayer; *obj.sg.* ~ 1386 [OE *gebed*]

bede *v.tr.* (1) offer 1666, 2085, 2173, 2775, 2781 (2) announce 2393; *1 pr.sg.* ~ 2173; *3 pr.sg.* **bedes** 2393; *3 pt.pl.* **beden** 2775, 2781. *See* **ut-bede** [OE *bēodan*]

bedel *n.* messenger of justice; *obj.pl.* **bedels** 266 [OF *bedel*]

beite, beyte *v.tr.* worry (with dogs); *inf.* 1841, *pass.inf.* 2331, *ger.* 2441 [ON *beita*]

belles *n.* church bells; *see* **on** *prep*.; *obj.pl.* ~ 242, 1107; *prep.pl.* ~ 390 [OE *belle*]

be(n) *v.intr.* be; *impers.:* hwat is þe (*ȝw*)? what is the matter with you? 453, 1952; *leuere* ~ be preferable 1194, 1424, 1672; ~ *nouht of* be altogether unconcerned about 123, 313, 838, *sim.* ~ *nouht a slo of* 850; *impers.:* ~ *wel* be glad 642, 1218, 2171, be amply furnished 274, be a splendid thing for 1694, *betere* ~ be better for 697; *impers.:* ~ *wo* be bitterly distressed 124, 854, 2746, rue 461; *phr.* ~ *ageyn* oppose 272, 2886; ~ *togydere* be united 1182; ~ *war of* notice 2140; ~ *wel* be in favour 2879; ~ *with* be on one's side 62; *yif he ne were* but for him 1975, *sim.* 2678 (*see* **ne were** *conj.*), *inf.* **ben** 272, 306, **be** 1668, 1931, 2068, 2322, 2788, 2886; *imper.pl.* **bes** 2247; *1 pr.sg.* **am** 167; *2 pr.sg.* **art** 527, 854; *3 pr.sg.* **is** 851, 908, 1384, *etc.* (agglut. with *ne*) **nis** 462, 1999, 2245, **es*** 2700; *see* **þis**; *1 pr.pl.* **aren** 620; *2 pr.pl.* **aren** 161, **are** 1629, **ar** 1882; *3 pr.pl.* **aren** 1147, 1322, 1350, **are** 1339; *3 pr.sg.subj.* **be** 520, 1077; *3 fut.sg.* **bes** 1745, 2008, **beth** 1261, 1262; *2 pt.sg.* **wore** 685; *3 pt.sg.* **was** 179, 481, *etc.*; *3 pt.pl.* **were** 414, 742, *etc.*, **ware** 400, 2256, **wore** 237, 718, 1054; *3 pt.sg.subj.* **were** 1975, 2678, **wore** 504, 1092; *1 perf.subj.* **were** would have been 1975; *3 perf.subj.pass.* **were** 1980, 2668; *p.p.* **ben** 2676 [OE *bēon*]

benes *n.* beans; *obj.pl.* ~ 770 [OE *bēan*]

beneysun *n.* grace at a meal 1724 [OF *beneisun*]

berd *n.* beard; *prep.sg.* ~ 702 [OE *beard*]

bere *n.* bear; *nom.sg.* ~ 574; *obj.sg.* ~ 1841, 2449; *prep.sg.* ~ 1839 [OE *bera*]

bere(n) *v.tr.* (1) carry 558, 582, 763, 806, 878, 939, 2553, *etc.* (2) wear 378, 1319, 2551, 2944 (3) give birth to 461, 975, 1169; *phr.* ~ *corune* be crowned 2944, be reigning monarch 1319; *god fey(th)* ~ be loyal to 2270, 2854, be devoted to the interests of 255; *inf.* **bere** 378, 806, 939, **beren** 255, 582, 763; *3 pr.sg.* **beres** 2324; *3 pt.sg.* **bar** 558, 816, 878, 940, 941; *3 pt.sg.subj.* **bore** 45, ? **bere** 975; *p.p.* **born** 461, 1169, 2856. *See* **up-bere** [OE *beran*]

bermen *n.* porters 869, 888; *obj.pl.* ~ 877 [OE *bǣrman*, f. on *bǣr* 'bier' (?)]

bern *n.* child 572. *See* **kradel-barnes** [OE *bēarn*]

berwen, burwe *v.tr.* (1) protect 2023 (2) save 698, 2871, save the life of 1427, 2680; *inf.* **berwen** 698, **berpen** 1427, **burwe** 2871; *3 pt.sg.* **barw** 2023, 2680 [OE *beorgan*]

best *adv. superl.:* see **wel** *adv.*

beste *a. superl.:* see **god** *a.*

beste *n.* animal; *nom.sg.* ~ 279, **best** 575, 945; *obj.sg.* **best** 2692 [OF *beste*]

bete *v.tr.* buffet 1900; *recipr.:* ~ *ayþer on oþer* (*dintes grete*) strike (heavy blows) at each other 2665; *intr.* rain blows 1877, 1917; *inf.* **bete** 2665, (*pass.*) 1900; *3 pt.pl.* **beten** 1877; *p.p.* **bet** 1917 [OE *bēatan*]

betere: see **wel**

beþe: see **boþe** *a. and adv.*

beye, byen *v.tr.* buy 969, 970, 1626, 1655, *absol.* 53; (*fig.*) pay for 2461*; *phr.* ~ *and sellen* 53, 1655; *inf.* **beye** 53, 1655, **byen** 1626; *3 pr.sg.* **beyes*** 2461; *3 pt.sg.* **bouthe** 969, 970; *p.p.* **bouth** 884 [f. an OE *byg-* in 2 pr.sg. *byg-est*, 3 pr.sg. *byg-eþ* (inf. *bycgan*)]

beyte: see **beite**

bi *prep.* (1) alongside 400, 883, 1964; at one's side 619; next to 2487 (2) along 2471, 2510 (3) in oaths: ~ *Crist* 2106, 2404, ~ *God* 2340, ~ *heueneking* 1938, ~ *þe Louerd* 1782; ~ *Seint Austin* 1774, ~ *Seint Dauy* 2868, ~ *Seint Iohan* 1113, 1722; ~ *þe fey . . .* 1667 (4) ~ *boþe halue* on both sides 2683 (5) ~ *þe pappes* as far as the nipples 2133 (6) ~ *þe heued* (*shuldre*) more a head taller 1702, head and shoulders taller 983 (7) (*temp.*) ~ *are-dawes* in days gone by 27, ~ *nither-tale* at dead of night 2026 (8) according to: ~ *hire wille* so far as her wishes were concerned 1131, ~ *his nauen* by name 1398, ~ *tale* in number 2027, ~ *mine wone* in my opinion 1712, 1973, (*sim.*) ~ *mine mone* 817; in accordance with: ~ *youre red* 2212 (9) (*means*): ~ *þe necke* 2047 (10) (*instr.*): ~ *his wif* 348. *See* **bi-stonde** [OE *bi*]

[**bicome**] *v.intr.* become; *imper.pl.* **bicomes** 2304; *3 pt.sg.* **bicam** 2255; *3 pt.pl.* **bicomen** 2258; *p.p.* **bicomen** 2265 [OE *becuman*]

bidden *v.tr.* (1) ask 529, 935, 938, 1669 (2) wish 1734, 2531 (*see n.*) (3) enjoin 399, 1227; command 165, 577, 669, 1046, 1416, 2306, 2397; demand 1155 (4) offer 484 (× **bede** *v.* offer, *q.v.*); *inf.* **bidden** 529; *1 pr.sg.* **bidde** 1734, 2531, **biddi** (*with agglut. pron.*) 484; *2 pt.sg.* **bede** 669, 2397; *3 pt.sg.* **bad** 165, 399, 577, 1046, 1227, 1416, 1669, 2306, *etc.* [OE *biddan*]

bidene *adv.*: *al* ~ in full 731, completely 2842 [ad. MFlem. *bedeene (medeen)* = MDu. *meteen* lit. 'in one']

bifalle *v.*; *impers.* happen; *inf.* ~ 2982; *3 pt.sg.* **bifel(le)** 339, 825 [OE *befallan*]

bifor, biforn *prep.*; (1) (*spatial*) beyond 1035 (2) under the impact of 2700 (3) in front of 1023, 1358, *phr.* ~ *min eyne* 1365 (4) in the front of 1813 (5) into the presence of 157, 246, 1696, 2053, 2378, 2453, 2464 [OE *beforan*]

big *a.* strong 1775 [unknown]

biginnen *v.intr.* (1) begin 826, 895, 1012, 1780 (2) proceed 230, 734, 1303, 1358, 1426, 1802; *tr.* begin 21; *inf.* **biginnen** 21; *2 pr.pl.* **biginnen** 1780; *3 pt.sg.* **bigan** 230, 734, 826, 895, 1426, 1802; *3 pt.pl.* **bigunnen** 1012, 1303 [OE *be-*, *biginnan*]

biginning *vbl.n.* opening; *prep.sg.* ~ 13* [ME *biginnen* v. + suff. -*ing*]

bihalue *v.tr.* surround 1835 [prob. OE **beh(e)alfian* = OHG *behalben*]

biheld *tr. 3 pt.sg.* looked up and down 1646*; *3 pt.pl.* **bihelden** scrutinized 2149 [OE *bih(e)aldan*]

[**bihote**] *v.tr.* promise; *2 pt.sg.* **bihetet** (*with agglut.* (*h*)*it*: *see* -**(e)t**) promised it 678; *p.p.* **bihoten** 565 [OE *bihātan*]

bihoue *n.* use: *prep.sg. to his* ~ for his benefit 1765 [OE **bihōf* in *bihōflic* a. 'useful']

bihoues *3 pr.sg.* (*impers.*) is incumbent on 583* [OE *bi-, behofian*]

bikenneth *3 pr.sg.tr.* makes known 1269, 1270 [ME *bi-* pref. + *kennen* v. 'make known']

[**bileue**] *v.intr.* remain; *imper.sg.* ~ 1229; *3 pt.sg.* **bilefte** 2964 [OE *belǣfan*]

bimene *v.tr.* signify 1260 [ME *bi-* pref. + *mēnen* v. < OE *mǣnan*]

binde(n), bynde *v.tr.* tie up; *inf.* **bynde** (*pass.*) 41, **binden** 1962, 2821 (*pass.*), **binde** 2050; *3 pr.pl.* **binde** 2584; *3 pt.sg.* **bounden** 2443, 2447; *p.p.* **bounden** 545, **bunden** 1429, **bunde** 2378. *See* **bynderes** [OE *bindan*]

binne *adv.* inside 585 [OE *binnan*]

birde, birþe: *see* **bire**

[**bire**] *v.* (1) *impers.*: *3 pr.sg.* **birþe** behoves 2102 (2) *with pers. subject*: *3 pt.sg.* **birde** had cause to 2762 [OE (*ge-*) *byrian*]

birþene *n.* load; *nom.sg.* ~ 808; *obj.sg.* ~ 901; *prep.sg.* ~ 903 [OE *byrþen*]

bise *n.* north wind 725 [perh. OF *bise* < Gmc **bīsa* 'whirlwind' in OHG *bisa*, MHG *bise*, OS *bisa*, MDu. *bise*]

biseken *v.tr.* entreat 2995 [ME pref. *bi-* + *sēken* < OE *sēcan*]

bi-souþe *prep.* on the south of 2829 [OE *be sūþan*]

[**bi-stonde**] *sep.v.tr.* (1) *3 pt.sg.* **bi-stod** stood alongside 476, 507 (2) *3 pr.sg.subj.* **stonde ... bi** help 2605–6 [OE *bī-standan*]

bistride *v.tr.* sit astride 2061 [OE *bi-, bestrīdan*]

biswike *p.p.* treated treacherously 1250 [OE *beswīcan*]

bitaken *v.tr.* hand over to 1227 [ME *bi-* pref. + ON *taka*]

bite *v.tr.* (1) bite (*pass.*) 2441 (2) drink 1732 [OE *bītan*]

bitechen *v.tr.* (1) hand over 203, 395, 559, 1409 (2) entrust to 1225, 2213; commit to the charge of 206, 384; formally commit 2318 (3) commend to the care of 2958; *inf.* **bitechen** 203; *imper.sg.* **biteche** 395; *1 pr.sg.* **biteche** 384; *3 pt.sg.* **bitaucte** 206, 559, **bitawchte** 1225, **bitawte** 1409, 1410, **bitauhte** 2213, 2318, 2958 [OE *betǣcan*]

bitwen(en) *prep.* between 749, 936, 1819, 2669, 2977; among 1834 [OE *betwēonan*]

blac *a.* black 48, clad in black 2522 (*see*

mon(e)kes); grimy 556 [OE *blæc* 'black']

blac *a.* white 311; fair-complexioned: *in phr.* ~ *and brown* fair and swarthy 1009 (sg.), (*þe*) *broune and . . . þe blake* (*pl.*) all and sundry 1910, 2182, 2250, 2848, *sim.* 2695 [OE *blāc* 'pale']

blakne *v.intr.* turn pale 2166 [ME *blāk* + inchoative suff. *-n-*; see n.]

blame *n.* disrepute 84, 1673, 2426, reprobation 1193 (*see* **bringe(n)**); transgression 2461 [OF *blame*]

blase *n.* flame 1255 [OE *blase*, *blæse*]

blawe, blowe *v.tr.* fan with a current of air: ~ *þe fir* 586, 588, 914; *inf.* **blawe** 588, **blowe** 914; *imper.sg.* **blou** 586 [OE *blāwan*]

blede *v.intr.* bleed: *on rode* ~ 103, 2404 [OE *blēdan*]

bleike *a.* pale; *phr.*: *see* **grene** *a.*; *nom.pl.* ~ 470 [ON *bleik-r* nom.sg.masc.]

blenkes *n.* tricks (*see* **make(n)** *v.*); *obj.pl.* ~ 307 [on **blenken, blenchen v.* < OE *blencan* 'cheat', or prim. ON **blenkja* > ON *blekka*]

blessed *p.p.* blest 1216 [OE *bletsian*]

blinne *v.intr.* desist 329, 2671; cease from effort 2368, 2375; *inf.* **blinne** 2368, 2375; *3 pr.sg.* **blinneth** 329; *3 pt.pl.* **blunne*** 2671 [OE *blinnan*]

blisse *n.* (1) general rejoicing 2188 (2) happiness 2936; *prep.sg.* ~ 2188, 2936 [OE *blīðs*]

blissed *p.p.* made glad 2874 [OE *blīðsian*, *blissian*]

bliþe *a.* glad 633, 887; happy 652, 778; joyous 2280; *nom.pl.* ~ 778, *obj. pl.* ~ 2280 [OE *blīðe*]

blod *n.* blood; *nom.sg.* ~ 216, 1851, 2745; *obj.sg.* ~ 1905; *prep.sg.* **blode** 432, **blod** 475, 499, 2687. *See* **herte-blod**. [OE *blōd*]

blome *n.* fairest flower 63 [ON *blómi*]

bloute *a.* soft; *obj.pl.* ~ 1911 [ON *blaut-r* nom.sg.masc.]

blowe: *see* **blawe**

bode *n.* summons (*cf.* **ut-bede**); *obj.sg.* ~ 2201, 2568 [OE *bod* 'command' × ON *boð* 'summons (to vassals, etc.)']

bodi *n.* body 84, 110, 996; physique 345; *periphr.* *his* ~ him 2311, 2733, ?363, *hire* ~ her 2846; *nom.sg.* ~ 363; *obj.sg.* ~ 2311, 2423, 2846; *prep.sg.* ~ 84, 110, 345, 996 [OE *bodig*]

bok *n.* book 2328; the Bible 487, 1419, 2308, 2312, 2373; the Mass-book 1083; 1174, 2218; *prep.sg.* **boke** 487, 2312, **bok** 1083, 1174, 1419, 2218, 2308, 2328, 2373 [OE *bōc*]

bold *a.* (1) valiant 107, plucky 450 (2) assured 193 (3) temerarious 64, aggressive 2310, forward 956; *phr.*: *see* **stille**; *nom.sg.* ~ 64, 107, 193, 450; *nom.pl.* **bolde** 956, *prep.pl.* **bolde** 2310. *See* **baldelike** [OE *bald*]

bole *n.* bull; *nom.sg.* ~ 2439; *obj.pl.* **boles** 2331 [ON *boli*]

bondeman *n.* peasant; *nom.sg.* ~ 32; *nom.pl.* **bondemen** 1017; *prep.pl.* **bondemen** 1309 [ON *bóndi* 'farmer', or LOE *bonda* < ON *bóndi*, + *man*]

bondes *n.* bonds; (*fig.*) pains 143; *nom.pl.* ~ 538, 2442; *prep.pl.* ~ 143, 636. *See* **dede-bondes**. [phon. var. of ME *band*, ad. of ON *band*]

bone *n.* request; *obj.sg.* ~ 1660 [ON *bón*]

bones *n.* frame (of the body); *prep.pl.* ~ 1297 [OE *bān*]

bor *n.* boar; *nom.sg.* ~ 1868, 1990; *obj.pl.* **bores** 2332 [OE *bār*]

bord *n.* (1) plank (in a wooden partition) 2107 (2) meal-table 99, 1723; *nom.sg.* ~ 1723; *prep.sg.* ~ 99, 2107 [OE *bord*]

borw *n.* guarantor 1668 [OE *borg*]

borw, boru, burw *n.* town; *prep.sg.* **borw** 848, 1015, 1645, 1758, 2087, 2827, **boru** 774; *obj.pl.* **borwes** 1294, 1445, **burwes** 2278; *prep.pl.* **burwes** 55, **borwes** 1631 [OE *burg*]

bote *n.* *phr.*: *non oþer* ~ no other expedient 1201; *obj.sg.* ~ 1201 [OE *bōt*]

bote *adv.*: *see* **but** *adv.*

boþe, boþen, baþe, beþe *a.* both (1) *absol.*: ~ 471 (2) *in appos. with pl.pron.*: *ye* ~ 1681, *he* ~ 2657, 2659, 2973, *us* ~ 695*, *hem* ~ 2544; *with n.*: *þe mayndnes . . .* ~ 2224; (2) *attrib. with pl.pron.*: ~ *ure liues* 698; *nom.pl.* **boþe** 2657, 2973, **boþen** 2659, **baþe 1337**, **baþe** 1681* (MS **beþe**); *obj.pl.* **baþe** 695* (MS **beþe**), 2544; *poss.pl.* **boþen** 698; *prep.pl.* **boþen** 471 [*baþe, boþe* ad. ON *bāð-ar* nom.masc., *báð-ir* nom.fem.; *boþen* ad. ON *báð-* × OE *bēgen* masc. 'both'; *beþe* ad. ON *bæþi* nom. & obj. neut. ? (*see* 360 *n.*)]

boþe, boþen *adv.* both 970, 989, 1097,

1105, 1219, 2036, *etc*.; **boþen** 173, 959; **baþe** 360* (MS **beþe**; *see n.*), 2585*, 2596 [as *boþe a.*]

bour, bowr *n.* (1) bedroom 2073, 2078 (2) lady's appartment 239; *obj.sg.* **bowr** 2073; *prep. sg.* **bour** 2078, **boure** 239 [OE *būr*]

bowes *n.* bows (as weapons); *prep.pl.* ~ 1749 [OE *boga*]

boyes *n.* ruffians; *obj.pl.* ~ 1900 [aph. < AN *embuié* p.p. 'fettered'; see n.]

brayd *pt.sg.intr.* started up 1283. *See* **utbrayde** [OE *bregdan*]

bred *n.* bread; *obj.sg.* ~ 463, 634, 644, 924, 1880 [OE *brēad*]

brede *n.* roast meat; *obj.sg.* ~ 98 [OE *brǣde*]

breken *v.tr.* break; *inf.* ~ 915, **breke** 1901, 1909 (*both pass.*); *3 pt.pl.* **broken** 1903, 1904; *p.p.* **broken** 1239. *See* **up-breke** [OE *brecan*]

brenne *n.* state of combustion; *prep.sg.* ~ 1240 (*see* **bringe(n)**) [ME *brenne* v. < ON *brenna* 'burn']

brennen *v.intr.* burn 595, 917; be burned 1163; *tr.* set fire to 2584; burn (at the stake) 2833, 2842, 2845; *inf.* **brennen** 917, **brenne** 1163; *3 pr.pl.* **brenne** 2584; *p.p.* **brend** 2833, 2842, 2845 [ON *brenna*]

brest *n.* chest; *prep.sg.* ~ 1031, 1649 [OE *brēost*]

bride *n.* bride; *nom.sg.* ~ 2132 [OE *brȳd*]

brigge *n.* bridge; *prep.sg.* ~ 876, 882* [OE *brycg* or ON *bryggja*]

brim *a.* furiously turbulent 2234 [OE *brēme*]

bringe(n) *v.tr.* bring 1235 *etc*.; conduct 1115; *phr.* ~ *bifore* bring into the presence of 2053, 2378, 2453, 2463*; ~ *upon* bring down on 65; ~ *in blame* bring into disrepute or reprobation 84, 1193, 2426; ~ *on brenne* kindle 1240; ~ *until huse* instal as wife 2914; *to wronge* ~ persuade to unjust courses 72; (*with p.p.* **brouth**) *to dede* ~ be on the verge of death 167; *to þe erþe* ~ interred 248; ~ *to* (*þe*) *grounde* laid low 1980, 2676; ~ *of liue* killed 513, 2413, dead 2130; ~ *to nouth* ruined 58; *in sorwe* ~ caused suffering to 336, (*refl.*) got (oneself) into trouble 2812; *to sorwe* ~ disgraced 57, plunged into misery 1373; *inf.* **bringen**

1115, 1193, 1235, **bringe** 72, **bringhe** 65; *p.p.* **brouth** 57, 84, 167, 248, 663, *etc*., **browt** 58, **brouct** 513. *See* **forthbringe** [OE *bringan*]

brini(e) *n.* coat of mail; *obj.sg.* **brinie** 1776, **brini** 2552; *obj.pl.* **brinies** 2611 [ad. ON *brynja*]

brisen *v.tr.* batter 1836 [OE *brȳsan*]

brith(e), bryth *a.* (1) (of the sun) radiant 2922; (of light) brilliant 590, 606, 1253, 1254, 2148 (2) glittering 2141, gleaming 2316, 2359, 2611; (3) (of a woman) lovely 2132; *comp.* **brithter** 2142 [OE *beorht*]

brith *adv.* brilliantly 2145 [OE *beorhte*]

brittene *v.tr.* (*pass.*) cut to pieces 2701 [OE *brytnian*]

brod *a.* broad 1648; wide in shape 897; *prep.pl.* **brode** 897 [OE *brād*]

broþer *n.* brother; *nom.sg.* ~ 1327, 2155; *obj.sg.* ~ 1397, 2349; *nom.pl.* **breþren** 2414 [OE *brōðor*; nom./acc.pl. *brōðru*, **brēðer* (Merc. *broeþre*)]

brouke *v.tr.* enjoy the use of; in mild oaths (*see* **so**): *So* ~ *I mi blake swire* 311; (*sim.*) ~ *finger or to* 1744, ~ *mi rith eie* 2546; *inf.* ~ 1744, 2546; *1 pr.sg.subj.* ~ 311 [OE *brūcan*]

broune, brown(e), brune *a.* dark-complexioned 1009, 1910, 2182, 2250, 2695, 2848; *in phr.* (*see* **blac** *a.*[2]) [OE *brūn*]

broys *n.* broth; *obj.sg.* ~ 925 [OF *brouetz* (?)]

bulder-ston *n.* large stone, (*orig.*) standing in a stream; *obj.sg.* ~ 1791 [MDu., MLG *bulderen* 'make a loud noise'; cf. OFris. *bulder-slek* 'loud blow', Sw. dial. *bullersten* 'large stone (that causes a rumbling noise in a stream')]

burgeys *n.* freeman of a borough 1329; *obj.sg.* **burgeis** 2467; *nom.pl.* **burgeys** 2013; *obj.pl.* ~ 2196* [OF *burgeis* < L *burgēnsis*]

burgmen *n.* citizens of a borough; *obj.pl.* ~ 2050 [OE *burhman*]

burwe: *see* **berwen**

burwes: *see* **borw**[2]

but *n.* cast (in the sport of putting the stone); *prep.sg.* ~ 1041 [ME *butten* v. (see **but** p.p.) or OF *bout* 'blow']

but *p.p.* thrust 1917 [OF *bouter*]

but, bute *prep.* except 111, 965, 1309, 2104 [OE *būtan* adv. and prep., < *be-ūtan* 'on the outside; without']

but, bote *adv.* only 722; (*with neg.*) *neuere* ~ no more than 723 [as **but** prep.]

but(e), buten *conj.* (*with neg.*) ~ if not 149; ~ þat with the proviso that 388 (*see n.*), ~ on þat with the single proviso that 505, except only that 963; ~ als except that 2023, except as 2032; unless 85, 691, 1150, 1160, (*sim.*) ~ y(i)f 2547, 2973; but 355, 729, 1206, 1280, 2957 [OE *būtan* conj.]

butere *n.* butter; *obj.sg.* ~ 644 [OE *butere*]

butte *n.* stubby-shaped fish; *obj.sg.* ~ 760 [ad. MDu. *but(te)* or MLG *but*]

buttinge *vbl.n.* thrusting; *obj.sg.* ~ 2323 [see **but** p.p.]

byen: *see* **beye**

bynderes *n.* burglars who tie up victims; *obj.pl.* ~ 2051. [on *binde* v.]

caliz *n.* cup used in the Eucharist; *obj.sg.* ~ 187, *prep.sg.* ~ 2712 [OF *caliz*]

callen *v.* (1) *intr.* shout 885, 888, cry out 230 (2) *tr.* summon 38, 2900 (3) *tr.* call in aid 1359 (4) *tr.* designate 746*, 748; *inf.* **callen** 748, 2900 (*pass.*), **calle** 38 (*pass.*), 230, 888 (*pass.*), **kalle** 1359; *3 pr.sg.* **calleth** 725; *3 pr.pl.* **calle** (*see* -(e)t) 746*; *3 pt.sg.* **kalde** 885 [ON *kalla*]

canst, kan: *see* **conne**

care: *see* **kare**

carl *n.* fellow 1790 [ON *karl*]

carte-lode *n.* cartload; *obj.sg.* ~ 896 [ON *kartr*; ME *lōde* 'burden' (< OE *lād* 'way; journey') × *lāde* v. 'load' < OE *hladan*]

castel *n.* castle; *obj.sg.* ~ 2277; *prep.sg.* ~ 412; *obj.pl.* **castles** 1322, 1443, **casteles** 397, 2366; *prep.pl.* **castels** 252 [ONF *castel*]

casten *v.tr.* throw 81, 519, 557, 568, 986, 1776; fling 1785, 1797; set roughly 2450; *inf.* **casten** 519 (*pass.*), **kesten** 81 (*pass.*), 1785, **keste** 2612 (*pass.*); *3 pt.sg.* **caste** 557, 568, 986, 1776, 1797; *3 pt.pl.* **keste** 2450 [ON *kasta*, perh. × *festen* (q.v.) < ON *festa*]

catel *n.* belongings 225; property 275, 2024, 2516, 2907, 2940 [ONF *catel* = Central OF *chatel* < L *capitale* a.]

cauenard *n.* wretch 2390 [*see n.*]

cayser(e), kaysere *n.* emperor; *phr.* king ne (*or*) ~ 353, 978, 1318, 1726 [ON *keisari*]

cerges, serges *n.* wax tapers; *nom.pl.* ~ 595, 2126 [OF *cerge* 'id.' < L *cēreus* a. 'waxen']

chaffare *n.* trading; *obj.sg.* ~ 1658 [OE *ceapfaru* = ON *kaupfǫr* 'voyage for trading']

chambioun *n.* fighting man; *nom.sg.* ~ 1008 (*see text, footnote*); *nom.pl.* **chaunpions** 1016, 1032, 1039, 1056 [OF *champiun*]

chanounes *n.* (ecclesiastical) canons; *obj.pl.* ~ 360 [OF *chanoine* × ME *canoun* < ONF *canonie*]

chapmen *n.* itinerant merchants; *nom.pl.* 51; *prep.pl.* 1640 [OE *cēapmon*]

charbucle-ston *n.* fiery gem believed to emit light in the dark; *nom.sg.* ~ 2146 [OF *charbucle* < L *carbunculus*; ME *stōn*]

chartre deed of manumission; *prep.sg.* ~ 677 [OF *chartre*]

chaste *a.* chaste 288 [OF *chaste*]

cherl *n.* (1) serf 262, 621, 685, 1093 (2) villain 2534; *nom.sg.* ~ 2534; *poss.sg.* **cherles** 1093; *nom pl.* **cherles** 621; *prep.pl.* **cherles** 262 [OE *ceorl*]

chese *n.* cheese; *obj.sg.* ~ 644 [OE *cēse*]

chesen *v.tr.* (1) choose 372 (2) distinguish (from similar objects) 2148; *3 pt.pl.* **chosen** 372 [OE *cēosan*]

chiche *a.* niggardly 1764*, 2942* [OF *chiche*, *chinche* 'niggardly', of uncertain origin]

child *n.* (1) boy 532, 537 (2) *pl.* children 348, 368, 474, 499, 957, 2935, 2979; *obj.sg.* ~ 532, 537; *nom.pl.* **children** 474, 957; *poss.pl.* **children** 499; *obj.pl.* **children** 348, 2935, 2979 [OE *cild*, pl. *cildru*]

chiste *n.* coffer; *prep.sg.* ~ 222. *See* **kiste**. [OE *cist*]

citte *3 pt.sg.tr.* hewed 943 [OE *cyttan*]

clad *p.p.a.* clothed; *phr.* ~ *ne* naked of any kind 2890. *See* **cloþe**. [OE *clǣðan*, p.p. *clǣdd*]

clapte *3 pt.sg.tr.* banged 1815, 1822 [OE *clappian*]

clare *n.* beverage made of wine, honey, and spices 1729 [OF *claré*]

clene *a.* pure 996 [OE *clǣne*]

clerc *n.* man in holy orders 33, 77*, 1030*, 2196, ecclesiastic 1178*; *nom.sg.* ~ 77*, 1030*, 1178*; *nom.pl.* **clerkes** 33; *obj.pl.* **klerkes** 2196 [OF *clerc*]

cleue *n.* bed-chamber; *prep.sg.* ~ 558, 597 [OE *cleofa* or ON *klefi*]

cleuen *v.tr.* split; *inf.* ~ 918; *3 pt.sg.* **clef** 2644, 2731 [OE *clēofan*]

closede *1 pt.sg.tr.* encompassed 1311 [OF *clos-*, subj. stem of *clore* < L *claudere*]

cloth *n.* (1) (piece of) cloth 185, 546 (2) piece of clothing 856, clothing 1145; (*pl.*) clothes 418, 969, 1234; *nom.sg.* ~ 856; *obj.sg.* ~ 185, 1145; *prep.sg.* ~ 546; *obj.pl.* **cloþes** 418, 969, **cloþen** 1234 [OE *clāþ*]

cloþe *v.tr.* clothe 1139; *refl.* put on one's clothes 1355; *inf.* **cloþe** 1139; *2 pt.sg.* **claddes** 2908: *3 pt.sg.* **cloþede** 420, **cladde** 1355; *p.p.* **cloþed** 972. *See* **clad**. [OE *clǣðan* (for *cladde(s)*), *clāðian* (for *cloþe* etc.)]

clubbe *n.* cudgel; *obj.sg.* ~ 2290; *prep.sg.* ~ 1928 [ON *klubba*]

clutes *n.* pieces of rag; *prep.pl.* ~ 548 [OE *clūt*]

clyueden *3 pt.pl.* ~ *on* clung to 1301 [OE *clifian*]

cok, kok *n.* cook; *nom.sg.* ~ 904, 922, 968, 2899; *obj.sg.* **kok** 881; *poss.sg.* **cokes** 1124, (*disj.*) **þe kokes** 1147; *prep.sg.* **kok** 892 [OE *cōc*]

cold, kold *n.* cold; *phr.*: *see* **fonge**; *obj.sg.* cold 857; *prep.sg.* **kold** 416, **cold** 449 [OE *cald*]

comen, komen *v.intr.* (1) come 1002, 1180, 1681, 1715, 1768 (2) arrive 864, 1204; *phr.* ~ **at** reach 2620; ~ *befor* present oneself before 156; ~ *intil helde* grow up 128; ~ *ner* be comparable with 991; ~ *of* descend from 2175; ~ *til* 1310, ~ *unto* 2827 reach (*cf.* **to-comen**); *inf.* **comen** 325, 2119, **komen** 1002; *imper.pl.* **comes** 1799, **cometh** 1886, 2248; *3 pr.sg.* **comes** 1768; *2 pr.pl.subj.* **comen** 1681; *3 pt.sg.* **kam** 767, 864, 933, 984, 991, 1022; *3 pt.pl.* **comen** 1018, **komen** 1204; *3 pt.sg.subj.* **come** 2563; *3 pt.pl.subj.* **keme** 1209; *p.p.* **comen** 1695, 1715, 2581, **come** 2575, 2795. *See* **ageyn-, forth-, on-, to-, up-**. OE [*cuman*]

conestable *n.* governor of a royal castle; *nom.sg.* ~ 2287; *obj.pl.* **conestables** 2367 [OF *conestable* < LL *comes stabulī*]

conne *v.* I *tr.* (1) know 773, 847; ~ *god red* know of an effective course of action

827 (2) feel: *þank* ~ be grateful 160, 2561 II *intr.* (3) have some knowledge: ~ *on* be expert in regard to 751 (4) know how (to) 93 (5) be able (to) 104, 112, 125, 369, 435; *1 pr.sg.* **kan** 160; *2 pr.sg.* **canst** 847; *3 pr.sg.* **kan** 104, 125; *3 pr.pl.* **kunne** 435; *2 pr.sg.subj.* **cone** 623, 624; *3 pt.sg.* **couþe** 93, 126, 653, 773, 827; *3 pt.pl.* **kouþen** 369 [OE *cunnan*]

conseyl *n.* advice; *obj.sg.* ~ 2863 [OF *conseil*]

corporaus *n.* cloth on which the consecrated elements are laid during the Mass; *obj.sg.* ~ 188 [OF *corporaus*]

corune *n.* crown; *obj.sg.* ~ 1320, 2945 (*see* **bere(n)**). *See* **croun(e)**. [AN *corune*]

coruning *vbl.n.* coronation; *prep.sg.* ~ 2949* [*corune* v. < AN *coruner*]

cote *n.* cottage; *obj.sg.* ~ 738, 1142 [OE *cote*]

couel, kouel, cuuel *n.* frock; *obj.sg.* **couel** 859; *prep.sg.* **couel** 769, 1145, **cuuel** 2905, **kouel** 965 [OE *cufle* or *cug(e)le*; see OED **cowl** sb.¹]

couere *v.intr.* recover 2041 [aph. f. *acouere* 'recover']

coupe *v.tr.* pay (dearly) for 1801; *p.p.* **keft** 2006 [ON *kaupa* 'buy'; OSw. p.p. *köft* = OIcel. *keypt-r*]

couth: *see* **quoth** 2607* *and textual footnote*

crake(de): *see* **krake(n)**

craude *3 pt.sg.tr.* begged for 634 [OE *crafian*]

crepen *v.intr.* sneak 68 [OE *crēopan*]

cri *n.* cry; *at one* ~ with one voice 2774; (*hauen*) *at his* ~ (have) at his beck and call 270 [OF *cri*]

‡**crice** *n.* anal cleft; *prep.sg.* ~ 2451* [ON *kriki* 'crack']

crie(n) *v.tr.* shriek in entreaty: ~ *'merci!'* 2502, 2773; beg loudly for: ~ *Godes ore* 2444; *inf.* **crien** 2444, **crie** 2773; *3 pt.sg.* **criede** 2502 [OF *crier*]

croiz *n.* cross; (1) the Cross '~' *kalle* invoke the Cross 1359 (*see n.*) (2) cross 1264, 1269, 2140; *nom.sg.* ~ 1269; *obj.sg.* ~ 1264, 1359; *prep.sg.* ~ 2140 [OF *croiz*]

croun(e), crune *n.* top of the head; *nom.sg.* **croune** 2658, *obj.sg.* **croune** 569, 1858, 1909; *prep.sg.* **croun** 903, **crune** 1815, 1906, 2663, 2735. *See* **corune**. [AN *corune*]

crus *a.* mettlesome; *nom.pl.* ~ 1967 [perh. ad. MLG *krûs*, MDu. *kruis*]

cunnriche: *see* **kinneriche**

cuppe *n.* goblet; *obj.sg.* ~ 14 [OE *cuppe*]

curt *n.* part of a castle 1686 (*see* **hey(e)**); *prep.sg.* ~ 1686 [OF *curt*, *cort*]

curteys *a.* (1) versed in the ways of high-born society 2876 (2) member of a noble household 2917; *obj.sg.* **curteyse** 2876 [OF *curteis*]

curteysye *n.* courtly behaviour 194 [OF *corteisie*]

dame *n.* (as title) dame 559, 566; (as form of address) madam 1718 [OF *dame*]

daþeit, datheit, datheyt *interj.* (1) *foll. by rel. cl.*: (*hwo*, *þat*, *þe*) a curse on (anyone who . . .) 296, 300, 927, 1126, 1800, 1888, 1915, 2048, 2448, 2512, 2605, 2758 (2) *emph.neg. in* ~ *on* not a single one 1996 [OF *dahait*, *dehet*, etc. < *De he ait* 'may he have the enmity of God']

day *n.* day 590, *etc.* (2) *pl.* lifetime 355; *phr.* *nicth and* ~ uninterruptedly 143; (*with adv.gen.sg.*) *dayes and nithes* 2354; *obj.sg.* **day** 143; *dat.sg.* **day** 868; *obj.pl.* **dawes** 2345, 2951, **dayes** 866 [OE *dæg*]

day-belle *n.* church-bell rung when day dawns; *nom.sg.* ~ 1133 [*day* + *belle* < OE *belle*]

ded *n.* death; *obj.sg.* ~ 1688; *prep.sg.* **dede** 167, **ded** 149, 2048, 2871; *obj. sg.* **dede** 2720 (*see n.*) [obsc.]

ded *a.* dead 232, 2008; *nom.pl.* **ded** 464 [OE *dēad*]

dede *n.* deed; *obj.sg.* ~ 551, 1357; *prep.sg.* ~ 180 [OE *dǣd*, *dēd*]

dede-bondes *n.* cerements; *prep.pl.* ~ 332 [calque on ON *dauðaband* 'grave-cloth']

deiled *p.p.* served out 1737* [ON *deila* 'distribute', etc. = OE *dǣlan*]

del *n.* part; *adv.phr.* *euere-il(c)* ~, *eueri* ~ completely 208, 1331, 2715; utterly 2470; in every particular 219, 1071, 1177, 1765, 2622, 2994; lock, stock, and barrel 1384, 1645, 2319; from top to toe 2503; *il* ~ in full 819; entirely 2113; lock, stock, and barrel 2484, 2515, 2910. *See* **euere-ichon, eueril** [OE *dǣl*, *dēl*]

demen *v.tr.* (1) adjudge 2468, 2766, 2813 (2) sentence 2821 (3) give judgment 2477, 2834, (*with cogn.acc.*) ordain 2489,

2839; *inf.* **demen** 2468; *1 pr.pl.* **deme** 2477; *2 pr.pl.subj.* **demen** 2813; *3 pt.pl.* **demden** 2821, 2834; *p.p.* **demd** 2489, 2766, 2839. *See* **rith** *n.* [OE *dēman*]

deplike *adv.* solemnly 1418 [OE *dēoplīce* lit. 'deeply']

dere *v.* (1) *tr.* injure 490, 575, 2311, harm 807 (2) *intr.* be harmful 649; *inf.* ~ 490, 575, 807, 2311; *3 pr.sg.* **dereth** 649 [OE *derian*]

dere *n.* shortage 825, (of food) 842 [OE *dēoru* = OHG *tiuri* 'preciousness; dearth']

dere *adv.* at a high price 1638, 1639 [OE *dēore*]

deserite *v.tr.* dispossess 2548 [OF *deseriter*]

deth *n.* death; *nom.sg.* 116, 354. *See* **ded** *n.* [OE *dēaþ*]

deuel *n.* Devil 446, 1189; *phr. a* ~*es lime* a limb of Satan 1410 [OE *dēofol*]

Deus *interj.* Oh God! 1313, 1651, 1931, 2097, 2115 [OF *Deus*]

deye(n) *v.intr.* die; *phr. liuen and* ~ 257 (*see n.*); *inf.* **deyen** 257, **deye** 168, 841; *3 pt.sg.* **deyede** 231, **deide** 402 [LOE *dēgan* or ON *deyja*]

dike *n.* ditch; *prep.sg.* ~ 2436; *prep.pl.* **dikes** 1924 [OE *dīc*]

dine *n.* uproar; *nom.sg.* 1861; *obj.sg.* ~ 1869 [OE *dyne*]

dinge *v.tr.* beat 215 (*pass.*), 227; *intr.* rain blows 1148; bang 2330; *inf.* ~ 215, 2330; *3 pt.sg.* **dong** 1148; *p.p.* **dungen** 227 [ON *dengja* wk.]

dint *n.* blow; *obj.sg.* ~ 1818, 2407; *prep.sg.* ~ 1808, 1970; *obj.pl.* **dintes** 1438; *prep.pl.* **dintes** 1863 [OE *dynt*]

dishes *n.* dishes; *obj.pl.* ~ 920 [OE *disc*]

dogges *n.* dogs; *nom.pl.* ~ 1840, *obj.pl.* ~ 1968, *prep.pl.* ~ 2441 [OE *docga*]

dom *n.* judgment (at law); *phr.*: *see* **demen, giue** *v.*, **make(n)**; *nom.sg.* ~ 2489, 2814, 2839; *obj.sg.* ~ 2474, 2820 [OE *dōm*]

Domesday *n.* the Day of Judgment; *prep.sg.* ~ 749, 2524 [OE *dōmes dæg*]

do(n) *v.tr.* (1) place 252, put 535, 660, 2367; lodge 412 (2) do 2391, 2419 (3) cause 185, 205, 412, 1170, 1351, 1841, 2038 (4) (*pass.*) *p.p.* ended 2355 (5) *intr.* act 17, do 1336 (6) *auxil.* (substitute for main v., in similes) 1839, 1914, 1995, 2290,

2699; (*reinforcing* an imper.) *do* ...
(*yeld*) pray ... 2717; *phr.* ~ *of* do
regarding 130, ~ *on frest* postpone 1338;
~ *þe gamen* go through the procedure
2251; *god* ~ show kindness to 2525; ~ *of
liue* kill 1806; ~ *scapes* do injurious
deeds 269; ~ *sham* dishonour 2425,
humiliate 2732, 2754, 2765, outrage 83,
1192, molest 56, do violence to 1936,
1940; *wel* ~ *with* treat handsomely 2864;
~ (*his etc.*) *wille* do what one pleases
954, 2424, do what someone else wants
525, 528; ~ *his herte wille* 70; ~ *wo* harm
2168, 2590; ~ *wrong* treat unjustly 76,
79; *inf.* **don** 117, 269, 535, 1192, (in
dones) 971, **do** 17, 252, 2251, 2765, *etc.*; 2
pr.sg. **dos** 2391; *3 pr.sg.* **dos** 1914, 1995,
2435, 2699, **doth** 1841; *imper.sg.* **do** 1336,
1351, 2717, *pl.* **doth** 2038; *2 pt.sg.* **dedes**
2394; *3 pt.sg.* **dede** 29, 56, 76, 185, 205,
212, 660, *etc.*; **dide** 710, *etc.*; *3 pt.sg.subj.*
dide 1940; *3 pt.pl.* **deden** 242, 954, 2307,
dide 2306; *p.p.* **don** 2355, 2525, **do** 1806.
See **on-do, undo** [OE *dōn*]
dore *n.* door; *obj.sg.* ~ 1783, 1797 [OE
duru and *dor*]
dore-tre *n.* wooden bar used to secure a
door; *obj.sg.* ~ 1807, 1969 [ME *dore* +
tre < OE *trēo*]
douhter, douther *n.* daughter; *nom.sg.*
douhter 120, **douther** 2868, **dowter**
258; *obj.sg.* **douther** 1080*, 2915; *dat.sg.*
douhter 2713; *nom.pl.* **douhtres** 2983;
obj.pl. **douhtres** 350, **douthres** 2980,
doutres 718 [OE *dohtor*]
doumbe *a.* dumb; *obj.pl.* ~ 543 [OE
dumb]
doun *adv.* down; *phr.* *up and* ~ everywhere 1631 [aph. form of *adoune*, q.v.]
[**doun-felle** *quasi-sep. v.tr.*] lay low; *p.p.*
doun-feld 1825 [ME *down* adv. + *fellen*
v. 'fell']
[**doun-sit(t)e** *quasi-sep.v.intr.*] sit down;
imper.sg. **sit** ... **doun** 926; *2 pr.pl.subj.*
doun-site 2810 [ME *doun* adv. + *sitten*
v. 'sit']
doutede *3 pt.sg.* was unequal to 709 [OF
douter v. 'fear']
douthe *n.* (1) fear 1378 (2) doubt 1332;
obj.sg. ~ 1332, 1378. *See* **haue** [OF
doute]
douthe *3 pt.sg.* was of value 704, was
worth having 834; *3 pt.sg.subj.* ~ might

be the best course 1185 [OE *dohte*, inf.
dugan 'avail']
douther: *see* **douhter**
doutres: *see* **douhter**
drad *p.p.* afraid 1670 [aph. f. *adrad*]
drake *n.* male duck 1242 [obsc.]
[**drawe**] *v.tr.* (1) drag 1926, 2478 (2) draw
(from a well) 943, (from a sheath) 1770,
2226, 2604; *intr.* (3) *refl.* ~ *to* make for
720; *phr.* ~ *blod* draw blood 2747; *of erþe*
~ recover from the dead 2162; *to þe peni*
~ convert into cash 706; *3 pt.sg.* **drou**
706, 720, **drow** 943; *p.p.* **drawen** 1770,
1926, 2162, 2226, 2604, **drawe** 2478. *See*
**forth-drawe, to-drawen, up-drawe,
ut-drawe, wit(h)drow** [OE *dragan*]
drawing *vbl.n.* pulling 235 [ME *drawen* +
-*ing*]
drede *n.* fear; *phr. see* **hauen**; *obj.sg.* 90,
181, 829, 1665, **dred** 478; *prep.sg.* **drede**
1170 [ME *dreden* v.]
[**drede**] *v.tr.* fear 2290, 2569, (*refl.*) 662,
2169; *imper.sg.* **dred** 662, 2169; *3 pt.pl.*
dredden 2290, **dredde** 2569 [aph. f.
adreden < OE *ondrǣdan*]
drem *n.* dream 1285, 1305 [OE *drēam*
'revelry, music' × ON *draumr* 'dream']
dremede *3 pt.sg.*; *impers.* ~ *me* I dreamt
1285, 1305 [*drem* n.]
dreinchen; *see* **drenchen**
drenchen *v.tr.* drown; *inf.* ~ 584, 1417,
1425, 2233, 2398, **dreinchen** 562,
drinchen 554; *p.p.* **drenched** 670, 674,
1369, **drenth** 520 [OE *drencan*]
dreng *n.* small landholder; *phr.* ~ *and
þeyn* 31*, 1328*, 2185, 2467, (*pl.*) 2195,
2261; *nom.sg.* ~ 31, 1328; *obj.sg.* ~ 2467;
prep.sg. ~ 2185; *nom.pl.* **drenges** 2261;
obj.pl. **drenges** 2195 [ON *dreng-r*
'young man']
drepe(n) *v.tr.* slay; *inf.* **drepen** 1784,
1866, **drepe** 1960; *3 pt.sg.* **drop** 2230; *3
pt.sg.subj.* **drepe** 506 [OE *drepan*]
dreping *vbl.n.* killing 2685 [*drepe(n)* v.]
drink *n.* drink; *prep.sg.* ~ 2458; *prep.pl.*
drinkes 1739 [OE *drinc*]
drinken *v.intr.* drink. *inf.* ~ 15, 459, 801
[OE *drincan*]
drit-cherl *n.* (as form of address) scum;
voc.sg. ~ 683 [ON *drit* 'excrement' +
ME *cherl*]
[**driue**] *v.* (1) *tr.* drive 726 (2) *intr.*
run 1794, 1873, speed 2703; *pr.part.*

driuende 2703; *3 pt.sg.* drof 726, 1794, 1873; *p.p.* driuen 2600. *See* ut-driue [OE *drīfan*]

drop: *see* drepe(n)

dubbe *v.tr.*: *phr.* ~ *to knith* knight (someone) by striking him on the shoulder (with a sword) 2043, 2315; *inf.* ~ 2043; *3 pt.sg.* dubbede 2315 [aph. f. OF *aduber*]

dun(e)-falle *quasi-sep.v.intr.* fall down; *inf.* ~ 889; *3 pt.sg.* fel (...) dune 1816, 2649; *3 pt.pl.* felle dune 2657; *p.p.* fallen dun 2659 [ME *dun*, *doun* adv. + *fallen* v.]

[dune-renne *quasi-sep.v.intr.*] flow down; *inf.* renne dune 1905 [ME *dun*, *doun* adv. + *rennen* v. 'run']

[dun(e)-sette *quasi-sep.v.tr.*] set down; *refl.*: *3 pt.sg.* sette ... dun 928; *3 pt.pl.* dune ... sette 2819, setten ... dun 2471; *p.p.* dun-set 2292 [ME *dun(e)*, *doun* adv. + *setten* v. 'set']

dunten *3 pt.pl.* buffeted 2449 [obsc.]

durste *3 pt.sg.intr.* ~ dared 65, 272; *3 pt.pl.* dursten 1867 [OE *dorste*; ME -*u*- after *shulde*, *muhte*]

dust *n.* dust; *prep.sg.* ~ 2833 [OE *dust*]

dwelle(n) *v.intr.* delay 810, 845, 1352, 2282; stay 4, 1186, 1221; pass some time 54; linger 1059, 1187, 1190, 1734, 2651; *inf.* dwellen 1186, 1187, dwelle 810, 1221, 2282, duelle 4; *1 pr.sg.* dwelle 2651; *1 pr.pl.* dwellen 1059; *2 pr.sg.subj.* dwelle 845, 1352; *3 pt.pl.* dwelleden 1190 [OE *dwellan*]

dwelling *vbl.n.* procrastination 1353 [ME *dwellen* + -*ing*]

eie, heie *n.* eye; *obj.sg.* eie 2546, eye 2726; *obj.pl.* heie 1153; *prep.pl.* eyne 681, 1274, 1365; eyen 1341, eyn 2172 [OE *ēage*]

eir, eyr *n.* heir; *nom.sg.* eir 410, 2236, 2540, eyr 289, 1096, 1116, 2158, 2302; *obj.sg.* eyr 110 [OF *eir*]

ek *adv.* also 1026, 1039, 1067, 1073, 2473, 2912, hec 2349. *See* ok [OE *ēc* < *ēac*]

eld *a.* old; *prep.sg.* (*str.*) eld 546; *nom.pl.* (*wk.*) helde 2473; (*superl.*) (*wk.*) heldeste 1397. *See* old [OE *ēald*]

elde, helde *n.* age; *phr.*: *see* comen; *prep.sg.* elde 2714, helde 128, 174, 387 [OE *eldu*]

eles *n.* eels; *obj.pl.* ~ 919; *prep.pl.* ~ 898 [OE *æl*, *ēl*]

elles *adv.* else 1193, 2591 [OE *elles*]

em *n.* uncle; *nom.sg.* ~ 1327 [OE *ēam*]

ende *n.* (1) end 247 (2) region 735; *prep.sg.* ~ 735, hende 247 [OE *ende*]

endinge *vbl.n.* death; *prep.sg.* ~ 3002 [OE *endung* × OE suff. var. -*ing*]

er *conj.* before 317, 1262, 2681; her 15; ~ þat 229 [OE *ǣr*]

erchebishop *n.* archbishop 1179 [OE *ærcebiscop*]

eritage *n.* heritage; *obj.sg.* ~ 2837 [OF *eritage*]

erl *n.* earl; *nom.sg.* ~ 31, 273, þerl 178 (see þe); *obj.sg.* erl 189; *poss.sg.* erles 881, 982, 2899; *prep.sg.* ~ 2184; *dat.sg.* ~ 206; *obj.pl.* erles 2195; *prep.pl.* erles 137 [OE *eorl*]

erldom *n.* earldom; *obj.sg.* ~ 2910 [OE *eorl* + *dōm*]

ern *n.* eagle; *nom.sg.* ~ 573 [OE *earn*]

erþe *n.* (1) earth 741 (2) the grave 248, 2162 (3) (the) earth 424, 2658; *prep.sg.* ~ 248, 424, 741, 2162, 2658 [OE *eorþe*]

erþe *v.intr.* dwell 740 [OE *eardian*]

es*: *see* be(n)

-es, ys, as *pers.pron.* them; *obj.pl.* ys 1175, as 1175; *encl. and agglut. in* dones 971, settes 785 [ad. MDu. *se* nom./acc.sg.fem., nom./acc.pl. 3 pers. pron. (unstr. and encl. form of *si* 'id.'), bes. red. and agglut. -*s*]

-(e)t *pron.* it; *encl. and agglut. obj.sg. in* bihetet 678, hauedet 715, hauenet 2006, youenet 1644; in MS *calleth* 746 (*see n.*) [ME (*h*)*it* < OE *hit*]

ete(n), hete *v.tr.* eat 460, 654, 657, 792, 908, *etc.*; *intr.* 642, 651, 658, 926, 930, 932; *inf.* eten 792, ete 460, 651, hete 642; *imper.sg.* et 926; *2 pr.sg.* etes 908; *3 pr.sg.* etes 2037; *pt.sg.* et 657, 1880, het 654; eten 658, 930, 932 [OE *etan*]

eþen: *see* heþen

eþer: *see* ayþer

eu(e)re, heuere *adv.* (1) always 17, 311 (2) ever 975, 2311 (3) *emph.* at all; (*in comp. cl.*) *more þan* ~ 793, 831; (*in rel. cl.*) al (*þat*) ~ 207, 705, 942, 1300, 1308; (*with prec. neg.*) 327, 714, 991; *colloc.*: ~ *yete* at any time so far 974. *See* neuer(e), eueremar [OE *ǣfre*]

euere-ichon, euerilkon *a.* every single one; *absolute*: 137, 1063, 2198; *with pron.*:

hem ~ 1997*. *See* **eueril, ilkan** [OE *æfre ylc* (beside *æfre ælc*) + *ælc ān*]

eueremar, eueremore *adv.* (1) in perpetuity 684, 2837 (2) ever 1127, at any time 301, 1972. *See* **neueremo, neuer(e)more** [cf. OE *æfre mā*; see **mo** and **more**]

eueril, euerilk *a.* every; *eueril* 2333, *euerilk* 2433; *euerilk a* every 2259; *of euere-il del* of every bit 1335; *phr.*: *see* **del**; *see* **euere-ichon** [OE **æfre ylc* bes. *æfre ælc*]

fader *n.* father 1225, 1327, 1404; *obj.sg.* ~ 1417; *prep.sg.* ~ 2492 [OE *fæder*]

faderles *a.* fatherless: *as n.* 75 [OE **fæderlēas* = OWM *feadurlēas*]

fadmede *1 pt.sg.* took into my embrace 1296 [OE *fæđmian < fæđmian*]

faile, fayle *n.*; *with(h)uten* ~ beyond a doubt (*or* absolutely) 179, unreservedly 2910 [OF *fail(l)e*]

falle *v.intr.* (1) fall 1303 (2) be overthrown 39 (3) drop down wounded or dead 2699* (*see n.*) (4) be appropriate 2360 (5) pertain 1178 (6) chance 351, 1010 (7) come by mischance 1674; *phr.* ~ *on þouth* (*impers.*) occur to 1191; ~ *at* (*to*) ... *fet* fall (prostrate) before 617, 1304, 2159, 2303; *imper.pl.* **falles** 2303; *3 pt.sg.* **fel** 351, 617, 1010, 1178, 1191, 2360, *pl.* **fellen** 1304, 2159, *3 pt.sg.subj.* **felle** 1674. *See* **dun(e)-falle** [OE *fallan*]

fals *a.* treacherous 2512 [LOE *fals < L falsus*]

falwes *n.pl.* ploughed fields 2510 [OE *fælging* 'fallows' + **fealh* n. and a. 'fallow'; see *OED*]

fare *n.* (1) journey 1338 (2) activities 2622; *obj.sg.* ~ 1338; *prep.sg.* ~ 2622 [OE *faru*]

fare(n) *v.intr.* (1) travel 51, 1632, sally out 2576 (2) act 2691, conduct oneself 2706 (3) get on 120; *phr.* ~ *after* go to fetch 2790; *on hunting* ~ go a-hunting 2383; ~ *with* busy oneself with 1656; *inf.* **fare** 51, 120, 2576, **faren** 1632; *3 pr.sg.* **fares** 2691; *2 pr.sg.subj.* **fare** 2706; *3 pt.sg.* **for** 2383; *3 pt.pl.subj.* **foren** 2381. *See* **þorw-fare** [OE *faran*]

fast *a.* firmly attached 711 [OE *fæst*]

faste *adv.* (1) firmly 1895; tightly 537, 639, 1786; (of sleeping) heavily 2129, soundly

662; securely 82, 2378 (2) searchingly 2149 (3) furiously 1677, 2690 [OE *fæste*]

fastinde *pr.part.intr.* fasting 866; *see* **yede** (*s.v.* **go**) [OE *fæstan*]

fauth: *see* **fyhte**

fawen *a.* delighted; *nom.pl.* ~ 2161 [OE *fagen*, bes. *fægen > fain*]

fayr *a.* beautiful 111, 288, 1720, 2769; handsome 344, 1705, 2157; of striking appearance 2301; *superl.* **fayrest(e), fairest** 200, 281, 1082, 1157 [OE *fæger*]

fayr(e), faire, feyre *adv.* (1) attractively 2921 (2) courteously 452 (3) in proper style 224, 2914 (4) successfully (?worthily) 786 [OE *fægre*]

fe *n.* (1) possessions 386, 564, 675, 1226, 2214 (2) property 44, 1431; *nom.sg.* ~ 1431; *obj.sg.* ~ 386, 564, 675, 1226, 2214 [OE *fēo*]

feble *a.* inferior 323, 2458 [OF *feble*]

feblelike *adv.* inadequately 418 [*feble* + suff. *-like*]

fede(n) *v.tr.* (1) feed 100, 420, 2908, provide with food 787, 907 (2) rear 322, nurture 622, 1433, 1694, 2238; *phr.* ~ *and fostre* nurture and bring up 1435, 2240; *inf.* **fede** 100, 322 (*pass.*), 622, **feden** 907; *3 pr.sg.* **fedes** 1694; *2 pt.sg.* **feddes** 2908; *3 pt.sg.* **fedde** 420, 787, 1433, 2238; *p.p.* **fed** 1435, 2240 [OE *fēdan*]

fel *a.* traitorous 1158* [OF *fel*]

felawes *n.pl.* comrades 1339 [LOE *fēolaga* wk.nom.sg. < ON *félagi* 'one who lays down money (in a joint undertaking)']

feld *n.* (1) country-side 2912 (2) field 1361 (3) field of battle 2635, 2686; *colloc.*: *see* **tun**; *prep.sg.* ~ 2635, 2686, 2912; **felde** 2036; *obj.pl.* **feldes** 1361 [OE *feld*]

felde *3 pt.sg.tr.* felled 1860; laid low 2695. *See* **doun-felle** [OE *fellan*]

feldem 2699: *see n.*

fele *a.* many 3000; *phr.* ~ *siþe(s)* on many occasions 779, again and again 1247, 1738 *siþes*, 2190, 2844, exceedingly 1278 [OE *fela*]

fele *adv.* very 2443 [OE *fela*]

‡**felede** *3 pt.sg.tr.* struck terror into 67 [ON *fæla* terrify]

felony, felounye *n.* breach of the feudal bond 444, 1091, 2990; *colloc.*: *see* **trayso(u)n** [OF *felonie* + med. L *felonia*; see 444 n.]

fen *n.* (1) marsh 2103 (2) mud 873; *prep.sg.*
~ 873, 2103 [OE *fen*]

fend *n.* diabolical wretch 506, 1412, 2230
[OE *feond*]

fer *adv.* far off 1864; from far 2342; *phr.* ~
and hende far and near 359, 2276; ~ *ne*
ner far nor near 2794 [OE *feor(r)*]

ferd(e) *n.* (1) army 2536, 2603, 2623, 2684,
2733, 2924 (2) body of men 2385; *nom.sg.*
ferde 2536; *prep.sg.* **ferd** 2385, 2603,
2623, 2733, 2924; *nom.pl.* **ferdes** 2684
[OE *ferd*, bes. *fierd*, *fyrd*]

fere *n.* consort 1215 [OE *ge-fēra*]

[**fere**] *v.intr.* go 151, 1679; *phr.* ~ *wel* be
virtuous 287 (*cf.* ME *wel-farinde*); ~
with treat 2412; *3 pt.sg.* **ferde** 287, 1679,
2412; *pl.* **ferden** 151 [OE *fēran*]

ferlik(e) *n.* matter for surprise or wonder
1259, 1850 [OE *fǣrlic* a. sudden]

ferne *a.* far-off 2032 [OE *feorran*]

ferne *adv.* far off 1865 [OE *feorran*]

ferþe *a.* fourth 1811 [OE *feorþa*]

ferþing *n.* farthing 821 (*see* **nok**); *attrib.*
879 [OE *feorðing*]

feste *n.* public festivities 2345, 2355 [OF
feste]

feste(n) *v.tr.* (1) keep securely (in
shackles) (*pass.*) 82, 1786; (*fig.*) hold in
duress 144 (2) endow (as a feudal lord)
2939 (*see n.*) [ON *festa*]

fete, fett *v.* fetch 643, 913, 938, (*pass.*) 316,
1245, 1716, 2038; *3 pr.sg.* **fetes** 2342 [OE
fetian]

fetere *v.tr.* shackle (*pass.*) 2759 [*feter*n.]

feteres *n.pl.* fetters 82, 2760, gyves 2481;
prep.pl. **feteres** 82, 1786, 2481, 2760 [OE
fetor]

fey *n.* good faith 1667; *phr. ghod* ~ *beren*
be loyal to (as a vassal) 255 (see **feyth**)
[OF *fei*]

***feyth** *n.* loyalty (as a vassal); *phr. god* ~
bere be loyal to (as a vassal) 2270, 2854
(*see* **fey**) [OF *feid*, i.e. /feiθ/, later > *fei*]

fif *a.* five 213; *pl.* **fiue** 213, **fyue** 1206 [OE
fif, pl. *fife*]

fifte *a.* fifth 1817 [OE *fifta*]

fiht *n. and v.*: see **fyht**

fikel *a.* disloyal (as subjects of a feudal
lord); *nom.pl.* **fikel** 1211, 2800 [OE *ficol*]

file *n.* (*fig.*) scum 2500 [ON *fȳla* 'stench;
worthless fellow', lit. 'foulness']

fille *n.*: *poss.a.* + ~ to one's heart's content; *obj.sg.* ~ 955 [OE *fyllu*]

[**fille**] *v.tr.* (1) fill 14, 934 (2) complete 355;
imper.sg. **fil** 14; *3 pt.sg.* **filde** 934; *p.p.*
fulde 355 [OE *fyllan*]

finde, fynde *v.tr.* (1) find 42, 220, 603,
1087, 1428, 2377 (2) encounter 49, 56;
inf. **finde** 220, 1087, **fynde** 42; *3 pt.sg.*
funde 49, *pl.* **funden** 56, 603; *p.p.*
funden 1428, **funde** 2377 [OE *findan*]

finger *n.* finger; *obj.sg.* ~ 1744 [OE *finger*]

fir, fyr *n.* fire; *obj.sg.* **fir** 588, 914, **fyr** 916;
prep.sg. **fir** 1163, 1255 [OE *fȳr*]

†**firrene** *a.* of fir-wood 2079 [ME *firr(e)*
(< OE *fyre or ON *fyri*) + suff. *-en*]

first *adv.* first 2251, 2658 [OE *fyrst*,
acc.sg.neut. of *fyrst* a.]

firste *a.* first 1053, 2091, 2389 [OE
fyr(e)st]

†**fir-sticke** *n.* faggot 967 [*fir* + *sticke* <
OE *sticca*]

fish *n.* fish; *coll.* ~ 763, 895; *obj.sg.* ~ 752;
obj.pl. **fishes** 883, 1394 [OE *fisc*]

fishere *n.* fisherman 750, 2231; *prep.sg.* ~
524 [OE *fiscere*]

fiuetene *a.* fifteen 2980 [infl. *fiue* for *fif-*
in OE *fiftēne*]

flaun *n.* custard- or cheese-cake; *obj.pl.*
flaunes 645 [OF *flaon*]

fle *v.intr.* (1) flee 492, 1426, 1432, 2237,
2417, 2870 (2) make one's escape 721,
1821, 1884. *Tr.* (3) flee from 1800; *inf.* **fle**
492, 1426, 1821; *3 pt.sg.* **fledde** 1432,
2237, 2870, *pl.* **fledden** 2417 [OE *flēon*]

flemen *v.tr.* banish 1161 [OE *flēman*]

flesh: see **fleys**

[**flete**] *v.intr.* float; *3 pr.sg.subj.* **flete** 522
[OE *flēotan*]

fleye *v.intr.* (1) fly (as if with wings) 1306
(2) hurtle 1792, 1814, 1828, 2636; *inf.* ~
1792, 1814, 1828, 2636; *1 pt.sg.* **fley** 1306.
See **of-fleye** [OE *flē(o)gan*]

fleys, flesh *n.* flesh; *prep.sg.* **fleys** 216,
flesh 782 [OE *flǣsc*]

flint *n.* stone of flint; *nom.sg.* ~ 2668,
prep.pl. ~ **es** 1864 [OE *flint*]

flo *v.tr.* flay; *inf.* ~ 613, 2496; *pt.sg.* **flow**
2503, *pl.* **flowe** 2434; *p.p.* **flawen** 2477*
[ON *flá*; OE *p.p. flawen*]

flod *n.* sea; *prep.sg.* ~ 522, 670, **flode** 1223
[OE *flōd*]

flok *n.* band of men; *prep.sg.* ~ 24 [OE
flocc]

flote *n.* group of people; *prep.sg.* ~ 739
[OF *flote*]

flour *n.* flower 1720, 2918 [OF *flour*]

fnaste *v.intr.* breathe 549 [OE **fnæstian*]

fo *n.* enemy; *prep.sg.* **fo** 1364, 2850; *obj.pl.* **foos** 67 [OE *fāh* a. + *gefā* n.]

fol *n.* imbecile 298; fool 2101; *dat.sg.* ~ 298; *nom.pl.* **foles** 2101 [OF *fol* n.]

fol *a.* foolish 307 [OF *fol* a.]

folc, folk *n.* (1) (the) people 438, 2317 (2) people 2106 (3) force of armed men 89, armed following 275; *coll.* **folk** 2106; *obj.sg.* **folk** 438, 2317, **folc** 89; *prep.sg.* **folc** 275 [OE *folc*]

[folwe] *v.tr.* (1) follow 1886, 2602 (2) pursue 1995; *imper.pl.* **folwes** 1886, 2602; *3 pt.sg.* **folwede** 1995 [OE *folgian*]

fonge *v.tr.* (1) *absol.* (*ger.inf.*) obtain (other goods) in exchange 764 (2) in *cold* ~: catch cold 857; *2 pr.sg.subj.* **fonge** 857 [OE *fang-* in *fangen* p.p. of *fon*]

for *prep.* (1) in the presence of 2948 (2) in exchange for (i.e. as ransom) 44 (3) in order to get 73 (4) *with ger. inf.*: for the purpose of 951; *hypercharacterized: for to* (+ *inf.*) = to 497, 1012, 1426, 1699, etc. (5) on behalf of 1688 (6) as being 1037 (7) because of 563, 1671, 1937 (*see* **þing**), (8) for the sake of 2522, 2883 (9) in spite of 2460 [OE *for*]

for *conj.* (1) because 455, 479 (2) for 601, 2041, 2528, 2865, 2905 [Cf. OE *for þon þe* as conj.]

for(en): *see* **fare(n)**

forbere *v.tr.* (1) spare 352, 2624 (2) omit (to visit) 765; *3 pt.sg.* **forbar** 765, 2624 [OE *forberan*]

forfaren *p.p.?intr.*: were ~ perish 1381 [OE *forfaran* intr. and tr.]

forgat *3 pt.sg.tr.* 2637, 2898, **foryat** 249 forgot [(*a*) OE *forgetan* × ON *geta*; (*b*) OE *forgetan*]

forgiue *v.* forgive 2719 [OE *forgefan* × ON *gifa*]

forhenge *v.tr.* hang 2725 [OE *for-* + *henge* < ON *hengja* caus.wk.v.]

forlor(e)n *p.p.* destroyed 581, 1425; altogether wasted 771 [OE *forlēosan* lose, p.p. *forloren*]

formede *3 pt.sg.tr.* fashioned 1169 [OF *fourmer*]

forsake *v.tr.* neglect 2779 [OE *forsacan*]

forsworen *p.p.intr.* perjured 1424 [OE *forswerian*]

forth *adv.* forward; (*with ellipse of v. of*

motion) ~ *away* sped away 1678; *see cpds. below* [OE *forþ*]

[forth-bringe] *sep.v.tr.*; *3 pt.sg.* **forth-broute** nurtured 2869 [OE **forþ-bringan**; cf. MDu. *vortbringen*]

[forth-cume] *sep.v.intr.*; *imper.sg.* **cum ... forth** come on 2065 [OE *forþcuman*; cf. MDu. *vortkomen*]

[forth-drawe] *quasi-sep.v.tr.*; *3 pt.sg.* **drow ... forth** produced 1633 [ME *forþ* + *drawe*; cf. MDu. *vortdragen*]

[forth-fere] *sep.v.intr.*; *3 pt.sg.* **ferde forth** set out 1945 [OE *forþfēran*]

forþi *conj.* (1) *co-ord.*: on that account 1195, 2501; accordingly 1432, 2909 (2) *subord.*: ~ (*þat*) because 2044 [OE *forþi*, *forþy*]

[forth-nime] *sep.v.intr.*; *imper.pl.* **nimes ... forth** set out 2595 [OE *forþniman*]

forthrith *adv.* straight forward 2691 [OE *forþrihte*]

[forth-saye] *sep.v.intr.*; *1 pr.pl.subj.* **saye* ... forth** tell on 338 [OE *forþsecgan*; cf. MDu. *vortzeggen*]

[forth-springe] *quasi-sep.v.intr.*; *3 pt.pl.* **sprongen forth** darted forward 871 [cf. MDu. *vortspringen*]

[forth-stirte] *quasi-sep.v.intr.*; *3 pt.sg.* **stirte forth** rushed forward 874, *pl.* 2610 [ME *forth* + *stirte* < OE *styrtan*]

forthward *adv.* from here on 732*, 1641 [OE *forþweard*]

[forth-wenden] *sep.v.intr.*; *3 pr.pl.subj.* **wenden forth** set out 1345 [OE *forþwendan*, *Battle of Maldon* 205; cf. *MED forth-wenden*]

forthwithal *adv.* along with (him) 2566 [*forþ mid* × *mid alle* < OE *mid ealle*, *mid eallum*]

forw *n.* furrow; *obj.sg.* ~ 1095 [OE *furh*]

forward *n.* compact 555; *to þat* ~ on condition 486; *obj.sg.* **forwarde** 555; *prep.sg.* **forward** 486 [OE *foreweard*]

forþi *adv.* for what reason 2579* [OE *for hwi*]

foryat: *see* **forgat**

fostred *p.p.tr.* brought up; *only in phr.* **fed and** ~ 1435, 2240 [OE *fostrian*]

fot *n.* (1) foot 101, 113, 617, 1023, 1200, 1304, 2447 (2) person: *in phr.* *euerilk* ~ every single one 2433 (*see* n.) (3) *as measure*: a foot 1055; *phr.*: *under fote* on foot 1200; *see* **falle, hand**; *obj.sg.* ~ 2433;

prep.sg. **fote** ~ 101, 113, 1200; *obj.pl.* fet 2447; *gen.pl.* fote 1055; *prep.pl.* fet 617, 1023, 1304 [OE *fōt*]

fouhten: *see* **fyhte** *v.*

foul(e): *see* **ful(e)**

foure (*card.num.*) *a.* four 817 (*see* **he** *pl.*), 1743 [OE *fēower*]

fourteniht *n.* fortnight 2285 [OE *fēowertȳne niht*]

fre, fri *a.* (1) free 262, 530, 563 (2) of noble disposition 2877, *fri* 1073; *phr.* ~ *and þewe* freemen and serfs 262 [OE *frēo*; *frī-* before front vowels in endings]

fredom *n.* freeman's status 632 [OE *frēodōm*]

freman *n.* man of free status 629, 630* [OE *frēoman*]

fremde *a.* unrelated by blood; (*sb. use*) *phr.*: *sibbe an* ~ 2278 [OE *frem(e)de*]

freme *v.tr.* do 441 [OE *fremian*]

frend(e) *n.* (1) friend 865, 2069, 2586 (2) kinsman 326, 375; *nom.sg.* **frende** 375; *obj.sg.* **frend** 865; *voc.pl.* **frend** 2586; *prep.pl.* ~ 326, 2069 [OE *freond*, pl. *freond, friend*; ON *frændi* 'kinsman', pl. *frænd-r*]

frest *n.* delay 1338; *phr.*: *see* **do(n)** [ON *frest* = OE *first, fyrst* 'time; delay']

fri: *see* **fre**

frie *v.tr.* censure 1999 [ON *frȳja* 'question; taunt']

fro *prep.* (1) from 16, 332, 663, 2663, *etc.*; away from 693 (2) concerning 279, about 2742 (3) (*direction*:) from 265, 939, 1741, 2112 [ON *frá* = OE *fram*]

fro *adv.*; *phr. to and* ~ backwards and forwards 2072 [ON *frá*]

ful *a.* full 2687; *obj.pl.* **fulle** 781 [OE *full*]

ful *adv.* (1) very 82, 308, 589, 652, 1188, 2178, *etc.* (2) altogether 6; (*emph.*) ~ (*swiþe*) *wel* 2114 [OE *full*]

fulde: *see* **fille**

ful(e), foule *a.* (1) dirty 556, 966, grubby 683, 1823; (*fig.*) squalid 627, 1159 (2) evil 2402 (3) loathsome 2045. *See* **fulike** [OE *fūl*]

fulike *adv.* humiliatingly 2750 [OE *fūllice*]

fyht, fiht *n.* combat 2669; *prep.sg.* **fyht** 2362, 2717 [OE *[ge]fiht*]

[**fyhte**] *v.intr.* fight; *3 pt.sg.* **fauth** 1991, *pl.* **fouhten** 2662 [LOE *fihtan* < *fehtan*]

fyn *n.* ending (of one's life) 22 [OF *fin*]

gad *n.* goad; *prep.sg.* ~ 279; *prep.pl.* ~ **gaddes** 1017 [ON *gadd-r*]

gadeling *n.* low fellow 1122 [OE *gædeling* companion]

gadred *p.p.tr.* mustered 2578 [OE *gad(e)rian*]

gaf: *see* **giue** *v.*

galle *n.* poison 40 [OE *galla*]

galues *n.* gallows; *prep.pl.* ~ 688; **galwes** 1162, 2509 [OE *galga*, pl. *galgan*]

galwe-tre *n.* gallows; *prep.sg.* ~ 43, 335, 696 [OE *galgtrēow*]

gamen *n.* (1) sport 468, 2136 (2) delight 2936, 2964 (3) merriment 1717 (4) frivolity 2578 (5) amorous sport 997 (6) proceedings 2251; *obj.sg.* ~ 2251; *prep.sg.* ~ 468, 1717, 2578, 2936, 2964, **game** 997 [OE *gamen*]

gan *auxil. of pt.*: ~ *crien* cried out for 2444 [aph. of *bigan* pt.sg.]

gange(n), gonge *v.intr.* (1) walk 370, 2042, 2060, 2284 (2) go 691, 797, 846, 1186, 1740, 2072; *phr. speken and* ~ speak and walk 370; *pr.part.* **gangande** 2284; *2 pr.sg.subj.* **gonge** 691, 2072. *See* **at-gonge, to-gange** [OE *gangan*]

gart(e) *pt.sg.tr.* (*with inf.*) caused 189, 1002, 1083, 1858, 2693; *pl.* **garte** 2505 [ON *gera*]

gate *n.* (1) road 847 (*see* **rith(e)**), 2510 (2) path: *in his* ~ 890; *obj.sg.* 847; *prep.sg.* ~ 890, 2510 [ON *gata*]

geet *n.pl.* goats 702* [OE *gǣt*, pl. of *gāt*]

genge *n.* (1) force of men 2384 (2) retinue 2354; followers 2363; dependents 787 (3) gathering 1736; *obj.sg.* ~ 787, 1736; *prep.sg.* ~ 2354, 2363, 2384 [OE *genge*]

gent *a.* resplendent 2140 [OF *gent*]

gest *n.* heroic tale in verse; *obj.sg.* ~ 2985; *obj.pl.* **gestes** 2329 [OF *geste* 'exploit(s)' (< L *gesta* 'acts, deeds'), whence 'story about heroic exploits']

gete(n) *v.tr.* (1) obtain 147, 793 (2) earn 798, 879 (3) win possession of 731 (4) be paid 909 (5) catch 1394 (6) beget 495, 2894, 2935, 2979 (7) (*absol.*) provide for (oneself) 931; *2 pr.sg.* **getes** 909; *3 pt.sg.* **gat** 495, 731, 879; *pl.* **geten** 2894, 2979, **gaten** 2935; *p.p.* **geten** 931 [ON *geta*]

gete *v.tr.* guard (*pass.*) 2763, watch over 2961 [ON *gæta*]

[**girde**] *v.tr.* gird; *3 pt.sg.* **girde** 2923; *p.p.* **girt** 2386 [OE *gyrdan*]

gisarm *n.* halberd 2554 [OF *gisarme*]

giue, gyue *n.* (1) gift (i.e. offering?) 357 (2) special privilege 2881 (*as cogn. accs.*) [*giue* v.]

giue *v.tr.* (1) give 418, 1312, 2881 (2) distribute 219, 220, 365 (3) deal 1818 (4) pronounce formally: *dom* ~ 2489 (5) (*refl.*) show oneself (to be): *gouen hem ille* were distressed 164 (*see n.*, *and* **yeue**); *1 pt.sg.* **gaf** 1312; *3 pt.sg.* **gaf** 219, 418, 1818; *pl.* **gouen** 164; *p.p.* **gouen** 220; **gyuen** 365, **giue** 2489 [OEN *giua*]

giueled *p.p.* heaped up 815 [apoph. var. of ONF *gaveler* 'heap up'; *see n.*]

glad *a.* cheerful; *phr.* ~ *and bliþe* 948 [OE *glæd*]

gladlike *adv.* with pleasure 806, 1761; ungrudgingly 907 [ME *glad* a. + -*like*]

glede *n.* live coal; *phr. so sparke of (on)* ~ 91, 871 (with *on* wrongly expanded < *o* < *of*) [OE *glēd* < Gmc *glōði-z*, on same root as *glow*]

gleiue, gleyue *n.* spear, ?halberd (*see OED glaive*); *obj.sg.* **gleiue** 1771; *prep.sg.* **gleyue** 1845, 1982; *obj.pl.* **gleyues** 1865; *prep.pl.* **gleyues** 267, 1749 [OF *gleive*]

glem *n.* ray of light 2123 [OE *glǣm*]

gleu *n.* entertainment 2333 [OE *glēow*- in infl. forms, bes. *glēo* nom.sg.]

glevmen *n.* musicians; *obj.pl.* ~ 2330 [OE *glēoman*]

glides *3 pr.sg.* flows 1852 [OE *glīdan*]

glotuns *n.pl.* villains 2105 [OE *gluton*]

gnede *a.* niggardly 97 [OE *gnēde* bes. *gnēaðs, gnēðe*]

go *v.intr.* (1) walk 542; go about 6, 2905 (2) go 851, 1781 (3) rush 2689, 2693 (4) come to an end 2263 (5) avail as ransom 44, 1431 (6) *with pres.part. of main v.*, *to express continuous action*: *yede fastinde* was continuously without food 866 (*see n.*); *phr.* ~ *ne speke* 113, ~ *and speken* 195, *speke ne* ~ 125 have the power of speech and motion; *see* **ride(n)**; *inf.* **go** 125, 542, 2689; *1 pr.sg.subj.* **go** 2098; *2 pr.sg.subj.* **go** 851; *imper.sg.* **go** 683, 684, *pl.* **goth** 1781; *3 pt.sg.* **yede** 6, 44, 866, 2905; *p.p.* **gon** 2263, 2693, **go** 1431 [OE *gān*]

god *n.* (1) property 2035 (2) profit 798 (3) advantage: *to* ~*e* advantageous 197 (4) *pl.* possessions 1222; *obj.sg.* ~ 798, 2035; *prep.sg.* **gode** 197; *obj.pl.* **gode** 1222 [sb. use of *god* a.]

god(e) *a.* (1) fine 98, 99; precious 2146; of high quality 14; dainty 303 (2) doughty 8 (3) virtuous 283 (4) of great account 7, worthy 852 (5) strong 710, 712, 761, 783 (6) fortunate: ~ *time* 2889 (*see n.*) (7) skilled 750, expert 1178; *superl.* **beste** (1) finest 1725 (2) doughtiest 87, 345, 1930, 1971 (3) worthiest 200, 1082; of most account 1751 [OE *gōd*, superl. *betsta*]

Goddot(h) *interj.* God knows! 607, 643, 797, 910, 1657, 2544 [red. *God wot*]

godemen *n.pl.* worthy men 1963 [ME *god(e)* + *man*]

gold *n.* gold; *phr. see* **red** *a.*; *nom.* ~ 44; *obj.* ~ 564, 675, 2142; *prep.* ~ 47, 73, 357*, 1263 [OE *gold*]

gold-ring *n.* ring of gold; *obj.sg.* ~ 1633, 1638, 1643 [ME *gold* + *ring*]

gome *n.* man 7 [OE *guma*]

gore *n.* fit of passion or rage 2498 [MDu. *gaer, gar* desire]

gos *n.* goose; *nom.sg.* ~ 1241; *obj.pl.* **gees** 703 [OE *gōs*, pl. *gēs*]

goulen *v.intr.* howl; *2 pr.pl.* ~ 454; *3 pt.pl.* **gouleden** 164 [ON *gaula*]

gram *a.* wrathful 2470 [OE *gram*]

graten *v.intr.* weep 241, 285, 329, 1391; *inf.* ~ 329; *pr.p.* **grotinde** 1391; *p.p.* **graten** 241, **igroten** 285. *See* **grete(n)** *v.*² [ON *gráta*]

graue *n.* grave; *prep.sg.* ~ 408 [OE *græf*]

grauntede *3 pt.sg.* granted 1155 [An *graunter* = OF *graanter, greanter*]

grede *v.tr.* cry 96, 2418, (*intr.*) 2704; *3 pt.sg.* **gredde** 2418 [OE *grǣdan*]

greme *v.tr.* anger 442 [OE *gremian*]

grene *n.*¹ stretch of greensward; *prep.sg.* ~ 2829, 2841 [sb. use of *grene* a.]

grene *n.*² sexual desire; *phr. leyke in* ~ disport oneself sexually 997 [ON *girni* 'desire, lust'; *see n.*]

grene *a.* pale; *phr.* ~ *and bleike* of sickly hue 470 [OE *grēne* 'green']

gres *n.* grass 2699 [EN *gres*, Da. *græs*, early Sw. *gräs*, bes. OIcel. *gras*]

gret(e) *a.* large (of lampreys) 772, 898; massive 1891; *comp.* **grettere** bigger 1894 [OE *grēat*]

grete *v.*¹ *tr.* (1) attack 1812, 2626 (2) salute 163, 452, 1213, 2291; *3 pt.sg.* **grette** 452, 1812, 2626, *pl.* **gretten** 1213; *p.p.* **igret** 163, **gret** 2291 [OE *grētan*]

grete(n) *v.*² *intr.* weep; *phr.* ~ *and goulen*

164, 454; 2 *pr.pl.* **grete** 454; *3 pt.sg.* **gret** 616, 1130, 2160; *3 pt.pl.* **greten** 164, 236, 415, 449, 2797 [OE *grētan* and/or *grēotan*]

greue *v.tr.* give offence to 2954 [F *grever*]

greyþe *v.tr.* (1) make ready 1763 (*pass.*), 2616 (2) get into trim 707, 715 (3) treat 2004; *3 pt.sg.* **greyþede** 707; *p.p.* **greyþed** 715, **greþed** 2004, **greþet** 2616 [ON *greiða* = OE *gerǣdan*]

greyue *n.* administrative official of a town; *voc.sg.* ~ 1772; *poss.sg.* (*disj.*) **þe greyues** the greive's house 1750; *obj.pl.* **greyues** 266 [ON *greifi* count]

grim *n.* (1) paroxysm of fury 2498 (2) frenzied excitement 2334: *phr.* ~ **greu** [MDu. *grimme* 'bitterness, hostility', or f. on ME *grim* a.]

grim *a.* (1) ferocious 2656 (2) wrathful 681 (3) vengeful 2399, 2762 (4) severe 155 [OE *grim(m)*]

grip *n.*¹ vulture; *nom.sg.* ~ 573 [med. L *gryp-em* 'griffin; vulture'; cf. OF *grip* 'griffin']

grip *n.*² ditch; *prep.sg.* ~ 2103; *prep.pl.* **gripes** 1925 [OE *grype*]

[**gripe**] *v.tr.* (1) grasp 1777, 1872, 1891, 1893 (2) lay hold of 1791, 1883; *imper.pl.* **gripeth** 1883; *3 pt.sg.* **grop** 1777, 1872, 1891, 1893, *pl.* **gripen** 1791 [OE *grīpan*]

grith *n.* (1) personal security 511 (2) state of peace 61 [OE *grip* < ON *grið*]

grith-sergeans *n.pl.* officers charged with keeping the peace 267 [OE *grip* + OF *seriantz*]

grom *n.* male child 791; young man 2473; *coll.* **grom** 2473 [obsc.]

gronge *n.* farmstead 765 [AN *graunge* = OF *grange*]

grotes *n.pl.* small pieces; *prep.pl.* ~ 472, 1415 [OE *grot*]

grotinde: *see* **graten**

growen *v.intr.* (1) grow 1168 (2) arise 2334 (3) develop 2976; *3 pt.sg.* **greu** 2334, *pl.* **grewe** 2976 [OE *grōwan*]

grund *n.* (the) ground; *prep.sg.* ~ 1860, **grunde** 1980, 2676 [OE *grund*]

grunden *p.p.a.* sharpened by grinding 2504 [OE *grunden*, p.p. of *grindan*]

grundlike *a.* solemn 2014 [OE *grund* + ME a. suff. -*like*]

grundlike *adv.* (1) solemnly 2269, 2308 (2) in good earnest 652 (3) vigorously 2660 [OE *grund* + adv. suff. -*like*]

‡**grundstalwrþe** *a.* exceedingly strong 1028 [OE *grund* n. used attrib. as intensive, + OE *stælwierðe*]

halde, holde(n) *v.tr.* (1) rule 61, 109* (2) keep 1383 (3) retain 2807 (4) have possession of 2911 (5) refrain from contravening 29 (6) travel undeviatingly along 1202 (7) be true to 2527 (8) *refl.* remain 69; *phr.* ~ *in* (*his*) *hond* have possession of 1383; *intr.*: *phr.* ~ *til* be loyal to 1172; ~ *with* take the side of 2309; *inf.* **halde** 2309, **holden** 29, **holde** 1172; *3 pr.sg.* **haldes** 1383; *3 pt.sg.* **held** 61, 109*, 2527, 2911, *pl.* **helden** 69, 1202; *p.p.* **halden** 2807 [OE *hǎldan*]

half *a.* half; *obj.sg.* ~ 2371*. *See* **haluendel** [OE *half*]

halle *n.* hall; *prep.sg.* ~ 157, 239, 1068 [OE *hall*]

hals *n.* neck; *prep.sg.* ~ 521, 671, 2511 [OE *hals*]

halte *a.* lame; *obj.pl.* ~ 543 [OE *halt*]

halue *n.pl.* sides; *bi boþe* ~ on both sides 2683 [OE *half*]

haluendel *n.* (to the extent of) the half part 460 [OE *halfan dæl* (acc. sg.)]

hamer *n.* hammer; *prep.sg.* ~ 1878 [OE *hamor*]

hand, hond *n.* hand 50, 95, 152, 235, 333, 380, 383, 637, 936, 1235, 1311, 1690, 1887; *fig.* possession 203, 251, 295, 610, 727, 1095, 1343, 1383, 2318, 2366, 2515, 2932, power 438, 1001, governance 1405, 2296; *phr.* ~ *and fet* hand and foot 1962, hands and feet 2447; *see* **halde, haue, onleye, wringen** *v.*, **wringing**; *obj.sg.* **hand** 1690; *prep.sg.* **hond(e)** 203, 438, 727, 1001, 1095, 1343*, 1405, 1887, 2296, 2318, 2366, **hand** 380, 610, 2515; *obj.pl.* **handes** 95, 235, 383, **hondes** 152, **hond** 1962, 2447; *prep.pl.* **hondes** 333, 936, 1235, **hond** 1311. *See* **hend** *n.pl.* [OE *hand*]

hand-ax *n.* axe for use with one hand in battle; *obj.sg.* ~ 2554 [prob. OE *hand-ax*]

hand-bare *a.* empty-handed 767 [OE *hand* + *bær* a. 'bare']

hand-dede *n.* (strength in) violent deeds; *prep.sg.* ~ 92 [*see n.*]

handel, handlen *v.tr.* (1) take up in one's hands 587 (2) wield 347 [OE *handlian*]

hange(n) *v.* hang (on a gallows); *tr.* 335

(*pass.inf.*), 613, 696, 2511; *intr.* 2047; *inf.*
hangen 335, 613, 696; **hange** 2047; *3
pt.pl.* **henge** 2511 [OE *hangian* or ON
hanga]

hard *a.* (1) tough 1993 (2) severe 143;
obj.sg. ~ 1993; *prep.pl.* **harde** 143 [OE
heard]

harde *adv.* (1) violently 568 (2) tightly 640
[OE *hearde*]

hare *n.* hare; *obj.sg.* 1995 [OE *hara*]

harping *vbl.n.* playing on the harp; *obj.sg.*
~ 2326 [OE *hearpung*, with var. suff.
-*ing*]

harum *n.* matter for regret 1984, 2410
[OE *hearm*]

hasard *n.* a game played with dice;
prep.sg. ~ 2327 [OF *hasard*]

hated(e) *v.tr. 3 pt.sg.* abominated; ~ 40,
1189 [OE *hatian*]

haue *v.tr. and auxil.* have; *phr.* ~ *kare of* be
concerned on behalf of 121, 836; ~
douthe (*offe*) doubt (regarding) 1332, ~
douthe and kare (*offe*) be apprehensive
and concerned about 1378; ~ *dred* be
afraid 478, ~ *drede* (*of*) fear 90, 181, be
concerned about 829, 1665; ~ *in honde*
have in one's hand 1887, *fig.* (*with
poss.pron.*) have in one's control 2365–6,
absol. be about one's business 1021; ~
sorwe grieve 238; ~ *under hond* hold
sway over 2296; *see* **cri**; *1 pr.sg.* **haue**
2370, 2873; *2 pr.sg.* **haues** 689, **hauest**
849; *3 pr.sg.* **haues** 1953, 1981, 1983,
1985, 1987, 2242, 2530, 2807, **haueth**
1286, 1353, 2033, 2999, **hauet** 565,
haueþ 1267; *1 pr.pl.* **hauen** 1222, **haue**
457 (2), 2800; *2 pr.pl.* **hauen** 2996; *3
pr.pl.* **hauen** 2006 (*see* **(-e)t**); *2 sg.imper.*
haue 1332, 1660, 1665; *1 pt.sg.* **hauede**
2907; *3 pt.sg.* **hauede** 90, 226, 829, 1643,
1675, 2771; *pl.* **haueden** 181, 1205, 1238,
2766, 2772, 2991, **aueden** 163 [OE *haf*-
in 2 & 3 pr.sg. *hafast*, *hafaþ* of *hæbban*]

hayse *n.* well-being 59. *See* **at** [OF *aise*]

he *3 pers.pron.masc.sg.* he 63, 78, 110, *etc.*;
obj.sg. **him** 575, 602, 985, 1750, 2315,
2409, *etc.*; *gen.sg.* **his** (. . .) *þat* of him
(. . .) who 728, 1257; (*partitive, with foll.
num.*) *his þre* three of him 1894 (*see n.*);
prep.sg. **him** 141, 1685, 1877, 1935, *etc.*;
dat.sg. **him** 225, 969, 1694, 1940, *etc.*; (*of
disadv.*) 1865, 1978, (*ethic*) for his part
286, 634. *See* **his(e)**, **he** *3 pers.pron.pl.*,
þei [OE *hē*]

he *3 pers.pron.pl.* they; *nom.pl.* **he** 54, 449,
555, 942, 1205, 1737, 1917, *etc.*, (*in appos.
to num.*) ~ *foure* 'four of them' 817;
obj.pl. **hem** 40, 376, 412, 1189, 1351,
1708, *etc.*, (*in appos. to num.*) *hem þre*
'three of them' 1808, 1970, *refl.* **hem**
1199, 1212, 1246; *gen.pl.* **here** 'of them'
2069, (*agglut.*) **ilker** 'each of them' 2353;
prep.pl. **hem** 367, 1697, 1902, 2433, *etc.*;
dat.pl. **hem** 1185, 1899, 2561, 2957. *See*
here *poss.*; **þei** *pers. pron.* [OE *hēo*]

hede *imper.sg.*; (*as interj.*) here! 2390 [OE
hēdan 'take heed']

heie: *see* **hey(e)**

heie *n.*: *see* **eie**

helde: *see* **elde** *n.*

helden: *see* **halde**

hele(n) *v.tr.* restore to health 1837; make
whole (a wound) 2059. *See* **holed**. [OE
hǣlan]

heles *n.pl.* heels; *obj.pl.* ~ 899 [OE *hǣla*
bes. *hēla*]

helle *n.* hell; *prep.sg.* ~ 16 [OE *hell*]

helle-pine *n.* the torment of hell; *prep.sg.*
~ 405 [OE adj. gen. *helle* + OE *pīn*; cf.
MHG *helle-pīne*]

helm *n.* helmet; *obj.sg.* ~ 379, 625, 1654;
obj.pl. **helmes** 2613 [OE *helm*]

helpen *v.tr.* help 902, 1713, 2596; *phr.* ~
doun help (someone) to put down 902;
intr. help 166, 649, 1973; *phr.*: *als helpe
God!* so help me God! 1973; *3 pr.sg.*
helpeth 166; *3 pr.sg.subj.* **helpe** 1973;
imper.pl. **helpes** 2596; *p.p.* **holpen** 902
[OE *helpan*]

hemp *n.* hemp; *obj.sg.* ~ 783 [OE *henep*]

hend *n.pl.* hands; *obj.pl.* ~ 2445; *prep.pl.* ~
505, 1413, 2070, 2229 [ON *hend-r*,
nom.pl. of *hǫnd*]

hende *n.* duck 1242 [OE *ened*]

hende *a.* skilful 2629; amiable 1105, 2878;
comely 1705, 2915; of sound character
1422 [aph. for *yhende* < OE *gehende* a.
'at hand']

hende *adv.* near; *phr. fer an*(*d*) ~ far and
near 359, 2276 [OE *gehende* adv.; as in
hende a.]

hendeleik *n.* graciousness, courtly qualities; *prep.sg.* ~ 2794 [ME *hende* a. + ON
suff. -*leikr* = OE suff. *lāc*]

henge(n) *v.tr.* hang 1923, (on a gallows)
43, 1430, 2435, 2481, 2545; *intr.* hang
2487; *pass.inf.* 43, 2435, 2545; *p.p.*

henged 1430, 1923, 2481 [ON *hengja* 'cause to hang']

henne *n.* hen 703, 1241; *obj.pl.* **hennes** 703 [OE *henn*]

henne *adv.* hence 844, 1781, 1800 [OE *heonan*]

her: *see* **er** *conj.*

her *n.* hair; *prep.sg.* ~ 1925. *See* **hor** [OE *hǽr, her*]

herboru *n.* housing; *prep.sg.* ~ 743 [early ME, perh. < OE **hereborg* 'protection for an army'; cf. ON *herbergi*, OHG *heriberga*]

herborwed *p.p.* accommodated 743 [early ME, perh. < OE **herebeorgian*; cf. ON *herbergja* 'give lodging to', OHG *heribergōn*]

her(e) *adv.* here 21, 690, 845, 1059, 1881, 2207, *etc.* [OE *hēr*]

here *n.* force of men raised for pillage, or for invasion (by sea) 346, 379, 2154, 2581, 2943; military invasion 66; *phr. hunger ne* ~ famine nor pillage 66; *see* **ut-lede** *v.*; *uten-laddes* ~ force of men brought from abroad 2154, 2581; *obj.sg.* **here** 66, 346, 379; *prep.sg.* ~ 2154, 2943 [OE *here*]

here *poss.a.pl.* their 919, 1017, 1309, 1414, 1911, 2152, 2223, 2412, 2660, 2992, *etc.* *See* **he** *pers.pron.pl.*, **þei** *pers.pron.pl.* [OE *heora*]

here(n) *v.tr.* hear 4, 286, 465, 732, 887, 1070, 1641, 1642, *etc.*; *intr.* listen 733; *inf.* **heren** 1641, 1642, 2280, **here** 732, 733, 2329; *3 pt.sg.* **herde** 286, 465, 868, 887, 1070, 1669, 2398, *pl.* **herden** 150. *See* **y-here.** [OE *hēran*, bes. *hīeran*]

hering *n.* herring; *obj.sg.* ~ 759 [OE *hǽring, hēring*]

her-inne *adv.* in this place 458 [OE *hēr-inne*]

herkne *v.tr.* listen; *imper.sg.* ~ 1286, *pl.* **herknet** 1 [OE *hercnian, heorcnian*]

hermites *n.* hermits; *prep.pl.* ~ 430 [OF *(h)ermite*]

hernes *n.*[1] *pl.* brains 1809 [prim. ON **hernon-* > ON *hjarni*]

hernes *n.*[2] ears; *prep.pl.* 1918 [ON *heyrn* 'hearing; ear', with subst. of root-vowel in ME *hēren* 'to hear']

hernpanne *n.* skull; *obj.sg.* ~ 1992 [ME *hern (n.*[1] above) + *panne* 'skull']

her-offe *adv.* about this 2586 [ME *her* + disyll. *offe* < *of* + adv. *-e*]

hert *n.* hart 1873 [OE *heorot, heort*]

herte *n.* heart 70, 479, 2055, 2226; affection 1706; *poss.sg.* ~ 70; *prep.sg.* ~ 2055, 2226, hert 479 [OE *heorte*]

herte-blod *n.* heart's blood; *obj.sg.* ~ 1820 [OE *heortan* gen. sg. + *blōd*]

hertelike *adv.* from the heart 1348; with great spirit 2749 [ME *herti* + *like*]

hetelike *adv.* with fury 2656 [OE *hetelīce*]

heþede ?*p.p.* strictly enjoined 552*; *see* 545–55 n. [OE *ǽþan*]

heþen, eþen *adv.* from here 1086; away from here 684, 691, 846, 2728 [ON *heðan*]

heu *n.* colour 2919 [OE *hēo(w)* bes. *hīw*]

heued *n.* head 1907; *obj.sg.* ~ 2644; *prep.sg.* ~ 379, 625, 1654, 1702, 1760, 2643; *prep.pl.* **-es** 1908 [OE *hēafod*]

heuene *n.* Heaven; *prep.sg.* ~ 62, 246, 1277 [OE *heofon*]

heueneking *n.* the King of Heaven; *prep.sg.* heueneking 1938 [OE *heofoncyning*, with subst. of ME adj. gen. *heuene* < OE *heofona*]

heueneriche *n.* the kingdom of Heaven; *prep.sg.* ~ 133, 407 [OE *heofonrice* × ME *heuene* as in **heueneking**]

heui *a.* heavy 809, oppressive 2457 [OE *hefig*]

hew *3 pt.sg.*; *intr.* ~ *on* slashed at 2730 [OE *hēow*, inf. *hēawan* 'cut']

hey(e), heie *a.* (1) high 1290, 2074 (2) tall 988, 1072, 1084; *phr. þe* ~ *curt* inner part of a castle (including the great hall) 1686 (*see* n.); *þe* ~ *se* the open sea 720; *see* **lowe** *a.*; *superl.* **hexte** tallest 1081; *nom.sg.* **hey** 1072, 1290; *prep.sg.* (*prec. by def. art.*) **heye** 720, 1686, 2074; *nom.pl.* **heye** 959, 1325, 2472, 2768, 2946; *prep.pl.* **heye** 2432 [OE *hēh*, bes. *hēah*; *superl. hēhsta*, bes. *hīehsta*]

heye *adv.* high 43, 335, 696, 1152, 2545, 2613 [OE *hēh*, bes. *hēah*; *hege*, bes. *heage*]

hey(e)like *adv.* with solemn ceremony 1330, 2320 [OE *hēhlice*]

heyman *n.* an exalted personage 1261, 1262, magnate 231; *nom.sg.* ~ 1261, 1262; *prep.pl.* **heymen** 231 [*hey* a. + *man*]

hidden *pt.pl.refl.* hid themselves 69; *p.p.*

hyd hushed up 1060 [OE *hȳdan*]

hider *adv.* hither 869, 886, 1432, 2248; *as
command, with ellipse of* come (*see OED
forth adv.* 5): *hider* come here! 886, ~
forth come over here! 869 [OE *hider*]

hides *n.pl.* skins; *prep.pl.* ~ 919 [OE *hȳd*]

hil: *see* **hyl** *n.*

hile *v.tr.* cover 2083 [ON *hylja*]

himself *pron.* himself; (1) *emph.*: nom.sg.
  (God) himselue 432; (2) *refl.*: obj.sg.
  himself 2812. *See* **meself (miself),
  youself, self.** [ME *him* obj. and
  prep.sg. + *self a.*]

hine *n.pl.* servants 621 [OE *hīne* nom.pl.,
  with *-n* from gen.pl. *hīna* < *hīgna*,
  nom.pl. *hīgan*]

hire *poss.a.fem.* her; 127, 1100, 1234, 1746,
  2507, *etc.* [OE gen.sg. *hire*]

hire *n.*[1] wages 909, 911; *obj.sg.* **hire** 911
  [OE *hȳr*]

hire *n.*[2] ?attractive (young) woman 998
  [cf. Icel. *hýra* fem.n. '(female) beloved'.
  See n.]

his(e) *poss. a. and pron. masc.* his; *sg.* **his**
  148, 1283, 1383, 1672, 1753, 1947, *etc.*;
  hijs 47, **hise** 479, 990, 1046, 1671, 2092,
  2158, *etc.*; *pl.* **his** 137, 505, 1851, 2089,
  2414, *etc.*, **is** 2480, **hise** 138, 333, 1197,
  1206, 2372, 2698, *etc.*, (*as sb.*) his men
  1929, *etc.*; (*disj.*) **his** 2514, 2838, **hise**
  2019 [OE gen.sg. *his*, as a. with pl. *hise*]

hof: *see* **[up-heue]** [OE *hōf*, 3 pt.sg. of
  hebban 'raise']

hok *n.* hook 1103, fishing-hook 753;
  prep.sg. ~ 753, 1103 [OE *hōc*]

hol *a.* restored to health 2076 [OE *hāl*]

hold *a.* concerned for the welfare of 74
  [OE *hold* a. loyal]

hold(e): *see* **old**

holde(n) *v.*: *see* **halde**

hold(e)-oþes *n.pl.* oaths of fealty; *phr.* ~
  sweren 2782, 2817; *obj.pl.* **holde-oþes**
  2782, 2817 [OE *hold-āþ*]

hole *n.* hole 2440; socket (of the eye) 1814;
  prep.sg. **hole** 1814, 2440 [OE infl. *hol-e,
  hol-es*, bes. nom.sg. *hol*]

holed *p.p.tr.* made well 2040 [OE *hāl* a.;
  cf. *OED hale* v.[2] tr.]

holi *a.* holy 36, 431, 1362; *phr. Holi Kirke*
  Holy Church 36 [OE *hālig*]

hom *n.* home; *phr.* at ~ 790, 823; *prep.sg.*
  ~ 790, **home** 823 [OE *hām*]

hom *adv.* home 558, 779; back to oneself
  1299 [*hom* n.]

hond: *see* **hand**

hope *n.* expectation 307 [OE *hopa*]

hor *n.* hair; *drawing bi* ~ tearing of hair
  235 [ON *hār*]

hore: *see* **ore** *n.*[2]

horn *n.* horn 701, 780 (*see* **simenels**);
  prep.sg. **horn** 701, 780 [OE *horn*]

hors *n.* horse; *obj.sg.* ~ 94; *prep.sg.* **horse**
  370; *obj.pl.* **hors** 702, 1223 [OE *hors*]

horse-knaue *n.* boy employed to tend
  horses 1020 [ME *horse* (adj.gen.) < OE
  hors, + *knaue* < OE *cnafa* 'boy']

hosen *n.pl.* stockings; *obj.pl.* ~ 861, 970.
  See **osed** [OE *hosa*]

hoslen *v.* administer the sacrament to
  212 (*pass.*), 362; *p.p.* **hos(e)led** 364, 2599
  [OE *hūslian*]

hoten *p.p.* named 106, 284 [OE *-hāten*,
  p.p. of *hātan*]

hul *n.prep.sg.* 2688; *obsc.*; *see* n.

hund *n.* dog 2332, 2436, hunting-dog
  1995; *prep.pl.* **hundes** 2332 [OE *hund*]

hundred *num.* (*a.*) hundred 1634 [OE
  hundred]

hunger *n.* hunger; *phr.*: *see* **here** *n.*;
  obj.sg. ~ 66, 653; *prep.sg.* ~ 416, 449, 636,
  842, *hungre* 2455 [OE *hungor*]

hungre(n) *v.impers.* be afflicted with
  hunger; *3 pr.sg.* **hungreth** 455, 464;
  pt.sg. **hungrede** 655 [OE *hyngr(i)an* remodelled on ME *hunger* n.]

hus, hws *n.* house; *obj.sg.* **hus** 741, **hws**
  1142; *prep.sg.* **huse** 2914. *See* **milne-
  hous** [OE *hūs*]

hw, hwou *adv.* how 120*, 287, 288*, 828,
  961, 962, 1647, 2412, 2947, 2987, 2988
  [OE *hū*]

hwan *conj.* (1) when 67, 312, 447, 566, 658,
  772, *etc.*, **huan** 932, **wan** 220, **quan(ne)**
  134, 162, 204*, 240, 286 (2) **hwan þat**
  seeing that 2809 [OE *hwanne*, bes.
  hwenne]

hware *adv.* where 1882, 2241, 2580 [OE
  hwǣr, hwār, and *hwara, hwar*]

hwar-of *adv.* from which 2977, of whom
  2981 [OE *hwār, hwara, hwar* + *of*]

hwat, wat *interr.pron.* (1) what? 117, 597,
  1138, 1260, 1787, 1931, 1952, 2705; ?1933
  (*see* n.) (2) who? (of what sort?) 1779 (3)
  in dep. clauses: what 1184, 1185, 1282*,
  2120, 2203, 2394 (4) *as excl.* what next?
  2548 [OE *hwæt*]

hwat *adv.* somewhat; *correl.* ~ *for* . . .
  what with . . . 636 [OE *hwæt*]

hwat *pt.*: *see* **quath**

hwel *n.* whale 756 [*see n.*]

hwere *conj.*: *see* **hweþer**

hwere *interr.adv.* where? 1084 [OE *hwǣr*]

hweþer, weþer, hwere, hwor *conj.* (1) *introd. a direct question*: is it a fact that ...? **weþer** 292, **hweþer** 294, **hwor** 1120 (2) *introd. a dep. question*: whether **hweþer** 2099 (3) *introd. an adv. cl.*: whether **hwere** 550 [OE *hweþer* bes. *hwæþer* 'which of two?'; **hwere** < infl. *hweþr-es* etc.; **hwore** < ON *hvár-r*]

hwi, qui *interr.adv.* why? 454, 1651 [OE *hwi* instr. of *hwæt*]

hwil *conj.* while 301, 363, 538, 1127, 1439, 2438, **wil** 6 [OE *þa hwile þe* 'during the time that']

hwile *n.* time 1831, short time 723; *prep.sg.* ~ 723, 1831 [OE *hwīl*]

hwil-gat *adv.* how 837 [OE *hwilc* + ME *gate* < ON *gata* 'road']

hwit, with *a.* white 48, 1145, 1730 [OE *hwīt*]

hwo, wo *interr.pron.* who? 172, 1953, 2031; *indef.pron.* whoever 79, 296, 300, 927, 2048, 2284, 2605 [OE *hwā*]

hwor: *see* **hweþer**

hwore-so *conj.* wherever 1350 [OE *hwar(a)*, *hwār* or ON *hvár* + OE *swā*]

hwo-so, wo-so *indef.pron.* (1) **wo-so** whoever 4, 76, 83, 197, **hwo-so** 1034 (2) **wo-so** if anyone (+ *subj.*) 473; *obj.sg.* **wom-so** 197 [OE *swā hwā swā*]

hwou: *see* **hw**

hyl, hil *n.* (1) hill 1288 (2) heap 893; *prep.sg.* **hyl** 893; **hil** 1288 [OE *hyll*]

Ich, I, Y *I pers.pron.sg.* I; *nom.sg.* **Ich** 3, 121, 388, 635, 794, 807, 915, *etc.*, **Ic** 298, **Hic** 304, 305, **I** 119, 384, 492, 581, 656, *etc.*, **Hi** 487, 2128, **Y** 21, 117, 494, 654, 797, 924, *etc.*, (*agglut.*) **biddi = bidde I** 484, **haui = haue I** 2003; *obj.* **me** 486, 495, 805, *etc.*; *dat.* ~ 132, 642, 678, 694, *etc.*; *prep.* ~ 171, 293, 491, 515, 536, *etc.* [OE *ic*]

ilkan, ilkon *separative pron.* each one 1771, 1843, 2109, 2358; *nom.* **ilkan** 1771, 2358; *with pl.n. or pron.*: *nom.* 1843, *obj.* 2109 [OE *ylc* + OE *ān*]

ilk(e) *separative pron.* each; ~ *of you* 1443, 2997; (*recipr.*) *ilc oþer* each other 1057, ~ ... *oþer* each ... the next man 1922 [OE *ylc*]

ilke, il *a.*[1] (1) every 822, 1741; *phr. on ~ wise* in every way 2960, with every means 1862; *dat.sg.* **ilke** 822, **il** 1741; *prep.sg.* **ilke** 1862, 2960. *See* **del, euereichon, eueril, ilkan** [OE *ylc*]

ilke *a.*[2] same 1088, 1216, 2675, 2680, 2841, 2888 [OE *ilca, ilce*, always infl. wk. in this sense]

ilker: *see* **he** *pers.pron.pl.*

ille *n.* injury 1953 (*see* **make(n)**) [*ille a.* < ON *ill-r*]

ille *adv.* (1) far from well 1166 (*see* **like**) (2) in disturbed fashion 164, 1130 (*see* **giue** *v.*, **yeue**) [ON *illa* adv.]

in *prep.* (1) (*loc.*) in 340, 562, 670, 735, 925, 1317, *etc.*, as a member of 8, 24 (2) (*position*) on 424, 974, 1102, 1823, *etc.* (3) clothed in 2905 (4) in a state of 2934 (5) in the course of: ~ *game* by way of 997, ~ *grene* prompted by 997 (6) (*temp.*) in 28, 45, 276, 339 (7) (*motion or dir. to*) into 68, 336, 519, 1193, 1845, 2318, *etc.* [OE *in*]

in, inne *adv.* in 221, 936, 1716, **inne** 763, 2523, **ine** in it 1420 [OE *in(n)*; ME **inne** (*a*) < OE *innan* expr. movement from, (*b*) < OE *inne* expr. loc.]

inch *n.* inch; *obj.sg.* ~ 1035 [OE *ynce*]

[in-late] *sep.cpd.tr.* let in; *imper.sg.* **lat** ... **in** 1773 [OE *inlǣtan* × ON *láta í*]

[in-leye] *quasi-sep.cpd.tr.* †set (a ship) on a course; *inf.* **leyn in** 719 (*see n.*) [prob. ad. ON *leggja inn* 'id.']

inow *a. and adv.*: *see* **ynow**

intil *prep.*; (*motion*) (1) into 251, 438, 1311, 2688 (2) to 128, 726, 1927, 2238 [OE *in* adv. + ON *til* 'to']

into *prep.*; (*motion*) (1) into 157, 203, 246, 535, 1002 (2) as far as 139, 265, 1086; (*temp.*) until 2873 [OE *in* adv. + OE *tō*]

ioie *n.* (1) happiness 663, 1279, 1316, 2964 (2) merry-making 2322, 2335 (3) joyous welcome 1210, 1238, (*with indir.obj.*) 1108; *phr.*: *see* **make(n)** [OF *joie*]

ioiinge, ioying *n.* rejoicing 2088, 2950 [OF *joir* + OE vbl.n. suff. *-ing*]

ioupe *n.* loose tunic 1768 [OF *jupe*]

is: *see* **be(n)**

it *neut.pron.sg.* it; *nom.sg.* **it** 590, 664, 709, 825, 976, 1020, *etc.*, (*proleptic*) 592, 724; *obj.sg.* **it** 708, 818, 936, 1048, 1794, 1915, *etc.*, (*proleptic*) 665, *agglut.* **-et: bihet** 678, **hauedet** 715, **youenet** 1644, **hauenet** 2006 [OE *hit*]

iuel, yuel *n.* (1) wickedness: *with ~ e* with wicked intent 50, 995, 1690 (*see* **on-leye**) (2) harm 2222 (3) sickness 114, 144, 148; *nom.sg.* **iuel** 114, **yuel** 2222; *prep.sg.* **iuele** 50, 1690, **yuele** 995; **iuel** 148, **yuel** 144 [OE *yfel*]

iuele, yuele *adv.* (1) severely 2756 (2) far from well 132 (*see* **like**) [OE *yfel*]

iustise *n.* (1) (king's) judge 1629, 2203; justice in eyre 263 (*see* 263–9 *n.*); justiciar 2959 [OF *justise*]

kables *n.* ropes; *obj.pl.* 711 [ONF *cable* < med. L *capŭlum* 'rope with which animals are caught']

kalde: *see* **callen**

kam: *see* **comen**

kan: *see* **conne**

kandel *n.* candle; *obj.sg.* ~ 586 [OE *candel*]

kare, care *n.* anxiety; *obj.sg.* 121, 836, 1378, 2063; *phr.*: *see* **haue** [OE *caru*]

‡**kaske** *a.* vigorous; *nom.pl.* 1842 [ON *karsk-r* 'brisk, bold']

kaysere: *see* **cayser(e)**

keft: *see* **coupe**

keling *n.* cod; *obj.sg.* 758 [unknown]

keme: *see* **comen**

kempe *n.* champion; *prep.sg.* 1037 [OE *cempa*]

kene *a.* bold 1833, valiant 2116; *see* **arwe** [OE *cēne*]

kepte *3 pt.sg.* kept watch on 880 [OE *cēpan*]

keste(n): *see* **casten**

keuel *n.* gag; *obj.sg.* ~ 548, *prep.sg.* ~ 638 [ON *kefli*]

keyes *n.* keys; *nom.pl.* 1304 [OE *cǣg*, *cǣge*]

kichin *n.* kitchen; *prep.sg.* 937 [OE *cycene*]

kid *p.p.* noised about 1061 [*kiðen* < OE *cȳðan* 'make known']

kilþing *n.* ?liquor for tippling; *obj.pl.* ~ 1737 [see n.]

kin, kyn *n.* (1) breed; *Kaymes* ~* the brood of Cain 2046 (2) (*coll.*) relatives 393, 414 (3) sort: *none ~ es* 862, 1141, *neuere ~es best* 2692; *poss.sg.* **kines** 862, 1141, 2692; *dat.sg.* **kin** 393; *prep.sg.* **kyn** 414 [OE *cynn*]

kindlen *v.tr.* kindle 916 [ON *kynda* 'id.' + freq. suff. *-le*]

king *n.* king; *nom.sg.* ~ 184, 609, 1272,

1335, 1404, *etc.*; *obj.sg.* ~ 163, 353, 1123, 2320; *poss.sg.* ~**es** 258, 1116, 1268, 2515; *prep.sg.* **king** 2475, 2953; *dat.sg.* (*of disadv.*) ~ 2484; *nom.pl.* ~**es** 2981 [OE *cyning*]

kinneriche *n.* kingdom; *obj.sg.* **cunn-riche** 2319; *prep.sg.* **kinneriche** 977, **kuneriche** 2401, **kunerike** 2805 [OE *cynerice* × OWN *kunung* 'king'; cf. *kun-rik*]

kippe *v.tr.* pick up 895; *see* ***up-kippe**, **ut-kippe** [ON *kippa* 'pull; snatch']

kirke *n.* church 36; *prep.sg.* ~ 1133, 1356; *obj.pl.* ~*s* 2584 [ON *kirkja*]

kiste *n.* coffer; *prep.sg.* ~ 2019. *See* **chiste** [ON *kista*]

kiste(n) *3 pt.sg.*(*pl.*)*tr.* kissed 1280, 2163 [OE *cyssan*]

knaue *n.* (1) boy 308, 409, 477, 560, 950, 1074, 1088, 2178; *phr.*: *see* **knith**; (2) servant 1124, 1147; *obj.sg.* ~ 308, 409, 560; *prep.sg.* ~ 1074. *See* **horse-knaue** [OE *cnafa*]

knawe *v.tr.* (1) acknowledge 2786 (2) know 1403*, 2208 (3) ascertain 2058 (4) realize 2150 (5) know of 2469; *inf.* ~ 2786; *2 pr.pl.* ~ 1403*, 2208; *3 pt.pl.* **kneu** 2469, **knewen** 2150; *p.p.* **knawed** 2058 [OE *gecnāwan*]

kne *n.* knee; *phr.*: *see* **sette**; *obj.pl.* **knes** 1903; *prep.pl.* **knes** 451, 1212, 2253 [OE *cnēo* neut., acc.pl. *cnewa*]

knele *v.intr.* kneel 1321; *3 pt.sg.* **knelede** 482 [OE *cnēowlian*]

knif *n.* dagger; *obj.sg.* ~ 479, 498, 2555; *prep.sg.* ~ 1366, 2485, 2494, 2504; *prep.pl.* **kniues** 1770 [LOE *cnīf*, ad. ON *knīfr*]

knith, knict *n.* knight; *phr.* ~ *ne knaue* 458; *nom.sg.* **knith** 1698, 2187, 2286, *etc.*; *obj.sg.* **knith** 458, 2347; *prep.sg.* **knith** 2043, 2186; *nom.pl.* **knictes** 239, 371, **knithes** 1069, 2121; *obj.pl.* **knithes** 2050, 2196, **knihtes** 2353, **knictes** 366; *prep.pl.* **knictes** 262 [OE *cniht*]

kok: *see* **cok**

kold: *see* **cold**

komen: *see* **comen**

kope, cope *n.* cloak; *prep.sg.* **kope** 429; *prep.pl.* **copes** 1958 [perh. OE *cāpe = med. L *cāpa*, ON *kápa*]

kor(e)n *n.* corn; *nom.sg.* **korn** 462; *prep.sg.* ~ 781, **koren** 1880 [OE *corn*]

kouel: *see* **couel**

‡**kradel-barnes** *n.pl.* infants in the cradle

1913 [OE *cradol* + OE *bearn* or ON *barn*]

krake(n), crake *v.tr.* break; *phr. croune(s)* ~ 569, 1858, 1909; *inf.* **kraken** 915, **krake** (*pass.*) 1858; **crake** (*pass.*) 1909; *3 pt.sg.* **crakede** 569 [OE *cracian*]

kranes *n.pl.* cranes 1727 [OE *cran*]

krike *n.* creek; *obj.sg.* ~ 709 [14c. F *crique*]

kuneriche, kunerike: *see* **kinneriche**

‡kunrik *a.* of exalted lineage 2144 [ON *kynrik-r* a. × *kun-* in *kunerike* n.; see **kinneriche**]

kynemerk *n.* birthmark attesting royal descent 605 [OE *cynemearc*, perh. × ON *merki*]

lac *n.* blemish; *phr. withuten* ~ 191, 2220 [ad. MDu. *lac* or MLG *lak* 'deficiency, fault']

[lacche] *v.tr.* (1) receive 745 (2) incur 1674, sustain 1989; *3 pt.sg.* **laute** 745; *3 pt.sg.subj.* **lauthe** 1674; *p.p.* **lauth** 1989 [OE *læccan*]

[lace] *v.tr.* lace up (*pass.*) 2612* [OF *lacier*]

ladde *n.* fellow, man of inferior status, retainer 891, 1768, 1787, 1842, 1898, 2194, 2257, (?) young man 1009, 1016, 1039, 1063, 2325; *nom.sg.* ~ 1009, 1768, 1787; *obj.sg.* ~ 2194; *n.pl.* **laddes** 1016, 1842, 2257, **ladden** 1039; *obj.pl.* **laddes** 891; *prep.pl.* **laddes** 1063, 1898, 2325. *See* **uten-laddes** [subst. use of p.p. *-lăd* (inf. *lēden*)]

lame *a.* maimed 1939 [OE *lama*]

lamed *p.p.* maimed 2756 [*lame* a.]

large *a.* open-handed 97, 2942 [OF *large*]

laste *v.intr.* (1) be available 538, 2438 (2) remain serviceable 2606 [OE *læstan*]

laste *a. superl.* (1) lagging behind the others 1896 (2) *quasi-sb.*: *at þe* ~ finally 638, at the last moment 1678 [OE *latost*, superl. of *læt* a. (cf. late *adv.*)]

last *adv. superl.* most recently 679 [OE *latost; see* **laste** *a.*]

late *adv.* belatedly; *to* ~ 692, 846 [OE *late* adv.]

late(n) *v.tr.* (1) leave 1926 (2) leave off 240 (3) allow 486, let 2063, 2652 (4) grant 17 (5) cause 92, 252; *intr.* (6) desist 2448, 2501 (7) neglect 2380 (8) stop speaking 328; *inf.* **laten** 328, **late** 1658; *imper.sg.* **lat** 1266; *2 pr.sg.subj.* **late** 486, *3 pr.* **late** 17; *3 pt.sg.* **let** 2063, 2448, 2501, **lete** 92,

leth 252, 2652, *pl.* **leten** 2380; *p.p.* **laten** 240, 1926. *See* **in-late** [ON *láta*]

lath *n.* harm; *obj.sg.* ~ 76 [OE *lāð*, sb. use of *lāð* a. neut.sg.]

lathe *n.* enmity 2719, animosity 2977; *nom.sg.* ~ 2977; *obj.sg.* ~ 2719 [OE *lǽððu*, f. on *lāð* a.]

lauhwen *v.intr.* laugh; *pr.part.* **lauhwinde** 947; *3 pt.sg.* **low** 904, *pl.* **lowen** 1057 [OE *hlæhhan*, bes. *hlehhan*]

laumprei, laumpre(e) *n.* lamprey; *þe grete* ~ 772, *grete* ~*s* 898 large variety of lamprey; *obj.sg.* **laumprei** 772; *nom.pl.* **laumpreys** 1728; *prep.pl.* **laumprees** 898 [AN *laumpreie* = OF *lampreie* > OF *lamproie*]

[laut(he)]: *see* **[lacche]**

lawe *n.* (1) law 28, 2816 (2) commandment: *in Godes* ~ in accordance with the ordinance of God 1182, 1217; *prep.sg.* ~ 1182, 1217, 2816; *nom.pl.* ~**s** 28 [LOE *lagu* fem. < ON *lagu* (> OIcel. *lǫg*) neut.pl.]

lawe *a.*: *see* **lowe** *a.*

lax *n.* salmon; *nom.sg.* ~ 1728; *obj.sg.* ~ 755; *prep.pl.* **laxes** 897 [OE *lax*, bes. *leax*]

leche *n.* physician; *nom.sg.* ~ 1837, 2058 [OE *lǽce*]

led *n.* cauldron; *prep.sg.* ~ 925 [OE *lēad* 'lead']

lede(n) *v.tr.* (1) take 320, 1685 (2) escort 1687, 1692 (3) (*refl.*) conduct one's life 786 (4) treat 2988 (5) have at one's disposal 2574 (6) carry on: ~ *wesseyl* 1247; *inf.* (*pass.*) **leden** 320, **lede** 1685; *3 pr.sg.* **ledes** 2574; *3 pt.sg.* **ledde** 786, 1687, 1692, *pl.* **ledden** 1247; *p.p.* **ledde** 2988. *See* **vt-lede** [OE *lǽdan*]

lef, leue *a.* dear 910; precious 431; (*quasi-sb.*) *as form of address*: *ya, leue, ya!* right, old fellow! 1889, *ye, lef, ye!* right, sir! 2607 (see **ya, ye**); *indecl.coll.*: *phr. lef and (ne) loth* all (none) 261, 440, 2274, 2314, 2380, 2776; *voc.sg.* **lef** 2607, **leue** 1889; *prep.sg.* **leue** 431. *Comp.* **leuere:** *see* **be(n)** [OE *lēof(a)*]

leite *v.tr.* search for; *ger.inf.* (*nouth*) *to* ~ amply in evidence 2442 [ON *leita*]

leme: *see* **lime**

lem(m)an *n.* beloved (of either sex); *voc.sg.* ~ 1284, 1313, 1323; *dat.sg.* ~ 1192 [OE *lēof* + OE *mann*]

lende *v.intr.* land 734 [OE *lendan*]

lene *v.tr.* give (the use of) 2073 [OE *lænan*]

lenge *n.* ling (fish) 833 [13c.; cf. MDu. *lenghe*, *linghe* (1599, Kiliaen, *Etymologicum Teutonicae Linguae*)]

lenge *v.tr.* prolong 1735, 2364 [OE *lengan*] **lengere**: *see* **longe** *adv.*

leoun, leun *n.* lion 574, 1868, 2691* [OF *leon*, *lion*]

lepe *v.intr.* (1) rush 1778; ~ *forth* rush forward 1897; ~ . . . *til* run to 892 (2) jump 2617; *3 pt.sg.* **lep** 892, 1778, *pl.* **lopen** 1897, 2617. *See* **up-lepe** [OE *hlēapan*]

ler *n.* cheek; *prep.sg.* 2919 [OE *hlēor*]

lere(n) *v.* (1) *tr.* instruct 2593 (2) *intr.* learn 798, 824; *inf.* **leren** 798, **lere** 824, 2593 [OE *læran* 'teach']

lese *v.tr.* set free; *3 pr.sg.subj.* ~ 333 [OE *lēsan*, bes. *līesan*]

lesse: *see* **litel**

let(e): *see* **late(n)**

leteres *n.pl.* inscribed words 2482 [OF *lettre*]

lette *v.tr.* (1) prevent 2254; raise difficulties about 1165; obstruct 2820 (2) *intr.* refrain 2446, 2628 [OE *lettan*; *in* (2), × OE *lætan*]

leue *n.* (1) permission 1627 (2) permission to depart: *aske* ~ 2953, *geue* ~ 2957 (3) farewell: ~ *take* 1388; *obj.sg.* ~ 1388, 1627, 2953, 2957 [OE *lēaf*]

leue *v.*[1] *intr.* remain; *p.p.* **leued** 225 [OE *læfan*]

leue *v.*[2] *tr.* grant; *3 pr.sg.subj.* 334, 406, 2808 [OE *lēfan* bes. *līefan*]

leue *v.*[3] *intr.* believe; *3 pr.sg.* **leues** 1782, 2106 [OE *(ge)lēfan* bes. *(ge)līefan*]

leuedi *n.* (1) feudal mistress 171, 293, 1121, 1275, 2798 (2) woman of high social status 239, 1237; *voc.sg.* ~ 2798; *nom.pl.* **leuedyes** 239 [OE *hlæfdige*]

leue(re): *see* **lef**

lewe *a.* warm 498, 2922 [OE **hlēow* a. in *hlēowe* adv.]

leye *v.*[1] *tr.* (1) place 2840, ~ *in graue* bury 408 (2) relinquish 229 (3) spread (a table) for a meal 1723 (4) *intr.* ~ *on* rain blows on 1908; *2 pt.sg.* **leidest** 637; *3 pt.sg.* **leyde** 229, *pl.* **leyden** 1908; *p.p.* **leyd** 408, 1723, 2840. *See* **[in-leye]**, **[on-leye]** [OE *lecgan*]

leye *n.* falsehood; *phr. withuten* ~ in fact 2118 [OE *lyge*, re-formed in ME on *leye* *v.*[2]]

leye *v.*[2] *tr.* (1) assert falsely 2011 (2) swear falsely; *phr.* ~ *oth* perjure oneself 2010* (*see n.*); *1 pr.sg.* ~ 2010*, 2011 [(1) OE *lēogan* (2) OE *āþ alēogan* × ON *ljúga eið*]

leyk *n.* (1) sport 1022 (2) game 2327; *obj.sg.* ~ 1022, 2327 [ON *leik-r* = OE *lāc*]

leyke(n), layke *v.intr.* (1) play 469, romp 951, 955 (2) sport amorously 998 (3) enter into athletic contests 1012; *phr.*: *see* **grene** *n.*[2]; *inf.* **leyken** 951, **leyke** 998, **layke** 1012; *3 pt.pl.* **leykeden** 955 [ON *leika*]

lich *a.* resembling 2156 [aph. < OE *gelīc*]

lif *n.* life; *phr.*: *see* **bringe(n), do(n)**; *on liue* alive 281, 695, 794, 1207, 1218, 2271, *o liue* 2866; *adv.gen.sg.* **liues** alive 509, 1004, 1308, 1920, 2855; *obj.sg.* **lif** 349, 2493, **lyf** 1367, **liue** 2893; *prep.sg.* **liue** 281, 332, 513, **lif** 2862, 2934; *obj.pl.* **liues** 698 [OE *līf* neut.]

lift *a.* left 2131, 2636 [OE *lyft* 'weak']

liften *v.tr.* lift 1029, 1031. *See* **up-lifte** [ON *lypta* 'raise' (i.e. orig. 'cause to be in the air [*lopt*]'; cf. OE *lyft* 'sky']

ligge(n) *v.intr.* (1) lie 883, sprawl on the ground 877 (2) lie idle 803 (3) languish 1375 (4) be lodged 330; *inf.* **liggen** 803, **ligge** 877, 883, 1375; *3 pr.sg.* **liggeth** 330. *See* **lye(n)** [ON *liggja* or OE *licgan*]

like *v.impers.* please; *phr. yuele* ~ 132, ~ *ille* 1166 be displeasing; *3 pt.sg.* **likede** 1166 [OE *līcian*]

lime *n.* limb; *phr. deueles* ~ imp of Satan 1410; *leme or lif* 2556; *pl.* genitals: *phr. of* ~*s spille* castrate 86; *obj.sg.* **leme** 2556; *prep.pl.* **limes** 86 [OE *lim*, pl. *leomu*]

line *n.* cord 539, fishing-line 783; *prep.sg.* ~ 539; *obj.pl.* ~**s** 783 [OE *line* and OF *ligne*]

lite *a.* little 276, small 1731, 1856 [OE *lyt* n., a., adv. and ON *lítt* adv. < *líttet* neut.sg. of *lítell* a.; or perh. red. of ME *litel*]

litel *a.* (1) small 6, 481, 950, 2015 (2) little 687, 1859; *phr. for* ~ for two pins 687; *litle and mikle* (lit. those of low and of high status) one and all 2015; *comp.* **lesse**: *phr.* ~ *and more* (lit. those of lower and of higher status) one and all 1014 [OE *lytel*, comp. *læssa*]

lith, lict *n.* (1) ray of light 589, 597, 599, 2094, 2111 (2) light: ~ *of day* daylight 664 (3) a light 577; *obj.sg.* **lict** 577, **lith** 2094 [OE *lēoht*, *lĕht*]

lith *a.*[1] fleet 1943 [OE *līht*, *lĕoht*, *lĕht*]

lith *a.*[2] bright 594 [OE *lēoht*, *lĕht*]

lith *v.tr.* (1) kindle 586 (2) *intr.* shine 534 [OE *līhtan*]

liþ *n.* band of men; *prep.sg.* **liþe** 1337* [ON *lið* 'a host', cogn. with *līða* 'go (on an expedition)']

lith *n.* people; *phr.* **lond and ~** domains and vassals 2516 [ON *lýð-r* 'people' = OE *lēode*]

lith *n.* travelling 1339 [ME *līðe* v. 'journey']

liþes *n.* last joints (i.e. tips) of the toes; *obj.pl.* ~ 2164 [OE *lið*]

liþes, lyþes *imper.pl.intr.* listen 1401, 2205, 2577 [ON *hlýða* 'listen', rel. to OE *hlēoðor* 'hearing; music']

‡**littene** *v.intr.* dwindle 2702 [after *litlen* v.intr. 'diminish', with v.suff. *-nen*]

liue(n) *v.intr.* live 199, 355, *phr.* **~ and deyen** 257; be alive 2045, 2873; *pt.pl.* **lieueden** 1300, *subj.sg.* **liuede** 2045, *p.p.* **liued** 2873 [OE *lifian*]

lof *n.* loaf of bread; *obj.sg.* 654 [OE *hlāf*]

loke(n) *v.intr.*: **~ on** 680, 2727, **~ til** 1042 gaze at; observe 1713; go and see 598; behold 2580; *fig.* make sure 1352, 1681, 2813; *tr.* observe 2293, 2301; watch over 376; *2 pr.sg.* **lokes** 2727; *imper.pl.* **loke** 1681, 1713, **lokes** 2241, 2293, 2301, 2580, 2813; *pt.sg.* **lokede** 680, 1042 [OE *lōcian*]

loken(e) *p.p.pl.a.* fastened up: **~ kope(s)** 429, 1958 [OE *locen* 'locked']

lond *n.* (1) land (as distinct from sea) 722, 737 (2) country 340*, 697, 1161, 1200, 1382, 2032 (3) domains 65*, 2352, 2911; *obj.sg.* ~ 1200, 2911; *prep.sg.* **-e** 65*, 697, 722, 1161, **lond** 737, 1382 [OE *land*]

long *a.*[1] (1) long 267 (2) tall 988, 1064, 1649; *prep.pl.* **longe** 267 [OE *lang*]

long *a.*[2]; *phr.* **~ on** depending on 802 [aph. < *ylong* < OE *gelang*]

long(e) *adv.* for a long time 241, 843, 2587; **so ~** (. . . *til*) for as long as the time till 172; *comp.* **lengere** any longer 810 [OE *lange*; OE *lengra* comp.a., for OE *leng* comp. adv.]

longes *3 pr.sg.intr.* pertains 396, 1444 [f. on *lang* a.[2]]

lopen: *see* **lepe**

loth *a.* hateful; *in phr.* **lef and** (*ne*) **~**: *see* **lef**. *See* **lath** *and* **lathe** [OE *lāð*]

loude *adv.* loudly 96, 2080 [OE *hlūde*]

loue *n.* (1) affection 1762 (2) charity; *phr.* **for ~ ne for sinne** out of charity nor out of pity 2376 (*see n.*) (3) love (in marriage) 2968, 2975; *prep.sg.* ~ 1762, 2376 [OE *lufu* and *lufe*]

loue(n) *v.tr.* love; *inf.* **louen** 196, **loue** 1710; *2 pr.sg.* **louest** 1664; *3 pr.pl.* **louen** 1348; *3 pr.pl.* **louede** 35, 71, 349, 1708; *3 pt.pl.* **loueden** 956, 958, **louede** 30 [OE *lufian*]

louerd *n.* (1) (feudal) lord 64*, 483, 620, 1214, 1222, 1230, 1885 (2) husband 1746 (3) (the) Lord 228* (*see n.*), 1360, 1376, 1782; *obj.sg.* ~ 1746; *prep.sg.* ~ 1782 [OE *hlāford*]

louerdinges *n.pl.* (1) (as form of address): sirs 1402 (2) rulers 515 [OE *hlāfording*]

loupe *v.intr.* run 1802. *See* **lepe** [ON *hlaupa*]

low, lowen: *see* **lauhwen**

lowe *n.* hill 1292, 1700; *prep.sg.* ~ 1292 [OE *hlāw*]

lowe, lawe *a.* of humble status; *phr.* **heye and ~** one and all 959, 1325, 2432, 2472, 2768, 2946 [ON *lág-r*]

lowe *adv.* in low tones 2080 [*lowe* a.]

lurken *v.intr.* hide 68 [f. on **lūr-* in MLG *lūren* 'lie in wait' + suff. *-k-*]

luue-drurye *n.* process of courtship 195 [OE *lufu*, *lufe* + OF *druerie* 'amorous relationship']

lye(n) *v.intr.* (1) lie 475, 570, 674, 1810, 2135 (2) lie ill 142 (3) lie asleep 576, 591, 1965 (4) lie in bed 1248, 2133, lie abed 813 (5) have coitus 998 (6) lie idle 823; *3 pr.sg.* **liþ** 674; *3 pt.sg.* **lay** 142, 570, 576, 591, 790, 813, 823, 1248, *pl.* **leyen** 475, 2133, **leye** 1965, **lay** 1810. *See* **ligge(n)** [OE *licgan*]

lyþe *n.* relief; *obj.sg.* ~ 147 [ME *līðe* a. 'mild; calm' < OE *līðe* a.]

mait, mayt(h): *see* **may**

make *n.* mate (in marriage); *prep.sg.* ~ 1151 [OE *gemaca* or ad. ON *maki*]

make(n) *v.tr.* (1) build 738, 741, fashion 761, 783 (2) create 436, 962 (3) compose 5, 23 (4) lay and kindle 914 (5) carry out 445 (6) cause 38, 39, 41, 1168, 1909, 1912, cause to be 677, 1442, 1911, 1954 (7) bring about 2462 (8) arrange 2889 (9) *refl.* proceed to be 1246; *phr.* ~ *blenkes* play tricks on 307; ~ *þe dom* pass sentence 2474; *ille* ~ do injury (*with dat.*) 1953; ~ *ioie* (*with dat.*) greet very cordially 1108, ~ *ioie* receive very cordially 1210, ~ *ioie* (*absol.*) provide a cordial welcome 1238; ~ *manrede* do homage to 2249; ~ *oth* formally swear on oath 2273; ~ (*his*) *quiste* settle (his) bequests 218, 365; ~ *strout* wrangle 1040; *inf.* **maken** 741, 783, 914, **make** 445, 761, 2249, **mak** 1442; *3 pr.sg.* **maketh** 307, **makes** 1168, 2462; *imper.sg.* **make** 677; *3 pt.sg.* **made** 38, 39, 41, 218, 738, 1108, **maude** 436; *pl.* **makeden** 555, **maden** 1040, 1210, 1911, **made** 1246, 1909, 1912, 2474; *p.p.* **imaked** 5, **maked** 23, 365, 962, 1238, 1953, **mad** 1954 [OE *macian*]

makerel *n.* mackerel; *obj.sg.* ~ 759 [OF *maquerel*]

male *n.* bag; *prep.sg.* ~ 48 [OF *male*]

malisun *n.* malediction; *obj.sg.* ~ 426 [OF *maleisun*]

man *n.* (1) man 9, 24, 45, *etc.* (2) vassal: *his* ~ 2255, 2265, *pl. hise men* 2258, 2304 (3) *as indef.pron.*: **man** one 40, 601, 1782, 2449; *reduced to* **men** (*with sg.v.*): 390, 648, 725, 901, 1192, 1841 *etc.*; *nom.sg.* **man** 1117; *dat.sg.* **man** 1111; *prep.sg.* **man** 24; *voc.pl.* **men** 1, 2; *nom.pl.* **men** 902, 2258, 2473; *obj.pl.* **men** 37; *prep.pl.* **men** 435, 1696 [OE *mann*]

mani *a.* many; *nom.sg.* ~ 1008, 1009, 1698; *obj.sg.* ~ 1003, 2176, 2239; *prep.sg.* ~ 1714; *obj.pl.* ~ 883; *prep.pl.* **manie** 2460 [OE *mænig*]

manrede *n.* feudal homage; *obj.sg.* ~ 484, 2181, 2249, 2266, 2268, 2313, 2775, 2781, 2817, 2848, 2851, **manred** 2173 [OE *manræden*]

mast *n.* mast (of a boat or ship); *nom.sg.* ~ 987; *obj.sg.* ~ 710 [OE *mæst*]

maugre *prep.* (*governing gen.*): ~ *þin* in spite of you 1129, 1790 [OF *maugré* < *malgré*]

may *pret.-pres.v.* (1) can, be able to 26, 427, 705, 804, 1706, 1900 (2) be capable of 642, 792 (3) be in a position to 801 (4) have occasion to 478, 571 (5) be at liberty to 1219, 1220; *1 pr.sg.* **may** 792, 804; *2 pr.sg.* **mayth** 642, **mait** 690, **mayt**

853, 1220; *3 pr.sg.* **may** 427 (*see n.*) 801, 1986, 2097, 2115; *2 pr.pl.* **mowen** 11, 12; *3 pr.pl.* **moun** 2588, 2589; *1/2/3 pr.sg.subj.* **mowe** 676, 2075, 175; *1 pr.pl.subj.* **moun** 460; *3 pt.sg.* **micthe** 42, **micte** 220, 221, 232, 233, 253, 571, **mithe** 1706, 1900, **mowcte** 210, **mouthe** 1710, 2059, 2090, 2147, 2254, **moucte** 705, **mouhte** 2491, 2550; *3 pt.pl.* **moucte** 257, **mouthe** 2020, **mithen** 1930, 2018; *1 pt.sg.subj.* **mouthe** 2039; *3 pt.sg.subj.* **mouthe** 478, 2031, 2071, 2147, 2611, 2665, **mithe** 2025, 2120, 2499; *3 pt.pl.subj.* **mouthen** 1184, 2040 [OE *mæg*, pl. *magon*; LOE pt.sg. *muhte*, pl. *muhton*, bes. *mihte*, *mihton*]

mayden *n.* (1) young unmarried woman 2, 33 (2) girl 111, 467 (3) (male) virgin 996; *nom.sg.* ~ 996; *prep.sg.* ~ 111; *voc.pl.* **maydnes** 2; *nom.pl.* **maydnes** 33; *obj.pl.* **maydnes** 467 [OE *mægden*]

mayster *n.* (1) commander 2029, 2386 (2) employer 1046, 1048 (3) (as form of address:) sir 1136 [OE *mægester* and OF *maistre*]

me: see **Ich**

mede *n.* reward 102, 686, 2902; deserts 119, 2403 (*see* **yelde**); a bribe 1636; *obj.sg.* ~ 102, 119, 686, 1636, 2403, 2902 [OE *mēd*]

meine, meyne *n.* household; *obj.sg.* **meine** 828, **meyne** 835 [OF *meyné*]

meke *a.* humble 946, 1067 [EME *mēoc*, ad. prim. ON **meuk-* > ON *mjúkr* 'soft; pliant']

mele *n.* grain ground into powder; *prep.sg.* ~ 781 [OE *melo*]

mele *v.intr.* speak 2060 [OE *mǣlan*]

mene *v.tr.* signify 598, 2115; *3 pr.sg.* **menes** 598 [OE *mǣnan*]

merci *n.* mercy; *obj.sg.* ~ 96, 615; *prep.sg.* ~ 271 [OF *merci*]

mere *n.* mare; *obj.sg.* ~ 2505; *poss.sg.* ~ 2479; *prep.sg.* ~ 2450 [OE *mēre* bes. *miere*]

meself, miself *pron.* myself; *emph.*: *nom.sg.* **miself** 2043, **I meself** in person 1668*; **I ... miself** 1932, 2098, 2251; *prep.sg.* **meself** 123. *See* **himself, youself, self** [OE *me* acc.sg. + *self* a., dat.sg. + *sylfum*; ME *mē* > *mi* in unstressed position]

messe *n.* Mass; *obj.sg.* ~ 243, 1177 [OF *messe*]

messe-bok *n.* missal (containing the service of the Mass for the whole year); *obj.sg.* ~ 186; *prep.sg.* ~ 391, 2711 [ME *messe* + OE *bōc*]

messe-gere *n.* objects used in the celebration of the Mass; *obj.sg.* ~ 188; *prep.sg.* ~ 389, 1079, 2218 [ME *messe* + ON *gervi*]

meste: *see* **michel**

mester *n.* occupation; *obj.sg.* ~ 824 [OF *mestier*, *mester*]

met *p.p.* (*impers.*) appeared in a dream 1286 [OE *mǣtan*]

mete *n.* (1) food 146, 650, 657, 790, 799, 908, 927, 1244, 1725 (2) *pl.* dishes 2341; *obj.sg.* ~ 146, 650, 657, 853, 2037; *prep.sg.* ~ 1733; *nom.pl.* metes 2341 [OE *mete*]

mette *3 pt.sg.tr.* encountered 1811, 2625 [OE *mētan*]

meyne: *see* **meiné**

michel, mikel, mik(e), muchel *a.* (1) large 934, 1024, 1026, 2384 (2) great 238, 661, 829, 2034, 2054, 2055; a great deal of 510, 729, 730; abundant 1108, 2111; lavish 2337 (3) *absol.* much 221, 816; *nom.sg.* **mikel** 1026, **mike** 961, 1745, 2337, **mik** 2343; *obj.sg.* **michel** 510, 729, 730, 829, 934, **mikel** 221, 238, 1040, 1108, 2034, 2035, 2054, 2055, 2111; *prep.sg.* **muchel** 661, **mikel** 647, 2384, **mike** 1762. *Comp.* **more** (1) taller 983, 1702 (2) a larger amount 831; *superl.* **moste** (1) biggest 1288 (*see* **on** *num.*) (2) greatest 423, 2322; **meste** (1) tallest 984 (2) greatest 233 [OE *micel* and *mycel*; *māra*; *mǣst* and LOE *māst*]

michel, mikel, mikle *adv.* much 60, 122, 2570; *comp.* **more**: (1) more 1711 (2) any more 945 (3) in addition 1270; *superl.* **mest**: (*to form superl. of a.*) most 946 [OE *māre* comp. a. (neut.sg.nom. acc.); OE *mǣst*]

micth *n.* strength; *prep.sg.* ~ 35 [OE *miht*]

middel *n.* middle; *phr.* þe ~ of þe nith 2093; *prep.sg.* ~ 2093 [OE *middel* n.]

middelerd *n.* the earth; *prep.sg.* ~ 2245 [OE *middaneard*, with subst. of *middel* a. for *middan*]

middel-nicht *n.* midnight; *prep.sg.* ~ 576 [OE *middelniht*]

mihte(n): *see* **may**

mik(e), mikel: *see* **michel**

milce *n.* mercy; *prep.sg.* ~ 1362 [OE *milts* < *milde* a. + OE suff. *-s*]

mile *n.* mile; *obj.sg.* ~ 722, 1832, 2499 [OE *mīl*]

milk *n.* milk; *obj.sg.* ~ 644 [OE *milc* (bes. *meolc*)]

milne-hous *n.* a building for milling; *prep.sg.* ~ 1968 [OE *mylen* + *hūs*]

mi(n) *poss.a.* my; *nom.sg.* (*bef. cons.*) **mi** 120, 387, 565, 1076, *etc.*; *obj.sg.* (*bef. cons.*) **mi** 528, 1367, *etc.*; *prep.sg.* (*bef. cons.*) **mi** 170, 799, 1364, 2547, *etc.*, **my** 639, **mine** 1973, (*bef. h*) **min** 1311; *voc.pl.* **mine** 2419; *nom.pl.* ~ 514, 1295; *obj.pl.* ~ 385, 2707; *prep.pl.* ~ 1297, 1304, (*bef. h*) **min** 637; (*disj.*) mine *prep.sg.* **min** 2078; *dat.sg.* ~ 2086; *sb.* my men (people) **mine** 2084; *phr.* me and ~ 295, 1960 [OE *min*, gen. sg. of *ic*]

‡**mine** *n.* game played with dice; *prep.sg.* ~ 2327 [OF *mine*]

miracle *n.* a miracle 500 [OF *miracle*]

mirke *a.*: *wk.* dark 404 [ON *myrk-r* nom.sg.masc.]

[**misdon**] *v.intr.* transgress 337, 2799; *tr.* wrong 1372; ill-use 993; *1 pt.sg.* **misdede** 1372; *3 pt.sg.* **misdede** 337, 993; *p.p.* **misdo** 2799 [OE *misdōn*]

miself: *see* **meself**

misferde *3 pt.pl.*: *intr.* ~ *with* were maltreating 1870 [OE *misfēran*]

misgos *2 pr.sg.*: *intr.* transgress 2708 [ME pref. *mis-* + *gon*]

misseyde *3 pt.sg.*: *tr.* affronted 49, 994*; *p.p.* **misseyd** insulted 1689 [ME pref. *mis-* + *sayen*]

miþe, myþe *v.tr.* conceal 653, 1279; dissemble 949 [OE *mīðan*]

‡**mixed** *a.* vile 2534 [ME *mix* 'vile wretch' < OE *mix* 'dung' bes. *meox*, + adj. suff. *-ed* < OE *-ede*]

mo *a. comp.* more (numerically) 1743, 1847, 2683, 2741; **withuten** ~ only 1743 [OE *mā* adv.]

mo *adv.* more; (*see* **neueremo, eueremar**) [OE *mā* comp.adv.]

mod *n.* heart; *prep.sg.* ~ 1704 [OE *mōd* 'courage; anger' etc.]

moder *n.* mother 975, 1389; *prep.sg.* ~ 1389 [OE *mōder*]

mone *1 pr.pl.* must, shall 841 [ON *munu* inf., *1 pr.pl. munum*]

‡**mone** *n.* opinion; *phr.* bi mine ~ 817

[*mēne* v. 'believe' × *won* n. 'opinion';
see n.]

mone *n.* moon; *phr. under ~ on earth* 373;
obj.sg. ~ 403, 534,1315 [OE *mōna*]

mon(e)kes *n.pl.* monks; ~ *blake* Benedictine monks 2522; *obj.pl.* ~ 243, 360,
2585; *prep.pl.* ~ 430 [OE *munuc*]

more: *see* **michel** *a.*

morwen *n.* morning; *prep.sg.* ~ 812, 1132,
1921, 2191, 2670 [OE *morgen*]

moste: *see* **michel** *a.*

[**mot**] *v.* (1) be allowed to 18, 406 (2) may
19, (in wishes) 1744, 2546; *1
pr.sg.subj.*(*opt.*) **mote** 1744, 2546; *3
pr.sg.subj.* ~ 19, 406; *pr.pl.subj.* **moten** 18
[OE pret.-pres.v. *mōt*, pt. *mōste*]

moun: *see* **may**

mouþe, mouth *n.* mouth; *prep.sg.*
mouþe 113, **mouth** 433, 592, 1257 [OE
mūþ]

mouthe, mouhte, moucte: *see* **may**

mowe *v.intr.* give blows with scything
motion 1853 [OE *māwan*]

mowe(n): *see* **may**

muchel: *see* **michel**

naked *a.* naked 6, 854, 1950, 1954, 2133
[OE *nacod*]

nam: *see* **nime**

name *n.* name; *nom.sg.* ~ 342, 2030; *obj.sg.*
~ 745 [OE *nama*]

[**name**] *v.tr.* name; *p.p.* **named** 1752 [OE
(*ge*)*namian* or ME *name* n.]

namore *n.* nothing further 2488 [as
namore *adv.*]

namore, nomore *adv.* (1) no longer 2364,
2531, **nomore** 1058 (2) in no greater
degree **nomore** 999 (3) no more 1867
[OE *nā* (emph.neg.) adv. < *ne ā* 'not
ever' + OE *māre* comp.adv.]

nauen *n.* name 1398*, 2530* [ON *nafn*]

nay *adv.*; *phr. seyen ~* refuse 2887 [ON *nei*
= OE *nā*]

nayl *n.* (1) toenail or fingernail 2164 (2)
nail 713, 858; *prep.sg.* ~ 858; *obj.pl.*
nayles 2164 [OE *nægl*]

ne *adv.* not 522, 804, 1087, 1706, 2284, 2793,
etc.; *with another neg.*: 501, 865, 1244,
2024, 2637, *etc.*; *with two other negs.*: 1372;
in consec. cl. after neg. main cl.: 57, 81, 91,
100, 250, 724, ?766 (*see* n.), 768, 2202,
2265, 2273, 2283, 2289, 2381, 2447, 2503,
2687, 2780, 2804, 2900. *See* **neþeles, ne
were** *conj.* [OE *ne*]

ne *conj.* nor 50*, 2778, 2886, 2906, *etc.*;
without prec. neg.: 420, 549, 1431; *correl. ne
. . . ne* neither . . . nor 73, 2376, 2492 [OE
ne]

necke *n.* neck; *obj.sg.* ~ 1824; *prep.sg.* ~
1823, 2047, 2757 [OE *hnecca*]

nede *n.* (1) crisis 9, 25, 1693, 1971, 2422,
2895 (2) state of need 647, 2904; *prep.sg.*
~ 9, 25, 647, 1971, 2422, 2895, 2904;
prep.pl. **nedes** 1693 [OE *nēd* bes. *nīed,
nȳd*]

neme: *see* **nime**

ner *adv.* near 991; nearly 1950, 2670, *wel* ~
very nearly 2413 [ON *nær* comp. of
ná-]

nese *n.* nose 2451 [ad. MDu. or MLG
nese]

nesh, neys *a.* soft 217, 2744 [OE *hnesce*]

neth, net *n.*[1] net; *prep.sg.* 753; *prep.pl.*
netes 784 [OE *net*(*t*)]

neth, net *n.*[2] (1) ox 809, 1027, 1892 (2)
cattle 701, 782, 1223; *obj.sg.* **net** 1892;
poss.sg. **netes** 782; (*coll.*) *obj.pl.* 701, 1223
[OE *nēat* neut.]

neþeles *adv.* nevertheless 1109, 1659 [OE
nā emph.neg. + instr. *þe* + *læs*]

neue *n.* fist; *phr.*: *see* **sette**; *prep.sg.* ~
2406; *prep.pl.* **neues** 1918 [ON *hnefi*]

neuer(e) *adv.* (1) never 90, 976, 1340, 1439,
1830, 1990, *etc.* (2) *emph.*: at all 944, (*with
neg.*) 132, 1211, 1372 (3) ‡ = **no(n)** *a.*: ~
kines best no animal of any kind 2692;
colloc. ~ *but* no more than 723; ~ *her*
never before 541; ~ *non* absolutely
none 1639, 2180, 2346, 2697, ~ *on* not a
single one 2272, 2282; ~ *a* (+ *n.*) not a
single 2686; ~ . . . *so* (+ *a.*) in however
great a degree 80, 1117; ~ *yete* never
495, 997, 1044, 2155, 2335, 2974, 2976
[OE *næfre*]

neueremo *adv.* never 511, 2051, 2723.
[OE *næfre* + OE *mā*; see **eueremar,
mo,** and **more**]

neuer(e)more, neuremore *adv.* (1)
never again 673, 2598 (2) ever again 2777
(3) never 297, 488, 493, 994. *See* **eueremar** [cf. OE *næfre* + OE *mā*; see **mo**
and **more**]

newe *a.* (1) new 263 (2) fresh 2462, 2975
[OE *nēowe*, bes. *ni*(*o*)*we*]

newe *adv.* freshly 2921 [OE *nēowe*]

ne were *conj.* (*in conditional cl.*) had not
2414* [see n.]

newhen *v.tr.* approach 1867 [OE (LONth.) *genēhwian*]

ney *adv.* (1) close 2620 (2) nearly 464, 641. *See* **ner** [OE *nēah*]

neys: *see* **nesh**

neyþer, noþer, noyþer *adv.*; *neyþer . . . ne* neither . . . nor 458, 765*, 833, 861, 1144; *sim. noþer . . . ne* 2624, *noyþer . . . ne* 2698 [(*a*) and (*c*): *noþer* × *eiþer* < OE *ǣghwæþer* (*b*) OE *ne* + OE **ōðer* < **ōhwæðer*]

neyþer *conj.*; (*correl.*) ~ . . . *ne* neither . . . nor 2971–2 [see **neyþer** *adv.*]

[**nime**] *v.tr.* (1) receive 2266 (2) seize 2582 (3) *intr.* go 1932, 2601, 2791, ~ *in . . . to*, ~ *until* depart for 1337, 2931; *phr. in armes* ~ enfold in a wrestling grip 985; *1 pr.sg.* **nime** 1932, *subj.pl.* ~ 2601; *imper.pl.* **nimes** 2595; *3 pt.sg.* **nam** 901, 985, 2931; *pl.* **nomen** 2791, *subj.* **neme** 2202; *p.p.* **nomen** 2266, **numen** 2582. *See* **forth-nime, ageyn-nime** [OE *niman*]

nis: *see* **be(n)**

nith, niht *n.* night; *phr.*: *adv.gen.sg.* **dayes and nithes** day and night 2354; *obj.sg.* **nith** 1755; *poss.sg.* **nithes** 2101; *prep.sg.* **nith** 404, 1248, **niht** 2670; *obj.pl.* **nihtes** 3000; *prep.pl.* **nithes** 2049. *See* **tonicht** [OE *niht*]

nither-tale *n.* the dead of night; *prep.sg.* ~ 2026 [ON *náttar-þel*: gen.sg. of *nátt* 'night' + *þel* 'bottom; core']

no *interj.* no! 1801 [OE *nā, nō < ne + ā* ever]

noble *a.* (1) of illustrious birth 1944 (2) magnificent 1264 [OF *noble*]

noblelike *adv.* in fine style 2641 [*noble* a. + suff. *-like* < OE *-līce*]

nok *n.* scrap; *colloc. a ferþinges* ~ a fraction of a farthing 821 [obscure; see n.]

noman *pron.* no-one 72, 223, 985, 1114, 1115 [OE *nān mann*]

nomore *adv.*: *see* **namore**

no(n) *a.* no; *nom.sg.* (*bef. cons.*) **no** 225, 462, 1244, 1758, 2962, non 64, 950, (*bef. h*-) **non** 1020, (*in pause*) 1837, 1907; *obj.sg.* (*bef. vowel*) **non** 686, 1201, (*bef. cons.*) **no** 147, 459, 657, 865, 2024, 2085; *poss.sg.* **none** in ~ *kines þinge* belongings of any sort 1141 (*see n.*); *prep.sg.* (*bef. cons.*) **no** 1644, 1836, 1937, 2578. *See* **nouth** *adv.* [OE *nān*]

non *pron.*; *nom.sg.* **non** none 1639, 2160, 2180, 2346, 2568, 2803, no one 272, 1920, 2697, 2764, 2820, *etc.*; *obj.sg.* **non** no one 352, 935, 938; *nom.pl.* **none** none 2104, (*in appos. to pl.pron.*) **he non** 2201; (*foll. by of* + *poss. a.* + *n.*) *sg.* **non** no one 325, 413, 2069, (*foll. by of* + *poss.a.*) *pl.* **none** none 2084. *See* **oþer** *pron.* (4) [OE *nān*]

norþ *n.* north; *prep.sg.* ~ 434, 725 [OE *norþ* adv. and as first el. of cpds.]

norþ *adv.* north 1256*: *see* **suth**; [OE *norþ* adv.]

north *a.* north 735 [as **norþ** *n.*]

nose *n.* nose 2824. *Cf.* **nese** [OE *nosu*]

note *n.* nut; *obj.sg.* ~ 419; *prep.sg.* **nouthe** 1333 [OE *hnutu*]

noþer: *see* **neyþer**

noþing *n.* nothing 2077, 2254 [OE *nān þing* (both declined)]

nou: *see* **nu** *adv.*

nouth, nowt *n.* nothing 313, 649; ~ *buten* only 149; *obj.sg.* **nowt** 579. *See* **outh** *n.* [as **nouth** *adv.*]

nouth, no-wicth, nowt(h), *adv.* (1) *emph.* not at all **nouth** 1372, **no-wicth** 97, **no-with** 1764, 2501; *simply . . . not* **nouth** 329 (2) not 653, 967, 1346, 2339, 2738, 2930, *etc. See* **ne** *adv.*; **outh** *adv.* [OE *nōwiht < ne ōwiht* with emph. *ō* 'ever' + *wiht* 'anything']

nouthe: *see* **note**

noyþer: *see* **neyþer**

nu *conj.* now that; *correl. nu . . . nu* 2847–50 [OE *nū* conj.]

nu, nou, now *adv.* now 161, 791, 1363, 2065, 2301, 2593, *etc.* [OE *nū* adv.]

numen: *see* **nime**

nunnes *n.* nuns; *obj.pl.* ~ 2585 [OE *nunne*]

nyne *card.num.* nine 872, 1011 [OE *nigon*]

nytte *v.tr.* use 942 [OE *nyttian*]

o: *see* **on** *prep.*

o-bon(e) *p.p.a.*; *phr. wel* ~ well accoutred 2356, 2572; *iuele* ~ in poor condition 2506, in poor circumstances 2526* [ad. OEN *of bóin*; see n.]

odrat *p.p.a.* afraid 1154. *See* **adrad**. [OE *ofdrǣd*, p.p. of **ofdrǣdan* 'terrify']

of *prep.* (1) (*motion*) from 216, 697, 858, 1283, 1890, *etc.*, (*with prec. adv.*) *vt* ~ out of 155, 725, (*prec. by a.*) *hol* ~ recovered from 2076 (2) (*origin*) from 2288 (3)

because of 181, 277, 2161 (4) (*agency*) by
?184, 436, 1979, 2599 (5) (*material*) (out)
of 539, 783, 859 (6) (*descriptive*) 14, 664 (7)
concerning 23, 84, 313, *etc*., regarding
2007, 2370, 2527, in regard to 107, 180,
345, 743, on behalf of 829, 838, 1665 (8)
(*definition*) 340, *etc*. (9) (*obj.gen.*) 278, 615
(10) (*partitive*) something of 92, (*foll. by
poss.*) ~ *his* 222 (11) singled out among:
~ *alle þinge* 71 (12) belonging to 381, (*in
group gen.*) 885. *See* **offe** [OE *of*]

of *adv.* off; *see* 919 *n.*, **of-tirue, o-bon(e),
odrat** [OE *of*]

offe *prep.*; (*agency*) by 435. *See* **her-offe,
þer-of** [*of* + *adv. -e*]

of-fleye *quasi-sep.v.intr.* be severed
swiftly; *inf.* ~ 2752. *See* **fleye** [cf. MDu.
afvliegen 'id.' (esp. of parts of the body)]

offrende *n.* (religious) offering; *obj.sg.* ~
1387 [OF *ofrende*]

[**of-plette**] *quasi-sep.v.tr.* strike off; *inf.* **of
... plette** 2445; *3 pt.sg.* **of ... plette**
2627; *p.p.* **of-plat** 2756 [*of* adv. + MDu.
pletten 'strike' × ME *platte*; see 2614 n.]

[**of-sle**] *quasi-sep.v.tr.* strike off; *p.p.* **of-
slawen** 2677 [OE *ofslēan* 'kill']

ofspring *n.* descendants; (*coll.*)*obj.sg.* ~
2566 [OE *ofspring*]

oft(e) *adv.* repeatedly 214, 226, 227, 885,
1038 [OE *oft*]

[**of-tirue**] *quasi-sep.v.tr.* peel off; *3 pt.pl.*
tirueden of 604 [see 604 n.]

ok *adv.* also 187, 200, 880, 1082, 1389, 1818,
2225, 2327 [ON *ók*]

old, hold *a.* (1) aged; *see phr.* (2) in long
use: **hold** 1145 (3) in age: **hold** 192, 259,
417 (4) past: **holde** 2461, **old** 2462; *phr.*:
yunge and holde 957, *yung ... holde* 30 one
and all [OE *ald*]

on, o, a *prep.*; (*position*) (1) on 383, 1288,
1387, 1430, 2131, ~ *knes* 1303, fixed on
839, with one's hands on (in making an
oath) 389, 391, 1083, 2218, etc. (2) attached to 1103 (3) situated on 321 (4) in
832, 1223, 1350 (5) (*temp.*) at (the time
of) 1921, 2191, during 1248, *o nith(es)* in
the night 1252, 2049, 2083, within 1831,
1859, 1874 (6) (*manner*) in: ~ *gamen* in
sport 1717, ~ *ilke* (*mani*) *wise* 1714,
1862, 2960 (7) (*state*) ~ *liue* living 363,
695, 1207, (*emph.*) in the world 281,
2271, (*oath*) *bi God* ~ *liue* 794; ~ *two*
asunder 471, 1824, 2731, *a two* 1414,

2644; (*with ger.*) to engage in 2383 (*see*
fare(n)); *see* **bringe(n)** (8) (*motion towards*) on 1839, 1877, 2330, on to 1301, at
904, into 1191 (9) regarding 751 (*see*
conne) (10) upon 1364, 1902. *See*
1933 *n.*; **lif, up, upon** [OE *on*]

on *adv.* in 391, 1782; *see* 347 *n.* [OE *on*]

on (1) *num.* one; *nom.sg.* **a** 2083, **on** 1801,
2029, 2264; *obj.sg.* **on** 762, 1985, ?1996;
(*adv.*)*gen.sg.* **ones**: *see* at (2) *n.* one
thing 505, 963 (*see* **but(e)**) (3) *pron.* ~ *þe
moste* uniquely large 1288; *þat* ~ that
single one 2448; *see* **neuer(e)** (4) *a.*
alone: (*in appos. to pers. pron.*) *he ... one*
by himself 1974, *him one* single-handed
816, 937, (*with num.*) *one foure* four un-
escorted 1743; *nom.sg.* **one** 1154, 1974;
obj.sg. **one** 2434; *dat.sg.* **one** 816, 937;
prep.sg. **on** 425, **a** 1808, 2135; *nom.pl.*
one 1743. *See* **a¹, euere-ich on, ilkan**
[(1), (2), (3) OE *ân*; (4) OE *āna* wk.a.]

[**on-come**] *sep.v.tr.* come upon; *p.p.*
comen ... on 116 [OE *oncuman* =
ON *koma á* (*ákvama* n.), MDu. *aen-
komen*]

on-do *sep.v.tr.* put on; *inf.* **don ... on** 971;
ger.inf. **on for to don** 588, **for to don
on** 578; *3 pt.sg.* **dide ... on** 860 [OE
ondōn; see 578 n.]

ones *adv.*: *see* **on** *num.*, **at**

[**on-haue**] *quasi-sep.v.tr.* be wearing (a
garment, etc.) *1 pr.sg.* **onne-haue** 1146
(*see* 347 *n.*) [See 1146 n., and cf. MDu.
aenhebben 'id.']

onlepi: *see* **anilepi**

[**on-leye**] *sep.v.tr.* lay on; *phr.* **onne
handes leye** use force on 1941, *hand
with iuele* ~ do physical violence to 50,
995, 1690; *pt.sg.* **on ... leyde** 50, 995,
subj. **onne ... leyde** 1941; *p.p.* **onne-
leyd** 1690 (*see* 347 *n.*, 1676 *n.*) [OE
onlecgan; see 50 n.]

onne *prep.* (?): in 2106 (*see* 347 *n.*) *See* **on-
leye, on-sitte** [extended f. of OE *on*,
after OE *inne bes. in*]

onon: *see* **anon**

on-ride *sep.v.tr.* ride upon; *inf.* ~ 347* (*see
n.*) [OE *onridan*: *see* 347 n.]

[**on-sitte**] *sep.v.tr.* be seated on; *3 pt.sg.*
onne-sat 1676 (*see n.*) [OE *onsittan*]

open *a.* open; *phr. caste(n) þe dore* ~ 1783,
1797 [OE *open*]

or *conj.* or 48, 573, 769, 1690, 1934, *etc.* [red. of *oþer* conj.]

or *adv.* (1) before 1044 (2) first 729, 2783 [ON *ár*]

or *conj.* before 417, 1357, 1689, 2456, ~ *þat* 1679*, 2263 [ON *ár*]

or *prep.* before 1045, 1790 [ON *ár*]

ore *n.*¹ (1) oar 712, 1872, 1887 (2) starboard 719 (*see n. and* **in-leye**); *obj.sg.* ~ 1872, 1887; *prep.sg.* ~ 719; *obj.pl.* **ores** 712 [OE *ár*]

ore, hore *n.*² mercy; *phr. Cristes* ~ 153, 2798; *Godes* ~ 211, 2444; *obj.sg.* **hore** 153, **ore** 211, 2444, 2798 [OE *ár*]

†osed *a.* having donned hose 972 [on *hose n.*]

oth, oþ *n.* oath; *phr.*: *grete oþes swere* swear solemn oaths 2014, 2232; *see* **leye** *v.*²: *obj.sg.* ~ 260, 314, 2010, 2273, 2527; *obj.pl.* **oþes** 2014, 2232. *See* hold(*e*)-oþes [OE *áþ*]

oþer *a.* (1) second: (*þet*) ~ *day* 880, (*þat*) ~ (*broþer*) 2350, *þe toþer* (*sister*) 411 (*with metanalysis of þet oþer*), (*þe*) oþer (*day*) (the) next day 1756 (2) different 575, 834, 911, 1201, 1357, 1628, ... *þan* 628 (3) additional 1987*, (*with num.*) ~ *two* 1805, ~ *þrinne* 762, *oþre fiue* 2414, *sixti oþer* 1769 two (*etc.*) others; *nom.sg.* **oþer** 575; *obj.sg.* ~ 490, 564, 1357, 2352, 2553; *prep.sg.* ~ 628, 1628; *nom.pl.* ~ 1769; *obj.pl.* ~ 1748, 1987*, 2835 [OE *ōðer*]

oþer *pron.* (1) *correl.* ~ ... ~ the one ... the other 2971* (2) *reciprocal*: *see* **ilk(e)** (3) *pl.* (the) rest: (*þe*) oþ(*e*)*re* 1785, 1833, 2417 (4) anyone else 1126; *non* ~ anything else (= otherwise) 2491; *nom.sg.* **oþer** 2491, 2971*; *obj.sg.* ~ 1126; *prep.sg.* ~ 2971*; *nom.pl.* **oþ(e)re** 1833, 2417; *obj.pl.* **oþre** 1785 [OE *ōðer*]

oþer *conj.* (1) or 788 (2) (*correl.*) ~ ... *or* either ... or 94, 2000 [OE *ōðer*]

ouer *prep.* (1) towering above 987, (*fig.*) above 293 (2) further than 1054, 1063 (3) across 2510 [OE *ofer*]

oueral *adv.* everywhere 38, 54 [OE *ofer eall*]

ouer-fare *v.* (1) *tr.* make one's way across 1379 (2) *intr.* pass from one 2064 [OE *oferfaran*]

[ouer-fleye] *sep.v.tr.* fly across; *1 pt.sg.* **fley ouer** 1306 [OE *oferflēon*]

ouer-ga, ouer-go *v.intr.* go unheeded 314, 2221 [OE *ofergān*]

ouer-gange *v.tr.* conquer 2588 [OE *ofergangan*]

ouertake *v.tr.* get within reach of 1817, 1857, 2696; *3 pt.sg.* **ouertok** 1817 [OE *ofer* + ON *taka*]

ouerþwert *adv.* cross-wise 2823 [*ouer* adv. + *þwert* adv. < ON *þver-t*, neut.sg. of *þver-r* a.]

oune *a.* own 375, 2429 [OE *āgen*]

oure *n.* shore; *prep.sg.* ~ 321 [OE *ofer*]

outh *n.* anything; *obj.sg.* ~ 704. *See* **nouth** *adv.* [OE *āht*; see **outh** *adv.*]

outh *adv.* (*emph.*) at all 1190, 1790. *See* **nouth** *adv.* [adv. use of acc.sg. of OE *āht* < *ā̄*, *ō* 'ever' + *wiht* 'creature; thing']

page *n.* page (in training for knighthood) 1731 [OF *page*]

palefrey *n.* saddle-horse (as distinct from war-horse); *obj.sg.* ~ 2061 [OF *palefrei*]

panier *n.* basket; *obj.sg.* ~ 814; *obj.pl.* **paniers** 761, 806 [early F *panier*]

pappe *n.* breast; *prep.pl.* **pappes** 2133 [ideo.; cf. mod. Norw. and Sw. dial. *pappe* 'nipple']

parlement *n.* conference, called by regent, of all earls and barons of England; *prep.sg.* ~ 1007, 1180 [OF *parlement* 'speaking']

†parred *p.p.* hemmed in 2440 [cf. MDu. *parre* 'fenced-in area', OE *pearroc* 'fence or hurdles to enclose a space'; see *OED parrock*]

parted *p.p.* dispersed 2963 [F *partir*]

passe *v.tr.* traverse 1377 [F *passer*]

pastees *n.pl.* pies; *obj.pl.* 645 [OF *pastée* p.p.a.]

Pater Noster *n.* (single utterance of) the Lord's Prayer 2998 [L *pater noster* as opening words of the Lord's Prayer]

†pateyn *n.* plate used in the Eucharist; *obj.sg.* ~ 187; *prep.sg.* 2712* [OF *patene*]

patriark *n.* bishop; *prep.sg.* ~ 428 [OF *patriarche*]

paþ *n.* path; *prep.sg.* **paþe** 2382, 2391; *obj.pl.* **paþes** 268 [OE *pæð*]

payed *p.p.* satisfied 184 [OF *paier* 'please; satisfy']

†pelle *v.intr.* hasten 811 [unknown]

peni *m.* penny 777, 1173, 2148; cash 706

(*see* **drawe**); *obj.sg.* ~ 2148; *prep.sg.* ~ 706; *nom.pl.* **penies** 1173; *obj.pl.* **penies** 777 [OE *penig*]

per *n.* equal; *nom.sg.* ~ 990; *obj.sg.* ~ 2242, 2793 [OF *per*]

pike *v.tr.* (*pass.*) caulk 708 [OE *pícian* 'coat with pitch']

pine *n.* suffering 540, distress 1375; *prep.sg.* ~ 540, 1375. See **helle-pine** [OE **pīn* < L *poena*; implied in OE *pīnian* v.]

pine *v.tr.* inflict suffering on 1959 [OE *pīnian*]

piping *vbl.n.* playing of pipes; *obj.sg.* ~ 2326 [OE *pīpian* + ME suff. *-ing*]

place *n.* settlement; *obj.sg.* ~ 744 [OF *place*]

plattinde: *see* **plette**

plawe *v.intr.* frolic 951. See **pleye** [OE (A.) *plagian*]

playce *n.* plaice; *prep.pl.* **playces** 897 [OF *plaiz*]

pleinte *n.* (1) lament 134 (2) complaint 2962; *obj.sg.* **pleynte** 134 [OF *plainte* < med. L *plancta* < p.p. of L *plangere* + OF *plaint* < L *planctus*]

plente *n.* (1) abundance 1243, 1730 (2) abundant number 1174 [OF *plenté*]

plette *v.intr.* hurtle; *pres.pret.* **plattinde** 2283; *3 pt.pl.* **plette** 2614. See **of-plette** [ad. MDu. *pletten* 'strike' × ME *platten* < OE *plættan* 'id.']

pleye *v.intr.* play 952. See **plawe** [OE *plegian*]

plith *n.* harm 1371, 2003; *obj.sg.* ~ 2003; *prep.sg.* ~ 1371 [OE *pliht* 'danger']

plow *n.* plough; *prep.sg.* ~ 1018 [LOE *plōh* (in obl. forms with [ɣ] foll. by vowel)]

poke *n.* sack 556; bag 770, 781; *prep.sg.* ~ 556, 770; *obj.pl.* **pokes** 781 [ad. either ONF *poque* = OF *poche* or ON *poki*]

pol *n.* pool; *prep.pl.* **poles** 2102 [OE *pōl*]

polk *n.* puddle 2686 [dim. of *pōl*]

pope *n.* pope; *prep.sg.* ~ 428 [OE *pāpa*]

pouere *a.* (1) penurious; (*sb.*) penurious persons 101 (2) of wretched quality 2458 [OF *povre*]

pourelike *adv.* meanly 323 [OF *povre* + ME suff. *-like* < OE *-líce*]

prangled *p.p.* tightly gagged 640 [on MDu. *prangen* 'press, squeeze' + ME freq. suff. *-le*]

prest *n. priest; nom.sg.* ~ 391, 1030; *prep.sg.*

~ 429, 1830, 2599; *nom.pl.* **prestes** 33; *obj.pl.* **prestes** 243, 2584; *prep.pl.* **prestes** 359 [OE *prēost*]

preye, preie *v.tr.* (1) beseech 169, 1344, 1441 (2) pray for 153, 211; *1 pr.sg.* **preie** 1441; *imper.sg.* **prey** 1344; *3 pt.sg.* **preide** 209, **preyede** 211, *pl.* **preyden** 153 [OF *preier*]

preyse *v.tr.* praise; *ger.inf.* to be praised 60 [OF *preisier*]

pride *n.* pomp; *prep.sg.* ~ 2947 [LOE *prўde*]

priken *v.intr.* ride (spurring one's horse) 2640 [OE *prician*]

priorie *n.* priory; *obj.sg.* ~ 2523, 2582 [OF *pris*]

pris *n.* worth; *prep.sg.* ~ 283 [OF *pris*]

prud *a.* arrogant 302 [LOE *prûd*]

pulten *3 pt.pl.intr.* ? cast 1024 (*see n.*)

pund *n.* pound (in money); *obj.sg.* ~ 2616; *n.pl.* ~ 1634 [OE *pund*]

put *n.* cast (with the stone, in a game); *obj.sg.* ~ 1056 [**putten** v.]

putten, puten *v.* (1) *tr.* cast (the stone, in a game); ~ (*þe ston*) 1045; *intr.* ~ *wit* (*sc. þe ston*) 1032, 1052; *absol.* 1034 (2) *intr.* thrust 1845; *inf.* **putten** 1034, 1045 (*pass.*), **puten** 1052; *3 pt.pl.* **putten** 1032, 1845 [LOE **putian*, in *putung*]

putting(e) *n.* the game of casting the stone; ~ *of ston* 2325; *obj.sg.* **putting** 2325; *prep.sg.* **puttingge** 1043, **putting** 1058 [**putten** v.]

pyment *n.* spiced wine 1729 [OF *piment*]

quaked *p.p.* trembled convulsively 135 [OE *cwacian*]

*qual *n.* jellyfish; *obj.sg.* ~ 754 (*see n.*) [Cf. Du. *kwal* 'jellyfish', G and LG *Qualle* 'basket-fish']

quan(ne): *see* **hwan**

quath *3 pt.sg.* said 607, 643, **hwat** 1651, 1879, **wat** 596; **quoth** 922, 1931, 2097, 2169, 2607*, 2724, *etc.*, **quot** 1955, 2809, **quod** 1889, **quodh** 1801 [OE *cwæþ*, 3 pt.sg. of *cweðan*]

queme *a.* (one's) pleasure 130, satisfactory 393 [OE *gecwēme* × *cwēman*]

quen(e) *n.* queen; *nom.sg.* **quen** 293, 1275, 2788, 2967, **quene** 183; *prep.sg.* **quen** 2761; *nom.pl.* **quenes** 2983 [OE *cwēn*]

quic, quik *a.* (1) alive 613, 2589; *phr. þe day þat he was* ~ *and ded* the day of his death

1406 (*see* 257 *n.*), 2211 (2) vigorous 1349 [OE *cwic*]

quic *adv. al* ~ ?on the instant 2642 [*quic a.*]

quiste *n.* testamentary arrangements; *nom.sg.* ~ 365; *obj.sg.* ~ 218 [*see n.*]

quod(h): *see* **quath**

quot: *see* **quath**

radde: *see* **rede(n)**

ran: *see* **renne**

rank *a.* self-willed 2562* [OE *ranc* 'haughty; arrogant', or *ad.* ON *rakkr* 'slender; bold' < prim. ON **rank-*]

rath *n.* (1) a source of help 75 (2) course of action: *phr. to* ~ *e* (*ben understood*) + *dat. of adv.* be one's course of action 694*, 2543; *nom.sg.* ~ 75; *prep.sg.* **raþe** 2543. *See* **red** *n.* [ON *ráð* = OE *rǣd*]

rathe, rothe *v.tr.* (1) guide: *phr. wisse and* ~ 361* (2) advise 1336, 2586*; *phr. wile(n) and* ~ 1682*, 2818; *inf.* **raþe** 361*, 1336, 2586*; *1 pr.sg.* **raþe** 1682*; *2 pr.pl.* **rothe** 2818. *See* **rede(n)** [ON *ráða*]

raþe, rathe *adv.* quickly 358, 2008, 2392, 2595, 2938 [OE *hraþe*]

[**recke**] *v.intr.* feel pity; *3 pr.sg.subj.* ~ 2048, 2512, 2758 [OE *reccan*]

red *n.* (1) advice 184, 1407, 2212, 2872, counsel 180 (2) course of action 518, 827, 1195, *to* ~*e* (*ben understood*) + *dat. of adv.* be one's course of action 118 (3) remedy 148, 1205; *phr.:* *see* **conne**, **take(n)**; *obj.sg.* ~ 148, 518, 827, 1195, 1205, 1407, 1834; *prep.sg.* ~ 180, 2212, 2872, **rede** 184. *See* **rath** [OE *rǣd*]

red *a.* (1) (*of gold*) red: *gold* ~ 1263, ~ *gold* 47 (2) red-haired 1687; (*as byname*) *þe Rede* 1398 [OE *rēad*]

rede(n) *v.tr.* (1) guide: *phr. wisse and* ~ 104, *so God me* ~! 688, 2086, 2901 (2) advise 1354 (3) read (aloud) 244; *inf.* **rede** 104, **reden** (*pass.*) 244; *3 pr.sg.subj.* **rede** 688, 2086, 2901; *3 pt.sg.* **radde** 1354. *See* **rathe** *v.* [OE *rǣdan*]

refte: *see* **reue(n)**

regne *v.intr.* prevail 2587 [OF *regner*]

renne *v.intr.* (1) speed 1162 (2) stream 216, 1851; *phr.* ~ *on blode* stream with blood 432; *tr.* (3) cover in running 1832; *inf.* ~ 1832; *3 pt.sg.* **ran** 216, 432, 1851 [ON *renna*]

rest *n.* (1) sleep 145 (2) rest 944; *obj.sg.* ~ 145, 944 [OE *rest*]

reue *n.* local official; *prep.sg.* ~ 1628 [OE *gerēfa*]

reue(n) *v.tr.* (1) plunder 2005 (2) deprive of 94, 2484, 2992; *phr.:* ~ + *dat. of disadv.* + *hise* (*etc.*) *lyf* 480, 1368, 2224, 2395, 2486, 2591, take from 1673; *inf.* **reuen** 480, 2992, **reue** 2591; *2 pt.sg.* **reftes** 2395; *3 pt.sg.* **refte** 94, 2224, 2486; *p.p.* **reft** 2005, 2484 [OE *rēafian*]

reures *n.* despoilers; *obj.pl.* ~ 2105 [OE *rēafere*]

rewe *v.tr. impers.* be moved with pity 497, 503, 968; *inf.* **rewe** 497, 968; *3 pt.sg.* **rewede** 503 [OE *hrēowian*]

rewnesse *n.* pity; *obj.sg.* **reunesse** 2228; *prep.sg.* **rewnesse** 502 [OE *hrēowe a.* + ME *-nes*]

ribbes *n.* ribs; *obj.pl.* ~ 1901 [OE *ribb*]

riche *a.* (1) mighty 341, powerful 1442 (2) affluent 676; *phr.* ~ *and pou(e)re* one and all 138, 237 (3) valuable 2940 (4) lavish 2902 (5) luxurious 2346, sumptuous 1763 [(1) OE *rīce*; (2) OE *rīce* + OF *riche*; (3)–(5) OF *riche*]

richelike *adv.* luxuriously 421 [OF *riche* + ME suff. *-like* < OE *-līce*]

ricth(e): *see* **rith** *n.*, **rith(e)** *a.*

ricthwise *a.* virtuous 37* [OE *rihtwīs*]

ride(n) *v.* ride; (1) *intr.:* ~ (*up*)*on* (*ani, a*) *stede* 10, 26, 623, 1759, 2062, 2896; *on horse* ~ 370; *go ne* ~ (take the field) on horseback or on foot 2778, ~ *and go* mounted and on foot 2849 (2) *tr.* ~ *stede* 1972; *inf.* **riden** 10, 26, 370, 623, 1759, 2896, **ride** 1972, 2062, 2778, 2849. *See* **on-ride** [OE *rīdan*]

rig *n.* back; *prep.sg.* 1776 [ON *hrygg-r*, or unassib. f. of *-gg-* (before OE back vowels in endings) in OE *hrycg*]

riht ?*v.* aim a blow at 1827 (*see n.*) [ad. MDu. *richten*]

rike *n.* kingdom; *prep.sg.* ~ 290 [prob. ON *ríki*]

ring *n.* ring (in coat of mail) 2741; *obj.pl.* **ringes** 2741 [OE *hring*]

ringen *v.tr.* ring; *inf.* (*pass.*) ~ 242, 1107; *3 pr.sg.* **ringes** 390; *p.p.* **rungen** 1133 [OE *hringan*]

rippe *n.* basket; *prep.sg.* ~ 894 [ON *hrip*]

rise *v.intr.* (1) stand up 2204 (2) move

above the horizon 1956 (3) develop 2978; *inf.* ~ 2204, 2978; *3 pt.sg.* ros 1956. *See* **up-rise** [OE *rīsan*]

rith, ricth *n.* (1) justice as prescribed by law: *phr. demen him* ~ pass on him the sentence required by law 2468, 2766, 2813 (2) justice 78; *phr. soth ant* ~ 36 (3) just dealing 71 (4) rightful property 395, 1100, 1384, 2992 (5) *adv.dat. to* ~ as it should be 109; *nom.sg.* **rith** 1384, 2992; *obj.sg.* **ricth** 36, 71, 78, 395, **rith** 2468, 2813; *prep.sg.* **ricth** 109 [OE *riht*]

rith(e), ricthe *a.* (1) direct: *þe* ~ *gate* 847 (*sti* 1202*, *wei* 773) (2) just 2474 (3) proper 2718, 2926 (4) rightful 289*, 2236, 2540, 2770 (5) right (as distinct from 'left') 605, 1813, 2141, 2409, 2546, 2726 [OE *riht*]

rith(e) *adv.* (1) directly 1906 (2) precisely 2980, exactly 1823, 2495; *phr.* ~ *þare* at that very place 2255, 2833 (3) altogether 2388, fully 1702, 2343, penetrating deep 2743 (4) properly 420 (5) correctly 2612. *See* **forthrith** [OE *rihte*]

†**ritte** *v.intr.* carve 2496 [ideo. f. Gmc *rit-*; *see n.*]

robben *v.tr.* rob 1959 [OF *rob(b)er*]

rode *n.* cross (of Christ); *prep.sg.* ~ 103, 431, 1358, 2404 [OE *rōd*]

rof *n.* roof 2083 [OE *hrōf*]

‡**romanz-reding** *vbl.n.* reading aloud of romances 2328 [OF *ramanz* + ME *reding*]

rop *n.* rope; *prep.sg.* ~ 2508; *obj.pl.* **ropes** 784 [OE *rāp*]

rore *v.intr.* roar; *inf.* ~ 2497, 2500; *3 pt.sg.* **rorede** 2439 [OE *rārian*]

rose *n.* rose 2920 [OF *rose*]

roser *n.* rose-bush; *prep.sg.* 2920 [AN *roser* = OF *rosier*]

rothe: *see* **rathe** *v.*

rowte *v.intr.* shriek 1912 [ON *rauta*]

runci *n.* riding-horse 2570 [OF *ronci* bes. *roncin*]

salte *a.* salt; *prep.sg.* ~ 1306 [OE *s(e)alt*]

salue *n.* healing ointment; *prep.sg.* ~ 1836 [< infl. f. of OE *sealf*, perh. × *saluen* v. < OE *sealfian*]

same: *see* **shame**

samen *adv.* together 467, 980, 1718, 2135, 2577, 2772 [OE *samen* bes. *somen*]

samened *p.p.* united 2891 [OE *samnian*]

saue *a.* unharmed 2227, preserved 561* [< infl. f. of OF *sauf*]

sauteres *n.* the penitential psalms 244 (*see n.*) [OF *sautere*]

saw(en): *see* **se(n)**

say: *see* **se(n)**

sayse, seyse *v.tr.* (1) ~ *in* put in legal possession of 2519 (2) ~ *in* (*til*) (*his*) *hond* take (formal) possession of 251, 2514, 2932, *inf.* (*pass.*) **sayse** 251; *1 pr.sg.* ~ 2519; *3 pt.sg.* **seysed** 2932; *p.p.* **seysed** 2514 [OF *saisir, seisir*]

scabbed, skabbed *a.* covered with scabs 2450, 2506 [ON *skabb-r* (= OE *sceabb*) > MSw. *skabb-er*, mod. Sw. *skabb* + suff. *-ed* < OE *-ede* 'having, characterized by']

scaþe *n.* (1) damage 1353; harmful deed 269: *see* **do(n)** *phr.* (2) matter for regret: *it is of him mikel* ~ it is a great pity about him 2007; *nom.sg.* ~ 2007; *obj.sg.* ~ 1353; *obj.pl.* **scaþes** 269 [ON *skaði*]

schal: *see* **shal**

sche: *see* **she**

schireue *n.* sheriff; *nom.sg.* **shireue** 2287; *obj.pl.* **schireues** 266 [OE *scīr-gerēfa*]

scho: *see* **she**

schrifte *n.* absolution; *obj.sg.* ~ 1830* [OE *scrift*]

‡**schulle** n. plaice; *obj.sg.* ~ 760 [MDu. or MLG *schulle, scholle*]

se *n.* sea; *obj.sg.* ~ 1377; *poss.sg.* **seis** 321; *prep.sg.* **se** 535, 720, 1306, **she** 519 [OE *sǣ*]

se(n) *v.tr.* see; *inf.* **sen** 1274, **se** 1022, 1986, 2082; *2 pr.sg.* **sest** 534; *1 pr.pl.* **sen** 1218; *2 pr.pl.* **sen** 168; *1 pr.sg.subj.* **se** 2098; *3 pt.sg.* **say** 882, **saw** 476, 2109, (*coll.*) **sawe** 1183, **sau** 2411, *pl.* **sowen** 958, 1056, **sawen** 2256, **sawe** 1963, 2144, 2431; *1 pt.subj.sg.* **sowe** 1324; *3 pt.subj.sg.* **sawe** 473 [OE *sēon*]

seckes *n.* sacks; *prep.pl.* ~ 2020 [OWN *sekk-r*]

segges *n.* cuttle-fish; *prep.pl.* ~ 897 [OF *sèche*; *see n.*]

seken *v.tr.* seek 1630; *intr.* search 1086; *inf.* ~ 1630; *1 pt.sg.subj.* **southe** 1086 [OE *sēcan*]

sele *n.* seal; *obj.sg.* ~ 756 [OE *sel-* in infl. forms of *sēlh*]

self *a.* (*emph.*): *nom.sg.* **(God)** ~ God himself 245; *see* **himself; meself, y(o)uself** [OE emphatic a. *self*]

seli *a.* innocent 477, 499 [OE *sǽlig*]
selkouth, selc(o)uth *n.* extraordinary phenomenon 2120; extraordinary thing 124; remarkable incident 1060 [ME *selcouþ* a.]
selkuth *a.* extraordinary 1285 [OE *seldcūþ* a., lit. 'seldom known']
selle(n) *v.tr.* sell; *phr. beye and* ~ 53, 1655; *inf.* **sellen** 53, **selle** 705, 1655, *ger.inf.* ~ 764; *3 pt.sg.* **solde** 700, 704, 818; *p.p.* **sold** 776, 1639 [OE *sellan*]
selthe *n.* happiness 1339 [OE *sǽlð*]
sembling *vbl.n.* coming together of people 1019 [*semblen* v., aph. f. of *assemblen*; or ad. OF aph. *sembler*]
[**seme**] *v.* (1) be fitting (*impers.*) 977, 1653, 2917, (*pers.*) 979 (2) *intr.* seem 1650; *3 pr.sg.* **semes** 2917; *3 pt.sg.* **semede** 1650; *3 pt.sg.subj.* **semede** 977, 1653 [ON *søma*]
sende *v.tr.* (1) send 1181, 1750, 2275, 2761; ~ *word* command (by messenger) 2393 (2) ~ *after* send for 136, 358, 523, 1104, 1134; ~ *unto* send a message 1935; *inf.* (*pass.*) ~ 523; *3 pr.sg.* **sendes** 2393; *1 pr.sg.subj.* **sende** 1935; *3 pt.sg.* ~ 136, 358, 1750, 2275, 2761, **sente** 1134; *p.p.* **sent** 1181 [OE *sendan*]
sene *a.* evident 657 [OE *gesēne*]
serga(u)nz, seriaunz *n.pl.* (1) retainers 1930, 2067, 2089, 2092 (2) men-at-arms 2362, 2372 (3) tenant by military service under the rank of knight 2117; *nom.pl.* ~ 2067, 2092; *obj.pl.* ~ 1930, 2089, 2117, 2362, 2372 [OF *serganz*, AN *-aunz*]
serges: *see* **cerges**
serk *n.* shirt; *obj.sg.* ~ 604 [OE *serc, serce* or ON *serk-r*]
seruen *v.*¹ *tr.* (1) minister to (as a servant) 1231 (2) worship 2523; *inf.* 1231, 2523 (*ger.*) [OF *servir*]
[**seruen**] *v.*² *tr.* deserve 1915; *3 pt.pl.* seruede 1915 [aph. f. OF *deservir*]
sette *v.tr.* (1) seat 162, 1287 (2) *refl. o(n) knes* ~ kneel down 451, 1212, 2253 (3) *intr.* (of the sun) sink below the horizon 2672 (4) *tr.* place 785; *phr. neue under hern* ~ strike (someone) under the ear with one's fist 1918; *sim.*: ~ *a dint with þe neue* 2406 (5) *tr.* fix a time for: ~ *day* appoint a day 2572 (6) put to a particular use: *wel set* wisely laid out 908, 2037; *3 pt.sg.* **sette** 451, 2406, 2253, 2572, **set**

785 (*see* **-es**), *pl.* **setten** 1212; *p.p.* **set** 162, 1287, 1918, 2037. *See* **dun(e)-sette** [OE *settan*]
seuene *card.num.* seven 2126 [OE *seofon*]
seuentenþe *ord.num.* seventeenth 2560 [OE *seofontēne* + suff. -(*e*)]
seuenþe *ord.num.* seventh 1826 [OE *seofoþa* × ME *seuene*]
se-weres *n.* enclosures for catching fish 785* (*see n.*) [LOE ‡*sǽwǽre* < *sǽ* + *were* 'weir']
seyen *v.tr.* (1) say 117, 376, 456, 648, 1214, 1314, *etc.* (2) recount 2994* (3) formally pronounce 2839; *inf.* **seyen** 2887; *2 pr.sg.* **seyst** 2009; *3 pr.sg.* **seyt** 648; *3 pt.sg.* **seyde** 117, 159, 1314, **seide** 1284, *pl.* **seyden** 376, 456, 1214; *p.p.* **seyd** 1282, 2839, 2994*, **seid** 1787. *See* **forthsaye** [OE *seg-* in 2 and 3 pr.sg. of *secgan*]
seyl, sayl *n.* sail; *obj.sg.* **seyl** 712; *prep.sg.* **seyl** 855, 2508, **sayl** 859 [OE *segl*]
shal *v.* (1) ought to 292, 294, 601, must 582, 584, 2000, 2197, 2279, 2487 (2) *fut. auxil.* 21, 1232, 1784, 1801, 2082, 2219, *etc.* (3) be destined to 608, 609, 610, 612–15, 2177, 2295 (4) be about to 587, 1767, 2225; *1 pr.sg.* **shal** 582, 584, **schal** 21; *2 pr.sg.* **shalt** 630, 2081, 2179, (*agglut.*) **shaltou** 1801; *3 pr.sg.* **shal** 1972, 2077; *1 pr.pl.* **shole** 1789; *3 pr.pl.* **sholen** 1232, 1234, 1236; *3 pt.sg.* **sholde** 2000; *1 pt.sg.subj.* **shude** 1080; *2 pt.sg.subj.* **sholdest** 2713; *3 pt.sg.subj.* **shulde** 198, 587, 2219, 2225, **sholde** 190, 292, 294; *pl.* **sholde** 1767, **sholden** 2197 [OE *pret.-pres.v. sceal* 1 and 3 pr.sg.; *scealt* 2 pr.sg.; *sculon* pr.pl.; *sceolde, sceoldon* 1 and 3 pt.sg., pt.pl.]
shame *n.* (1) dishonour 1666, 1674, disgrace 2462 (2) humiliation 2732, 2754, 2765 (*see* **do(n)** *phr.*) (3) violence 56, 1936, 1940, (to a woman) 83, 1192, 2085 (4) matter for reproach 800; *phr.*: *seye* ~ insult 1942; *see* **do(n)**; *nom.sg.* ~ 800; *obj.sg.* ~ 56, 1192, 1674, 1940, 2462, 2732, *etc.*, **same** 1942 [OE *sceamu*]
shamelike *adv.* humiliatingly 2463, 2826, 2828 [OE *sceamlice*]
shankes *n.* legs; *obj.pl.* ~ 1904 [OE *sceanca*]
shape *v.tr.* (1) create 424, 1102 (2) form: *wel shaped* 1648; *3 pt.sg.* **shop** 1102; *p.p.*

shaped 424, **schaped** 1648 [inf. reformed on OE *sceapen*, p.p. of *sc(i)eppan*]

shar 3 *pt.sg.tr.* cut 1414 [OE *scær*, inf. *sceran*]

sharpe *a.* sharp 2323, 2646 [OE *scearp*]

shawe, shauwe, shewe *v.tr.* (1) examine 2057* (2) see 1854*, 2785; scrutinize 1699*; gaze at 2137 (3) reveal 1402* (4) declare 2207; *inf.* **shaue** 1402*, **shawe** 1854*, *ger.inf.* **for to** ~ 1699*, 2785, **for to shewe** 2137; *p.p.* **shawed** 2057* [(1) *shewe* < OE *sceáwian* (with falling dipth.); (2) ME *shawe*, *showe* < OE *sceáwian* (with stress-shifted rising dipth.)]

she, sho 3 *pers.pron.fem.sg.* she; *nom.sg.* (1) **she** 174, 282*, 292, 567, 1119, 1237, 1673, *etc.*, **sche** 1722 (2) **sho** 112, 125 (2), 128, 129, 288, 337, 650, 1164, *etc.*, (*in rhyme*) 1233, **scho** 126; *obj.sg.* **hire** 172, 206, 333, 1106, 1236, 1687, *etc.*; *gen.sg.*: *see* **hire** *poss.a.fem.*; *dat.sg.* **hire** 130, 300, 1108, 1666, 2718, 2917, *etc.*; *prep.sg.* **hire** 121, 285, 1096, 1258, 1665, 1717 [OE *héo*; gen.dat.sg. *hire*]

sheld *n.* shield; *colloc.* ~ *and* (*ne*) *spere* 489*, 625, 1654, 2552; *obj.sg.* ~ 489*, 625, 1654, 2552, 2731 [OE *sceld*]

shende *v.tr.* (1) put to shame 2750 (2) bring destruction on 1423 (3) ruin 2846; 3 *pt.sg.* **shente** 2750; *p.p.* **shend** 2846 [OE *scendan*, caus.v. f. on *scam-* in *scamu*]

shep *n.* sheep; *poss.sg.* **shepes** 782; *obj.pl.* **shep** 701 [OE *scép*, bes. *sceap*]

sheres *n.* scissors; *obj.pl.* ~ 858* [OE *scéar*, pl. *sceára*]

shewe: *see* **shawe**

shides *n.* pieces of wood split for kindling fire; *obj.pl.* ~ 918 [OE *scíd*]

shilde 3 *pr.sg.subj.tr.* keep away 16 [OE *scildan*]

shine *v.intr.* shine 404, 2145; 3 *pt.sg.* **shon** 2145 [OE *scínan*]

ship *n.* sailing-vessel; *nom.sg.* ~ 736; *obj.sg.* ~ 707 [OE *scip*]

shir *a.* brilliant 589, 1254 [OE *scír*]

shir *adv.* brightly 917 [OE *scíre*]

shireue *n.* high administrative official with justiciary and fiscal duties; *nom.sg.* ~ 2287; *obj.pl.* **schireues** 266. *See* **reue** [OE *scírgeréfa*]

shirte *n.* shirt; *prep.sg.* ~ 769 [OE *scyrte*]

sho: *see* **she**

sho *v.tr.* provide shoes for 1139; *p.p.* **shod** 972 [OE *sceo(ge)an*]

shof 3 *pt.sg.tr.* pushed 872, 893 [OE *sceáf*, with stress-shifted diphth., < *sceaf* 3 pt.sg. of *scúfan*]

shole(n): *see* **shal**

shon *n.* shoes; *obj.pl.* ~ 861, 970 [OE *scó(h)*, gen.pl. *scóna* bes. nom. acc.pl. *scós*]

shop: *see* **shape**

shoten, schoten 3 *pt.pl.* (1) (*intr.*) ~ *on* rushed at 1839, **scuten** 2432 (2) (*tr.*) *with dat. of disadv.*: **schoten** hurled 1865 [OE *scéotan*]

shrede *n.* morsel of food; *obj.sg.* ~ 99 [OE *scréade*]

shride *v.tr.* (1) clothe 979 (2) wear 964; *ger.inf.* **to** ~ 964; *p.p.* **shrid** 979 [OE *scrýdan*]

shriue *v.tr.* (1) hear confession from 2490, 2599 (2) confess and impose penance on 212, 227, 362, 364; *inf.* ~ (*pass.*) 212, *ger.inf.* **for to** ~ 362; *p.p.* **shriuen** 227, 364, 2599, **shriue** 2490 [OE *scrifan*]

shrud *n.* clothes; *prep.sg.* ~ 303 [OE *scrúd*]

†shudre-blade *n.* shoulder-blade; *prep.sg.* ~ 2645 [cf. MLG *schulder-blat*]

shuldre, sholdre *n.* shoulder; *prep.sg.* **shuldre** 605, 1263, 2141, **sholdre** 2739; *prep.pl.* **shuldren** 983, **sholdres** 1648, 1819 [OE *sculdor*, pl. *sculdru*]

shuldreden 3 *pt.pl.tr.* nudged (with the shoulder) 1057 [on *shuldre* n.]

sibbe *n.* kindred; *phr.* ~ *an fremde* kindred and unrelated persons alike 2278 [OE *sibb*]

side, syde *n.* side of the body; *prep.sg.* ~ 127, 1845, 1981; *prep.pl.* **siden** 371, **sides** 1851 [OE *síde*]

sike *v.intr.* sigh 291 [OE *sícan*]

sikerlike *adv.* assuredly 422, 626, 2708; beyond question 2302, 2872 [LOE *sicerlíce*]

sikernesse *n.* sworn promise to refrain from prejudicial actions 2857 (*see n.*) [calque on med. L *securitas*]

siking *vbl.n.* sighing 234 [*sike* v. + suff. *-ing*]

siluer *n.* silver; *obj.sg.* ~ 819, 1224; *prep.sg.* ~ 73 [OE *silfor*, *silfr-es*, *-e* + ON *silfr*]

simenels *n.pl.* loaves of bread or buns made of fine wheaten flour; ~ *with þe horn* 780 *see* n. [AN or OF *simenel* 'bread or cake of the finest flour', f. on L *simila* 'fine wheaten flour']

singe(n) *v.tr.* intone 243; declaim (to music) 2329; (*pass.*) 2329; *intr.* chant 391; *3 pr.sg.* **singes** 391 [OE *singan*]

sinne *n.* (1) sin 536, 1381, 1421, 2462; (2) a pity 1977; pity 2376, 2628; *obj.sg.* **sinne** 536, 1421; *prep.sg.* ~ 1381, 2376, 2628 [OE *synn*]

sire, syre *n.* (1) as form of address to male superior 2010, *leue* ~ 910, ~ *erl* 2862 (2) (feudal) lord 310, 1230 [OF *sire*]

sister *n.* sister; *obj.sg.* ~ 411; *nom.pl.* **sistres** 1232; *obj.pl.* ~ 1366, 1409, 1413 [ON *systir*]

sitte, site *v.*[1] *intr.* (1) sit down 366, 399, 923, 1767 (2) remain seated 1739 (3) ~ *and* (*wesseylen*) sit continuously (tippling) 2099 (4) run aground (*lit.* take up a position) 736 (5) continue 2345 (6) ~ (*him*) *up* raise himself into a sitting position 634; *phr.* ~ *on knes* kneel down 2710 (*cf.* **sette** (2)); *inf.* **site** 366; *imper.sg.* **sit** 923; *2 pr.sg.* **sittes** 1317; *3 pr.pl.* **sitten** 2099; *3 pt.sg.* **sat** 399, 567, 634, 736, 2345, *pl.* **seten** 1767; *p.p.* **seten** 1739. *See* **atsitte, doun-sit(t)e** [OE *sittan*]

[**sitte**] *v.*[2] *tr.*: *3 pt.sg.* **sat** flouted 2568 [aph. f. of *atsitte*, or ON *sitja*; see n.]

siþe, syþe *n.* occasion; (*with prec. num.*) 213, 1053, 2163; *phr.*: *see* **fele** *a.*; *prep.sg.* **siþe** 1053; *gen.pl.* ~ 779, 1247, 2190, **syþe** 2844; *instr.pl.* **siþes** 213, 1278, 1738, **syþes** 2163 [OE *siþ*]

siþen *conj.* after 1989 [OE *siððan*]

siþen *adv.* afterwards 399, 472, 727, 1367, 1415, 1811, 2261, **siþe** 1815 [OE *siððan*]

sixe *card.num.* six 1825 [OE *siex, six*]

sixtene *card.num.* sixteen 891 [OE *sixtiene, sextēne*]

sixti *card.num.* sixty 1748, 1769 [OE *siex-, sextig*]

sket *adv.* quickly 1927, 1961, 2304, 2494, 2514, 2575, 2737, 2840 [prim. ON **skéot-* > *skjótt*]

skirming *n.* fencing; *obj.sg.* ~ 2324 [OF *eskirmir*]

slawen: *see* **slo(n)**

slenge *v.tr.* throw; *inf.* ~ 2436; *p.p.* **slenget** 1924 [ON *sløngva, sløngja* wk.]

slep *n.* sleep; *prep.sg.* ~ 1283 [OE *slēp*]

slepen *v.intr.* sleep; *inf.* ~ 2109; *2 pr.sg.* **slepes** 1284; *imper.sg.* **slep** 661, 662; *3 pt.sg.* **slep** 1281, *pl.* **slepen** 2129 [OE *slēpan*]

sleues *n.* sleeves; *prep.pl.* ~ 1958 [OE *slēfe*]

sley, sleie *a.* (1) discerning; *obj.pl.* **sleie** 2117 (2) resourceful 1085 [ON *slœgr* 'clever']

slike: obscure; *see* 1158 n.

slo *n.* sloe; *nom.sg.* ~ 850; *obj.sg.* ~ 2052 [OE *slā(h)*]

slo(n) *v.tr.* (1) strike 2604, 2634, 2690 (2) kill 501, 512, 1365, 1413, 1746, 1808, 1970, 2071, 2167, 2433, 2544, 2589 (3) *absol.* strike 2604, 2690 (4) *intr.* ~ (*upo*) charge (at) 2597 (5) *intr.* ~ *togidere* clash in battle 2684; *inf.* **slon** (*pass.*) 2544, **slo** 512, 1365, 1413, 1746, 2071, 2167, 2604; *2 pr.sg.* **slos** 2707; *imper.pl.* **slos** 2597; *2 pt.sg.* **slowe** 2070; *3 pt.sg.* **slou** 501, **slow** 1808, 1970, 2634, *pl.* **slowe** 2433, 2684; *p.p.* **slawen** 1929, 2631, 2748 [(1) *inf.* and pres. stem < LOE *slā* or ON *slá*; (2) OE *slôh, slôgon, slagen*]

smerte *a.* painful 2056 [OE *smeart* a. × *smeortan* v.]

smerte *adv.* painfully 215 [on ME *smert(e)* a.]

smite *v.tr.* strike; *inf.* **smite** 1855; *3 pr.sg.subj.* **smite** 1888; *3 pt.sg.* **smot** 1677, 1824, 1829, **smoth** 2655 [OE *smitan*]

smith *n.* 1877 [OE *smiþ*]

†**so** *n.* tub; *obj.sg.* ~ 934 [ON *sá-r*]

so *A. adv.* (1) thus 339, 351, 1010, 2138, in this fashion 2452, 2680 (2) *predic.* with *be*: 19, 1077 (3) *continuative: and* ~ in this way 2187 (4) likewise 748, 2609 (5) just like 91, 1852, *etc.*, as much as 349, 1708 (6) ~ . . . *so* (*with a.*) so . . . as 2156, (*with v.*) so (well) as 1991 (7) *als* . . . *so* as . . . proportionately 992 (8) (*temp.*) then 2859. *B. conj.* (9) (*manner*) just as 2290, 2449 (10) (*temp.*) *al* ~ . . . ~ *see* (8) *and* **al so** *conj.* (2) (11) as if 1778, 1897, *etc.* (12) ~ *þat* (*consequence*) 742, 1070, *etc.* (13) ~ *þat* (*manner*) 324, 1812, *etc.* (14) (*introd. oaths*) as I hope 311, 1744, 1976 (15) (*concessive*) ~ *as* ‡although 337 [OE *swā*]

†**sobbing** *vbl.n.* sobbing 234 [ME *sobben*,

ideo. f. on Gmc *suƀ- 'sip' as in OE *sufl* '*condiment*', with *-eu-* grade in OE *séofian* 'sigh; lament']

softe *a.* mild 992 [OE *sõfte*]

softe *adv.* (1) comfortably 305 (2) quietly 2619 [OE *sõfte*]

somdel, sumdel *adv.* somewhat 240, 497, 1055, quite 450, rather 2307, 2951 [OE instr. *sume dǽle*]

sond *n.* beach 736, shore 709; *obj.sg.* ~ 709; *prep.sg.* ~ 736 [OE *sand*]

sone *n.* lad; *voc.sg.* ~ 661, 840, 857; son *prep.sg.* ~ 246; *obj.pl.* **sones** 1344, 1400, 2980; *prep.pl.* **sones** 763, 1197 [OE *sunu*]

sone *adv.* (1) at once 57, 78, 86, 971, 986, 1355 (second), 1356, 2374 (2) quickly 700; *emph.colloc.* ~ *anon*; *see* **anon** [OE *sõna*]

sone *conj.*: ~ *so* as soon as 664; (*with ellipsis of so*) *correl.* ~ . . . *sone* as soon as . . . immediately 1355 [OE *sõna swã . . . swã*]

sor *n.* (1) physical pain 1989 (2) grief 234; *obj.sg.* ~ 1989 [OE *sãr* n.]

sor *a.* grievous 1818 [OE *sǽr* a.]

sore, sare *adv.* (1) painfully 2443, 2648, bitterly 1391 (2) grievously 152, 214, 401, 455 (3) mightily: ~ *smite* 1855, 1888, 2639, ~ *slow* 2634 (4) exceedingly 503, 1670, 2166 [OE *sãre*]

sori, sory *a.* (1) distressed 151, 477, grieved 1249, 2542 (*see* **sorwful**) (2) vile 2230* [OE *sãrig*]

sorwe *n.* (1) grief 233, misery 57, 663, 1373, distress 2055, 2064 (2) matter for grief 473 (3) distressing situation 1881; *see* **bringe(n)** [OE *sorg-* in inflected forms]

sorwful, sorful a.: *only in phr. sorful and sori* sorrowful 151, dismayed 2542, *sory and sorwful* distressed 1249 [OE *sorhful*]

soth *n.* the truth; *phr. for* ~ truly 274; *nom.sg.* ~ 2016; *obj.sg.* ~ 36, 2009; *prep.sg.* ~ 274 [OE *sõþ*]

soth *a.* true 648, 2017 [OE *sõþ* a.]

soþlike *adv.* truly 276 [OE *sõþlíce*]

soule *n.* soul; *phr. his* ~ *hold* concerned for his salvation 74; *obj.sg.* ~ 245, 1423; *poss.sg.* ~ 1976; *dat.sg.* ~ 74 [OE *sãwol*]

soupe, supe *v.intr.* take supper 1766, 1767 [OF *soper, super*]

south *adv.* south; *phr.* †*norþ and* ~ in all directions 1256* [OE *sũþ*]

sowel *n.* any food eaten with bread; *bred and (ne)* ~ 768, 1144, 2906 [*sufl-*, infl. form of OE *sufol, sufel*]

span-newe *a.* as new as chips of wood 969 [ad. ON *spánný-r* 'id.']

spare *v.tr.* (1) refrain from punishing 2814* (2) exempt 1907 (3) have mercy on 1996, 2692 (3) be niggardly with 1241 (4) be sparing in the use of 899; *inf.* ~ 1996; *3 pr.sg.* **spares** 2692, **spareð** 2814*; *3 pt.sg.* **sparede** 899; *p.p.* **spared** 1241, 1907 [OE *sparian*]

sparke *n.* spark; *so* ~ *of (on) glede* 91, 871 [OE *spærca*]

sparkede *3 pt.sg.intr.* sparkled 2145 [on *sparke* n.]

speche, speke *n.* (1) style of speech 947 (2) power of speech 229 (3) report 1066*, 1071*; *nom.sg.* **speke** 1066*; *obj.sg.* ~ 1071*, **speche** 229; *prep.sg.* **speke** 947 [OE *spǽc, spéc*, with unassib. /k/ bef. back vowels in endings]

spede *v.intr.* (1) be successful 757, 1198, distinguished oneself 93 (2) get what one wants 1635; *ger.inf.* ~ 1635; *3 pt.sg.* **spedde** 757 [OE *spédan*]

speke *n.*: *see* **speche**

speke *v.intr.* speak 113, 125, 372, 679, 1069; *inf.* ~ 113, 125; *1 pt.sg.* **spak** 679; *3 pt.sg.* ~ 2969, *pl.* **speken** 1069, **spoken** 372; *p.p.* **speken** 2370 [OE *specan*]

spelle *n.* story; *prep.sg.* ~ 338 [OE *spel(l)*]

spelle *v.intr.* (1) discourse 2531 (2) narrate one's tale 15 [OE *spellian*]

sperd(e) *p.p.* shut up 414, 448 [ad. MDu. *sperren*]

spere *n.* spear; *colloc.*: *see* **sheld**; *obj.sg.* ~ 347, 380, 489*, 625, 1654, 2552; *prep.sg.* ~ 2300, 2653 [OE *spere*]

speu *3 pt.sg.tr.* vomited forth 1820 [obsc. rel. to OE *spíwan* to spit]

spille *v.tr.* destroy 2423 (*pass.*); *of limes* ~ castrate 86 (*pass.*) [OE *spillan*]

spired *p.p.intr.* made inquiries 2621 [OE *spyrian*]

spore, spure *n.* spur; *obj.sg.* **spore** 2570; *prep.pl.* **spures** 1677 [OE *spora, spura*]

sprawleden *3 pt.pl.intr.* were spread-eagled 475 [OE *spreawlian*]

sprede *v.tr.* (1) hold up in surrender 95 (2) *intr.* open 2921; *p.p.* **sprad** 2921 [OE *sprǽdan*]

springe *v.intr.* (1) dash 91, 871 (2) be bruited abroad 960 (3) dawn 1132; *3 pt.sg.* **sprong** 91, 960, *pl.* **sprongen** 871; *p.p.* **sprungen** 1132 [OE *springan*]

sprote *n.* twig; *obj.sg.* ~ 1143 [OE *sprota* 'shoot']

spuse(n) *v.tr.* (1) join in marriage 1176 (2) wed 1124, 1171, 1267, 2876 (3) *absol.* get married 2888 [OF *espuser*]

spusing(e) *vbl.n.* (1) marriage 1165, 2887, 2889 (2) the marriage service 1178 [*spusen* v.]

stac *n.* haystack 815 [ON *stakk-r*]

staf *n.* (1) pole (used as weapon) 1891; (2) symbolic rod used in ceremonial investiture 2518 (*see* 2517 *n.*); *obj.sg.* ~ 1891; *prep.sg.* ~ 2518 [OE *stæf*]

stake *n.* post; *prep.sg.* ~ 2831 [OE *staca*]

stalworþe *a.* (1) robust 905 (2) doughty; *superl.* **stalworþeste** 25 [OE *stælweorðe*]

stalworþi *a.* doughty 24, 2028 [*stalworþe* + *-y* < OE adj. suff. *-ig*]

stan-ded *a.* stone-dead 1816 [ME *stan* + *ded*]

standeth: *see* **stonden**

star *n.* sedge; *obj.sg.* ~ 940 [OIcel. **star(r)a-* (> *storr*), Sw. *star*, Da. *star*]

stare *v.intr.* (1) gaze intently 1038 (2) glare 508; *pr.part.* **starinde** 508; *3 pt.pl.* **stareden** 1038 [OE *starian*]

stark *a.* (1) (of a weapon) stout 380 (2) physically powerful 1016, 1025, 2028; *colloc.* ~ *and strong* 989 (3) mighty 341, 2180; *colloc. strong and* ~ 609, 1272, 2536 [OE *stærc*]

stede *n.* place; *nom.sg.* ~ 745; *prep.sg.* ~ 142; *prep.pl.* **stedes** 1847 [OE *stede*]

stede *n.* charger; *phr.: see ride(n)*; ~ 10, 26, 88, 623, 2062, 2550; *obj.sg.* 1676, 2358; *prep.sg.* ~ 10, 26, 88, 2062, 2193, 2387, 2641, 2703; *prep.pl.* **stedes** 2573, 2617 [OE *stēda*]

stel *n.* steel; *prep.sg.* ~ 2504, 2760 [OE *stēle*]

stem *n.* ray of light 592 [OE *stēam*]

sternes *n.* stars; *prep.pl.* ~ 1810 [ON **sterna* (> **stéarna* > *steárna* > OIcel. *stjarna*]

stert *n.*[1] tail; *prep.sg.* ~ 2824 [OE *steort*]

stert *n.*[2] moment of time; *prep.sg.* ~ 1874 [rel. to *stirte* v.]

steuene *n.* voice; *obj.sg.* ~ 1276 [OE *stefn*]

sti *n.* road; *obj.sg.* ~ 1202* (*see* **rith(e)** *a.*); *prep.sg.* ~ 2619 [OE *stīg*]

sticke, stikke, stike *n.* stick (for firewood) 915; 1143, 1239; *obj.sg.* **stikke** 1143; *obj.pl.* **stickes** 915, **stikes** 1239 [OE *sticca*]

stille *a.* (1) motionless; ~ *als a ston* 929 (2) quiet 165; *colloc.* ~ *and bolde* the quiet and the aggressive 956, 2310 [OE *stille*]

stirte *3 pt.sg.intr.* hastened 1050, 1697. *See* **forth-stirte, up-stirte** [OE *styrtan*]

stith *n.* anvil; *prep.sg.* ~ 1878 [ON *steði*]

stiward *n.* seneschal; *nom.sg.* ~ 667 [OE *stīg, stī, weard*]

ston *n.* (1) stone 570, 929 (*see* **stille** *a.*) 1024, 1045, 1051, 1062 (2) gem 1634; *nom.sg.* ~ 929, 1634; *obj.sg.* ~ 1045, 1051, 1062; *prep.sg.* ~ 570, 1024 [OE *stān*]

stonden *v.intr.* (1) stand 680, 890, 904, 1898, 2138, 2241 (2) loiter 690 (3) be situated 321 (4) (of beam of light) be emitted 592 (5) (*impers.*) (*awe*) ~ (fear) be felt 277 (*see n.*) (6) (*impers.*) ~ *wel* be happily placed 2984; *inf.* **stonden** 690; *3 pr.sg.* **standeth** 321, **stondes** 2241, 2984; *3 pt.sg.* **stod** 592, 680, 904, *pl.* **stoden** 2138, stode 890, 1898 [OE *standan*]

stonden *3 pt.pl.tr.* stoned 1864* [on *ston* n.]

stor *a.* numerous 2384 [ON *stór-r*]

storie *n.* tale; *obj.sg.* ~ 1642, 1735 [AN *estorie*]

stormes *n.* storms; *prep.pl.* ~ 1379 [OE *storm*]

stra *n.* straw; *obj.sg.* ~ 315, 466 [ON *strá*]

strangest: *see* **strong**

strangle *v.tr.* strangle; *3 pr.pl.* **strangleth** 2585; *p.p.* **strangled** 641 [OF *estrangler*]

strem *n.* stream 2688 [OE *strēam*]

strenes *3 pr.sg.tr.* begets 2984 [OE *(ge)strēonan*]

strengþe *n.* physical strength; *prep.sg.* ~ 991 [OE *strengþu*]

strie *n.* witch, sometimes a nocturnal succubus 999 (*see n.*) [OF *estrie* + med. L *striga*]

striue *v.intr.* be recalcitrant 2272 [OF *estriver*]

strong *a.* (1) powerful 80, 1272, 2536 (2) severe 114, 842, 1987 (3) heinous 443 (4) reprehensible 803; *phr.: see* **stark**; *superl.* **strangest** 200, 1082 [OE *strang*]

stronglike *adv.* violently 135 [*stranglice*]

strout *n.* wrangling; *obj.sg.* ~ 1040 [OE **strut*, or f. on *stroute* v.]

stroute *v.intr.* behave obstreperously 1780 [OE *strūtian*]

stund, stounde* *n.* space of time 1859, 2298* (*see* **vmbe**); *prep.sg.* **stund** 1859, **stounde** 2298* [OE *stund*]

sturg(i)un *n.* sturgeon; *nom.sg.* ~ 1728; *obj.sg.* ~ 754 [AN *sturgeon*]

suere: *see* **swere**

sum *a.* (1) some or other 1093; (*pl.*) some 1784, 1845 (2) ~ ... ~ one ... another 1844, 1966; (*pl.*) some ... others 1924; *nom.sg.* **summe** 1966; *nom.pl.* **summe** 1845, 1924, 1925; *obj.pl.* **summe** 1784 [OE *sum*]

sumdel: *see* **somdel**

sunne-bem *n.* shaft of sunlight 593, 2124 [OE *sun(ne)bēam*]

supe: *see* **soupe**

super *n.* supper; *obj.sg.* ~ 1763 [sb. use of OF *super* v. 'take supper']

sure *adv.* bitterly; ~ *keft* paid dearly for 2006 [f. on *sur* a. < OE *sūr* 'sour']

suth *n.* south; *phr.* norþ *and* ~ 434; *see* **norþ, south** [OE *sūþ* adv.]

svich: *see* **swilk**

swain: *see* **sweyn**

swannes *n.* swans; *nom.pl.* ~ 1727 [OE *swan*]

swerd *n.* sword; *obj.sg.* ~ 1760, 1803, 1826, 2646, 2734, 2751; *prep.sg.* ~ 2604, 2626, 2632, 2636; *obj.pl.* **swerdes** 1838, 2660; *prep.pl.* ~ 1770 [OE *sweord*]

swere, suere *v.tr.* (1) take an oath 189, 204, 254, 398, 1078, 2308 (2) assert solemnly 648, assert 2368; *phr.* ~ *an oath* pledge on oath 1119; ~ *grete opes* swear solemnly 2014, 2232, 2338, 2853; *inf.* ~ **swere** 254, 1078, 2232, 2853, **suere** 189; *3 pr.sg.* **suereth** 648; *3 pt.sg.* **swor** 398, 1119, 2368, *pl.* **swore** 2014, 2308; *1 pt.subj.sg.* **swore** 2338; *p.p.* **sworn** 204, **sworen** 580 [*swerian*]

swete, suete *a.* (1) delectable 2928 (2) gracious 1389 [OE *swēte*]

sweyn, sueyn, swain *n.* attendant on knight 32, 1329, 2196, *etc.*; *colloc.* knict *and* ~ 343, 371, 1698, 2186, 2262, 2428, 2624; *nom.sg.* **swain** 32, **sweyn** 1329, 1698; *obj.sg.* ~ 2428, 2624, **sueyn** 343; *nom.pl.* **sweynes** 371, 2262; *obj.pl.* ~ 2196 [ON *sveinn*]

swike *n.* traitor; *nom.sg.* ~ 423, 552, 627, 1159, 2402, 2483, 2806; *obj.sg.* ~ 2452; *nom.pl.* **swikes** 2991; *obj.pl.* ~ 2835 [OE *swica* wk., nom. acc. pl. *swican*]

swikedam *n.* treason; *obj.sg.* ~ 2469 [OE *swicdōm* × *swic(e)* n. 'deceit']

swikel *a.* treacherous 1109 [OE *swicol*]

swillen *v.tr.* rinse 920 [OE *swilian*]

swilk, suilk, svich (a) *dem.a.* of this kind 60, (**svich**) 1119; (*foll. by dep. cl.*) on such a scale 2685; (*with correl.* **so**) of the same kind 2124 (b) *pron.* things of that kind 645; (*anticipatory*) to this effect 2784; (*with dep. rel.* **als**) those things 1626 [OE *swilc*]

swin *n.* swine; *poss.sg.* **swines** 782; *obj.pl.* **swin** 702, 1228 [OE *swīn*]

swinge *v.tr.* scourge; *inf.* (*pass.*) ~ 214; *p.p.* **swungen** 226* [OE *swingan*]

swink *n.* (1) grievous affliction 2457 (2) toil 802, exertions 771; *obj.sg.* ~ 771; *prep.sg.* ~ 802, 2457 [OE *swinc*]

swinken *v.intr.* toil; *inf.* ~ 799, 800; *3 pt.sg.* **swank** 789 [OE *swincan*]

swire *n.* neck; *obj.sg.* ~ 311 [OE *swīra*]

swiþe *adv.* (1) very 111, 341, *etc.* (2) quickly 140, 602, speedily 2279 (3) at once 585, 683, 691, 1773, 1799, 2595, 2728 [OE *swīðe*]

swot *n.* blood 2663 (*cf. OED sweat*, sb. I. 1) [OE *swāt*]

swungen: *see* **swinge**

syþe: *see* **siþe**

syþe *n.* weapon with a curved blade (as on early war-chariots); *obj.sg.* ~ 2554; *prep.sg.* ~ 2700 [OE *sīðe*]

tabour *n.* small drum; *prep.sg.* ~ 2330 [OF *tabour*]

take(n) *v.tr.* (1) catch 754 (2) carry off 354, 446 (3) (*fig.*) seize 114 (4) accept (as one's own responsibility) ~ (*on me, him*) 536, 1421, accept (as wife) 1150, 1217, 2875, receive 2181, 2851 (5) get 820 (6) enter upon: *phr.* ~ *red* follow a course of action 518, concert a plan 1195, 1834; ~ *under fote* set out to traverse 1200; *phr.* leue ~ take (one's) leave 1388; *inf.* **taken** 518, 1421, **take** 2181; *3 pr.sg.* **taken** 1834; *2 pr.sg.subj.* **take** 1150; *3 pr.sg.subj.* **take** 446; *2 pt.sg.* **toke** 1217; *3 pt.sg.* **tok** 114, 467, 754, 820, 1388, 2851, *etc.*; *pl.* **token** 1195, 1200; *p.p.* **taken** 2268 [LOE *tacan*, ad. ON *taka*]

taleuaces *n.* large shields; *prep.pl.* ~ 2324 [OF *talevas*]

tarst *adv.* first; *þo* ~ only then 2689 [red. of *at arst* < OE *æt* + OE *ǣrest*]

tauhte *3 pt.sg.tr.* entrusted 2215 [OE *tǣcan*, or aph. < *be-techen* 'entrust']

tayl *n.* tail; *prep.sg.* ~ 2479, 2507 [OE *tægl*]

tel *n.* (cause for) reproach: *wituten* ~ irreproachably 191, 2220 [OE *tǽl*]

telle *v.tr.* (1) recount 3 (2) count 777, count out 1173, 2616 (3) ~ *for* account 1037; reckon on (it) **tel** 1349* (MS *til*); *p.p.* **told** 777, 1037, **tolde** 1173 [OE *tellan*]

ten *card.num.* ten 872, 2415, 2430 [OE *tēn*]

tendre *a.* tender 217, 2744 [OF *tendre*]

tene *n.* affliction; *obj.sg.* ~ 730 [OE *tēona*]

ter *n.* tear 285 [OE *tēar*]

tere *v.tr.* smear with tar 708 [ME *tere* n. < OE *teoru*; repl. OE *tyrwan*]

teth *n.* teeth; *prep.pl.* ~ 2407 [OE *tōþ*]

teyte *a.* spirited 1842; eager 2332 [ON *teit-r* 'cheerful; glad']

theyn: *see* **þayn**

thusand: *see* **þousind**

tid *n.* time; *dat.sg.* ~ 2101 [OE *tīd*]

tiding *n.* news; *nom.sg.* ~ 1927. See **tiþandes** [LOE *tīdung*; see *OED* tiding sb.]

til (MS): *see* **telle**

til *prep.* (1) to 141, 865, 894, 1197, 1289, 1307, 1802, 1848, 2280 (2) for 762 (3) till 1756, 2239 [ON *til* 'to' or ONth. *til* 'to']

til *conj.* till 378, 930, 1341, 1885, 2453; ~ *þat* till 174, 387, 900, 1440, 2377, 2600, 2631, 2672 [red. < *til þat*]

tilled *p.p.* won over 438 [OE *tyllan* in *fortyllan* 'draw away']

time *n.* (1) era 45 (2) life-time 28 (3) point of time: *phr.* †*god* ~ auspiciously 2889 (*see n.*); *prep.sg.* ~ 28, 45 [OE *tīma*]

tinte *3 pt.sg.tr.* was deprived of 2024 [ON *týna* 'destroy; lose']

tirueden: *see* **of-tirue**

tith *p.p.* intended 2991* [OE *tyhtan*]

tiþandes *n.* news; *obj.pl.* ~ 2280 [ON *tiðendi*]

to *n.* toe; *obj.sg.* ~ 1744; *prep.sg.* ~ 1848; *obj.pl.* **tos** 899, 2164 [OE *tā*, pl. *tān*]

to *card.num.*: *see* **two**

to *prep.* (1) (*motion and direction*): to 142, 558, 666, 720, 848, 937, 1162, 1337, 1778, 1898, 2559, 2897, *etc.* (2) (*extent*) as far as 64, 1029, 1031 (3) (*loc.*) at: ~ *þe* (*þi, his*) *fet* 617, 1321, 2303 (4) (*temp.*) till 576, 805 (5) (*purpose*) for 1235, 1765, for the making of 784, for the use of 739; for the purpose of, in order to: (*a*) *in ger.inf.* ~ + *v.* 264, 326, 763, 1022, 1394, 1715, 2135, 2847, *etc.*, 60, 1999 (*b*) *in hyper-*characterized *ger.inf. for* ~ + *v.* 102, 270, 362, 445, 588, 798, ?1299, 1427, 1635, 1959, *etc.*; as regards 951, 1199 (6) *hence as gramm. sign of inf.*: (*a*) *in* ~ + *v.* 78, 291, 542, 798, 938, 1169, 1374, 1650, 1802, *etc.* (*b*) *in for* + ~ + *v.* 329, 800, ?978, 1293, 1426, 1780, 2496, *etc.* (7) (*result*) cause to end in: *turne* ~ 1316 (8) (*resulting condition or status*) ~ *grotes* to pieces 1415, ~ *knith* as a knight 2043, 2315, ~ *make* as spouse 1151, ~ *wiue* as wife 2865, by way of ~ *rede* 118 (*see* **red** *n.*), ~ *raþe* 694*, 2543 (*see* **rath**), ~ *gode* 197 advantageous (9) (*human relations*) towards 2399, to 75 (10) (*object of action*) to 230, for 2362 (11) (*with intr. v.*) for 1178, 2360, to 1401, 1667, *etc. See* **into, þer-to, vnto** [OE *tō*]

to *adv.*[1] too 690, 692, 846, 1059, 2651, **al** ~ altogether too 302 [OE *tō* prep.]

to *adv.*[2] (*dir.*): ~ *and fro* backwards and forwards 2072 [OE *tō* adv.]

to-brised *p.p.tr.* bruised black and blue 1951 [OE *tō-brȳsan*]

[**to-comen**] *sep.v.tr.* (1) reach 325, 413, 2962 (2) come to 1325, 2557; *inf.* **comen** (...) **to** 325, 413, 2557, **to ... comen** 1325; *3 pt.sg.* **to ... cam** 900, **kam to ... 933**; *3 pt.sg.subj.* **come ... to** 2962 [OE *tō-cuman in *tō-cumende* pr. part.; cf. *tō-cyme* n.]

†**to-cruhsse** *v.tr.* shatter 1993 [ME *prep.* *to-* *pref.*[2] + OF *croissir*]

today *adv.* today 426 [OE *tō dæg*]

to-deyle *v.intr.* take part in; *3 pr.pl.* ~ 2100 [ME *to-* pref.[2] + ON *deila*, repl. *to-dele* < OE *tō-dǣlan*]

to-drawen *p.p.tr.* torn to pieces 2002 [ME *to-* pref.[2] + *drawen*]

†**to-frusshe** *v.tr.* smash 1994 [ME *to-* pref.[2] + *frusshe* < OF *froissier*]

[***to-gange**] *sep.v.tr.* approach; *inf.* **to (putting) gange** set about 1058 [Cf. OE *tō-gang* 'access; approach', and see **to-go**]

togidere *adv.* together 1129, 1182, 2684, 2892 [< ME *togidere* < *togedere* < OE *tōgædere*]

[***to-go**] *sep.v.tr.* approach; *3 pt.sg.* **to-yede** made his way to 766 (*see n.*) [Cf. OE *tō-gang* 'access; approach'; MDu. *toe-gaen* v. 'approach', *toe-gang* n. 'id.']

to-hewen *p.p.tr.* cut to pieces 2002 [OE *tō-hēawan*]

tomorwe(n) *adv.* tomorrow 530, 1128*, 2012, 2181 [OE *tō morgen(ne)*]

tonicht, tonith *adv.* (1) tonight 533 (2) last night 1956, 2004 [OE *tō niht*]

to-riue *v.* (1) *tr.* reduce (someone's clothing) to tatters 1954 (2) *intr.* split asunder 1793; *3 pt.sg.* **to-rof** 1793; *p.p.* **to-riuen** 1954 [ME *to-* pref.² + *riue* ad. ON *rífa*]

to-shiuere *v.tr.* break in pieces 1994; *p.p.* **to-shiuered** 2668 [ME *to-* pref.² + *shiueren* ad. MDu. *scheveren*]

totede *3 pt.sg.intr.* peered 2107 [OE ‡*totian*]

to-tere *v.tr.* (1) tear to pieces 1840 (2) reduce (someone's clothing) to tatters 1949, 2022; *p.p.* **to-torn** 1949, 2022 [OE *tō-teran*]

to-turuen *v.tr.* strip clean 919 (*see n.*) [ME *to-* pref.² + *tiruen*]

to-tused *p.p.tr.* dishevelled 1949 [ME *to* pref.² + ME *tusen* < OE **tūsian* = OHG *zir-zūson* pull to pieces]

toþer: *see* **oþer** *a.*

toun: *see* **tun**

tour *n.* tower; *prep.sg.* ~ 448, 2074 [LOE *tur* ad. OF *tur*]

toward *prep.* towards 2139 [OE *tōweard*]

to-yede: *see* **to-go

trayso(u)n, tresoun *n.* treason 312; *colloc. trechery,* ~, *and felony* 444, 1091, 2990 (*see* **felony** *and* 444 *n.*) [AN *treis(o)un, tres(o)un*]

trayt(o)ur, traitour *n.* traitor 319, 666, 693, 2758 [OF acc.sg. *trait(o)ur* (nom. *traitre*)]

tre *n.* (1) tree 1430, 1720 (2) wooden beam 1023, 1822, 1844, 1883, 1893, 1966, 2033; *nom.sg.* ~ 1023; *obj.sg.* ~ 1883, 1893, 1966; *prep.sg.* ~ 1430, 1720, 1822, 1844, 2033 [OE *trēow*]

trechery *n.* disloyalty to a feudal lord 443, 1090, 2989; *colloc.:* see **trays(o)un** [OF *trecherie*]

trewe *a.* faithful 179, 1757; *superl.* **trewest** 374 [OE *trēowe*]

tristen *v.intr.* trust 253 [obsc. rel. to *traisten* < ON *treysta*, and to *trusten*]

tro *v.tr.* (1) trust 2863 (2) credit 2339* (*see n.*); *inf.* ~ 2863; *p.p.* **trod** 2339* [OEN *tróa* (= OWN *trúa*)]

trome *n.* band of men; *prep.sg.* ~ 8 [OE *truma*]

trone *n.* firmament (of Heaven); *prep.sg.* ~ 1317 [OF, AN *trone* 'id.']

trowe *v.tr.* believe; *inf.* ~ 1657; *3 pt.sg.* **trowede** 382. *See* **tro** [OE *trēowian* with stress-shift in diphth. of *trēowian* and red. of diphth. bef. *-w-*]

trusse *v.tr.* pack up 2018 [OF *trusser*]

tuenti *card.num.* twenty 259 [OE *twentig*]

tumberel *n.* porpoise; *obj.sg.* ~ 758 [OF *tomber* to fall + *-erel* after *makerel*; see n.]

tun *n.* town; *colloc. boþe in* ~ *and ek in felde* 2036, 2912; *obj.sg.* ~ 765; *prep.sg.* ~ 1002, 1632, 2036, 2264, **toun** 1751, **towne** 2912; *obj.pl.* **tunes** 397, 1445, 2278 [OE *tūn* 'enclosed area']

tunge *n.* tonge; *colloc. speken wit* ~ 369; *prep.sg.* ~ 369 [OE *tunge*]

turbut *n.* turbot; *obj.sg.* ~ 755 [OF *tourbout*, AN *turbut*, or MDu. *turbot*]

turnen *v.tr.* (1) lead 154 (2) ~ *to* cause to end in 1316; *3 pr.sg.subj.* **turne** 1316 [OF *turnian* or OF *turner*]

turues *n.* strips of peat; *obj.pl.* ~ 940 [OE *turf*]

twelf *card.num.* twelve 788; *pl.* twelue 1055*, 2456* [OE *twelf*]

two, to *card.num.* two 350; **to** 2665*; *on* ~, *a* ~: *see* **on** *prep.* [OE *twā*]

þan *dem.pron.:* see **þat** *dem.pron.* and **wiþ** *prep.*

þan, þanne *conj.*¹ when; **þan** 232, 354, 534*, 902, 979, 2714, *etc.,* **þanne** 260, 650, 1298, 1386, 1841, 2659, *etc.;* þanne ... þan(ne) when ... then 980, 1204 [OE *þanne, þænne*]

þan, þanne *conj.*² (1) *conjunctive particle (after comp.)* than: **þan** 793, 984, 1101, 1832, 1957, 2118, *etc.,* **þanne** 1655, 1934, 1940; than that 1673; than if: **þan** 945, **þanne** 1868 (2) *(after oþer)* than: **þan** 628 [as **þan, þanne** conj.]

þank *n.* thanks; *phr. God* ~ thanks to God 2006; *see* **conne**; *obj.sg.* ~ 160, 2561 [OE *þanc*]

þankede *3 pt.sg.tr.* gave thanks to 2190, 2844 [OE *þancian*]

þare: *see* **þer(e)**

þarne *v.tr.* (1) be deprived of 2493, 2836 (2) be without 1914; *inf.* ~ 2493, 2836;

3 pr.sg. **þarnes** 1914; (*p.p.* **þarned** (MS) 1688: *see* **þoled**) [ON *þarna* 'be without' < *þarfna*]

þat *dem.pron.* that 566, 802, 1274, 1801, 2114, 2393, *etc.*; *prep.sg.* **þan** 532. *See* **wiþ** *prep.* (2) [OE *þæt* neut.nom.sg.; *þam* dat.sg.m. and n.]

þat *dem.a.* that 287, 477, 555, 693*, 1000, 1269, *etc.*; ~ **ilke** + *n.* 1088, 1216, 2675, 2680, 2841, 2888; **þet (oþer day), þe (toþer sister), þat (oþer broþer), þe (oþer day)** the: *see* **oþer** *a.* (1) *nom.pl.* **þo** those 2045; *prep.pl.* **þo** 1919 [OE *þæt* neut.nom.sg.]

þat *conj.* that; *in* (1) *noun cl.* (*a*) *as subj.* 461, 692, *as obj.* 789, 1342, 2219, 2565, *etc.* (*b*) *in appos.* 642, 1306, *as obj. of prep.* ('the fact that') 2004 (*c*) *periphr. after* **it** 648 (2) *cl. of reason* 1119, 1705 (3) *cl. of purpose or desire* 272, 388, 520, 1237, 1766, *etc.* (4) *exclamatory cl.* 572, 1656, 1879, *etc.* (5) *cl. of cause* 867 (6) *cl. of result* 356, 709, 1194, *etc.*, *so* ~ 641, 1859; *foll. by subject* + *neg.* 57, 91, 250, 724, 768 (*see* 767–9 *n.*), 1022, 1858, 2160, 2273, 2283, 2289, 2381, 2447, 2687, 2900; *no expr. subj.* 1997, 2503, *no subj. or neg.* 65; *dep. on neg.* + *so* + *a. in main cl.*, *& foll. by subj.* + *neg.* 81, 100, 952, 1993; *no foll. neg.* 2688, 2699 (*see n.*) (7) *in cpd. conj. but* (*on*) ~ provided only that 388, 505; except only that 963; *hwil-gat* ~ 837, *til* ~ 623, 882, *yif* ~ 377, 733 [OE ðæt]

þat *indecl.rel.pron.* who, that, which; (1) *introd.adj.cl.* 45, 400, 1267, 1322, 2370, 2434, *etc.*; *with antec.* **þat** 2016, *om.* (< **þat ... þat**) that which 382, 396, 669, 1669, 2992, *etc.*; *with pers.pron. as antec.* *gen.sg.* **his ... þat** 728, 1258, *gen.pl.* **here ... þat** 2069; *dat.sg.* **þat** 2030 (2) *with foll. pers.pron. marking case*; *gen.sg.* ~ ... **his(e)** whose 28, ?1809; *obj.pl.* ~ ... **hem** whom 2967–8 [OE *þæt* neut.sg.nom.]

þaue, thaue *v.tr.* (1) concede 296 (2) stand firm under 2697; *inf.* **þaue** 2697; *3 pr.sg.subj.* **thaue** 296 [OE *þafian*]

þayn, thayn, theyn *n.* man ranking above ordinary freeman, usually with non-heritable land (*in Hav., solely in colloc. with* **dreng**); *nom.sg.* **þayn** 31*, 1328*; *obj.g.* **thein** 2467; *prep.sg.* **thayn** 2185; *obj.pl.* **theynes** 2195 [OE *þegn*]

þe *indecl.rel.* who; (*with antec. om., as*

indef.pron.) him who, *i.e.* anyone who 1915 [*þe* < *þe þe* 'he (etc.) who', < OE *sē* (etc.) *þe*]

þe *indecl.def.art.* the; *nom.sg.* ~ 106, 345, 960, *etc.*; *agglut. in* **þerl** 178 (*see* **erl**); (*after voiceless cons.*) **te** 87; *obj.sg.* **þe** 102, 426, 536, *etc.*; *dat.sg.* ~ 206; *prep.sg.* ~ 279, 402, 554, *etc.*; *nom.pl.* ~ 474, 538, 953, *etc.*; *obj.pl.* ~ 150, 543, *etc.*; *prep.pl.* ~ 75, 252, 390, *etc.* [OE nom.sg.m. *se* (def.art.), by anal. with forms with *þ*-]

þe *n.* thigh; *obj.sg.* ~ 1951; *prep.sg.* **þhe** 1985; *obj.pl.* **thes** 1904 [OE *þē(oh)*]

þede *n.* national community; *prep.sg.* ~ 105, 2891 [OE *þéod*]

þef *n.* thief; *nom.sg.* **þhef** 2290*; *obj.sg.* **þef** 2435; *voc.pl.* **þeues** 1781; *nom.pl.* **þeues** 1957; *obj.pl.* theues 41 [OE *þéof*]

þei *3 pers.pron.pl.* they; *nom.* ~ 414, 1021, 1196, 2615, 2662, 2671, 2768, **þey** 1006, 1038*, 2557, 2893; *gen.pl.* **þere** 1351. *See* **he** *3 pers.pron.pl.* [ON *þei-r*, gen.pl. *þeira* (? × ME *here* in *þere* 1351)]

þei, þey *conj.* although 1683*, 1967, **þey** 808, 993, 1166, 2502. *See* **þou** *conj.*, **thow** *adv.* [OE *þéah*]

þenke *v.tr.* (1) think 504, 507, 1870, 306 (*intr.*), 1074 (2) devise 312, 443 (3) regard as: *phr.* ~ *nowt of* attach no importance to 579; *2 pr.sg.* (*with agglut.* þu) **þenkeste** 579; *3 pr.sg.* **þenkes** 306; *3 pt.sg.* **þoucte** 504, 507, **þouthe** 443, **þowthe** 1870, **þouthte** 1074; *p.p.* **þouth** 312 [OE *þencan*]

þenne *adv.* thence 778, 1186, 1196 [obsc. < OE *þanon*]

þer(e), þare, þore *adv.* (1) there 234, 500, 523, 740, 866, 1005, 1198, 1947, 2238, *etc.*, **þare** 2740, 2830, **þor(e)** 742, 1015, 1034, 1045, 2013, 2336, 2481, 2511 (2) in that regard 1999 [OE *þær, þār(a)*]

þer(e) *conjunctive adv.* (1) (*relation*) where 142*, 158, 318, 330, 413, 449, 721, 1741, 2529, 2559 (2) (*reason*) since 804 [OE ðǽr]

þer-after *adv.* after that 135, 2943 [OE ðǽr æfter]

þer-bi *adv.* near the spot 2013 [OE ðǽrbi]

þer-biforn *adv.* before that time 656 [OE ðǽr beforan]

þer-fore *adv.* (1) in exchange for it 777 (2) because of that 2446, 2448 (3) for the sake of it 3000 [OE ðǽr + *fore*]

þer-fram, þer-fro *adv.* (1) away from them 55 (2) from (doing) it 2254 [OE *ðær* + (1) OE *fram*, (2) ON *frá*]

þer-inne, þer-hinne (1) *adv.* in it 535, 660, 752, 1322, 2180, 2933, *etc.*, in them 2367, **þer-hinne** in it 322; (*sep.*) **þer . . . inne** in it 852, in them 808 (2) *cpd.adv.* there inside, in there 589, 594, 1252, 1701, 1703, 1731, 2091 (*sep.*) **þer . . . inne** 595 [OE (1) *ðærin* (2) OE *ðær inne*]

þerl: *see* **þe** *def. art.*

þerne *n.* girl; *dat.sg.* ~ 298 [ON *þerna*]

þer-of *adv.* for it 315, 1627, to it 1096, about that 1069, regarding it 2410, 2527; **þer-offe** of it 1332, 1334, for it 466, regarding it 1378, 2339; about it 372 [OE (1) *þærof*, (2) *þærof* + ME adv. *-e*, after *-inne* etc.]

þer-on *adv.* on it 186, 189 [OE *ðæron*]

þer-tekene *adv.* in addition to that 2879 [OE *ðær tō eācan*]

þer-til *adv.* to it 396, in that direction 1042; **þor-til** to it 1444 [*þer, þor* + *til*]

þer-to *adv.* (1) to it 1050 (2) for that purpose 4 (3) in addition to that 2913 [OE *ðærto*]

þer-þoru *adv.* (1) through it 2828 (2) by that means 1099 [*þer* + *þoru*]

þer-(o)ute *cpd.adv.* there outside 1779, 1810 [OE *ðærūte*]

þer-wit(h) *adv.* (1) with it 1032, 1047, 1656 (2) by it 640*, 641* (3) by means of it: **þor-wit** 100 [OE *þærwið* × OE *þār*]

þer-yen *adv.* against that 2272 [OE *ðær ongēan*]

þet: *see* **þat** *dem.a.*

þeþen *adv.* from there 2499, 2630* [ON *þeðan*]

þeu *n.* serf; *phr.* ~ *and fre* serf and freeman 2206, *fre and þewe* 262 [OE *þēow*]

þewes *n.* moral qualities; *prep.pl.* ~ 282 [OE *þēaw*]

þey: *see* **þei** 3 *pron.pl.*

þey: *see* **þei** *conj.*

þicke *a.* massive 1649 [OE *þicce* a.]

þicke *adv.* in great number 1173 [OE *þicce* adv.]

þider *adv.* thither 851, 1013, 1014, 1022, 2279 [OE *þider*]

þi(n) *poss.a.* your (*sg.*); *nom.sg.* **þi** (*bef. cons.*) 1663, 2066, *etc.*; *obj.sg.* (*bef. cons.*) **þi** 1266, 1660, *etc.*; *prep.sg.* (*bef. cons.*) **þi** 2078, *etc.*, (*bef. h*) **þin** 1343; *dat.sg.* (*bef.*

cons.) **þi** 2085; *nom.pl.* (*bef. cons.*) **þine** 621, 2067, *etc.*; *prep.pl.* (*bef. cons.*) **þi** 1321, (*bef. vowel*) **þin** 1274, (*bef. h*) 2070; (*disj.*) *nom.sg.* **þin** 1331; *nom.pl.* **þine** 620 [OE *þin*, poss.a., gen.sg. of *þū*]

þigge *v.tr.* beg 1374 [OE *þicgan*]

þing *n.* (1) reason; *phr. for no* ~ on no account 1937 (2) matter 1403 (3) deed ?66 (*see n.*) (4) creature 2866 (5) article (of food and drink): *see* **kilþing** and 1737 *n.*: (6) possessions 1141, 2022 (7) something valued; *phr. of alle* ~ *e* above everything 71; *obj.sg.* **þing** 1403; *prep.sg.* ~ 1937; *obj.pl.* ~ 2022, **þinge** 1141; *prep.pl.* **þinge** 71 [OE *þing*]

þinke *v.impers.*; seem 197, 1287, 1709, 2170, ?2136; *phr. to gode* ~ seem advantageous 197; *god* ~ seem fit 256; 3 *pr.sg.* **þinkes** 2170; 3 *pt.sg.* **þouthe** 1287, 1709, **þoucte** 197, 256, **þouth** 2136 [OE *þyncan*]

þis *dem.pron.* this; *nom.sg.* ~ 1260, 1313, 2115, 2483; *red. of* ~ **is** 607 [OE *þis* nom. acc.sg.neut.]

þis *dem.a.* this; *nom.sg.* ~ 2209, 2884, *etc.*; *obj.sg.* ~ 260, 1338, 1736, *etc.*; *prep.sg.* ~ 647, 1074, 2391, *etc.*; *nom.pl.* ~ 1146, **þise** 2482; *obj.pl.* **þise** 1884 [OE *þis* nom. acc.sg.neut.]

þisternisse *n.* darkness; *nom.sg.* ~ 2192 [OE *þēosternes*]

þo *dem.a.pl.* those; *nom.* 2045; *prep.* 1919 [OE *þā* nom. acc.pl. of *þæt*]

þo *conj.* when 1021 [OE *ðā*]

þo *adv.* then 291, 540, 931, 1700, 1861, 2521, *etc.* [OE *ðā*]

þoled *p.p.* endured 1688* [OE *þolian*]

þore: *see* **þer(e)**

þorn(e)bake *n.* skate; *obj.sg.* ~ 760, 833 [?ME *þorn* + *bak*]

þor-til: *see* **þer-til**

þoru, þorw, þoruth, þuruth *prep.* piercing 1983, 2409, 2673; throughout 1066; (*as agent*) by means of 367, 1074, 2675, 2787, 2872; by the agency of 628, at the hands of 632; *phr.* ~ *and* ~ right through 775 [OE *þurh*]

[þoru-go] *sep.v.tr.*; *p.p.* **gon . . . þoru** traversed 849 [OE *þurhgān*]

þoruth: *see* **þoru**

þoruthlike *adv.* searchingly 681 [ME *þor(u)ȝ* + *-like* adv. suff. < OE *-līce*]

þorw-fare *sep.cpd.tr.*; *ger.inf.* **to faren**
þorw 264 [OE *þurhfaran*]

þor-wit: *see* þer-wit(h)

þou, þow *conj.* though 124, 299, 2178,
2338; even if 1086, if 1259; *see after*
þouth, þei *conj.* [ON *þóh (> þó)]

þou, þu *2 sg.pers.pron.* you; þou 560, 846,
agglut. -(*t*)*ow*, -*te*: **shaltow** 1323, 1801,
wiltu 682, 906, **wilte** 528, 1136,
þenkeste 579; *obj.* þe 646, 1267, *etc.*;
obj.gen. þin 1129, 1790 (*see* **maugre**);
dat. þe 855, 1227, *etc.*; *prep.* þe 628,
1345, *etc.* [OE *þū*]

þousind, thousande *card.num.* (*n. and a.*)
thousand 127, 2682, **thousand** 2356,
2361, 2372, **þhousend** 1974 [OE
þūsand, þūsend]

þouth *n.* (1) mind 122, 839, 1191 (*see*
falle) (2) what is in one's mind 2170 (3)
anxiety 2054 (4) intention 2784; *nom.sg.*
~ 839; *obj.sg.* ~ 2054, 2170; *prep.sg.* ~
122, 1191 [OE *þoht < þōht*]

thow *adv.* nevertheless 1670. See þou
conj., þei *conj.* [As for þou conj.]

þral *n.* serf 527, 685, 1098, 2565, 2590;
wretch 1159, 1409; *obj.sg.* ~ 2565, *dat.sg.*
~ 1409, *obj.pl.* (?) 2590 [OE *þrǣl < ON
þrǽll*]

þrawe *n.* (1) hour (as point of time) 1216
(2) space of time 276; *nom.sg.* ~ 1216;
prep.sg. ~ 276 [OE *þrāg*]

þre *card.num.* three 385, 2067, 2213; *hem* ~
three of them 1808, 1970; *his* ~ three
such as him 1894 (*see n.*) [OE *þrēo*]

þredde: *see* þridde

þrette *3 pt.sg.intr.* uttered menaces 1164
[OE *þrēatian*]

þridde, þredde *ord.num.* third 868, 2634
[OE *þridda*]

þrie *adv.* obscure (*see n.*): 731 [?OE *ðriga*
'three times']

þrinne *card.num.* three 717, 762, 1978,
2092 [LOE *þrinna < ON þrinn-r*]

þriste(n) *v.tr.* (1) press 639; cram 2020 (2)
poke 1153; *p.p.* þrist 639 [ON *þrýsta*]

þriue *v.intr.* (1) make one's fortune 514
(2) turn out well 280 [ON *þrífa*]

þrotes *n.* throats; *obj.pl.* ~ 471, 1414 [OE
þrote]

þu: *see* þou *pron.*

þurte *3 pt.sg.intr.* had occasion to 10 [OE
þorfte × þurfon pr. pl.]

þuruth: *see* þoru

þus *adv.* in such fashion 1780, 1953, 2049,
2706 [OE *ðus*]

þus-gate *adv.* in this fashion 786, 2420,
2587 [ME *þus* + *gate* n. way]

ueneysun *n.* venison 1727 [OF *veneisun*]

vmbe *prep.* around; *adv.phr.* ~ **stounde**
from time to time 2298* [ON *um stund*
'for a time' × ON *umb (> um)*]

umbistode *3 pt.tr.* were besetting 1876
[ME cpd. verb-pref. *umbe-* (*um* < ON
um(b)), after MDu. *ombe-* > *omme-* in
e.g. *ommestaen* 'surround'; *bi-* subst. for
be-; OE *standan*]

vmbiyeden *3 pt.pl.tr.* thronged round
1843* [as prec.; cf. MDu. *ommegaen*
'surround'; OE *ymbegān*]

vnbliþe *a.* unhappy 141 [OE *unblīþe*]

unbounden *3 pt.pl.tr.* untied 602 [OE
unbindan]

vncloþede *3 pt.pl.tr.* undressed 660 [ME
un- + *cloþes* n.]

under *prep.* under 1918 (*see* **sette** *phr.*)
phr. (*token*) ~ *fote* (set out to traverse)
on foot 1200; ~ *God* of all mankind 423,
973; ~ *hond* under one's rule 2296 (*see*
haue *phr.*); ~ *mone* on earth 373, 1157,
2792 [OE *under*]

underfong *3 pt.sg.tr.* realized 115 [OE
underfōn]

understonde *v.tr.* receive 2815, (into
one's house) 1761; accept (in wedlock)
1160; *2 pr.sg.subj.* ~ 1160; *3 pt.sg.* **understod** 1761 [OE *understandan*]

undertake *v.tr.* (1) accept (in wardship)
377 (2) set out on 665; *3 pt.sg.* **undertok**
665, *subj.* ~**e** 377 [*under* + *take*]

undo *v.tr.* (1) open (the door) 1772, 1773
(2) cut through 2740; *inf.* (*pass.*) ~ 2740;
imper.sg. ~ 1772, 1773 [OE *on-, undōn*]

unker *pers. pron.* (*gen.dual*) of you two;
eþer ~ 1883 [OE *uncer*, gen. of *wit* 'we
two', instead of *incer* gen. of *git* 'you
two']

‡vnkeueleden *3 pt.pl.tr.* ungagged 602
[*un-* + ON *kefla*]

unkyndelike *adv.* (of marriage) beneath
one's station 1251 [OE *ungecyndelīce*]

vnornelike *adv.* derogatorily 1942 [OE
unornlīc a.]

unride *a.* (1) painful 1982, 1986, 2674 (2)
massive 1796 (3) inelegant 965 (4)

numerous 2948; *superl.* **vnrideste** 1986
[OE *ungerȳde*]
vnrith *n.* injustice; *prep.sg.* ~ 1370 [OE
unriht]
until *prep.* (*motion*) to 2914, 2931, **huntil***
2841. *Cf.* **intil** [ON *und* (in *undz* < *und*
+ *es*) 'as far as' + *til*]
vnto, unto *prep.* (1) (*usually motion*) to
1420, 1686, 1799, 1935, 2087, 2382, 2475,
2647, 2827, 2953, *etc.* (2) till 1434 [on
until, with synon. *to* subst. for *til*]
unwraste *a.* dilapidated 548; in poor
condition 2822 [OE *unwrǣst*]
uoyz *n.* voice; *obj.sg.* ~ 1265 [OF *voiz*]
up *adv.* (1) aloft (i.e. on a higher floor)
1068, 2074 (2) ashore: *see* **up-come**; *phr.*
~ *and down* everywhere 1631; ~ *o londe*
in the country districts 764. *See* **up-**
[OE *yp(p)*]
[**up-bere**] *quasi-sep.v.tr.*; *3 pt.sg.* **bar up**
lifted up 896 [ME *up-* + *bere*]
[**up-breke**] *quasi-sep.v.tr.*; *3 pt.pl.* **broken
up** forced open 1961 [ME *up-* +
breken; cf. MDu. *opbreken*]
[**up-come**] *sep.v.intr.* (1) grow up: *p.p.* **up
... cumen** 1436-7 (2) land: *p.p.* **comen
up** 2541 [LOE *ūpcuman*]
[**up-drawe**] *sep.v.tr.* pull up; *3 pt.sg.* **up-
drow** 933, **drou up** 737 [Cf. MDu.
opdragen, MLG *updragen*, MSw.
updragha]
[**up-heue**] *sep.v.tr.* raise; *3 pt.sg.* **hof up**
2751 [OE *ūphebban*]
[***up-kippe**] *quasi-sep.v.tr.*; *3 pt.sg.* **kipte
up** quickly lifted 1051, snatched up 2639
[ON *kippa upp*; cf. **ut-kippen**]
[**up-lepe**] *sep.v.intr.* jump up; *inf.* **up ...
lepe** 2193; *3 pt.sg.* **lep up** 1943, [OE
ūphlēapan; cf. MDu. *oploopen* 'jump up']
[**up-lifte**] *quasi-sep.v.tr.* lift up; *3 pt.sg.*
lifte up 1807 [cf. MSw. *uplyfta*, MDa.
oplyfte]
upo: *see* **upon**
upon *cpd.prep.* (1) *loc.*: on 47, 736, 2062,
2387, 2641, 2822; on top of 1292; with
one's hand on 1079 (2) *manner*: by way
of 468 (3) *motion*: on to 1776, 2635 (4) *distrib.*: so as to make 893 (5) *dir.*: against
65, **upo** 2597 [OE *ūp* adv. + *on* prep.;
cf. ON *upp á*, with stress on the prep.]
[**up-rise**] *quasi-sep.v.intr.* get up; *imper.sg.*
ris up 585, 598* [see *OED* uprise v.; cf.
OE *ūp-arisan*, MDu. *oprisen*, MLG
uprisen]

[**up-sitte**] *sep.v.intr.* get into sitting position (from recumbent one); *3 pt.sg.* **sat
... up** 634 [OE *ūpsittan*; cf. MDu.
opsitten]
[**up-stirte**] *quasi-sep.v.intr.* jump up; *3
pt.sg.* **stirt up** 398, 813, 1148, 1775, 2737,
vp ... stirte 567, *pl.* **stirten up** 1965,
stirten ... up 600, **stirt up** 2257 [ME
up + *stirte* < OE *styrtan*]
ure *poss.a.* our; *nom.sg.* 607, 1225, 1885,
hure 843; *obj.sg.* **vre** 2294; *prep.sg.* **vre**
597, **hure** 338; *nom.pl.* **hure** 1232; *obj.pl.*
ure 2591 [OE *ūre*, gen.pl. of *wē*]
ure *partitive gen.*: *see* **we**
ut *adv.* out 2729. *See* **ut of**, *and cpds. in* **ut-**
[OE *ūt*]
ut-bede *sep.v.tr.* call out for military service; *phr. ferd* ~ 2549*. *See* **bede** *v.*
[calque on ON *bjóða út*]
[**ut-brayde**] *quasi-sep.v.tr.* pull out (a
sword); *3 pt.sg.* **brayd ut** 1826 [ME *out*
+ *brayde*]
[**ut-drawe**] *sep.v.tr.* pull out; *3 pt.sg.* **vt-
drow** 1795, 2633, **drow ut** 2734; *3 pt.pl.*
ut-drowen 2660, **drowen ut** 1838; *p.p.*
ut-drawe(n) 1803, 2632 [LOE *ūt-
dragan*, Chron. s.a. 1083]
[**ut-driue**] *sep.v.tr.* drive out; *3 pt.pl.*
driue ... ut 1967 [OE *ūtdrīfan*; cf. *ūt-
drǣf(ere)*]
uten *a.* used up 843 (*see n.*) [ad. ON *úti* (of
time) 'at an end' or MDu. *ute* 'used up']
uten-laddes *n.* men brought from abroad:
colloc. ~ *here* 2154, 2581; *adj.gen.pl.* ~
2154, 2581. *See* **here** *n.*, **ladde**, **vt-lede**
[cf. OE *ūt-lǣdan* sep.v.]
[***ut-kippe**] *quasi-sep.v.tr.* pull out; *3 pt.sg.*
kipt ut 2408 [cf. MDu. *utekippen*]
vtlawes *n.* outlaws; *obj.pl.* ~ 41 [LOE
ūtlaga ad. ON *útlagi*]
vt-lede *sep.v.tr.* lead to war; *inf.* 89, **leden
uth** 346, 379. *See* **uten-laddes** [OE *ūt-
lǣdan*]
ut of *cpd.prep.* (1) (*dir.*) from (a confining
space) 1257, 1814, 1947, 1968, (a habitat)
1179, 1277, 2870, (a physical condition)
so as to be free from 155 (2) (*position*)
outside 2122 [OE *ūt* adv. + *of* prep.
'from', in sequence *ut of* (see
Bosworth–Toller *ūt*)]
utrage *n.* intolerable conduct; *prep.sg.* ~
2838 [OF *outrage* (< *oltrage* < **ultra-
gium* f. on L *ultra* 'beyond'), reinterpreted as ME *out-* + *rage*]

[†**ut-sprede**] *quasi-sep.v.intr.* open out; *p.p.* **sprad ut** 2921 [ME *out-* + *spreden*; see *OED* out-spread v., and cf. MDu. *utespreiden*]

[†**ut-þriste**] *quasi-sep.v.tr.* poke out; *inf.* **þrist ut** 2726 [ME *out-* + ON *þrysta*; see *OED* out-thrust v.]

Note. Words containing initial þ ('wyn') are so few that they are entered as if spelt with *w*.

wa: *see* **wo**
wade *v.intr.* pass 2646 [OE *wadan*]
wagge *v.tr.* brandish 89 [ideo. f. on OE *wagian*]
waiten *v.intr.* (1) *intr.* lie in wait 512, 2071 (2) *tr.* guard 1755; *inf.* ~ 512, 1755 (*pass.*), **wayte** 2071 [ONF *waitier* guard, watch, lie in wait for]
waken *v.intr.* (1) stay up at night 3000 (2) wake up 2094 (3) *tr.* watch over 631; *inf.* ~ 631; *3 pt.sg.* **wok** 2094; *p.p.* **waked** 3000 [(1) OE *wacian* wk. (2) OE *wæcnan* str. and *wæcnian* wk. (3) OE *wacian* × *weccan* caus. wk.]
wakne *v.intr.* wake up 2165 [OE *wæcnan* str. + *wæcnian* wk.]
wantede *3 pt.sg.intr.* was lacking 713, 1244 [ON *wanta* > *vanta*]
war *a.* aware; *phr.* ben ~ 789, ben ~ of notice 2140 [OE *wær*]
warant *n.* protector 2068 [ONF *warant* bes. OF *garant*]
ware *n.* (collective) merchandise; *obj.* ~ 1630; *prep.* ~ 52, 766 [OE *waru* (coll.)]
warie *v.tr.* curse; *3 pr.sg.subj.* ~ 433; *p.p.* **waried** 434 [OE *wærgan*]
warne *v.tr.* warn 2835 [OE *warnian*]
warp *3 pt.sg.tr.* cast 1062 [OE *weorþan*]
was: *see* **be(n)**
washen *v.tr.* wash 1234 [OE *wæscan*, *wascan*]
wastel *n.* cake; *obj.sg.* 879; *obj.pl.* **wastels** 780 [OF (NE) *wastel*, bes. OF *g(u)astel*]
wat: *see* **quath**
water *n.* water; *colloc. wind and* ~ air and water (as elements) 1361; *nom.sg.* ~ 1852, 2344; *obj.sg.* ~ 913, 933, 938, 1235, 1361 [OE *wæter*]
wawe, wowe *n.* wall; *prep.sg.* **wawe** 474, 2471, **wowe** 1964, 2079 [OE *wāg*]
waxe *v.intr.* (1) grow (physically) 792 (2)

develop into 281 (3) become 302; *3 pt.sg.* **wex** 281; *p.p.* **waxen** 302, 792 [OE *wæxan*]
wayke *a.pl.* puny; *colloc. stronge and* ~ 1013 [ON *weik-r* > *veik-r*]
we *1 pers.pron.pl.* we 328, 457, 620, 1059, 1890, 2477; *obj.* **us** 1773, 2083, 2296, 2588; *partitive gen.* (**boþen**) **ure** of us (both) 698; 2592 (*twice*); *dat.* **us** 22, 455, 459, 461, 2591; *prep.* **us** 2803, **vs** 103. *See* **ure** *poss.a.* [OE *wē*]
wedde *v.tr.* marry; *inf.* ~ 1114; *p.p.* **wedded** 2771, **weddeth** 1128 [OE *weddian*]
wede *n.coll.* (1) clothing 323, 862 (2) armour 94; *obj.* ~ 94, 862; *prep.* ~ 323 [OE *wǣd* + *wǣde* < coll. *gewǣde*]
wede *v.intr.* run amok 2388, 2642. *See* **wod** [OE *wēdan* 'go mad; rage']
wei *n.* (1) road 953 (2) route 773 (*see* **rith(e)** *a.*); *obj.sg.* ~ 773; *prep.sg.* **weie** 953 [OE *weg*]
weilawei *interj.* alas! 462, 571 [OE *wei lā wei* < *wā lā wā* × ON *wei* > *vei*]
wel *n.* well-being; *phr. for* ~ *ne for wo* neither in prosperity nor in adversity 2778 [OE *wela*]
wel, wol *adv.* (1) handsomely 2864 (*see* **do(n)**), 2939, liberally 646, 801, 930, 1395 (2) with due care 190, 209, 2153, 2219, 2299, scrupulously 29, 2527 (3) in due form 218, 1382, 2320, (*phr.*) *faire and* ~ 224, 1176, 1433; very properly 183 (4) happily 2984 (*see* **stonden**), fortunate 1694 (*see* **be(n)**), in favour 2879 (*see* **be(n)**) (5) profitably 818, (*colloc.*) *wol* ~ very profitably 776, to good purpose 908 (6) with ample reason 2762 (7) adequately 2356, 2572, thoroughly 977, 2621, 2993, normally 2042, 2075 (8) without difficulty 2081 (9) successfully 1382 (10) competently 916, 920 (11) confidently 2340, 2483 (12) fully 1070, 1290, 1403, 2076, 2208, amply 757, 2880, 2908 (13) beyond a doubt 119, 1324, 1385, 2709, 2716 (14) (*intens.*) very much: (*colloc.*) ~ *wilen* 2227, (*with num.*) fully 891, 1748 (15) (*colloc.*) *ful* ~ very well 29, 916, 949, 1188, 2060, 2174, *etc.*; *comp.* **betere** better 109, 697 (*see* **be(n)**), 1759; *superl.* **best** best 376, most 354* [OE *wel*, *bet(e)ra*, a., *betst*]
welde *v.tr.* (1) hold sway over 129, 1360 (2)

have at one's disposal 2035 (3) *refl.* be responsible for oneself 175 (4) handle: (*colloc.*) *wepne* ~ 1437; *inf.* ~ 129, 175, 1437, 2035; *3 pr.sg.* **weldes** 1360 [OE *weldan* v. wk. I]

welkome *interj.* welcome 1214, 1215 [OE *wilcuma* n. 'someone whose arrival gives pleasure' > ME *wel-* 'well' + *kome* inf. or imper. See *OED welcome* sb.¹]

welle *n.* (1) spring 1852 (2) well 933; *prep.sg.* ~ 933, 1852 [OE *wella* n. and *welle* n.]

wel-ner *adv.* very nearly 2413 [ME *wel* adv. + ON *nær* comp. 'nearer' > positive 'near']

wende *v.tr.* (1) turn right round 2139*, 2451, 2824 (2) *intr.* be alienated 1706 (3) go 1345, 1347, 1441, 2630; *inf.* ~ 1347, 1706, 2630; *2 pr.pl.subj.* ~ 1441; *3 pr.pl.subj.* **wenden** 1345; *p.p.* **went** 2139*, 2451, 2824. *See* **awey-go** [OE *wendan*]

wene *v.tr.* (1) think 524, 599, 656, 841, 1092, 1261 (2) hope 1198, 2548 (3) intend 1804; *1 pr.sg.* **wene** 656, 841, 1261; *2 pr.sg.* **wenes** 599, (*agglut.*) **wenestu** 1788; *3 pt.sg.* **wende** 524, 1092, 1804, *pl.* **wenden** 1198, 2548 [OE *wēnan*]

wepen *3 pt.pl.intr.* wept 152, 401 [OE *wēpan*]

wepne *n.* weapon; *obj.sg.* ~ 89; *obj.pl.* ~ 1437, 2360; *prep.pl.* ~ 93, 275 [OE *wǣpn*, pl. *wǣpn(u)*]

werd, worde *n.* world; *nom.sg.* **werd** 2969; *obj.sg.* ~ 1291; *prep.sg.* ~ 2242, 2336, 2793, **worde** 1350 [OE *weorold*, *woruld*]

were *v.tr.* defend 2153, 2299 [OE *werian*]

werk *n.* (1) deed 34 (2) labour 867; *prep.sg.* ~ 867; *prep.pl.* **werkes** 34 [OE *werc*]

werwed, wirwed *p.p.tr.* throttled 1916, 1922 [OE *wyrgan*]

werne *v.tr.* refuse 927, 1346; *inf.* ~ 1346; *3 pr.sg.subj.* ~ 927 [OE *wernan*]

werse *a.comp.* more wicked 1101, 1135 [ON *wersi* > ON *verri*]

wesseyl *n.* a toast (in liquor) 1247 (*see* **lede(n)**) [ME *wes heil* 'good luck!' < ON *wes heill* > *ves heill*]

wesseylen, wosseylen *v.intr.* quaff toasts; *3 pr.pl.* **wesseylen** 2099; *p.p.* **wosseyled** 1738 [*wesseyl* n.]

weþer: *see* **hweþer**

wicke, wike, wikke *a.* (1) evil 66 (*see n.*) 269, 689, 693, 2104, 2105 (2) wicked 319, 425, 666, 2402 (3) disreputable 1159 (4) malicious 1193 (5) disastrous 1407 (6) shabby 966, 2459, 2826 [ME *wikke* a., perh. < OE *wiccig* (*Pet. Chron. wicci*), f. on *wicc-* in *wicca* 'witch']

wicth: *see* **with** *a.*¹

wide *a.* (1) ample 1958 (2) gaping 1846 [OE *wīde*]

wide *adv.* (1) far and wide 960 (2) to its full extent 1797 [OE *wīde*]

wider *adv.*; *interr.* whither? 1140 [OE *hwider*]

wif *n.* (1) woman 1714, 2856 (2) wife 348, 699, 2861, 2865, married woman 2; *obj.sg.* ~ 1714; *poss.sg.* **wiues** 699; *prep.sg.* **wif** 348, 2861, **wiue** 2865; *nom.pl.* **wiues** 2; *prep.pl.* **wiues** 2856 [OE *wīf*]

with *n.*: *see* **nouth** *adv.*

wik(k)e: *see* **wicke**

wil *a.* at a loss 864, ~ *of* altogether at sea regarding 1043 [ON *vill-r* 'having lost one's way']

wil *conj.*: *see* **hwil**

wilde *a.* unfrequented 268 [OE *wilde*]

wile *v.tr., absol., etc.* (1) want 456, 906, 1136, 2388, 2642, *etc.*, ask for 922 (2) wish 269, 367, 520, 824, 1077, 1298, 1827 (? *see n.*), *etc.* (*pret.subj.*) should like 799, 855, 2995; (3) be willing 100, 317, 525, 867, 998, 1732 (4) intend 469, 1806, be about to (as intention) 3 (5) (*auxil. of fut.*) will 485, 536, 695, 806, 1221, *etc.* (6) (*auxil. of mood*) would 575, 1421, 2438, 2786; *colloc.* ~ *wel* be strongly disposed to 2227; *1 pr.sg.* **wile** 3, 15, 485, 581, 922, 1682, *etc.*, **wille** 388, **wole** 494, 1151; *2 pr.sg.* **wilt** 1120, 1221, (*agglut.*) **wiltu** 682, 906, **wilte** 528, 1136; *3 pr.sg.* **wile** 4, 352, 649; *1 pr.pl.* **wile** 1237; *2 pr.pl.* **wilen** 921, 2818; *3 pr.pl.* ~ 1346; *2 pr.sg.subj.* **wile** 2863; *3 pt.sg.* **wolde** 100, 317, 525, *etc.*, *pl.* **wolden** 1187, 2167, **wolde** 269, 1806, 1962; *1 pt.sg.subj.* **wolde** 799, 855, 1937, *pl.* **wolden** 456 [OE *willan*]

wille *n.* (1) wish(es) 70, 85, 525, 528 (*see* **do(n)**), 1675 (2) what one pleases 954, 2424 (*see* **do(n)** *phr.*); *phr. at his* ~ at his pleasure 271; *bi hire* ~ in accordance with her wish 85, if she could have had her way 1131; *colloc.* god ~ goodwill 601; *Godes* ~ God's will 1167; *nom.sg.* ~

1167; *obj.sg.* ~ 525, 528, 601, 954, 1675, 2424; *prep.sg.* ~ 85, 271, 1131 [OE *willa*]

wimman, wymman *n.* woman; *nom.sg.* **wimman** 1721, 2714, **wman** 174, 281; *obj.sg.* **wimman** 1140, 1169; *prep.sg.* ~ 1745, **wymman** 1157 [OE *wifman*]

win, wyn *n.* wine; *nom.sg.* **win** 1730; *prep.sg.* **wyn** 2342 [OE *win*]

wind *n.* wind; *nom.sg.* ~ 724; *obj.sg.* ~ 1361 [OE *wind*]

winde *v.tr.* wrap; *inf.* ~ 221; *p.p.* **wnden** 546 [OE *windan*]

winne *n.* happiness; *(adv.) with (muchel)* ~ (very) happily 661, 2966 [OE *wynn*]

winne *v.tr.* (1) gain possession of 1323 (2) earn 853 [OE *winnan*]

winter *n.pl.* years 192, 259, 417, 788, 2239 [OE *winter*]

wirchen *v.tr.* (1) bring about 510, 1353, inflict on 2454; *phr.* see **wo** *n.* and *a.* (2) *intr.* act 2811; *p.p.* **wrouth** 1353, **wrowht** 2454, **wrouht** 2811 [OE *wyrcan*]

wis *a.* sagacious 180, 282, 288, 1422, 1636 [OE *wis*]

wise *n.* way; *on ilke* ~ in every conceivable way 1862; *on his* ~ in the form that he prescribed 204; *prep.sg.* ~ 204, 1714, 1862 [OE *wise*]

wislike *adv.* undoubtedly 274 [OE *wislice*]

wisse *v.tr.* guide; *phr.* ~ *and rede* 104, ~ *and raþe* 361* [OE *wissian*]

wissing *n.* guidance; *prep.sg.* ~ 2903 [on *wisse* v.]

wite *v.tr.* guard 560, protect 405; *imper.sg.* ~ 560; *3 pr.sg.subj.* ~ 405 [OE *witan* + *witian* (in *bewitian*)]

wite(n) *v.* know; *phr. see* **Goddot(h)**; *God it woth* God is my witness 2528, *God it wite* may God be my witness 517, *þat wite þw* may thou be my witness 1317 *(see 1316 n.)*; *inf.* **witen** 2787, **wite** 367, 626, 2202; *1 pr.sg.* **woth** 119, 213, 654; *2 pr.sg.* **wost** 527, 583, 1385, 2709; *3 pr.sg.* **woth** 2528; *2 pr.pl.* **wite** 2809; *2 pr.sg.subj.* **wite** 1317; *3 pr.sg.subj.* **wite** 517, 695; *3 pt.sg.* **wiste** 223, 358, 1281, *pl.* **wisten** 1184, 1185, 1188, 1201 [OE *witan*]

witerlike *adv.* undoubtedly 672 [ON *vitrliga* × ME -*like*]

with, wicth *a.*[1] (1) doughty 1652, 1693, 2044, 2348 (2) strong 1009, 1065, **wicth** 344; *superl.* **wicteste** doughtiest 9 [obsc.]

with *a.*[2] white 48, 1145, **hwit** 1730 [OE *hwit*]

wiþ, with, wit* *prep.* (1) sitting next to: *(ete)* ~ 1662, 1719 (2) *(with dem., as conj.)* ~ *þan* provided that 532; ~ *þat* on condition that 1221, in order that 19 (3) to: *(speke)* ~ 326, 679, 1628, 2389 (4) *(of behaviour towards)* to 1871, 2412, 2706; at 2166 (5) in regard to 93, 903 (6) in someone's estimation 2879, 2883 (7) on someone's side 62, 2309 *(see* **halde** *phr.)* (8) along with 998*, 1307, 1441, 1685, 1769, 2065, 2357, *etc.* (9) having 701, 780, 1958, bearing 52, 766, wearing 429, equipped with 267, 1749, 1770, 2573 (11) *(with n.; as adv. of manner)* with 35, 661, 995, 1090, 1370, 1762, 2088, 2656, *etc.* (12) *(instr.)* by means of 113, 333, 433, 677, 1274, 1413, 1677, 1822, 1918, *etc.*, *wiþe* 1052 (13) *(agency)* by 144, 2325, 2332, 2441, 2490, 2667 [OE *wiþ*; and cf. **in, inne** adv. and **onne** prep.]

withal *adv.* as well 755. *See* **forthwithal** [modif. of EME *mid alle* < OE *mid ealle*, *mid eallum*]

with-drow, piþdrow *3 pt.sg.tr.* held back 498; *refl.* drew back 502 [*wiþ* + *drawe*]

with-held *3 pt.sg.tr.* retained 821, 2357, 2363 [*wiþ* + *holde*]

with-inne *prep.* (1) into 2537 (2) *(temp.)* within 1334 [OE *wiþinnan*]

withsitten *v.tr.* oppose 1684 [*wiþ* + *sitten*]

wit(h)uten *prep.* (1) except for 425* (2) lacking 2861 (3) *(with n., as neg.adv.) phr.:* ~ *hende* eternally 247, ~*faile* unfailingly 179, ~*leye* it is true to say 2118 [OE *wiþūtan*]

wlf *n.* wolf; *nom.sg.* ~ 574 [OE *wulf*]

wluine *n.* she-wolf; *nom.sg.* ~ 574 [MDu. *wolvinne* (= OE *wylfen*)]

wman: *see* **wimman**

wo, wa *n.* (1) misery 541 (2) misfortune: *phr.* ~ *wurþe (impers.)* 2222 (3) harm 1745: *phr. wirchen* ~ wreak harm 510 (*cf.* **wo** *a. phr.*) (4) physical injuries 2076 (5) plaint 465 [OE *wā*]

wo *a.* very miserable: *phr. do ful* ~ (+ dat.) 612, 2590, *ful* ~ *wirche* 2454 give (someone) hell [< impers. use of OE *wā* n.]

wo *adv.:* *see* **be(n)**

wod *a.* (1) in a frenzy 508, 1778, 1897, 2610 (2) frenziedly eager: *phr. to fyht ~ e* 2362 (3) enraged 1849; *pl.* **wode** 1897, 2362, 2610 [OE *wōd*]

wodes *n.obj.pl.* woods 268; *colloc. ~ and wonges* 397, 1445, *~ and feldes* 1361 [OE *wuda* acc.pl.]

wok: *see* **waken**

wol: *see* **wel**

wold 1933; *obscure (see n.)*

wolde: *see* **wile**

wolle *n.* wool; *prep.sg. ~* 701 [OE *wull*]

wombes *n.* bellies; *obj.pl. ~* 1912 [OE *wamb*]

wom-so: *see* **hwo-so**

won *n.* (1) opinion: *bi mine wone* in my judgement 1973, I should think 1712 (2) abundance: *adverbial phr. ful god won* in great number 1025, 1838, in abundance 2326, thick and fast 1908, 2730, with great force 1792, as hard as they could go 2618; *prep.sg.* **wone** 1712, 1973 [ON *wān > ván*]

wone *v.intr.* dwell; *3 pr.sg.* **woneth** 105; *3 pr.sg.subj.* **wone** 247, *3 pr.pl.* **wone** 1326 [OE *wunian*]

wone *a.* wont 2152, 2298 [OE *gewuna*]

wonges *n.* pieces of unenclosed land in an open-field system; *obj.pl. ~* 397, 1445; *phr.: see* **wodes** [OE *wang*]

word *n.* (1) speech 107 (2) report 960 (3) bidding *(see* **sende**) 2393 (4) word 2011; *nom.sg. ~* 960; *obj.sg. ~* 2011, 2393; *prep.sg. ~* 107 [OE *word*]

wore: *see* **be(n)**

worth *n.* amount; *obj.sg. ~* 1333 [OE *weorþ* n.]

worth *a.* of the value of 967, 1634 [OE *weorþ* a.]

worþe, wurþe, wrþe *v.intr.* (1) come about 2222 *(see* **wo** *n.)* (2) *(as pass.auxil.)* be 434, 1103, 2874; *3 pr.sg.subj.* **worþe** 1103, 2874, **wrþe** 434, **wurþe** 2222 [OE *weorþan*]

wo-so: *see* **hwo-so**

wosseyled: *see* **wesseylen**

w(o)unde *n.* wound; *obj.sg.* **wunde** 1981; *prep.sg.* **wounde** 1979; *nom.pl.* **wundes** 2057; *obj.pl.* **wundes** 1846, 1899, 1987, **woundes** 1978, 2039 [OE *wund*]

woundede *3 pt.sg.tr.* wounded 2743; *pl.* **woundeden** 2430 [OE *wundian*]

wrastling *vbl.n.* wrestling; *obj.sg. ~* 2325 [on *wrastle* v. < OE *wrǣstlian*]

wrathe *n.* (1) anger 2720 (2) friction 2978; *nom.sg. ~* 2978; *obj.sg. ~* 2720 [OE *wrǣðð̆u*]

wreieres *n.* persons who bring accusations 39; *phr.: ~ and* **wrobberes** *(see Appendix A)* 39 [OE *wrēgere*, f. on *wrēgan* 'accuse']

wreken *v.tr.* avenge; *inf.* **wreken** 327; *imper.sg.* **wreke** 1364; *3 pr.sg.subj.* **wreke** 544; *p.p.* **wreken** 2369, 2993, **wreke** 1885, 2850 [OE *wrecan*]

wringen *v.tr.* (1) twist (to squeeze water out of) 1234 (2) (of hands) twist and press together in distress 152; *inf. ~* 1234; *3 pt.pl.* **wrungen** 152 [OE *wringan*]

wringing *vbl.n.* (of hands) convulsive twisting and pressing together in distress 235 [on ME *wringen*]

writ *n.* (1) written record 2487 (2) summons to attend court or official assembly 136, 150, 2276; *nom.sg. ~* 2487; *obj.pl.* **writes** 136, 150, 2276 [OE *writ*]

writen *p.p.tr.* inscribed 2482 [OE *wrītan*]

wrobberes *n.* persons given to stirring up strife *(see Appendix A)*; *obj.pl. ~* 39 [ideo.; f. on *wrobbe* v., apoph. var. of *wrabbe* v. < Gmc *wrab̄-* 'twist; be contentious']

wrong *n.* (1) evil deeds 72 (2) injustice 76, 79 *(see* **do(n)** *phr.)*; *(adv.phr.) with mikel ~e* very unjustly 2807; *obj.sg. ~* 76, 79; *prep.sg.* **wronge** 72, 2807 [sb. use of ~ a. < LOE *wrang* < ON *wrang-r > rang-r* 'awry; unjust']

wros *n.* corners; *prep.pl. ~* 68 [ON *wrá > vrǭ*]

wroth *a.* (1) angry 1118 (2) *(recipr. use)* **wroþe** at loggerheads 2974 [OE *wrāþ*]

wrouht, wrouth, wrowht: *see* **wirchen**

wrþe: *see* **worþe**

wunde: *see* **w(o)unde**

wurþe: *see* **worþe**

wydues *n.* widows; *nom.pl. ~* 33; *dat.pl.* **widuen** 79 [OE *widewe* wk., nom.acc.pl. *widewan*]

ya, ye *interj.* (1) yes, indeed!: *ya* 2010 (2) right! *(phr.) ya, leue, ya!* 1889; *ye, lef, ye* 2607* [*gēa*, with *(a)* rising diphthong > *yā (b)* falling diphth. > *yē*]

yare *a.* ready; *nom.sg. ~* 2575*; *nom.pl. ~* 1392, 2789, 2955 [OE *gearu*, pl. *gearwe*]

yaren *v.tr.* put in trim 1351 [OE *gearwian*]

yat *p.p.* acceded to 1675* [ON *játta*, or LOE *gēatan* < ON *játta*]

ye: *see* **ya**

ye *2 pers.pron. pl.* you; (1) *nom.pl.*: ~ 732, 1128, 1641, 1779, 2586; *obj.* **you** 1442, 2578; *dat.* **you** 1402, 2579, **yw** 453; *prep.* **you** 2816 (2) *polite use for sg.*: *nom.* **ye** 921, 2806; *obj.* **you** 911, 1627, 2800; *dat.* **you** 913; *prep.* **you** 1362, 1629*. *See* **y(o)ure**. [OE *gē*]

yede: *see* **go**

yeft *n.* distribution of gifts 2337 [on *yeue* v.]

yelde *v.tr.* (1) pay: *phr.* ~ *þe þi mede* pay you your deserts 2403 (2) reward 804 (3) hand over 2713, 2718; *3 pr.sg.subj.* ~ 804; *imper.sg.* **yeld** 2718 [OE *geldan*]

yeme(n) *v.tr.* (1) take care of 131, 172, 182, 209, 368, 392, look after 175* (*refl.*), 631 (2) nurture 305 (3) have charge of 2214, 2277 (4) rule 2961 (5) guard 268, 324, 1754* (6) protect 2153, 2299; *pt.pl.* **yemede** 2277; *p.p.* **yemed** 305 [OE *gēman*]

yer *n.* year; *prep.sg.* ~ 1334 [OE *gēar*, *gēr*]

yerd *n.* farmyard; *prep.sg.* ~ 703 [OE *geard*]

yerne *3 pr.sg.subj.tr.* desire 299 [OM *geornan* (ONth. *giorna*, OWS *giernan*)]

yerne *adv.* (1) eagerly 881 (2) willingly 1347 (3) assiduously 153, 211 [OE *georne*]

yet(e) *adv.* (1) in addition 2365, 2834 (2) (*reinf.* **(n)euere**: till now 974, 997, 1044, 1289, 2335, by no means 495 (3) still 2830 (4) in time to come 1261, 1320, once more 2041 [OA *gēt(a)*]

yeue *v.tr.* (1) give 304, 924, 1635, 1636; part with 1644; bestow (a woman) in marriage 1080, 1110, 1126, 1251 (2) distribute 224 (3) grant 22, 2035 (4) deal 1846, 1899 (5) give (a straw, etc.) (for): ~ *nouth a stra* (*note, slo*) 315, 419, 466, 2052 (6) *intr.*: *refl.* show oneself (to be) *yaf hire ille* was distressed 1130* (*see* **giue** v. and 164 *n.*); *inf.* **yeue** 924, 1080; *1 pr.sg.* **yeue** 2052; *3 pr.sg.subj.* **yeue** 22, 300, 1126, 2035; *imper.sg.* **yif** 675, *pl.* **yeueþ** 912; *3 pt.sg.* **yaf** 315, 419, 466, 1130*, 1635, 2352, *pl.* **yeuen** 1846; *p.p.* **youen** 224, 304, *agglut.* **youenet** 1664. *See* **giue** v. [OE *gefan*]

yf: *see* **yif**

yhere *v.tr.* hear all about 11 [OE *gehēran*]

yif, yf *conj.* (1) **yif** if 509, 1935, 2045, 2425, 2678, 2709, **yf** 513, 1190, 1742, 2041; **yif þat** 377, 2562, **yf þat** 2040; but **yif** unless 2547 (2) whether 2788 [OE *gif*]

ylere *v.tr.* get to know 12 [OE *gelǣran* teach × ME *lerne* < OE *leornian*]

ynow, inow *a.* (1) in abundance 564, in large numbers 1019, (*pl.*) a great many 2683 (2) enough 912, 932; *nom.sg.* **inow** 1019, *obj.sg.* **ynou** 564, **inow** 912, 932; *nom.pl.* **ynowe** 2683 [OE *genōge*, oblique cases and nom. acc.pl. of *genōg* a.]

ynow *adv.* exceedingly 707, **inow** 905, 1796 [OE *genōh*]

y(o)ure *poss.a.* your; *nom.sg.* **yure** 171; *obj.sg.* **youre** 1417; *dat.sg.* ~ 2249; *prep.sg.* ~ 2212; (*polite use to one person*) *nom.pl.* **youre** 2802 [OE *ēower* gen. of *gē* 'you (pl.)']

youres *poss.pron.* (*disj.*) yours; (*honorific use to one person*) 2799, 2802 [OE *ēower* + poss. ending -*s*, modelled on *his*]

y(o)uself *2 pl.refl.pron.* yourselves 2426, 2596. *See* **himself, meself (miself), self** [OE 2 pl.pers.pron.acc. dat *ēow* + OE emph. a. *self*]

ys: *see* **-es**

yse *v.tr.* finally see 334 [OE *gesēon*]

yunder *adv.* to that place 923 [OE *geond(an)* prep., cf. *geon* a., and suff. in OS *gendra* a. on this side, MLG *ginder*, Goth. *jaindrē* 'thither' and *hidrē* (= OE *hider*)]

yung *a.* young; *colloc.* ~ *and (ne; or)* old 957, 1640, 1934, *etc.*; *nom.sg.* **yung** 112, *obj.sg.* **yunge** 716; *nom.pl.* **yunge** 957; *obj.pl.* **yunge** 368 [OE *geong*]

yungemen *nom.pl.* young men 1010 [see *OED young man* and *yeoman*]

INDEX OF NAMES